Social Work in the
21st Century

Adventures in Social Research: Data Analysis Using SPSS® for Windows™ by Earl R. Babbie and Fred Halley

Critical Thinking for Social Workers: A Workbook by Leonard Gibbs and Eileen Gambrill

Adventures in Criminal Justice Research: Data Analysis Using SPSS® for Windows™ by George Dowdall, Earl R. Babbie, and Fred Halley

Exploring Social Issues Using SPSS® for Windows™ by Joseph F. Healey, Earl R. Babbie, and Fred Halley

Race, Ethnicity, Gender, and Class: The Sociology of Group Conflict and Change by Joseph F. Healey

Race, Ethnicity, and Gender in the United States: Inequality, Group Conflict, and Power by Joseph F. Healey

Aging: Concepts and Controversies by Harry R. Moody

Diversity in America by Vincent N. Parrillo

The McDonaldization of Society, Rev. ed., by George Ritzer

Expressing America: A Critique of the Global Credit Card Society by George Ritzer

Shifts in the Social Contract: Understanding Change in American Society by Beth Rubin

Worlds of Difference: Inequality in the Aging Experience, 2nd ed., by Eleanor Palo Stoller and Rose Campbell Gibson

The Pine Forge Press Series in Research Methods and Statistics
Edited by Kathleen S. Crittenden

- **Investigating the Social World: The Process and Practice of Research** by Russell K. Schutt

- *A Guide to Field Research* by Carol A. Bailey

- *Designing Surveys: A Guide to Decisions and Procedures* by Ronald Czaja and Johnny Blair

- *How Sampling Works* by Richard Maisel and Caroline Hodges Persell

- **Social Statistics for a Diverse Society** by Chava Frankfort-Nachmias

- *Regression: A Primer* by Paul Allison

- *Experimental Design and the Analysis of Variance* by Robert Leik

- *Program Evaluation* by George McCall

Social Work in the 21st Century

University of Pennsylvania

Eileen Gambrill
University of California at Berkeley

PINE FORGE PRESS
Thousands Oaks, California
London ■ New Delhi

For information, address:

 Pine Forge Press
A Sage Publications Company
2455 Teller Road
Thousand Oaks, California 91320
(805) 499-4224
E-mail: sales@pfp.sagepub.com

Sage Publications Ltd.
6 Bonhill Street
London EC2A 4PU
United Kingdom

Sage Publications India Pvt. Ltd.
M-32 Market
Greater Kailash I
New Delhi 110 048 India

Production: Melanie Field, Strawberry Field Publishing
Copy Editor: Carol Dondrea
Interior Designer: Lisa Mirski Devenish
Typesetter: Christi Payne, Book Arts
Cover Designer: Ravi Balasuriya
Production Management: Scratchgravel Publishing Services
Print Buyer: Anna Chin

Printed in the United States of America
97 98 99 00 01 10 9 8 7 6 5 4 3 2 1

Library of Congress Cataloging-in-Publication Data
Social work in the 21st century / edited by Michael Reisch, Eileen
   Gambrill.
        p.   cm.
    Includes bibliographical references and index.
    ISBN 0-8039-9091-X (p : alk. paper)
    1. Social service—Forecasting.   2. Twenty-first century—
Forecasts.   I. Reisch, Michael, 1948– .   II. Gambrill, Eileen
D., 1934– .
HV40.S619   1997
361.3' 2–DC21   96-45367
                                                                           CIP

To the social workers of the past who looked toward the future, and to those of the future who can learn from the past.

About the Editors

Michael Reisch is Professor of Social Work and director of the doctoral program at the University of Pennsylvania School of Social Work. He has published and presented widely on social policy, community organization, social service administration, and the history and philosophy of social welfare. He currently chairs the Peace and Social Justice Committee of the National Association of Social Workers and the Commission on Educational Policy of the Council on Social Work Education.

Eileen Gambrill is Professor of Social Welfare at the University of California at Berkeley. She is the author of *Critical Thinking in Clinical Practice* (1990) and *Social Work Practice: A Critical Thinker's Guide* (1997). She is interested in professional decision making and plays a leading role in encouraging inclusion of content on critical thinking in social work curricula.

About the Publisher

Pine Forge Press is a new educational publisher, dedicated to publishing innovative books and software throughout the social sciences. On this and any other of our publications, we welcome your comments.

Please call or write us at:

Pine Forge Press
A Sage Publications Company
2455 Teller Road
Thousand Oaks, CA 91320
Phone: (805) 499-4224
E-mail: sales@pfp.sagepub.com

Visit our new World Wide Web site, your direct link to a multitude of on-line resources:

http://www.sagepub.com/pineforge

Contents

Part III
Theories, Knowledge, and Values and the Social Work Profession / 297

Preface

This is a book about the future of social work practice and the social work profession. We recognize that attempting to predict the future is a precarious challenge, particularly in these uncertain and rapidly changing times. Perhaps it is a task better left to writers of science fiction rather than social and behavioral scientists. A cursory review of the prophesies written a century ago would certainly lead to this conclusion. Yet, because a primary role of social work is the generation of knowledge for action, and all actions have consequences beyond their immediate impact, the profession must be as concerned with the future as it is with learning from the past and deciphering the present.

This book's purpose is to stimulate a constructive, creative discussion among students, faculty, and practitioners about this future. One requisite for such a discussion is a multifaceted analysis of contemporary U.S. society, national and global changes currently under way, and the mission and roles of social work in this changing context. Another is a candid consideration of different possible futures. Considering these assumptions, we have encouraged authors to be provocative and to raise alternative possibilities. At the same time, we have attempted to keep in mind that what may seem ludicrous and improbable today may soon come to be everyday parts of our lives in this unpredictable world.

The essays that follow are all original contributions written by leading figures in social work education and practice. They reflect diverse projections about and recommendations for the future. For example, in the final section, "The Social Work Profession," David Austin argues that the profession of social work will grow in the future, while David Stoesz suggests that it will be absorbed into broader human service programs that now exist side by side with those of social work on many campuses. One projection, therefore, suggests that social work will expand in the future. Another suggests that social work will decline in influence and status as a profession, if not lose its professional identity entirely. Essays by Jerome Wakefield and Tomi Gomory present different views and recommendations regarding the future relationship of psychiatry and social work. One advocates for closer interaction; the other calls for total separation.

We have encouraged authors to describe their points of view clearly and to discuss the potential consequences of their views for social work practice and education. Thus, although we sought candor and the presentation of provocative ideas, we did not equate either quality with simply pronouncing a controversial perspective. In order to stimulate critical analysis and dialogue, authors must clearly describe their positions. Related arguments must also be clearly explained. As the history of the 20th century demonstrates, in spite of careful planning, unintended consequences will occur and unforeseen developments are inevitable. As Sir Karl Popper has pointed out, if thinking about a problem carefully in the beginning can avoid some unwanted consequences—such as harm to clients—is it not better to do so?

With these thoughts in mind, we have tried to prepare a book that helps readers to consider the future of social work in relation to demographic, economic, social, and political trends in the United States and, to a lesser extent, in the world as a whole. Although we have included topics that are often ignored or given limited attention, such as the role of religious organizations in providing services, we have also omitted topics that could easily have been included, on such issues as family structure, the physical environment, the future of cities, the impact of technology, and the potential consequences of epidemic diseases such as AIDS/HIV. We have tried to avoid being mystified and shackled by contemporary political, cultural, and scholarly fashions or labels. Terms like *freedom, responsibility, social justice, diversity, multiculturalism,* and even *social welfare* have different meanings for different people in different eras and contexts. If we are serious about formulating models of practice and education for the next century that focus on helping people in need, we must avoid the use of vague, or ill-defined, terms or slogans, whatever their ideological origins. We must clarify and candidly examine the consequences of the concepts and values that are proposed as guides to our work. This book attempts to follow this advice and make a small contribution to this broader effort.

The book is intended for both undergraduate and graduate students in social work and related fields. It is divided into three major parts, each with a brief introductory essay. These introductions are designed to guide the reader, to connect the essays to the book's larger themes, and to draw out their implications for social work practice and education. Each essay is also preceded by a headnote that identifies its major themes and provides brief biographical information about the authors.

Part I reviews certain major characteristics of the external environment, including demographic changes, economic and political trends, developments in international social welfare and the nonprofit sector in the United States, and the changing character of poverty. These essays would be particularly useful in the opening sessions of courses such as Introduction to Social Work or U.S. Social Policy.

Part II has two sections. The first contains essays on many, but not all, of the major policy issues that affect the social work profession and its clients. These include domestic developments in child welfare, health care and mental health care, Social Security and Medicare, family violence, the workplace, and juvenile justice, as well as recent trends in the international arena. These essays would be valuable for introductory courses on social policy and policy analysis, or in advanced courses on the specific topics covered.

Essays in the second half of Part II address different arenas of social work practice. Some are broadly framed, such as the essays on prevention, community organizing, social work and the law, practice with marginalized populations, and occupational social work. Others focus on more specific areas, such as Jane Isaacs Lowe's essay, "A Social-Health Model," or Stephanie Hochman's essay, "School–Community Collaboratives." Other essays examine topics that receive less attention in the literature, such as the role of religious congregations in the provision of services and multicultural community organizing. These entries could be utilized in introductory practice courses or advanced courses on the specific fields of practice covered. We have tried to strike a balance between essays concerned with *what is* with those that discuss *what might be* in the years ahead.

Part III also has two sections. The first consists of essays that examine certain aspects of the knowledge and value bases of the profession, their relationship to practice and education, and the ethical issues that are emerging as we approach the 21st century. They are particularly well suited for courses on social work research and social work practice, and for advanced courses on social work theory and social work education.

The essays in the concluding section present different perspectives on the prospects for the social work profession in the decades ahead. They reveal considerable differences in how the authors view the profession's history and contemporary reality, and extract widely varying lessons for the future.

Our work taught us much about the breadth of the social welfare field and the innovations that are already under way. We have tried to present pieces of many different futures. We hope these essays will stimulate lively debate in classes that discuss the nature of the social work profession, as well as in faculty meetings and informal exchanges.

Acknowledgments

We want to express our appreciation to the authors who have contributed to this volume and thank our many colleagues whose enthusiasm about a "future-oriented" book encouraged us to undertake this project. We want to acknowledge the contributions of those who reviewed drafts of the manuscript and helped shape its content and form: Sadhna Diwan, Georgia State; Philip Farmer, Stephen F. Austin University; and Phillip Popple, Western Michigan University. We would also like to thank Sharon Ikami of the University of California at Berkeley, and Pat Frederick-Burns and Janet Geel of the University of Pennsylvania for their secretarial support and computer expertise.

Michael Reisch
Eileen Gambrill

Part I
The External Environment

Even before Mary Richmond instructed social workers to "get to individuals by way of their social environments" in her 1917 classic, *Social Diagnosis,* social workers have been concerned with the context that influences individual and social problems and in which those problems have to be addressed. The earliest analyses of the causes of poverty and human suffering by Charles Loring Brace (1873), Amos Warner (1894), Robert Hunter (1904), W. E. B. DuBois (1899), and Homer Folks (1894) underscored the importance of such issues as unemployment, low wages, physical and mental health, and family composition in influencing the life chances and well-being of the clients of social service agencies. Despite the influence of intrapsychic explanations for human behavior since the 1920s, a distinguishing characteristic of 20th-century social work has been its emphasis on environmental factors in understanding the human condition.

It seemed appropriate, therefore, to begin a book on social work in the 21st century by exploring some of the major environmental factors that will shape practice and education in the years ahead. The difficulty, of course, lies in determining which factors will have the greatest impact. Reflecting on the past century, it is clear that economic, political, cultural, and technological events have all had an impact on the evolution of social policy and social work practice.

Given this difficulty, we relied on several complementary criteria in making our selection of topics: (1) those influences that have consistently shaped the policy and practice environment of social work, such as the economic and political contexts; (2) those influences that affect the nature of the client populations with whom social workers will work, such as demographic issues and societal views of poverty and human need; and (3) those influences that affect the institutional context in which social policies are created and implemented, such as international developments and the roles of government and nongovernmental institutions. (Some of the essays fall into more than one of these categories.) Reluctantly, we excluded some important issues, such as changes in the physical environment (e.g., global warming, the erosion of the ozone layer, the destruction of the rain forests), threats to public health (e.g., the AIDS/HIV epidemic, the Ebola virus, and other potential bacterial pandemics), technological developments (e.g., computers), and the combined impact of war, militarism, and terrorism. Although the consequences of these issues may influence social work practice, we felt an analysis of their implications for the future would necessarily be either too broad or too speculative and might carry this book too far from its intended focus. Space limitations also played a role in our selection of topics to be covered.

Because social work is a profession that focuses on people and their needs, the lead essay by Martha Ozawa, "Demographic Changes and their Implications," plays a vital role in this volume by addressing two critical questions: What will be the composition of the U.S. population in the next century? and What are the implications of this new population mix for social welfare? Unlike political and economic influences, demographic trends cannot be changed by policy shifts in the short term. Although Ozawa acknowledges two oft-cited significant demographic shifts—the aging of the population and its increasing racial and ethnic diversity—as being of great concern to the public and policymakers, she focuses her essay on the dramatic impact such demographic changes will have on the nation's children. By looking at the combined effects of these demographic shifts, her analysis points out some significant implications for social policy and practice in the decades ahead. In sum, these are:

- By the mid-21st century, the United States will have a burgeoning elderly population that will still be two-thirds white, being supported by fewer workers, about 50% of whom will be persons of color. A few years later, the majority of American workers will be persons of color, as will nearly 60% of the nation's children.

- By 2050, the United States will have to provide education and social supports for this nonwhite majority of children to enable them to earn average wages that are $1^1/_2$ times the current average worker— *just to maintain Social Security benefits at their current levels.*

- Unless there are dramatic improvements in the level of economic and social supports provided for children, particularly children of color, they will be economically worse off in the mid-21st century than they are today. Unless current cutbacks in social welfare spending are reversed, Ozawa argues, the nation is on a self-destructive econodemographic course.

The essays that follow offer different levels of hope and skepticism about the ability of the United States to make the structural changes needed to respond to this inexorable demographic reality. They also present different interpretations as to how social workers will be affected by external environmental forces and different prescriptions as to what they might do in response to these changes. The authors seem to agree, however, on two critical points: the significance of growing economic and social inequality as a determinant of the quality of life in the next century, both in the United States and abroad, and the failure of current ideological, economic, and political systems to provide adequate solutions to this central problem.

In her essay, "The Future Economic Landscape," Nancy Rose argues that current economic conditions are the consequences of four interrelated trends that began two decades ago: corporate restructuring, economic globalization, increased unemployment and underemployment, and a growing elitist orientation of U.S. economic and social policies. These trends have produced a widening gap in income and wealth, a decline in the standard of living for working people, and "the ongoing reality of gender and racial discrimination." She believes they are likely to continue unabated unless a powerful political opposition to the status quo appears. Her conclusions provide an economic complement to Ozawa's demographic warnings.

John Longres provides another spin on this emerging social reality in his essay "The Impact and Implications of Multiculturalism." He asserts that the present fight over multiculturalism has its roots in the nation's failure to resolve what Gunnar Myrdal called "the American dilemma," and what W. E. B. DuBois prophetically termed the "problem of the color line" nearly a century ago. It emerged from the desire of disadvantaged racial and ethnic groups to obtain access to the political and economic mainstream without sacrificing their unique cultural heritage. The ultimate measure of multiculturalism as a strategy, Longres argues, can only be found, therefore, in its ability to produce economic and social justice. Yet, the "mainstreaming" of multiculturalism and its successes in championing the cause of cultural separation, have been accompanied by a decline in its commitment to justice concerns. According to Longres, multiculturalism "is on the verge of becoming just one more method for dealing with private troubles," and not a particularly effective one at that. He challenges this tendency to become bogged down in a nationalistic celebration and reification of culture and argues "that cultural amalgamation is not only possible but desirable . . . [to] end ethnic stratification as we know it in contemporary America." Social workers can promote this end by breaking down "binary thinking," maintaining our emphasis on social and economic justice, and focusing on intergroup relations as the core of multicultural practice.

Mark Stern is similarly concerned with the implications of the physical, socioeconomic, and ideological barriers that have developed between low-income Americans who are disproportionately from racial and ethnic minorities, and the largely white middle and upper classes. Ironically, these barriers have emerged in an era when "the work life, family life, and cultural perspective of the poor and the 'mainstream' are more alike . . . than at any time in this century." In his essay, "Poverty and Postmodernity," Stern reassesses the validity of our century-old materialist definition of poverty and argues that the twin realities of social/cultural convergence and neo-social Darwinist obsessions with race will shape our definition of poverty in the 21st century.

Like Longres, Stern paints a more hopeful view of the future than do Ozawa and Rose. He argues that growing social and cultural similarities will "undercut a racial definition of the politics of rich and poor," while economic and social gaps between whites and persons of color will continue to narrow. Simultaneously, the new multiracial demographic reality may revise the nation's bipolar view of race, which has heretofore prevented the formation of interracial coalitions between the African-American poor and the white working class. Stern concludes that "the values which social workers have championed in the past—diversity, tolerance and social justice—will be even more central to the debate of the next century," particularly as cuts in social welfare spending, which disproportionately affect racial and ethnic minorities, are likely to continue for the foreseeable future. Like Longres, Stern warns that unless we are able to overcome the burden of racism, the prospects for achieving these values are remote.

James Midgley's essay, "Social Work in International Context," places the above dilemmas in the broader, global setting. He argues that internationalism will not only be desirable in the next century, but that it will be essential to address those locally based individual and social problems that social workers confront on a daily basis. Midgley cites several developments in support of his thesis. He concurs with Rose that economic globalization "has been accompanied by new social problems which social work needs to address." These include an increase in the incidence of absolute poverty in many developing nations and growing economic and social stratification in industrialized countries. Economic problems have, in turn, led to family disintegration, various forms of violence, and the spread of self-destructive and antisocial behavior. In addition, the economic and political effects of globalization are producing an unprecedented migration of populations. This migration not only creates new social problems, it exacerbates class and ethnic tensions in those countries, like the United States, that attract large numbers of immigrants, and makes local public health concerns international in scope. Finally, it is now widely acknowledged that the effects of global environmental changes can only be successfully addressed through international cooperation.

Midgley exhorts social workers to develop an authentic commitment to internationalism through expanding the parameters of their research, incorporating knowledge about international developments and issues into curriculum, increasing their involvement with international social welfare agencies and organizations, and, above all, by expanding their frame of analysis to incorporate an internationalist perspective. These changes, Midgley maintains, will not only contribute to the resolution of persistent social and economic ills, they will also enable social workers to take advantage of new opportunities to expand their knowledge base, improve their repertoire of skills, and enhance their professional status.

Instead of looking at the commonalties implicit in an internationalist perspective, Eleanor Brilliant's essay, "Nonprofit Organizations, Social Policy, and Public Welfare," examines what might be termed the "exceptionalist" aspect of U.S. social welfare: the unique importance that the non-profit sector has played in the development and implementation of social policies and services. She believes that many social workers have misconstrued recent conservative attacks on the welfare state as implying a linkage between the role of the voluntary sector and the maintenance of a residual approach to social welfare. Yet, since the 1960s, the growing partnership between government and non-profit organizations has promoted the growth of welfare state provisions and has been to the mutual benefit of clients and social service professionals. She argues that attacks on the welfare state have been accompanied by restrictions on both charitable giving and advocacy by voluntary sector organizations. The results have been a diminution of the much-heralded capacity of the non-profit sector to compensate for cutbacks in public welfare expenditures.

Brilliant asserts that in the 21st century social workers need to reexamine the role of non-profit organizations in the development and implementation of social policies and programs in order to take advantage of the connection between public policy and tax policy, promote altruism and community responsibility, mobilize people at the grassroots level to oppose harmful social policies, and promote the values of diversity and freedom of choice. This reexamination requires social workers to ask hard questions as to how to apportion responsibilities to create the most effective public-private synthesis and to consider new means to achieve the profession's social justice goals. Brilliant's conclusion complements that of John Longres: In order to be effective in the 21st century, social workers will have to pay more attention to community process, group participation, and shared leadership in the formation of viable social policy alternatives.

Whereas Brilliant emphasizes the need for social workers to reassess the historic relationship between public and private sectors, Michael Reisch's discussion, "The Political Context of Social Work," analyzes the meaning of three interrelated contemporary political trends for the future of U.S. social welfare: changes in the ideological content of politics, changes in the distribution of political power, and changes in popular attitudes about politics and the role of government. He argues that a "mythology of simplicity" has shaped both recent policy debates and the analysis of those debates by pundits on all points of the political spectrum. The reality, he argues, is far more complex and ambiguous, reflecting neither a clear philosophical direction for the nation, nor a single emerging pattern of political behavior.

Reisch asserts that the very fluidity of the U.S. political scene in the decades ahead makes it imperative for social workers to incorporate a political dimension into their practice and education for both altruistic and self-interested motives. Social workers should not merely react to political developments at the local and national level. They can shape these developments by serving as interpreters of the environment to both policymakers and the public, advocates for groups that lack power and resources, and mediators between institutions and communities in the public, non-profit, and for-profit sectors. These are roles that, at times, social workers have effectively played throughout the 20th century. Reisch concludes that we will need to make them consistent, ongoing elements of our practice in the next century if we are to develop effective solutions to the problems generated by the emerging demographic and economic reality in the United States and the world.

Demographic Changes
and Their Implications

Martha N. Ozawa

The author describes demographic trends, projects these into the next century, and discusses their implications, including economic differences and social service needs. She highlights the difficult decisions that will have to be made to protect the development of children around the world. Martha N. Ozawa, Ph.D., is Bettie Bofinger Brown Professor of Social Policy at the George Warren Brown School of Social Work, Washington University, St. Louis, MO. One of her specialties is providing clear, evidence-based descriptions of large databases and drawing out their implications for social problems and related social welfare policies. She has published widely in the social work literature. Her publications include: Income Maintenance and Work Incentive: Toward a Synthesis *(1982), and* Women's Life Cycle and Economic Insecurity: Problems Proposals *(New York: Praeger, 1989).*

In his seminal work on social welfare spending, Lampman (1984) stated that among several factors that shape social policy, demographic changes are a major one. Other factors include structural changes in society stemming from urbanization, industrialization, and families; the public's increasing demand for a higher quality of education and health care; the development of new approaches to ensure income and health security, such as social insurance; changes in political institutions, such as in the political party system and in suffrage; and the rise in interest groups.

Indeed, the effects of future demographic changes on social welfare policy should be of great concern to the public and to policymakers. The U.S. population is aging, albeit not at as fast a rate as in Japan or other industrialized countries, such as the United Kingdom and Germany (Ozawa and Kono, 1995). Moreover, the U.S. population is becoming increasingly diverse, racially and ethnically, so much so that by the middle of the 21st century, Caucasians are expected to make up only about half the population.

Because both the age composition and racial-ethnic composition of the U.S. population will change, the future well-being of American children is expected to be affected the most radically. This chapter focuses on the prospects for American children in the 21st century. From what racial and ethnic groups will they come? When will white children cease to be the majority? How will the economic well-being of American children be affected by the demographic changes in the coming five decades? And, to what extent will children become more worse off than adults and elderly persons? Finally, what will be the implications for social welfare policy in the next century?

Demographic Changes

Changes in the U.S. Population

Age composition. According to the latest projections reported by the U.S. Bureau of the Census (1993a), the United States is expected to undergo rapid demographic changes in its age composition and racial-ethnic composition. Whereas changes in the age composition of the population are not unique to the United States (other industrialized countries are also undergoing them), changes in the racial-ethnic composition are unique to the United States, making the country a truly diverse society. Tables 1, 2, and 3 summarize these changes. For the purpose of this chapter, racial-ethnic populations are identified, first, by dividing the population into the Hispanic and non-Hispanic populations and then by dividing the non-Hispanic population into the non-Hispanic white, non-Hispanic black, non-Hispanic American Indian, and non-Hispanic Asian populations. Thus, all the populations in these tables are mutually exclusive. Hereafter, non-Hispanic whites, non-Hispanic blacks, non-Hispanic American Indians, and non-Hispanic Asians are called whites, blacks, American Indians, and Asians. All data are based on the intermediate assumptions on fertility, life expectancy, and net migration.

The United States population is expected to grow from 263 million in 1995 to over 392 million in 2050, when it will be composed of 206 million whites, 88 million Hispanics, 56 million blacks, 38 million Asians, and 3.7 million American Indians. Although the annual rate of growth of the U.S. population, which will range from 0.95 percent during 1995–2000 to 0.54 percent in 2040–2050, will be moderate (see Table 4), changes in the age composition will be profound. As Table 2 indicates, the pro-

portion of persons aged 65 and over will increase from 12.8 percent in 1995 to 20.7 percent in 2040 and then decrease slightly to 20.4 percent in 2050. In 2050, the proportion of elderly persons within each racial-ethnic population will be as follows: white, 26.0 percent; Hispanics, 14.1 percent; blacks, 13.6 percent; American Indians, 12.6 percent; and Asians, 15.6 percent. With regard to the rate of increase in the proportion of elderly persons, the Hispanic population will experience the fastest rate and the black population will experience the slowest rate.

In contrast, the proportion of children in the population will shrink from 26.2 percent in 1995 to 23.4 percent in 2050. Particularly noticeable will be the drop in the proportion of white children, from 23.7 percent of the white population in 1995 to only 18.9 percent in 2050. American Indian children will be at the other extreme: In 2050, 31.8 percent of the American Indian population will be children, compared to 35.2 percent in 1995. In terms of the speed of decline in the proportion of children, the white population will experience the fastest rate and the black population will experience the slowest rate.

The proportion of the population aged 18 to 64 (generally called the working-age population) will also decline: from 61.0 percent in 1995 to 56.2 percent in 2050. Like the situation of children, the speed of decline in the proportion of those aged 18 to 64 will be the fastest for the white population and the slowest for the black population. However, the speed of change in the proportion of those of working age will not be as fast as that for children or for elderly persons.

Racial-ethnic composition. Changes in the racial-ethnic composition of the population are expected to be dramatic. As Table 3

TABLE 1

Projections of the U.S. Population, by Age, Race, and Hispanic Origin: 1995 to 2050
(numbers in thousands; resident population)

Year	Total	Hispanic	Non-Hispanic			
			White	Black	American Indian	Asian
All persons						
1995	263,434	26,798	193,900	31,648	1,927	9,161
2000	276,241	31,166	197,872	33,741	2,055	11,407
2005	288,286	35,702	200,842	35,793	2,190	13,759
2010	300,431	40,525	203,441	37,930	2,336	16,199
2020	325,942	51,217	208,280	42,459	2,641	21,345
2030	349,993	62,810	210,480	46,934	2,960	26,810
2040	371,505	75,130	209,148	51,489	3,314	32,424
2050	392,031	88,071	205,849	56,346	3,701	38,064
Under age 18						
1995	69,035	9,467	45,945	10,290	678	2,655
2000	71,789	10,938	45,949	10,864	709	3,328
2005	73,123	12,357	44,682	11,374	732	3,978
2010	73,618	13,543	42,978	11,698	758	4,641
2020	77,776	16,473	41,842	12,808	859	5,795
2030	83,038	19,654	41,375	14,024	948	7,037
2040	86,794	22,623	39,622	15,256	1,053	8,241
2050	91,754	25,754	38,827	16,692	1,176	9,306
Aged 18 to 64						
1995	160,750	15,799	119,250	18,697	1,122	5,882
2000	169,130	18,303	122,348	20,052	1,198	7,230
2005	178,193	20,977	125,839	21,420	1,287	8,669
2010	186,709	24,064	128,178	22,954	1,380	10,132
2020	194,818	29,997	125,033	25,061	1,506	13,220
2030	196,780	35,540	116,772	26,531	1,651	16,286
2040	207,697	42,287	115,017	29,084	1,849	19,459
2050	220,168	49,865	113,425	32,002	2,058	22,817
Aged 65 and over						
1995	33,649	1,532	28,705	2,661	127	624
2000	35,322	1,925	29,575	2,825	148	849
2005	36,970	2,368	30,321	2,999	171	1,112
2010	40,104	2,918	32,285	3,278	198	1,426
2020	53,348	4,747	41,405	4,590	276	2,330
2030	70,175	7,616	52,333	6,379	361	3,487
2040	77,014	10,220	54,509	7,149	412	4,724
2050	80,109	12,452	53,597	7,652	467	5,941

Note: The American Indian population includes American Indians, Eskimos, and Aleuts. The Asian population includes both Asians and Pacific Islanders. Persons of Hispanic origin may be of any race.

Source: Derived from U.S. Bureau of the Census (1993a, Table 2, pp. 12–55).

TABLE 2

Percentage Distribution of the U.S. Population, by Age: 1995 to 2050

Year	Total	Hispanic	White	Black	American Indian	Asian
			Non-Hispanic			
			White	Black	American Indian	Asian
Under age 18						
1995	26.2	35.3	23.7	32.5	35.2	29.0
2000	26.0	35.1	23.2	32.2	34.5	29.2
2005	25.4	34.6	22.2	31.8	33.4	28.9
2010	24.5	33.4	21.1	30.8	33.6	28.6
2020	23.9	32.1	20.1	30.2	32.5	27.1
2030	23.7	31.3	19.7	29.9	32.0	26.2
2040	23.4	30.1	18.9	29.6	31.8	25.4
2050	23.4	29.2	18.9	29.6	31.8	24.4
Aged 18 to 64						
1995	61.0	59.0	61.5	59.1	58.2	64.2
2000	61.2	58.7	61.8	59.4	58.3	63.4
2005	61.8	58.8	62.7	59.8	58.8	63.0
2010	62.1	59.4	63.0	60.5	59.1	62.5
2020	59.8	58.6	60.0	59.0	57.0	61.9
2030	56.2	56.9	55.5	56.5	55.8	60.7
2040	55.9	56.3	55.0	56.5	55.8	60.0
2050	56.2	56.6	55.1	56.8	55.6	60.0
Aged 65 and over						
1995	12.8	5.7	14.8	8.4	6.5	6.8
2000	12.8	6.2	14.9	8.4	7.2	7.4
2005	12.8	6.6	15.1	8.4	7.8	8.1
2010	13.3	7.2	15.9	8.6	8.5	8.8
2020	16.4	9.3	19.9	10.8	10.5	10.9
2030	20.1	12.1	24.9	13.6	12.2	13.0
2040	20.7	13.6	26.1	13.9	12.4	14.6
2050	20.4	14.1	26.0	13.6	12.6	15.6
All persons						
1995	100.0	100.0	100.0	100.0	100.0	100.0
2000	100.0	100.0	100.0	100.0	100.0	100.0
2005	100.0	100.0	100.0	100.0	100.0	100.0
2010	100.0	100.0	100.0	100.0	100.0	100.0
2020	100.0	100.0	100.0	100.0	100.0	100.0
2030	100.0	100.0	100.0	100.0	100.0	100.0
2040	100.0	100.0	100.0	100.0	100.0	100.0
2050	100.0	100.0	100.0	100.0	100.0	100.0

Note: The American Indian population includes American Indians, Eskimos, and Aleuts. The Asian population includes both Asians and Pacific Islanders. Persons of Hispanic origin may be of any race.

Source: Derived from U.S. Bureau of the Census (1993a, Table 2, pp. 12–55).

TABLE 3

Percentage Distribution of the Population, by Race and Hispanic Origin: 1995 to 2050

| Year | Total | Hispanic | Non-Hispanic | | | |
			White	Black	American Indian	Asian
			All persons			
1995	100.0	10.2	73.6	12.0	0.7	3.5
2000	100.0	11.3	71.6	12.2	0.7	4.1
2005	100.0	12.4	69.7	12.4	0.8	4.8
2010	100.0	13.5	67.7	12.6	0.8	5.4
2020	100.0	15.7	63.9	13.0	0.8	6.5
2030	100.0	17.9	60.1	13.4	0.8	7.7
2040	100.0	20.2	56.3	13.9	0.9	8.7
2050	100.0	22.5	52.5	14.4	0.9	9.7
			Under age 18			
1995	100.0	13.7	66.6	14.9	1.0	3.8
2000	100.0	15.2	64.0	15.1	1.0	4.6
2005	100.0	16.9	61.1	15.6	1.0	5.4
2010	100.0	18.4	58.4	15.9	1.0	6.3
2020	100.0	21.2	53.8	16.5	1.1	7.5
2030	100.0	23.7	49.8	16.9	1.1	8.4
2040	100.0	26.1	45.7	17.6	1.2	9.5
2050	100.0	28.1	42.3	18.2	1.3	10.1
			Aged 18 to 64			
1995	100.0	8.9	74.2	11.6	0.7	3.7
2000	100.0	10.8	72.3	11.9	0.7	4.3
2005	100.0	11.8	70.6	12.0	0.7	4.9
2010	100.0	12.9	68.7	12.3	0.7	5.4
2020	100.0	15.4	64.2	12.9	0.8	6.8
2030	100.0	18.1	59.3	13.5	0.8	8.3
2040	100.0	20.4	55.4	14.0	0.9	9.4
2050	100.0	22.6	51.5	14.5	0.9	10.4
			Aged 65 and over			
1995	100.0	4.6	85.3	7.9	0.4	1.9
2000	100.0	5.4	83.7	8.0	0.4	2.4
2005	100.0	6.4	82.0	8.1	0.5	3.0
2010	100.0	7.3	80.5	8.2	0.5	3.6
2020	100.0	8.9	77.6	8.6	0.5	4.4
2030	100.0	10.9	74.6	9.1	0.5	5.0
2040	100.0	13.3	70.8	9.3	0.5	6.1
2050	100.0	15.5	66.9	9.6	0.6	7.4

Note: The American Indian population includes American Indians, Eskimos, and Aleuts. The Asian population includes both Asians and Pacific Islanders. Persons of Hispanic origin may be of any race.

Source: Derived from U.S. Bureau of the Census (1993a, Table 2, pp. 12–55).

indicates, the U.S. population will be transformed, declining from 73.6 percent white in 1995 to 52.5 percent white in 2050. However, the proportions of all other racial-ethnic populations will rise. Notably, the proportion of Hispanic persons will surpass that of black persons by 2010 and will zoom to 22.5 percent in 2050. Though relatively small in absolute terms, the Asian population is expected to grow at the fastest rate: from 3.5 percent of the U.S. population in 1995 to 9.7 percent in 2050. In contrast, the proportion of the black population will grow at the slowest rate: from 12.0 percent of the U.S. population in 1995 to 14.4 percent in 2050.

The decline in the proportion of white children will be drastic. Whereas white children constituted 66.6 percent of all children in 1995, they will make up only 42.3 percent of all children in 2050. In short, by 2030, white children will cease to be the majority group. In contrast, the proportions of all other groups of children will increase. For example, the proportions of Hispanic and Asian children will surge from 1995 to 2050: from 13.7 percent to 28.1 percent for Hispanic children and from 3.8 percent to 10.1 percent for Asian children. In terms of the speed of growth in proportion, Asian children will experience the fastest rate, and black children will experience the slowest rate.

The proportion of white elderly persons among all elderly persons will decline from 85.3 percent in 1995 to 66.9 percent in 2050, indicating that they still will be the majority group over 50 years from now. Meanwhile, the increase in the proportion of other elderly groups will be considerable. In particular, the proportion of Hispanic elderly persons will more than triple: from 4.6 percent in 1995 to 15.5 percent in 2050; and the proportion of Asian elderly persons will almost quadruple: from 1.9 percent in 1995 to 7.4 percent in 2050.

Causes of Differential Rates of Change

Behind the dramatic changes in the age composition and the racial-ethnic composition of the population are the differential rates of growth among the racial-ethnic groups.

As Table 4 indicates, from 1995 to 2050, the white population will experience consid-

TABLE 4

Population Change, by Race and Hispanic Origin: 1995 to 2050

Year	Total	Hispanic	Non-Hispanic			
			White	Black	American Indian	Asian
1995 to 2000	0.95	3.02	0.41	1.28	1.29	4.39
2000 to 2005	0.85	2.72	0.30	1.18	1.27	3.75
2005 to 2010	0.83	2.53	0.26	1.16	1.29	3.27
2010 to 2020	0.82	2.34	0.24	1.13	1.23	2.76
2020 to 2030	0.71	2.04	0.11	1.00	1.14	2.28
2030 to 2040	0.60	1.79	−0.06	0.93	1.13	1.90
2040 to 2050	0.54	1.59	−0.16	0.90	1.10	1.60

Note: The American Indian population includes American Indians, Eskimos, and Aleuts. The Asian population includes both Asians and Pacific Islanders. Persons of Hispanic origin may be of any race.

Source: U.S. Bureau of the Census (1993b, Table K, p. xxiii).

erably lower rates of growth than will any other racial-ethnic population; in fact, from 2030 and beyond, it will decline. Although the other racial-ethnic populations will also grow at a slower rate in the coming decades, considerable differences in the rates of growth of the white population and the other racial-ethnic populations will remain. For example, the Asian population will experience an annual growth rate of 4.39 percent from 1995 to 2000, or more than 10 times the rate for the white population (0.41 percent), and will increase at an annual rate of 1.6 percent from 2040 to 2050, whereas during that 10-year period, the white population will decrease at an annual rate of 0.16 percent. In fact, from 2040 to 2050, all other racial-ethnic populations will increase at a faster rate than of the white population during the 1995–2000 period.

A population increases or decreases depending on how many births and deaths occur and what the net immigration (the number of immigrants minus emigrants) is. Table 5 presents the contributions by each racial-ethnic population to the nation's births, deaths, and net immigration.

As Table 5 shows, the number of births among the white population will constitute an increasingly smaller percentage of all births in the United States in the coming decades. Whereas white births represented 63.2 percent of all births in 1995, they will be only 40.5 percent in 2050—or a 36 percent decline. Taking the size of the white population into account (see Tables 1 and 3), the contribution of white births to the total births in the United States will decrease from 85.9 percent of the equal share in 1995 to 77 percent of the equal share in 2050. (The equal share is the number of births that are expected from a particular racial-ethnic population if births occur proportionately.) In contrast, the number of

deaths among the white population will be 66.0 percent of all deaths in the United States in 2050, compared with 81.4 percent in 1995— or a 19 percent decline. Again taking the size of the white population into account, white deaths will be 26 percent more than the equal share in 2050, compared with 11 percent in 1995. That the white population will have increasingly more deaths relative to its population reflects the accelerating aging of this population.

As for net immigration, the white population will contribute significantly less than its equal share: During 1995–2050, the net immigration of whites will represent only 21.9 percent of the total net immigration in the United States.

Throughout the next half century, births among the other racial-ethnic populations will be relatively more numerous, deaths will be relatively less numerous, and net immigration will be significantly greater. The only exceptions to this generalization will be as follows: Asian births will be smaller than the equal share in 2050, black deaths will be fewer than the equal share in 2050, and the net immigration of the American Indian and black populations during 1995–2050 will be smaller than their equal shares.

The case of the Hispanic population illustrates how racial-ethnic populations contribute to the net growth of the U.S. population. In 1995, Hispanic births were 15.9 percent of all births, or 56 percent more than the equal share, whereas in 2050, Hispanic births will be 29.4 percent of all births, which will be 31 percent more than the equal share. With regard to deaths, the reverse will be true: In 1995, Hispanic deaths were 4.5 percent of all deaths (only 44 percent of the equal share), but in 2050, they will be 13.5 percent of all deaths (60 percent of the equal share). From 1995 to 2050, Hispanic net immigration will account for 36.6

TABLE 5

Percentage Distribution of Births, Deaths, and Net Immigration, by Race and Hispanic Origin: 1995 to 2050

Year	Total	Hispanic	Non-Hispanic			
			White	Black	American Indian	Asian
			Births			
1995	100.0	15.9	63.2	16.1	0.8	3.9
2000	100.0	17.5	60.1	16.6	0.9	4.8
2005	100.0	19.0	57.5	17.0	1.0	5.5
2010	100.0	20.3	55.4	17.3	1.0	6.0
2020	100.0	22.9	51.6	17.5	1.0	7.0
2030	100.0	25.5	46.8	18.3	1.1	8.2
2040	100.0	27.6	43.5	18.8	1.2	8.8
2050	100.0	29.4	40.5	19.4	1.3	9.4
			Deaths			
1995	100.0	4.5	81.4	12.6	0.4	1.1
2000	100.0	5.3	79.8	13.0	0.4	1.4
2005	100.0	6.0	78.6	13.2	0.4	1.8
2010	100.0	6.7	77.2	13.3	0.5	2.2
2020	100.0	8.3	74.0	14.0	0.6	3.2
2030	100.0	9.8	71.4	14.2	0.6	4.0
2040	100.0	11.4	69.1	14.1	0.6	4.8
2050	100.0	13.5	66.0	14.1	0.6	5.8
			Net immigration			
1995–2050	100.0	36.6	21.9	6.9	0.0	34.5
			Net increase in the population			
1990–1995	100.0	30.3	38.1	16.0	0.9	14.7
1995–2000	100.0	34.1	31.0	16.3	1.0	17.5
2000–2005	100.0	37.7	24.7	17.0	1.1	19.5
2005–2010	100.0	39.7	21.4	17.6	1.2	20.1
2010–2020	100.0	41.9	19.0	17.8	1.2	20.2
2020–2030	100.0	48.2	9.1	18.6	1.3	22.7
2030–2040	100.0	57.3*	—	21.2*	1.6*	26.1*
2040–2050	100.0	63.0*	—	23.7*	1.9*	27.5*

Note: The American Indian population includes American Indians, Eskimos, and Aleuts. The Asian population includes both Asians and Pacific Islanders. Persons of Hispanic origin may be of any race.

*These percentages do not total 100 percent because of the declining size of the white population.

Source: U.S. Bureau of the Census (1993a, Tables L and O, pp. xxiii and xxxi).

percent of the total net immigration in the United States.

The bottom part of Table 5 indicates the contributions of each racial-ethnic population to the net growth in the U.S. population when births, deaths, and net immigration are taken into account. It clearly shows that Hispanics and Asians will be two major sources of the growth in the U.S. population.

Dependency Ratio

The dependency ratio is an important indicator of the extent to which society needs to support persons who are presumed to be out of the labor force. There are two kinds of dependency ratios: the child dependency ratio and the old dependency ratio. The former is the ratio of children (aged 0 to 17) to persons aged 18 to 64, and the latter is the ratio of the elderly (those aged 65 and over) to those aged 18 to 64. The sum of the two ratios is called the "total dependency ratio." Table 6 presents the dependency ratios for the U.S. population and for each racial-ethnic population.

The U.S. population will experience persistent increases in the old dependency ratio from 1995 to 2050. In 2050, it will have 36.4 elderly persons per 100 working-age persons, compared with 20.9 elderly persons per 100 working-age persons in 1995. In contrast, the child dependency ratio will first decline from 42.9 in 1995 to 39.4 in 2010, will start increasing in 2020, will reach 42.2 in 2030, and will settle at 41.7 in 2050.

As a result of the confluence of these two ratios, the total U.S. dependency ratio will decrease from 63.9 in 1995 to 60.9 in 2010, but will increase sharply to 78.9 in 2040 and then decrease slightly to 78.1 in 2050, indicating a 22 percent increase in the total dependency ratio from 1995 to 2050. That is, in 2050, the United States will have 78.1 children and elderly persons per 100 working-age persons,

compared with only 63.9 such persons in 1995.

All the racial-ethnic populations will generally experience increasing old dependency ratios and somewhat zigzagging child dependency ratios in the coming decades. However, the levels of these ratios in a given year will differ considerably across various populations. For example, the white old dependency ratio will be by far the highest among all racial-ethnic populations throughout the next 50-odd years, and the white child dependency ratio will be by far the lowest. With these demographic forces offsetting one another, the total white dependency ratio (81.5) will be the highest among all racial-ethnic populations in 2050, whereas it was the second lowest in 1995, next only to the Asian population.

It is generally believed that as long as the total dependency ratio stays constant, a country does not necessarily need to increase social welfare spending (Adamchak & Friedman, 1983; Cowgill, 1981; Schulz, 1995). However, one can argue that the change in the age composition of the dependent population affects the extent of social welfare spending. Table 7 presents the impending changes in the ratio of elderly persons to children.

As Table 7 shows, the number of elderly persons per 100 children will increase continuously from 48.7 in 1995 to 88.7 in 2040 and then decrease slightly to 87.3 in 2050, indicating an 80 percent increase from 1995 to 2050. Among the racial-ethnic populations, the rate of increase in the ratio of elderly persons to children will be highest among the Hispanic population and lowest among the black population. In spite of such a rapid increase in this ratio, the Hispanic population will still have a smaller ratio (48.3) in 2050 than the white population did (62.5) in 1995. In 2050, the number of white elderly persons per 100

TABLE 6

TABLE 6

Dependency Ratios, 1995 to 2050

| Year | Total | Hispanic | Non-Hispanic | | | |
			White	Black	American Indian	Asian
			Child dependency ratio			
1995	42.9	59.9	38.5	55.0	60.4	45.1
2000	42.4	59.8	37.6	54.2	59.2	46.0
2005	41.0	58.9	35.5	53.1	56.9	45.9
2010	39.4	56.3	33.5	51.0	54.9	45.8
2020	39.9	54.9	33.5	51.1	57.0	43.8
2030	42.2	55.3	35.4	52.9	57.4	43.2
2040	41.8	53.5	34.4	52.5	56.9	42.4
2050	41.7	51.6	34.2	52.2	57.1	40.8
			Old dependency ratio			
1995	20.9	9.7	24.1	14.2	11.3	10.6
2000	20.9	10.5	24.2	14.1	12.4	11.7
2005	20.7	11.3	24.1	14.0	13.3	12.8
2010	21.5	12.1	25.2	14.3	14.3	14.1
2020	27.4	15.8	33.1	18.3	18.3	17.6
2030	35.7	21.4	44.8	24.0	21.9	21.4
2040	37.1	24.2	47.4	24.6	22.3	24.3
2050	36.4	25.0	47.3	23.9	22.7	26.0
			Total dependency ratio			
1995	63.9	69.6	62.6	69.3	71.7	55.7
2000	63.3	70.3	61.7	68.3	71.5	57.8
2005	61.8	70.2	59.6	67.1	70.2	58.7
2010	60.9	68.4	58.7	65.2	69.3	59.9
2020	67.3	70.7	66.6	69.4	75.4	61.5
2030	77.9	76.7	80.2	76.9	79.3	64.6
2040	78.9	77.7	81.8	77.0	79.2	66.6
2050	78.1	76.6	81.5	76.1	79.8	66.8

Note: The American Indian population includes American Indians, Eskimos, and Aleuts. The Asian population includes both Asians and Pacific Islanders. Persons of Hispanic origin may be of any race.

The sum of the parts does not necessarily add up to the total because of rounding errors.

Source: Derived from U.S. Bureau of the Census (1993a, Table 2, pp. 12–55).

white children will reach 138, the highest ever in U.S. history.

As the proportion of elderly persons increases, the proportion of the old-old (those aged 85 and over) will also increase. From 1995 to 2050, the proportion of the old-old will increase from 1.2 percent in 1995 to 4.8 percent in 2050 (not shown in Table 2). This increase may well mean that per capita social welfare expenditures for the elderly will rise. In addition, these greater expenditures will have to be met by a smaller number of workers per each

TABLE 7

The Number of Elderly Persons per 100 Children: 1995 to 2050

			Non-Hispanic			
Year	Total	Hispanic	White	Black	American Indian	Asian
1995	48.7	16.2	62.5	25.9	18.7	23.5
2000	49.2	17.6	64.4	26.0	20.9	25.5
2005	50.6	19.2	67.9	26.4	23.4	28.0
2010	54.5	21.5	75.1	28.0	26.1	30.7
2020	68.6	28.8	99.0	35.8	32.1	40.2
2030	84.5	38.8	126.5	45.5	38.1	49.6
2040	88.7	45.2	137.6	46.9	39.1	57.3
2050	87.3	48.3	138.0	45.8	39.7	63.8

Note: The American Indian population includes American Indians, Eskimos, and Aleuts. The Asian population includes both Asians and Pacific Islanders. Persons of Hispanic origin may be of any race.

Elderly persons are those aged 65 and over; children are those under age 18.

Source: Derived from U.S. Bureau of the Census (1993a, Table 2, pp. 12–55).

elderly person, requiring greater productivity and earning power from each future worker. This dynamic, chain-type economic relationship between generations will make it imperative for the society to produce stronger and more productive children who will not only fare better at school but be healthier both physically and mentally. Producing generations of such children will require greater per capita social welfare spending for children. Thus, the increase in the proportion of the elderly within the population of dependents will cause social welfare spending to increase, even if the total dependency ratio stays the same. In reality, the United States will face not only a greater total dependency ratio in 2020 and thereafter, but a persistently increasing proportion of the elderly within the dependent population in the coming five decades. As a result, the country will inevitably have to spend more for social welfare, either under public or private auspices.

One needs to be aware of the underlying assumption made by the author. She assumes that elderly persons will continue to be defined as those aged 65 and over. As elderly persons become healthier and thus stay physically capable of working past age 65, the definition of the elderly may change. If so, the age composition within the dependent population will surely change, and the total dependency ratio will be smaller than what is projected in this chapter.

In fact, under the Old-Age Insurance program, the primary retirement age is scheduled to increase to 67 by 2027, thus practically redefining the age at which a person is considered old. On the other hand, the decision to retire does not depend solely on what the Old-Age Insurance program provides under the law. It depends also on what employer-provided pension programs provide and on individuals' preference to retire at a certain age. If anything, employer-provided pension programs generally encourage workers to retire early (Hall & Johnson, 1980; Quinn & Burkhauser, 1994; Stock & Wise, 1990; Wiatrowski, 1993), an employment practice that is contrary to the intent of the Old-Age Insurance program. At any rate, governmental data show that the proportion of workers who retire early has consistently increased over the years (Social Security Administration, annual). Thus, whether future workers stay employed beyond age 65 will depend heavily on whether the American economy is strong enough to absorb aging workers and whether aging workers prefer work over retirement. It seems acceptable, therefore, to assume that, for the foreseeable future, the elderly are defined as those aged 65 and over.

Summary and Agenda

The foregoing discussion indicates that the U.S. population is aging and becoming more racially diverse. There will be fewer workers to support each retiree, and the workers will increasingly come from populations other than the white population. Thus, in 2050, there will be only 275 working-age persons for each 100 elderly persons, compared with 478 such persons in 1995 (derived from Tables 1 and 6). The 2050 racial divide will be 66.9 percent white versus 33.1 percent other racial-ethnic group among the elderly, 51.5 percent white versus 48.5 percent other racial-ethnic group among those of working age, and 42.3 percent white versus 57.7 percent other racial-ethnic group among children (see Table 3). Hence, in 2050, the elderly, a great majority of whom will be white, as they were in 1995, will be supported by fewer workers, about half of whom will be either Hispanic or nonwhite. And only a few years after 2050, the majority of American workers are expected to be Hispanic or nonwhite, given the demographic composition of the population of children in 2050.

With the projected demographic changes, the issue will be how the shrinking population of workers can support the increasing population of elderly people. More pointedly, will

Hispanic and nonwhite workers be able to increase their earning power, not just to reach the level of the current white workers, but to exceed it? In 2050, the ultimate issue will be whether the United States can nurture Hispanic and nonwhite children so that they, who will replace white children, will be educated and nurtured into workers who can earn far more than the current white workers. Van de Water (1984) noted that by the time the baby-boom generation retires, the earning power of the average worker must be more than $1^1/2$ times greater than that of the current average worker just to provide the same level of Social Security benefits as are currently provided.

Effects of Demographic Changes on the Economic Status of Children

The economic status of children in relation to that of other age groups is an important indication of how effectively society channels its resources to nurture and educate its children. This section reviews the current economic status of children and compares it to that of the adult and elderly populations. It then presents the author's estimate of the degree to which the projected demographic changes will affect the future economic status of children. The economic status of children, adults, and elderly persons is defined as the money income of households from which these people come. To adjust for different household sizes, household incomes are transformed into poverty ratios. The poverty ratio of 2, for example, means that a person comes from a household with an income that is twice the poverty line.

According to the author's analysis of the economic status of these groups of persons, based on wave 3 of the 1991 panel of the Survey of Income and Program Participation (U.S. Bureau of the Census, 1992), indicates that American children live under considerably

TABLE 8

Poverty Ratio of Persons, by Age, Race, and Hispanic Origin: 1991

| | | | Non-Hispanic | | | |
Year	Total	Hispanic	White	Black	American Indian	Asian
Children	2.53	1.58	2.87	1.68	1.44	2.88
Adults	3.65	2.45	3.93	2.54	2.65	3.76
Elderly	3.03	2.00	3.19	1.96	1.64	3.63
All persons	3.28	2.11	3.57	2.19	2.19	3.50

Note: The American Indian population includes American Indians, Eskimos, and Aleuts. The Asian population includes both Asians and Pacific Islanders. Persons of Hispanic origin may be of any race.

Source: Derived from U.S. Bureau of the Census (1992); U.S. Bureau of the Census (1993a, Table 2, pp. 12–5; 1993b, Table 1, pp. 2–3).

disadvantaged economic circumstances relative to those of adults and elderly persons. Table 8 shows the economic status, measured in average poverty ratios, of these three groups in 1991.

As Table 8 indicates, there is a great disparity in the economic statuses of children, adults, and elderly persons in the United States. American children, on average, live at 2.53 times the poverty line, compared with 3.65 times the poverty line for adults, and 3.03 times the poverty line for elderly persons. Within the population of children, Hispanic, black, and American Indian children live under especially disadvantaged conditions. The average poverty ratio is only 1.58 for Hispanic children, 1.68 for black children, and 1.44 for American Indian children.

Asian children have the highest economic status relative to that of Asian adults; they live at 77 percent of the poverty ratio of Asian adults. In contrast, American Indian children, who live at only 54 percent of the poverty ratio of American Indian adults, have the lowest economic status.

White children live at 90 percent of the poverty ratio of elderly white people, which is the highest percentage among all racial-ethnic populations of children. At the other extreme,

Hispanic children live at only 79 percent of the poverty ratio of Hispanic elderly persons, and Asian children live at 79.3 percent.

The relative economic deprivation of American children has been noted by numerous analysts. For example, Rainwater and Smeeding (1995) showed that among all children in Western, industrialized countries, American children have the highest poverty rate (defined as the percentage of those who live in households with incomes below half the median household income). In addition, Smeeding, Torrey, and Rein (1988) found that the ratio of the poverty rate of children to that of elderly persons was higher in the United States than in any other industrialized country except Canada and Sweden, which indicates that American children are considerably worse off than are American elderly persons. Moreover, Ozawa and Kono (1995) found that the proportion of Japanese children who live at the level of national minimum household expenditures (equivalent to public assistance payment levels) is actually smaller than that of Japanese elderly persons.

If the current economic status of American children seems bad, future demographic changes will make it even worse. Suppose the

TABLE 9

Effects of Demographic Changes on the Economic Status of the U.S. Population, 2050

	Poverty Ratio in 1991	Poverty Ratio Targeted for 2050	Poverty Ratio Actually Achieved in 2050*	Percentage Difference Between the Goal and the Achievement
Children	2.53	5.06	4.55	−10.1
Adults	3.65	7.30	6.73	−7.9
Elderly persons	3.03	6.06	5.82	−3.9
All persons	3.28	6.56	6.05	−7.8

*Under the assumption that each racial-ethnic population will succeed in doubling its average poverty ratio by 2050.

Source: Derived from U.S. Bureau of the Census (1992); U.S. Bureau of the Census (1993a, Table 2, pp. 12–55; 1993b, Table 1, pp. 2–3).

United States sets the goal of doubling the national average poverty ratio by 2050. Also suppose that each racial-ethnic population succeeds in doubling its average poverty ratio. What will happen to the national average? Because the white population will be gradually replaced by other racial-ethnic populations, it is expected that the nation as a whole will not succeed in doubling its average poverty ratio although each racial-ethnic population will double its own average poverty ratio. This discrepancy will result from the demographic changes. How much discrepancy will there be in 2050? Table 9 presents the results of the author's data analysis, which was based on the projected demographic changes from 1991 to 2050 (U.S. Bureau of the Census, 1993a, 1993b).

As Table 9 shows, as each racial-ethnic population of children increases its average poverty ratio by 100 percent by 2050 (thus doubling its average poverty ratio), the average poverty ratio of the entire population of children will come short of the target by 10.1 percent. In comparison, the entire populations of elderly persons and of adults will come short of the target by only 3.9 percent and 7.9 percent, respectively. In addition, the average

poverty ratio of the entire population of children, adults, and elderly persons will come short of the target by 7.8 percent.

A further analysis indicates that for the population of children to double its poverty ratio by 2050, the poverty ratio of each racial-ethnic population of children in 2050 must be 2.3 times that of 1991, compared with 2.1 times the 1991 poverty ratio required for each racial-ethnic population of elderly persons and 2.2 times the 1991 poverty ratio required for each racial-ethnic population of adults. Also, for the U.S. population to become twice as well off in 2050 as it was in 1991, the average poverty ratio of each racial-ethnic population in 2050 will have to be 2.2 times that of 1991.

Why does the improvement of the economic status of each racial-ethnic population not translate into a commensurate improvement for the entire population? The answer is simple. Except for the Asian population, the other racial-ethnic populations—Hispanics, blacks, and American Indians—all started from considerably lower poverty ratios in 1991 than did the white population. Thus, as these populations gradually displace the white population, they will push down the national average poverty ratio, although their

TABLE 10

Effects of Demographic Changes on the Relative Economic Standing of Children, 2050

Year	Children's Poverty Ratio as a Percentage of Adults'	Children's Poverty Ratio as a Percentage of Elderly Persons'
1991	69.3	83.5
2050	67.6	78.1

Source: Derived from U.S. Bureau of the Census (1992); U.S. Bureau of the Census (1993a, Table 2, pp. 12–55; 1993b, Table 1, pp. 2–3).

own average poverty ratios will increase at the same rate as does the white population's.

Because the adverse effects of demographic changes on the average poverty ratio of children will be greater, this poverty ratio will lag further behind those of adults and elderly persons if each racial-ethnic population of children is allowed to improve its poverty ratio only at the same rate as that for adults and elderly persons, which in this case is doubling the 1995 poverty ratio by 2050. Table 10 presents the results of the data analysis.

As Table 10 shows, from 1991 to 2050, the average poverty ratio of children will decline from 69.3 percent to 67.6 percent of the average poverty ratio of adults and from 83.5 percent to 78.1 percent of the average poverty ratio of elderly persons. In fact, the same decline in the relative economic status of children will result no matter what rate of increase in the poverty ratio is assumed. Thus, if there is no improvement in the poverty ratio of each racial-ethnic population of children, adults, and elderly persons from 1991 to 2050, the population of children will be worse off in 2050 than it was in 1991 by 10.1 percent, and children's average poverty ratio will decline from 69.3 percent to 67.6 percent of that of adults and from 83.5 percent to 78.1 percent of that of elderly persons.

These results indicate that as the racial-ethnic composition of the U.S. population changes over the years, the economic fortune of children will further decline in relation to other age groups. Children will fare worse than adults or elderly persons because the change in the racial-ethnic composition of the country will be the greatest among them.

In addition, with regard to the change in the age composition of the U.S. population, children will constitute a smaller proportion of the population in the coming decades (see Table 2). If there is a smaller proportion of American children in the future and if these children are raised in increasingly deteriorating economic circumstances relative to those of adults and elderly persons—which certainly can happen—then the United States will indeed be in a self-destructive econodemographic condition.

Effects of Other Demographic Changes and Economic Changes

The foregoing discussion on how demographic changes will affect the economic status of children presents only part of the story. In addition, changes in the living arrangements of children will have an adverse effect on their economic status. According to U.S. government data, the proportion of white children who lived only with their mothers increased from 6.1 percent in 1960 to 19.5 percent in 1991. Furthermore, the proportions of black children and of Hispanic children who did so increased from 19.9 percent in 1960 to 54.0 percent in 1991 and from 19.6 percent in 1980 to 26.6 percent in 1991, respectively (data for Hispanic children prior to 1980 are not available; U.S. House of Representatives, 1993, pp. 1119, 1122–1123).

Since the poverty rate of children (the percentage of children who are poor) who live only with their mothers has been high but relatively steady,[1] the surge in the poverty rate of children has been caused not by their high poverty rate but by the increase in the proportion of children who live only with mothers.

The increasing inequality in earnings among people of different age groups and between the better educated and the less educated have further compounded the deterioration of the economic status of children. According to the Committee on Ways and Means of the U.S. House of Representatives (1993, p. 596), men aged 16 to 24 who worked year-round full time in 1989 earned only 87 percent of the wages earned by their counterparts in 1978, whereas men aged 45 to 54 who worked year-round full time in 1989 earned 105 percent of the wages of their counterparts in 1978. College graduates earned 37 percent more than did high school graduates in 1978, but 53 percent more in 1989 (Murphy & Welch, 1993). Because children tend to live in households headed by relatively young workers, the deterioration in the earnings of young workers has adversely affected children. Also, because black and Hispanic parents have lower educational achievement[2] than do white parents and thus are overrepresented among low-wage workers, the growing disparity in earnings of the better educated and the less educated has adversely affected the economic status of black and Hispanic children.

All these forces—both demographic and economic—have adversely affected the economic status of children over time, as is dramatically indicated by the increasing poverty rate of children. Figure 1 shows the poverty rate of all children, compared with the poverty rates of elderly persons and all persons from 1959 to 1992. Figure 2 shows the poverty rates of white, Hispanic, and black children from 1975 to 1991. The poverty rates in these figures are based on the U.S. official poverty line (see Social Security Administration, 1994, Table 3.E1).

It is clear from Figures 1 and 2 that the poverty rate of children has been rising since 1969. Furthermore, it surpassed the poverty rate of the elderly in 1974, and climbed to 21.9 percent in 1992, or 1.7 times that of the elderly in that year (U.S. House of Representatives, 1994, p. 1158). Moreover, the poverty rate of black children was continuously the highest among all groups of children from 1975 to 1991. In addition, the poverty rate of Hispanic children was 40.4 percent in 1991, a record high since 1976, when data became available. The poverty rate of white children, though historically low compared with those of the other two groups of children, reached 16.8 percent in 1991, the highest since 1983 (U.S. House of Representatives, 1993, p. 1218).

Discussion and Conclusions

Demographic changes, over which individual children have no control, are expected to affect the economic standing of future generations of children. Compared with other forces, demographic changes are powerful and thus cannot be controlled, steered, or changed by legislation in the short term. The only course a

[1]During the past three decades, the poverty rate of all children who lived in female-headed families ranged from 48.6 percent in 1979 to 58.2 percent in 1966. Among white children, it ranged from 38.6 percent in 1979 to 47.1 percent in 1983 and 1991; among black children, it ranged from 63.1 percent in 1979 to 76.6 percent in 1966; among Hispanic children, it ranged from 64.3 percent in 1989 to 72.4 percent in 1985, during the period 1973–1991 for which data are available for the Hispanic group. (U.S. House of Representatives, 1993, p. 1220).

[2]In 1993, 81.5 of white persons aged 25 and over completed four years of high school or more, compared to 70.4 percent of their black counterparts and 53.1 percent of their Hispanic counterparts (U.S. Bureau of the Census, 1994, Table 232, p. 157).

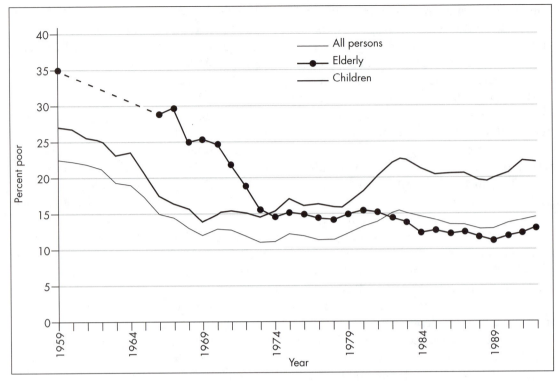

Figure 1 Poverty Rates by Age: 1959–1992

Source: U.S. House of Representatives (1994, Table H-4, p. 1158).

nation can take is to have a clear understanding of what its age composition and racial-ethnic composition will be in the coming decades and deal with the effects of the impending demographic changes in the years ahead.

A country's overriding concern should be the well-being of children because it is obvious that a society such as the United States, which raises children in measurably undesirable economic conditions, cannot expect to sustain high living standards for its population for long. There may be many reasons why the United States has placed its children in such dire circumstances. Recent economic changes are one reason; changes in the living arrangements of children are another. But, more important, whereas the United States established a clear social policy with regard to the well-being of elderly persons by enacting the Social Security Act in 1935 and its amendments in later years, it did not establish such a policy for children. The differential treatment of children and elderly persons as dependent populations is reflected in federal spending for the two groups. In 1990, the federal government spent only $1020 per child, compared with $11,350 per elderly person (U.S. House of Representatives, 1992, pp. 1579 and 1583). The government's failure to ensure a national minimum of income and health security for children, as it did for the elderly, will continue to

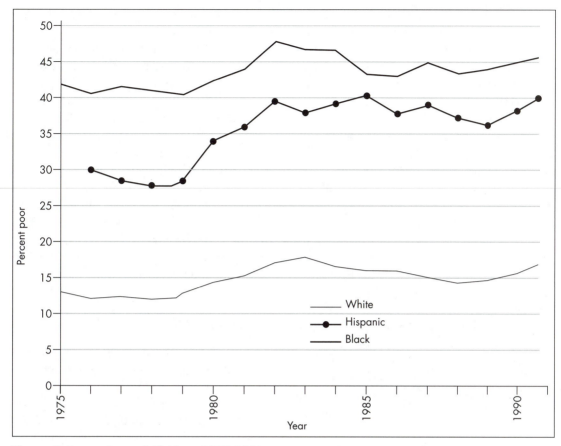

Figure 2 Poverty Rates of Children: 1975–1991

Note: Persons of Hispanic origin may be of any race.

Source: U.S. House of Representatives (1993, Table 68, p. 1218).

perpetuate the relative misery of American children, which will be compounded by the continuing demographic changes in the coming decades.

As long as many policymakers and politicians are busy attempting to downsize the federal role in social welfare spending and to eliminate welfare as it has functioned in the past, the nation will have no way of nurturing and educating its children far better than it has done. More pointedly, unless the United States, either under private or public auspices, chan-

nels more resources to children—especially to Hispanic, black, and American Indian children—the economic conditions of children will not only continue to deteriorate and to be worse than those of other age groups, but the inequality in children's economic status will continue to widen—and it is already considerably greater than that in most other industrial countries (Rainwater and Smeeding, 1995). Such greater inequality in economic standing among children can be expected to continue in the future unless Hispanic, black, and American Indian children are allowed to progress economically at a faster rate than do white children because these groups of children will increase proportionately more than will white children and because they are significantly worse off than white children are today.

The issues the United States faces seem clear: Is the nation ready to channel more resources to its children? Is it ready to do so in a way that will address the well-being of Hispanic, black, and American Indian children with greater fiscal force and commitment? And, if so, how can it do so?

Under the political heat of the "Contract with America," "downsizing government," and the inability of American civilization to survive "unless the government stops feeding women and children born out of wedlock," can this nation see the demographic imperative that lies ahead? In the future, social welfare spending for the elderly will inevitably increase as the aging of the population accelerates, and each child must be invested in with greater intensity as the proportion of children declines. In a broader perspective, the American public needs to know that the country's glory and preeminence in the world cannot be recaptured by depriving and destroying its offspring. The future of the United States lies in the recognition of these truths.

As the federal government retreats from its responsibility for caring for children and relinquishes its authority over many social welfare programs to the states, the role of local and state governments in educating and caring for the nation's children will be critical. Yet, income security of children can be ensured adequately and equitably only by the federal government. Furthermore, the financial responsibility for funding many social welfare programs for children will have to rest primarily with the federal government if all children are to be served with equal care and equal resources, regardless of where they live.

Social workers will be strong witnesses to the changing demographic and economic environment of children across the country. They will see American children living in a truly diverse society with greater economic inequality. Through practice in serving children individually, in developing child welfare programs, and in advocating new policies on behalf of children, they will ultimately contribute to the development of a nation with a hospitable environment that allows all children to grow, that is strong economically, and that is once again a proud country.

REFERENCES

Adamchak, D. J., & Friedman, E. A. (1983). Societal aging and generational dependency relationships: Problems of measurement and conceptualization. *Research on Aging* 5: 319–338.

Cowgill, D. O. (1981, April). Can we afford our aging populations? Paper prepared for the Conference on Economics of Aging, Kansas City, MO.

Hall, A., & Johnson, T. R. (1980). The determinants of planned retirement age. *Industrial and Labor Relations Review,* 33: 241–251.

Lampman, R. J. (1984). *Social welfare spending: Accounting for changes from 1950 to 1978.* New York: Academic Press.

Murphy, K. M., & Welch, F. (1993). Industrial change and the rising importance of skill. In S. Danziger and P. Gottschalk (Eds.), *Uneven tide: Rising inequality in America* (pp. 101–132). New York: Russell Sage Foundation.

Ozawa, M. N., and Kono, S. (1995). Child well-being in Japan: The high cost of economic success (Innocenti Occasional Papers, EPS 46). Florence,

Italy: International Child Development Center, UNICEF.

Quinn, J. F., & Burkhauser, R. V. (1994). Public policy and the plans and preferences of older Americans. *Journal of Aging & Social Policy*, 6: 5–20.

Rainwater, L., & Smeeding, T. M. (1995). Doing poorly: The real income of American children in a comparative perspective (Luxembourg Income Study Working Paper Series No. 127). Syracuse, NY: Maxwell School of Citizenship and Public Affairs.

Schulz, J. H. (1995). *The economics of aging* (6th ed.). Westport, CT: Auburn House.

Smeeding, T., Torrey, B. B., & Rein, M. (1988). Patterns of income and poverty: The economic status of children and the elderly in eight countries. In J. L. Palmer, T. Smeeding, and B. B. Torrey (Eds.), *The vulnerable* (pp. 89–119). Washington, DC: The Urban Institute Press.

Social Security Administration. (annual). *Annual statistical supplements, annual, to the Social Security Bulletin*. Washington, DC: Author.

Social Security Administration. (1994). *Annual statistical supplements, 1994, to the Social Security Bulletin*. Washington, DC: Author.

Stock, J. H., & Wise, D. A. (1990). The pension inducement to retirement: An option value analysis. In D. A. Wise (Ed.), *Issues in the economics of aging* (pp. 205–229). Chicago: University of Chicago Press.

U.S. Bureau of the Census. (1992). *Survey of income and program participation (SIPP) 1991 panel wave 3 core microdata file*. Washington, DC: Author.

U.S. Bureau of the Census. (1993a). *Population projection of the United States, by age, sex, race, and Hispanic origin: 1993 to 2050*. Current Population Reports, P25–1104. Washington, DC: U.S. Government Printing Office.

U.S. Bureau of the Census. (1993b). *U.S. population estimates, by age, sex, race, and Hispanic origin: 1980 to 1991*. Current Population Reports, P15–1095. Washington, DC: U.S. Government Printing Office.

U.S. Bureau of the Census. (1994). *Statistical abstracts of the United States, 1994* (114th ed.). Washington, DC: U.S. Government Printing Office.

U.S. House of Representatives, Committee on Ways and Means. (1992). *1992 Green book: Overview of entitlement programs*. Washington, DC: U.S. Government Printing Office.

U.S. House of Representatives, Committee on Ways and Means. (1993). *1993 Green book: Overview of entitlement programs*. Washington, DC: U.S. Government Printing Office.

U.S. House of Representatives, Committee on Ways and Means. (1994). *1994 Green book: Overview of entitlement programs*. Washington, DC: U.S. Government Printing Office.

Van de Water, P. N. (1984). Social-security financing: An overview of the issues and options. In C. D. Campbell (Ed.), *Controlling the cost of social security* (pp. 59–79). Lexington, MA: Lexington Books.

Wiatrowski, W. J. (1993). Factors affecting retirement income. *Monthly Labor Review*, 16(3): 25–35.

The Future Economic Landscape

Implications for Social Work Practice and Education

Nancy Rose

Since the late 1890s, social workers have recognized the central role that economic developments play in creating and responding to individual, family, and community needs. Early social work curricula included classes taught by leading economists and representatives from both industry and labor. Today, however, although economic changes are dramatically shaping the environment of social work practice, few social workers possess even a rudimentary knowledge of economics. This essay by Nancy Rose, professor of economics and director of the Women's Studies program at California State University, San Bernardino, critically analyzes some of the underlying trends that have shaped the U.S. economy since the mid-1970s and are likely to continue shaping into the 21st century. The primary trend, Rose argues, is the increasing gap in income and wealth between the rich and everyone else. This is a consequence of four factors: corporate restructuring through deindustrialization, downsizing, and outsourcing; ongoing global restructuring and internationalization of corporations; increased unemployment and underemployment; and government policies involving interest rates, taxes, trade, and the money supply that have favored owners over workers and the upper class over all others.

Rose is well-suited for the task, possessing an MSW from the University of North Carolina and a PhD in economics from the University of Massachusetts. She has published widely on women, welfare, and government work programs, and has been active in the women's movement and the welfare rights movement since the early 1970s.

When I was asked to write a short essay on what social workers should know about the economic landscape in the 21st century, I saw it as a challenging project. Understanding the most significant economic trends is clearly important for knowledgeable social workers because everything happens in the context of the economy—in a sense, it forms the base of the society. Projecting the future is actually relatively straightforward. What we need to do is to look at the underlying trends that have characterized the economy since the mid-1970s because these trends are likely to continue into the 21st century unless a political movement is sufficiently organized to challenge the status quo.

In writing this essay, I am hoping to be able to counter one of my pet peeves. Because economics is often described in a manner that makes it seem difficult to understand, economic policies are typically explained as though they are in the interest of working people when this is far from the truth. The most common example is policies about interest rates.

Briefly, the Federal Reserve Board raises interest rates in order to "cool off" the economy—to prevent inflation from increasing.

I would like to thank Mayo Toruño, Eileen Gambrill, and Michael Reisch for helpful comments on earlier versions of this essay.

This is explained as being "good for the economy" and, more broadly, "good for America." But whether or not this is good for you depends on your class status. When interest rates are raised, it becomes more expensive to borrow money. Consumers feel this when they try to obtain a mortgage to purchase a home or a loan to buy a car, and sometimes they need to postpone major purchases because of it. Business owners experience this when considering whether they should borrow money to invest in new buildings and machinery—that is, in capital goods. When investments are not undertaken because of the higher cost of borrowing, fewer jobs are created and unemployment rises. Increased numbers of people out of work makes it more difficult for those with jobs to get raises in wages and better working conditions because more people are willing to take their jobs. This is clearly *not* good for the average working person—though it can help owners by keeping wage costs lower.

Thus, perhaps the most critical implication of this essay for social work education is the importance of understanding the fundamentals of how the economy works in order to be able to look beyond the rhetoric and know what is really going on.

Growing Inequality in Income and Wealth

The most important trend to be aware of is the continually increasing gap in income and wealth between the rich and everyone else. Data from the Congressional Budget Office shows that the richest 1% of the population, which is projected to have an average after-tax income of $438,000 in 1996, now receives 12% of total national after-tax income (Shapiro, 1995). The top 20%—those usually referred to as "high income"—have a projected after-tax income averaging $89,000 in 1996, which is approximately one-half of the total national income (Shapiro, 1995).

The data regarding the changes in income between 1977 and 1992 tells a sobering story of the expansion in this inequality. As a result of the policies and trends that will be discussed below, the inflation-adjusted income (i.e., income measuring actual purchasing power) of the top 1% of the population rose a full 91% during these years! The income of the top 20% of the population increased 28% during these 15 years. In contrast to these gains, the income of the middle quintile remained about the same and the income of the bottom fifth of the population fell 17% (Shapiro, 1995).

This decline in the standard of living for working people can be seen in the falling purchasing power of wages. Whereas median wages (adjusted for inflation) increased 60% from the end of World War II through their high point in 1972, they have decreased approximately 20% since that time (Council of Economic Advisors, 1995, table B-45). In contrast, those at the top have seen their incomes rise substantially. A *Business Week* survey of the pay of chief executive officers (CEOs) found that, whereas their average pay was 42 times as high as that of the average factory worker in 1980, this differential more than tripled by 1995 so that the average CEO received 141 times as much as the average factory worker ("That Eye-Popping Executive Pay," 1994; "How High Can CEO Pay Go?" 1996).

Clearly illustrating the ongoing reality of gender and racial discrimination is the fact that income gaps have continued between women and men, and between people of color and whites. In 1994, median income for blacks was only 60% as much as it was for whites, and median wages for women were 74% as high as they were for men (for full-time, year-round workers). This has a direct impact on poverty rates and helps account for the abysmal fact that for at least the past 20 years (since the statistics began to be reported), approximately half of all families headed by African-American women have been below a seriously underestimated poverty line (Council of Economic Advisors, 1996, table B-29). Further, although the income gap between women and men narrowed from 59% in the late 1970s to the current 74%, this is not due to the success of right-wing policies, but to the more precipitous decline in wages for men compared to women and to the success of a cohort of women who have managed to do relatively well.

Although factors such as inferior education for people of color and occupational segregation for women are often acknowledged as contributing to these income gaps, the underlying causes are rarely recognized. In a nutshell, people of color have built this country, typically receiving low wages and working under hazardous conditions, a status maintained through some of the institutions challenged by affirmative action, which is currently under fierce attack by an array of forces. For women, their "place" has historically been seen as the home, where their work has not been recognized as real work because they have not been paid for it (unless they work in someone else's home); when they work for wages, they have not been taken as seriously as men and therefore not paid wages commensurate with their skills (see Amott and Matthaei, 1991).

In sum, the United States is increasingly becoming a society of a smaller group of wealthier people, primarily white, tightly holding on to what they perceive as belonging to them, while at the other end increasing numbers of people are worrying about whether they will be able to pay their bills.

Underlying Economic Trends

Why have the rich become so much richer at the expense of everyone else? The answer lies in four underlying and interrelated economic trends: (1) corporate restructuring, from deindustrialization (closing factories) in the 1970s to downsizing (layoffs) and outsourcing (purchasing parts from other companies) in the 1980s and 1990s; (2) continued global restructuring and internationalization of businesses, spurred, in part, by policies such as NAFTA (North American Free Trade Agreement); (3) increased unemployment and underemployment and the substitution of relatively secure, higher-wage jobs with lower-wage, often part-time and/or temporary, jobs; and (4) government policies that have favored owners over workers and the rich over everyone else.

These trends began in the mid-1970s, grew during the 1980s, and mushroomed in the 1990s. It is helpful to understand that they are responses to a long-term economic decline that reflects changes in the institutional structure of the economy (see Bowles, Gordon, and Weisskopf, 1990). This decline is reflected in a myriad of statistics, the most critical of which is a fall in the average rate of profit (profits divided by the value of plant and equipment) from its peak in 1966. Most important for this essay, these trends are likely to continue to characterize the economic landscape into the 21st century.

Let's look at these trends in further detail.

Corporate Restructuring

Although the term *restructuring* sounds technical and innocuous, its consequences have been far from that. Deindustrialization, which began in the wake of the severe recession of 1973–1975, has eliminated millions of manufacturing jobs, as factories have been converted into office buildings, shopping malls, or simply torn down (see Bluestone and Harrison, 1982, and Harrison and Bluestone, 1990). Often, plants with unionized work forces have been shut down, with the firms reopening in nonunion, lower-wage areas in the United States or in Third World countries.

By the 1980s, and through the 1990s, downsizing became an increasingly common mechanism by which to reduce total wage costs and boost profits. This often occurred in the wake of mergers and acquisitions (M&As), in which companies bought each other out, sometimes creating behemoth corporations as a result. Although the layoffs in the 1970s affected primarily blue-collar workers, these more recent rounds have also hit white-collar workers—and people who thought they would have their jobs for the rest of their lives have found themselves out of work. The largest downsizings during the 1990s have included a 1991 cut by General Motors of 70,000 workers, a 1993 I.B.M. reduction of 63,000, and AT&T's announcement in December 1995 that it was laying off 40,000 workers (*The Nation,* January 22, 1996, 3). Although the former workers face uncertain economic futures, owners applaud the increase in profits. This is often reflected in stock prices, which tend to increase in the wake of the layoff announcements (see Henwood, 1996).

An increasingly common tactic accompanying downsizing has been outsourcing, whereby companies contract out the production of parts to other firms instead of having them produced by workers at the parent company. These outside firms produce the parts at a lower cost, in large part by paying lower wages. In March 1996, General Motors' layoffs, in conjunction with outsourcing of brake parts to a nonunion company in South Carolina, led to a successful strike by the United Auto Workers—a bright spot in an otherwise gloomy picture of a decline in union strength.

By the 1990s, the epitome of restructuring occurred in the form of the "virtual corporation." A play on the term *virtual reality,* these generally highly profitable entities are composed of a core of (high-salaried) managers and staffed by "contingent" workers—temporary, often part-time, and easily expendable.

Global Restructuring

From the end of World War II until the mid-1970s, the United States was the most powerful country in the world, and therefore able to set the terms of the international monetary and trade systems. This hegemonic status was signified by the dollar's position as the basis of these systems. (Most importantly, many international transactions were carried out in dollars because it was the most desired currency, effectively forcing others to borrow dollars from the United States.) This situation ended in the early 1970s when the United States was forced to abandon the gold exchange standard and OPEC (the Oil Petroleum Exporting Countries) raised the price of oil. Since that time, the United States has not had as much control over world affairs in general, or the international monetary and trade systems in particular. Although the major capitalist countries meet annually to try to develop coordinated economic and trade policies, this group has no ability to enforce decisions.

The main response of the United States to this trend has been remilitarization. After declining from a peak during the Vietnam War, military expenditures (adjusted for inflation) slowly began to increase in the late 1970s and grew a full 50% between 1980 and their high point in 1987 (Council of Economic Advisors, 1996, table B-2). This trend picked up again in the mid-1990s. In spite of the deep cuts proposed for all social programs, both the Clinton administration and congressional Republicans plan increases in military expenditures over the next few years. In fact, Republicans voted in December 1995 to give the Pentagon $7 billion more than the $260 billion it had requested (*The Nation,* December 25, 1995, 812).

Other responses to this international environment have included the development of free-trade agreements, and the expansion of free-trade zones and production in Third World countries. Accords such as NAFTA (North American Free Trade Agreement) decrease import tariffs (taxes on goods coming into a country) and generally make it even easier to conduct business in other countries. In the wake of NAFTA, even more U.S. firms have opened plants in Mexico, especially *maquiladoras,* along the border with the United States, that take advantage of the much lower wages and higher unemployment and people's resultant desperation to work (see "A New Wave of *Maquiladoras,*" 1995, and Enloe, 1995).

Unemployment and Underemployment

Both corporate and global restructuring have contributed to the third underlying trend, as there has been a marked increase in unemployment and in underemployment (when people are employed in jobs below their skill level and/or do involuntary part-time work). Although the overall unemployment rate remained below 4% of the labor force during the mid to late 1960s, those figures are long gone. Since the economic crisis began in the mid-1970s, unemployment rates have remained above 5%, and have risen to 7%, 8%, and 9% during recessions (Council of Economic Advisors, 1995, table B-40).

One result of racial discrimination has been consistently higher unemployment rates for people of color compared to whites. In fact, during both good and bad economic times, rates for blacks have been 2 to $2^1/2$ times as high as they have been for whites. In 1995, for example, unemployment rates were 4.9% for white males and 4.8% for white females, compared to 10.6% for black males and 10.2% for black females. In addition, unemployment rates have consistently been approximately three times as high for youth aged 16 to 19 (Council of Economic Advisors, 1996, table B-39).

As troubling as these rates are, the official unemployment rates understate the extent of joblessness. First, only those who are actively looking for work are counted—people who become "discouraged" and drop out of the labor force are not even included. Further, people who have jobs below their skill level or who work part-time but would prefer full-time employment are counted as fully employed (instead of only partially employed). This higher real unemployment is reflected, in part, in the steady decline in labor force participation rates for men, as greater numbers of males have simply dropped out of the legitimate economy. (The aging of the population has also contributed to this decline, which began following World War II.) Although rates for white men fell from 83.4% in 1960 to 80% in 1970, 78.6% in 1980, and 75.7% by 1995, the drop for African-American men has been much steeper—from 83.0% in 1960 to 76.5% in 1970, 71.3% in 1980, and 69.0% by 1995 (Council of Economic Advisors, 1996, table B-36).

The most important result of high unemployment and underemployment has been an increase in jobs that are less safe and more tedious, that pay lower wages, and, in general, that contribute to more widespread economic insecurity and poverty. People become more willing to accept low-wage, part-time and/or temporary jobs—if they don't, someone else will. And if those with jobs voice complaints, they can easily be replaced.

Right-Wing Economic Policies

The main government response to the deteriorating economy has been implementation of right-wing economic policies, commonly known as supply-side economics, designed to boost profits. There have been five main types of policies.

Tax cuts—in both personal income and corporate profits—are considered the foundation of supply-side economics. According to supply-side theory, tax cuts will lead people to save more. Capitalists will use the additional savings to invest in plant and equipment, thereby creating more jobs as the fruits "trickle down" from those at the top to everyone else. However, in the past, instead of producing increased investment in plants and equipment, the extra income was used primarily for luxury consumption and financial speculation (see Bowles, Gordon, and Weisskopf, 1990). In fact, one result of the ensuing frenzy of speculation was increased instability in financial institutions—from the 500-point fall in the Dow Jones average in October 1987 to the many failures of savings and loans (S&Ls) and banks.

Tax cuts also contributed to the increase in income inequality discussed at the beginning of this essay. Although the effective federal income tax rate (taxes as a percentage of income) remained at 16.5% for the bottom 80% of families between 1977 and 1992, it fell from 35.5% to 29.3% for the top 1%. While taxes on corporate profits averaged 45% in the 1950s,

they have fallen almost by half to approximately 24% today (Folbre, 1995).

The second policy has been remilitarization, discussed earlier, which sought to help restore the premier position of the United States internationally. Bolstered by military ventures such as the invasion of Grenada and the Gulf War, remilitarization would help create a "good business climate" in less developed countries and thereby help ensure the profitability of multinational corporations (corporations with branches in more than one country).

The third response has been the tight monetary policy of the Federal Reserve. This began in earnest in October 1979 and led to the deep recession of 1981–1982, as overall unemployment rose above 10% of the labor force. Higher unemployment effectively helped discipline workers, and contributed to the increase in part-time, temporary work and to the fall in wages. It also took pressure off prices and lowered inflation, which had been high by historical U.S. standards—close to or over 10% from 1974 through 1981 (Council of Economic Advisors, 1996, table B-56).

The fourth type of response has put workers more directly on the defensive. This has been done through three sets of policies that began in 1978 and 1979 and increased under the Reagan administration. The "safety net" of social welfare programs was shredded as a variety of programs—most importantly AFDC and unemployment compensation—were constricted and funding was slashed (see Greenstein, 1984). These cuts have intensified under the current Republican onslaught (see the essay by Mark Stern in this volume). This policy has eviscerated the "cushion against unemployment" and increased the "cost of job loss," as people have less to fall back on if they're unemployed and so are more willing to accept lower wages and worse working conditions.

Workers were also put on the defensive through anti-union policies. Beginning with the defeat of labor law reform in 1978, policies quickly heightened under the Reagan administration. Soon after taking office in 1981, Reagan fired the striking PATCO (Professional Air Traffic Controllers Organization) workers, and appointed people who were generally opposed to labor unions to serve on the NLRB (National Labor Relations Board, which was established in 1935 to protect the rights of workers to organize unions of their own choosing and bargain collectively). This anti-union atmosphere contributed to a fall in union membership as a percentage of all employees, from about 30% in 1954 to 10.4% in 1996 (Folbre, 1995; Hornblower 1996).

In addition, the purchasing power of the minimum wage was severely eroded. This undermined wages for all low-wage workers because the minimum wage serves as a floor for low wages in general; when it is raised, other low wages also usually increase. Throughout the 1980s, the minimum wage remained at $3.35 per hour; it was raised by the federal government to only $4.25 in 1990 to $4.75 in 1996. Yet prices continued to climb, so that the purchasing power of the minimum wage fell 30% from 1981 through 1995 (Council of Economic Advisors, 1996, table B-56). Viewed from another angle, in order to simply have the same purchasing power that it had at its peak in 1968, the minimum wage would have to be increased to $7 per hour (in 1995 dollars).

The final component of right-wing economic policies has been deregulation. Explained as cutting unnecessary red tape and thereby allowing businesses to pursue profits more freely, some of the protections provided by OSHA (Occupational Safety and Health Administration), the EPA (Environmental Protection Agency), and the Equal Employment Opportunity Commission (EEOC) were undone. Budgets were cut and, as with the NLRB, the Reagan administration appointed "foxes to guard the chicken coops," as people were appointed to head agencies whose missions they opposed. We see the results in increased industrial hazards, continuing environmental degradation, and attacks on affirmative action. In addition, deregulation of specific industries—for example, airlines and trucking—has contributed to mergers and downsizing, as more profitable firms have bought out less profitable ones (see Bowles, Gordon, and Weisskopf, 1990).

Implications for Social Work Practice, Education, and Research

The trends described in this essay are likely to continue into the 21st century unless opposition to the right-wing policies that have allowed them to flourish is sufficiently organized. This has implications for social work practice, education, and research.

The main implication for social work education is the importance of including a basic knowledge of economics as part of the curriculum. Most helpful is a progressive political economic perspective because mainstream theories often justify the status quo without providing a critical look (see the "Helpful Sources" at the end of this essay). Understanding how the economy works—and doesn't work—can be empowering. Such understanding can help one make sense of economic gyrations and of policies that otherwise simply seem to be mean-spirited, can help social workers better understand the societal causes of some of the problems manifested by individuals, and can help one articulate a vision of a just society.

This is particularly important because the continuation of the trends discussed in this essay means a likely increase in income inequality, poverty, and social dislocation, and an accompanying rise in tension, violence, and racism. Pat Buchanan's strong showing in his bid for the 1996 Republican presidential nomination, based on a combination of economic populism and sexist, racist, nativist, and homophobic rhetoric and proposals, was a forceful public testament to the power of these ideas.

Further, in terms of practice, social workers will likely be called on to deal with some of the manifestations of the increased stress of unemployment and economic insecurity, in both the accompanying heightened child abuse, alcoholism, and depression, as well as in the general societal tension and violence. In addition, if current trends of reduced government expenditures on social programs continue, which is also probable, social workers will most likely be called on to do more and more with fewer and fewer resources. This is a clear prescription for burn-out.

There are also implications for community organizing. Instead of accepting the common scapegoats—primarily welfare mothers and undocumented workers—and the racism and sexism underlying their choice as targets, we can help people understand where the problem really lies: in an economic system based on profits that favors the rich. This also calls for the articulation of an alternative vision of economic and social welfare policies, which I will briefly sketch.

I should begin by saying that, although almost two decades of right-wing domination make these policies seem unrealistic at this time, it is important to have a long-range

vision of what would characterize a just society. In place of supply-side, trickle-down policies that favor the rich and corporations, we need "bubble-up" policies that get money into the hands of those at the bottom of the economic ladder. As we saw during the Great Depression of the 1930s, such policies have a "percolator effect," as the money is quickly spent on goods and services, inducing business owners to expand production and hire more workers. Thus, it is far more likely to lead to economic expansion than the welfare for the rich and corporations that characterizes supply-side policies.

Instead of basing investment and disinvestment decisions solely on expected profits, capitalists need to be accountable to local communities. Such accountability could involve complying with policies that mandate advance notice of layoffs and several months severance pay, as well as policies facilitating worker and/or public ownership of businesses. Social workers throughout the United States have, no doubt, seen the effects on towns when thousands of employees are laid off, thus undermining individual workers as well as the viability of the towns themselves. Such a situation was clearly depicted in Michael Moore's film, *Roger and Me*, which documented the devastating effects of General Motor's plant closings in Flint, Michigan.

Economic security could be enhanced through family policies, labor market policies, and job creation programs. These would be based on recognizing both women's work in the home as socially useful labor and society's responsibility for children, and would enable both women and men to combine work in the home with wage-labor while maintaining an adequate standard of living. Family policies should include replacing income-tested AFDC with a family allowance as payment for the work of raising children, federally funded health care, subsidized child care, expanded family leave (for example, paying 90% of the person's wages for six months), and an adequate supply of low-cost housing. The United States could simply copy policies that have been implemented in all of the other industrialized countries (except South Africa). These programs should be provided by the federal government, as opposed to state and local governments and/or private companies, and should be universalized so that the poor are not stigmatized.

Labor market policies should include increasing the minimum wage and indexing future raises to the rate of inflation, expanding the EITC (Earned Income Tax Credit) for the working poor, invigorating affirmative action, implementing a pay equity policy to help close the income gaps between women and men and between people of color and whites, and undoing the damage done to labor unions since the late 1970s. Rounding these out would be expanded employment and training programs and a job creation program, with the government creating jobs—with voluntary participation and payments connected to labor market wages—for those who are not absorbed by the private sector.

We have examples in our own history of innovative programs that attempted to provide for working people. This is especially true of job creation programs, which were part of the economic and social landscape through the Works Progress Administration (WPA) in the 1930s and Comprehensive Employment and Training Act (CETA) in the 1970s. Even though they are typically dismissed as failures, millions of people were put to work on a wide variety of projects: constructing buildings and roads, running community arts and recreation programs, providing additional services for hospitals and police departments,

and sewing clothing and canning food. In fact, criticisms that the WPA and CETA provided unnecessary "make-work" can be countered by understanding the constraints imposed on the programs to prevent them from becoming "too attractive" to workers and from offering alternatives to the logic of production-for-profit. For example, the programs were supposed to provide useful work but not replace normal government workers. However, this easily led to the conclusion that if the work were truly necessary, the government would do it, and that it must therefore be "make-work" (see Rose, 1994 and Rose, 1995).

Comprehensive programs could build on proposals that were developed, but never enacted, by federal entities from the 1930s through the 1970s. Proposals made in 1942 and 1943 by the National Resources Planning Board, a federal-level planning agency, as well as the original versions of the 1935 Social Security Act, the Employment Act of 1946, and the 1978 Humphrey–Hawkins Act, all had a much broader vision—that everyone has the right to enjoy socially useful work and freedom from poverty—than the constricted legislation that eventually came into being (see Rose, 1995).

These programs would be expensive, but the money could easily be found. It can come from: rescinding the tax breaks for corporations and the rich, which have been implemented since 1981; seriously cutting military expenditures; requiring those responsible for the failures of banks and savings and loans to end their dependency on the government and pay for the bailouts themselves; and a tax on the sale of assets held less than a year (which would also discourage speculation).

Bringing these ideas into the public discourse will involve expanding the boundaries of what is seen as mainstream debate. In place of the mean-spirited vision that has dominated recent policies, we need one that treats people with respect. Instead of policies that increase income for the rich at the expense of everyone else, we need policies that are grounded in meeting people's basic needs.

Helpful Sources about the U.S. Economy

Michael D. Yates, *Longer Hours, Fewer Jobs* (New York: Monthly Review Press, 1994), is an excellent brief history of the role of unemployment in the U.S. economy. It is part of the Cornerstone Series of short, easily accessible books about various social, political, economic, and historical phenomena.

Nancy Folbre and the Center for Popular Economics, *The New Field Guide to the U.S. Economy: A Compact and Irreverent Guide to Economic Life in America* (New York: New Press, 1995), has one-page explanations on a range of topics, including the economics of the environment, health care, education, and welfare, as well as the global economy, government budgets and macroeconomics, and the economic situations of owners, workers, women, and people of color. Filled with charts, graphs, and cartoons, and including a helpful glossary of terms, it imparts a great deal of information in an easily understandable manner.

Samuel Bowles, David M. Gordon, and Thomas E. Weisskopf, *After the Wasteland: A Democratic Economics for the Year 2000* (Armonk, NY: M. E. Sharpe, 1990), is probably the best all-around book about the U.S. economy since World War II. Based on the theory of social structures of accumulation, it explains the rise and subsequent decline of the economy and develops policies for a democratic economic system. Numerous graphs and charts illustrate the history and theory.

David M. Gordon, *Fat and Mean: The Corporate Squeeze of Working Americans and the Myth of Managerial "Downsizing"* (New York: The Free Press, 1996), is a very readable book that locates the main cause of declining wages in bloated corporate bureacracies—"fat and mean" instead of "lean and mean"—and develops alternative policies based on incentives and wage-led productivity growth.

Bennett Harrison and Barry Bluestone, *The Great U-Turn: Corporate Restructuring and the Polarizing of America* (New York: Basic Books, 1990), is another accessible book that focuses on the deindustrialization and right-wing economic policies of the 1980s and the resultant increase in income inequality.

Dollars and Sense (One Summer Street, Somerville, MA 02143) is a progressive economics journal that began publication in the early 1970s. Currently published bimonthly, the articles are short and written for noneconomists. In addition to the journals, the publishers put out *Real World Macro* and *Real World Micro,* extremely useful collections of articles about the micro- and macroeconomy, as well as various readers about, for example, women in the global economy, the banking system, and the Contract with America.

Mayo Toruño, *The Political Economics of Capitalism* (Ames, Iowa: Kendall-Hunt, 1994), is a more theoretical book that synthesizes Marxist, neo-Ricardian, and Keynesian economics. For those seeking a more thorough understanding of the workings of the economy, this is a good introductory text.

Finally, in my book, *Workfare or Fair Work: Women, Welfare, and Government Work Programs* (New Brunswick, NJ: Rutgers University Press, 1995), each chapter (aside from the introductory first chapter) looks at a decade from the 1930s through the 1990s (with the 1940s and 1950s combined), beginning with a description of the economy, the social and political environment, and the economic situation of women and people of color.

REFERENCES

Amott, Teresa L., and Julie A. Matthaei, *Race, Gender, and Work: A Multicultural Economic History of Women in the United States* (Boston: South End Press, 1991).

Bluestone, Barry, and Bennett Harrison, *The Deindustrialization of America: Plant Closings, Community Abandonment, and the Dismantling of Basic Industry* (New York: Basic Books, 1982).

Bowles, Samuel, David M. Gordon, and Thomas E. Weisskopf, *After the Wasteland: A Democratic Economics for the Year 2000* (Armonk, NY: M. E. Sharpe, 1990).

"Bunker Bill," *The Nation* (December 25, 1995): 812.

Council of Economic Advisors, *Economic Report of the President* (Washington, DC: U.S. Government Printing Office, various years).

Enloe, Cynthia, "The Globetrotting Sneaker," *MS.* (March/April 1995): 10–15.

Folbre, Nancy, and the Center for Popular Economics, *The New Field Guide to the U.S. Economy: A Compact and Irreverent Guide to Economic Life in America* (New York: New Press, 1995).

Greenstein, Robert, *End Results: The Impact of the Federal Policies Since 1980 on Low-Income Americans* (Washington DC: Center on Budget and Policy Priorities, 1984).

Harrison, Bennett, and Barry Bluestone, *The Great U-Turn: Corporate Restructuring and the Polarizing of America* (New York: Basic Books, 1990).

Henwood, Doug, "The Dow and the Joneses," *The Nation* (April 1, 1996): 3–4.

Hornblower, Margot, "Labor's Youth Brigade," Time (July 15, 1996): 44–45.

"How High Can CEO Pay Go?" *Business Week* (April 22, 1996): 100–106.

"A New Wave of *Maquiladoras*," *Business Week* (June 26, 1995): 30.

"A Real Budget Vote," *The Nation* (January 22, 1996): 3.

Rose, Nancy E., *Put to Work: Relief Programs in the Great Depression* (New York: Monthly Review Press, 1994).

Rose, Nancy E., *Workfare or Fair Work: Women, Welfare, and Government Work Programs* (New Brunswick, NJ: Rutgers University Press, 1995).

Shapiro, Isaac, *Unequal Shares: Recent Income Trends Among the Wealthy* (Washington, DC: Center for Budget and Policy Priorities, November 1995).

"That Eye-Popping Executive Pay: Is Anybody Worth This Much?" *Business Week* (April 25, 1994): 52–58.

The Impact and Implications of Multiculturalism

John F. Longres

A conversation between two social work students:
White female: *Am I a racist if I won't marry a man of another race?*
Black female: *No. I would never consider marrying a white man.*

Few could deny that a current buzz word of the nineties is multiculturalism. We live in a multicultural society in which people have different values and norms. Professor Longres takes a critical look at the impact and implications of current approaches to multiculturalism and makes suggestions for the future. He suggests that multiculturalism discard cultural pluralism in favor of culture amalgamation and that intergroup relations be the focus of multicultural practice. John F. Longres is professor and associate dean at the School of Social Work, the University of Washington, Seattle, WA. He is the editor of the Journal of Social Work Education *and has published widely in the area of social work. He is the author of* Human Behavior in the Social Environment *(Itasca, IL: Peacock, 1990).*

Multiculturalism is arguably the most important issue in the social services today. It offers both an explanation and a solution to the problems confronting clients of color and those who would serve them. As such, it affects policy, program development, and the delivery of direct services. This essay defines multiculturalism, critically assesses it, and proposes to redirect it.

The Societal Context of Multiculturalism

Ethnic divisions have been a major source of conflict throughout the world, and in the United States such divisions have been with us from the beginning. Although ethnic conflict is reflected in economic inequality, the former is nevertheless independent of the latter. Economic conflict pits owners, management, and the professional classes against the skilled and unskilled labor they hire. Conflict shows up as disputes in the workplace and over the distribution of wealth and income in a society. Ethnic struggles, on the other hand, are struggles over national and cultural identity: the language we speak, the holidays we celebrate, the legal and religious systems we espouse, and, in more general terms, the social mores and traditions we follow. They are also struggles over national physical identity: the phenotype of our gods and mythical heroes; the physiognomy of our idealized selfhood, our beauty queens and conquering heroes; the physical image we project to the world of nation states. Ethnic struggles are intimate and often carry a sexual connotation. They take place close to home, in the development of neighborhood and friendship cliques. Not unusually, they are also quarrels about the nature of home and the proper household, over the suitability of marital and sexual partners, and over the definition of bloodlines.

Ethnic struggles, like economic struggles, lead to stratification, systems of ranking where some ethnic groups stand over others, determining the culture and defining the phenotype and in the process commanding a greater share of the social, political, and material rewards produced by society. In the United States, peoples from northern and western European nations have come to dominate, followed by those from southern and eastern Europe, and under them the various "people of color" from Latin America, Asia, Africa, and North America. The weapons of ethnic struggles may be violent and brutal: Africans were enslaved and Native Americans were driven from their lands, to cite but two examples. Regardless of level of brutality, the weapons of ethnic struggles always include words: ethnocentric ideas and beliefs, prejudice, and negative stereotyping. In this war of words, the dominant usually exalt themselves, while denigrating the culture and very being of the dominated.

The Multicultural Response

This is the context of multiculturalism as we know it today in the United States: It is the response of the intellectual leaders of subordinated ethnic groups, their solution to the denigration experienced at the hands of "European Americans." Although it burst onto the scene during the past two decades, it is not a new idea. Echoes of it were expressed earlier in this century and, in fact, its roots lie in the 17th-century concept of the *Volkgeist* (spirit of the people), developed by Herder and other German romantic philosophers (Finkielkraut, 1995). Like its predecessors, multiculturalism is bathed in an ethnic revival, and so it is not surprising that its principal expression is the celebration of past and present, real and putative, cultural traditions. Its present incarnation is born out of the failure of American institutions to successfully incorporate people of color—what Gunnar Myrdal appropriately called the American dilemma (1944). A country built on the philosophy that all are created equal still treats a significant number of individuals unequally. A country built on the principle of individual achievement still judges individuals by the parental phenotype. America promised equal economic, political, and social opportunity but failed to keep its promise for people of color.

Although multiculturalism means many things to many people, it is possible to piece together one prominent and common meaning. I will describe this—though later I will call attention to another meaning that is slowly emerging and that I believe may be, in the end, a more fruitful way of thinking about multiculturalism—but that is getting ahead of myself.

The most prominent meaning of multiculturalism is economic and political integration coupled with cultural separation. Members of marginalized ethnic groups want greater opportunity for participating and enjoying the benefits of our economic and political institutions. They argue that they were left out of the economic and political mainstream and want a chance to move into it. However, members of marginalized ethnic groups also want greater opportunity for maintaining their unique heritage. In the cultural arena,[1] they argue that they were forced to assimilate into Anglo-European ways and want no more of it. Multiculturalism takes the idea of "a nation of immigrants" away from the melting pot and into the mosaic. As European Americans maintained the color line by shutting the door on social and sexual integration, people of color have responded in kind. They demand that their cultural patterns be recognized as unique and allowed to flourish unencumbered by expectations of acculturation. They may consent to biculturation, the ability to move easily between the dominant world and their own, but they eschew full cultural integration. They want to protect their culture by keeping to themselves, marrying among their own, and raising children who will continue their traditions.

Theoretical support for multiculturalism is based on cultural relativity and social constructivism. Multiculturalists argue that culture emerges out of a process of social interaction. As a result, there is no one type of social organization; no one way by which the cultural achievements of one group may be judged superior to those of another; no universal standard by which to evaluate the beliefs, values, traditions, and lifestyles developed by societies. Moreover, there is no ineluctable evolutionary progression from primitive to advanced society. Those groups that dominate ethnic and racial hierarchies do so not because of intrinsic worth but because they have managed to seize power. Cultures may be different but they aren't better.

A second theoretical support is to be found in the related concepts of ethnic identity and self-esteem. Multiculturalists commonly assert that prejudice and discrimination place people from subordinated groups at risk for low self-esteem, which in turn makes it difficult for them to achieve in school and in the workplace. A strong ethnic identity is believed to be the corrective for this. Only when people know about the accomplishments of their group and have a strong allegiance to its traditions and values can they have the confidence to succeed.

The Social Service Response

Multiculturalism is clearly influencing the social services. Because a major goal is to gain access to the resources that allow for success, people of color see the welfare industry as a means to an important end. But they also see it as an industry that has contributed to their denigration and, moreover, to the demise of their cultural heritage. People of color, therefore, both need and distrust the social services and, as a result, the welfare industry and the university programs that educate those who would work in them have become arenas of multicultural wars. These wars pit those who would deliver "traditional" services, the services associated with an oppressive past, against those who would advocate for a liberated future through multiculturalism.

From the point of view of people of color, many successes are evident. In spite of hostility to multiculturalism in the larger environment, no serious challenge is evident among leaders in social work education and practice (Van Soest, 1995). Social workers now daily proclaim their commitment to cultural diversity and pluralism, and "assimilation" has become anathema. In social work education, for instance, accreditation standards have mandated supportive content on racial and ethnic groups for well over two decades.

[1]There is no consensus on the meaning of the term *culture*. Here it is used to describe those traditions—including, but not limited to, linguistic, religious, and familial—that have been inbued with value among people who consider themselves a community.

During this period, phrases such as "ethnic sensitive" and "cultural competence" have become commonplace. Although the meaning of such terms remains vague, in one way or another they refer to designing policies and programs that can meet the twin objectives of economic and political integration through the celebration of cultural differences.

At the same time, researchers continue to document the various ways by which policies and programs limit access, discriminate, or otherwise provide inferior service. They have shown that cultural background influences the way clients identify problems, and seek and accept help and, conversely, how those operating from a European mind-set can easily misperceive culturally different behavior (Green, 1995). Helping professionals and the students who would succeed them have been scrutinized for evidence of prejudice and stereotyping. Practitioners and students of color are cautioned to rid themselves of internalized racism and assimilationist tendencies. As an indication of the overriding success of multiculturalism, university courses, in-service training, texts, and articles in professional journals on multicultural practice issues have proliferated. In the beginning, ethnic-sensitive practice was promoted as an alternative to mainstream or "monocultural" practice. Today, although the rhetoric of "nontraditional" lingers, ethnic sensitivity is in fact the mainstream, and there is every reason to believe that it will continue to be so into the foreseeable future.

A Critique of Multiculturalism

The ultimate test of multiculturalism is its ability to significantly improve the status of people of color—that is, to produce economic and social justice. In particular, we must be concerned about its ability to help those historical minorities that have been mired in high rates of poverty or subjected to systematic exclusion from the social mainstream. Yet, it is in this very area that the potential of multiculturalism may be questioned. Van Soest (1995) notes that a hidden debate in the otherwise apparent success of multiculturalism is the inability of social work to rally around the cause of economic and social justice. Regardless of whether justice is defined as equality, equity, or simply equal opportunity, a profession committed to social and economic justice would develop very different programs, services, and educational models from those that presently exist. The welfare industry has historically been unable to rise above a focus on private troubles and the development of myriad talk therapies to deal with them. At best, we end up putting Band-Aids on the subordinated. At worst, we regulate and control them. Any way you look at it, we continually fail to create the opportunities or the within- and across-group connections necessary for collective success.

As multiculturalism went from alternative to mainstream, its commitment to social and economic justice became increasingly muted. Although some multiculturalists have cried out for activism (Dean, 1977; Hardy-Fanta, 1986), the major ethnic-sensitive models of today (Lum, 1996; Green, 1995; De Anda, 1984; De Hoyos et al., 1986; Devore & Schlesinger, 1994), although acknowledging racism and a history of discrimination, devote relatively little attention to methods for social and economic justice. Even specialized ethnic agencies, whose renaissance is rooted in civil rights movements, don't appear to have a very clear social reform focus (Iglehart & Becerra, 1995). This, of course, is the history of the profession. We have long struggled to determine if social reform is indeed part of our mission. But that is just the point. Multiculturalism, which promised reform, is on the verge of becoming just one more method of dealing with private troubles. It is becoming, in Steinberg's (1995) words, part of a more general "retreat from racial justice in American thought and policy."

Even with regard to private troubles, it is not clear that multiculturalism is particularly effective. Direct service providers promote cultural sensitivity on the assumption that social work, although effective with white, middle-class Americans, is not effective with people of color. Unfortunately, no evaluation studies exist to support this assumption. No studies can be found that compare "ethnic-sensitive" and "non-ethnic-sensitive" models of practice. Videka-Sherman (1988), in her review of mental health evaluation studies, points out that most fail to report client racial characteristics. Although there are "grounds for optimism" (Rubin, 1985), it is far from clear that social work practice is effective regardless of population. The popularity of multicultural approaches to direct service, like so many other approaches, rests largely on their potential.

Process evaluations suggest that multiculturalism is associated with increased satisfaction (Gomez, 1985) and increased use of services, but this may be a dubious success. Much of the social work discussion of multiculturalism assumes that people of color are "underserved" in the social services, yet this is not the case when the broad array of social services is taken into account. Witness the disproportionate numbers using public welfare, child welfare, and criminal justice services. People of color are also increasingly evident in community mental health services, where the term *underserved* is most commonly used (O'Sullivan, Peterson, Cox, and Kirkeby, 1989). In terms of the larger society, where the debate over multiculturalism rages, the overrepresentation of people of color in the social services is used as evidence that social services, however ethnically sensitive, are irrelevant to the economic and political advancement of people of color.

Multiculturalism has been more successful in championing the cause of cultural separatism. Almost all approaches to ethnic sensitivity start from the premise of "cultural pluralism," or what Van Soest refers to as the "increasing concern that cultural amalgamation might not be possible or desirable" (1995, p. 55). It will be my objective to challenge this tenet of multiculturalism—that is, to argue that cultural amalgamation is not only possible but desirable and a key toward achieving an end to ethnic stratification as we know it in contemporary America.

Multiculturalism is becoming bogged down in nationalism, the celebration and reification of culture. It needs a good dose of reflective, critical analysis if it is to get back on track. It substitutes slogans like "celebrate diversity" for critical analysis. Diversity is a fact of life and as such is neither intrinsically good nor bad. Human societies have developed a wide range of cultural patterns, but must we celebrate them all? Anyone concerned with the place of women, gays and lesbians, and the disabled in society must surely be wary of an exaggerated concern for cultural self-determination. For instance, should we celebrate patriarchal institutions, including the circumcision of women, their cloistering behind veils, marrying them off at age 12, and the like?

Jayasuriya (1992) calls attention to the difference between sociological and cultural relativity. Cultural relativity argues that people may develop an endless variety of normative patterns, each one equally valuable. Sociological relativity acknowledges that people may develop an endless variety of norms but reserves the right to question their relative worth. Multiculturalists need to turn their attention to helping sort out what should and should not be celebrated.

Although multiculturalists rely on social constructivism, they have used it largely as a critique of the universalistic claims underpinning Western dominance and often fail to turn its lens inward. If all cultures were truly of equal merit, why should we fight so hard to have our children preserve their heritage? Why limit their friends and sexual partners to their group? Why not let them pick and choose and, in the process, help piece together a new and unifying American culture? It is only when the aim is to demonstrate that *our* way is better than *their* way, that we feel the need to conserve a heritage.

Ethnocentrism has many causes, but a major one is found in its connection with self-esteem. To the extent that self-esteem is rooted in ethnic identity—and it is—in-group favoritism and the derogation of out-group members follows automatically (Brown, 1986). There is, therefore, a basic contradiction in multiculturalism: Although we wish to celebrate difference, we end up celebrating ourselves at the expense of others. When we raise our children to defend their heritage against its possible corruption, we are teaching ethnocentrism. When we create social services that work to preserve a cultural heritage, we ferment and deepen ethnic competition and hostility.

In a society marked by ethnic stratification, it is not surprising that the study of culture has become an exercise in proving the superiority of one group over another. Claims of a "culture of poverty" among the "underclass" are matched by claims of a "culture of strength and resistance" among "oppressed people." As all cultures are marked by tensions and contradictions, weaknesses and strengths, neither description is entirely accurate. We should not condone the derogation of culture, but neither should we romanticize culture through "political correctness" (Gross, 1995). Although political correctness is no more associated with multiculturalism than it is with those who would challenge it, it ultimately weakens the analytic potential of multiculturalism. To work for economic and social justice, we need to look at both the external and internal contexts of group life. We need to understand how racism and ethnocentrism limit social and economic success, but we also need to know how individual and group adaptations may themselves make overcoming oppressive circumstances more difficult.

Toward the Future of Multiculturalism

American society is racked by increasing ethnic and racial hostilities. It is also racked by class and gender hostilities and by hostility rooted in sexual orientation and physical abilities. The role of the welfare industry, at least as I see it, is to intervene in these hostilities in a way that ensures that American society will continue to function in relative harmony and stability. A basic function of the social services is to advocate for the subordinate against the dominant—that is, to achieve social and economic justice, not just across ethnic and racial groups, but within them as well. This goal will not be achieved if multiculturalism continues to espouse cultural separation and if cultural relativity and the need to develop strong ethnic identities continues to be its cornerstone.

I propose that we reconsider the melting pot. Ethnic and racial minorities are right to reject assimilation—giving up one heritage in favor of that of another—but we should not reject amalgamation. The melting pot promised that all groups would blend into one and in the process create a unique culture that would be a combination of all of them. Multiculturalism should be taken from the social to the psychological, from the structure of our environment to the structure of our inner selves. Having melted, we become not another but each other.

Melting pots take time, yet over the history of the United States it is clear that we are producing one. Immigrants from Europe, once considered physically and culturally different, have melted into a more or less indistinguishable mass. Even at the level of religion, crossgroup progressive and orthodox ideologies constitute a greater bond than the historical division among Catholic, Protestant, and Jew (Hunter, 1991) . We should not, however, underestimate the melting being done by "people of color."[2] Many, perhaps even a majority of, Native Americans are of mixed heritage. The rates of out-marriage by Asian- and Latino-Americans continue to be very high. African Americans have lower rates, but even among them, the rates are relatively high and increasing (U. S. Bureau of the Census, 1994). Americans are becoming darker and our culture increasingly resembles our different backgrounds. American culture is hardly a simple recreation of English or even European culture. That it has been greatly influenced by Western traditions is readily apparent. That it is being influenced by non-Western traditions should be equally apparent.

---

[2] The concept of race presumably refers to biological differences among groups of people. Anthropologists are clear, however, that there are no pure races, and every classification system, including that used by the U.S. Census, is ultimately arbitrary, expressing not a racial but a political reality. The term "people of color," which is not an official designation, has become popular, and in everyday usage can refer to just about anyone, regardless of phenotype, whose origins are in some way connected to Africa, Asia, or Latin America including the Caribbean.

We should not minimize the difficulties of the melting pot. Racism is real and it works especially against the amalgamation of African Americans. We will need to get over our cultural traditions—owned as much by white as by black Americans—of dividing our world into black and white. We should be heartened in this regard by the growth of the "biracial" or "multiracial" identity movement (Wright, 1994). People of mixed heritage are demanding that they be able to incorporate identities that reach into all their parental backgrounds; that they be able to mark all the boxes that apply. This movement has major implications and is the basis for a redefinition, not only of multiculturalism, but of ethnic-sensitive social service practice.

Multiculturalism should discard cultural pluralism in favor of cultural amalgamation. Ours is indeed a culturally plural nation and we must always celebrate our origins. This does not mean, however, that we must conserve them. This point of view is beginning to be expressed in the social work literature. Gould (1995) contends that we have misconstrued multiculturalism and that we should work to build a "multicultural identity for all groups" and leaders, quoting Hartman (1990), who "find their identities in the synthesis of groups." The role of social workers in an increasingly melted America, as Fong, Spickard, and Ewalt (1995) suggest, is to break down the binary thinking that leads us to force clients into single categories that engulf them in an ethnic role.

The quest for social and economic justice, however, should continue to form the basis of multicultural thinking. This requires us to direct our attention to the use of all existing opportunities and to work to create new opportunities for social and economic achievement when they are lacking. But it also means that we need to devise approaches that allow us to advance justice and the melting pot by effectively managing cross-group conflict.

I suggest that intergroup relations be the focus of multicultural practice. Presently multiculturalism is directed at providing relevant services to individuals and families. We cannot altogether do away with these, but we can add to them a focus on cross-group relations—that is, on building, through our services and practice methods, bridges over which separated communities may become one. We can help different groups explore their common human needs. We can help different groups identify with and support their common familial, educational, and occupational aspirations. We can encourage integrated living patterns and cross-group friendships. In short, mediation models and models of between-group conflict resolution should be the special focus of those who would define the future of multicultural practice.

The first wave of multiculturalism brought us renewed respect for all the diverse ethnic origins we find in the United States. The second wave should fulfill the promise for social and economic justice and lead us to a more unified America.

REFERENCES

Brown, R. (1986). Social Psychology. 2nd ed. Free Press, pp. 541–585.

Dean, W. R., Jr. (1977). Back to activism. *Social Work* 22(5), 369–374.

De Anda, D. (1984). Bicultural socialization: Factors affecting the minority experience. *Social Work* 29(2), 101–108.

De Hoyos, G. et al. (1986). Sociocultural dislocation: Beyond the dual perspective. *Social Work* 31(1), 61–68.

Devore, W., & Schlesinger, E. G. (1994). Ethnic-Sensitive Social Work Practice. 3d ed. Merrill.

Finkielkraut, A. (1995). The Defeat of the Mind. Columbia University Press.

Fong, R., Spickard, P. R., & Ewalt, P. L. (1995). A multiracial reality: Issues for social work. (Editorial). *Social Work* 40(6), 725–728.

Gomez, E. (1985). A study of psychosocial casework with Chicanos. *Social Work* 30(6), 477–482.

Gould, K. H. (1995). The misconstruing of multiculturalism: The Stanford debate and social work. *Social Work* 40(2), 198–205.

Green, J. W. (1995). Cultural Awareness in the Human Services: A Multi-Ethnic Approach. 2d ed. Allyn & Bacon.

Gross, E. R. (1995). Deconstructing politically correct practice literature: The American Indian case. *Social Work* 40(2), 206–214.

Hardy-Fanta, C. (1986). Social action in Hispanic groups. *Social Work* 31(2), 119–123.

Hartman, A. (1990). Our global village. (Editorial). *Social Work* 35, 291–292.

Hunter, J. D. (1991). Culture Wars: The Struggle to Define America. Basic Books.

Iglehart, A. P., & Becerra, R. M. (1995). Social Services and the Ethnic Community. Allyn & Bacon.

Jayasuriya, L. (1992). The problematic of culture and identity in social functioning. *Journal of Multicultural Social Work* 2(4), 37–58.

Lum, D. (1996). Social Work Practice and People of Color: A Process Stage Approach. 3d ed. Brooks/Cole.

Myrdal, G. (1944). The American Dilemma. Harper & Bros.

O'Sullivan, M. J., Peterson, P. D., Cox, G. B., & Kirkeby, J. (1989). Ethnic populations: Community mental health services ten years later. *American Journal of Community Psychology* 17, 17–30.

Rubin, A. (1985). Practice effectiveness: More grounds for optimism. *Social Work* 30(6), 469–476.

Steinberg, S. (1995). Turning Back: The Retreat from Racial Justice in American Thought and Policy. Beacon.

U. S. Bureau of the Census (1994). *Statistical Abstract of the United States: 1994*. 114th ed. Government Printing Office.

Van Soest, D. (1995). Multiculturalism and social work education: The non-debate about compet-ing perspectives. *Journal of Social Work Education 31*(1), 55–66.

Videka-Sherman, L. (1988). Meta-analysis of research on social work practice in mental health. *Social Work 33*(4), 325-338.

Wright, L. (1994, July 25). One drop of blood. *The New Yorker 70*(22).

Poverty and Postmodernity

Mark J. Stern

Over the past century, poverty has been a central concept in the development of U.S. social policies and the social work profession. This reading examines the question as to whether the dominant view of poverty in the 20th century—defining it in terms of material deprivation and inadequate consumption—might be coming to an end. Mark Stern, professor of social welfare and history at the University of Pennsylvania, takes the position that the materialist perspective underestimates the role of two sets of choices in shaping the reality of poverty in the late 20th century. One involves what he terms the "postmodern" choices people who are poor have made about their lifestyles and domestic situation that have increased their risk of poverty. The other involves the choices our society has made to allow certain social groups to remain in poverty, despite our possession of the means and methods to prevent it. Stern argues that, although the work life, family life, and cultural perspective of the poor and nonpoor are more alike today than at any time in this century, current policy debates over poverty are obscured by the growing physical segregation of the poor and the increasing reliance on racial ideologies to justify a neo-social Darwinism. This contradiction will shape how we define and respond to poverty in the next century.

Dr. Stern's publications include Dependency and Poverty: Old Problems in a New World *(with June Axinn),* Society and Family Strategy: Erie County, New York, 1850–1920, *and* The Social Organization of Early Industrial Capitalism *(with Michael Katz and Michael Doucet). He is currently completing research projects on the history of poverty since World War II and on the social impact of arts and cultural institutions in Philadelphia.*

Poverty has been a central concept in the development of social work over the past century. As a measure of economic deprivation, it is important in itself. Moreover, we view it as an underlying cause of a whole range of problems with which professionals must grapple daily—poor health, family stress and breakdown, weakened community structure, and political and social apathy and anomie.

Indeed, the centrality of poverty to the profession makes it difficult to recall that our conceptualization of poverty is relatively new. The notion of defining the idea of poverty in material deprivation and inadequate consumption really did not arise until the waning decades of the 19th century (Ruggles, 1990). It was only during the heroic years of the Progressive period that the focus on material needs as the primary indicator of a social problem gained general acceptance (Ruggles, 1990; Zelizer, 1994).

Before the victory of a materialist definition of poverty, the dominant view of deprivation focused on the poor's moral constitution. The two central figures in the melodrama of 19th-century philanthropy—the pauper and the tramp—were worrisome because of their moral failings, not their material deprivation. The policy prescriptions of the period—ending "outdoor" relief, confining the poor to the almshouse, and jailing the tramp—were championed because they addressed the "root causes" of poverty, which their advocates assumed were lodged in the moral constitution of the poor (Katz, 1989).

Many of these policy initiatives, labeled "welfare reform" by today's conservatives, are back in favor. It might be useful to ask if their newfound popularity is an indicator of some profound social change. Could it be that the importance of a materialist definition of poverty is—with the century—coming to its end?

It is this question that lies at the center of this essay. I first examine the successes of the past century in addressing material poverty, arguing that American society passed through a critical threshold during the 1940s and 1950s—a threshold in which poverty moved from an economic to a political phenomenon. I then examine some of the theories of contemporary poverty, particularly the idea that postindustrial economic changes are responsible for poverty's current guise.

I take the position that this perspective underestimates the role of agency in the realities of poverty in the later 20th century. On the one hand, the poor themselves have made a set of "postmodern" choices about their lifestyle and domestic situation that have increased their risk of poverty—a startling shift from the cultural patterns of earlier in the century. On the other hand, Americans have collectively made a set of choices to allow certain social groupings to remain in poverty, even though we clearly have the means and the policy technologies to prevent it. Two sets of choices—those of the poor and those of the rest of society—define poverty as we move into the next century.

It is important to emphasize the importance of agency because in many ways the dilemmas faced by the poor and nonpoor have converged over the past several decades. As I shall argue below, the work life, family life, and cultural perspective of the poor and the "mainstream" are more alike today than at any time in this century. These powerful forces should be at the center of our discussion of poverty.

But the trend toward convergence has been obscured by geography and ideology. On the one hand, the powerful drive toward segregation documented by Douglas Massey and Nancy Denton in *American Apartheid* (1993) continues to construct a physical barrier between poor minorities and the white middle- and upper-classes. On the other hand, racial ideologies, which had relied on a *cultural* justification for the past half century, have now been reinforced by the new vogue for neo-social Darwinism. The controversy over the *Bell Curve* illustrates the influence of this trend (Fraser, 1995; Herrnstein and Murray, 1994). These twin realities—social pushes toward convergence and the racial obsession—will define poverty in the next century.

Managed Poverty: The Success and Failures of Poverty Policy

Between World War II and the 1970s, American poverty went through a fundamental change. Earlier in the century, poverty was an economic category; people were poor because they could not earn enough. By the 1970s, the poverty rate was primarily a function of politics. Several groups that had historically had poor labor market position and high poverty—the older and the disabled—had seen their poverty rates decline rapidly. At the same time, women with children, a group that had historically had little presence in the labor market, could not translate a rapid increase in its work effort into a reduction of poverty (Katz, 1989; Stern, 1991, 1993; Tobin, 1994).

By the last quarter of the 20th century, then, poverty had become a managed phenomenon. An activist federal government had formulated a set of income-maintenance policies that had fine-tuned its ability to help some groups escape poverty and others to remain incarcerated. Thus, after this watershed, the trends and future of poverty became primarily a political and cultural issue.

The best indicator of this transformation is the rapid decline in poverty among full-time workers. On the eve of World War II, nearly a third of household heads who worked full-time did not earn a living wage. Over the next several decades, the full-time, poverty wage worker almost disappeared. True, among women and people of color, the percentage of the population that worked full-time and still lived in poverty remained substantially higher, but by 1980, there was clear convergence of the patterns among men and women, whites and people of color (Axinn and Stern, 1988; author's calculations based on U.S. Census public-use samples).

By the same token, the coming of Social Security during the New Deal and its dramatic expansion during the 1950s and 1970s meant that two populations that had historically had very high poverty rates, the elderly and people with disabilities, achieved dramatic declines in poverty even though their labor force participation actually declined. For example, in 1949 the poverty rate of people over the age of 65 was 55 percent; forty years later it had fallen to 15 percent (author's calculations based on U.S. Census public-use samples).

Yet, as these groups achieved success, other groups experienced just the opposite phenomenon. As these latter entered the labor force in greater numbers and secured better earnings, shifts in public assistance and unemployment insurance worked to undercut their success. African Americans and female householders were most notable in this regard. For example, during the 1980s, the earnings poverty rate of all African Americans declined from 46 to 41 percent, but reductions in public transfer programs left their poverty rate virtually unchanged. African-American female householders—the major focus of contemporary welfare reformers—absorbed the brunt of these shifts. Even as their labor force participation increased from 47 percent in 1960 to 58 percent in 1990, their poverty rate stagnated.

America had achieved a politically managed system of poverty. The rise and fall of poverty rates were a product of a set of political forces and choices. Some groups emerged from these processes as clear winners and others as losers.

To look toward the future, then, one would need a perspective that integrates the political and the economic. Ironically, in many circles, just the opposite has occurred. The dramatic restructuring of the economy since the 1970s has captured the imagination of social scientists and policy analysts. A set of arguments that links these postindustrial transformations to the poverty trend have captured the political center.

The Postindustrial Explanation of Poverty

Until a society produces enough to provide for all of its members—both those who work and those who are dependent—poverty is inevitable. This iron linkage provides the starting point for postindustrial explanations of poverty. It argues that, just as the industrial era produced clear trends in income and poverty, so too will a postindustrial economy.

John Kasarda's work poses the most straightforward statement of this position. According to Kasarda, a mismatch has developed between the skills and educational needs of the economy and the abilities of the labor force. Most critically, central cities, which have lost virtually their entire industrial sector, are now dependent on a high-education and high-skill postindustrial sector. The old industrial work force—black, white, and brown—no longer has the right skills to take up these jobs. The emergence of chronic joblessness and high poverty in isolated city neighborhoods is a direct outcome of these economic forces (Kasarda, 1983, 1989).

Although Kasarda's analysis is the most parsimonious statement, the postindustrial theoretician who has had the greatest impact on poverty policy is William J. Wilson (Wilson, 1987). Building on Kasarda, Wilson sees the development of economic isolation as the first step in a broader process of social isolation. Joblessness provokes a broader set of cultural and behavior problems in America's African-American urban neighborhoods. As men lose their economic foothold, women no longer have any incentive to marry them; the "breakdown" of the black family begins. As chronic joblessness spreads, crime and drugs become attractive alternatives to "mainstream" pursuits. Finally, an ideology of racial exploitation provides the black middle class with a rationalization for affirmative action and the black poor with an explanation of their failure. Thus, for Wilson, the postindustrial transformation sets loose a set of broad cultural forces that are ultimately devastating.

The postindustrial hypothesis has been extremely persuasive for policymakers looking for an explanation of the declining effectiveness of traditional approaches to dependency. However, it is built on a faulty empirical foundation. First, economic disruptions of industrial restructuring have affected all ethnic groups. Whites have lost more ground in blue-collar industrial employment than have people of color. Second, even when people of color did enjoy greater opportunities for industrial employment, there is little evi-

dence that it was a ticket to economic security. With the exception of a couple of industrial centers, particularly Chicago and Detroit, African Americans never enjoyed either the benefits of industrial employment that the postindustrial theoreticians have granted them or the increases of poverty since the 1970s (Bane and Jargowsky, 1991; Stern, 1991, 1993).

Wilson's starting point caused many of his problems. Having made his reputation with *The Declining Significance of Race*, Wilson set out to develop a postindustrial theory of poverty that would demonstrate that class and economic forces—not racism and racial discrimination—were responsible for the plight of the urban poor (Wilson, 1978). Judged by this standard, his work has been a colossal failure. The work of most poverty researchers, including Christopher Jencks, Massey and Denton, and even two of Wilson's students, has convincingly demonstrated the centrality of racism to the current structuring of poverty (Jencks, 1992; Massey and Denton, 1993; Neckerman and Kirschenman, 1991).

Thus, where the postindustrial theory of the underclass sees contemporary poverty as a product of new structural forces, the reality of the black and brown jobless is rooted in the oldest of structural realities: racial discrimination. What is new is the cultural context within which chronic joblessness plays itself out. Postmodern work and family patterns, to which we now turn, have become a more central element in the social construction of the poor.

Postmodern Poverty

A postmodernist account of trends in poverty differs from the postindustrial version in two ways. First, it focuses on the declining significance of a purely materialist conception of poverty. This realization leads to a second difference: A postmodern perspective on poverty emphasizes the similarity between the poor and the rest of society. The power of the postindustrial emphasis on the "underclass" is to draw a sharp and often lurid distinction between the poor and the mainstream. As I have argued elsewhere, much of the drive for drawing this distinction derives from the impact of postmodern social change, with respect to work and family, on the clarity of the mainstream. As work and family histories have become more disrupted and less predictable, all of us have become less mainstream. By defining the "underclass" as more deviant, we are able to redefine the mainstream so that it includes the broken careers and marriages that now are commonplace across the social structure (Stern, 1993).

Yet, if the argument in this paper is correct, at least part of this image is wrong. The poor are not marginal to our society, but in some essential ways they are more like the rest of us than we would like to know. The structural realities that have been transforming the lives of all Americans and their associated cultural trends will work to pull the poor and nonpoor together over the next half century.

At work, the impact of these changes is already clear. The recent increased emphasis on the "downsizing" of America underscores the impact of globalization and the increased contingency of work (Frank and Cook, 1995; Harrison and Bluestone, 1988; Piore and Sabel, 1984). The poor have always had to live with the constant threats of economic disruption and unemployment. At the height of the New Deal order, the middle class and a large part of the working class saw this threat recede.

Now, it is back in full force for a larger share of the work force than has been the case for at least half a century. The proportion of householders who were employed full-time for the entire year was lower in 1989 than at any time since the Depression. Furthermore, since 1959—when nearly a third more whites than blacks (59 percent vs. 43 percent) were employed full-time for the full year—there has been a marked narrowing of the gap between ethnic groups. The narrowing, however, has been accomplished through a decline in the proportion of whites fully employed, not an improvement in the status of blacks or Latinos (Axinn and Stern, 1988; author's calculations from U.S. Census public-use samples).

Changes in work interact with changes in the family. We use the proportion of female-headed households in the population as an index of family disruption. Certainly the increase in the proportion of female-headed families among African Americans is a notable trend, particularly now that roughly half of black families have a female head. However, the female-headed family has increased nearly as rapidly among other ethnic groups as well. Since 1950, the proportion of families that are headed by a female has increased by about $2^{1}/_{2}$ times among African Americans and by about 3 times among non-Hispanic whites. According to the U.S. Census Bureau, by 1990, about 2 in 7 white families were female-headed.

The changes in family and work have been duly noted in the poverty debate. However, postmodern cultural changes have been peripheral to the discussion of the future of poverty. Conservatives have been more willing than others to raise the implications of cultural change and, for them, these changes have been seen as uniformly negative. Charles Murray, Gertrude Himmelfarb, William Bennett, and Lawrence Mead, to name only the best known, have seen the erosion of "virtue"—especially the importance of "personal responsibility"—as central to their indictment of the welfare state and modernity (Bennett, 1993; Himmelfarb, 1983, 1995; Mead, 1986, 1992).

In the coming century, the intellectual left must formulate a more balanced way of connecting the undeniably important changes in our culture to social welfare. In her recent study, *The Social Meaning of Money* (1994), Viviana Zelizer argues that part of progressivism was to tie a material definition of poverty to a cultural framework that stressed the virtues of security, rationality, responsibility, and planning. The idea of a budget and the rational allocation of resources was an intrinsic part of this redefinition (Zelizer, 1994).

Yet, as we stumble into the next century, these progressive values have come into conflict with an emergent postmodernity. When sociologists like Ulrich Beck speak of a "risk society," they suggest that the search for security, rationality, and a future orientation are now in conflict with other values, ones that stress self-fulfillment, the present, and unpredictability. The quest for risk may now be as important as the quest for security. As a society in which people leave "good" jobs to seek self-fulfillment, in which women leave their husbands in spite of the fact that this increases their risk of poverty, and in which young women choose to have a child rather than chase the illusive reward of delayed gratification is one that is much harder to manage (Beck, 1992; Beck, Giddens, and Lash, 1994; Giddens, 1992).

A set of powerful forces are working to pull together the lives of the poor and the nonpoor. Insecure and uncertain work, which has always been the lot of the poor, has now spread up the job ladder. A disrupted and unstable family life, which has usually been identified with the poor, is now common across the social structure. Finally, the quest for individual happiness and the attraction of risk has rooted itself more deeply in the lives of the poor and nonpoor. Thus, work, family, and culture are exerting a pressure toward convergence of the life-worlds of the poor and nonpoor.

Yet, at the same time that these pressures converge, other tendencies are working in the opposite direction. On the one hand, the politics of poverty has changed radically. The alliance of the poor, workers, and sections of the middle class, which was the hallmark of liberalism and progressivism, has come undone. These tendencies have to be reinforced by the persistence of race consciousness and division.

The politics of poverty has been a victim of its own success. The political successes of the New Deal era were a product of a coalition that included elements of the poor and nonpoor. Throughout the 1940s, 1950s, and 1960s, the relative deprivation of a large segment of the working class provided fertile ground for policy initiatives that more closely allied the poor and nonpoor. A quick examination of the legislative histories of major welfare initiatives of this era underline the fact that policy for workers and policy for the poor were quite similar until the late 1960s. The core of the American welfare state was the social insurances that dominated American social policy from the Great Depression until the 1970s. These programs—old age and survivors insurance, unemployment insurance, and disability insurance—addressed the everyday concerns of working people and served to build a set of common interests that forged the New Deal coalition of the era (Weir, 1995; Weir, Orloff, and Skocpol, 1988).

Economic realities have undercut the political logic of social insurance. First, the rise in real incomes from World War II until the 1970s meant that the gap between the economic well-being of the average American and that of the poor increased. Thus, the gap between social policy directed at these two groups grew.

The social insurances were designed for social groups who found themselves living at or near poverty. By offering a floor, these programs did much to increase the economic security of the postwar generation. A factory or clerical worker earning perhaps twice the poverty level knew that unemployment, old age, or disability would not reduce his earnings dramatically. Social insurance promoted a community of interest between the poor and near-poor.

Today, this same basis for solidarity is less viable. The computer technician, factory worker, or administrative assistant earning perhaps $40,000 a year can no longer count on the social insurances alone to offer protection. To some extent, this is a consequence of the decisions to privatize the welfare state during the 1950s. More to the point, a set of programs justified on an individualistic logic of cost-benefit (that each recipient should gain more than they contribute) simply could not keep up with the most affluent 60 percent of the labor force (Weir, Orloff, and Skocpol, 1988).

The schism between the poor and the nonpoor is, of course, reinforced by race. As the material condition of the poor and the nonpoor diverged during the early postwar years, the cultural basis of their solidarity was undercut as well. As we look toward the next century, in fact, the centrality of race promises to increase. In recent years, segregation has resulted in an increased racial homogeneity of municipalities. Cities with large African-American populations have become less white; rural and suburban areas have remained overwhelmingly white. This trend, combined with the devolution of power from the federal government to state and local governments, strength-

ens the stranglehold of racial inequality (Massey and Hajnal, 1995; Weir, 1995).

The implications for poverty of the new politics of race can be seen in the current welfare reform debate. The core of the materialist vision of progressive reform—that increasing benefits would allow the poor to find better jobs and maintain a more stable family life—was directly challenged by the guaranteed income experiments of the 1970s (Bane and Ellwood, 1994). A central finding of those experiments—that many poor women used increased economic independence to get out of unhappy marriages—opened up the cultural debates about "traditional" family values. With the materialist vision severely dented, an alternative vision of welfare reform, based not on improving the economic security of the poor but on using the poor's economic vulnerability to change their values and culture, asserted itself. The welfare reform proposals of the Clinton administration and congressional Republicans—notwithstanding their substantial differences—underline the extent to which issues of culture and values have displaced a concern for material well-being (Ellwood, 1996; Handler, 1995).

Thus, in spite of the forces reducing the gap between the cultural realities of the poor and nonpoor, the politics of poverty have moved in the opposite direction. The key means of securing the alliance of the poor and nonpoor—the development of the social insurances—has been divorced from poverty policy. At the same time that issues of entitlement and fairness continue to drive the debate over Social Security and Medicare, the politics of welfare has turned to issues of personal responsibility and cost-cutting. To no one's surprise, this division has been reinforced by that of race.

Imagining the Future of Poverty

In the face of a declining progressivism and an assertive conservatism, it is easy to imagine where the future might lead. The chronically poor will find themselves increasingly isolated in declining urban centers and rural enclaves. With the abolition of an entitlement for welfare, the informal economy—half criminal, half quasi-legal—will continue to boom. Under the weight of increasing demands, social institutions—the schools, social services, and health services—will slowly decline or flee. Our central cities will become the townships of America's apartheid.

Certainly, this is the image many of us have in mind as we ponder poverty in the next century. The postindustrial image of poverty has been successful insofar as it has projected the image of the poor as marginal to our society. We are left with the image of the majority of America as a walled community, protected—albeit at a cost—from the specter of the poor.

Yet, if we realize that this is wrong, that the forces affecting the poor are the same as those affecting the rest of us, we can open up an alternative line of reasoning. The materialist conception of poverty, and the progressive worldview of which it was a part, led us to look for materialist ways of bringing the poor and nonpoor into political coalition. For the better part of half a century, it did this admirably.

The breakdown of the politics of social welfare and its reinforcement by the politics of race, make it difficult to imagine an alternative to the conservative domination of the debate over policy. Yet, a number of trends may yet work to our advantage.

Most importantly, convergence of the realities of work, family, and culture will continue to undercut a racial definition of the politics of rich and poor. Gaps that separated blacks, whites, and Latinos by hours worked, earnings, and family structure are likely to continue to decline as we move through the next century. Nor are the broader cultural forces, whatever the political rhetoric of "personal responsibility," likely to be reversed.

At the same time, the changing demographics of race may highlight the underlying convergence of ethnic groups. The progressive approach to welfare was formulated at a time when a multiethnic image of American society was common; the United States was seen as an amalgam of a variety of different "races": Nordic, Italian, Hebrew, and so on. Thus, the imagery of class and solidarity could work as a means of overcoming these divisions, either in the union movement of the 1930s or the war effort of the 1940s. The triumph of a bipolar view of race, black and white, during the 1950s and 1960s served to sharpen the lines between the black poor and the white working class.

In the next century, a new multiethnic image of America will reassert itself. The impact of Asian and Latin American immigration is likely to continue. On the one hand, this reality may work to divide people of color, as was evidenced in the Los Angeles riots of 1992. On the other hand, conservative policies are likely to help identify common ground among different ethnic groups; this could work to undercut the political isolation of the African-American poor.

Take the role of the Catholic church. Catholic communitarianism was critical to the labor insurgency of the 1930s and its populist rhetoric. The Church was more likely to find itself and its parishioners on the conservative side of many of the social debates of the 1960s and 1970s. Yet, in the past decade, the strengthening of Catholic social values (for example in the Bishop's Letter on Economic Justice) and the increase in the number of poor Latino Catholics has led the Catholic church to play a prominent role in many of the social justice issues of the 90s (Fraser and Gerstle, 1989; Katz, 1989).

For social work practitioners, the struggles of the next century are likely to be particularly trying. The moral fervor and antigovernment rhetoric that has fueled the conservative offensive of the past two decades has cast service providers as the defenders of the status quo. In reaction to the moral absolutism of our opponents, we defend the poor and existing welfare programs. Or, as is the case with the Clinton administration, we may try to coopt the language of the Right—"real" welfare reform, "real" family values—for a different set of ends.

We must avoid the lure either to accept the moral absolutes of the Right or to trim our sails in front of the apparent force of political sentiment. The values that social workers have championed in the past—diversity, tolerance, and social justice—will be even more central to the debate of the next century. At the same time, the bureaucratic structures for service delivery that our professional ancestors championed are likely to give way to the demand for services that are more responsive to community concerns. When our values come into conflict with the institutional settings in which we find ourselves—as they do in the cases of the welfare, educational, and child welfare systems—it is the values, not the existing institutions, that demand our allegiance.

Underlying social realities do have a way of affecting their representation in culture and politics. Americans may continue to deny the convergences around work, family, and culture because of race. We have used the stereotype of the underclass to obscure the powerful forces that are pushing black, white, and brown Americans in the same direction. The racial fixation, too, will continue to affect what happens in the field of social welfare policy. As we have noted, if it were not for cuts in transfer payments, the poverty rates of blacks and whites would have converged during the 1980s. The use of racially specific cuts in public programs is likely to continue to influence the realities of poverty into the next century.

Still, it is unlikely to dominate. The new social realities that we all confront in our daily life open us to different ways of making sense of our society. In the face of rapid social and cultural change, we are apt to look for fixity and reassurance. The power of the past—or more accurately the imagined past—is apparent in the popularity of fundamentalism: whether peddled by the Christian Coalition or the Nation of Islam. Yet, the realities of work, family, and culture will continue to undercut fundamentalism, especially as more attractive ways of making sense of contemporary society emerge.

The cultural perspective of the fin de siècle often is Manichean; it is full of foreboding and promise, gyrations between wild optimism and deep pessimism. Certainly, as we look toward poverty after the year 2000, this is likely to be our stance. The ways we live and the values we share and act upon have probably never been more similar than they are today. Yet, the burden of past and present racism continues to cast a shadow over the promise of the future. Until we are able to overcome it, the prospects for addressing poverty—among all ethnic groups—are unlikely to succeed.

REFERENCES

Axinn, June, and Stern, Mark J. (1988). *Poverty and Dependency: Old Problems in a New World*. Lexington, Mass: Lexington Books.

Bane, Mary Jo, and Ellwood, D. (1994). *Welfare Realities: From Rhetoric to Reform*. Cambridge, MA: Harvard University Press.

Bane, Mary Jo, and Jargowsky, Paul. (1991). In Christopher Jencks and Paul E. Peterson, eds., *The Urban Underclass*. Washington, DC: Brookings Institution.

Beck, Ulrich. (1992). *Risk Society: Towards a New Modernity*. Translated by Mark Ritter. London and Newbury Park, CA: Sage Publications.

Beck, Ulrich, Giddens, Anthony, and Lash, Scott. (1994). *Reflexive Modernization: Politics, Tradition, and Aesthetics in the Modern Social Order*. Cambridge, England: Polity Press.

Bennett, William J. (1993). *The Book of Virtues: A Treasury of Great Moral Stories*. New York: Simon and Schuster.

Ellwood, David T. (1996). "Welfare Reform As I Knew It." *The American Prospect* 26 (May–June): 22–29.

Frank, Robert H., and Cook Philip J. (1995). *The Winner-take-all Society: How More and More Americans Compete for Ever Fewer and Bigger Prizes, Encouraging Economic Waste, Income Inequality, and an Impoverished Cultural Life*. New York: Free Press.

Fraser, Steve, ed. (1995). *The Bell Curve Wars: Race, Intelligence, and the Future of America*. New York: Basic Books.

Fraser, Steve, and Gerstle, Gary, eds. (1989). *The Rise and Fall of the New Deal Order, 1930–1980*. Princeton: Princeton University Press.

Giddens, Anthony. (1992). *The Transformation of Intimacy: Sexuality, Love, and Eroticism in Modern Societies*. Stanford: Stanford University Press.

Handler, Joel F. (1995). *The Poverty of Welfare Reform*. New Haven: Yale University Press.

Harrison, Bennett, and Bluestone, Barry. (1988). *The Great U-Turn: Corporate Restructuring and the Polarizing of America*. New York: Basic Books.

Herrnstein, Richard J., and Murray, Charles. (1994). *The Bell Curve: Intelligence and Class Structure in American Life*. New York: Free Press.

Himmelfarb, Gertrude. (1983). *The Idea of Poverty: England in the Early Industrial Age*. New York: Alfred Knopf.

_____. (1995). *On Looking into the Abyss: Untimely Thoughts on Culture and Society*. New York: Alfred Knopf.

Jencks, Christopher. (1992). *Rethinking Social Policy: Race, Poverty, and the Underclass*. Cambridge, MA: Harvard University Press.

Kasarda, John. (1983). "Entry-level Jobs, Mobility and Urban Minority Unemployment." *Urban Affairs Quarterly* 19 (September): 21–40.

_____. (1989). "Urban Industrial Transition and the Underclass." *Annals of the American Academy of Political and Social Science* 501 (January): 26–47.

Katz, Michael B. (1989). *The Undeserving Poor: From the War on Poverty to the War on the Welfare*. New York: Pantheon.

Massey, Douglas S., and Denton, Nancy A. (1993). *American Apartheid: Segregation and the Making of the Underclass*. Cambridge, MA: Harvard University Press.

Massey, Douglas S., and Hajnal, Zoltan L. (1995). "The Changing Geographic Structure of Black-White Segregation in the United States." *Social Science Quarterly* 76 (September): 527–542.

Mead, Lawrence M. (1986). *Beyond Entitlement: The Social Obligations of Citizenship*. New York: Free Press.

_____. (1992). *The New Politics of Poverty: The Nonworking Poor in America*. New York: Basic Books.

Neckerman, Kathryn M., and Kirschenman, Joleen. (1991). "Hiring Strategies, Racial Bias, and Inner-City Workers." *Social Problems* 38 (November): 433–447.

Piore, Michael J., and Sabel, Charles F. (1984). *The Second Industrial Divide: Possibilities for Prosperity*. New York: Basic Books.

Ruggles, Patricia. (1990). *Drawing the Line: Alternative Poverty Measures and Their Implications for Public Policy*. Washington, DC: Urban Institute Press.

Stern, Mark J. (1991). "Poverty and the Life-Cycle, 1940–1960." *Journal of Social History* 24 (Spring): 521–540.

_____. (1993). "Poverty and Family Since 1940." In Michael B. Katz, ed., *The "Underclass" Debate: A View from History*. Princeton: Princeton University Press.

Tobin, James. (1994). "Poverty in Relation to Macroeconomic Trends, Cycles, and Policies." In Sheldon H. Danzinger, Gary D. Sandefur, and Daniel H. Weinberg, eds., *Confronting Poverty: Prescriptions for Change*. Cambridge, MA: Harvard University Press.

Weir, Margaret. (1995). "In the Shadows: Central Cities' Loss of Power in State Politics." *Brooking Review* (Spring): 16–19.

Weir, Margaret, Orloff, Ann, and Skocpol, Theda, eds. (1988). *The Politics of Social Policy in the United States*. Princeton: Princeton University Press.

Wilson, William J. (1978). *The Declining Significance of Race: Blacks and Changing American Institutions*. Chicago: University of Chicago Press.

_____. (1987). *The Truly Disadvantaged: The Inner City, the Underclass, and Public Policy*. Chicago and London: University of Chicago Press.

Zelizer, Viviana. (1994). *The Social Meaning of Money*. New York: Basic Books.

Social Work in International Context
Challenges and Opportunities for the 21st Century

James Midgley

For the first time in human history, our lives are no longer defined solely by the local environments in which we live. Despite the recent resurgence of nationalism and ethnic conflict, many believe that an international world system will inexorably replace the local community and even the nation-state as the primary basis for social identity. Such trends are already apparent in such diverse areas as economic development, computer and communications technology, and popular culture. James Midgley, dean of the School of Social Welfare at the University of California, Berkeley, discusses the major challenges and opportunities facing social work in the new international order and considers some of the ways the profession can enhance its international relevance. He analyzes the impact of challenges in such areas as economic globalization and the social problems it is generating. He points out how globalization can provide social work with new opportunities to expand its knowledge base, increase its practice effectiveness at both the international and domestic levels, create a greater shared identity among social workers around the world, improve international professional collaboration, and produce a greater commitment to respond collectively to the challenges of the interdependent world of the future.

James Midgely is the author of eight books on international and comparative social welfare and has contributed to many leading social policy, social work, and development studies journals. He served as associate vice chancellor for research and economic development at Louisiana State University from 1993 to 1996 and as dean of the School of Social Work at LSU from 1986 to 1993, and has been on the faculty of the London School of Economics and the University of Capetown.

For most of human history, people's lives have been framed by the localities in which they live. Today, the process of globalization is creating an international world system that, many believe, will replace the local community and nation-state as the primary basis for social identity. Global economic forces arising from international capital flows and enhanced communications now exert greater influence than ever before. These forces dictate trends in domestic economies; international political cooperation is improving; and popular culture is increasingly subject to foreign influences. Despite the resurgence of nationalism and ethnic conflict in many parts of the world, the trend toward internationalism will continue, and it is not inconceivable that a truly global human society will eventually emerge.

As social work enters the 21st century, it too must face the challenges of globalization. Although the social work profession has not ignored these challenges, much more needs to be done if it is to be adequately prepared for the new international order that will emerge in the next century.

This chapter discusses the major challenges and opportunities facing social work in the new international order. It considers some of the ways the profession can enhance its international relevance. These include the need to improve international content in social work education, the exchange of practice ideas and innovations, and the strengthening of international professional associations. Also important is the need to inculcate an authentic commitment to internationalism in social work.

Challenges and Opportunities of Globalization

Although international events have always impinged on the lives of ordinary people, the process of globalization is now having a major impact around the world. This impact is perhaps most strongly felt in economic affairs, where global capital movements are undermining the ability of governments to manage their domestic economies effectively (Bluestone and Harrison, 1982; Lash and Urry, 1987; Reich, 1991). Conventional Keynesian methods of stimulating economic demand, creating employment, and counteracting inflation are increasingly unable to direct domestic economic trends. The Western industrial economies have faced new challenges as traditional economic activities based on manufacturing have declined. Falling demand for low-skilled labor has exacerbated the problem, creating serious structural difficulties in the labor markets of many industrial nations. The global economy has also created new challenges for low-income countries. Although these countries are able to benefit from the demand for low-cost labor, skills and expertise commensurate with global economic demands are also required. In this new climate, nations will have to be much more flexible, competitive, and responsive if they and their citizens are to prosper.

Although globalization has been applauded by some, it has been condemned by others. Although some welcome the growing interdependence of economies, nations, and cultures, others reject the view that increased internationalization has positive implications for humanity. In addition to eliciting different normative responses, the trend toward globalization has been accompanied by new social problems that social work needs to address. The process of globalization has also created new opportunities for social work to expand its knowledge base, improve its practice skills, and enhance its development as a profession. Social work should not only respond to the problems associated with globalization but seize the opportunities that have arisen from increasing international interdependence.

The Social Problems of Globalization

Numerous new social problems have emerged as a result of globalization. For example, as the global economy has expanded, the incidence of poverty and deprivation in many parts of the world has increased (World Bank, 1990). Whereas some nations, particularly in Eastern Asia, have benefited from the expansion of the global economy, many people in the world's poorest nations have been left behind, and the incidence of absolute poverty in many African, Asian, and Central and South American countries has increased. These problems have been exacerbated by the imposition of structural adjustment programs in many parts of the Third World (Watkins, 1995). Structural adjustment refers to the policies adopted at the prompting of the International Monetary Fund and World Bank by developing countries seeking international credit to stabilize their economies. These policies involve trade liberalization, increased deregulation, and retrenchments in public expenditures. In addition, many middle- and low-income families in the industrial countries have also suffered as a result of economic globalization. The transition to a postindustrial economy in Europe and North America has created a dearth of employment opportunities for unskilled or semiskilled workers, with resulting blight in large urban areas (Bluestone and Harrison, 1982; Wilson, 1987). High unemployment in these areas has been accompanied by family disintegration, poverty, despair, violence, and drug abuse. Whereas multinational firms and investors in the centers of global economic power have enjoyed unprecedented prosperity, incomes for many ordinary people have stagnated.

Globalization has also created massive new population movements, which have resulted in dislocation and problems of cultural adaptation and acceptance. Although Europe, North America, and other economically developed regions of the world have traditionally attracted the majority of international migrants, migration flows to Eastern Asia, the Middle East, and other regions with employment opportunities have increased rapidly. The number of illegal migrants entering these regions has also increased. Large-scale migration has created new social problems that are not yet properly recognized in social work circles. In addition to the problems of cultural adjustment, which have been within the purview of social work practice for some time, problems such as the exploitation of women migrants (particularly in domestic service), the harsh treatment of illegal migrants, and the growing attachment of racist sentiment to social policy issues affecting migrants need to be addressed (United Nations, 1993).

Paradoxically, globalization has also fostered increased ethnic conflict and violence in many parts of the world. This problem is related to the growth of migration, but it is also a function of the tensions accompanying economic, political, and social integration. Acts of racist violence have increased significantly as the European community has become more integrated. However, incidents of large-scale ethnic conflict often have their roots in the early phases of globalization, when the European powers subjected the peoples of Africa, Asia, and Central and South America to global imperial rule. Many incidents of ethnically based violence are the result of political struggles and upheavals resulting from the European imperial system. Similar forces are at work in the Balkans and the former territories of the Soviet Union today. As a result of these events, entire nations are now experiencing massive suffering, and large numbers of families and even whole communities have been dislocated. The global refugee problem may not be a new one, but it now exists on a huge scale (United Nations, 1993).

Social work needs to respond to the social problems caused by globalization. The problems of poverty, inner city decay, unemployment, and increasing despair in the industrial countries are a direct consequence of global economic change and the unwillingness of governments to address these problems in ways that integrate displaced people into the productive economy rather than discarding them. Social work also needs to be more active in providing services to immigrant ethnic minorities and promoting a better understanding of the advantages of cultural diversity. Although the profession has previously worked with refugee populations, more needs to be done to enhance social work's effectiveness in this growing field of practice.

Opportunities of Globalization

Although it is imperative that social work enhance its capacity to contribute to the amelioration of these social problems, the profession can also benefit by responding to the many positive opportunities created by globalization. Globalization has created new opportunities for social workers in different parts of the world to share experiences and learn from each other. Increased reciprocal contacts not only benefit individual practitioners but assist social work's development as a profession and, we hope, equip it to exert greater international influence.

Globalization offers new opportunities for social work to expand its knowledge base. By engaging more actively in international activities, social work educators can enhance their understanding of pressing contemporary social problems. Problems such as AIDS, homelessness, substance abuse, and child neglect have critical international dimensions that, if properly understood, can provide deeper insights into etiological and related issues. For example, the World Health Organization's effective dissemination of information on international AIDS research has undoubtedly promoted a better understanding of this tragic condition (Midgley, 1993). Another example comes from narcotic control efforts, which, as Oppenheimer (1993) has shown, can benefit when domestic policies are critically reviewed in the light of international experience. Academic knowledge can also be enhanced through international exchanges. Comparative research allows hypotheses to be tested more widely and promotes a more accurate conceptual knowledge base within the profession.

Enhanced knowledge can, in turn, inform practice and increase its effectiveness at both the international and domestic levels. Social workers can increase their practice effective-ness by critically examining and adapting practice innovations emanating from other countries. Although international exchanges in social work have long been characterized by unilateral transfers, particularly from the industrial to the developing countries (Midgley, 1981), there is growing evidence that more discerning transfers of practice innovations are being made (Kendall, 1995; Martinez-Brawley and Delevan, 1993; Midgley, 1989; 1994). In addition, efforts are being made to reverse the conventional transfer of practice wisdom from the industrial to the developing countries by advocating increased "learning from the Third World" (Midgley, 1990; Midgley and Simbi, 1993).

Globalization can also facilitate social work's efforts to enhance its own professional development. Greater international contacts will contribute to a greater shared identity among social workers, improved opportunities for collaboration, and a greater commitment to respond collectively to the challenges of an interdependent world. The steps that have been taken to foster international professional collaboration through international social work associations such as the International Federation of Social Workers and the International Association of Schools of Social Work (Healy, 1995a) need to be augmented. These efforts will not only help social work to attain international professional recognition but increase its ability to affect international policy-making and address the new social problems associated with globalization. However, to make a contribution of this kind, social work must renew its international commitments and enhance its international relevance.

Responding to the Challenge

It is often claimed that social work is characterized by a narrow parochialism that has inhibited its engagement in international activities (Healy, 1995b). However, this assertion is only partially correct. Although it cannot be claimed that social work is sufficiently committed to internationalism, the profession has not been inattentive to international issues. Indeed, social work has benefited from international exchanges from its very beginning. The emergence of casework and settlement work as prime social work practice methods in the United States at the end of the 19th century owed much to British innovations. Similarly, the writings of American social workers such as Mary Richmond in the early 20th century were widely adopted in Britain and in other parts of the world where social work was emerging as a profession. The first international professional social work associations were founded in the 1920s (Healy, 1995a), and by mid-century, schools of social work had been created in several Anglophone territories and in some Latin American countries (Midgley, 1981; Resnick, 1995). The creation of schools of social work in different parts of the world fostered social work professional recognition, and employment opportunities for social workers in both government and non-profit agencies proliferated. By the 1980s, social work was well established internationally in both the Western industrial countries and the nations of the Third World. Following the collapse of Soviet communism, social work spread to regions where the profession was previously unknown.

Despite these achievements, social work is not fully prepared to respond to the challenges and opportunities of globalization. Too few social work courses include international content, practitioners are seldom aware of innovations in other countries and international exchanges remain underdeveloped. Greater efforts are needed to ensure that the profession is able to address the pressing social problems associated with globalization. Similarly, much more needs to be done to ensure that social work fully exploits the opportunities afforded by increased internationalization.

This requires that social work enhance its efforts to inculcate an international outlook among its students and that practitioners become more aware of the way international events affect their daily practice. Steps need to be taken to improve international exchanges and encourage social workers to become more involved in the activities and programs of international agencies. The professional associations should also be strengthened so that they will be more able to exert international influence. Also, if social work is to respond effectively to the challenges and opportunities of globalization, it will need to foster an authentic commitment to internationalism as a value system. However, it is not certain that social work is ready or able to make a commitment of this kind. As Healy (1995b) pointed out in a recent article, social work in the United States has retreated from its earlier commitment to internationalism. Ways must be found to revitalize this commitment, not only within American social work, but within the profession as a whole. Only in this way will social work be able to respond to the demands of an emerging global society in the new century.

Enhancing Relevance to Global Challenges
Previous efforts to enhance an international focus in social work have been led by social work educators, and it is appropriate that they play this role. However, leadership has come from a few committed social work educators, and much more needs to be done to enhance the curriculum and expose students to international developments.

Some research has been undertaken into the efforts of schools of social work to promote a greater awareness of international issues among students (Healy, 1995b). Although the findings of this research are mixed, there is cause for optimism. Surveys have found that international course content is now offered at many schools of social work in both the United States and other countries, and that inclusion of international material has increased over the years (Healy, 1995b). However, these findings should not foster complacency because it appears that international course content is very uneven, dependent on the availability of interested faculty and often taught sporadically. Despite the progress that has been made, schools of social work around the world have not made a strong commitment to internationalism, and they do not adequately prepare students for professional practice in an increasingly interdependent world (Healy, 1995b).

However, efforts are being made to enhance international content in the professional social work curriculum. The Council on Social Work Education in the United States has recently modified its curriculum policy statement, which now recognizes the importance of including appropriate content to increase students' awareness of international issues. Several schools of social work have expanded international teaching and students are now regularly exposed to developments in other countries. This trend has been accompanied by more frequent international exchanges of students and faculty and by the creation of formal links between schools in different countries.

One example of the expansion of international course content comes from the University of Pennsylvania School of Social Work, where the curriculum permits students to specialize in social development involving a sub-

stantial amount of international course content. In addition, the school has developed appropriate teaching materials. The book *Internationalizing Social Work Education: A Guide to Resources for a New Century,* which was prepared by Professor Richard Estes (1992), covers the field concisely and is an extremely useful resource document that should be widely used.

Efforts are also being made to enhance international awareness in the arena of professional practice. Although evidence shows that practitioners are more interested in international social work than before, few are able to link international events to their everyday practice. As Healy (1995b, p. 433) notes: "They do not recognize the relevance of knowledge about the profession, policy and practice beyond national borders." And yet, as was suggested earlier, many of the problems social workers deal with are directly related to the trend toward globalization. Social workers who provide services to AIDS victims, or who work with impoverished inner city children, or who provide counseling to minority immigrant families all deal with problems that have profound international links.

To promote a greater understanding of the role of international events in social work practice, the National Association of Social Workers has actively promoted greater international contacts among practitioners in different parts of the world. It has given leadership in "twinning" the NASW local chapters with professional groups in other nations. By 1992, 21 of the association's 55 chapters had established links with international counterparts. NASW has also sponsored the publication and dissemination of information about social work practice in other countries. In 1992, the association hosted the World Assembly, a major gathering of social work educators and practitioners from around the world in Washington, D.C., and marked the event by the publication of the book *Profiles in International Social Work,* the first comprehensive overview of professional social work around the world (Hokenstad, Khinduka, and Midgley, 1992).

Promoting international professional cooperation plays an obvious role in fostering international awareness in social work, but care must be taken to ensure that international exchanges are truly reciprocal. This issue has been the subject of much debate over the last two decades, and it is clear that there is a greater appreciation of the need to avoid the one-sided transfers that characterized much of social work's previous international development. Nevertheless, the problem has not been fully resolved, and continued vigilance is needed if social workers are to benefit from truly reciprocal international exchanges. Through mutual respect and reciprocal sharing, the profession can become truly international and better equipped to make a positive contribution to ameliorating pressing global social needs (Midgley, 1994).

A good example of the positive exchange of international professional experience is provided in the account by Martinez-Brawley and Delevan (1993) of a project that involved the transfer of practice innovations from England to the United States. The British "patch" model of social work practice was believed to be appropriate to the needs of rural social work in the United States. This approach involves the decentralization of public social services to small, local, community-based teams of social work practitioners who become intimately familiar with the people and with the neighborhoods in which they work (Hatch and McGrawth, 1980). It is claimed that this approach is a far more responsive practice alternative to conventional bureaucratic social service delivery systems. By carefully study-

ing the British system, and with the full cooperation of British experts, the lessons of the British experience were successfully adopted in rural Pennsylvania.

Social workers in the industrial countries are able to benefit from the extensive experience of their Third World colleagues with developmental forms of social work. The developmental approach (Lowe, 1995; Midgley, 1995, 1996) offers an exciting opportunity for the profession to transcend conventional remedial and maintenance-based approaches and to engage in forms of practice that address pressing material needs by promoting economic growth. One field in which fruitful exchanges of this kind are already taking place is micro-enterprise development. As this approach becomes more popular, social workers in the United States are finding that they have much to learn from the experiences of their Third World colleagues (Balkin, 1989; Else and Raheim, 1992).

Another way of enhancing the internationalization of social work is through the engagement of social workers in international agencies. Although social workers have been employed in these agencies in the past, more needs to be done to increase their participation in these bodies. However, employment opportunities of this kind are only likely to become available when the profession has demonstrated its ability to train personnel with the requisite knowledge and skills, and when the profession's commitment to internationalism is more widely recognized and appreciated. The active engagement of professional associations in promoting social work's international relevance is critically important.

Greater effort is also needed to strengthen the activities of the international professional associations. As noted earlier, social work is fortunate in having two major international professional associations, which are responsible for promoting greater international awareness and engagement in the profession. However, the activities of these international bodies are not always emulated at the national level. In addition, both organizations require more financial and organizational support, and their activities need to be more widely advertised. The International Association of Schools of Social Work has experienced severe fiscal problems in recent years, and more extensive involvement from social work educators is needed if it is to remain viable. These associations also need to play a more active role at the international level in seeking to influence governments and in promoting policy positions compatible with the profession's values.

As has been shown, it will not be difficult for social work to increase its efforts to engage more effectively in forms of professional education and practice that enhance its commitment to internationalization. The opportunities and prospects for greater social work involvement in international activities are excellent. The profession has already made a significant commitment to internationalism. As the 21st century draws near, a stronger commitment by the profession as a whole is urgently needed. Only in this way can social work successfully cope with the demands of the new international order of the future.

REFERENCES

Balkin, S. (1989). *Self employment for low-income people.* New York: Praeger.

Bluestone, B., and Harrison, B. (1982). *The deindustrialization of America.* New York: Basic Books.

Else, J. F., and Raheim, S. (1992). AFDC clients as entrepreneurs: Self-employment offers an important option. *Public Welfare* 50 (4): 36–41.

Estes, R. (Ed.). (1992). *Internationalizing social work education: A guide to resources for a new century.* Philadelphia, PA: University of Pennsylvania School of Social Work.

Hatch, R., and McGrawth, M. (1980). *Going local: Neighbourhood social services.* London: Bedford Square Press.

Healy, L. (1995a). International social welfare: Organizations and activities. In R. Edwards et al. (Eds.), *Encyclopedia of social work.* 19th edition (pp. 1499–1510). Washington, DC: NASW Press.

Healy, L. (1995b). Comparative and international overview. In T. D. Watts, D. Elliott, and N. S. Mayadas (Eds.), *International handbook on social work education.* (pp. 421–440). Westport, CT: Greenwood Press.

Hokenstad, M. C., Khinduka, S. K., and Midgley, J. (Eds.). (1992). *Profiles in International Social Work.* Washington, DC: National Association of Social Workers.

Kendall, K. (1995). Foreword. In T. D. Watts, D. Elliott, and N. S. Mayadas (Eds.), *International handbook on social work education* (pp. xiii–xvii). Westport, CT: Greenwood Press.

Lash, S., and Urry, J. (1987). *The end of organized capitalism.* Cambridge: Polity Press.

Lowe, G. R. (1995). Social development. In R. Edwards et al. (Eds.), *Encyclopedia of social work.* 19th edition (pp. 2168–2172). Washington, DC: National Association of Social Workers.

Martinez-Brawley, E. E., and Delevan, S. M. (1993). *Transferring technology in the personal social services.* Washington, DC: NASW Press.

Midgley, J. (1981). *Professional imperialism: Social work in the Third World.* London: Heinemann Educational Books.

Midgley, J. (1989). Social work in the Third World: Crisis and response. In P. Carter, T. Jeffs, and M. Smith (Eds.), *Social work and social welfare yearbook I* (pp. 33–45). London: Open University Press.

Midgley, J. (1990). International social work: Learning from the Third World. *Social Work* 35: 295–301.

Midgley, J. (1993). The challenge of international social work. In M. C. Hokenstad, S. K. Khinduka, and J. Midgley (Eds.), *Profiles in international social work* (pp. 13–28). Washington, DC: NASW Press.

Midgley, J. (1994). Transnational strategies for social work: Towards effective reciprocal exchanges. In R. G. Meinert, J. T. Pardeck, and W. P. Sullivan (Eds.), *Issues in social work: A critical analysis* (pp. 165–180). Westport, CT: Auburn House.

Midgley, J. (1995). *Social development: The developmental perspective in social work*. Thousand Oaks, CA: Sage.

Midgley, J. (1996). The developmental perspective in social welfare: Transcending residual and institutional models. *Social Work Practice*, 2–8.

Midgley, J., and Simbi, P. (1993). Promoting a developmental focus in the community organization curriculum: Relevance of the African experience. *Journal of Social Work Education*, 29: 269–278.

Oppenheimer, G. M. (1993). To build a bridge: The use of foreign models by domestic critics of U.S. drug policy. In R. Bayer and G. M. Oppenheimer (Eds.), *Confronting drug policy* (pp. 194–226). New York: Cambridge University Press.

Reich, R. B. (1991). *The work of nations*. New York: Alfred Knopf.

Resnick, R. P. (1995). South America. In T. D. Watts, D. Elliott and N. S. Mayadas (Eds.), *International handbook on social work education*. (pp. 65–86). Westport, CT: Greenwood Press.

United Nations. (1993). *Report on the world social situation 1993*. New York: Author.

Watkins, K. (1995). *The Oxfam poverty report*. Oxford: Oxfam.

Wilson, W. J. (1987). *The truly disadvantaged: The inner city, the underclass and public policy*. Chicago: University of Chicago Press.

World Bank. (1990). *World development report, 1990: Poverty*. Washington, DC: Author.

Nonprofit Organizations, Social Policy, and Public Welfare

Eleanor L. Brilliant

*Social policy is . . . centered on those institutions that
cause integration and discourage alienation.*

Kenneth Boulding, 1967

Unique among industrialized nations, the nonprofit, or voluntary, sector has played a critical role in the development of social welfare and the social work profession in the United States. Yet, according to Eleanor Brilliant, many social workers continue to view voluntary sector activities as essentially pre-New Deal phenomena. Today, however, a variety of circumstances have stimulated a reexamination of the relationship between nonprofit organizations and public policies. These include recent efforts by conservatives to dismantle the American welfare state. In this essay, Brilliant, professor of social work at Rutgers University, reviews the role of the nonprofit sector in the United States, discusses the impact of the new conservatism on voluntary associations, and considers the implications of her analysis for the voluntary sector and the social work profession in the decades ahead. She argues that in the next century social workers must develop both philosophical rules and practice principles that will help clarify expectations about the respective roles of the public and private sectors in regard to the general welfare. This will require social workers to pay more attention to community process, group participation, and shared leadership in the development of its policy and practice paradigms.

Dr. Brilliant is a member of the Scholar's Advisory Council of the Indiana University Center on Philanthropy and the author of The United Way: Dilemmas of Organized Charity. *She will soon publish a book that analyzes the public policy impact of the Peterson and Filer Commissions on the role of the American nonprofit sector, and is engaged in research on the empowerment of women through fund-raising and organizational activity.*

Introduction

In the Introduction to a posthumous edition of essays by Richard Titmuss, S. M. Miller (1987) suggested that in Titmuss's book *The Gift Relationship* (1971), the author had opened the door to voluntarism as an aspect of social policy. In fact, Titmuss had argued that the voluntary giving of blood in Great Britain produced a better product than the market system in the United States. Although this gift occurred in the context of the government-run National Health Service, Titmuss emphasized his finding that the voluntary, altruistic, gift of blood to strangers resulted in greater quantity and higher quality than the commercial selling of blood.

At about the time that Titmuss died (1974), the idea of a "third sector," separate from government and business, and including a range of philanthropic and voluntary (nonprofit) organizations, was being conceptualized in the United States and Britain (Commission on Private Philanthropy and Public Needs, 1975). Regrettably, we cannot know how Titmuss might have related this concept of a voluntary sector to his social policy paradigm. However, in an earlier seminal essay, Titmuss (1963) had proposed that social policy and redistribution of wealth should be analyzed in relation to three different programmatic categories: social welfare, occupational welfare, and fiscal welfare. Because philanthropic contributions are closely linked to tax policies in the United States, voluntary, nonprofit activity could be viewed as a subgroup of fiscal welfare under this schema. In any case, the connection between tax policies and support for voluntary nonprofit organizations suggests questions about the role of these organizations in American society today and in the future.

Despite the fact that the origins of social work are closely intertwined with the history of voluntarism, in the years since publication of *The Gift Relationship*, social workers in this country have on the whole been reluctant to include voluntary activity as part of their social policy paradigm. Many social work activists and scholars seem to view charity and voluntary activity as essentially pre-New Deal phenomena. Some apparently believe that nonprofit agencies contribute to the limitations of a residual welfare system in the United States (McInnis-Dittrich, 1994) and, by implication, that the reluctant welfare state described by Wilensky and Lebeaux (1965) results from our commitment to voluntarism.

In recent years, however, a growing number of social work educators and scholars have become interested in the relationship among the various sectors in our complex economy and in the role of public-private entities in social welfare provision particularly (Brilliant, 1974; Gilbert, 1995; Kamerman and Kahn, 1989; Kramer, 1981; Wedel, Katz, and Wick, 1979; Wenocur and Reisch, 1989). Other authors incorporate the related notion of a common good or of community into their policy paradigm (Schorr, 1986); or emphasize the significance of integrative social relationships (Gil, 1992). Stoesz and Karger (1992) and Smith and Lipsky (1993) are among those who more recently have attempted to assess the role of voluntary organizations in their analysis of a fragmented social welfare system. In effect, social workers are joining with scholars in other disciplines who have been asking similar questions. In doing so, they are also concerned with perhaps the most difficult question of all about nonprofit organizations: Cui bono? For whose benefit? (Clotfelter, 1992; Gronjberg, 1993).

Political, economic, and social circumstances are encouraging social workers to confront the profession's ambivalence about nonprofit organizations in a welfare state.[1] Conservatives, acting as if they had a popular mandate, have attempted to dismantle the American welfare state. The "Contract for America," proposed by Representative Newt Gingrich (1994), was directed not only at cutting program expenses, but at the whole idea of entitlements, rights, and basic supports. In effect, new conservatives propose that services under private auspices should be substituted for public programs and policies, even while

---

[1]The author confronted this early on in her academic career. When she discussed her interest in voluntarism with a colleague in a major social work program in New York, she was told that this focus would be dangerous to her career and professional advancement. I want to express my appreciation to Rutgers for not making this warning a prediction.

they are cutting the supports for voluntary organizations. Consequently, it has become apparent that as we enter the 21st century social work also must be concerned with the place of voluntary activity in a welfare state.

Why is this so? Why should social workers care about the fate of voluntary organizations when decreased public dollars threaten essential public welfare programs for poor families and children? In this essay, I begin by reviewing the role of the nonprofit sector in our society and its significance for social welfare and the common good in the United States (Ford Foundation, 1989). I then discuss the new conservativism and its impact on voluntary associations. In conclusion, I consider the implications of my analysis for social work in the 21st century.

The Third Sector: Scope, Purposes, and Taxes

Terminology regarding the third sector is problematic, but, in general, the terms *voluntary sector, nonprofit sector,* and *third sector* are used interchangeably, and I will follow this practice here (Brilliant, 1995). *Philanthropy* is usually used in a similar way, although arguably it has a somewhat different connotation related to the giving of money or, more specifically, contributions by the rich to a variety of "charitable" activities. Overall, voluntary sector organizations are characterized by diversity, with evident religious and secular particularism in regard to ideological views or targeted populations (e.g., feminist self-help groups or ethnic art museums). Organizations of the nonprofit sector vary enormously in range and scale, including mutual benefit associations and political organizations, as well as hospitals, universities, and donor organizations such as foundations (Brilliant, 1995; Van Til, 1988).

Most tax-exempt organizations are non-profit, but some types of nonprofit organizations are not tax-exempt. One expert in tax law points to the complexity of the different terms and suggests that " 'nonprofit organizations' are usually a matter of state law," whereas "tax-exempt organization" is a concept of federal law (Hopkins, 1992b, p.3). In contrast with for-profit corporations, nonprofit organizations operate under a "distribution constraint," which prevents private inurement to individuals. Although they may make a profit, in contrast to businesses (which are expected to benefit owners), nonprofits *are not permitted to distribute profits or gains* to interested parties such as board members or staff. They are expected to plow surpluses from any of their activities (including permissible related businesses) into their public interest functions (Hansmann, 1987; Hopkins, 1992b; Simon, 1987).

The theoretical rationale for tax privileges and benefits enjoyed by third-sector organizations is defined variously in terms of economic needs (i.e., they represent a response to market failure in the delivery of needed services, or they exist because service recipients lack adequate evaluative knowledge); as a response to government failure (i.e., problems of choice, lack of adequate voter support for special services or for amounts of services); or as part of basic constitutional guarantees of free speech, religion, and the right of assembly (Brilliant, 1990; Douglas, 1983; Weisbrod, 1988).

The size and scope of the third sector is usually defined in terms of the official list of the U.S. Internal Revenue Service (IRS), whose master file contains an updated count of active tax-exempt organizations with recent annual revenues of over $25,000 annually. In 1993, the number of such organizations in the IRS master file was 1,118,000, but the actual number may be considerably larger because churches and smaller organizations do not have to register with the IRS (Hodgkinson, Weitzman, Toppe, and Noga, 1992). Overall it is estimated that nonprofit organizations represent about 6 percent of our gross national product and employ about 8 million people (1990) (Hodgkinson, Weitzman, Noga, and Gorski, n.d.).

Two categories of the IRS master list of tax-exempt organizations are most directly related to social welfare and social work—the group defined as charitable 501(c)(3) organizations and the related group of 501(c)(4) civic leagues and social welfare organizations. In 1993, there were are an estimated 575,690 of the former and 142,325 of the latter, and together they made up about two-thirds of all nonprofit organizations on the tax-exempt master list. The first group of "charitable" organizations is defined as including religious, scientific, educational, literary, and other activities, as well as activities defined specifically as charitable. It therefore includes most of the service-providing agencies with which social workers are associated and in which they usually work (such as hospitals and family service agencies, as well as the intermediary funding groups that provide support for those organizations, such as foundations and federated fund-raising organizations). The related category of 501(c)(4) organizations encompasses groups that have social welfare purposes but are essentially not direct service agencies. This category includes organizations that engage in extensive lobbying and advocacy activities, such as the National Association for Colored People (NAACP), the American Association for Retired People (AARP), and Common Cause. The 501(c)(3) and (c)(4) groups together have been referred to as the "independent sector" (Hodgkinson et al., 1992). They have also been

the major target for attacks by conservatives in Congress in the late 1990s (National Committee for Responsive Philanthropy, 1995).

Nearly all organizations on the tax-exempt list, including the 501(c)(4) group, receive some exemption from local and state taxes based on historical tradition and the notion that there is a degree of public interest in their activities. However, organizations in the 501(c)(3) "charitable" category are in a sense special under our tax laws, and they generally enjoy a second tax benefit; that is, their donors may receive a deduction (from taxable income) for contributions to these organizations. These organizations are expected to meet particular public purposes and to have independent governing systems. Under current tax laws, organizations defined as charitable are limited in the amount of lobbying they can carry out, but with the exception of the delineated group of private foundations, limitations on lobbying have been, on the whole, interpreted loosely (Hopkins, 1992a).

The "double" tax benefit for charitable organizations has been justified since its origins in the early 20th century because of the particular public purposes these organizations serve (Hopkins, 1992a). However, both liberals and conservatives recognize that charitable deductions benefit the giver as well as the receiver; they can also be considered as subtracting potential dollars from the public exchequer. Since 1974, tax dollars "lost" as a result of tax-deductible contributions have been counted along with other tax preferences (for dependents or interest on home mortgages) as "tax expenditures" in the official federal budget (Goode, 1977; U. S. Congress, 1994). This has happened despite the fact that economists have apparently argued successfully that charitable contributions result in more dollars going to the public good than are subtracted by deductions from taxable income

(Feldstein and Taylor, 1975). An estimated 82 percent of federal tax expenditures benefitted individuals, and between 1971 and 1988, tax expenditures' share of public costs increased from 22 percent ($52 billion) to 28 percent (or $289 billion) although the real value of the different exemptions varies (Moon, cited in Gilbert, 1995). Attention is often focused on tax policies that result in disparate and inequitable tax preferences for wealthier individuals and groups, and indeed, under the current system, the cost of charitable giving is on the whole considerably less for individuals in higher income brackets. It is questionable, however, whether this is adequate justification for replacing our present (moderately) progressive tax system with a new system of flat taxes, which would almost certainly provide even more benefit for the rich (Johnston, 1996).

The Shadow State: Services, Advocacy, and Social Reform

Government and voluntary organizations have been closely linked since the early days of our republic (Persons, Osborn, and Feldman, 1976). However, it was really only after the New Deal and, indeed, since the explosion of government funding in the 1960s, that the federal government has become, directly and indirectly, a major supporter of local voluntary organizations (Brilliant, 1990; Weisbrod, 1988). In any case, the relationship between government and nonprofit organizations is complex and variable, depending on the political climate, the kind of organization receiving the funds, and the use to which it is believed the funds are being put. This follows from the range of purposes the sector encompasses in the pursuit of diversity and choice in our society.

The partnership role of government and charitable organizations has particular significance for human services. Primary evidence for the partnership derives from the amount of support that charitable nonprofits receive from government, which is estimated to be more than one-third or as much as 37 percent of their total income in 1995 (Hodgkinson, Pollak, and Salamon, 1995). This money comes directly via grants from the federal government, as well as more indirectly through local or state government or payments that go initially to individuals. It is not given without "strings"; funds are expected to be used for legitimately defined public purposes stipulated in laws and regulations that enable grants and contracting for private (for-profit as well as not-for-profit) organizations. Extensive use of contracting is certainly part of the reason that case management has become such an important service delivery technology in mental health, disability, and public welfare programs, where counseling and vocational rehabilitation (for example) may be among the many contracted services. Nonetheless, since the early 1970s, the phenomenon of contracted services has raised concerns, including the question of accountability for meeting public goals (Brilliant, 1974; Demone and Gibelman, 1989; Kamerman and Kahn, 1989) and whether the use of private organizations will inevitably mean devolution of government responsibility (Bendick, 1989; Starr, 1989).

During the 1970s and into the 1980s, contract relationships between the voluntary sector and government expanded until new issues emerged as a result of retrenchments in federal support for social welfare programs under the Reagan administration. Not counting health, it was estimated that support for nonprofit organizations dropped by 27 percent between 1980 and 1984 (Salamon, 1995, p. 159). Still, in the 1980s, government appeared to spend considerably less on direct human service provision than did organizations in the nonprofit sector. In 1987, government was reported to have spent $87.1 billion in providing human services, in contrast to $238.7 billion spent by the entire nonprofit service sector (incuding hospitals and educational and cultural institutions), with $36.6 billion spent by social and legal service organizations alone (Salamon, 1995, p. 117). More reent calculations of mandated services (for welfare recipients) under the Family Service Act of 1988 would undoubtedly reveal increased costs for contracted services by nonprofit agencies.

The end of the Reagan-Bush era of the 1980s presented policy analysts with something of a paradox. On the one hand, concern was expressed that, in developing a symbiotic relationship with the state, the nonprofit sector had lost its independence and was essentially serving as a shadow state (Wolch, 1990). On the other hand, criticism of the trend toward privatization of the welfare state was increasing. In this sense, privatization included not only voluntary agencies but related for-profit activities. It was noted that even with the federal cutbacks, voluntary human service agencies increased in number and total expenditures as they made up for the loss of federal revenues. In this regard, state and local revenues were helpful but not sufficient. In the early 1980s, human service agencies increased their reliance on fees, sales, and other marketing devices that seemed to undermine their nonprofit purposes. There was also a marked growth in the use of for-profit organizations in the delivery of human services (Salamon, 1995). Salamon and others decried the increasing privatization of the social services in the United States and elsewhere (Salamon, 1993; Starr, 1989). However, by the end of the 1980s, it had become increasingly clear that there was a distinction between federal government *payments* (expenditures) for human services (day care, health and mental health care, and legal assistance), which most social workers consider essential, and federal (or other) government *provision* of all services, which could be more debatable. Meanwhile, privatization in the form of for-profit activity continued to grow.

By the mid-1990s, a serious antiwelfare state paradigm had reemerged in the United States. Conservatives in Congress and outside demanded lower government spending, and focused on reduced federal support for social welfare programs in any form. Individuals and families were supposed to become less dependent on welfare by renewed work efforts, while at the same time massive spending reductions were proposed for a wide range of service programs (apart from direct welfare) that would affect the elderly, the poor, and other disadvantaged people. Voluntarism was hailed as the alternative to public social welfare programs and private (for-profit and nonprofit) agencies were supposed to provide the new safety net for vulnerable populations.

Closer examination of the intended cutbacks reveals the absurdity of this idea. In the fall of 1995, the umbrella organization Independent Sector estimated that planned reductions in an initial Senate bill would result, by 2002, in a cumulative reduction of $961 billion in funding for federal programs of interest to nonprofit organizations, including health, income assistance, education training, social services, and community and regional development (Hodgkinson et al., 1995). In order to estimate the impact of these cutbacks on the voluntary sector, Independent Sector surveyed a sample of 108 organizations (with 306 programs in 31 states) to determine how they would be affected by these proposed funding reductions. About 91 percent (98) of the organizations received federal funding; one-third of the participants were family service agencies; most were human service–related agencies, although a few arts and cultural agencies were included. Overall, the proposed reductions were expected to cause these agencies to have a gap in revenue of about 10 percent of their total spending, or $121 million, by 2002. Not surprisingly, legal services, which were under special attack in the Congress, reported an expected 90 percent funding reduction. Above and beyond anticipated and planned increased giving, the study concluded that "these organizations would have to increase charitable contributions by 120 percent to offset the reduction in federal funding" (Hodgkinson et al., 1995, p.11). After extended congressional negotiations with the White House, it was still feared that the projected balanced federal budget would result in a loss for nonprofits of between $140 to $150 billion in revenues by the year 2002 (Freudenheim, 1996).

These draconian cuts were expected to be modifed before final passage of the bill. Even so, as we enter the 21st century, social welfare policy is likely to be framed in the context of a generally conservative climate in which the nonprofit sector will continue to lose revenues at the same time as major public program expenditures are reduced. For social policy, the impact of the partnership relationship is evident: If one-half of the partnership suffers losses, so does the other. Public decreases cause private reactions. In compensation, therefore, in the next millenium, we will probably see more human service business organizations or profit-making activities by nonprofit human service agencies. Although these are allowable under the law—if they are related to the public interest purposes of the organization—the pursuit of profits tends to distort selection of clients and agency service goals. Consequently, continued cutbacks in public funds may result in a geometric decrease in services to the most needy—those who cannot pay for them—in the nonprofit sector as well as the public sector.

Proposed decentralization of responsiblity to local government levels will also increase existing disparities in services for the poor, as demonstrated by differences among state-determined welfare benefits under AFDC (Committee on Ways and Means, U.S. House of Representatives, 1994). Current discrepancies in tax support for local public schools have certainly had this effect, and recent research also demonstrates a correlation between low charitable contributions and low public expenditures in local regions (Wolpert, 1995).

Advocacy, Freedom of Speech, and Dissent

So far, we have discussed the relationship between nonprofit organizations and the public sector largely in terms of their partnership in providing human services. However, there are other significant ways in which the public and private-not-for-profit sector relate to each other, and which appear to be in great jeopardy at the end of the 20th century. Indeed, if the price of liberty is eternal vigilance, this vigilance will be needed as we enter the next century, with fundamental values of free speech and voluntary association still threatened. To amplify: Relationships between organizations of the voluntary sector and the private sector can be considered on a continuum. These relationships range from government control and policy determination (e.g., tax policies) to partnerships between public and private organizations to advocacy and lobbying for public services by voluntary agencies to autonomy and independence to expression of active difference, dissent, and social movement (nonprofit) organizations. Overall, it is the range of organizations at the latter end of the continuum that particularly characterizes civil liberties and that, therefore, should be of great concern to social workers. The notion of a civil society, existing freely in public and private spaces outside of the voting process, is basic to a democratic state. This notion includes protecting the rights of many different organizations—for example, dissenting groups of feminists, people of color, students proposing ethnic studies, and gay and lesbian rights groups—groups that permit freedom of expression or "voice" for the great diversity of people in our country. A variety of voices is embedded in the freedom to choose with whom we associate, how we express our beliefs, and where we worship. The organizations we choose, in effect, become the vehicles through which we speak freely without fear of government control or censorship, and by which we advocate for interests that may not be represented adequately in our formal governmental structure. Beyond our own country, rights related to advocacy and lobbying are fundamental to the idea of a civil democratic society that America exports to other nations, including Eastern Europe (Brilliant, 1995).

In the United States, advocacy and lobbying are carried out by most nonprofit organizations, as well as by business organizations. However, curiously, the current attack on such activities is almost entirely directed at the organizations of the nonprofit sector and, in particular, at the 501(c)(3) charitable category, which includes most human service agencies, and at its close relation, the 501(c)(4) group. This is highly problematic on two accounts. In the first place, lobbying and advocacy activities can and should be practiced by workers in direct service agencies, who are all too aware of the needs and deprivations of their clients (Wineman, 1984). Currently, advocacy and lobbying are permitted under current tax regulations for 501(c)(3) organizations as long as such activity is not on behalf of particular candidates for office (Hopkins, 1992a; 1995). Second, even

more latitude for advocacy and political activity is permitted by 501(c)(4) organizations, whose defined purpose includes such actions, as well as by some other nonprofit organizations such as professional associations.

Arguably the most critical function of nonprofit organizations in our country will always be the protection of group diversity and individual choice—so as to guarantee the kind of civil society in which different beliefs can be expressed and pursued, even to the point of dissent with the government.[2] Nonetheless, throughout this century (and before) there have been repressive periods when this freedom has been attacked. Indeed, in the 1950s, during the McCarthy era, congressional committees investigated so-called subversive activities by foundations, including Ford and Rockefeller (Cuninggim, 1972). Later, in the Tax Reform Act of 1969, limitations were placed on the political actions of a defined group of "private" foundations. In the 1980s, two attempts were made to limit advocacy and lobbying by a broader group of nonprofit organizations. Restrictions were placed on organizations that received federal grants (OMB Circular A-122, 1981), and advocacy groups were eliminated as potential recipients of the federal workers' fund-raising campaign (the Combined Federal Campaign) (Brilliant, 1990).

---

[2]Large foundations in our country have enormous resources (an estimated $189.2 billion in assets) as well as powerful stakeholders. Although "private" foundations are somewhat limited by tax laws, which constrain them from political actions, many continue to provide funding for progressive activities. In addition, a whole group of grass roots alternative funds are organizing around issues affecting women, the environment, gays and lesbians, and people of color. These latter are inherent forces for social change within the scope of philanthropy, which I am exploring in two studies, and particularly in a study of women's funding organizations. For figures on the overall size of U.S. foundations, see Renz and Treiber (1995, pp. 1–2.)

In the waning years of the 20th century, renewed attacks on charitable and social welfare agencies by the Right suggest continuing threats to our basic freedoms. In August 1995, what amounted to a "charity gag rule" was proposed by Republican representatives Ernest Istook (Oklahoma), David McIntosh (Indiana), and Robert Ehrlich (Maryland). This legislation would have severely limited expenditures of private funds for political activity (lobbying and advocacy) by charitable organizations that received any federal grants (Arenson, 1995). The bill passed the House of Representatives but did not pass in the Senate. Other legislation was also proposed to limit activities of the 501(c)(4) organizations, although this was directed only at more powerful organizations, and specifically at the AARP—probably because it was an effective advocate for programs that conservatives were targeting for cuts, such as Medicare (National Committee for Responsive Philanthropy, 1995). Evidence suggests that efforts to limit the advocacy and lobbying activities of nonprofit sector organizations in the social welfare–related 501(c)(3) and 501(c)(4) categories will continue into the next century, along with other challenges to the idea of tax exemption at the state and local level.

Concluding Thoughts About the Future

Most social workers recognize a professional obligation to advocate for people's rights, to organize for protection of those rights, and even to lobby for social policy reforms. This kind of activity can take place in human service organizations, more easily through work in coalitions and advocacy groups, and also through our professional organizations (CSWE and NASW). To do this, however, social workers need to develop their advocacy skills and learn how to use community organization strategies in grass roots lobbying. I would also argue that, in order to combat attacks on the welfare state from the radical Right, social work education must reinforce the connection between policy and practice. Making this connection effectively will continue to have major consequences for our profession, our clients, and the future welfare of our society. Furthermore, social work educators cannot act as if social movements are totally foreign to social work activities. If we do so, we will be unable to create professionals who can be leaders in organizing new policy strategies with emerging groups. Indeed, in preparation for the next millenium, we need to strengthen our political skills at all levels, beginning with developing the capacity of practitioners to influence decision making in their own organizations. [Some of the language being proposed for the new professional Code of Ethics (1996) suggests awareness of this need.]

Challenges facing the American welfare state require social workers to reexamine the place of nonprofit organizations and philanthropic activity in social policy, social service delivery and planning for community needs—for both pragmatic and conceptual reasons, including the strong connection between public policy and tax policy; the altruistic spirit of caring for our neighbors and the need for community responsibility, which must be considered along with recognition of rights, entitlements, and contract relationships; the need to account for and use the power of the great foundations for the general welfare; the need for grass roots organizing and lobbying to oppose harmful public policies; and the value attached to diversity and freedom of choice in our society. Review of the Titmuss paradigm may help us to enter the 21st century with a sharper perspective on philanthropy and voluntary activity in relation to basic social policy goals of economic equity and wealth redistribution.

Social work in the next century requires philosophical rules and practical procedures that help clarify expectations about the public and private sectors in regard to the general welfare. Even if the mixed political economy of American welfare has evident benefits in terms of values of choice and diversity, we will need to know how to apportion responsibilities for an effective mix. Apart from economic supports for poor and vulnerable individuals through (public) income transfers, there is, arguably, no inherent reason why social services cannot be delivered through nonprofit organizations, provided that an effective government partnership with nonprofit organizations is maintained. But the record of nonprofit organizations in serving needy populations appears to be uneven (Clotfelter, 1992), and therefore we need to develop better tools of accountability for public goals by the public monitoring of private actions. In any case, we need to participate in practical and theoretical examinations of the nonprofit sector, including discussions about "disaggregating" the sector in regard to the status of some fee-collecting institutions such as hospitals (Hansmann, 1987). In general, social workers need to do more extensive research on who uses what services, under what conditions, and with what benefit.

Finally, a renewed commitment to social justice for the future means using a new lens to look at ways to achieve these goals. The evidence suggests that, to be effective in the 21st century, social work will have to incorporate more attention to community process, group participation, and shared leadership as part of its policy paradigm. We cannot by ourselves guarantee social and economic equity, but we

should help protect freedom and opportunity for those groups who fight for these rights and who promote the public good. We must also develop ways to join with them in common cause.

REFERENCES

Arenson, K. W. (August 7, 1995). Legislation would expand restrictions on political advocacy by charities. *New York Times*, p. A-10.

Bendick, M., Jr. (1989). Privatizing the delivery of social welfare services: An idea to be taken seriously. In S. B. Kwmerman and A. J. Kahn (Eds.), *Privatization and the welfare state* (pp. 97–120). Princeton: Princeton University.

Brilliant, E. (1974). Private or public: A model of ambiguities. *Social Service Review* 47: 384-396.

Brilliant, E. (1990). *The United way: Dilemmas of organized charity.* New York: Columbia University Press.

Brilliant, E. (1995). Voluntarism. In R. L. Edwards (Ed.), *The encyclopedia of social work*, (19th ed., Vol. 3 (pp. 2469–2482). Washington, DC: NASW Press.

Clotfelter, C. T. (Ed.). (1992). *Who benefits from the nonprofit sector?* Chicago: University of Chicago Press.

Commission on Private Philanthropy and Public Needs. (The Filer Commission). (1975). *Giving in America: Toward a stronger voluntary sector.* Washington, DC: Government Printing Office.

Committee on Ways and Means, U.S. House of Representatives. (1994). *Background materials on major programs under the jurisdiction of the committee on ways and means.* Washington, DC: Government Printing Office.

Cuninggim, M. (1972). *Private money and public service: The role of foundations in American society.* New York: McGraw-Hill.

Demone, H. W., Jr., and Gibelman, M. (Eds.). (1989). *Services for sale: Purchasing health and human services*. New Brunswick, NJ: Rutgers University Press.

Douglas, J. (1983). *Why charity? The case for the third sector*. Beverly Hills, CA: Sage Publications.

Feldstein, M. S., and Taylor, A. (1975). The income tax and charitable contributions: Estimates and simulations with the Treasury tax files. In *Research Papers of the National Commission on Private Philanthropy and Public Needs* (pp. 1419–1440). Washington, DC: U.S. Treasury Department, 1977.

Ford Foundation. (1989). *The common good: Social welfare and the American future*. New York: Author.

Freudenheim, M. (February 5, 1996). Charities aiding poor fear loss of government subsidies. *New York Times*.

Gil, D. (1992). *Unravelling social policy: Theory, analysis and political action towards social equality*, 5th ed. Rochester, VT: Schencken.

Gilbert, N. (1995). *Welfare justice: Restoring social equity*. New Haven, CT: Yale University Press.

Goode, R. (1977). The economic definition of income. In Joseph Pechman (Ed.), *Comprehensive income taxation*. Washington, DC: Brookings Institution.

Gronjberg, K. A. (1993). *Understanding nonprofit funding: Managing revenues in social services and community development organizations*. San Francisco: Jossey-Bass.

Hansmann, H. B. (1987). Economic theories of nonprofit organizations. In W. W. Powell (Ed.), *The nonprofit sector: A research handbook* (pp. 27–42). New Haven, CT: Yale University Press.

Hodgkinson, V. A., Pollak, T. H., and Salamon, L. M. (1995). *The impact of federal budget proposals upon the activities of charitable organizations and the people they serve, 1996–2002: The 100 nonprofit organizations study*. Washington, DC: Independent Sector.

Hodgkinson, V. A., Weitzman, M. S., Noga, S. M., and Gorski, H. A. (n.d.). *National summary: Not-for-profit employment from the 1990 census of population and housing*. (Preliminary Findings). Washington, DC: Independent Sector.

Hodgkinson, V. A., Weitzman, M. S., Toppe, C., and Noga, S. M. (1992). *Nonprofit almanac 1992–1993: Dimensions of the independent sector*. San Francisco: Jossey-Bass.

Hopkins, B. R. (1992a). *Charity, advocacy, and the law*. New York: John Wiley & Sons.

Hopkins, B. R. (1992b). *The law of tax-exempt organizations*, 6th ed. New York: John Wiley & Sons.

Hopkins, B. R. (1995). *The law of tax-exempt organizations, 1995 cumulative supplement*, 6th ed. New York: John Wiley & Sons.

Johnston, D. C. (January 21, 1996). How a flat tax would work, for you and for them. *New York Times*, p. 3.

Kamerman, S. B., and Kahn, A. J. (Eds.). (1989). *Privatization and the welfare state*. Princeton: Princeton University Press.

Kramer, R. M. (1981). *Voluntary agencies in the welfare state*. Berkeley: University of California Press.

McInnis-Dittrich, K. (1994). *Integrating social welfare policy and social work practice*. Pacific Grove, CA: Brooks/Cole.

Miller, S. M. (1987). Introduction: The legacy of Richard Titmuss. In Brian Abel-Smith and Kay Titmuss (Eds.), *The philosophy of welfare: Selected writings of Richard M. Titmuss* (pp. 1–17). London: Allen & Unwin.

Moon, A. (1989). Analysis of tax expenditures. Ph.D. dissertation. University of California, Berkeley.

National Committee for Responsive Philanthropy (NCRP). (Fall 1995). War on nonprofits continues unabashed but charities help in key victory on Istook amendment. *Responsive Philanthropy*, p. 1.

Office of Management and Budget. (1981). Circular A-122. Washington, DC: Government Printing Office.

Persons, J. P., Osborn, J. J., Jr., and Feldman, C. F. (1976). Criteria for Exemption Under Section 501(c)(3). In *Research papers of the National Com-*

mission on Private Philanthropy and Public Needs (pp. 1909–2044). Washington, DC: U.S. Treasury Department, 1977.

Renz, L. S., and Treiber, R. R. (1995). *Foundation giving: Yearbook of facts and figures on private, corporate, and community foundations.* New York: The Foundation Center.

Salamon, L. M. (1993). The marketization of welfare: Changing nonprofit and for-profit roles in the American welfare state. *Social Service Review* 67, (1), March: 16–39.

Salamon, L. M. (1995). *Partners in public service: Government-nonprofit relations in public service.* Baltimore, MD: Johns Hopkins.

Schorr, A. L. (1986). *Common decency: Domestic policies after Reagan.* New Haven, CT: Yale University Press.

Simon, J. (1987). The tax treatment of nonprofit organizations: A review of federal and state policies. In W. W. Powell (Ed.), *The nonprofit sector: A research handbook* (pp. 67–98). New Haven, CT: Yale University Press.

Smith, S. R., and Lipsky, M. (1993). *Nonprofits for hire: The welfare state in the age of contracting.* Cambridge, MA: Harvard University Press.

Starr, P. (1989). The meaning of privatization. In S. B. Kamerman and A. J. Kahn (Eds.), *Privatization and the welfare state.* (pp. 15–48). Princeton: Princeton University Press.

Stoesz, D., and Karger, J. (1992). *Reconstructing the American welfare state.* Lanham, MD: Rowman & Littlefield.

Titmuss, R. M. (1963). *Essays on the 'welfare state,'* 2d. ed. London: Allen & Unwin.

Titmuss, R. M. (1971). *The gift relationship: From human blood to social policy.* New York: Pantheon.

U.S. Congress, Joint Committee on Taxation. (November 9, 1994). *Estimates of federal tax expenditures for fiscal years 1993–1994.* (JCS-6-94).

U.S. House of Representatives, Committee on Ways and Means. (1994). 103rd Congress, 2nd Sess. *Overview of entitlement programs.* (1994 Green Book). Washington, DC: Government Printing Office.

Van Til, J. (1988). *Mapping the third sector: Voluntarism in a changing social economy.* New York: Foundation Center.

Wedel, K. R., Katz, A. J., and Wick, A. (Eds.). (1979). *Social services by government contract: A policy analysis.* New York: Praeger.

Weisbrod, B. (1988). *The nonprofit economy.* Cambridge, MA: Harvard University Press.

Wenocur, S., and Reisch, M. (1989). *From charity to enterprise: The development of American social work in a market economy.* Urbana: University of Illinois Press.

Wilensky, H. L., and Lebeaux, C. N. (1965). *Industrial society and social welfare,* Rev. ed. New York: Free Press.

Wineman, S. (1984). *The politics of human services: Radical alternatives to the welfare state.* Boston: South End Press.

Wolch, J. R. (1990). *The shadow state: Government and voluntary sector in transition.* New York: Foundation Center.

Wolpert, J. (1995). *Who's supporting the safety net?* Cleveland: Mandel Center for Nonprofit Organizations, Case Western Reserve University. (Discussion Paper Series).

The Political Context
of Social Work

Michael Reisch

Social work and politics were intertwined even before the profession had a name. Discussions of the future of social work must inevitably consider the changes that are under way and anticipated for the political context of social policy development and social work practice. This essay by Michael Reisch, professor of social work at the University of Pennsylvania, analyzes the contemporary political environment and discusses the implications of current trends in three major areas. He argues that many analyses of American politics are based on myths about our history—a desire to seek simple explanations for complex phenomena; the isolation of politics from its broader economic, social, and cultural context; and a tendency to predict the future based on linear projections of contemporary reality.

*Reisch has an MSW from Hunter College School of Social Work and a PhD in social history and the history of ideas from the State University of New York at Binghamton. He has served on the faculties of the State University of New York at Stony Brook; the University of Maryland; the University of California, Berkeley; San Francisco State University; and the New Bulgarian University; and as a campaign manager and political consultant to local, state, and federal candidates. He is currently writing two books—*Politics and Social Work *and* Radicalism and Repression in Social Work History *—and is engaged in research for a multicultural history of social welfare in the United States.*

Introduction: Social Work and Politics

More than at any time in this century, politics and social work are inextricably connected. During the past two decades, political changes have shredded the veil of consensus, which hid long-standing ideological divisions within the American electorate. Philosophical attacks and fiscal cutbacks have forced social workers to defend our underlying assumptions about human need and human nature, and the effectiveness of programs of social intervention in the political arena at the national, state, and local levels.

Politics are no longer, however, confined to electoral campaigns, legislative hearings, or newspaper editorials. They appear openly in agency board meetings, in staff conferences, and, ultimately, in the day-to-day decisions that affect worker–client relationships and the quality of services that agencies provide. Ironically, even in the face of this politicization of the practice environment, most social workers have been reluctant to enter the political fray as individuals and in organized groups. Attitudes about the relationship between professionalism and politics partially explains this reluctance—so do ignorance of the political process and fear of the risks involved in political activity (Chambers, 1965; Ehrenreich,

1986; Haynes and Mickelson, 1991; Reisch, 1993a; Specht and Courtney, 1994; Walkowitz, 1988; Wenocur and Reisch, 1989). Yet, politics and social work have been intertwined even before the profession had a name. Unless we recognize how politics shapes the creation of many of the social policies and institutions we often take for granted, we will never comprehend the intrinsically political nature of the work we do.

For example, the inability of social work's traditional clientele to purchase service by themselves and their lack of political power to influence policy decisions has made them unusually dependent on external political support from elites and especially vulnerable to the expectations of sponsors regarding ideological and behavioral conformity. Social work's dependence on such political support has placed the profession at the mercy of political forces throughout its history (Reisch and Wenocur, 1986).

This essay is based on the assumption that in the 21st century the survival of the social services, the well-being of clients and communities, and the ability of social workers to derive satisfaction from our careers depend on the integration of political action into a broader pro-social welfare strategy. Political knowledge and skills should become as much a part of every social worker's repertoire as skills in assessment and intervention with individuals and families (Abramovitz, 1993; Fisher, 1995). Understanding the contemporary political context is an initial step in this direction because of the critical role that government has played in the evolution of U.S. social policies and the expansion of the social work profession. Making projections about the future, however difficult, is a second, equally vital step.

Politics, Government, and Social Work: A Brief History

In the United States, government began to play an active role in social welfare during the 17th century at the village level. During the 18th century, counties began to take responsibility for the provision of public relief for the poor. After independence and throughout the 19th century, public sector responsibility expanded upward to the state level, particularly in the form of institution-building (Axinn and Levin, 1992; Popple and Leighninger, 1990; Trattner, 1995).

As a result of industrialization, urbanization, and overall population growth and change, there was a dramatic increase in social needs at the end of the 19th and during the first decades of the 20th century. A broader definition of the role of government began to emerge during this so-called Progressive Era, culminating in the social insurance programs of the 1930s and the 1960s. Major factors influencing this expanded government role included an increase in poverty among individuals and families as a consequence of economic developments beyond their control; unprecedented demographic changes, such as the growth of the elderly population; new family configurations (e.g., the higher number of female-headed households); the increasing complexity and geographic mobility of U.S. society, which broke down traditional community ties and values; and the inability of private sector agencies to address these issues adequately (Axinn and Levin, 1992; Chambers, 1965; Davis, 1967; Fisher, 1980; Popple and Leighninger, 1990; Trattner, 1995).

Although social workers had been involved in local, state, and national politics since the late 19th century—as advisors to presidential candidates like Theodore Roosevelt, allies of reform mayors like New York's Seth Low, and adversaries of city aldermen—the primary objective of their involvement prior to the 1930s was institution-building directed at selected social problems at the state and county levels, particularly those that focused on so-called deviant populations (Chambers, 1965; Davis, 1967). The creation of large public welfare bureaucracies by the New Deal, however, transformed the size and scope of the social work profession and its relationship to U.S. politics. For most of the rest of the 20th century, the major political focus of the social work profession has been the promotion of an expanded role for government as a tool of economic and social intervention on behalf of vulnerable groups and the population as a whole (Axinn and Levin, 1992; Ehrenreich, 1986; Trolander, 1975; Wenocur and Reisch, 1989).

Although the awareness of social need receded somewhat in the immediate postwar period, government intervention in the social services accelerated rapidly in the 1960s and 1970s, as did the reliance of social workers on supportive relationships with political leaders, particularly within the Democratic Party. During this period, which saw the passage of such landmark legislation as Medicare and Medicaid, SSI, Title XX, the Community Mental Health Act, and the Older Americans Act, as well as the expansion of Social Security benefits, a broad political consensus seemed to have emerged among liberals and conservatives. This consensus recognized that some limited form of a "welfare state" was a minimum requirement of modern society to ensure basic social protection, improve the quality of life, increase equality of opportunity, and help correct the flaws in the market economy. Although evidence of this consensus exists

through the mid-1970s, the defeat of President Nixon's Family Assistance Plan in 1970 by a coalition of liberals and conservatives in the Congress may have signalled the beginning of its demise (Axinn and Levin, 1992; Edsall and Edsall, 1991; Fraser and Gerstle, 1989; Trattner, 1995).

Nevertheless, from the 1960s until the mid-1990s, the structure of federal social insurance programs remained largely unchanged, although block grants and funding cuts in the 1980s reduced their effectiveness in alleviating poverty. By 1967, the federal government surpassed state and local governments as the primary funder of social welfare, and despite recent "welfare reform" legislation passed by the Congress, it continues to play this preeminent role today. Over 12% of the labor force now works in the human services field. Total annual government spending now exceeds $1 trillion. This represents about 20% of the U.S. Gross Domestic Product and over 50% of all government spending. Although this statistic is somewhat misleading—as much of this spending goes to individual and institutional providers through the Medicare and Medicaid programs—it is clear that the politics of social welfare has a major impact on the political economy of the nation (Axinn and Levin, 1992; Ehrenreich, 1986; Plotke, 1996; Popple and Leighninger, 1990; Reisch and Wenocur, 1982; Specht and Courtenay, 1994; Trattner, 1995).

Since the mid-1970s, however, the prevailing consensus on social welfare has been attacked and ultimately shattered by conservatives and, more recently, by neo-liberals, who have challenged the existence of these minimum requirements and their underlying assumptions. As wages have stagnated for the working class and middle income population, and as universal services appeared to shift in the public's mind toward more selective services (often associated with populations of different racial and ethnic backgrounds), conservatives have reaped political capital by focusing on the burden of high taxes, the need for a balanced budget and deficit reduction, mistrust of the efficacy of government intervention, incipient racism among the electorate, class prejudice, and economic insecurity. Consequently, during the past two decades, social workers have directed much of their political energies toward the defense of the limited welfare state that had been created during the previous half century (Carmines and Stimson, 1989; Edsall and Edsall, 1991; Ehrenreich, 1986; Haynes and Mickelson, 1991; Phillips, 1990; Simon, 1994).

The Contemporary Political Landscape

At the close of the 20th century, U.S. politics are in such a state of flux that any serious attempt to make meaningful predictions about the political future would be the height of hubris. Every election appears to herald a new national trend, while each new public opinion poll underscores the volatility of the electorate. This essay is being written before the November 1996 elections, which pundits are touting as a benchmark event that will either confirm or reverse recent political developments (e.g., the "Republican Revolution" of 1994). Although the latest polls point to the possibility of a "mixed outcome" in the balloting—that is, Democratic control of the presidency and Republican control of the Congress—recent political history emphasizes the importance of waiting until the votes are counted before projecting the future political direction of the nation.

In this uncertain context, it is risky to project the political future based largely on inten-sive analyses of recent voting patterns (as this author has done in the past for local, state, and congressional candidates). The safer, if less dramatic, option is to identify key features and trends on the political landscape, assess the validity of these developments, make some projections about their future impact, and discuss their possible implications for social work practice and education. These trends can be placed in three general categories: (1) the role that ideology plays in U.S. politics and in the ideological content of politics; (2) the distribution of political power and the nature of political discourse; and (3) changes in popular attitudes about politics and the role of government and their influence on political behavior. A close examination of these trends reveals that the political context of contemporary social work is far more complex than a cursory glance would indicate. The "mythology of simplicity" that many politicians and voters seek has never been less valid than today.

Changes in Ideology

A major feature of the U.S. political landscape during the past two decades has been the appearance of an ideological reorientation of the electorate. To put it simply, on a number of major policy issues, the political "center" seems to have moved significantly to the right (or conservative) end of the political spectrum. Various factors have been cited as producing this shift, including the decline of liberal and progressive social movements since the 1960s, the growing weakness of organized labor, and the effects of increasing racial and class stratification, particularly in major metropolitan areas (Barlett and Steele, 1992; Bellah et al., 1985; Carmines and Stimson, 1989; Edsall and Edsall, 1991; Etzioni, 1993;

Greenberg, 1995; Hagstrom, 1988; Huckfeldt and Kohfeld, 1989; Phillips, 1990; Terkel, 1988). The shift is most notable around such issues as crime, welfare spending, and so-called social issues (abortion rights, family values, and so on). It is illustrated by the Clinton Administration's embrace of many positions formerly identified with the Republican Party. Although election year strategy plays a role in this political posturing—the tactic of controlling the political center has been a long-established dictum of American politics—there is no denying that the interpretation of the mood of the electorate as more conservative on social and cultural issues plays a role in the policy positions articulated by leaders of both major parties.

Perhaps the most negative of recent ideological changes are the growing racialization of politics and the increasing comfort felt about the public expression of political sentiments that reflect gender biases and homophobia. These are best exemplified by the appeal of candidates like Patrick Buchanan and David Duke to voters' prejudices, fears, and insecurities. Even more temperate politicians have succumbed to the pressure to seek scapegoats for the nation's widespread insecurities about the economy, crime, and the environment. Previously unacceptable ideas about race, class, ethnicity, gender, and religion have once again permeated our political vocabulary, and outmoded concepts like "illegitimacy" have crept back into the discourse that shapes public policy decisions (Barlett and Steele, 1992; Blumenthal, 1988; Edsall and Edsall, 1991; Faludi, 1991; Gallup Poll, 1995; Greenberg, 1995; Hill and Jones, 1993; Lind, 1995; The Nation, 1995; Phillips, 1990; Saloma, 1989).

Yet, the supposed conservative "tilt" of U.S. politics ignores several key points. First, to a considerable extent, the United States has always been a conservative country, if conservatism is defined in terms of such values as individualism and individual rights, a preference for marketplace over governmental solutions to economic and social problems, and a belief that state and local governments are closer, and hence more responsive to popular will. Through this lens, the period of liberal ideological hegemony in U.S. politics, from roughly 1935–1975, can be viewed as an aberration, the consequence of particular historical and economic circumstances (Axinn and Levin, 1992; Barlett and Steele, 1992; Ehrenreich, 1986; Etzioni, 1993; Fraser and Gerstle, 1989; Huckfeldt and Kohfeld, 1989; McElvaine, 1987; Morone, 1991; Phillips, 1990; Plotke, 1996; Smith, 1988).

Second, the notion that there is a common American ideology is itself somewhat suspect. Opinion polls demonstrate significant differences among the voting age population on many issues based on geographic region, social class, generation, gender, race, religion, and education, and political party affiliation. These polls also reveal that the ideological implications to be gleaned from respondents are not crystal clear and depend more on the agenda of the polltakers and the phrasing of the poll's questions. For example, a majority of voters favors reductions in welfare spending, while simultaneously supporting an increase in social provision for poor children and families (Gallup Poll, 1995).

Third, on many issues, Americans across the political spectrum have become more "liberal" during the past generation. Whereas the political center may have shifted to the right, the entire political spectrum has shifted somewhat to the left. For example, there is now widespread support for the preservation of such social welfare programs as Medicare and Social Security, for increased aid to public education, for legislation to preserve the physical environment, for reducing the military budget, and, despite some political rhetoric to the contrary, for the protection of the civil rights of women, persons of color, and gays and lesbians. The label "liberal" may have become a dirty word in U.S. politics, but many of the positions associated with a liberal perspective have become mainstream. This underscores the shifting nature of the ideological spectrum in the United States and the inaccuracy of oft-repeated political epithets. A key factor in the persistent use of such labels may be the extent to which certain policies or programs are regarded as "universal" in nature—that is, of benefit to the society as a whole—or viewed as "selective"—solely benefiting either so-called special interests or some long-stigmatized group. This distinction has significant implications for the development of social policies in the next century (Barlett and Steele, 1992; Blumenthal, 1988; Brownstein, 1994; Etzioni, 1993; Greenberg, 1995; Hagstrom, 1988; Lind, 1995; McElvaine, 1987; *National Journal*, 1988; Phillips, 1990).

Changes in the Distribution of Political Power and the Nature of Political Discourse

During the past two decades there has been a significant shift in the distribution of political power in the United States, a trend that will probably continue into the 21st century. This shift is the complement to similar shifts in the distribution of economic power, which have been long documented (Rifkin, 1995; Sale, 1976), and is the by-product of major developments in communication and informational technology. The primary cause of this shift, however, is not ideology, but demographics. Those states that have more conservative political traditions, less powerful labor and social movements, and weaker concentrations of political power among communities of color have gained representation in Congress

through reapportionment (U.S. Bureau of the Census, 1991). One major consequence of this shift at the national level has been the transfer of political power from the industrial Northeast and Midwest to Southern and Western states. The "Republican Revolution" of 1994, therefore, was influenced more by census patterns in the 1980s than by political decisions in the 1990s (Greenberg, 1995; Lind, 1995; Phillips, 1990).

At the same time, there has been a transfer of power within states from urban to suburban areas. Combined with a general decline in the economic significance of cities and the increased concentration of low-income persons of color in inner city neighborhoods, this transfer has led to the dominance of rural/suburban coalitions on many policy issues and to the reduction of electoral power (and, hence, influence on policy) of racial and ethnic minorities. Patterns of voter participation have produced and exacerbated this development, which can be generally characterized as favoring the promotion of conservative fiscal policies (e.g., the maintenance of low-income, energy, and corporate tax rates) that reflect biases against urban areas and urban populations (Carmines and Stimson, 1989; Edsall and Edsall, 1991; Etzioni, 1993; Greenberg, 1995; Hill and Jones, 1993; Huckfeldt and Kohfeld, 1989; *The Nation*, 1995; Phillips, 1990).

In some ways, this shift is a return to the political patterns of the United States prior to the emergence of the "New Deal coalition," which dominated American politics from the 1930s through the 1960s (Fraser and Gerstle, 1989; Plotke, 1996). Although suburban voters tend to be more accepting of the conditions of modern life than their rural counterparts of earlier generations, they are often as isolated from the realities of urban social issues as their rural forebears. One major difference in contemporary politics is that suburban voters' views of urban reality are primarily formed by the images conveyed by the media, especially television (Devitt, 1996; Putnam, 1996). Another difference is that the economic and social forces producing this return to a pre–New Deal political reality appear to be exacerbating the political isolation of low-power, often underrepresented, populations. Whereas the period of 1935–1975 might be characterized as one of unrealized hopes and crushed expectations, the mood of the past two decades and the unforeseeable future is one of growing hopelessness and the lack of any expectations for positive change. This has contributed substantially to the explosive situation that currently grips the nation's cities (Barancik and Shapiro, 1992; Barlett and Steele, 1992; Edsall and Edsall, 1991; Hill and Jones, 1993; Lind, 1995; Phillips, 1990).

A second major element in the shift in political power is the presence of a weakened, but lingering, two-party system. Leaving aside questions as to whether there are substantive differences between the Republican and Democratic parties, and whether a structural reorganization of political parties along the lines of emerging ideological and social movements would be desirable, there is ample evidence that the role the Democratic and Republican parties play, *as organizational entities*, has been considerably diminished. Both candidates and elected officials are increasingly reluctant to define themselves in terms of their party affiliation and seek, instead, to identify themselves either as political independents or as affiliated with an organization or cause outside of mainstream politics. This has caused the virtual disappearance of "ticket voting" in elections and the erosion of party solidarity in legislative arenas. As more Americans define themselves as political independents, as opinion polls show less evidence of philosophical solidarity among nearly every constituent group, and as an antipolitics mood grips the country, the impetus for politicians to define themselves as outside of politics and organized political parties becomes stronger (Blumenthal, 1988; Greenberg, 1995; Hagstrom, 1988; Huckfeldt and Kohfeld, 1989; McElvaine, 1987; Morone, 1991; Phillips, 1990).

This impetus is strengthened by the growing, well-documented, and complementary roles of money and the media in shaping the nature and outcomes of political campaigns. Politicians are less dependent on the resources or organizational clout of the major parties to win nomination or election. Campaigns, especially at the state and national levels, are increasingly fought over the airwaves or electronic superhighway, not in neighborhoods or suburban shopping malls. Although this has freed candidates and elected officials from oaths of fealty to party bosses, it has made them more dependent for their political survival on wealthy individual and corporate contributors (Devitt, 1996; Phillips, 1990; Public Citizen, 1995; Putnam, 1996).

Much has been written about the corruption of politics that this "marriage" of money and technology has produced. Several consequences are particularly noteworthy, however, and justify repetition in this essay. First, the reliance on media-dominated campaigns, with their associated astronomical costs, exacerbates the exclusionary aspects of American politics. Presidential candidates, Congress, and state legislatures are becoming more and more the domain of the super-wealthy. Over 20% of the members of Congress, for example, are millionaires, compared with less than 1% of the population (*Roll Call*, 1996). Millionaire (even billionaire) presidential candidates are now the rule rather than the exception. Ironically, recent "reforms" such as term limits and restrictions on legislators' outside earned income will further disadvantage average Americans who may be considering a public-service career. Consequently, our elected officials are becoming less like the rest of us and more out of touch with people's everyday issues. Efforts to pass genuine campaign finance reform have failed regardless of which party holds a majority in Congress.

Second, the importance of fund-raising for political survival forces legislators, particularly those serving two-year terms, to spend far more time raising money than raising issues and listening to the concerns of those who can assist their campaigns instead of those who need their assistance. Legislators spend fewer days in their district offices dealing with constituents and more time on the phone seeking funds, often from contributors who live outside their districts. This erodes the concept of representation at the heart of the democratic process, heightens the cynicism of Americans about politicians and the efficacy of politics itself, and diminishes the legitimacy of the nation's political institutions and, ultimately, of democracy as a form of government (Barlett and Steele, 1992; Carmines and Stimson, 1989; Devitt, 1996; Etzioni, 1993; Gallup Poll, 1995; Lind, 1995; Morone, 1991; Phillips, 1990).

Third, the media/money marriage shapes the nature of policy debates in two significant ways. The medium of television (and through its influence, radio and newspapers to some extent as well) places a premium on image over substance, on the appearance of the messenger rather than on the nature of his or her message. It also requires complex and often intractable issues to be boiled down to mere "soundbites" and political homilies. Although politicians from Ronald Reagan to Ross Perot have benefited from this "mythology of simplicity," it has prevented serious and multisided discussions of the nation's economic and social problems and fed the desire for quick, painless fixes to our country's ills. The decline of public intellectuals (who have been replaced in our culture by ratings-hungry talk show hosts and unruly shouting matches by self-styled political pundits) has further contributed to this problem (Devitt, 1996; Phillips, 1990).

Finally, the money/media marriage has distorted policy dialogue in the country by narrowing the range of issues that is placed on the political agenda and framing those issues that are discussed in terms sympathetic to those who pay for their presentation. The debates over health-care reform and environmental regulations are prime examples of these tendencies. This trend favors those interest groups with the deepest pockets, who are able to sustain long-term financial commitments to candidates, such as multinational corporations, and powerful single-issue organizations, like the NRA and the Christian Coalition, who are able to mobilize large numbers of constituents on behalf of their cause (Frankel, 1996; Greenberg, 1995; Morone, 1991; Phillips, 1990; Saloma, 1989).

Changing Views of Politics

In the past generation, in response to these changes in the political process, assorted political scandals (from Watergate to Whitewater), and the decline of a sense of community and civic virtues in American life, attitudes toward politics have shifted dramatically (Bellah et al., 1985; Etzioni, 1993; Phillips, 1990). Since the late 1970s, unstinting attacks on "big government" as the cause of the nation's persistent ills have also affected people's faith in the political process as a means to solve the nation's problems. In the early 1960s, 76% of all Americans trusted that government would usually "do the right thing" when it came to addressing important social or economic problems. By the early 1990s, only 29% of the population felt the same way. Surveys since the early 1990s have revealed that an average of 62% of respondents, regardless of political affiliation, disapprove of the way Congress is doing its job. This disapproval rating is 26 points higher than it was two decades ago during President Nixon's impeachment proceedings (Gallup Poll, 1995).

These shifting attitudes have influenced voting patterns, public awareness of policy issues, and participation in the nonvoting processes of citizenship (attendance at public meetings, for example). The proportion of adult Americans who vote or even register to vote has declined steadily in recent decades, particularly among young persons and people of color. Explanations for this decline range from deliberate restrictions on the processes of voter registration to intentional harassment of voters in certain districts to the general cynicism and apathy about politics that afflict a passive, television-saturated public (Devitt, 1996; Piven and Cloward, 1989; Putnam, 1996). These developments have serious implications for the field of social work because of its reliance on government intervention as a major vehicle of social change and its long-time promotion of democratic values and processes. Both appear to be threatened by recent political trends.

Early in the next century, therefore, the U.S. political system will confront the following fundamental issues that will have profound implications for social workers, their clients, their agencies, and their communities:

1. Has the advent of a global economy, computers, and communications technology rendered existing political systems irrelevant, if not obsolete? If so, in what forms will people's hopes, fears, and aspirations be expressed? If not, how will our political system adapt its local focus to an international environment?

2. What will be the long-term political impact of the increasing physical separation of American communities on the basis of race and class? How will the American party system respond to these dramatic changes in our communities? Will a permanent system of "political apartheid" emerge in this context?

3. What will be the role of government as its relationship to private and non-profit organizations is fundamentally changed?

4. What will be the future of social work in a world that lacks any ideological or political counterweights to the dominance of free market approaches to social welfare?

Implications for Practice and Education

A half century ago, Bertha Reynolds (1951-1987) made a compelling case for the ongoing involvement of social workers in political activity: "The philosophy of social work cannot be separated from the philosophy of a nation, as to how it values people, and what importance it sets upon their welfare . . . . [We are] faced with a choice between contradictory forces in our society: those which are moving toward the welfare of the people . . . and those which destroy human life in preventable misery and war, and relieve poverty only grudgingly to keep the privileged position they hold." These words have a clear message for social workers today: We cannot divorce our practice from the political debates that rage around us. We cannot retreat to hermetically sealed agencies that operate in moral and political vacuums.

The absence of a political framework for our practice has a deleterious effect on our daily work, whatever the level of intervention or arena. First, it compels us to accept the political vocabulary of others who may not share our values and social concerns. Second, it compels us to accept the problem definitions of others, even to accept others' view as to what constitutes a social condition worthy of attention. Third, it often leads us to accept as inevitable the reality of fiscal austerity and place our professional integrity on the line by attempting to deal with spiraling and increasingly complex human needs with shrinking resources. This increases chronic tensions between workers and clients (Lewis, 1976–1977; Reisch, 1993a).

The linkage of politics and social work requires social workers to reconceptualize the nature of our practice roles to include elements with which they may be unfamiliar and initially uncomfortable. The first of these is *partisanship*—fighting a battle against a defined "enemy" and identifying openly with the plight of groups in positions of power and resource disadvantage. This role challenges some of our tacit assumptions about professionalism, particularly those that compel social workers to seek the approval of elite sponsors for economic, political, and ideological support. The second role is one that involves the active pursuit and use of *power* to manipulate the environment and obtain a desired benefit for a constituent population (Fisher, 1995; Reisch, 1993b).

The following are some suggestions for practitioners and educators to adopt in the rapidly changing and unpredictable political environment of the future:

- Identify and publicize impediments to the delivery of quality social services and those working conditions that interfere with service delivery or create hardships for clients and workers at all levels of practice.

- Use both intra- and interorganizational groups to strengthen the political efforts of our agencies and schools.

- Link efforts to improve our agencies' services to larger underlying issues in our advocacy, political, and public education work—for example, by engaging in research on the impact of public policies on poverty and inequality.

- Work for increased political action within established professional organizations such as NASW and CSWE, while creating activist social work organizations to complement the efforts of mainstream professional associations.

- Form internal support groups in agencies and schools to discuss the political aspects of practice and education.

- Enter power entities, especially those that establish social policy priorities such as political parties, while building stronger relationships with low-power clients around issues that they define as important and helpful.

- Reemphasize the role of the political environment in the conceptual frameworks and modes of intervention that underlie our practice, scholarship, and teaching (Abramovitz, 1993; Fisher, 1995; Haynes and Mickelson, 1991; Reisch, 1993a, 1993b).

Conclusion

Contemporary events underscore the importance of political acts, big and small, in shaping both policy development and the environment of social work practice. In recent years, advocacy and political action have helped eradicate ignorance and myths around such areas as child abuse, family violence, and AIDS. Yet, these modest successes have also revealed that social workers have our own set of myths. For example, we have long operated under the illusion that compassion alone will produce change. Although compassion motivates some people to act and think differently, it is insufficient to transform the deep-rooted institutional indifference of our society. The history of social welfare demonstrates that political power, in combination with education and moral indignation, has produced the major policy advances of the 20th century (Chambers, 1965; Davis, 1967; Ehrenreich, 1986; Fisher, 1980; Trolander, 1975; Wenocur and Reisch, 1989).

Political action can also serve as a reaffirmation of the values that motivated most social workers to enter the field. It can serve as a means to increase worker and client competence and, therefore, as a linkage between an agency's empowerment strategy and the demands of the political environment. Political action can facilitate intraagency and intracommunity cooperation. By the very demands it creates for improved data, more extensive public education programs, greater media and technological skills, and stronger ties to constituents and communities, political action can produce long overdue intraorganizational change in social service agencies. Political action can serve as a catalyst for the redistribution of resources and power within an agency and a redefinition of the nature of its work. Finally, political action, by externalizing client, worker, and agency problems and focusing them on a mutually agreed upon target, can help workers and clients overcome the battering they receive daily from a hostile environment.

The major role for social workers in political action is as educators. We can educate clients and constituents about their rights and about the resources available to them. We can educate our colleagues about the institutional forces that constrain our practice efforts. We can educate policymakers and the general public about the conditions of the lives of people with whom we work and about the effects of societal intervention on these conditions. We can, therefore, make a major contribution to eliminating the ignorance and apathy that so often shape contemporary American politics.

In the final analysis, if power is the ability to determine alternatives (Bottomore, 1981)—and politics are about nothing if not power—social workers need to understand and become involved in the political process in order to enhance our effectiveness and expand clients' capacity for self-determination. To paraphrase Camus, finding meaning in such activity may seem absurd in the present context, but it is the very struggle against this absurdity that can provide the ultimate meaning for our work. It may be that such struggle also offers us the only hope for producing lasting change in the future.

REFERENCES

Abramovitz, Mimi. (1993). "Should All Social Workers Be Educated for Social Change? Pro," *Journal of Social Work Education*, volume 29, pp. 6–11.

Axinn, June, and Levin, Herman. (1992). *Social Welfare: A History of the American Response to Need*, 3d ed., New York: Harper and Row.

Barancik, Scott, and Shapiro, Isaac. (1992). *Where Have All the Dollars Gone? A State-By-State Analysis of Income Disparities over the 1980s.* Washington, DC: Center on Budget and Policy Priorities.

Barlett, Donald, and Steele, James. (1992). *America: What Went Wrong?* Kansas City, MO: Andrews and McMeel.

Bellah, Robert et al. (1985). *Habits of the Heart: Individual and Community in American Life*. Berkeley: University of California Press.

Blumenthal, Sidney. (1988). *Our Long National Daydream: A Political Pageant of the Reagan Era*. New York: Harper and Row.

Bottomore, Thomas. (1981). *A Dictionary of Marxist Thought*. Cambridge, MA: Harvard University Press.

Brownstein, Ronald. (1994). "Nation Seeking Common Standards for Social Policies," *Los Angeles Times*, August 8, p. A-5.

Carmines, Edward G., and Stimson, James A. (1989). *Issue Evolution: Race and the Transformation of American Politics*. Princeton, NJ: Princeton University Press.

Chambers, Clarke. (1965). *Seedtime of Reform: American Social Service and Social Action, 1918–1933*. Minneapolis: University of Minnesota Press.

Davis, Allen F. (1967). *Spearheads for Reform: The Social Settlements and the Progressive Movement, 1890–1914*. New York: Oxford University Press.

Devitt, James. (1996). "The Effect of Critical News Coverage on Public Confidence in Institutions." Unpublished paper presented at the American Association for Public Opinion Research Conference, Salt Lake City, Utah, May 17.

Edsall, Thomas Byrne, and Edsall, Mary D. (1991). *Chain Reaction: The Impact of Race, Rights, and Taxes on American Politics*. New York: W. W. Norton.

Ehrenreich, John. (1986). *The Altruistic Imagination: A History of Social Policy and Social Work in the United States*. Ithaca, NY: Cornell University Press.

Etzioni, Amitai. (1993). *The Spirit of Community: Rights, Responsibilities and the Communitarian Agenda*. New York: Crown.

Faludi, Susan. (1991). *Backlash: The Undeclared War Against American Women*. New York: Crown Publishers.

Fisher, Jacob. (1980). *The Response of Social Work to the Depression*. Cambridge, MA: Schenkman.

Fisher, Robert. (1995). "Political Social Work," *Journal of Social Work Education*, volume 31, pp. 194–203.

Frankel, Max. (1996). "What Quo for the Quid?" *New York Times Magazine*, February, pp. 24, 26.

Fraser, Steven, and Gerstle, Gary, eds. (1989). *The Rise and Fall of the New Deal Order, 1930–1980*. Princeton, NJ: Princeton University Press.

The Gallup Poll. (1995). *Public Opinion 1994*. Wilmington, DE: Scholarly Resources.

Greenberg, Stanley. (1995). *Middle Class Dreams: Politics and Power of the New American Majority*. New York: Times Books.

Hagstrom, Jerry. (1988). *Beyond Reagan: The New Landscape of American Politics*, New York: W. W. Norton.

Haynes, Karen, and Mickelson, James. (1991). *Affecting Change: Social Workers in the Political Arena*, 2d ed. White Plains, NY: Longman.

Hill, H., and Jones, E. J., eds. (1993). *Race in America: The Struggle for Equality*. Madison: University of Wisconsin Press.

Huckfeldt, Robert, and Kohfeld, Carol Weitzel. (1989). *Race and the Decline of Class in American Politics*. Urbana and Chicago: University of Illinois Press.

Lewis, Harold. (1976–1977). "The Cause in Function," *Journal of the Otto Rank Society*, volume 2 (2), pp. 17–25.

Lind, Michael. (1995). *The Next American Nation: The New Nationalism and the Fourth American Revolution*. New York: Free Press.

McElvaine, Robert S. (1987). *The End of the Conservative Era: Liberalism After Reagan*. New York: Arbor House.

Morone, James. (1991). *The Democratic Wish: Popular Participation and the Limits of American Government*. New York: Basic Books.

The Nation. (1995). Special Issue on "Black Politics," October 30.

National Journal. (1988). "Reagan's Legacy: The Paradox of Power," May 14, no. 20.

Phillips, Kevin. (1990). *The Politics of Rich and Poor: Wealth and the American Electorate in the Reagan Aftermath*. New York: Random House.

Piven, Frances Fox, and Cloward, Richard. (1989). *Why Americans Don't Vote*. New York: Pantheon.

Plotke, David. (1996). *Building a Democratic Political Order: Reshaping American Liberalism in the 1930s and 1940s*. New York: Cambridge University Press.

Popple, Philip R., and Leighninger, Leslie. (1990*). Social Work, Social Welfare and American Society*. Boston: Allyn and Bacon.

Public Citizen. (1995). "Report Concerning Political Action Committee (PAC) Contributions Received by Members of the U.S. House of Representatives and the U.S. Senate," January–September. Washington, DC: Public Citizen.

Putnam, Robert D. (1996). "The Strange Disappearance of Civic America," *The American Prospect*, no. 24, Winter, pp. 34–48.

Reisch, Michael. (1993a). "Lessons from the History of Social Work for Our Time," *Jewish Social Work Forum*, volume 29, pp. 3–27.

Reisch, Michael. (1993b). "The Social Worker in Politics as Multi-Role Group Practitioner." In S. Wenocur, et al., eds., *Social Work with Groups: Expanding Horizons*. New York: Haworth Press.

Reisch, Michael, and Wenocur, Stanley. (1982). "Professionalization and Voluntarism in Social Welfare: Changing Roles and Functions," *Journal of Voluntary Action Research*, volume 11, nos. 2–3, April–September, pp. 11–31.

Reisch, Michael, and Wenocur, Stanley. (1986). "The Future of Community Organization in Social Work: Social Activism and the Politics of Profession-Building," *Social Service Review*, volume 60 (1), pp. 70–91.

Reynolds, Bertha. (1987). *Social Work and Social Living*. Silver Spring, MD: National Association of Social Workers. (Originally published in 1951.)

Rifkin, Jeremy. (1995). *The End of Work*. New York: Random House.

Roll Call. (1996). Washington, DC: U.S. Congressional Printing Office.

Sale, Kirkpatrick. (1976). *Power Shift*. New York: Vintage Press.

Saloma, John J. III. (1989). *Ominous Politics: The New Conservative Labyrinth*. New York: Hill and Wang.

Simon, Barbara Levy. (1994). *The Empowerment Tradition in American Social Work: A History*. New York: Columbia University Press.

Smith, R. M. (1988). "The 'American Creed' and American Identity: The Limits of Liberal Citizenship in the United States," *Western Political Quarterly*, volume 41, pp. 225–251.

Specht, Harry and Courtney, Mark. (1994). *Unfaithful Angels: How Social Work Abandoned Its Mission*. New York: Prentice-Hall.

Terkel, Studs. (1988). *The Great Divide: Second Thoughts on the American Dream*. New York: Pantheon.

Thompson, J. J. (1994). "Social Workers and Politics: Beyond the Hatch Act," *Social Work*, volume 39, pp. 457–465.

Trattner, Walter. (1995). *From Poor Law to Welfare State*, 5th ed. New York: Free Press.

Trolander, Judith. (1975). *Settlement Houses and the Great Depression*. Detroit: Wayne State University Press.

United States Bureau of the Census. (1991). *The 1990 Census of the United States of America*. Washington, DC: U.S. Government Printing Office.

United States Bureau of the Census. (1995). *Statistical Abstract of the United States*. Washington, DC: U.S. Government Printing Office.

Walkowitz, Daniel. (1988). *Professionalizing Social Workers: The Social and Ideological Construction of Women's Work, 1900–1930*. Seattle: University of Washington Press.

Wenocur, Stanley, and Reisch, Michael. (1989). *From Charity to Enterprise: The Development of American Social Work in a Market Economy*. Urbana, Illinois: University of Illinois Press.

Part II
Policy and Practice

A. Policy Issues

The essays in the first half of Part II examine some critical policy arenas that will influence social work practice in the years ahead. There are three striking things about this group of essays. First, they reveal that contemporary policy concerns are remarkably similar to those of a century ago. With few exceptions, the essays address economic and social issues that would be familiar to our professional ancestors. Second, the uniquely contemporary issues discussed by the essays—such as family violence, the long-term needs of the elderly, and international social development—have been placed on the policy agenda by a combination of demographic, social, and economic changes, and the concerted actions of social workers and their allies. Many of these developments could not have been forecast a hundred years ago. Third, the essays agree that most contemporary policies in the United States fail to address the root causes of individual and social problems or to respond adequately to a complex and rapidly changing environmental context.

The essays by Duncan Lindsey and Julia R. Henly on the future of child welfare and by Ira M. Schwartz on the juvenile court will particularly evoke a sense of déjà vu. Lindsey and Henly's opening assertion, "Something is amiss for children in the United States," was pointed out nearly as often by child advocates in the 1890s as it has been by their modern-day counterparts. These authors document this assertion with recent data on child poverty, foster home placement, and child abuse, but their most telling point is the strong interrelationship among these phenomena. Yet, despite compelling evidence that poverty is the most reliable predictor of child mistreatment, the central aim of child welfare policies since the 1970s has been identifying and protecting children at risk for abuse, and not the elimination of poverty. Lindsey and Henly assert that this is due to the persistence of a residual perspective within the child welfare system that over the past two decades has transformed it "into an investigative and protective service agency." The most recent manifestation of this transformation is the "family preservation movement," whose main component is the provision of "intensive casework" services.

After a careful examination of the most rigorous empirical studies of family preservation programs, Lindsey and Henly find that, despite their current popularity among professionals, there is little evidence that such programs work as intended. Their impact, Lindsey and Henly assert, is limited for two reasons: (1) their principal methodology, casework, frequently makes little difference in clients' lives, and (2) their underlying residual model is inappropriate to address the needs of low-income children and families in an increasingly competitive market economy. They conclude that an alternative to the historic fluctuation of the child welfare system between child protection and family preservation may be found in policies that have significantly reduced poverty among the elderly.

Like Lindsey and Henly, Ira M. Schwartz finds that the juvenile court has strayed in recent decades from its intentions of a century past due to a combination of conceptual flaws in its basic design and rising public concerns over juvenile crime. The original purpose of the juvenile court was to provide youth with an individualized system of justice in which a child's problems would be diagnosed and solved through corrective actions. This model, based on the legal principle of *parens patriae* dominated juvenile justice policy in the United States until the 1967 landmark *Gault* decision that "precipitated a 'due process revolution' that substantially transformed the juvenile court from a social welfare agency into a legal institution." More recently, state policymakers have revised statutes to emphasize the protection of the public and the punishment, rather than the rehabilitation, of juvenile offenders. In the 1990s, this has resulted in legislation in a majority of states that allows juveniles to be prosecuted as adults at younger ages.

Schwartz argues that these trends bode ominously for the future when the juvenile "at risk" population of 10- to 17-year-olds is projected to increase. He cites research that demonstrates the ineffectiveness of current punitive policies in reducing recidivism or deterring crime. In addition, such "get tough" policies, which break down the historic separation of children from adults, are likely to produce the increased brutalization of juveniles by adult offenders. The privatization of juvenile justice systems and the adoption of a managed care approach will also shape the future of the juvenile court. Although Schwartz believes that the court will survive into the 21st century, he concludes that it "must be a court of justice, and justice only."

Another policy area that involves both the social services and criminal justice systems is family violence. Whereas the protection of children from abusive adults has long been a concern of social workers, it is only in recent decades that this concern has included the protection of women who are abused by their male partners. The essay by Bonnie Yegidis points out the widespread nature of this social problem in the United States and around the world: 10–30% of American women are abused by their male partners, 7% of them seriously; over 100 million girls and women around the world have experienced genital mutilation alone. Family violence, Yegidis asserts, is more than a criminal justice issue. Three decades of data reveal its long-term physical, psychological, and emotional consequences. Yet, until the mid-1970s, "there were no social services specifically designed to prevent or provide early intervention to abused women in the United States." Ironically, it was feminist activists, not social workers, who initiated the development of the first shelters and safe houses for battered women and their children.

Yegidis argues that, because abuse is the result of a complex set of interacting variables, program models that combine educational, cognitive, and behavioral approaches have the greatest possibility of success. These would require social service agencies to work collaboratively with the courts and law enforcement officials to develop a systemic response to the problem. Finally, she points out that social workers have a great deal to learn from other countries, including those in the Third World, where creative approaches to violence against women are being developed. The ideas gleaned from such exchanges can enhance cross-cultural strategies in our nation in the years ahead.

In addition to the abuses that occur in the home, social workers have long been involved as advocates around the abuses that occur in the workplace. Social work pioneers such as Jane Addams, Florence Kelley, and Mary van Kleeck fought for limitations on child labor and for the creation of safer working environments. In combination with programs of "welfare capitalism" around the turn of the century and, more recently, the emergence of Employee Assistance Programs (EAPs), primarily to combat alcoholism, they have shaped contemporary policies and social work practice in the workplace.

Lawrence S. Root analyzes this development and discusses the significance of current economic and organizational trends for the future of EAPs, which have become a regular feature of human resources programming. These trends can be divided into "internal" and "external" programs, the latter (contracted out to outside agencies) being the more common approach.

Root believes that two underlying dynamics will shape the future of social work services in the workplace: (1) the growth of EAPs within private and non-profit organizations; and (2) the growing gap between good and bad jobs. The first trend will lead to a general increase in the existence of EAP services. The second will produce a two-tiered system in which employees in bad jobs will have minimal services, whereas those in good jobs will have comprehensive programs at their disposal. Both will use an "external" model, primarily for reasons of cost control and government regulation. Root asserts that these developments will require social workers to pay additional attention to issues of organizational behavior, the structure of labor market opportunities and demands, the special needs of employees, models of cost-benefit/cost-effectiveness analysis, and the legal and ethical issues involved in workplace policies and practice.

Just as the transformation of the labor market will influence policies and services within it in the next century, demographic and economic changes among the nation's elderly population will have dramatic effects on the ability of older people to address the multiple processes of aging. Neal Cutler's essay takes an innovative approach to the problems caused by the "graying of America" by examining the interrelationship of public policies to the financial issues of the life cycle. Cutler points out how multiple changes will shape the context in which Social Security and Medicare operate in the 21st century. One significant consequence of these changes is that "because of the intersection of several social, financial, and cultural trends, people have fewer years to accumulate the financial resources for a longer older-age expenditure period." Few participants in recent public policy debates have raised the problems this dynamic generates.

The critical issue, according to Cutler, is not "Is Social Security important?" but *For whom* is Social Security important?" Cutler cites evidence that—contrary to what he terms the "Rich Man, Poor Man" dialogue, and even contrary to the original intentions of the Social Security Act—Social Security now constitutes a cornerstone of economic security and financial well-being for middle-income Americans. The keys to ensuring the long-term survival and continued success of the system, Cutler argues, are a reexamination of the concept of early retirement eligibility and the linkage of Medicare eligibility to new Social Security retirement ages.

Stephen Gorin and Cynthia Moniz express similar concerns about the continuing viability of the nation's health-care system and the linkage between health, health care, and the economic well-being of individuals and families. They argue that the long-standing pillars of the U.S. health-care system—fee-for-service medicine, employment-based insurance, and government-funded programs (especially Medicare and Medicaid)—are being dramatically eroded by changes in the marketplace and public policy. The most significant of these changes are the growth of managed care, the decline of employment-based health insurance, the evolving structure of work, and cutbacks in government spending. In their view, these developments will produce a health-care system "based on oligopoly, limited regulation, and shrinking coverage or universal coverage through a single-payer system with managed competition."

Under the first scenario, the phenomenon of "corporate medicine" would dominate the health-care system. This would be characterized by the privatization of health services, increasing monopoly control of health-care institutions, the emergence of health-care conglomerates, the spread of Health Maintenance Organizations (HMOs), and "the regionalization and nationalization of health-care markets and services." The consequences, Gorin and Moniz argue, would be limitations on health-care coverage, an expansion of the uninsured population, and an increase in health-care costs. They prefer the second scenario, based on a single-payer system with managed competition. They believe this approach would have several benefits. It would eliminate administrative waste, expand coverage, and focus on a multidimensional model of health status that links health with employment, education, family support, and the physical environment, rather than merely with the provision of health-care services. This model would provide new opportunities for social workers in formulating health policy, working with multidisciplinary health-care teams, and researching the linkage between socioeconomic status and health.

Tomi Gomory analyzes the related field of mental health, but draws markedly different conclusions. He argues that the current mental health system is essentially a "comprehensive social control effort" that requires "an institutional structure for implementation." He asserts that the public mental health system can best be understood, therefore, as a bureaucratic entity similar to other large public systems. Gomory believes that through the support of the state, this system has expanded its hegemony over growing numbers of people and increasing forms of individual and social problems, despite little evidence of the efficacy of its methods.

Gomory proposes as an alternative policy solution a free-market mental health system based on vouchers. This approach would give clients greater control over the services they receive and contribute to their empowerment. He cites the success of the food stamp program as evidence of the potential for a system to work. Although he admits that his recommendations would probably put many mental health professionals, including social workers, out of work, the cost savings would justify such short-term hardships. Some of these savings could be spent on the provision of concrete services to clients, such as food, housing, physical health care, education, and social or employment skills training. Other savings could be used to find new jobs for those persons displaced by the policy changes he proposes.

Given the general consensus of the above essays that the nation's current social policies are seriously flawed, it is appropriate to conclude this section with an exploration of the lessons we can derive from analyzing the experiences of other contemporary societies. In their essay "Lessons from International Social Work: Policies and Practices," Nazneen Mayadas and Doreen Elliott discuss a paradigm shift that has occurred in the developing world, away from the remedial and medical models of Western social work toward a model of social development. This approach incorporates economic, social, and cultural systems and recognizes the often hidden social costs of poverty. They cite diverse examples of the social development perspective from Bangladesh, Great Britain, El Salvador, and Sri Lanka. They argue that the social development approach can be successfully applied to populations in the United States because of its "potential to integrate the dichotomy between" micro and macro methods and because "it offers a common ground" for social workers to develop a stronger professional identity.

Mayadas and Elliott also suggest specific areas of North American social welfare policy and practice that can benefit from the application of ideas developed in other nations. These include French child-care policies, Sweden's parental leave policy, and Britain's health-care system. Another lesson would involve the extension of community practice methods to address such problems as infant mortality, unemployment, and inadequate health care. Social workers in the United States should also recognize the benefits of international cooperation in combating public health issues, such as AIDS, and the advantages of using para-professionals in service delivery. Finally, Mayadas and Elliott point out that "an international perspective centralizes the role of culture [and] promotes diversity as a normal human condition." Given the dramatic demographic changes that are already under way in the United States, the adoption of an international perspective may be the profession's only hope of producing meaningful social change in the 21st century.

The Future of Child Welfare

Duncan Lindsey and Julia R. Henly

Concerns about the child welfare system are aired daily in the media as well as in professional sources. Currently, over 20 states are under federal sanction for failure to follow guidelines laid down by the federal government. Duncan Lindsey and Julia Henly provide suggestions for overhauling the child welfare system. A more extensive version of the proposal suggested can be found in Duncan Lindsey's recent book The Welfare of Children, *(1994), published by Oxford University Press. Duncan Lindsey is a professor in the School of Public Policy and Social Research, University of California at Los Angeles. He is the founding editor of* Children and Youth Services Review *and continues to function as its senior editor. He is one of the most eminent child welfare scholars in the country today. His web site address is www.childwelfare.com. Julia R. Henly is an assistant professor in the School of Public Policy and Social Research at UCLA. Her research is in the areas of poverty, welfare policy, and families.*

Something is amiss for children in the United States. Whether measured in terms of child abuse reports or foster care placements, an alarming percentage of American children are entangled in the child welfare system. Since 1985, foster care placements have been rising steadily, so that today more than a half a million children are estimated to be living in out-of-home care (Lindsey, 1994). In California, often regarded as a bellwether for the nation, the number of children in foster care has more than doubled in the last decade, reaching a total of almost 90,000 placements in 1995

(Berrick, 1994). In addition to rising foster care, during the last two decades the number of child abuse reports per thousand in the United States has more than quadrupled (McCurdy & Daro, 1993; Pelton, 1989). In California alone, more than 650,000 child abuse reports are received each year (Lindsey & Doh, 1996). Further, as Figures 1 and 2 illustrate, projections of child abuse reports extending through the end of the century do not suggest that this upward trend will change in the near future (Berrick, 1994; Lindsey & Doh, 1996).

Such negative indicators are not distributed randomly throughout the child population, but are noticeably concentrated among poor children. Over the years, research has steadily documented the association between poverty and child involvement with the welfare system (Gil, 1970; Pelton, 1981, 1989; Lindsey, 1994; Testa, 1992). Today, nothing better illustrates the close relation between the two than how foster care is financed. About one-half of all foster care placements nationally are funded by Aid to Families with Dependent Children Foster Care (AFDC-Foster Care) (Courtney, 1996). In California, the proportion is even higher, with approximately two-thirds of children in foster care being paid for through AFDC-Foster Care, indicating that the majority of foster care placements originate in low-income homes where families depend on public assistance (Illig, 1994).

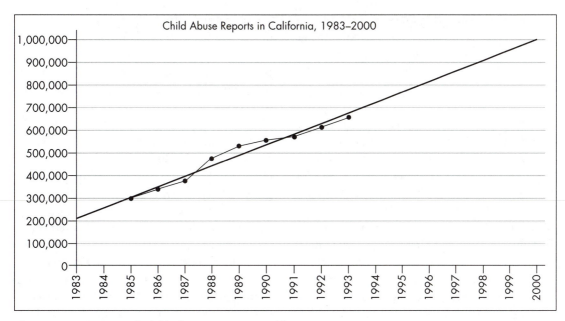

Figure 1 Projections of Child Abuse Reports in California
Source: Berrick (1994).

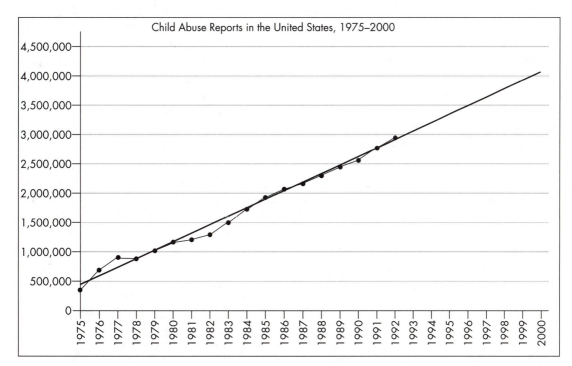

Figure 2 Projections of Child Abuse Reports in the United States
Source: Lindsey and Doh (1996).

Child poverty does far more than increase a child's risk of being abused or placed in foster care. Poverty—especially long-term spells of poverty—can instill a blight that will last a lifetime, for both the individual and society. For example, growing up in poverty greatly increases the child's chance of performing poorly in school; of becoming pregnant; and of getting involved in drugs, crime, and, eventually, the juvenile justice system—to name just a few of the negative indicators associated with poverty (Lindsey, 1994; National Research Council, 1993). In addition, children who experience long-term durations of poverty attain significantly lower education and income levels as adults (Corcoran, Gordon, Laren, & Solon, 1992; Duncan & Rodgers, 1988).

Given the strong association between poverty and involvement with the child welfare system, child welfare workers can expect their problems to increase as the future unfolds because child poverty is rising steadily. Whereas the poverty rate decreased briefly in the 1960s, it has since increased to the extent that by 1990 one-fifth of U.S. children were living below the poverty line (Danziger & Danziger, 1993). In California in 1970 about 12 percent of the state's children lived in poverty. By 1980, this number had increased to 15 percent. A decade later the poverty rate was 18 percent. In 1994, 28.6 percent of California's children were living in poverty (see Figure 3).[1]

Such trends for children take on heightened significance when compared with the situation for the elderly, who, during the same period, have seen their economic situation improve dramatically. Danziger and Weinberg (1994) report that in 1960 one-third of the elderly were poor (35.2 percent), but that by 1990 this number had declined to less than 13 percent. In 1994, less than 7 percent of the elderly in California could be said to live in poverty (Fay, 1994). The contrast with children could not be greater: Thirty-five years ago the poverty rate for seniors in the United States was significantly higher than the poverty rate for children. Today the national child poverty rate is *double* that for seniors. California's children are 4 *times* more likely to live in poverty than its seniors (Fay, 1994; Lindsey & Doh, 1996). Such a reversal of fortune for children is further confirmed by the fact that child poverty rates are higher than elderly poverty rates within racial groups. That is, African-American children are more likely to be poor than African-American elderly, Latino children poorer than Latino elderly, and white children more impoverished than white elderly (Danziger & Weinberg, 1994).

The trends in child poverty, which derive from inadequate income, are mirrored among trends in the distribution of wealth in the United States. In 1989, the top 1 percent of families owned 38.9 percent of all privately held wealth (Kennickell & Starr-McClurer,

---

[1]Overall poverty rates, although significant, mask important differences in the poverty rate by ethnicity. For example, whereas in 1990 about one-fifth of all American children lived in poverty, slightly over one-third of Latino children and two-fifths of African-American children—more than double the overall rate—lived in poverty (Danziger & Danziger, 1993). These poverty rates are particularly disturbing in light of the relatively positive position of Europe's children. In the United Kingdom, poverty rates are about 3 times lower than the U.S. overall poverty rate (7.4 percent), in (West) Germany, the rate is 7 times lower (2.8 percent), and in Sweden, the rate is 10 times lower than the American overall rate (1.6 percent) (Smeeding, 1992, as reported by Burtless, 1994). Put another way, whereas fewer than 2 Swedish children out of 100 and fewer than 8 out of 100 British children are poor, in America 35 out of 100 Latino-American children and 44 out of 100 African-American children live in poverty.

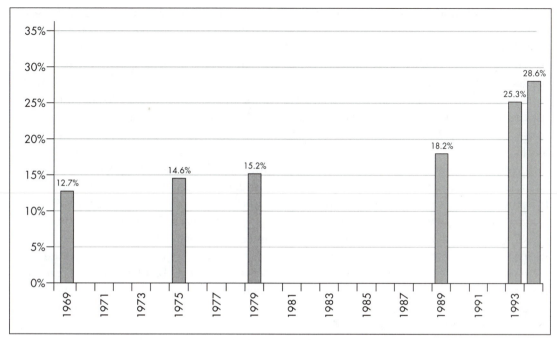

Figure 3 Child Poverty in California
Source: Lindsey and Doh (1996).

1994; Wolff, 1995). The next 19 percent owned 45.7 percent of all the privately held wealth. Thus, the top 20 percent of families owned 84.6 percent of all the wealth. The bottom 80 percent, which is an odd term, owned the remaining 15.4 percent. The bottom 20 percent were more likely to have negative net worth. When social and economic policies and programs result in this type of distribution of wealth, it is to be expected that many families, especially those at the bottom end of the distribution (primarily single mothers with children[2]) will have great difficulty.

[2]In California, more than 75 percent of AFDC recipients have children age 6 or under (Lindsey & Doh, 1996). More than half have a child 3 or under.

Despite evidence that poverty is the greatest predictor of child mistreatment (Gil, 1970; Jones & McCurdy, 1992; Lindsey, 1994; Pelton, 1989), the child welfare system steadfastly refuses to tackle the problem head on. Since the 1970s, the central aim of child welfare has remained one of identifying and protecting children at risk for abuse, making child welfare principally and foremost a child protective system (Kamerman & Kahn, 1990; Lindsey, 1994). Given this orientation, the system does little to ameliorate the impoverished conditions facing children, or the stressors inherent in such an environment. Little attention is paid to the long-term and multifaceted problems facing children who grow up in poverty. By limiting child welfare solely to investigative and protective functions, the system is simply not as far-reaching or helpful as it might be.

The reason for this narrow perspective is not hard to identify. From its inception, child welfare has been viewed from a *residual perspective* (Lindsey, 1994). Abandoned, orphaned, abused, or neglected children have traditionally been regarded in Western societies as social "leftovers," or "residual" children. Being without adequate family or other resources, they are to be provided for, if at all, as inexpensively and conveniently as possible. As Kadushin and Martin (1988, 673) noted, "In general, arrangements to provide institutional care for children were made for the convenience of the community, not out of the concern for the individual child. Provision of minimal care in the cheapest way was considered adequate care." Government aid, when provided, is usually minimal,

time-limited, and confined to highly selective forms of service directed to specific categories of need.

In the seventies, when public concern with child abuse led legislators to pass mandated child abuse reporting laws in all 50 states, the child welfare system was transformed into an investigative and protective service agency, wherein the residual perspective was narrowed and refocused to exclude everyone but the child suspected of being abused. Reform efforts such as the Permanency Planning movement, which research had shown had effectively reduced the growing numbers of children consigned (often indefinitely) to foster care, were abandoned in the scramble to identify and protect children who might be at risk of abuse. As a result, the numbers of children in foster care continued to grow (see Figure 4).

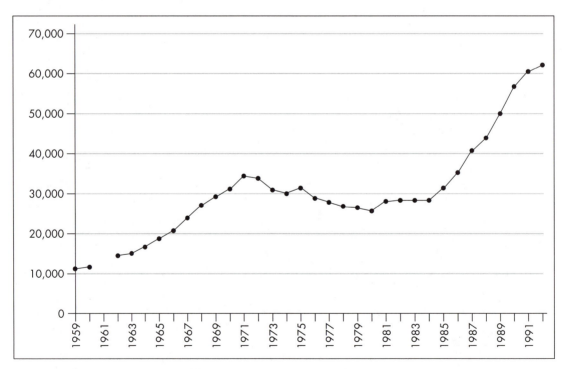

Figure 4 AFDC Foster Care in California

The Emergence of Family Preservation

After nearly three decades of investigating and prosecuting parents, and removing at-risk children to foster care, a movement known as "family preservation" has arisen, in which the emphasis has shifted from removing children to preserving families and preventing children from being removed. The axiom guiding the family preservation movement is the following: Too many children are being placed in foster care, when time-limited intensive services from a child welfare caseworker might otherwise have prevented their placement. Thus, family preservation dictates that every effort must be made to keep children with their biological family.

Although family preservation services differ from program to program, the main ingredient is the provision of "intensive casework" services. These are not tangibly different from those provided by the traditional casework approach, only that they are provided more intensively in a time-limited fashion. The family preservation approach is crisis-oriented, capable of responding to a family within 24 hours. Whereas traditional services are more long-term, family preservation services are provided for a shorter period of time, usually concentrated within a period of four to six weeks, but can be as long as five months in some programs. They include such things as teaching parenting skills, helping to obtain resources, resolving family conflict, counseling, and in-home monitoring of family members at risk, all of which, it is hoped, will maintain family stability and mend the problems of those families reported for child abuse and neglect (see Whittaker & Tracy, 1990, for review).

Claiming an innovative casework approach that focuses on helping families in a time of crisis to prevent unnecessary placement of children in foster care, the family preservation movement has attracted a wide following. Because the child protection system often failed to understand the importance of preserving the family, it is not surprising that this has been seen as a welcome development by many child welfare professionals. Overall the message is one of hope and belief in the possibility of mending the problems of families reported for child abuse and neglect. The response has been so great that today the momentum throughout child welfare is overwhelmingly toward the family preservation approach.

One of the great strengths of the family preservation movement has been its commitment to research—a commitment that has, in an era of increased demand for accountability, strengthened the attraction of family preservation for many people. In recent years, a number of evaluation studies have attempted to gauge the effectiveness of family preservation programs (e.g., Pecora, Fraser, Haapala, 1991; Schuerman et al., 1994; Schwartz & Au Claire, 1991; Yuan et al., 1990). The results vary dramatically depending primarily on the rigor with which the studies are conducted. In reviewing the research on family preservation, we conclude that the most rigorous empirical studies have yielded the *least* convincing evidence in favor of family preservation services.

One of the most comprehensive and rigorous evaluations of family preservation services was recently completed by a group of researchers at the University of Chicago. This study by Schuerman and colleagues (1994) focused on the effects of Illinois's family preservation program over a 3-year demonstration period. The study stands out for its care in documenting exactly what services the experimental group received in comparison to the control group. Each family in the study was randomly assigned to participate in one of two groups: (1) a 90-day family preservation program (i.e., treatment group); or (2) a traditional casework services program (i.e., control group). Findings reveal that, although families in the experimental group received almost *10* times more contact hours with a caseworker than did those acting as controls, *no significant differences* were found between the experimental and control groups in terms of subsequent child maltreatment, or in terms of the types and duration of out-of-home placements. In fact, in terms of placement prevention rates, the families within the treatment group experienced a slightly *lower* success rate than families within the control group. Seventy-seven percent of the treatment group avoided placement, whereas 81 percent of the control group avoided placement. In other words, families that received family preservation services had their children removed from their homes more frequently than families that received traditional (nonintensive) casework services. Schuerman and his colleagues concluded: "We find little evidence that family preservation programs result in substantial reductions in the placement of children. Claims to the contrary have been based largely on non-experimental studies which do not provide sufficient evidence of program effects."

A 1990 study by Yuan, McDonald, Wheeler, Struckman-Johnson, and Rivest examined the effects of family preservation programs within the state of California over a 3-year demonstration period. For the first two years of the study, a total of 709 families received family preservation services, but no control sample was utilized. During the third year, however, a substudy was conducted with both a treatment and control sample. The study offers two success rates (i.e., placement prevention rates): one for the first two years, and another for the third year. For the first two years, 85 percent of the families are reported as having avoided placement. Given the lack of a control group, the extent to which this result can be attributed to family preservation per se is unknown. For the third year, the treatment group experienced a 75 percent placement prevention rate, whereas the control group experienced an 80 percent placement prevention rate.[3] Given its more rigorous design, the third year substudy is the valuable part of this evaluation, and its results are quite comparable to those found by Schuerman and his colleagues (1994). From the California study, we can conclude that families in the treatment group experienced a lower success rate than families in the control group.

Thus, the major clinical trials of the family preservation approach have consistently found virtually no evidence of measurable impact of the program's approach. In 1996, two comprehensive reviews of all the major family preservation studies, each done independently and without knowledge of the other, came to the same conclusion: Family preservation programs have, overall, had no measurable impact on child safety or likelihood of foster care placement (Heneghan, Horwitz, & Leventhal, 1996; Lindsey & Doh, 1996). Heneghan, Horwitz, and Leventhal (1996) examined 46 program evaluations and found 10 that were scientifically credible. "Despite current widespread use of FPS to prevent out-of-home placements of children, evaluations of FPS are methodologically difficult and show no benefit in reducing rates of out-of-home placements of children at risk of abuse or neglect in 8 of 10 studies" (p. 535).

[3]The difference was not statistically significant.

They conclude, "Policy in this area has evolved more on faith than on fact" (p. 542).

Overall, the research suggests that family preservation, despite its strong following from both within and outside the child welfare community, is not a cure. The problems facing those families who come to the attention of the child protection system through reports of abuse or neglect appear not to be fundamentally altered by casework services, whether these be the intensive services offered by family preservation advocates, or the more traditional long-term casework services. The few studies that report otherwise are either flawed in their research methodology or are more appropriately regarded as "advocacy" or promotional studies than as objective research. Although the program may provide temporary relief for some families, its application is stymied through the inability to identify which families those might be.

Why Family Preservation Doesn't Work

The family preservation approach is limited for two reasons: (1) Its principle methodology, casework, too often makes very little difference, and (2) the residual model, which underlies the program, is a failed service distribution approach that is inappropriate for solving the problems children face in a highly competitive market economy that has become increasingly unsupportive to low-income families.

Casework. The casework method assumes that the client—in this instance, the parents of the child—are unable to manage their own affairs. The task of the caseworker is to collect information, analyze, and investigate the situation of the parent and child. The premise is that the child welfare social worker can identify the family's problems, figure out a solution, and develop a case plan to achieve remedy. Unfortunately, evaluation research on casework, conducted over several decades, suggests that this doesn't happen and that casework, despite its almost universal application in social welfare, fails to make any measurable and substantial difference for most families (Fischer, 1973; Mullen & Dumpson, 1972; Segal, 1972; Sheldon, 1986).

The difficult conclusion has to be that as long as generic casework services yield virtually no significant differences in the lives of clients, it may be unrealistic to expect different results simply by intensifying the same services and calling them "family preservation."

The residual model. Underlying family preservation is a residual perspective that at first glance seems to be the least expensive, most logical, commonsense approach to caring for children in need. In the long-term, however, the residual model doesn't work. A number of principal failings can be identified:

1. *The residual model waits until a problem occurs before intervening.* If we wait until a family is in crisis and their children are in "imminent need of placement," then we have waited too long. Service and support were undoubtedly needed well before the crisis. The case of teen parenting is a good example. Teen parenting has been linked to an increased risk of involvement with the child welfare system (e.g., see Testa, 1992). Family preservation services attempt to improve the teen's ability to function as a parent while neglecting the conditions that both led to her early motherhood and continue to impose stressors on her ability to parent. Yet, the research overwhelmingly demonstrates that the strongest predictor of teen parenting is, in

fact, one's socioeconomic status (Hayes, 1987). Altering a teenager's sense of life options, not simply providing intensive services after she has already become a parent, is necessary if we hope to reduce the risks to teen mothers and their children.

2. *The residual model offers minimal services.* Little is offered through the residual approach that can substantively change the situation of a family in difficulty. When family support services are provided, a delicate balance must be struck between ameliorating the suffering without appearing to reward the client for failure. As a consequence, support services are ratcheted down to a minimum. In 1970, more than 70 percent of families seen by the public child welfare system in California received some form of in-home or out-of-home service. In 1992, less than 6 percent received such services (Lindsey & Doh, 1996). For most families, child welfare contacts were limited to an investigation of the alleged abuse or neglect for which they were reported.

3. *The residual model places a premium on failure.* Residual services are not provided until the person demonstrates need. Because of limited resources each situation must be "means tested" to determine who qualifies for services. In the case of child protection, this means that little or nothing can be done until the child is reported for abuse. In fact, in California, family preservation services are provided only after a family has been reported for abuse and neglect. Those clients served are the ones most in need, most desperate, or most imperiled. In some sense, a system that targets the most disadvantaged cases can be viewed as a more efficient use of resources, but targeting can also create a perverse incentive to fail, as services are limited to those who are most in need.

4. *Residual services are ameliorative rather than curative.* Residual services may temporarily alleviate one or more problems, but they are fundamentally unable to restore long-term economic viability and opportunity for the individual. Family preservation views abuse and neglect as a problem that can be addressed within the family system. Thus, the family is the sole target of change—without simultaneous attention to the broader socioeconomic and neighborhood disadvantages underlying the parent's inability to parent or the child's ability to grow successfully (Lindsey, 1994; Schuerman, Rzepnicki, Littell, & Chak, 1993). Whereas poverty may be recognized as a factor related to a family's distress, family preservation services are focused on problems within the family system that produce that distress. The caseworker can teach parenting skills, provide a family with a new refrigerator, or counsel a family regarding strategies for managing anger and stress; however, he or she cannot attend to the poor quality schools and services within the family's neighborhood, high unemployment rates, and minimal public assistance benefits that remain after the short-term intensive services end. In a market economy, measures are needed that promote economic independence and self-reliance. Instead, the residual model provides services that create social and economic dependence. Frequently portrayed as a "safety net," like that deployed beneath a trapeze, for many, the services more closely resemble a trawler's net that traps and entangles those who fall into it.

5. *The residual model is corrosive to the human spirit.* The aim of a residual model is not to prevent the circumstances that lead up to a problem, but rather to find more adaptive ways to adjust to those circumstances. Such a model reinforces resignation and contentment with limited life options and can have a corrosive effect on the recipient's sense of competence and self-worth.

In sum, family preservation fails because, remaining in the domain of the residual paradigm, it does not address the fundamental problem that brings families and children to the attention of child welfare agencies to begin with—poverty. In our view, the study of child welfare can benefit from an examination of the broader systemic issues that affect families generally.

Placing Child Welfare in Its Broader Social Context

In recognizing a correlation between child poverty and the need for child protective services, it is imperative to attend to the direction of that correlation. Most children demand child welfare services *because of* the stressors that high poverty conditions produce. Until that fundamental condition is altered, it will be very difficult to provide more than short-term solutions to child welfare problems. Thus, a broader understanding is needed that will guide research into the mechanisms, processes, and causes that lead some families and their children—and not others—into poverty, and from there into the hopelessness and despair that invite intervention by the child welfare system.

Over the last 25 years, important economic and demographic shifts have occurred, as well as changes in policies affecting poor families,

that have had clear implications for children. Changing economic and labor market conditions, the increased urbanization of poverty, and reductions in safety net programs have all been recognized as important to understanding the declining position of American families (e.g., see Danziger & Danziger, 1993; Danziger & Gottschalk, 1995; Ellwood, 1988; Wilson, 1987). Despite overall economic growth, income and wealth inequality has increased dramatically, with most of the increase taking place in the 1980s (Danziger & Gottschalk, 1995; Danziger & Weinberg, 1994; Krugman, 1992; Wolff, 1992). The increased economic inequality has occurred in a climate where employers are relying increasingly on part-time and contingent workers and are less frequently providing health insurance and other benefits to their workers (Mishel & Bernstein, 1994), where relatively good paying jobs in the inner city have either been eliminated or have moved from inner city to suburban locations (Kasarda, 1989; Wilson, 1987), and where low-skilled unionized jobs, which provide substantially higher wages than other low-skilled jobs, have declined significantly in numbers (Freeman, 1994). More and more, the primary wage earner in poor families is employed in minimum wage or near minimum wage work, or in part-time or temporary employment, none of which afford a living that will lift a family out of poverty. Families have increasingly needed to rely on the income of two adults in order to maintain a reasonable standard of living. Moreover, AFDC benefits, the primary source of public assistance available to poor families, have declined in value by an average of 40 percent since 1970 (Lav, Lazere, Greenstein, & Gold, 1993). In the summer of 1996, the AFDC program was ended. Responsibility for income assistance to low-income families was turned over to the states with a projected reduction of benefits of $60 billion over five years. Thus, over the last two decades, wages as well as welfare benefits have eroded, increasing the economic insecurity of poor families.

During this same period, where the earnings of two adults have become more crucial to economic well-being, a demographic shift away from two-parent families has occurred. Single-parent families now make up a significant portion of all families in the United States. At any point in time, about one-quarter of all children live with only one parent. By the time a child reaches age 18, there is a 50 percent chance that she will have lived in a single-parent family for six years (National Research Council, 1993). Placing this demographic shift in the context of the changing economic trends described above, it is not surprising that single-parent families, in particular mother-headed families, are disproportionately poor (McLanahan & Sandefur, 1994). Women earn less than men, even controlling for educational attainment, and women are disproportionately employed in part-time and temporary jobs (Blank, 1994; Mishel & Bernstein, 1994).

Whereas a great many negative effects have been associated with single parenting, "low income or income loss is the single most important factor in accounting for the lower achievement of children in single-parent families" (McLanahan & Sandefur, 1994). Adjusting for the effects of socioeconomic status, the difference between child outcomes in single-versus two-parent families is greatly reduced. For example, once income is taken into account, the difference in drop-out rates and adolescent parenting rates between teens living in two-parent versus one-parent households drops by about 50 percent (McLanahan & Sandefur, 1994). Thus, single-parent families are disproportionately facing the task of raising children under economically disadvantaged circumstances, and this greater likelihood of economic hardship presents risks for children living in these families.

The changing economic and demographic climate has had a particular effect on large urban cities. The increased concentration of poverty in urban areas has resulted in a growing concern with the negative effects of such highly disadvantaged neighborhoods on residents (e.g., see Jencks & Mayer, 1990; Wilson, 1987, 1993). The study of "neighborhood effects" is an attempt to understand the independent effect of living in an area of concentrated poverty—with its corresponding high crime rate, limited and low-quality services, and high unemployment rates and welfare use among neighborhood residents. Despite methodological difficulties in measuring neighborhood effects independent of social class effects, recent research findings suggest that neighborhood characteristics are associated with increased rates of teen pregnancy and reduced levels of educational attainment (Brooks-Gunn, Duncan, Klebanov, & Sealand, 1993; Crane, 1991; Hogan & Kitagawa, 1985). In addition, residents of highly disadvantaged neighborhoods appear to be at increased risk of their children being placed in foster care (Berrick & Barth, forthcoming).

Can Progress for Children Be Achieved?

Progress *can* be made for children when the goal is clear and when effective methods of treatment and prevention can be identified. In 1920, for example, the U.S. Children's Bureau waged an all-out campaign to reduce infant mortality. The success of their effort was nothing short of miraculous. Because disease pathologies were coming to be understood, and serums and vaccines were being developed, immunization programs and other public health measures, such as the safe milk campaign, had a dramatic effect in all but eliminating diseases that had been contributing to the high infant mortality rates (Desowitz, 1987).

In the same way, the child welfare system must first identify and *acknowledge* the fundamental causes that bring families and children to its attention. Then it must identify and promote remedies that will bring real and lasting changes to that population. This requires replacing the residual approach with a broader structural perspective in which child welfare services are part of a universal public infrastructure designed to support child development and opportunity. There is no reason why real reforms cannot be implemented. In the same way that poverty among senior citizens was dramatically reduced in mid-century from almost 40 percent in 1965 to less than 10 percent today, so too can poverty among children be reduced or ended. Without structural reforms aimed at systematically ending poverty among children, attempts at reversing the deteriorating conditions of children are futile. What we will likely see in the future are ever greater numbers of children sinking into poverty, with more—not less—coming into the public child welfare system.

The Elderly May Offer a Solution

The success of Social Security in removing great numbers of the elderly from poverty has been recognized by a substantial body of literature (e.g., see Burtless, 1994; Danziger & Weinberg, 1994). Marmor, Mashaw, and Harvey (1990) describe Social Security as, "the most popular and successful social welfare program that America has ever launched" (p.

130). Before the government established Social Security, the elderly themselves were responsible for setting aside sufficient resources for their retirement. Such a noninterventionist strategy by the government resulted in high rates of poverty among the elderly. The steady decline in poverty among the elderly since the program's inception in 1935 as part of Roosevelt's Social Security Act can be explained almost entirely by its implementation.[4]

The Social Security program operates on a pay-as-you-go basis, with mandatory employer and employee contributions being paid to the government, and retired beneficiaries being paid from contributions collected from the current working generation. Benefits are only marginally related to contributions, and many current beneficiaries receive payments well in excess of what similar contributions to a private system would have entitled them to. Contrary to common perception, contributions to Social Security do not go into a special trust fund earmarked for the individual who has made the contribution. Instead, they go into a general fund from which they are distributed to current beneficiaries. Social Security thus represents a "social savings" approach to providing income protection for the elderly. There are no efforts to try to make Social Security unattractive or to discourage participation. Quite the contrary, Social Security stipulates universal coverage, providing benefits for all, irrespective of their income. A testament to the widespread effect of the Social Security program is the fact that over 92 percent of seniors are covered by the program

[4]This includes important later amendments that greatly expand the scope of the program—who was covered (e.g., widows; most occupations), the size of the monetary benefits (e.g., automatic cost of living adjustments), and the type of benefits (e.g., the addition of Medicare in 1965).

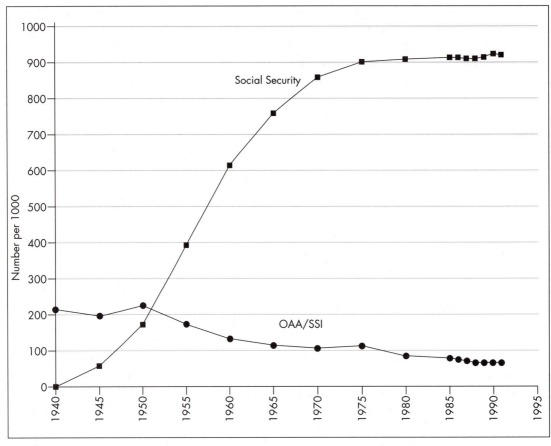

Figure 5 The Increasing Coverage of Social Security and the Declining Dependence on Welfare for the Elderly

(see Figure 5). The main reason for the decline of poverty among seniors, while poverty among children has increased, is the effectiveness of Social Security (see Figure 6).

As a social savings program, Social Security does not have the stigma of a "public assistance" program, but retains the dignity of an "earned pension." Advocates and partisans who fight on behalf of the elderly for improved Social Security benefits are not viewed as asking for charity, only demanding what their constituency has earned. Social Security enjoys wide support because it is viewed as an insurance program paid for by the beneficiaries (Aaron, 1982). The example of Social Security stands in stark contrast to that of AFDC—a means-tested targeted program that, although administered at far less cost to the government, is more stigmatizing for recipients, more punitive in its delivery, and without a strong lobby to protect its beneficiaries (see Handler & Hasenfeld, 1991, for a historical account of the development of AFDC policy).

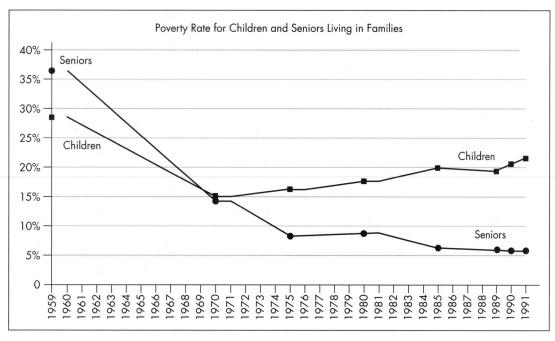

Figure 6 Poverty Rates for Children and Seniors, 1959–1991

Child's Future Security Account

The same "social savings" model that has proven so successful in providing for the economic needs of the elderly in the United States could provide the answer to breaking the cycle of poverty for children. Just as Social Security requires citizens to prepare for their retirement years by setting up a social savings account, a similar "child's future security" account might be created that would provide a savings account to ensure that young persons have the funds necessary to embark successfully on adult life at the age of 18, regardless of the economic situation they are born into.

At birth, all children, regardless of the current economic status of their family, would have a custodial account—a "Child's Future Security" (CFS) account—opened in their name, with an initial deposit by the government of $1000 at a bank or registered brokerage firm selected by the parent. Each year the account would receive an additional $500 deposited by the government from funds collected in the same fashion used by Social Security. The parents or child could, if they wished, contribute privately to the account, although such contributions would not diminish that made by the government. At age 18, the accumulated funds would be made available to the young person for approved career program expenditures, such as college tuition, vocational training, job-readiness programs, and so on. By the time the child reached 18, a typical CFS deposit could have an accumulated balance of almost $40,000 (Lindsey, 1994).

Given roughly 4 million births a year in the United States, new CFS accounts would cost an estimated $4 billion annually. Maintaining the annual contribution to the accounts for the other roughly 60 million children under the age of 18 would add another $30 billion, for a total annual cost of roughly $34 billion. Following start-up expenses, the program would be funded entirely by children repaying their benefits during adulthood, using a collection mechanism similar to that used by the Social Security Administration, in which a payroll contribution of less than one-half of 1 percent would be made by employee and employer. Because recipients of CFS would repay their benefits through payments made during their working adulthood, the Child's Future Security program represents an approach that, like Social Security, reinforces the broad social reciprocal contract between the generations. Further, the children would likely go on to pay substantially more taxes as productive citizens, and be less likely to incur social costs (i.e., welfare assistance or correctional system costs).

Ideally, CFS funds would be held in custodial accounts at private brokerage firms, where they could be invested in stocks, bonds, or mutual funds, in much the same way that retirement funds are invested in Individual Retirement Accounts (IRAs) in the United States or Registered Retirement Savings Plans (RRSPs) in Canada. Parents might select among approved mutual funds in which to invest their child's account balances. Children would be encouraged to participate in the investment decision-making process, perhaps receiving semiannual statements of their account balances that would reinforce the lessons of saving and investing. By working with their own funds, children would be learning lessons and habits that could serve them in our society throughout their lives. In a sense, the CFS account is conceived more as a "capital building" account than a "savings account," with a view that children will learn the skills of investing.

> In this manner, the child would establish a meaningful base for accumulating asset wealth and ownership in our economy. The United States is a free enterprise market economy in which virtually all business and industry are privately owned, with small public sector involvement. To participate meaningfully in the nation's wealth, individuals must come to know and understand early in their lives the procedures and instruments used to allocate and manipulate ownership and wealth. Today, most young people know very little about stock ownership, what it is, how it works, and the good of it. It is extremely important that children living in a free market economy not grow up alienated by ignorance of the very instruments of power and wealth that represent ownership in their society (Siegal, 1985).

The aim of the CFS account is not new. Economists and others have long recognized the value of such an approach (Haveman, 1988; Sherraden, 1990; Thurow, 1992). In 1968, Nobel Prize–winning economist James Tobin proposed:

> After high school, every youth in the nation—whatever the economic means of his parents or his earlier education—should have the opportunity to develop his capacity to earn income and to contribute to the society. To this end the federal government could make available to every young man and woman, on graduation from high school and in any case at the age of 19, an endowment of, for example, [roughly $20,000 in 1991 dollars].

> This proposal has a number of important advantages. Individuals are assisted directly and equally, rather than indirectly and haphazardly, through government financing of particular programs. The advantages of back-

ground and talent that fit certain young people for university education are not compounded by financial favoritism. Within broad limits of approved programs, individuals are free to choose how to use the money the government is willing to invest in their development. No individual misses out because there happens to be no training courses where he lives, or because his parents' income barely exceeds some permissible maximum.

We have presented an approach to child welfare that offers children the same social insurance we guarantee our seniors. Although the CFS alone cannot address the problems of eroding wages and deteriorating cities, such a strategy could instill hope and opportunity in millions of young people who otherwise face despair (Siegal, 1985). Even the poorest children would know that upon graduation from high school, opportunity would be waiting for them. The most important aspect of this approach may not be its financial benefits, which will be substantial, but its impact on personal and social development. CFS is not a panacea; however, it is a beginning. The security guaranteed by CFS, coupled with an increased governmental commitment to building and maintaining our community resources, would significantly improve the social context in which poor families live. It is poor children who make up the bulk of our child welfare system, and it is these children that would benefit most from such an approach.

Conclusion

Historically, the child welfare system has swung between two competing approaches: (1) protecting children by removing them from homes where they are being abused or neglected, and (2) making every effort to keep children in those homes, even when the facts indicate they are seriously at risk. When it appears that one approach is not working, we switch to the other. We continue with that approach until we become convinced that it, too, is not working, whereupon we switch back, "(re)discovering" the previous approach, which we take up again. And so we swing back and forth, and although changes in the child welfare system occur, no forward progress is ever made, only a continual swinging from side to side.

The problem isn't that the families served by child welfare agencies cannot manage their own affairs. The problem is that most of these families do not have adequate resources to manage their own affairs. Casework merely shifts control from the client to a therapeutic professional who becomes responsible for figuring out and helping solve the root causes of the client's difficulties. The approach not only blames the client for his or her failure and dysfunction (despite larger social and economic factors that might be causing it), it also encourages the worst kind of dependency, in which the client becomes captive to the solutions and approaches developed by the family preservation caseworker. The caseworker does not have a proven therapeutic treatment, unlike, for example, a physician. The caseworker has no magic pill, no pharmaceutical drug, no surgical operation that will restore the family to health. This is the fundamental, but overlooked, fallacy of such programs as family preservation: It lacks a scientifically proven treatment that will effect a cure. Family preservation advocates have attempted to wrap their approaches in scientific credibility. However, the objective and rigorous studies have consistently found that it fails to have any appreciable impact on reducing the risk of abuse or poverty children are exposed to.

Methods are required that economically empower the families who find themselves in need of child welfare services. Principally, children need to grow up in families that have adequate income to house, clothe, and feed them. If it ever hopes to succeed, the child welfare system must begin focusing on ways to place resources directly under the control and management of parents. Policies and programs must encourage independence and self-initiative. They must provide training and skill development to parents to improve their ability to obtain gainful employment and effectively participate in the economy. Because it is unrealistic to expect a lone mother to seek work at a low-paying job if she is unable to find affordable and decent child care, child welfare services must ensure adequate child care.

All this requires an approach different from that taken so far. The residual paradigm that has shaped child welfare's outlook and understanding for the last hundred years or more is a minimalist perspective that has failed, and will continue to fail, to make substantive advances in reducing poverty, abuse, and neglect among children.

Although efforts like family preservation appear to be new, in fact, only the wrapping is new. The core of such programs is casework, an old and ineffective approach to solving the problems of impoverished families. These programs provide jobs for cadres of caseworkers, who can be expected to be the most ardent defenders. But more than special interests must guide child welfare policies and programs. Insofar as family preservation has served as a vehicle for the hopes and aspirations of those who work in the child welfare system, it has renewed optimism and faith in the families served. Our concern is that such enthusiasm and good intentions will only continue to miss the mark in making headway against the mounting problems children face, especially in an era where there is no federal entitlement to economic security for poor children.

During the last several years, while the end of AFDC has been considered, the child welfare field was principally focused on the failed family preservation approach. Meanwhile, the most important protection available to poor children—AFDC—has been assailed and finally eliminated. It is unfortunate that during this crucial period child welfare was so distracted by such an ineffective and obsolete approach that only served the interests of a few (primarily its research grant recipients—i.e., its inventors and advocates). We hope that the future of child welfare will shed these failed approaches and focus on improving the economic opportunity and well-being of children following the lead of approaches that have worked so well for the elderly.

REFERENCES

Aaron, H. (1982). *Economic effects of Social Security*. Washington, DC: The Brookings Institution.

Berrick, J. D. (1994). *Child maltreatment in California*. Sacramento: California Family Impact Seminar.

Blank, R. (1994). The employment strategy: Public policies to increase work and earnings. In S. H. Danziger, G. D. Sandefur & D. H Weinberg (Eds.), *Confronting poverty: Prescriptions for change* (pp. 168–204). Cambridge, MA: Harvcard University Press.

Brooks-Gunn. J., Duncan, G. J., Klebanov, P. K., & Sealand, N. (1993). Do neighborhoods influence child and adolescent development? *American Journal of Sociology, 99(2)*, 353–395.

Burtless, G. (1994). Public spending on the poor: Historical trends and economic limits. In S. H. Danziger, G. D. Sandefur, & D. H. Weinberg (Eds.), *Confronting poverty: Prescriptions for change* (pp. 51–84). Cambridge, MA: Harvard University Press.

Corcoran, M., Gordon, R., Laren, D., & Solon, G. (1992). The association between men's economic status and their family and community origins. *Journal of Human Resources, 27(4)*, 575–601.

Courtney, M. (1996). Kinship foster care and children's welfare: The Califonia experience. *Focus, 17(3),* Spring, 42–48.

Crane, J. (1991). Effects of neighborhoods on dropping out of school and teenage childbearing. In C. Jencks & P. E. Peterson (Eds.), *The urban underclass* (pp. 299–320). Washington, DC: The Brookings Institution.

Danziger, S. K., & Danziger, S. (1993). Child poverty and public policy: Toward a comprehensive antipoverty agenda. *Daedelus.*

Danziger, S., & Gottschalk, P. (1995). *America unequal.* Cambridge, MA: Harvard University Press.

Danziger, S., & Weinberg, D. (1994). The historical record: Trends in family income, inequality, and poverty. In S. H. Danziger, G. D. Sandefur, & D. H. Weinberg (Eds.), *Confronting poverty: Prescriptions for change* (pp. 18–50). Cambridge, MA: Harvard University Press.

Desowitz, R. S. (1987). *The thorn in the starfish.* New York: W. W. Norton.

Duncan, G. J., & Rodgers, W. (1988). Longitudinal aspects of childhood poverty. *Journal of Marriage and the Family, 50,* 1007–1021.

Ellwood, D. (1988). *Poor support.* New York: Basic Books.

Fay, J. S. (1994). *California almanac,* 7th ed. Santa Barbara, CA: Pacific Data Resources.

Fischer, J. (1973). Is casework effective? A review. *Social Work 18,* 5–20.

Freeman, R. B. (1994). How much has de-unionization contributed to the rise in male earnings inequality? In S. Danziger & P. Gottschalk (Eds.), *Uneven tides: Rising inequality in America* (pp. 133–164). New York: Russell Sage Foundation.

Furstenberg, F. F., Jr., Brooks-Gunn, J., & Morgan, S. P. (1987). *Adolescent mothers in later life.* New York: Cambridge University Press.

Gil, D. (1970). *Violence against children.* Cambridge, MA: Harvard University Press.

Handler, J. F. & Hasenfeld, Y. (1991). *The moral construction of poverty.* Newbury Park, CA: Sage Publications.

Haveman, R. (1988). *Starting even: An equal opportunity program to combat the nation's new poverty.* New York: Simon and Schuster.

Hayes, C. (1987). *Risking the future: Adolescent sexuality, pregnancy, and childbearing,* Vol I. Washington, DC: National Academy Press.

Heneghan, A. M, Horwitz, S. M., & Leventhal, J. M. (1996). Evaluating intensive family preservation programs: A methodological review. *Pediatrics, 97,* 535–542.

Hogan, D. P., & Kitagawa, E. M. (1985). The impact of social status, family structure, and neighborhood on the fertility of black adolescents. *American Journal of Sociology, 90,* 825–855.

Illig, D. C. (1994*). California's process for resolving allegations of child abuse and neglect.* CRB-BB-94-004. Sacramento: California Research Bureau.

Jencks, C. & Mayer, S. E. (1990). The social consequences of growing up in a poor neighborhood. In L. E. Lynn, Jr., & M. G. H. McGeary, (Eds.), *Inner-city poverty in the United States.* Washington, DC: National Academy.

Jones, D., & McCurdy, K. (1992). The links between types of maltreatment and demographic characteristics of children. *Child Abuse and Neglect, 16,* 201–214.

Kadushin, A., & Martin, J. A. (1988). *Child welfare services,* 4th ed. New York: Macmillan.

Kamerman, S. B., & Kahn, A. J. (1990). Social services for children, youth, and families in the United States. *Children and Youth Services Review, 12.*

Kasarda, J. D. (1989). Urban industrial transition and the underclass. *Annals of the American Academy of Politics and Social Science, 501,* 26–47.

Kennickell, A. B., & Starr-McCluer, M. (1994). Changes in family finances from 1989 to 1992: Evidence from the Survey of Consumer Finances. *Federal Reserve Bulletin, 80,* 861–882.

Krugman, P. R. (1992). The rich, the right and the facts: Deconstructing the income distribution debate. *The American Prospect, 11,* 19–31.

Lav, I. J., Lazere, E., Greenstein, R., & Gold, S. (1993). *The states and the poor: How budget decisions affected low income people in 1992.* Washington, DC: Center on Budget and Policy Priorities.

Lindsey, D. (1994). *The welfare of children.* New York: Oxford University Press.

Lindsey, D. & Doh, J. (1996). *Family preservation, family support and California's children.* Sacramento: California Family Impact Seminar.

Marmor, T. R., Mashaw, J. L., Harvey, P. L. (1990). *America's misunderstood welfare state.* Basic Books.

McCurdy, M. A., & Daro, D. (1993). *Current trends in child abuse reporting and fatalities: The results of the 1992 annual fifty state survey.* Chicago: National Committee for the Prevention of Child Abuse.

McLanahan, S., & Sandefur, G. (1994). *Growing up with a single parent: What hurts, what helps.* Cambridge, MA: Harvard University Press.

Michael, L. & Bernstein, J. (1994). *The state of working America, 1994–1995.* Economic Policy Institute Series. Armonk: M. E. Sharpe.

Mullen, E. J., and Dumpson, J. R., eds. (1972). *Evaluation of social intervention.* San Francisco: Jossey-Bass.

National Research Council. (1993). *Losing generations: Adolescents in high risk settings.* Washington, DC: National Academy Press.

Pecora, P. J., Fraser, M., & Haapala, D. A. (1991). Client outcomes and issues for program design. In K. Wells & D. Biegel (Eds.), *Family preservation services* (pp. 3–32). Newbury Park, CA: Sage Publications.

Pelton, L. H. (1981). Child abuse and neglect: The myth of classlessness. In L. H. Pelton (Ed.). *The social context of child abuse and neglect* (pp. 23–38). New York: Human Sciences Press.

Pelton, L. H. (1989). *For reasons of poverty: A critical analysis of the public child welfare system in the United States.* New York: Praeger.

Pelton, L. H. (1994). Is poverty a key contributor to child maltreatment? In E. Gambrill & T. J. Stein (Eds.), *Controversial issues in child welfare* (pp. 16–28). Needham Heights, MA: Allyn & Bacon.

Schuerman, J. R., Rzepnicki, T., & Littell, J. (1994). *Putting families first: An experiment in family preservation.* Hawthorne, NY: Aldine De Gruyter.

Schwartz, I. M., & Au Claire, P. (1991). Family preservation services as an alternative to the out-of-home placement of adolescents: The Hennepin County experience. In K. Wells & D. Biegel (Eds.), *Family preservation services* (pp. 33–46). Newbury Park, CA: Sage Publications.

Segal, S. P. (1972). Research on the outcomes of social work therapeutic interventions: A review of the literature. *Journal of Health and Social Behavior 13,* 3–17.

Sheldon, B. (1986). Social work effectiveness experiments: Review and implications. *British Journal of Social Work 16,* 223–242.

Sherraden, M. (1990). Rethinking social welfare: Towards assets. *Social Policy 7,* 37–43.

Siegal, M. (1985). *Children, parenthood, and social welfare: In the context of developmental psychology.* Oxford: Oxford University Press.

Testa, M. F. (1992). Conditions of risk for substitute care. *Children and Youth Services Review, 14,* 27–36.

Thurow, L. C. (1992). *Head to head: The coming economic battle among Japan, Europe, and America.* New York: William Morrow.

Tobin, J. (1968). Raising the incomes of the poor. In K. Gordon (Ed.) *Agenda for the nation: Papers on diplomatic and foreign policy issues* (pp. 77–116). Washington, DC: The Brookings Institution.

Whittaker, J. K., & Tracy, E. M. (1990). Family preservation services and education for social work practice: Stimulus and response. In J. K. Whittaker, J. Kinney, E. M. Tracy, & C. Booth (Eds.), *Reaching high-risk families: Intensive family preservation in human services* (pp. 1–11). New York: Aldine de Gruyter.

Wilson, W. J. (1987). *The truly disadvantaged.* Chicago, IL: University of Chicago Press.

Wilson W. J. (1993). *The new urban poverty and the problem of race.* Tanner Lecture on Human Values, October 22, 1993. *Michigan Quarterly Review, 33*(2).

Wolff, E. N. (1992). Changing inequality of wealth. *American Economic Review, 82*, 552–558.

Wolff, E. N. (1995). How the pie is sliced: America's growing concentration of wealth. *The American Prospect, 22*, 58–64.

Yuan, Y. Y., McDonald, W. R., Wheeler, C. E., Struckman-Johnson, D., & Rivest, M. (1990). *Evaluation of AB 1562 in-home care demonstration projects: Final report.* Sacramento: Walter R. McDonald & Associates.œ

Juvenile Justice

Back to the Future, or Will We Learn from the Past?

Ira M. Schwartz

Social workers have had relatively little involvement with the criminal justice system. This is unfortunate given the intersection of many other problems with this system. This essay provides a brief overview of the juvenile justice system and suggests future roles for social workers. Ira M. Schwartz is currently dean of the University of Pennsylvania School of Social Work. Prior to that he was director of the Institute for Juvenile Research at the University of Michigan. He continues to pursue research concerning juvenile offenders. Recent publications include (In)justice for Juveniles: Rethinking the Best Interests of the Child *(New York: Free Press, 1989) and* Juvenile Justice and Public Policy: Toward a National Agenda *(New York: Macmillan, 1992).*

Introduction

In 1999, the juvenile court will be 100 years old. Instead of being a celebration, the 100th anniversary will be a bittersweet event.

The juvenile court is under attack and in danger of being put out of business. The public has lost confidence in the juvenile justice system's ability to respond effectively to the problems of serious, repeat, and violent young offenders. As a result, elected public officials are scurrying to enact legislation and implement policies designed to treat young offenders like adults. The cry that "adult-like crime deserves adult-like time" has caught on and is sweeping the nation.

A Brief History

The idea that troubled and troubling children should be managed separately from adults dates back to the early 1800s (Schlossman, 1977). The New York House of Refuge opened its doors to delinquent, dependent, and neglected youth in 1825 (Schlossman, 1977). Considered an important breakthrough, it spawned the establishment of similar facilities throughout the country. These institutions have been characterized by their managers as "a factory, a workhouse, a prison, a public school, a nursery, a hospital, a boarding school, a poorhouse, and an orphanage. That they were in a quandary is not surprising; the Refuge was any and all of these at the same time" (Schlossman, 1977).

Not long after they were created, the Houses of Refuge came under scrutiny and criticism. Scandals, fires, media exposés, and official investigations revealed an enormous gap between the reality of life and conditions in these facilities and the claims of their administrators. "Educational achievements were minimal; rehabilitative accomplishments were exaggerated; corruption was rife; political considerations intruded into the appointment process and inflated expenses; . . . vocational training programs amounted to no more than busywork or worse still, exploitation of cheap child labor for private profit; and finally, incarceration provided a perfect setting for mutual instruction and reinforcement of the norm and techniques of criminal behavior" (Schlossman, 1977). "By mid-century the inability of the . . . house to rehabilitate or even maintain order was becoming, at least in charity circles, a frequent topic of conversation" (Schlossman, 1977).

The Houses of Refuge eventually gave way to a new concept: the reformatory. These new institutions emphasized education, discipline, and a "homelike" environment. Often located in the country, their architectural design included cottages where children lived together in relatively small groups staffed by house parents (Platt, 1977; Schlossman, 1977).

The next major development in separating troubled children, and delinquents in particular, from adults was the creation of the juvenile court. The rise and promise of the social sciences during the Progressive Era led reformers to the concept of individualized justice. The vision was that "the juvenile court would employ varying degrees of procedural informality in order to assess the causes of delinquency—not what the child had done, but why he had done it" (Schlossman, 1977). Professional probation officers were employed to prepare reports for judges that, among other things, would carefully and systematically diagnose a child's problems and prescribe corrective actions and solutions. This approach was largely based on the medical model of diagnosis and treatment of patients. Detention centers were built to confine youth pending their appearance in court so they would not have to be confined in adult jails. Also, instead of relying almost exclusively on institutions for the care and treatment of delinquents, probation officers supervised and treated them in the community, preferably in their own homes, where the focus of intervention would include the family (Schlossman, 1977).

It took nearly a century for the reforms and fundamental components of the juvenile justice system outlined above to unfold. Although states today differ with respect to the upper age of juvenile court jurisdiction, the types and availability of intervention services and programs, and the way juvenile courts and youth detention and correction services are organized and administered, these basic components make up the core of every state's juvenile justice system. "The legal justification for the house of refuge and, later, juvenile court intervention was *parens patriae*, the right and responsibility of the state to substitute its own control over children for that of the natural parents when the latter were unable or unwilling to meet their responsibilities or when the child posed a community crime problem" (Feld, 1993). Embedded within the principle of *parens patriae* is the assumption that juvenile court judges should view themselves as if they are a friendly parent and make decisions that are "in the best interests of the child."

The *parens patriae* model dominated juvenile justice policy in the United States until the late 1960s. Then, in 1967, the U.S. Supreme court handed down the landmark *Gault* decision. In an attempt to address the abuses of power and discretion and virtual absence of legal safeguards that flourished under the *parens patriae* model, the Court mandated that juveniles be given many of the same due process and procedural protections accorded adults (287 U.S. 45[1932]). The *Gault* decision precipitated "a due process revolution" that substantially transformed the juvenile court from a social welfare agency into a legal institution (Feld, 1993). It was also "the first step in the convergence of the procedures of the juvenile justice system with those of the adult criminal process" (Feld, 1993). In addition, primarily in response to hardening public attitudes about juvenile offenders, policymakers in states revised the purpose clause of their juvenile statutes to emphasize protection of the public, punishment, and just desserts and deemphasized "the best interests of the child" and rehabilitation (Feld, 1993).

These developments, as significant as they were, did not anticipate the level of public fear and outrage about juvenile crime that emerged in the 1990s. Bombarded by almost daily media accounts of teenagers arrested for drive-by shootings, gang violence, carjackings, homicides, bringing guns to school, tourist killings, and the killing or maiming of innocent children from errant bullets, the public demanded that politicians and professionals take corrective action. Mounting public pressure, coupled with increasing disillusionment about the ability of the juvenile justice system to respond appropriately, prompted elected public officials in states throughout the country to enact legislation designed to try more juveniles in the adult criminal courts. As a result, legislation has been passed in more than half the states that has removed certain offenses from the jurisdiction of juvenile courts, allowed juveniles to be tried in the adult criminal courts at younger ages, and given prosecutors more discretion with respect to which court they could choose to prosecute young people. The cherished and long-held view that troubled and troubling children should be managed separately from adults was eroding.

The federal government has also weighed in on the side of more punitive measures for young people. "Both the Clinton administration and members of the 104th Congress have endorsed policies that would greatly facilitate the criminal prosecution of violent and repeat juvenile offenders in adult courts" (Council on Crime, 1996). Although the federal government has little to do with the management, policy development, and financing of state and local juvenile justice services, federal support for policies designed to treat juveniles as adults will have a significant impact in the states.

The Future of Juvenile Justice

The trend of implementing more punitive policies toward young offenders will probably increase in the years ahead. The juvenile "at-risk" population (10- to 17-year-olds) is projected to increase. Unless the behavior patterns of this age group change, the numbers of juveniles who can be expected to be referred to the juvenile and adult criminal courts will probably increase as well. As the juvenile crime problem worsens, state legislatures will continue to enact laws that will further erode the jurisdiction of the juvenile court. Eventually, lawmakers will have to face the question "Can a separate court for juveniles be justified?" In fact, state lawmakers in at least two states, Arizona and Michigan, are already confronting this issue.

In Michigan, in the late 1980s, conservative and liberal legislators collaborated on the development and enactment of a package of "get tough" measures targeted toward juveniles. Since that time, additional laws have been passed that propelled even greater numbers of young people into the state's adult criminal justice system. Now, some policymakers are asking whether the juvenile court should be abolished or whether its jurisdiction should be limited to misdemeanors and minor felony cases. Also, consideration is being given to transferring the state's youth training schools from the Michigan Department of Social Services to the Department of Corrections, the agency that administers the state's prison system. The rationale for the transfer is that the Department of Corrections would operate the facilities more like adult prisons than treatment centers. In Arizona, legislation has been introduced that would essentially eliminate the juvenile court. Although the legislation did not pass, the issue has been put on the public agenda in that state and will probably be raised again.

From a historical perspective, we have come full circle. Beginning in the early 1800s, social reformers directed their energy toward separating juveniles from adults. One hundred years later, we find an angry public and state and federal elected public officials demanding that we return to the old days. There is virtually no credible scientific evidence indicating that treating juveniles as adults will be effective in reducing recidivism or as a deterrent to committing crimes by others (Jones & Krisberg, 1994). In fact, what little evidence there is suggests these policies are likely to be counterproductive. For example, a recent study of juveniles sentenced to adult prisons in Minnesota indicated that 84% of those released returned to prison within five years. More than half returned to prison within two years (Executive Summary, 1995). A study in Florida indicated that juveniles released from Florida's prisons had significantly higher rates of recidivism than a matched group of adults (Schwartz, 1989).

While "get tough" policies are likely to prevail in the short run, the sentencing of juveniles to adult prison is problematic. Despite the best efforts of prison administrators, juveniles sentenced to adult prisons will be raped, sodomized, exploited, and brutalized by adult inmates. Violence and brutality are part of the reality of the American prison experience, and juveniles will be particularly vulnerable to these realities. Scandals will surface in the media that will be followed by official inquiries. This will lead to recommendations calling for juveniles to be separated from

adults and housed in facilities where they can be equipped with the knowledge and skills needed to survive in a 21st-century environment. Studies will also find that recidivism rates for juveniles released from adult prisons will be extraordinarily high. This will also generate support for developing separate and specialized correctional programs for young offenders.

The youth correction system of the future will, in all likelihood, be very different from the system that exists today. It must be credible, ensure that the public is protected, and have options for the management and supervision of violent and chronic offenders. There will be increased emphasis on privatization of services (for-profit and non-profit), as well as on outcomes and performance contracting with the private sector. The concept of managed care, which is so prominent in the healthcare field, will also probably emerge as a critical ingredient in the management and delivery of youth correction services. In Philadelphia, juvenile correctional officials announced their intentions to "privatize" the operation of the Youth Studies Center (the local juvenile detention facility). This will be the first large metropolitan area juvenile detention center in the country to be operated by a private for-profit or non-profit provider. In addition, they are also exploring the concept of capitated rates in contracting with providers of residential services for delinquent youth.

The State of Missouri is nationally recognized for having an enlightened and cost-effective youth corrections system. Unlike most other states, elected public officials and juvenile justice professionals in Missouri have resisted enacting policies designed to propel significant numbers of juvenile offenders into their adult prison system. Juveniles found guilty of serious violent crimes and who are chronic repeaters are confined in small, physically secure treatment units strategically located throughout the state and administered by the Missouri Department of Youth Services. Juvenile offenders who do not require secure custody confinement are managed in a diverse network of community-based programs that provide high levels of supervision and surveillance, and enriched treatment and educational opportunities. Recently, after reviewing the recommendations of a Governor's Task Force, the governor of South Carolina announced plans to restructure that state's juvenile justice system. The plans are remarkably similar to those implemented in Missouri.

When state policymakers realize that sending more juveniles into adult prison systems is both too costly and counterproductive, they will be forced to look for other and more promising options. States like Missouri and South Carolina will probably be the models they will turn to.

Despite the legislative assault on the juvenile courts, the juvenile court as an institution will survive. Although the court is plagued with serious substantive problems, the juvenile court concept enjoys broad support within the professional social and child welfare establishment. The juvenile court has been an influential advocate for services for troubled children and families. Also, most of the juvenile court's business consists of child welfare, domestic relations, children's mental health, and other related family matters. These are particularly complex and sticky issues that require special expertise that judges in other courts of general trial jurisdiction prefer be handled elsewhere.

Although the juvenile court will survive, I believe it will have to be a very different institution in the 21st century, particularly as it relates to the handling of delinquency matters. The juvenile court in the United States is a curious mixture; it is a legal institution and a social welfare institution. Although it has become more legalistic since the landmark *Gault* decision, it still has the trappings of a social welfare institution and many decisions or dispositions continue to be made based on "the best interests of the child."

My experience leads me to the conclusion that the juvenile court in the 21st century must be a court of justice, and justice only. Young people must be accorded all of the due process and procedural protections that adults have, in addition to the other protections the social and behaviorial sciences suggest are necessary. One such example is an unwavering right to counsel because of the research suggesting that juveniles do not understand the full implications of waiving their right to an attorney. In addition, the juvenile court of the future must demonstrate that it can handle all delinquency cases, including the most heinous and serious ones. If this does not happen, we will continue to see the juvenile court's jurisdiction eroded until the only cases left for the court to process are misdemeanors and status offenses. In addition, youth correction systems will have to demonstrate that they can manage the most serious delinquency cases. This will give the juvenile courts credible dispositional options for these youth, some of whom will have to be incapacitated for a considerable period of time.

Also, youth correction resources will have to be used more wisely. For example, incarceration in an institution, which is the most expensive intervention, should be reserved for those youth who must be confined because they are dangerous and pose a serious threat to the community and for those who cannot be managed in a less secure setting. All other delinquents should be managed in community-based programs and provided with appropriate supervision and educational, employment, and treatment services. Although this approach is inconsistent with the punitive policies currently being implemented in many states, it is a cost-effective strategy that is supported by the best available research and thinking in the field.

Implications for Social Work

The social work profession has essentially abandoned the fields of juvenile and criminal justice. Beginning in the 1970s, professional social workers started to leave juvenile and criminal justice agencies because they never really fit in or felt comfortable working in probation offices, detention centers, juvenile training schools, adult jails, and prisons. They were primarily attracted to the less coercive, more "professional," and more lucrative settings in the fields of health, mental health, child and family services, and private practice. Frankly, many of the non–social workers working in juvenile and criminal justice system were glad to see them leave. Judges, probation administrators and probation officers, and institutional superintendents often did not feel that social workers had much to offer, particularly those who were clinically trained and believed that psychotherapy was a cure for delinquency.

The exodus of social workers from juvenile and criminal justice was also impacted by the availability of federal Law Enforcement Assistance Administration (LEAA) funds for education and training in the justice fields. LEAA funds were primarily used to support the training of law enforcement officials and the establishment of undergraduate criminal justice programs in colleges and universities throughout the country. The graduates from these programs had no problem finding employment because state and local juvenile and adult criminal justice systems expanded greatly during the 1970s and 1980s. These systems continue to be one of the largest growth areas with respect to public and private sector employment today.

Although some may disagree, the absence of professional social workers and social work values in juvenile and criminal justice has been costly. The adult criminal justice system is strictly in the punishment and warehousing business. Unfortunately, the juvenile justice system has been pushed in this direction as well. Juvenile probation officers often lack the skills needed to help troubled youth and their families. They spend little time with the cases assigned to them and are mainly concerned with issues of surveillance and accountability (i.e., ensuring that orders of the court are obeyed). Staff in most juvenile detention and correction facilities are ill-trained and largely concerned with security and maintaining order. The conditions in many of these institutions are deplorable and the practices repressive. Despite rhetoric to the contrary, there is little emphasis on treatment and rehabilitation. When youth are released, they are rarely provided with the aftercare and transition services they need to adjust to community life. As a result, the rates of recidivism and failure for these young people are high.

It would be foolish to think that professional social workers by themselves could turn this situation around. However, the juvenile justice system in the United States would be more rational, humane, and effective if more social workers were employed in it. Professional social workers have the theoretical and practical knowledge needed to design, plan, implement, and evaluate programs. They have the skills needed to advocate for rational and humane policies and resources. At the interpersonal level, social workers have the skills needed to build effective working relationships with delinquent youth and their families. They can also work at the neighborhood and community levels where some of the more influential forces that impact on the lives of youth are located. In addition, the presence of social workers will help ensure that youth detention and correction programs are not abusive and that they operate in accordance with professional standards and practices.

Social workers are not going to gravitate to the juvenile justice field on their own. Schools of social work will have to serve as a catalyst for developing students' interest in juvenile justice by developing additional and more exciting field placements in juvenile justice agencies (e.g., in police departments, public defender and prosecuting attorneys offices, juvenile courts, probation departments, detention centers, training schools, and community-based programs). In developing such field placements, schools of social work will have to be sensitive to the privatization movement in juvenile justice and make sure that students have opportunities in both the not-for-profit and the growing for-profit sectors. Schools of social work will also have to recruit faculty with juvenile justice backgrounds and research interests who can inspire students and get them interested in working in the juvenile justice system as a career choice.

The juvenile justice field is challenging and has unlimited opportunities for social workers. Also, no domestic problem is more pressing than juvenile crime and violence. It is to be hoped that social workers will play a more significant role in helping to meet these challenges in the future than has been the case in the past.

REFERENCES

The Council on Crime in America. (1996). *The state of violent crime in America*. Washington, DC: The New Citizenship Project.

Executive Summary, Minnesota State Legislative Auditor's Office. (1995). *Residential facilities for juvenile offenders*.

Feld, B. C. (1993). *Justice for children*. Boston: Northeastern University Press.

Jones, M. A., & Krisberg, B. (1994). *Images and reality*. San Francisco: National Council on Crime and Delinquency.

Platt, A. M. (1977). *The child savers*. Chicago: University of Chicago Press.

Schlossman, S. L. (1977). *Love and the American delinquent*. Chicago: University of Chicago Press.

Schwartz, I. (1989). *(In)Justice for juveniles: Rethinking the best interests of the child*. Lexington, MA: Lexington Books.

Family Violence
Implications for Social Work Practice

Bonnie L. Yegidis

Family violence has existed for millennia as a means of social control, it is only recently that its effects have been considered a worthy subject of social concern. Bonnie Yegidis, professor and dean of the School of Social Work at the University of Georgia, explores the nature and extent of family violence at the end of the 20th century both in the United States and abroad. She presents different definitions of the problems and their implications for research and practice models. She concludes that those models which take a broad-based perspective on family violence will have the greatest utility in the future.

Dr. Yegidis was formerly professor and dean at the School of Social Work at the University of South Florida. She is the author or coauthor of numerous manuscripts that address the incidence and assessment of family violence, including methods of social work intervention.

Introduction and Historical Perspective

There is nothing new about women and children being abused physically, emotionally, and/or sexually by their husbands, fathers, and other relatives. The history of civilization is replete with references to the abuse of women and children. Physical abuse has been used historically as a means of social control, and such punishment has been viewed as the legitimate domain of the husband/father.

In African and Islamic cultures, there are numerous examples of the abuse of women by their husbands and/or their families to control them. For example, genital mutilation and infibulation is used in dozens of African cultures to control the sexuality of women and to ensure their virginity for marriage (Hicks, 1993; Lightfoot-Klein, 1989). Recent estimates have placed the number of girls and women worldwide who have been so mutilated, typically without anesthesia, at over 100 million (Crossette, 1995). In Islamic culture, adultery by wives has been punishable by death, such as is vividly documented in *The Stoning of Soraya M.* (Sahebjam, 1990). Thus, in Western and non-Western cultures and across generations of time, women have been abused by the men in their lives and by their families. And, such abuse has been viewed by traditional cultures as necessary, appropriate, and legitimate.

The issue of family violence is critical to American society. Estimates of abuse vary considerably depending on the definition applied and the methodology used in a given study. Also, because definitions of abuse vary among people and cultures, it is difficult to reach agreement about what constitutes abuse. However, national statistics estimate that between 10% and 30% of women are abused by their male partners. Of this amount, about 7%

is serious abuse (Straus and Gelles, 1986), abuse that is characterized by injury to the victim. The National Crime Victimization Survey (NCVS) produces estimates of the violence that victims are willing to report. According to this source, most violence between intimates is assault, the intentional inflicting of injury on another person. In 1992, according to the FBI, an estimated 1432 women were killed by intimates. Compared to males, females annually experienced over 10 times as many incidents of violence by an intimate (Bureau of Justice Statistics, 1994).

Violence between intimates is difficult to measure because this type of behavior typically occurs within the privacy of one's home. Also, victims are reluctant to report these crimes to law enforcement because of shame or fear of reprisals. In addition, victims tend to distort their responses to questions of abuse by researchers, so as to appear more socially acceptable. Finally, estimates of abuse vary considerably depending on the definitions of abuse applied and the methods of study. Definitions of abuse vary among people and among cultures, thus it is difficult to reach agreement across cultures of what constitutes abuse.

Legal definitions of abuse vary among states, with no real consistency in these definitions across the United States. However, in 1994, the Uniform Crime Reports added domestic violence as a distinctive criminal behavior. As part of the Violence Crime Control and Law Enforcement Act of 1994, the categories of stalking and domestic violence were added as part of the National Incident- Based Reporting system (Uniform Crime Reports, 1994). Although national data is not yet available from this source, it is expected to be available for researchers and policymakers by sometime in 1996.

For current study purposes, the operational definition provided by Straus is the one used most extensively in national research on this topic and is considered the standard in the field. In brief, Straus has conceptualized abuse in the Conflict Tactics Scale (1979) as being on a continuum of severity, from most to least. The scale measures the level of reasoning, verbal aggression, and violence used for conflict resolution by individuals. Based on this measure, used in two separate studies separated by a decade, family violence in the United States has remained fairly stable from 1975 to 1985. However, there has been a slight decline in parent to child abuse (630 per thousand children in 1975 to 620 per thousand children in 1985) and a similar decline in marital violence (121 per thousand couples in 1975, 113 per thousand couples in 1985). These are the only national studies to date that have used large survey-type designs to estimate the incidence of family violence in America.

The abuse of women and children takes a serious toll on the emotional well-being of families (Yegidis, 1992). There is about 30 years of data in the social sciences about the correlates and consequences of family violence. There is agreement in the research that physical abuse leads to injury of victims and carries the risk of homicide and/or suicide to the victim or perpetrator. In addition to the physical trauma that is typically sustained, abuse leads to numerous psychological symptoms in victims. Typical symptoms include depression, anxiety, irritability, fearfulness, withdrawal, and sometimes hopelessness. In addition, the literature has shown that growing up in abusive homes shapes how children will choose to resolve conflict in their own lives. However, the once widely accepted "cycle of violence" theory is being questioned in the more recent research on family violence (see, for example, Pressman, Cameron, and Rothery, 1989).

The literature in social work practice addressing family violence dates to the early 1960s. These early studies of family violence were conducted primarily by the case study approach and were designed to describe the characteristics of the abuser or the victims. The essence of these early studies was that abuse was pathological behavior that was appropriate for casework intervention (see, for example, L. Schultz, 1960).

Theory and Practice

Early social work practice with abused women was geared toward helping them understand how their behavior triggered the abuse. Women were led to believe that something about them or their behavior was actually at fault. Thus, locating the source of change within themselves should lead to a change in their partners. Casework was designed to keep families together by changing women's behavior or their perceptions about their partners. It is fair to say that early casework intervention was not oriented toward empowering women or helping them to develop better lifestyle alternatives for themselves and their children. And, there is no evidence to suggest that this form of intervention had any substantial impact on reducing family violence in communities.

In addition, there were no social services specifically designed to prevent or provide early intervention to abused women in the United States until the mid-1970s. In fact, the beginning of services for abused women and their children was a product of the women's movement, rather than a response by social service providers. The early work of feminists like Erin Pizzey helped shape the beginning of shelters and safe houses for battered women and their children. For the first decade of their existence, shelters were run by grass roots organizations, focused on helping victims of abuse find alternative housing, job training, and sources of income. More recently, shelter staff have included professional social workers, who have been used to provide counseling as well as resource development for victims of family violence. However, feminist theory continues to play a major role in our understanding of and response to the abuse of women.

Beginning in the early and mid-1970s, the literature in social work began to reflect an interest in the design and delivery of services for abused women and children, probably in response to the developing national awareness about the serious consequences of abuse on children. Each state approved legislation to outlaw the abuse of children and to specify teachers, physicians, social workers, and other professionals who come into contact with children as mandatory reporters. Consistent with this national awareness, the social work profession expanded its attention to meeting the needs of abused victims.

Within the last 20 years, the professional journals in social work have published hundreds of articles about practice with and for abusive families. Numerous models of practice have been developed, applied, and evaluated for work with abusive families. Most research has shown that models of practice that include the use of couples' counseling alone are not effective in treating or reducing the incidence of family violence (Deschner, 1984). The practice models that have shown to be most effective in treating and deterring abuse tend to use methodologies that are confrontive of the abuse, and that require abusers to change their behaviors. These types of models use primarily cognitive and behavioral methods of intervention. They are focused on changing attitudes and beliefs about gender roles and expectations, teaching methods for controlling arousal and aggression, and teaching alternative models of conflict resolution, including assertive communication.

Current and Future Trends

The models that have the greatest utility for social work are those that take a broad-based perspective of the nature of the problem. This is so because the research has shown consistently that abuse is the product of complex interacting variables about individuals and their environments. Thus, more simplistic models do not explain how and why abuse occurs, and models of intervention based on them are lacking. The "typical" abusive relationship is likely to be understood as a combination of inappropriate learning, environmental stress, economics, and poor coping skills. Thus a person-in-environment perspective is more useful in explaining abuse than, say, one that focuses solely on interpersonal dynamics or personality development. Intervention that is based on a person-in-environment perspective focuses on developing individual and family coping methods, while examining the effects that economics and institutional forms of oppression have on individuals and communities. Ecological theory is also useful here, as it takes into account the interaction of various levels of systems describing relationships or linkages that persons have with the family, community, and culture. Thus, intervention from these perspectives focuses on individual and/or group methods of treatment, as well as on developing community responses providing for appropriate types of prevention and treatment.

Community responses typically include the collaboration of social agencies, the courts, and law enforcement designed to ensure an overall effective response to family violence. These collaboratives are a recent phenomena in communities, developing from an increased sensitivity of communities to the failure of more traditional modes of intervention. In many communities around the country, for example, public awareness campaigns proclaiming zero tolerance for family violence have been developed. In addition, communities around the country are developing domestic violence task forces to evaluate the effectiveness of various forms of intervention and develop new models and protocols. These models, by and large, draw together law enforcement, the courts, domestic violence shelters, and individual service providers, including professional social workers. The goals of these task forces are many, including developing public awareness campaigns; designing training packages for law enforcement and court personnel, including encouraging arrest and mandatory treatment; and identifying preferred models of therapeutic interventions for individual providers and social service agencies. Professionally educated social workers have played a major role in shaping the development, and activities of these task forces, and may be expected to influence the development of policy and programming. Social workers will need to continue their presence on these community panels since our perspective on the problem is one that is not provided by other professions.

Some of the more promising intervention models that are being developed around the country use educational, cognitive, and behavioral approaches to stopping interpersonal violence. For example, the Men Stopping Violence Movement is a national, non-profit organization working to end violence against women (Men Stopping Violence, 1996). This organization conducts batterers' classes and has trained various professional and lay groups in their model. The approach, largely feminist in nature, holds batterers accountable for their behavior, while teaching them strategies to end their use of violence. The program also shows professionals how an educational model fits within an overall coordinated community response that includes the provision of social services and advocacy for abused women. Intervention for abused women also should provide an opportunity for them to explore their own histories of abuse and learn how these experiences, as well as others, may unknowingly set them up for establishing serial abusive relationships. Advocacy will continue to be a critical component of programming for abused women, as these women typically need help in finessing the legal and judicial parameters of community programming.

Other program models are in place throughout the nation. Most of these models provide for mandatory intervention for the batterer. In communities in which preferred, presumptive, or mandatory arrest is operational police policy, batterers are arrested, scheduled for a court appearance, and remanded for treatment. In most communities, treatment means a structured, several-month psychoeducational program designed to stop the violence. Typically, these programs will have been reviewed and approved by the local community collaborative.

The focus of social work intervention for the coming years will continue to be on prevention and early intervention. To be responsive to and a part of this process, social work educators should focus on preparing students for community-level practice interventions, as well as direct practice. It is at the community level that education, prevention, and early intervention programs are primarily designed. Being able to work with communities to design and deliver programs such as these are critical skills for effective service delivery in this domain. This suggests that the models under-

lying our education programs must include an appreciation of community-level factors that shape human behavior and social policy development, as well as an understanding of interpersonal dynamics. For many social work education programs, this will mean broadening the models underlying their curricula.

In addition, we would be wise to examine cross-cultural research on family violence in our educational programs. This is so because abuse varies in terms of its meaning within different cultures. To be responsive to working in diverse environments, it will become increasingly important to understand how violence is expressed and understood across people and cultures. Moreover, as was demonstrated in the recent teleconference on the challenge of violence worldwide (NASW, 1996), we have much to learn from developing nations. In various Third World nations, violence on intimates is shunned publicly. In our nation, the daily papers often report the murder of women by their partners, followed by acquittal.

Moreover, students will need to be exposed to working as members of cross-disciplinary teams. This is not a new concept for social work education. For decades, social work students and professionals have worked with psychologists, psychiatrists, and other professional helpers to design effective psychotherapeutic approaches to intervention. Within the field of family violence treatment and prevention, the composition and interest of these teams is different. It is now critical for social workers to be able to effectively interact with law enforcement personnel, judges, and lay individuals. The focus of interest within these teams is multifaceted, including an interest in the needs of children and families, but also an interest in preserving the safety of the community at large. Thus, social workers must be able to understand and respect the role of law enforcement, for example, in preventing and intervening with violent families. And, they must be able to understand and use the research developed by these groups. For example, numerous studies conducted within the last decade have suggested that presumptory or mandatory arrest may be an effective intervention for abusive families (see, for example, Berk & Sherman, 1988). Although there are conflicting data now on this point, as a short-run intervention, arrest has been shown to be effective for minor offenders. (Berk, Campbell, Klap, & Western, 1991). Being able to use these types of findings and know their limitations is critical in the design of social policies and programs aimed at reducing family violence.

Within social work education, there is a deep understanding of the effects of gender-based violence. The Women's Commission of the Council on Social Work Education is an important vehicle for the development of policy in social work education designed to prevent the abuse of women. During the last several years, the work of this commission has included developing models for curricular reform, as well as encouraging the development of policy aimed at preserving the rights of women faculty and students.

Developing a Global Response to Family Violence

As noted in the introductory paragraphs of this essay, family violence is a global problem. We primarily understand its effects as it impacts upon American families. However, developing international responses to the issue is more than warranted. The International Association of Schools of Social Work, Women's Caucus, held a symposium on Violence Against Women at the United Nations Fourth World Conference on Women in Bei-

jing in 1995. This symposium generated a resolution for consideration by the governments of the Fourth World Conference, identifying ten solutions for gender-based violence.

These solutions define desirable governmental actions in the domains of research, economics, politics, education, and health care. For example, educating all women about their legal rights and about laws that pertain to their status in society is one such solution. Continuing to press for these changes will be a challenge for international educators, but should have lasting implications for women around the world.

International efforts will grow in importance as technology expands our abilities to link with other nations. In addition to the work of international committees, the social work profession should strive to use the cross-cultural research on family violence produced by ethnographers and anthropologists. By developing a broader understanding of the issues underlying the expression of family violence, social workers will be better positioned to advise leaders on the development of national and international policies best suited to reducing violence against women and children.

REFERENCES

Berk, R. A., Campbell, A., Klap, R., & Western, B. (1991). The deterrent effect of arrest in incidents of domestic violence: A Bayesian analysis of four field experiments. *American Sociological Review, 57,* 698–708.

Berk, R. A., & Sherman, K. W. (1988). Police responses to family violence incidents. *Journal of the American Statistical Association, 83,* 73–76.

Bureau of Justice Statistics, Selected Findings. (1994). *Domestic Violence.* Washington, DC: Office of Justice Programs.

Crossette, B. (1995). Female genital mutilation by immigrants is becoming cause for concern in the U. S. *New York Times*, December 10, 1995.

Deschner, J. P. (1984). *The hitting habit: Anger control for battered couples*. New York: Free Press.

Hicks, E. (1993). *Infibulation: Female mutilation in Islamic Northeastern Africa*. New Brunswick and London: Transaction Publishers.

Lightfoot-Klein, H. (1989). *Prisoners of ritual: An odyssey into female genital circumcision in Africa*. New York and London: The Haworth Press.

Men Stopping Violence (1996). Atlanta, Georgia.

National Association of Social Workers. (1996). *Social work and the challenge of violence worldwide*. Chapel Hill: University of North Carolina Center for Public Television, the Benton Foundation, and the Council on Social Work Education.

Pressman, B., Cameron, C., & Rothery, M. (Eds.). (1989). *Intervening with assaulted women: Current theory, research and practice*. Hillsdale, NJ: Lawrence Erlbaum Associates.

Sahebjam, F. (1990). *The Stoning of Soraya M*. New York: Arcade Publishing.

Schultz, L. (1960). The wife assaulter. *The Journal of Social Therapy, 6*, (1–4), 103–112.

Straus, M. (1979). Measuring intrafamily conflict and violence: The conflict tactics scales (CTS). *Journal of Marriage and the Family, 41*, 75–88.

Straus, M., & Gelles, R. (1986). Societal change and change in family violence from 1975 to 1985 as revealed by two national surveys. *Journal of Marriage and the Family, 48*, 75–88.

Uniform Crime Reports for the United States. (1994). Washington, DC: Federal Bureau of Investigation, U. S. Department of Justice.

Yegidis, B. (1992). Family violence: Contemporary research findings and practice issues. *Community Mental Health Journal, 28*, 6, 519–530.

Social Work and the Workplace

Lawrence S. Root

Although people spend the largest portion of their waking hours at work, it is only recently that social workers have developed a regular role within the workplace. In this essay, Lawrence S. Root, professor in the School of Social Work, University of Michigan, and director of the Institute of Labor and Industrial Relations, writes that although social workers have long been concerned with problems of employment, their recent attention to the workplace stems from changes in both the labor market and the regulatory structure. Root, who also directs the Urban Entrepreneurship and Economic Development Program at the Institute, argues that employee assistance programs (EAPs) hold the greatest promise for the further integration of social services and employment issues. Their growth will be influenced by two underlying dynamics: an increasing acceptance of EAP services by corporations and non-profit organizations, and a growing gap between good and bad jobs.

Before becoming director of the Institute, Professor Root was director of the National Older Workers Information System, the co-director of the UAW-Ford Life/Educational Planning Program, and the director of the UAW-General Motors Educational Development Counseling Program. His graduate degrees are from Bryn Mawr College and the University of Chicago, and his research and teaching interests are in social welfare and employment.

Introduction

Social work practice takes its shape from the contours of the social and economic environ-ment. Protective services fill a gap when families fail to nurture the young or care for the infirm. Health and mental health services respond when assistance is needed to cope with the demands of daily living. Income support programs address the economic needs of those unable to achieve an adequate living through the institutions of employment.

This interplay between social work practice and its environment is nowhere clearer than in the practice of social work in the workplace. In the United States, social work services exist in employment settings because companies see that it is in their interest to help workers when personal problems interfere with work. Although problems of employment have been a traditional concern of social workers, a regular role for social work within the workplace is a recent phenomenon, growing out of specific programs and changes in both the labor market and its regulatory structure.

In this chapter, we consider the future of social work in the workplace. In so doing, we first address the nature of current workplace-based services. There are many *potential* roles for social workers, such as designing and implementing training programs, building effective work teams, developing corporate policies of disability management, and working on company–community partnerships. We shall focus, however, on employee assistance programs (EAPs) because they are the largest and most established mode of social work practice in the workplace. EAPs, by creating a social work role in industry, provide a basis for the further integration of social services and employment issues.

Following our discussion of current practice, we identify trends in the labor market and in human resource management. These provide a framework for thinking about the future of social work roles and the implications of such roles for education and practice.

The Emergence of Current Social Work Practice in the Workplace

Social work has traditionally addressed issues of employment. The settlement house movement was deeply concerned with the employment problems of the urban poor. Jane Addams was a leader in advocating limits on child labor and creating a safer working environment. Her efforts to reduce the phosphorus exposure of young women involved in making matches is only one example of early initiatives to introduce greater occupational safety. Other pioneering social workers shared these goals of addressing workplace problems. Mary van Kleeck, for example, headed up the specialization on "industrial research" at the New York School of Philanthropy and directed the newly formed Department of Industrial Studies of the Russell Sage Foundation (Ball, 1991). These social workers (and their contemporaries in the Charity Organization Societies) recognized that issues of employment were critical to well-being, and the inability to succeed in the labor market was a central concern of social work.

There are also precedents for current social work and workplace programs in the "welfare capitalism" of the late 1800s and early 1900s (Brandes, 1976). As companies struggled with

the changes experienced in industrialization, they instituted social programs reminiscent of earlier paternalistic patterns of feudal responsibility. These programs also reflected the new realities of modern production technologies and their implications for changes in the demands on labor and management. For example, increased use of expensive machinery in mass production demanded a disciplined, punctual work force. Idle machines were a major cost for employers. Worker protests and work stoppages were a growing problem.

Companies developed programs for their workers that resemble services now provided by government and non-profit agencies. It was not unusual for companies to employ "welfare secretaries" to help "Americanize" immigrant workers and to encourage regular habits in the home. Although welfare secretaries were not typically trained as social workers, that title was often associated with the group. The "social workers" of Henry Ford's Sociological Department made home visits to ensure that his workers lived moral lives and kept a clean home. Home visits and examination of the backgrounds of workers also could be used to combat the "disease of unionism."

It was also not uncommon for employers to provide housing for workers. For example, the Steinway Company moved its piano production to rural Queens to avoid labor problems the company associated with an unruly urban New York work force (Lieberman, 1995, p. 77). In other cases, whole communities were planned and created. The town of Pullman, built south of Chicago by the sleeping-car maker, was the best-known example, attracting visitors from around the world. It was actively promoted and popularly perceived as a model industrial village until labor conflicts and a bitter national strike laid bare the tensions inherent in joining the roles of employer and landlord (Buder, 1967).

Company programs encompassed a variety of other services, such as kindergartens and schools, recreational facilities, and medical care. In a later example, Kaiser shipbuilding created comprehensive medical services to meet the needs of workers in an underpopulated production area in the Northwest. That medical program became the prototype for modern HMOs.

Welfare capitalism provides examples of differing motivations and interpretations for workplace programs. Whether they are expressions of concern and benevolence on the part of companies or simply efforts to exert greater control over workers is an open question. This same ambiguity continues to exist in workplace programs today.

Contemporary social work practice in the workplace has more recent historical antecedents in occupational programs to combat alcoholism (Trice and Roman, 1972). These efforts received a federally supported boost in the 1970s, when occupational program consultants were funded to develop alcoholism programs throughout the country (Sonnenstuhl, 1986). Their goal was to develop programs to address problem drinking, which negatively affected job performance. Once established, these occupational alcoholism programs provided the basis for an expanded role for social services within the repertoire of employee services, evolving into what we now call "employee assistance programs" (EAPs).

EAPs are programs to assist employees (and sometimes their families) with personal problems that interfere with employment. Most EAPs are part of the organizational structure of management. In unionized set-tings, however, the union itself has been an important participant in the development of EAPs. Among craft unions, "member assistance programs" are often the sole responsibility of the union itself. Because members of craft unions often work for many different employers, the union itself provides the stable organizational relationship in their work lives. In industrial unions, the company rather than the union is usually the organizational focus for programs. But in such settings, the union is closely involved in the development of the programs and, usually, in the provision of services. For example, EAPs in the auto industry are the joint responsibility of company and union, with the mandate for services arising from collective bargaining.

Although EAPs began with a focus on substance abuse, they have now been extended to a broad range of problems. They address both the interests of the employee in solving his or her problems and the interests of the employer in maintaining a productive work environment. In addition to diagnosis and referral, EAPs typically provide a range of related services, such as outreach, marketing, and training of supervisors, as well as a variety of direct interventions (e.g., constructive confrontation with substance abusers, critical incident debriefing, and short-term treatment). As the responsibilities of EAPs have expanded, the expectations for practitioners have shifted to a broader set of responsibilities. Social workers have become the professional group most often providing EAP services, although by no means the only group involved.

EAPs can be divided into "internal" and "external" programs although there are many variations on this basic dichotomy. Internal EAPs are staffed by individuals who are regular employees of the company. Internal programs can have the advantage of greater integration into the workings of the company, leading to more effective organizational development and outreach.

External EAP services, however, are provided on a contractual basis by outside agencies. Initially, existing social service agencies developed contracts to provide these services. Subsequently, proprietary companies emerged who specialized in the provision of EAP services. Some of the larger EAP providers have national and even international operations. External programs are often thought to be more confidential because those providing the services are not employees of the company being served.

In practice, what appear to be structural advantages and disadvantages of internal versus external programs may be less important than the characteristics of the practitioners and the specifics of program implementation. For example, the presumed advantage of greater confidentiality in an external EAP can be compromised under pressure to satisfy the customer and have a contract renewed. And internal EAPs may remain marginal to the rest of the company operations, not fulfilling the promise of integration suggested by their structure.

As EAPs have gained in popularity, external EAPs have become the more common approach. This reflects the broader trend among businesses to outsource services rather than add new staff and departments. Contractual relationships have the advantage of limiting long-term commitments and increasing flexibility. We can expect this trend to continue, with the principle of outsourcing driving this structural decision rather than the programmatic advantages of internal versus external models.

EAP services are separate and distinct from treatment provided under the employee's health insurance plan. The structure of the EAP, however, can influence the design and utilization of health insurance. For example, an EAP may provide short-term counseling. Typically these sessions do not require a co-payment from the employee. In contrast, health insurance programs, particularly those related to mental health services, often call for significant co-payments. This difference in the cost may make the EAP more attractive to the employee than the mental health portions of the health insurance program. The availability of EAP services, by providing one vehicle for the provision of short-term counseling, can reduce the demand for more comprehensive coverage under the insurance program. An employer can elect to cut back on mental health coverage with the rationale that the EAP provides an alternative source of treatment.

The existence of EAPs frequently have other impacts on employee health insurance plans. Many EAPs are involved in cost-control efforts with regard to substance abuse and mental health treatment. They have become the employer's "in-house" professionals—individuals who can serve as informed intermediaries between the company and treatment agencies.

EAPs are now a common part of human resources programming. Sixty-two percent of those working in medium-sized or large firms are covered under EAPs (U.S. Bureau of the Census, 1995, Table 685). These EAPs vary widely in the nature of the services provided and in their specific role in the workplace. In some cases, an EAP is a comprehensive service, offering round-the-clock diagnostic and referral services, short-term treatment, and consultation on work–family problems. At the other extreme, an EAP may simply be a telephone number to an information and referral hotline. This wide variation in the level, intensity, and role of EAPs provides one clue to anticipating future patterns.

Future Directions for Services in the Workplace

I believe that two underlying dynamics will shape the future of social work services in the workplace: (1) an increasing acceptance of EAP services as a part of a human resource programming and (2) a growing gap between good jobs and bad jobs. The first dynamic will lead to an expansion of the existence of EAP services generally. The second dynamic will produce a two-tiered system, with basic, skeletal EAPs characteristic of low-paying jobs and comprehensive EAPs for the higher-paying jobs.

Looking at the first factor, we can expect to see human resource managers increasingly accept the basic premise of EAPs—that one role of human resource policy is to assist workers who are experiencing personal problems that interfere with work. Even if individual personnel directors would prefer to fire troubled (and troublesome) employees, EAP services will become an integral part of what constitutes enlightened, progressive, and effective human resource practice.

This acceptance of EAP services will be strongly influenced by practical considerations arising from government regulation and legal liability. In the 1960s and 1970s, substance abuse shifted in popular and legal thought from moral frailty to disability. Once substance abuse was seen as a medical condition, it became more difficult to fire an employee with an alcohol or other drug problem. With the passage of the Americans with Disabilities Act (ADA) in 1990, constraints on

personnel actions that may be related to an employee's disability tightened further. Having an EAP available to the work force provides one protection against the charge of failing to make reasonable accommodations for such disabilities.

The second dynamic, an increasing gap between pay/benefits at the upper and lower ends of the labor market, will further bifurcate the nature of EAP services. Current trends suggest that the job market will become increasingly polarized. On one end of the spectrum will be better-paying jobs in which employers compete with each other to retain valued employees. On the other end of the spectrum will be low-paying jobs, characterized by high turnover and vestigial or nonexistent employee benefits.

The evidence for this pattern can be seen in the expansion of part-time and contingent work and in the growing disparity in wage levels. Involuntary part-time employment (part-time employment when a full-time job is wanted) is growing. The number of "contingent workers" (temporary or "leased" employees) is also increasing sharply. This latter pattern has emerged clearly in recent years. "Personnel supply services," the industry providing temporary and "leased" workers, grew at the rate of 9.8 percent per year in the five years from 1989 to 1994. Although still representing only 2 percent of the work force, this increase was almost ten times that of employment growth generally (U.S. Department of Labor, 1995a).

The deterioration of wages at the lower end of the job market is also striking. Labor market data indicate that the wages of lower-paid workers have been decreasing sharply in purchasing power since the 1970s (Mishel and Bernstein, 1994; U.S. Department of Labor, 1995b). Although there is some debate about current trends, the impacts of technological change, corporate restructuring, and global competition are creating an environment in which companies aggressively seek to increase their competitiveness by reducing labor costs. We can expect increasing competition for workers with needed skills (usually those with advanced education or training) and deteriorating job conditions for others (Berlin and Sum, 1988; Reich, 1991; Rifkin, 1995).

These two dynamics—the increasing acceptance of EAPs as part of employment and the growing bifurcation of the job market—set the stage for future directions in social work services in the workplace. We can expect to see the emergence of a *two-tiered pattern*. EAPs will become more common generally, but vary enormously in their role and function depending on the employment context. Even in many lower-paying jobs, we will see "basic EAPs," with a focus on substance abuse. Higher-paying jobs will develop what we might call "deluxe EAPs," with an expanded set of programs designed to attract and retain valued workers in a competitive job market.

Basic EAP services will be broadly available in a variety of jobs. They will be intended to meet the needs of the employer in addressing personnel issues arising from the personal problems of employees and, when relevant, ensuring conformance with relevant government regulations on substance abuse (e.g., Department of Transportation regulations for truck drivers). Basic programs will include diagnostic/referral services and short-term treatment. These services will formally extend to mental health problems, but their raison d'être will be as the employer's response to regulations and liability associated with substance abuse in the workplace.

Both basic and deluxe EAPs will use an external model, with services offered by companies that specialize in workplace-based services. In industries with special government regulation of substance abuse (e.g., when public safety is a central concern), EAPs will be tailored to comply with those regulations.

At the other extreme, deluxe EAPs will provide comprehensive programs to employees in better-paying jobs, primarily full-time employees of medium and large firms. The variety of services offered in deluxe EAPs will expand, extending the trajectory of earlier growth—from substance abuse services to mental health generally to additional social support systems growing out of the personal needs of employees.

Deluxe EAP services will be provided through contracts with outside agencies, but large employers may also have internal personnel who will be responsible for coordinating and overseeing these programs. Thus, a role will emerge in such larger companies for an expert in social services on the executive level who can direct and coordinate a variety of employer-based social services. EAPs in large companies have begun this transition, often addressing conflicts associated with balancing the demands of work and family. For example, many EAPs, as workplace-based service professionals, play a pivotal role in developing child-care options for employees. On-site child-care programs are a highly visible but relatively rare manifestation. Much more common are child-care information and referral services for assisting employees with locating resources outside of the workplace.

In addition to the traditional range of services, we can expect new services to be incorporated into deluxe EAPs to address emerging needs of the work force, particularly those related to work–family pressures and the personal impact of corporate reorganization and downsizing. For example, we have recently seen an increase in programs to assist workers caring for aged parents. It is estimated that the incidence of such programs among companies with more than 100 employees increased from 3 percent in 1989 to 31 percent in 1993 (Kirk, 1995).

We can expect EAPs to expand into other community services, particularly when responding to the impacts of corporate restructuring. For example, school-related problems, such as arranging for schools when an employee is relocated to a new city, may become a regular part of the assisting role of the EAP. Companies may also find that it is useful to offer other transitional services when relocation is needed.

Deluxe EAPs will also become increasingly involved in cost control. During the 1980s and 1990s, restrictions on mental health reimbursement have grown as employers seek to lower their employment costs. In many cases, such cost control has been exercised through blanket restrictions or limits on selected services, such as arbitrary limits on the length of in-patient treatment for substance abuse (Root, 1991). Although such restrictions may achieve short-term savings, there may be significant long-term costs. Inadequate treatment may increase subsequent costs if the initial problem is not adequately addressed. Also, such restrictions can be costly in terms of employee morale. Resentment at arbitrary restrictions may undercut any positive aspects of having extensive employee benefits.

With mental health professionals available through EAPs, employers have the capacity to develop more targeted cost controls. Instead of arbitrary restrictions, EAP personnel can develop approaches that take into account the specifics of each individual situation. However, this difference can be subtle, and the overall effect may be to generate hostility toward the EAP—both from employees who feel their treatment options are restricted and from agencies whose treatment recommendations are second-guessed by EAPs suggesting less costly modalities.

Challenges Facing Social Work Teaching and Research

This chapter focuses on social work practice directed toward the workplace. But many of the issues discussed present a broader challenge to social work education. Workplace experiences have profound effects on a range of issues central to the concerns of social work. The pressures of work and family, for example, are inextricably linked. Most mothers with children now work, even those with children under school age. The pressures, rewards, programs, and policies of the workplace are taking on a greater and greater importance for family well-being. The clinician who fails to elicit information about the work life of clients is missing a major element of their social reality.

Social work education is incomplete without exposure to the realities of the workplace. Course material addressing the structure of job opportunities, the distribution of jobs among disadvantaged groups, the expectations of employers, the role of employee benefits, the dynamics of finding a job, and the impacts of job loss should be a central part of the curriculum.

The view of the future of social work and the workplace presented in this chapter also suggests a number of specific areas for further development in social work education and research. Many are common to other aspects of professional practice, but the context of the workplace creates specific challenges related to understanding the employer–employee relationship and its context:

1. *Organizational behavior and program innovation* Social workers often work in "host" environments—organizations, such as schools or hospitals, whose primary purpose is not social work. In order to work effectively with business organizations, social workers must understand the dynamics of organizations and how for-profit businesses operate. Program innovation in such a context requires a range of skills, including being able to assess needs in relation to the overriding goals of the organization and then to design, market, and implement programs to meet those goals.

2. *Structure of labor market opportunities and demands* As an ancillary service within the workplace, social work programs must reflect an understanding of the job opportunities and demands faced by employers who will be using their services. Detailed knowledge of specific jobs is less important than recognizing the nature of employment requirements and the interplay with the capabilities of and demands on employees.

3. *Identification of and response to special needs of employees* The conditions of employment involve specific performance imperatives. Institutional structures may create expectations in the social and physical environment that are problematic for individuals. The traditional person–environment focus of social work assessment is particularly well-suited to determining and addressing the needs of employees. For example, as companies continue to contract for services, the implications of job instability will become increasingly important. This may disrupt customary arrangements, such as job progression, away from more physically demanding

jobs as workers age. One result may be increased job insecurity for older workers.

4. *Cost-benefit/cost-effectiveness analysis* Even though most organizational practices are accepted on the basis of custom, programs must be able to demonstrate their contributions to the overall goals of the organization. This is particularly true for programs that may not be seen as central to the goals of the organization. EAPs and other services in the workplace must be prepared to assess their effectiveness in terms that can be understood by decision makers.

5. *Ethical issues and conflicting demands* Social workers in any context can find themselves confronting ethical dilemmas. In treatment agencies, policies may be at odds with what is best for an individual client. In the work setting, this conflict often appears in sharper contrast. The demands on the company for economic viability may lead to employment decisions that hurt individuals. EAP services, particularly with their growing cost-control role in mental health treatment, will inevitably face ethical questions when the goals of the company appear at variance with the "best interests" of the employee.

6. *Legal and regulatory framework for employment* The expansion of governmental rules and regulations concerning substance abuse and disability are examples of the growing complexity of the environment within which social workers operate in the workplace. As services (such as the accommodation of disabilities) become more involved with legal rights and responsibilities, developing a broad understanding of that environment is critical for effective practice.

Employment has been called the "master role" because it has such a pervasive impact on our identities and well-being. Although work played a central role in the formative stages of the social work profession, problems of employment have taken a subordinate position in contemporary practice. As a profession, we must reintroduce issues of the workplace into our professional consciousness. For those providing services in the workplace, the challenge will be to maintain a commitment to the welfare of the employee while respecting the legitimate demands facing the employer.

REFERENCES

Ball, Michael A. (1991). In Mary Jo Deegan, (Ed.), *Women in sociology*. New York: Greenwood Press.

Berlin, G., and Sum, A. (1988). *Toward a more perfect union: Basic skills, poor families and our economic future*. New York: Ford Foundation.

Brandes, S. D. (1976). *American welfare capitalism, 1880–1940*. Chicago: University of Chicago Press.

Buder, S. (1967). *Pullman: An experiment in industrial order and community planning, 1980–1930*. New York: Oxford University Press.

Kirk, M. O. (1995). Need extra care for an aging parent? Maybe the boss can help. *New York Times*, August 20, F9.

Lieberman, R. K. (1995). *Steinway and sons*. New Haven, CT: Yale University Press.

Mishel, L., and Bernstein, J. (1994). *The state of working America, 1994–95*. Armonk, NY: M. E. Sharpe.

Reich, R. B. (1991). *The work of nations*. New York: Vintage.

Rifkin, J. (1995). *The end of work*. New York: Tarcher/Putnam.

Root, L. S. (1991). Cost controls in mental health services: Context and role of the professional. *EAP Quarterly, 7*, 2 (Winter), 1–14.

Sonnenstuhl, W. J. (1986). *Inside an emotional health program*. Ithaca, NY: ILR Press.

Trice, H. M., and Roman, P. M. (1972). *Spirits and demons at work: Alcohol and other drugs on the job*. Ithaca: New York State School of Industrial and Labor Relations.

U.S. Bureau of the Census. (1995). *Statistical abstract of the United States, 1995* (115th edition). Washington, DC: Government Printing Office.

U.S. Department of Labor. (1995a). *Employment and earnings*. (Total and SIC 736 employment). August 1992, March 1995, December 1995.

U.S. Department of Labor. (1995b). A surge in growing income inequality? *Monthly Labor Review, 118*, 8, 51–61.

The Financial Gerontology Birthdays of 1995–1996

Social Security at 60 and the "Baby" Boom at 50

Neal E. Cutler

The recent anniversaries of the passage of Social Security and Medicare has prompted numerous reflections on the underlying assumptions of these landmark acts, their survival in the next century, and a cluster of controversial policy issues around them. This essay by Neal Cutler, a professor in the School of Social Work at the University of Pennsylvania, asks social workers and gerontologists to examine another central issue: How can we educate future generations about these programs in a climate of increasing uncertainty about the viability of both public and private retirement income systems? Cutler argues that recent policy changes have been motivated more by the anticipation of demographic changes than by any inherent defects in these programs. He analyzes the future prospects for aging Boomers, poses hard questions about the preservation or modification of the concept of retirement in the 21st century, and makes a compelling case for the elderly to acquire "financial literacy" as a tool of economic well-being.

Dr. Cutler is a Senior Fellow of the Leonard Davis Institute of Health Economics; a Fellow of the Institute on Aging, the Gerontological Society of America, and the Employee Benefit Research Institute's Educational Research Foundation; and Research Associate at the Population Studies Center. He has published extensively on the topics of financial gerontology and serves on the editorial boards of Aging Today *and the* American Journal of Alzheimer's Care and Research.

In 1995 and 1996, the young field of social gerontology celebrated several real and symbolic birthdays. 1995 was not only the 60th birthday of Social Security, but the 30th birthday of Medicare, of Medicaid, and of the Older Americans Act. A second major component of this national mood of celebration is another stream of birthdays, which began on January 1, 1996. On that day, the first Baby Boomer "officially" inaugurated the middle-aging of the Boom as she celebrated her 50th birthday. During each of the 19 years from 1996 through 2014, an average of 4,000,000 men and women will also celebrate that important birthday transition into the graying of the population. And so it is appropriate that we consider Social Security in the context of these multiple interacting birthdays.

As is typical on birthdays and anniversaries, our focus is largely reflective and retrospective, and it is appropriate to reflect on some of the key facts of Social Security over the past decades. But simultaneously, Social Security represents a cluster of controversial policy issues. The demographic, economic, and political environment have all changed dramatically since 1935, and so a central question for social work and social gerontology arises: Given the changing context and the enduring importance of Social Security, how can we both understand and educate maturing individuals and families, especially middle-aging Boomers who are confronted with increasing uncertainties in both public and private retirement income systems?

Introductory Concepts: Two Varieties of Aging, Financial-Political Controversies, and the Human Wealth Span

The "graying of America" is affected by two varieties of aging. **Population aging** refers to the number and proportion of older people in a population, independent of how long any of those people might live. In 1900 there were 3.1 million people aged 65+ in the United States, representing 4% of the population. By 1995 the 32 million Americans age 65 and older represented 13% of the population. Gerontology, however, is not simply the study of old people, but *the study of the multiple processes of aging*, including middle aging. In the context of Social Security and the financial anticipation of retirement, therefore, it is especially important to keep in mind that as of January 1, 1996, 76 million Boomers began "officially" moving into middle age and on to old age (Cutler, 1992a).

A second variety of aging is **individual aging**. Independent of how many older people there are in society, individual aging refers to how long each of those older people is likely to live. Life expectancy in older age has been increasing. For example, in 1940 there was a 7% chance that a person celebrating his or her 65th birthday would live to age 90. By 1980 the probability that a 65-year-old would live to age 90 and older had tripled to 24% (Taeuber and Rosenwaike, 1992). Clearly

the implications of these patterns of aging are dramatic for Social Security: Individual aging and population aging "magnify" or "multiply" each other, as millions and millions of Boomers will live longer than their parents and grandparents did.

Partly because of individual aging and population aging, but also because of other societal dynamics, major public and private programs connected to aging—Social Security, Medicare, employer pensions—are in various stages of political-financial trouble. Observers of differing political perspectives generally agree that we probably won't be able to count on these programs in the same way as in the past. At the same time, it's often reported that the Baby Boom is a generation of prolific spenders, not savers, and that they're not appropriately anticipating and planning for their own retirement and financial future. Although there is conflicting research on this question, it is an important and continuing theme of the overall debate (CBO, 1993; EBRI, 1994a).

Over the course of the 20th century, *the human wealth span* (Gregg and Cutler, 1991; Cutler, 1996a) has been changing. The *wealth span* model offers a heuristic view of the financial stages of the life cycle, divided between the years individuals and families accumulate financial resources and the years during which those resources will be spent in retirement. The balance between the two basic stages—their relative length—is shifting. Because we stay in school longer, start careers later, and retire earlier, the *accumulation stage* has gotten shorter. But because we retire earlier and live longer, the *expenditure stage* has gotten longer. In other words, we have a relatively shorter period of time in which to accumulate financial resources that have to last for a longer period of time.

In sum, multiple changes are taking place both in Social Security and in the context within which Social Security operates. The country is "getting older," but this means both that larger numbers of people than in the past will become old (population aging) *and* that those people will, on average, live longer than did older people in the past (individual aging). At the same time, because of the intersection of several social, financial, and cultural trends, people have fewer years to accumulate the financial resources for a longer older-age expenditure period. And both the accumulation and expenditure stages of the wealth span are now taking place in a political-financial environment that points to a reduction in public responsibility and a concomitant increase in individual responsibility for later-life financial and retirement preparation.

On the occasion of these important birthdays and in the context of these fundamental trends, what should we say about the coming changes in Social Security? In this fluid political climate it would be inappropriate to even attempt to predict with any certitude which of the many proposed changes in Social Security eligibility rules or benefit levels will emerge as public policy in the next few years. Instead, we can use the occasion of these birthdays to identify one especially important question whose consideration is highly likely to prove important and useful to social work and social gerontology. Specifically, our analysis will focus briefly on *the early retirement eligibility age* in Social Security *and the likelihood that it will change.* Because recent labor force trends and public opinion polls document continued preference for "earlier than normal" (i.e., age 65) retirement (EBRI, 1994b), early retirement continues to be an especially important ele-

ment of the larger political and financial context of Social Security and its future.

But before looking ahead, we focus on a brief retrospective of some of the financial and demographic trends that have taken place during Social Security's own 60-year "wealth span."

Social Security As a Middle-Class Success Story

A fundamental characteristic of Social Security is that it was never intended to be the only or even the primary source of retirement income for most older men and women. Rather, for most people, it was intended to provide a relatively modest income resource on which individuals and families could build a more complete plan for their retirement income security (Schulz, 1995). As is well-recognized, however, the goal of a well-funded "3-legged stool" of retirement income—including Social Security, employer pensions, and personal savings—has not been achieved by all Americans. At the same time, Social Security benefits have increased substantially over the past 25 years, with the fortunate result that Social Security has kept many older people out of poverty, and for others it has become the largest single component of their financial resources.

By receiving so much credit for reducing old-age poverty, Social Security is often perceived as a program whose primary value is to serve the poorest groups of society. In one sense this is an apt description: For the poorest fifth (quintile) of older families in the United States (Income Group I in Table 1), Social Security provides more than 80% of their total annual income. At the other extreme, for the wealthiest quintile, Social

TABLE 1

Social Security as a Share of Total Income of Older (age 65+) Households (1992)

	Income Group (*quintiles*)	% of income
I	$0–$7,000	82%
II	$7,000–$11,000	77%
III	$11,000–17,600	62%
IV	$17,600–29,000	46%
V	over $29,000	24%
All older (65+) families		58%

Source: Social Security Administration

TABLE 2

Growth of the Older (age 65+) Population, 1940 to 2030

	1940	1960	1980	2000	2010	2020	2030
In millions	9.0	16.3	25.6	35.3	40.1	53.3	70.2
% of population	7%	9%	11%	13%	13%	16%	20%

Source: U.S. Census Bureau

Security provides only about 24% of annual income.

Typically overlooked in this "Rich Man, Poor Man" dialogue, however, is that Social Security provides a substantial share of predictable income security for the American middle class. That is, the critical question for social and financial analysis is *not* "Is Social Security important?" but *"For whom* is Social Security important?" In answer to this latter question, Table 1 shows that for middle-income older families (the middle quintile), Social Security constitutes over 60% of their annual retirement income, and Social Security provides almost half (46%) of the income for the fourth quintile. But even this "cash value" may understate the overall importance of Social Security.

The late Dr. Davis W. Gregg, founding director of the Boettner Institute and long-time president of the American College of Life Insurance, often told the story of a close friend of his whose retirement income came from a combination of stock dividends, pension payments, and Social Security. Despite the fact that Social Security was not the largest monthly check, it was seen as the most important piece because of its predictability. Similarly, for many middle-income men and women, Social Security doesn't make them rich, but it pro-

vides the focal point of a sense of economic security and financial well-being. As several financial and gerontological analysts have noted (e.g., Doyle, 1992), money has a personal or subjective meaning as well as an objective economic meaning. By providing the guaranteed core of a systematically designed financial strategy, Social Security is as much a middle-class success story as it is successful in keeping less wealthy older families out of poverty.

Multiple Crystal Balls

There can be little doubt that despite its successful track record there are predictable bumps and curves in Social Security's future roadway. The United States has become a substantially older country since the early 1940s, when the first cohort of older Americans qualified for Social Security benefits. In 1940, as Table 2 shows, there were only 9 million persons age 65 and older, a number that will quadruple to 35 million by the year 2000. By the time the last Baby Boomer turns 65 in 2029, the United States is projected to have 70 million senior citizens, representing a fifth of the national population.

From a demographic perspective, the real "engine" of these social and economic trends is the birth (then) and aging (now and in the future) of the Baby Boom. Yet the number of maturing Boomers is only one of the age-related demographic stresses pressuring the Social Security system. In addition, as noted earlier, because of increasing old-age longevity, these future Boomer beneficiaries will "live in the system" for a longer period of time. Consequently, the pressures on Social Security reflect a larger number of aging persons who are living longer than previous cohorts of Social Security beneficiaries. Inflation, taxes, economic growth, individual health status, and the cost of health care—each of these represents an additional set of question marks and challenges. In the context of all of this, how do we plan for the future, both for ourselves and for our family, friends, and clients, with regard to Social Security, aging, and financial planning?

Obviously, the financial gerontology and social work research projects that will be completed in the next two years will not be able to answer this question in a complete way. Instead, from all of the issues, speculations, questions, and potential Social Security changes that are likely to affect financial planning, we consider one change that has three important characteristics: (1) It is directly relevant to future planning; (2) the appropriate research data are currently available; and (3) it's an area where Social Security changes are likely to take place in the near future. The policy change that meets these three criteria is *early retirement* eligibility within the Social Security system.

In recent years there has been substantial discussion about raising the Social Security retirement age from its traditional age, 65. Indeed, in 1983 Congress did raise the age for full benefits in the future to age 67, a change that will be phased in starting in the year 2003. Recent proposals to raise the age to 70 have also been heard. For most Americans, however, the age of full benefits, whether 65 or 67 or 70, is less important than the age of early retirement benefits. In 1956 women and in 1961 men were given the opportunity to retire at age 62 with actuarially reduced Social Security benefits (see Doyle et al., 1992, chapter 4).

Since that time, substantially more people have retired at age 62–64 than have waited to age 65, and the trend in early retirement is rather striking. In 1965 only 30% of new Social Security beneficiaries were age 62–64; in 1980 this had risen to 52%, and by 1990 to 66%. Looking at same data from the "other side," in 1960 virtually 100% of new beneficiaries were age 65 or older. By 1980 it was 48% and by 1990 only 34% of new Social Security retirees waited until age 65. Early retirement has become a central element of the Social Security story.

Early Retirement vs. No Retirement: It's a Matter of Choice

In 1986 Congress eliminated age-based mandatory retirement in all but a few occupations. Now men and women cannot be forced to retire simply because they have come to their 65th birthday. This means that we have two sets of laws influencing retirement decisions. Social Security enables early retirement, and the Age Discrimination in Employment Act outlawing age-based mandatory retirement allows people to choose to work until they may be quite elderly. One may well wonder if a society whose public policies simultaneously encourage both early retirement *and* delayed retirement isn't simply to be called "schizophrenic." Perhaps so, but a more appropriate answer would be that the underlying policy theme is choice. Current retirement policy gives the individual the choice to retire early or retire later (or not at all!).

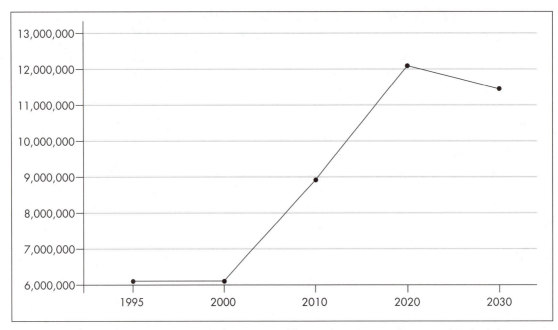

Figure 1 When Baby Boomers Become the "Young-Old"—Early Retirement (age 62–64) Eligibility, 1995 to 2030

Source: U.S. Census Bureau, Current Population Reports

Public opinion polls and Social Security records indicate that the predominant national pattern of millions of individual choices is fairly clear: Over the past three decades, more and more Americans have chosen to retire as early as they possibly can, and for many it is the availability of the early Social Security retirement option at age 62 that opens the door to planning this kind of future. In this context, a national debate focusing on age 67 or 70 as the age for full Social Security benefits misses the point because most people choose to retire and take their benefits much earlier than age 65, 67, or 70. What then is likely to happen in the next few years? It seems probable that as policymakers consider alternative ways of financially protecting Social Security, the early retirement age rules will be seriously scrutinized. The trend in Figure 1 shows how the aging of 76 million Baby Boomers will swell the ranks of those eligible for early retirement at age 62 to 64.

The first Boomer (born in 1946) will celebrate her 62nd birthday in 2008, and the last Boomer (born in 1964) will turn 62 in 2026. The increase in the size of the 62–64 age group over these years is dramatic. Over the period 2008 to 2026, between 8 and 12 million people each year become eligible for new Social Security benefits *under the current early retirement rules*. This is not to suggest, of course, that every person at this age will in fact choose to retire early. Yet it is important to keep in mind that the percentage of new Social Security beneficiaries who have chosen to retire early at age 62–64 has remained fairly steady at about 66% since 1985.

Policymakers are likely to look at these demographics from the perspective of how many dollars would be saved if Social Security benefits are simply not available at these younger ages. After all, if the logic of raising the full-benefits Social Security retirement age to age 67 or 70 is that people are living longer and healthier lives, then the same reasoning applies to the younger end of old age. Alternatively stated, if "young-old" is 62 when "old" is 65, then if 65 is raised to 67 (or 70), shouldn't "young-old" be redefined as 64 or older? At the very least, it's probable that the public policy debate will move in this direction.

The implication of these alternative scenarios for Social Security is reasonably clear. If government demographers and actuaries interpret these population trends as suggested here, it follows that new proposals to raise the retirement age will include raising the early retirement age as well. Consequently, Boomers currently in their forties and fifties who prefer early retirement *realistically should not plan to receive Social Security income at age 62.* Planning in anticipation of such changes would include such questions as:

- Will changes in early retirement eligibility be phased in over several years, as currently planned changes in full retirement eligibility are being phased in?

- What is likely to be the youngest age at which Social Security will offer early retirement benefits?

- What will be the reduced amount of the early retirement Social Security benefit?

- And given these changes in both the lowered benefit amounts and delayed availability of those benefits, what other financial accumulation and planning must be done, if early retirement remains a personal and family goal?

Early Retirement and "Financial Literacy"

A second and very important implication of changes in early retirement planning concerns Medicare and family health insurance. It is important to remember that under current Social Security retirement rules, Medicare eligibility does not come until age 65, even for a person who exercises his or her early retirement option at age 62. Among the future uncertainties, therefore, is how Congress might link Medicare eligibility to new Social Security retirement ages. If Medicare eligibility remains linked to a full-benefits age that rises to age 70, then the planning for an age 62 early retirement will have to include several years of health insurance financing prior to Medicare eligibility (Cutler, 1992b).

Unfortunately, the public's knowledge of these important health insurance and retirement issues is not very well developed. In early 1996, as part of our new *Financial Literacy 2000* research initiative, we tested the financial knowledge of a nationally representative sample of 1000 adults. Two of the items were directly linked to questions of early retirement and health insurance. Respondents were presented with series of statements and asked to identify each as either a "fact" or a "myth." Figure 2 documents the seriousness of the situation, indicating the percentage of the public that correctly answered two Medicare/health insurance items and, for comparison, showing the responses to two of the more general retirement finance items included in the Financial Literacy survey. The text of these four statements as presented to the respondents during the interview is as follows:

> When it comes to saving for retirement, it is better to put your money into an account that pays compound interest than into an account that pays simple interest.

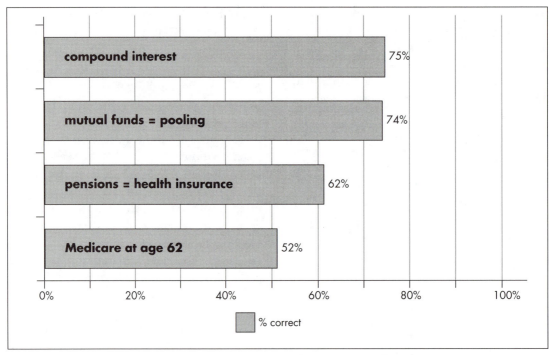

Figure 2 Financial Literacy: Basic Knowledge versus Health Insurance and Medicare

Source: University of Pennsylvania, *Financial Literacy 2000.*

When you purchase shares of a mutual fund, your money is invested in several different stocks or bonds.

If you begin receiving Social Security at age 62, you are eligible for Medicare benefits at the same time.

Employers who provide pension plans are also required to provide health insurance to their retirees.

Figure 2 shows that a sizable majority of the public understands some of the basic principles of saving and investing: Most know what a mutual fund is and know about compound interest (although it is not especially encouraging to see that a quarter of the public does not know that compound interest is better than simple interest). But compared to even a 75% baseline of financial literacy,

public knowledge about important health finance issues is low. Only 62% correctly know that *employers who offer a pension are not required to also provide retiree health insurance.* And given public preference for early retirement plus the high cost of health care, even more frightening is the fact that barely half the public correctly knows that *you are not eligible for Medicare at age 62 even if you choose early Social Security retirement at age 62.*

In Sum . . . .

It's been argued that Social Security is one of the most successful public policies ever enacted in the United States—if not *the* most successful. Indeed, the policy and finance debates concerning Social Security over the past several years have been stimulated more by the anticipated effects of the changing demographics of population aging than by any inherent defects of the program. Thus, even as its administrative and fiscal problems are acknowledged, the American public continues to see Social Security as a national success story that has benefitted middle-class Americans as well as the poor (Public Agenda, 1994). But there's no doubt that additional changes are coming. It's been our goal in this discussion to take note of some of the history and to modestly identify some of the trends that are likely to have a direct impact on how Social Security influences future retirement plans.

There are multiple challenges—political and financial, public and individual—that any prudent crystal ball gazer would identify, and from which we have selected only one for additional analysis. Clearly the early retirement piece of the future Social Security picture is both important and challenging to a growing number of aging Boomers. As such, it will remain as one of the central concerns for social work, gerontology, business, and public policy over the next years and decades.

REFERENCES

Congressional Budget Office. 1993. *Baby Boomers in Retirement: An Early Perspective.* Washington, DC: Author.

Cutler, N. E. 1992a. "The Emerging Dynamics of Financial Gerontology: Individual Aging and Population Aging in the New Century." In N. E. Cutler, D. W. Gregg, and M. P. Lawton (Eds.), *Age, Money, and Life Satisfaction: Aspects of Financial Gerontology* (pp. 1–21). New York: Springer Publications.

Cutler, N. E. 1992b. "Employee Benefits and the Retirement Decision." *Journal of the American Society of CLU & ChFC,* 46 (July): 26–28.

Cutler, N. E. 1996a. "Davis W. Gregg's Model of the Human Wealth Span: Defining the Theory and Practice of Financial Gerontology Over a Life Time and Across Historical Time." In L. A. Vitt and J. K. Siegenthaler (eds.), *Encyclopedia of Financial Gerontology* (pp. 359–367). Westbury, CT: Greenwood Press.

Cutler, N. E. 1996b. "Pensions." In J. E. Birren (ed.), *Encyclopedia of Gerontology,* 2d ed. San Diego, Academic Press.

Devlin, S. J., and Cutler, N. E. 1996. "Financial Literacy 2000." *Journal of the American Society of CLU & ChFC,* 50 (July): 32–37.

Doyle, K. O. (ed.). 1992. *The Meanings of Money.* Special Issue of *American Behavioral Scientist,* 35 (July/August).

Doyle, R. J., Tacchino, K. B. , Kurlowicz, T. R., Cutler, N. E., and Schnepper, J. 1992. *Can You Afford to Retire?* Chicago: Probus Publishing. [Chapter 4: Early Retirement].

Employee Benefit Research Institute. 1994a. *Baby Boomers in Retirement: What Are Their Prospects?* EBRI Special Report SR-23, EBRI Issue Brief Number 151. Washington, DC: Employee Benefit Research Institute.

Employee Benefit Research Institute. 1994b. *Retirement Confidence in America: Getting Ready for Tomorrow.* EBRI Special Report SR-27, Issue Brief 156, Washington, DC: Employee Benefit Research Institute.

Gregg, D. W., and Cutler, N.E. 1991. "The Human 'Wealth Span' and Financial Well-Being in Older Age." *Generations,* Winter.

Public Agenda. 1994. *Promises to Keep: How Leaders and the Public Respond to Saving and Retirement.* New York: Public Agenda in collaboration with the Employee Benefit Research Institute.

Schulz, J. A. 1995. *Economics of Aging,* 6th ed. Dover, MA: Auburn House.

Taeuber, C. M., and Rosenwaike, I. 1992. "A Demographic Portrait of America's Oldest Old." In R. M. Suzman, D. P. Willis, and K. G. Manton (eds.), *The Oldest Old* (pp. 17–49). New York: Oxford University Press.

Social Work and Health Care in the 21st Century

Stephen Gorin and Cynthia Moniz

Despite the failure of recent reform efforts, perhaps no area of U.S. social policy is changing as rapidly as health care or has as powerful an impact on so many Americans. The growth of the managed care system, the erosion of employment-based insurance, and government cutbacks in health-care spending are breaking down the old system of health-care delivery and creating a new one for the next century, whose shape is yet to be determined. Stephen Gorin and Cynthia Moniz see the choice ahead as between oligarchically based health care, with shrinking coverage, or universal coverage through a single-payer system with managed competition. Either outcome will produce dramatic transformations for social workers in the health-care field. Gorin and Moniz argue that these changes will create opportunities for social workers to play a leading role in policy formulation, to work as members of community-based health-care teams, and to engage in research on the connections between socioeconomic status and health.

Stephen Gorin is associate professor and Cynthia Moniz is associate professor and director of the Baccalaureate Program at Plymouth State College in the University System of New Hampshire. Dr. Gorin served as a member of the White House Health Professionals Review Group, which advised President Clinton's Health Care Task Force, and the National Advisory Council of the Center for Mental Health Services in the U.S. Department of Health and Human Services. Dr. Moniz has written and spoken on health-care reform. She is a trustee of the NASW Legal Defense Service and a consulting editor of the Journal of Baccalaureate Social Work.

As the 21st century approaches, the U.S. health-care system is in a period of flux and transition. In 1994, Congress seemed on the verge of enacting universal health-care coverage, which would have enabled the United States to join the other industrialized nations in providing health care to all its citizens. This effort failed, however, and universal coverage has disappeared from national debate. Despite this, the U.S. health-care system continues to face serious problems.

This essay examines the realities of and projects future developments for the U.S. health-care system. Section one considers current trends and problems with the system. The growth of managed care, the erosion of employment-based insurance, and the shrinking role of government provide the context in which future efforts to shape our health-care system will unfold.

Section two examines the challenges social workers will face in helping to build a new health-care system in the 21st century. In our view, the breakdown of the old system will give way to health care based either on oligopoly, limited regulation, and shrinking coverage or on universal coverage through a single-payer system with managed competition. Whichever scenario prevails, social work in health care will change dramatically.

Current Trends in the Health-Care System

For the past four decades, the U.S. health-care system has been rooted in three institutions: fee-for-service medicine, employment-based insurance, and government programs, particularly Medicare and Medicaid. These are now undergoing fundamental change.

The Growth of Managed Care

The fee-for-service system, in which individual practitioners charge patients based on services provided, dates from the birth of the medical profession in the United States. Starr (1982) points out that physicians "had no more desire to be dominated by private corporations than by agencies of government" and opposed the development of corporate medicine. For years, the AMA and many physicians vigorously resisted the introduction of group practices, such as Kaiser-Permanente and the Health Insurance Plan of New York (HIP) (Starr, 1982).

During the early 1970s, the Nixon Administration promoted health maintenance organizations to rein in health-care inflation and expand access to care (Rothfeld, 1976). In 1973, Congress enacted the Health Maintenance Organization (HMO) Act, which helped initiate the managed care revolution. Although Kaiser-Permanente and HIP employed their own staff under one roof, today managed care refers to a range of cost-cutting approaches, including independent practice associations, "gatekeeper" plans, and utilization review (Iglehart, 1994; Starr 1994).

During the early 1990s, the continued acceleration of costs led to a rapid expansion of managed care plans, particularly those operating on a for-profit basis (Iglehart, 1995). Currently, approximately two-thirds of the workers with insurance belong to managed care plans, and three-fourths of physicians have associated with managed care networks (Eckholm, 1995). Although managed care may have reduced health-care inflation, it has also generated controversy (Enthoven and Singer, 1995). The spread of managed care has limited the ability of hospitals to serve uninsured people and raised concern that managed care gives providers an incentive to underserve patients (Preston, 1996; Relman, 1992). In response to criticism from both physicians and consumers, managed care organizations have abandoned "a range of cost-cutting practices that reward doctors and hospitals for limiting care" (Freudenheim, 1996b).

The Erosion of Employment-Based Insurance

The employment-based system of health insurance dates from the late 1940s. Originally, Roosevelt had hoped to include national health insurance as part of the Social Security Act of 1935. The failure of this effort, along with the imposition of wage controls during World War II, accelerated bargaining between labor and management over health insurance (Starr, 1994). By 1993, 90 percent of those with health-care coverage received it through an employer (White House Domestic Policy Council, 1993).

However, evidence suggests that the employment-based system may be eroding. Between 1990 and 1994, the fraction of the population (employees and dependents) insured by employers fell from 61 percent to 56.8 percent (Flint, Yudkowsky, and Tang, 1995; Thorpe et al., 1995). At the same time, employment has declined in industries that have traditionally offered health insurance and increased in those that have not (Wiatrowski, 1995). The growth of part-time and temporary, or "contingent," work has also contributed to the erosion of employment-based insurance (Wiatrowski, 1995). In addition, many employers have shifted the costs of insurance to employees.

A more long-term threat to employment-based insurance lies in the evolving structure of work itself. The reorganization of production, and the mechanization of all areas of the economy, have reduced demand for labor at every level, including professional and managerial (Head, 1996; Rifkin, 1995). During previous periods, displaced workers found jobs in newly emerging industries; today, however, unemployment is a problem in almost every sector. According to Rifkin (1995), "we have entered a new phase in world history . . . in which fewer and fewer workers will be needed to produce the goods and services for the global population." These trends raise the possibility of a world without work and the end of employment-based health insurance (Aronowitz and DiFazio, 1994; Rifkin, 1995).

The Changing Role of Government

The third cornerstone of our health-care system is the federal government. In 1965, Congress enacted Medicare and Medicaid, which extended health-care coverage to older adults, people living in poverty, and individuals with disabilities. At the time, health-care advocates envisioned these programs as steps toward universal health-care coverage. In 1993, President Clinton introduced the Health Security Act, which would have provided health insurance to all citizens.

The election in 1994 of a Republican Congress transformed the health-care debate from one of establishing universal coverage to one of cutting existing programs, particularly Medicare and Medicaid. The Republicans initially proposed reducing Medicare spending by $270 billion and Medicaid spending by $182 billion between 1996 and 2002 (Dewar, 1995). They have also sought to turn Medicaid into a block grant, ending coverage to all eligible individuals, and to expand Medicare to include medical savings accounts.

Although the immediate future of Medicare and Medicaid will hinge on the outcome of the 1996 election, it seems clear the nation cannot sustain current levels of spending on these programs. Under the current system, federal and state Medicaid expenditures could surpass $230 billion by the year 2000 (Wolfe, 1996). The Social Security and Medicare Boards of Trustees (1996) recently reported that Medicare will become bankrupt in 2001.

Although Congress and the president will likely resolve the short-term difficulties of Medicare, the long-term problem of absorbing the baby boom generation will prove much more difficult. The Trustees have called for an independent advisory commission to address this issue. According to the Public Trustees, who represent both political parties, preserving Medicare will require changes in health education and prevention and "a wide range of . . . delivery alternatives and financing options" (Social Security and Medicare Boards of Trustees, 1996). This would result in a fundamental transformation of our health-care system.

The Health-Care System in the 21st Century

In light of current trends, two scenarios may be envisioned for the U.S. health-care system in the 21st century. Scenarios are tools "for considering how interacting sets of trends might lead to a range of conditions in the future" (Bezold, 1996). Scenarios emerge out of disorder, or chaos, as old systems break down and new, more complex systems develop (Prigogine and Stengers, 1984; Warren, Franklin, and Streeter, 1996).

Under the first scenario (S1), a relative handful of for-profit managed care corporations would dominate the system, and the uninsured population would grow to previously unacceptable levels. Federal funding for health-care services, and protection for consumers, would be sharply reduced and limited. Under the second scneario (S2), the United States would have a single-payer system with (nonprofit) managed competition. This would be accompanied by a shift in focus from health care to health and the separation of health-care coverage from employment.

Scenario One

Under S1, what Starr (1982) has called "corporate medicine" would dominate our health-care system. He identified five aspects of this phenomenon: (1) a shift from nonprofit to profit-making organizations; (2) horizontal integration, or the takeover of previously independent institutions by large corporations; (3) the emergence of health-care conglomerates, involved in a wide range of markets and activities; (4) vertical integration, or the emergence of organizations encompassing a broad continuum of care, such as health maintenance organizations (HMOs); and (5) the regionalization and nationalization of health-care markets and services. These trends lead to oligopoly, or what the *New York Times* calls "managed care empires" (Freudenheim, 1996b; Weil, 1994).

This would have a profound impact on quality, coverage, and cost. In recent years, much attention has focused on the quality of health care, as measured by appropriateness, effectiveness, and other factors (Newhouse et al., 1993; Roos and Roos, 1994). Evidence suggests that corporate medicine, with its emphasis on profit, competition, and cost-reduction, may have an adverse impact on quality (Zwanziger and Melnick, 1996). According to Kane, Turnball, and Schoen (1996): "Market success appears at best only weakly linked to quality of care provided. Plans with relatively poorer reputations continue to grow." Moreover, as Miller (1996) notes, our ability to measure quality is at a primitive stage and, without pressure from the federal government, is unlikely to advance. Blumenthal (1996) concludes that, under a for-profit system, competition may lower quality of care for chronically ill people, older adults, low-income people, and others.

Under S1, health-care coverage would become more limited. Shrinking federal involvement, combined with the erosion of employer-based insurance, would result in a dramatic increase in the uninsured population. Thorpe and colleagues (1995) estimated that the 1995 congressional Medicaid proposal would expand the uninsured population to between 48.7 million and 66.8 million in 2002.

Finally, S1 could increase health-care costs. Although health-care inflation has slowed in recent years, it has not disappeared (Aaron, 1994; Levit, Lazenby, and Sivarajan, 1996). This slowdown may be largely due to the recession of the early 1990s and one-time savings from managed care (Foster Higgins, 1995). Because an oligopolist, by definition, can influence prices, the emergence of managed care empires will likely undermine efforts to control costs (Adams and Brock, 1986). In addition, as Reinhardt (1996) notes, despite conventional wisdom, managed care's reliance on reducing hospital care may ultimately increase overall health-care spending.

Scenario Two

S1 may have built-in limits. For example, Goldsmith (1994) argues that vertical integration has neither lowered costs nor increased quality. He predicts that the current wave of mergers and buyouts will eventually unravel, with companies "shedding fixed cost and capacity, reducing administrative cost, and spinning off health-related businesses" (Goldsmith, 1994).

Political factors are also at work. As we have seen, under S1, health insecurity will grow. At some point, this will likely reach crisis proportions, and demand for universal coverage will emerge. One way of achieving universal coverage would be through an employment-based system, such as President Clinton's Health Security Act. However, given trends toward "the end of work," this approach does not seem feasible. A more likely approach to universal coverage is a single-payer with (nonprofit) managed competition.

This approach, which builds on the work of Paul Starr, Arnold Relman, Michael Rachlis and Carol Kushner, and others, combines regulation and competition with universal coverage. Managed competition refers to a model of health-care delivery advanced by Alain Enthoven (1993). Enthoven envisioned a system that would rely on government to encourage and regulate competition among groups of providers to restrain the growth of health-care costs. Studies showed that (nonprofit) staff-model HMOs were superior to fee-for-service in cost, quality, and distribution of resources; they were also more likely to stress prevention and early diagnosis (Newhouse et al., 1993). Consumers would choose among provider groups, which would offer standard benefit packages. Consumers would also receive information on the quality of the provider groups and would choose among them based on the best combination of price and quality. The discipline of the market would pressure higher-cost or lower-quality plans to alter their behavior.

Enthoven (1993) also stressed that managed competition is not a "free market," which he believed cannot work in health care. Government is needed to structure the market and enforce the rules of competition. The Clinton Administration built on Enthoven's idea of managed competition in developing its Health Security Act.

Under a single-payer system, the government, whether federal or state, serves as sole insurer, thus eliminating duplicative and wasteful administrative spending. A single-payer has enabled Canada to provide universal coverage and control costs (Marmor, 1994). The single-payer also negotiates fees, or global budgets, with providers; it is financed through the tax system. In recent years, however, Rachlis and Kushner and others have proposed sweeping changes in the delivery of Canadian health care. These include a shift to capitation, emphasis on prevention, reliance on outpatient and community-based facilities, consumer participation, a team approach to health care, and the expansion of nonphysician and nontraditional services (Rachlis and Kushner, 1994). Although they do not use Enthoven's language, Rachlis and Kushner essentially suggest incorporating (nonprofit) managed competition into the Canadian system of government insurance and universal coverage.

In the United States, Arnold Relman (1992), the longtime editor of the *New England Journal of Medicine*, has proposed a similar model. He advocates state or regional single-payers, which would insure all individuals and determine payments to providers. The latter would be organized in group-model HMOs, which would compete based on quality. Providers would negotiate salaries with HMO boards. The federal government would license and help in the organization of the HMOs. The HMOs would also receive a global budget that they could spend as they chose.

Relman also believes that providers should operate strictly on a nonprofit basis. According to him, for-profit HMOs often undermine physicians' morale by giving them incentives to limit care to patients and permitting "business managers to decide the conditions under which the doctors work" (Relman, 1992). He concludes that a single-payer with a system of nonprofit HMOs would yield significant savings in both the administrative and delivery systems (Relman, 1992).

The heart of S2 is a transition from health care to health. Our current system is based on what Evans and Stoddart (1994) call a "thermostat" model, which assumes that health status is largely linked with diagnosis and medical treatment. However, medical care may not be the major factor in the health of populations. In the West, broad sociological factors, such as rising incomes, improved nutrition, and smaller families, played a much larger role in declines in mortality than advances in health care (Fogel, 1994; McKeown, 1994; Reves, 1985). Scholars have also found that inequality has a profound impact on health (Wilkinson, 1994).

The idea of health, as distinct from health care, has gained increasing attention. During the 1950s, the World Health Organization defined health as "the state of complete physical, mental, and social well-being, and not merely the absence of disease or injury" (Evans and Stoddart, 1994). In the 1970s, the idea of holistic medicine emerged, emphasizing the roles of mind and body in "wellness" (Rowley, 1995). In 1990, the Public Health Services of the U.S. Department of Health and Human Services established Healthy People 2000: National Health Promotion and Disease Prevention Objectives (1996). The Public Health Service recognized the need to expand prevention programs and promote healthy lifestyles to create a healthy population.

More recently, Evans and Stoddart (1994) proposed a multidimensional model of health status. According to them, the key determinants of health are physical and social environments, biological endowment, individual responses, and national wealth. From this perspective, they closely link health status with employment, education, family support, and the physical environment (Gorin and Moniz, 1996). This newer model emphasizes systems, interconnections, and complexity. The transition from health care to health is thus a transition from a system that narrowly focuses on disease and illness to one that considers individuals in their biopsychosocial context.

Social Work Under Scenario One

As described above, a key feature of S1 is the expansion of for-profit health care. In 1993, Gibelman and Schervish (1993) noted that "contrary to historical patterns, the for-profit sector has evolved into a major employer of social workers." Traditional sites of social work practice, such as nursing homes, home health agencies, hospitals, and clinics, are increasingly organized on a for-profit basis (Freund and McGuire, 1991; Macarov, 1991). Critics argue that for-profit health and welfare services have many drawbacks, including commercialization and standardization of care, false economies, and oligopoly (Karger and Stoesz, 1994).

For-profit corporations may also choose clients selectively, "according to criteria of organizational performance—as opposed to client need" (Karger and Stoesz, 1994). This exacerbates existing inequalities and fosters development of a two-tiered system of care (Blumenthal, 1996). Social workers in for-profit organizations may face conflict between the demands of their employers and the ethics of their profession (Macarov, 1991). On the other hand, as Marmor, Schlesinger, and Smithey (1994) point out, the distinction between for-profit and nonprofit organizations should not be exaggerated. From a social work perspective, the fundamental problem with S1 is the lack of both universal coverage and federal regulation of the marketplace.

Under S1, social work's historic commitment to poor and oppressed people would face serious challenge. Social work could enter an era like the 1920s, when, as Trattner (1994) notes, disillusion with reform, and the "conservative climate of the postwar years," led social workers to focus on the individual and professionalism. According to Reamer (1992), in recent years, entering social workers have had a "limited commitment to the profession's traditional concern with social justice and public welfare." In health care, the difficult conditions of S1 could lead social workers to abandon their commitment to universal coverage and advocacy for underserved populations.

Social Work Under Scenario Two

In contrast with S1, S2 could result in a broad expansion of social work practice. With universal coverage, social work may play an even greater role than it does now in the health-care arena. New roles for social work could also emerge from the transition from health care to health. In particular, social workers could play an increasingly important role in community-based care and health research, and health promotion and disease prevention.

Community-Based Care and Health Research
Managed care has transformed the role of hospitals in the health-care system. Capitation has lowered rates of hospitalization, reduced lengths of stay, and led to an expansion of out-

patient care (Reinhardt, 1996). Many hospitals have either closed or merged with others. Capitation has also helped shift the system's focus from individuals to groups and populations (Freeman and Trabin, 1994). Because hospitals have been a major arena for medical social workers, these developments will have a dramatic impact on the profession (Gibelman and Schervish, 1993).

In the 21st century, medical care will primarily be delivered on an ambulatory and outpatient basis (Ross, 1995; Schreiber, 1996). Regional teaching hospitals will provide emergency services and intensive care, but new technologies, medicines, and scientific breakthroughs will further reduce the role of traditional hospitals in the spectrum of health care. Rowley (1995) predicts that "the hospital might not be a place at all"; services would be spread throughout the community, in "workplaces, shopping malls and the home" (Rowley, 1995).

These changes will create new opportunities for social work practice at several levels. First, with their biopsychosocial perspective, social workers could play a leading role in formulating health policy. The transition from health care to health could create opportunities for social workers to redesign broader health-related social welfare policies, including income maintenance, employment, housing, and education.

Second, social workers could work in the emerging network of community health sites. Clancy (1996) envisions (the coming of) "multiservice health care center social workers," who would manage services "provided in . . . multiple community outpatient centers and . . . healthy living communities." These facilities would serve as the nexus of health activities, providing treatment and promoting wellness. Social workers could work as members of health-care teams, coordinating all aspects of a client's treatment and care.

Third, the new focus on the health of groups and populations will provide important research opportunities for social workers. In recent years, researchers have focused on the links between socioeconomic status and health (Evans, Barer, and Marmor, 1994; Moss, 1995). At the 1996 Annual Program Meeting of the Council on Social Work Education, Dr. Norman B. Anderson, director of the Office of Behavioral and Social Sciences Research of the National Institutes of Health, called on social workers to collaborate with other professionals to examine the links among education, income, occupation, and other factors and health status. Social workers have long understood the importance of interactions between individuals and their social environment (Germain and Gitterman, 1995). In the 21st century, the profession will be able to shape health policies and programs based on its contributions to biopsychosocial research.

Health Promotion and Disease Prevention

The transition from fee-for-service to capitation and health care to health will bring about new emphasis on health promotion and disease prevention (Freeman and Trabin, 1994). Under S2, health promotion and disease prevention would include changing the social factors that influence people's lives. Implementing such a strategy could expand opportunities for social workers. First, social workers could serve as health planners, counselors, educators, advocates, and health promotion experts in public health departments, community-based clinics, centers, and networks, and an array of social settings. Second, social workers could collaborate with other professionals to design social welfare policies that promote healthy populations. This would increase the demand for social workers in community mental health, school social work, child welfare, adult day care, and other areas.

Social Work Education Under S1

If, as suggested above, social work enters a period similar to the 1920s, schools would face pressure to adjust to the new reality. Issues of social justice and inequality would no longer play a central role in the social work curriculum. In the absence of universal coverage, schools would focus on the needs of the relatively affluent insured population and on preparing students to work in for-profit managed care organizations. Edinburg and Cottler (1995) predict that managed care will bring "an increase in fiscal management of care at the expense of clinical management." In this context, students would need training in the use and development of outcome measures, business and finance, administration, and research (Warren, 1996).

Social Work Education Under S2

Under S2, social work education would address the social determinants of health, and students would learn to intervene in ways that improve socioeconomic status. Social workers would help eliminate health-related problems, including poverty, crime, and social violence. This would require active involvement in biopsychosocial research and expanded content on research in the social work curriculum.

In the area of skill development, emphasis would be placed on communities and community-based interventions. Social workers would join multidisciplinary networks working in communities to provide health and welfare services. They would need planning, advocacy, and organizing skills to ensure that all segments of the community have access not only to health-care services, but also to economic opportunities, adequate housing, educational resources, and social supports.

Conclusion

Prediction is fraught with difficulty. Unanticipated and apparently random events can have enormous consequences. In a matter of weeks, a butterfly beating its wings in South America can precipitate a tornado in the midwestern United States (Shroyer, 1993). Social reality is perhaps even more unpredictable than the natural world. In this paper, we have used current trends to predict future possibilities. We have envisioned alternative scenarios for the health-care system and social work. Scenario one would clearly conflict with the values of social work, whereas scenario two would advance them. The challenge for social workers in the 21st century could be to bring about the opportunities envisioned in the second scenario.

REFERENCES

Aaron, H. J. (1994). Thinking Straight About Medical Costs. *Health Affairs, 5,* 7–13.

Adams, W., and Brock, J. W. (1986). *The Bigness Complex: Industry, Labor and Government in the American Economy.* New York: Pantheon Press.

Aronowitz, S., and DiFazio, W. (1994). *The Jobless Future.* Minneapolis: University of Minnesota Press.

Bezold, C. (1996, February). On Futures Thinking: Trends, Scenarios, Visions and Strategies. Military Health Services System 2020 Working Group Symposium. Unpublished paper.

Blumenthal, D. (1994, Spring). The Vital Role of Professionalism in Health Care Reform. *Health Affairs, 13,* 1, 252–256.

Blumenthal, D. (1996, Summer). Effects of Market Reforms on Doctors and Their Patients. *Health Affairs, 15,* 2, 170–184.

Clancy, C. A. (1996). Beyond 2000: The Future of Hospital-Based Social Work Practice. In P. R. Raffoul and C. A. McNeece (Eds.), *Future Issues for Social Work Practice* (pp. 66–73). Needham Heights, MA: Allyn & Bacon.

Dewar, H. (1995, June 24). GOP Pushes Compromise on Budget: Congress Prepares for Tax Cut Battles. *Washington Post,* A6.

Eckholm, E. (1994, December 18). While Congress Remains Silent, Health Care Transforms Itself. *New York Times,* 1.

Edinburg, G. M., and Cottler, J. M. (1995). Managed Care. In R. L. Edwards (Ed.-in-Chief), *Encyclopedia of Social Work* (19th ed., Vol. 2, pp. 1635–1642). Washington, DC: NASW Press.

Enthoven, A. C. (1993). The History and Principles of Managed Competition. *Health Affairs,* Supplement, 24–48.

Enthoven, A. C., and Singer, S. J. (1995, Spring). Market-Based Reform: What to Regulate and by Whom. *Health Affairs, 14,* 1, 105–119.

Evans, R. G., Barer, M. L., & Marmor, T. R. (Eds.). (1994). *Why Are Some People Healthy and Others Not? The Determinants of Health Populations.* Hawthorne, NY: Aldine De Gruyter.

Evans, R. G., and Stoddart, G. L. (1994). Producing Health, Consuming Health Care. In P. R. Lee and C. L. Estes (Eds.), *The Nation's Health* (4th ed., pp. 6–13). Boston: Jones and Bartlett.

Flint, S. S., Yudkowsky, B. K., and Tang, S. S. (1995, November). Children's Medicaid Entitlement: What Have We Got to Lose? *Pediatrics, 96,* 5, 967–970.

Fogel, R. W. (1994, April). *Economic Growth, Population Theory, and Physiology: The Bearing of Long-term Processes in the Making of Economic Policy.* Working Paper No. 4638. Cambridge: National Bureau of Economic Research.

Foster Higgins. (1995, February 14). *National Survey of Employer-sponsored Health Plans.*

Freeman, M. A. and Trabin, T. (1994, October 5). *Managed Behavioral Health Care: History, Models, Key Issues and Future Course.* Rockville, MD: U.S. Center for Mental Health Services, SAMHSA.

Freudenheim, M. (1996a, May 19). H.M.O.'s Cope with a Backlash on Cost Cutting. *New York Times*, 1.

Freudenheim, M. (1996b, April 2). Managed Care Empires in the Making. *New York Times*, D1, D8.

Freund, P. E. S., and McGuire, M. B. (1991). *Health, Illness, and the Social Body: A Critical Sociology*. Englewood Cliffs, NJ: Prentice-Hall.

Germain, C. B., and Gitterman, A. (1995). Ecological Perspective. In R. L. Edwards (Ed.-in-Chief), *Encyclopedia of Social Work* (19th ed., Vol. 1, pp. 816–824). Washington, DC: NASW Press.

Gibelman, M., and Schervish, P. H. (1993). *Who We Are: The Social Work Labor Force as Reflected in the NASW Membership*. Washington, DC: NASW Press.

Goldsmith, J. C. (1994, September–October). The Illusive Logic of Integration. *Healthcare Forum Journal*, 26–31.

Gorin, S., and Moniz, C. (1996). From Health Care to Health: A Look Ahead to 2010. In P. R. Raffoul and C. A. McNeece (Eds.), *Future Issues for Social Work Practice* (pp. 58–65). Needham Heights, MA: Allyn & Bacon.

Head, S. (1996, February 29). The New, Ruthless Economy. *The New York Review of Books, 43*, no 4.

Iglehart, J. K. (1994). The American Heath Care System: Managed Care. In P. R. Lee and C. L. Estes (Eds.), *The Nation's Health*. (4th ed., pp. 231–237). Boston: Jones and Bartlett .

Iglehart, J. K. (1995). A Conversation with Leonard D. Schaeffer. *Health Affairs, 14*, 4, 131–142.

Kane, N. M., Turnball, N. C., and Schoen, C. (1996, January). *Markets and Plan Performance: Private Summary Report on Case Studies of IPA and Network HMOs*. The Commonwealth Fund.

Karger, H. J. and Stoesz, D. (1994). *American Social Welfare Policy: A Pluralist Approach*. New York: Longman.

Korten, D. C. *When Corporations Rule the World*. West Hartford and San Francisco: Kumarian Press and Berrett-Koehler Publishers.

Levit, K. R., Lazenby, H. C., and Sivarajan, L. (1996, Summer). Health Care Spending in 1994: Slowest in Decades. *Health Affairs, 2*, 130–144.

Macarov, D. (1991). *Certain Change: Social Work Practice in the Future*. Silver Spring, MD: NASW Press.

Marmor, T. R. (1994). Patterns of Fact and Fiction in Use of the Canadian Experience. In T. R. Marmor, *Understanding Health Care Reform*. New Haven, CT: Yale University Press.

Marmor, T. R., Schlesinger, M., and Smithey, R. W. (1994). Nonprofit Organizations and Health Care. In T. R. Marmor, *Understanding Health Care Reform*. New Haven, CT: Yale University Press.

McKeown, T. (1994). Determinants of Health. In P. R. Lee and C. L. Estes (Eds.), *The Nation's Health* (4th ed., pp. 6–13). Boston: Jones and Bartlett.

Miller, R. H. (1996, Summer). Competition. *Health Affairs, 15*, 2, 107–120.

Moss, N. E. (1995, Summer). Social Inequalities and Health. *Health Affairs, 14*, 2, 318–321.

Newhouse, J. P., and the Insurance Experiment Group. (1993). *Free for All? Lessons from the RAND Health Insurance Experiment*. Cambridge, MA: Harvard University Press.

Preston, J. (1996, April 14). Hospitals Look on Charity Care As Unaffordable Option of Past. *New York Times*, 1, 36.

Prigogine, I., and Stengers, I. (1984). *Order out of Chaos: Man's New Dialogue with Nature*. Toronto: Bantam Books.

Rachlis, M., and Kushner, C. (1994). *Strong Medicine: How to Save Canada's Health Care System*. Toronto: HarperCollins.

Reamer, F. G. (1992). Social Work and the Public Good: Calling or Career? In P. N. Reid and P. R. Popple (Eds.), *The Moral Purposes of Social Work: The Character and Intentions of a Profession* (pp. 11–33). Chicago: Nelson-Hall.

Reinhardt, U. E. (1996, Summer). Perspective: Our Obsessive Quest to Gut the Hospital. *Health Affairs, 15*, 2, 145–154.

Relman, A. S. (1992, August). *The Choices for Health Care Reform*. Camp Hill, PA: Pennsylvania Blue Shield Institute.

Reves, R. (1985). Declining Fertility in England and Wales as a Major Cause of the 20th Century Decline in Mortality. *American Journal of Epidemeology, 122*, 112–126.

Rifkin, J. (1995). *The End of Work*. New York: Random House.

Roos, N. P., and Roos, L. L. (1994). Small Area Variations, Practice Style, and Quality of Care. In R. E. Evans, M. L. Barer, and T. R. Marmor (Eds.), *Why Are Some People Healthy and Others Not?* New York: Aldine De Gruyter.

Ross, J. W. (1995). Hospital Social Work. In R. L. Edwards (Ed.-in-Chief), *Encyclopedia of Social Work* (19th ed., Vol. 2, pp. 1365–1377). Washington, DC: NASW Press.

Rothfeld, M. (1976). Sensible Surgery for Swelling Medical Costs. In Health/PAC, D. Kotelchuck (Ed.), *Prognosis Negative: Crisis in the Health Care System*. New York: Vintage Books.

Rowley, W. (1995). Health Care Delivery in the 21st Century: Trends and Predictions. Military Health Services System 2020 Working Group Symposium. Unpublished paper.

Schreiber, J. (1996, April 28). Curbside Medical Service Is Envisioned: Paramedics, EMTs Would Treat, Release. *Boston Sunday Globe*, NH 1, 4.

Shroyer, J. A. (1993). *Quarks, Critters, and Chaos— What Science Terms Really Mean*. New York: Prentice-Hall General Reference.

Social Security and Medicare Boards of Trustees. (1996, June). *Status of the Social Security and Medicare Programs: A Summary of the 1996 Annual Reports*.

Starr, P. (1982). *The Social Transformation of American Medicine*. New York: Basic Books.

Starr, P. (1994). *The Logic of Health Care Reform*. New York: Penguin Books.

Thorpe, K. E., Shields, A. E., Gold, H., Altman, S. H., and Shactman, D. (1995, November). Anticipat-ing the Number of Uninsured Americans and the Demand for Uncompensated Care: The Impact of Proposed Medicaid Reductions and Erosion of Employer-Sponsored Insurance. Unpublished study. Waltham, MA: Brandeis University.

Trattner, W. I. (1994). *From Poor Law to Welfare State: A History of Social Welfare in America*. New York: Free Press.

U.S. Department of Health and Human Services, Public Health Services. (1996). *Healthy People 2000 Midcourse Review and 1995 Revisions*. Sudbury, MA: Jones and Bartlett.

Warren, K., Franklin, C., and Streeter, C. L. (1996, February 18). Chaos, Complexity and Social Work Research. Unpublished article.

Warren, R.V. (1996, May). *Focus Group Exploration of Social Work Skills Needed for the Managed Care Environment*. Washington: NASW.

Weil, T. P. (1994, October 15). Managed Care and Networks: Resulting in Virtual Monopolies and State Regulation as a Public Utility? *Rate Controls/Supplement, 18*, no. 10A, 5–8.

Wennberg, J. E. and Keller, R. (1994, Spring). Regional Professional Foundations. *Health Affairs, 13*, 1, 257–263.

White House Domestic Policy Council. (1993). *Health Security—The President's Report to the American People*. Washington, DC.

Wiatrowski, W. J. (1995, June). Who Really Has Access to Employer-provided Health Benefits? *Monthly Labor Review*, 36–44.

Wilkinson, R. G. (1994). The Epidemiological Transition: From Material Scarcity to Social Disadvantage? *Daedalus, 4*, 61–77.

Wolfe, B. (1996, Spring). A Medicaid Primer. *Focus, 3*. 1–6.

Zwanziger, J., and Melnick, G. (1996, Summer). *Health Affairs, 15*, 2, 185–199.

Mental Health Services

Tomi Gomory

[Psychiatric] bureaucrats are like other men.
This proposition sounds very simple and straightforward,
but the consequences are a radical departure from
orthodox economic theory.

If [psychiatric] bureaucrats are ordinary men, they will
make most of . . . their decisions in terms of what benefits
them, not society as a whole. Like other men, they may
occasionally sacrifice their own well-being for the wider
good, but we should expect this to be exceptional behaviour.

[In contrast] most of the existing literature on the
machinery of government assumes that, when an activity is
delegated to a bureaucrat, he will . . . make decisions in the
public interest regardless of whether it benefits him or not.

Tullock, 1976, p. 26

The mental health industry consumes billions of dollars. Social workers comprise a significant part of it. The industry is based on the too often unexamined assumptions that there is such a thing as mental illness, that we know what it is, and that there are services that have been found to be helpful. This essay argues that these premises are faulty, based on both logical and evidentiary grounds. Given professionals' concerns to help and not harm (e.g., impose unreliable and invalid pathological labels), this perspective is an important one to air. Tomi Gomory, MSW, is currently completing his doctoral studies in the School of Social Welfare, University of California at Berkeley. He is the recipient of a National Institute of Mental Health Doctoral Fellowship. His current areas of research include a critical review of outcome claims of PACT-type community programs, which target the "severely mentally ill," conceptual and situational analysis of the historical changes in the public mental health system, and an evaluation of the impact on social work of justificationary philosophic frameworks—logical positivist: heuristic paradigm, postmodernism, relativist—versus a fallabilist evolutionary epistemology. Mr. Gomory's practical experience includes directing the San Francisco component of the federal model project The Homeless Family, co-sponsored by the Robert Wood Johnson Foundation.

In line with Thomas Szasz (1965), I claim that, like sexual intercourse between consenting adults, voluntary psychiatric intercourse between consenting adults, based on the contractual assent of the parties, is no business of any one but the individuals involved, in this case the client and the therapist. Such contractual psychiatric services generally entail agreement, treatment, and fee payment between a professional and a person who is—sometimes unfortunately and derogatorily labeled the "worried well" by the public mental health establishment—seeking help in the context of private practice.

Alternatively, I claim that society's concern should be, and this essay's is, with a critical review of the public mental health system, a vast bureaucracy, because it is funded by our tax dollars to the tune of approximately $29 billion annually (Manderscheid & Sonnenschein, 1993, p. 115, table 6.9a) and because it often "treats" its clients against their will (Gomory, 1995; Szasz, 1987, 1994). Such an approach requires close scrutiny.

The theses of this paper are the following: (1) Political necessity required nation-states (for example, in Europe) to set up social control policies to contain the social agitation and unrest of marginal populations of dependents—such as the poor, the mad, the physically sick, the criminal, the loafer, the socially inept—which entailed institutionalization of this highly heterogeneous group. (2) Such institutions created large bureaucracies with their own agendas. (3) People labeled mad or insane were, over time, separated from this group and provided their own institutional setting (in the United States, these were ultimately called state mental hospitals) with its own theoretical framework—a metaphorical use of the 19th-century medical model (Boyle, 1990; Szasz, 1961, 1963, 1976)—and a profession (alienists/psychiatrists) that claimed therapeutic success—control or cure of various mental disorders—based on this frame-

work. The fact that a special bureaucracy was created to handle the problem of "mad" deviants ensured that the bureaucrats who took on the professional role of "mad doctors" would do all in their power to "legitimate" this position and the accompanying authority (see, on bureaucratic behavior, for example, Niskanen, 1971; Tullock, 1965). This they have done with a vengeance for well over 150 years in America.

Beyond this administrative effort, which, as I discuss in what follows, has been an unqualified success, these psychiatric professionals have also asserted expertise in two roles: first as social control agents for the state and second as experts uniquely qualified to handle a problem they have invented out of whole cloth and defined as the medical problem of mental diseases. This article will in brief—due to the constraints of the short essay format—review the history of the development of these issues, evaluate the success of the two expert skills claimed by institutional psychiatric professionals, discuss current trends, and make some suggestions for the future of this system using client outcome and demand for services as guiding principles.

Social work has had a vital if subsidiary role to play in the provision of public mental health services from the very beginning, as Dorothea Dix's focal role, delineated below, will show. Although my analysis will deal primarily with the role played by psychiatrists, because that professional group defines and runs the system, it should be kept in mind that we, as one of its leading support professions, bear a major responsibility for all that is good and bad about it. This, of course, also means that we can play an essential role in changing the current system in the coming century, if we believe, as I do, that this system is in need of much improvement.

Historical Review and Institutional Development

This essay is not the place to comprehensively document the full development of the current institutional system of care for the "mentally ill" out of the earlier system of social control applied to all categories of dependents, as it has been well documented previously by such experts as Scull (1981, 1989, 1993), Porter (1983, 1987, 1990), Bynum (1982, 1985), Castel (1988), and Skultans (1979). Nevertheless, a brief review is in order.

The historical development of mental health systems, including their institutional state-run bureaucracies, can be traced to 16th-century European nation-states' desire to maintain internal order. For example in England,

> [i]ncreasing population, coupled with the growing commercialization of agriculture and the spread of enclosures, [which] was spawning a volatile "army" of vagrants, beggars and idlers . . . forced . . . the Tudor monarchs . . . to supplement religious with secular control of the poor. (Scull, 1993, pp. 12–13)

By 1601, under the Poor Law Act,

> the poor, including the insane poor, . . . were now acknowledged to be a secular rather than a religious responsibility. (p. 15)

As the old Tudor paternalistic order in England shifted in the 18th and 19th centuries to a free-market economic and social system, the growing middle class became more and more alienated from the traditional noninstitutional responses to the poor. At the same time, the dramatic increase of those on temporary or permanent poor relief to nearly 1 million individuals rapidly reduced the inclination of most citizens to simply tolerate such conditions. The use of

> [w]orkhouses, asylums, and the like were . . . expected to provide an efficient and economical solution to the problem [of poverty, insan-

ity, and dependence in general]. (Scull, 1993, pp. 33–34)

This large aggregation of impoverished "dependents" was divided in short order into those who were able-bodied, and therefore able to work, and those who were infirm for various reasons, and could not (p. 37). The odd behavior of "lunaticks" exacerbated the conditions in workhouses and speeded up the collection of private funds for setting up separate charity asylums for these "distracted" individuals (p. 39). By the time the 18th century drew to a close and the next began, the existence of insane asylums created the impression, which was encouraged by the individuals (alienists) running them, that some expertise was available to treat the inmates even though no scientific evidence could be provided for such claims (see Scull, 1993, pp. 41–42).

Scull has persuasively argued that the American institutional system of care for the insane can be traced directly to the above system, as first developed in England (Scull, 1993, pp. 95–117). It subsequently took on some unique American characteristics, as discussed by Rothman (1990) and, from a somewhat different perspective, by Grob (1973, 1983). This American system has been in place at least since the third or fourth decade of the 19th century (Rothman, 1990).

Dorothea Dix, one of social work's patron saints, led the early lobbying in America for state-funded asylums for the insane. Although well intentioned, her selling and marketing of state-run institutions was based on two dubious premises: first, that such asylums were the most cost-effective means of treatment, and second, that insanity was a highly curable phenomenon.

> Again and again in her crusade . . . [she] was to draw upon such claims. . . . Repeatedly she informed state legislatures that "all experience

shows that insanity reasonably treated is as certainly curable as a cold or a fever." She drew upon the elaborate statistics provided by her allies among the asylum superintendents . . . to provide estimates to the penny of the money to be saved by "a combination of medical and moral treatment" in an asylum. (Scull, 1989, p. 112)

This lobbying in the 1800s for state institutional treatment, asserting superior cost effectiveness based on unreliable or false statistics (Rothman, 1990, pp. 131–133) and high "cure rates" based on the obviously false claim of curing insanity—since we seem to be no closer even today to knowing what any of the asserted major mental illnesses are or how to cure them (for example, see Shore, 1993, p. 3, on schizophrenia)—is very similar to the politicking and claim making being done by the mental health establishment currently for another form of community mental health treatment. This latter, called Assertive Community Treatment—which has equally little empirical evidence to back its claim (Gomory, 1995)—is, paradoxically, the precise opposite of institutional treatment, being done with the client in his own place of residence.

In summary, the treatment of a particular group of deviants or dependents—those referred to as insane, mad, or mentally ill—grew out of the political necessity to control a large heterogeneous population, who, because of poverty, physical illness, poor educational opportunities, societal economic reorganization, absence of social skills, sometime criminal activity, and various other deviant behaviors, were perceived as threats to the general welfare of society. This comprehensive social control effort, naturally requiring an institutional infrastructure for implementation, subsequently became allied—for those exhibiting "hard to fathom" deviant behav-

ior—with the more socially benign causal explanations of medicine, which implied this group's amenability to "scientific" treatment (Grob, 1983; Rothman, 1990; Scull, 1993).

Bureaucratic Behavior Is Separate from Assigned Professional Role

The best way to understand the public mental health system and its functioning is to view it as a bureaucratic entity much like any of our other large public systems—for example, those involved with public education or public health or the provision of social welfare. Simply because certain people work in professions whose alleged role is to help other people with various human difficulties—thus, the by-now-clichéd and, I believe, presumptuous self-identification of these professions as the "helping professions"—does not mean that these professionals operate any differently—that is, on a loftier moral plane with higher ethical standards—than any other group of individuals in society who provide a professional service. By eliminating this assumption of ultra virtuous behavior, and thereby normalizing the helping professions as being like other professions, we may be able to analyze the claims and asserted successes of the public mental health system just by examining the evidence (Szasz, 1977, 1984, 1988, 1994).

Like all bureaucracies, the public mental health system's chief aim is to remain in power and grow, and its bureaucrats,

[a]s a general rule, . . . find that . . . possibilities for promotion increase, . . . power, influence, and public respect improve . . . if the bureaucracy in which [they] work(s) expands . . . . He gains more, however, if *his* Ministry [agency] expands, and more yet if the *sub*-division [profession] in which he is employed expands. (Tullock, 1976, p. 29)

As in other groups of professionals, along with self—not selfish—interest[1] there may also be a genuine desire to help the population that is the target of the professionals' claimed expertise (Tullock, 1976, p. 28). Regardless, claims for the success of treatment will be ubiquitous. These claims should not be accepted naively or uncritically; they must be open to empirical testing and have undergone severe tests—attempts to falsify theoretical hypotheses or empirical interventions (Miller, 1994)—and have passed them, in order for us to accept these tentatively as helpful or "successful" (Popper, 1962). The key is to evaluate claims of success or effectiveness against the available empirical evidence, separate from the rhetoric of the bureaucracy's propaganda asserting that it is helping its designated population.

The Nature of the Behemoth

Institutional psychiatry is a massive bureaucracy in the United States. According to the National Institute of Mental Health, as of 1988, it employed over 600,000 workers nationally, including 30,000 psychiatrists, 30,000 psychologists, 58,000 social workers, and 85,000 registered nurses (Manderscheid & Sonnenschein, 1993, p. 38). The population it claims to serve is the estimated 4 to 5 million "seriously mentally ill" in the United States (p. 255). Of these individuals, 1.7 million are further labeled, in vague and obscure fashion, as the "severely mentally ill" (Attkisson, 1992, p. 562), about 900,000 of whom are in institutions and the rest of whom are reported to live in community settings or are homeless.

[1]For clarification of the distinction between the two, see Hayek (1980, pp. 113–116).

The annual tax dollars spent on funding this system is well in excess of $29 billion (see p. 163, this article). The research into its "Sacred Symbol" schizophrenia (Szasz, 1976)—only one of an ever-expanding list of mental disorders (Kirk and Kutchins, 1992)—exceeds $100 million per year (Shore, 1993, p. 2). An important additional cost to taxpayers is the payment of SSDI and SSI monthly benefits by the Social Security Administration to the almost 1.4 million individuals who have been found administratively to be mentally disabled and unable to work; this totaled at least $630 million in 1991 alone (Manderscheid & Sonnenschein, 1993, p. 224).

The accurate evaluation of the empirical claims of this institutional enterprise is crucial because of the costs and benefits accruing to various groups of citizens based on the presumption of the scientific validity of psychiatry. It is crucial for those who pay taxes because the system's substantial cost is funded almost entirely by public tax dollars, and it is crucial for those—some of whom may also be taxpayers—who are clients, particularly the 900,000 "severely mentally ill" citizens who are institutionalized (many of them against their will) because of the human costs incurred in emotional and spiritual deprivation, loss of physical freedom and autonomy, and the brain damage resulting from the iatrogenic effects, such as tardive dyskinesia, of this "helpful" therapy (Breggin, 1979, 1983, 1991; Whitaker, 1993). These costs have to be weighed against the benefits received by the hundreds of thousands of workers employed within the system, the benefits received in the form of disability checks handed to the "scientifically" diagnosed clients, and the possible therapeutic effects that may result from the psychiatric interventions.

What's the Evidence

In order to prognosticate[2] about this system's future, we have to separate out the social control role from the alleged therapeutic role and evaluate each for efficacy.

Social control was the original rationale for the system (Scull, 1993) and continues to be of central importance in its present version. The need to keep deviant and marginal groups in line, in order to avoid excessive social unrest, is today just as much a part of our society as it was in the past. The striking difference is the type of explanatory spin we put on our methods of control. We have turned almost all of our social control efforts over to those experts who claim to solve these problems therapeutically (Conrad & Schneider, 1992; Szasz, 1984, 1988, 1994).

The therapeutic octopus is insatiable. Scores of books have documented the transformation of what used to be considered volitional behaviors, requiring self-control and personal responsibility, into emotional disorders or illnesses ripe for treatment. Some of these acts—no longer considered such—are: random youth violence, now considered a public health concern; sexual offenses cured by castration; profligate gambling, now an addiction; ditto for indiscriminate drug, tobacco, and alcohol use, or homelessness—no longer seen as the possible consequence of personal characteristics like antisocial behavior, resulting in the alienation of support from family and friends, or the lack of social skills, poor educational history, or disinterest in societal expectations, resulting in few economic opportunities.

The mental health system, with the active cooperation of the state, has been exceptionally successful in increasing its hegemony over more and more deviant behaviors and, consequently, more and more people. If, as the available evidence suggests, the authority of mental health professionals extends over such diverse populations as young self-starving women (anorexics); people who sexually assault children (pedophiles); the homeless (a condition due, primarily, to mental illness); poor students (learning disabled); bored or physically very active children (attention deficit disordered); those who don't want to have sex with their wives, husbands, or partners (the sexually dysfunctional), those exhibiting poor judgment in their choice of lifestyles or use of various chemicals (sex addicted, codependent, gambling addicted, shopping addicted, alcohol addicted, drug addicted, food addicted, sports addicted); those who steal (kleptomaniacs); those who kill (schizophrenics); those who contemplate, threaten, or choose to end their lives (suicidally insane); then ultimately the vast majority of the population will fall under this system's jurisdiction, with its accompanying definition of social problems and its preferred methods of "treatment and cure" (all these "disorders" are discussed in Breggin, 1991; Conrad & Schneider, 1992; Szasz, 1980, 1984, 1985, 1987, 1988, 1992, 1994)—excepting perhaps only the psychiatric experts themselves.

How many could escape being diagnosed as the helpless victim of at least one of the literally hundreds of putative mental disorders (Kirk & Kutchins, 1992, pp. 199–200) listed in institutional psychiatry's sacred text, the *DSM*, currently in its fourth revision (Ameri-

---

[2]For the difficulties of predicting future occurrences based on our present knowledge, see the ingenious essay of W. W. Bartley (1990), in which he states, "To create knowledge is not to fathom or command it or own it. . . . After their birth, bodies of knowledge remain forever unfathomed and unfathomable. They remain forever pregnant with consequences that are unintended and cannot be anticipated. . . . They are autonomous" (p. 32).

can Psychiatric Association, 1994)? According to the psychiatric establishment, major mental illness is not only a serious problem but one that is on the rise. It is claimed that a "total of 15 million or more Americans" (Attkisson, 1992, pp. 562) have experienced a major mental disorder at least once in their lives. The experts are suggesting here that we have only tapped, to use a too well worn cliché, the tip of the mental illness iceberg. There lies before institutional psychiatry an untold wealth of potential future populations of mentally dysfunctional people, especially ripe for the labeling now because the diagnosing of the "severely mentally ill" has shifted from clinical to functional criteria (pp. 561–562).

Now, as to this system's *claim to scientifically help the clients* under its control, the evidence is clear. In the 150 some odd years of its existence, "scientific" psychiatry's many thousands of psychiatric researchers have been unable to find any meaningful, critically well tested evidence that even tentatively corroborates the existence of mental illnesses (Bentall, 1990; Boyle, 1990; Lewontin, Rose, & Kamin, 1984; Szasz, 1961, 1976, 1977, 1984, 1987). When reviewing the original research, what we find are tens of thousands of studies discussing volitional behaviors as if they were like physical illnesses, or studies purporting to be examining these "diseased" behaviors in scientific ways in order to find "treatments" for them, or twin/family studies searching for the genetic causality of various mental disorders. The result of all this frantic activity can be summed up in one word: *failure*—failure of all the various studies to withstand a critical scrutiny of their claims for the reliability and validity of their experimental constructs and measures, or their inability to replicate successfully research and outcomes (Boyle, 1990; Lewontin, Rose, & Kamin, 1984).

To be sure, I am not suggesting—nor is anyone who has criticized this system's approach to human problems saying—that annoying, bizarre, violent, or hard-to-fathom behavior does not exist. What is being asserted is that these behaviors are never mental diseases. They are the volitional acts of individuals who are always free to act otherwise than they do (Flew, 1987; Szasz, 1987). The truth is that in the 19th century we did find a physical disease that had psychiatric (behavioral) symptoms. This was neurosyphilis—earlier called general paralysis of the insane (GPI)—which, along with much else, was appropriated from medicine by psychiatrists and used as the paradigmatic model for mental diseases (Boyle, 1990; Szasz, 1976). This disorder had a physiological origin and, if untreated, led to death (Quetel, 1990). In sharp contrast, none of the putative mental disorders have ever been shown to have physiological causes or to have unambiguous courses leading to death if left untreated. Obviously, if they were shown to have physiological causes, they no longer would be considered "mental" and then a real doctor—a neurologist for brain diseases, for example— would be needed to treat the disease. Put directly, psychiatric researchers have not been able to scientifically demonstrate in any psychiatric populations the existence of a discreet, non-randomly occurring "mental symptom and sign" syndrome, the minimum needed to claim a disease construct (Boyle, 1990; Engle & Davis, 1963).

The mental health system is an unqualified bureaucratic success when it comes to social control and a similar dismal failure when it comes to its scientific pretensions. Nevertheless, due to society's need to exert control over marginal dependent populations—in our case, the "lunatick's" of yesteryear—and the resultant bureaucracy's organizational survival needs, as explained earlier, the system has survived and thrived.

What Is the Future of the Public Mental Health System?

If left to its own bureaucratic devices, the mental health system is sure to continue to proliferate unchecked and unchanged as long as institutional support remains for its ideology and methods. This system has a very powerful lobby, based in the first instance on the hundreds of thousands, if not millions, of people whose livelihoods are derived from it, and in the second instance based on the entrenched system of agencies whose very existence depends on the claimed validity of the psychiatric belief system. The following are just a few of these organizations: the National Institute of Mental Health, all the state and local mental health departments, all those agencies evaluating and paying mentally disabled clients, all state-run and subsidized mental health institutes and hospitals, and, of course, all the educational institutions responsible for educating all of the various mental health professionals in the system. Based both on the political and economic clout of this lobby, I believe that the immediate dismantling of the system, although preferred, is a pragmatic impossibility.

However, if the proper treatment of personally and socially troubled people is an important goal for all of society—because they are seen not as a client population in need of social engineering, but as equal members of it, with the attendant rights and responsibilities—then we may be able to respond to that goal by altering the present system to genuinely "empower" this group.

The policy solution I propose is a free-market system of mental health based on vouchers. The use of vouchers as fee payment for services places the purchasing power and control over the system directly into the hands of the system's clients (customers). This, I suggest, is real empowerment. The entire public mental health service system and any other public or private group or individual who would like to offer services—psychiatric or social—would be free to compete for the voucher dollars of this "mentally ill" population. The clients would be free to select any and all agencies and spend, in vouchers, up to whatever amount is currently being spent per client in the existing system, on those agencies deemed by them to provide helpful services. Those agencies that could not attract clients or would not alter their services to be more responsive to clients' needs would simply be allowed, as it were—using Marx's felicitous phrase—to wither away.

The idea of vouchers as a funding mechanism is not new or radical—consider our extensive federal food stamp program, for example. Nevertheless, it would be revolutionary in public mental health. It's the application of the free market to goods or services that, in part or whole, is usually considered to be appropriate for government subsidies. The free market has proven itself to be the best mechanism for helping individuals select, according to their own preferences, the goods and services they deem necessary for their well-being, by operating as an unplanned, spontaneous, self-organizing informational system (Hayek, 1978, 1980).

The alternative, central planning or a command economy based on Marxist/Leninist doctrine, has been empirically falsified by the collapse across the globe of all but the most repressive regimes professing this ideology. These are rapidly being replaced by democratic governments based on the free market, enthusiastically supported by the previously repressed and impoverished citizens of these new democracies.

It is remarkable how little the schools of social welfare and their various social policy scholars learned from this tragic lesson. They fervently go on teaching their students and extolling in social policy texts the superiority of the public system of social welfare services—the system's policies are, of course, centrally planned[3]—without any evidence that they are superior to market institutions. I would like to suggest a more appropriate social policy approach. In an open society (Popper, 1971), no public interventions or programs should be undertaken except where the market has been tried and found wanting, and then only continued if the public intervention is found to be superior. The problem here, of course, is that experts of all kinds are loath to give up their power to the lay public, as witnessed by the hew and cry, fomented and led by educational bureaucrats, concerning school vouchers, which would return power over that system to the parents.

Unlike community mental health experts' efforts to evaluate program effectiveness, most of which have been miserable failures (Gomory, 1995), "mental health" vouchers will provide immediate feedback as to what services actually work for the clients by allowing the clients to vote with their feet, and as a con-

sequence also confer real autonomy on them, a key outcome all psychiatric services profess to be after. This system would, I venture, meet with strong resistance from the experts. They will undoubtedly claim that this population is unable, because of its diminished mental status, to make good choices about appropriate treatment—sometimes called denial of their illness. My response is simple. The system cannot have it both ways. If, for example, when diagnosing schizophrenia, psychiatrists claim to accept that clients are accurately and truthfully reporting their hallucinations and delusions—these symptoms are the sine qua non of this "disease"—thus serving the psychiatrists' needs for diagnosis, they cannot then turn around and assert that clients are incapable of truthfully and accurately choosing interventions or services that are helpful for their problems, when the results are disadvantageous—the likelihood of reduced employment—for the very same psychiatrists. Either the clients are capable of accurate and truthful reporting or they are not.

I believe that the proposed voucher system, here only sketched in its bare outline, is a worthy alternative to the very expensive, ineffective, pseudoscientific system now in place. It would quickly eliminate most programs that are not sufficiently patronized by the clients—no great loss because most of these programs lack any scientific standing anyhow—saving millions, perhaps billions of our tax dollars. A part of these savings could still be spent on some psychiatric research, perhaps of the kind being done mostly in England on psychological symptomology, such as visual or auditory hallucinations or delusional beliefs, which, contrary to the psychiatric medical modelers' claim, appears to occur in all populations, normal or deviant, and conse-

[3]Program development, funding, regulation, and oversight of the major social programs in the United States are centrally planned or micromanaged by the federal executive and legislative branches, and such agencies as HUD, HEW, HHS, and the Social Security Administration (Wilson, 1989).

quently is open to research without necessitating the problematic assumption of underlying mental illness (Boyle, 1990, pp. 196–216). This type of research has the potential to produce successful symptom-reducing treatments, which could be offered to clients where appropriate (Boyle, 1990).

The psychiatric experts have also had to back away from the great successes claimed in the past for their paradigmatic intervention, psychotropic medication. By even their own accounts, drugs are turning out to be at best "effective" in only 30–40% of psychiatric clients, with about as many clients iatrogenically brain damaged[4] by their use (Breggin, 1983; Shore, 1993, pp. 113–141). The experts currently claim that the major mental illnesses primarily affect,

> thought processes, perception, sense of self, and volition. The resulting disturbances usually disrupt routine daily functioning in all areas, including work, social relationships, and self-care. (Attkisson, 1992, p. 562)

Such problematic behavior appears in most marginal populations of dependents, not just those labeled psychiatric (Szasz, 1994), thus undermining the claim for psychiatric nosology both as a reliable and valid classificationary mechanism and as a means of targeting specific treatments for particular disorders. The entire psychiatric nosological system, which is without empirical support (Boyle, 1990; Kirk & Kutchins, 1992), should be dismantled. This would effectively eliminate

institutional psychiatry's claim to explanatory authority over deviant human behavior, freeing the system to experiment with daring new approaches to cope with difficult behaviors, open to severe tests by attempted "refutations" and critical debate, the only way that we ever really make scientific progress (Popper, 1962).

The implementation of these recommendations for change would probably at first put many people, including social workers, out of jobs and would have other potentially negative consequences for those reliant on the old system for their livelihood. Although there is no reason to bemoan the elimination of meaningless jobs that are burdens on the taxpayer and useless to the client, in order to ameliorate some of the personal difficulties of being unemployed, I would recommend spending some of the savings reaped by the voucher system on a one-time job-retraining effort aimed at those unemployed workers of the old system who could not find alternate positions utilizing their skills elsewhere in the new free-market service environment.

Some of the remaining savings could be spent on providing start-up monies for groups interested in offering concrete services, such as food, housing, physical health care, education, and various types of social and employment skills training, to the client/customers. These are the types of services that appear to best help all marginal dependents, including "the mentally disturbed," become more functional. These are also the types of services in which the social work profession can claim genuine expertise, making us, potentially, the leading profession in the new environment—assuming, of course, that we are willing to reconsider, based on the overwhelming empirical counterevidence, our dogmatically held professional distaste for the free market.

---

[4]Tardive dyskinesia, an often irreversible central nervous system disorder, causing involuntary facial, tongue, and jaw movements, is the major effect after sedation of psychotropic drugs, the most frequently provided treatment by institutional psychiatrists for "major mental illness." Only some 30 years after it had been recognized as brain damaging did institutional psychiatry begin to acknowledge and disclose the problem (Brown & Funk, 1986).

REFERENCES

Articles

Attkisson, C. (1992). Clinical services research. *Schizophrenia Bulletin, 18* (4), 561–626.

Brown, P., & Funk, S. C. (1986). Tardive dyskinesia: Barriers to the professional recognition of an iatrogenic disease. *Journal of Health and Social Behavior, 27* (June), 116–132.

Bynum, W. (1982). Theory and practice in British psychiatry from J. C. Prichard (1786–1848) to Henry Maudsley (1835–1918). In T. Ogawa (Ed.), *History of Psychiatry* (pp. 196–216). Osaka: Taniguchi Foundation.

_____. (1985). Physicians, hospitals, and career structures in eighteenth century London. In W. F. Bynum & R. Porter (Eds.), *William Hunter and the Eighteenth Century Medical World* (pp. 105–128). Cambridge: Cambridge University Press.

Engle, R. L. (1963). Medical diagnosis II: Present, past, and future. *Archives of Internal Medicine, 112*, 116–125.

Engle, R. L., & Davis, B. J. (1963). Medical diagnosis I: Present, past, and future. *Archives of Internal Medicine, 112*, 108–115.

Flew, A. (1987). Must naturalism discredit naturalism? In Gerald Radnitzky & W. W. Bartley, III (Eds.), *Evolutionary Epistemology, Rationality, and the Sociology of Knowledge* (pp. 401–421). La Salle, IL: Open Court.

Gomory, T. (1995). Evaluating the training in community living model. *Working Paper.*

Porter, R. (1983). The rage of party: A glorious revolution in English psychiatry? *Medical History, (27)*, 35–50.

_____. (1990). Foucault's great confinement. *History of the Human Sciences, (3)*, 47–54.

Whitaker, H. A. (1993). Special issue: Tardive dyskinesia and cognitive dysfunction. *Brain & Cognition. 23*, September.

Zuriff, G. E. (1996). Medicalizing character. *The Public Interest, 123* (Spring), 94–99.

Books

American Psychiatric Association. (1994). *Diagnostic and statistical manual of mental disorders: DSM IV.* (4th ed.). Washington, DC: Author.

Bartley, W. W. (1990). *Unfathomed knowledge, unmeasured wealth.* La Salle, IL: Open Court.

Bentall, R. P. (Ed.). (1990). *Reconstructing schizophrenia.* London: Routledge.

Boyle, M. (1990). *Schizophrenia—a scientific delusion?* London: Routledge.

Breggin, P. (1979). *Electro-shock: Its brain-disabling effects.* New York: Springer.

_____. (1983). *Psychiatric drugs: Hazard to the brain.* New York: Springer.

_____. (1991). *Toxic psychiatry.* New York: St. Martin's Press.

Castel, R. (1988). *The regulation of madness: The origins of incarceration in France.* Berkeley: University of California Press.

Conrad, P., & Schneider, J. W. (1992). *Deviance and medicalization.* Philadelphia: Temple University Press.

Grob, G. (1973). *Mental institutions in America: Social policy to 1875.* New York: Free Press.

_____. (1983). *Mental illness and American society, 1875–1940.* Princeton: Princeton University Press.

Hayek, F. A. (1978). *The constitution of liberty.* Chicago: The University of Chicago Press.

_____. (1980). *Individualism and economic order.* Chicago: The University of Chicago Press.

Kirk, S. A., & Kutchins, H. (1992). *The selling of DSM.* New York: Aldine De Gruyter.

Lewontin, R. C., Rose, S., & Kamin, J. (1984). *Not in our genes.* New York: Pantheon Books.

Manderscheid, R. W., & Sonnenschein, M. A. (Eds.). (1993). *Mental health, United States, 1992.* Rockville, MD: U. S. Department of Health and Human Services.

Miller, D. (1994). *Critical rationalism: A restatement and defence.* Chicago: Open Court.

Niskanen, W. A. (1971). *Bureaucracy and representative government.* New York: Aldine-Atherton.

Popper, K. R. (1962). *Conjectures and refutations: The growth of scientific knowledge.* New York: Basic Books.

_____. (1971). *The open society and its enemies.* Princeton: Princeton University Press.

Porter, R. (1987). *Mind forg'd manacles: A history of madness in England from the Restoration to the Regency.* London: Athlone.

Quetel, C. (1990). *History of syphilis.* Cambridge, UK: Polity Press.

Rothman, D. J. (1990). *The discovery of the asylum.* Boston: Little, Brown.

Scull, A. (Ed.). (1981). *Madhouses, mad-doctors, and madmen: The social history of psychiatry in the Victorian era.* Philadelphia: University of Pennsylvania Press.

_____. (1989). *Social order/mental disorder: Anglo-American psychiatry in historical perspectives.* Berkeley: University of California Press.

_____. (1993). *The most solitary of afflictions: Madness and society in Britain 1700–1900.* New Haven: Yale University Press.

Shore, D. (Ed.). (1993). *Special report: Schizophrenia 1993.* Rockville, MD: U.S. Department of Health and Human Services.

Skultans, V. (1979). *English madness: Ideas on insanity 1580–1890.* London: Routledge and Kegan Paul.

Szasz, T. (1961). *The myth of mental illness.* New York: Hoeber-Parker.

_____. (1963). *Law, liberty, and psychiatry.* New York: Collier Books.

_____. (1965). *The ethics of psychoanalysis: The theory and method of autonomous psychotherapy.* New York: Basic Books.

_____. (1976). *Schizophrenia: The sacred symbol of psychiatry.* New York: Basic Books.

_____. (1977). *The manufacture of madness.* New York: Harper & Row.

_____. (1980). *Sex by prescription.* Garden City, NY: Doubleday Anchor.

_____. (1984). *The therapeutic state: Psychiatry in the mirror of current events.* Buffalo, NY: Prometheus Books.

_____. (1985). *Ceremonial chemistry: The ritual persecution of drugs, addicts and pushers.* Holmes Beach, FL: Learning Publications.

_____. (1987). *Insanity: The idea and its consequences.* New York: John Wiley & Sons.

_____. (1988). *The theology of medicine: The political-philosophical foundation of medical ethics.* Syracuse, NY: Syracuse University Press.

_____. (1992). *Our rights to drugs: The case for the free market.* New York: Praeger.

_____. (1994). *Cruel compassion: Psychiatric control of society's unwanted.* New York: John Wiley & Sons.

Tullock, G. (1965). *The politics of bureaucracy.* Washington, DC: Public Affairs Press.

_____. (1976). *The vote motive.* London: The Institute of Economic Affairs.

Wilson, J. Q. (1989) *Bureaucracy.* New York: Basic Books.

Lessons from International Social Work

Policies and Practices

Nazneen S. Mayadas and Doreen Elliott

There has long been an interest in international social work. This interest has increased apace. In this essay, Nazneen Mayadas and Doreen Elliott place current activities and future potentials in a developmental context. Nazneen S. Mayadas is a professor of social work at the University of Texas at Arlington. She served as chief of social services with the United Nations High Commissioner for Refugees. Recent coedited books include The World of Social Welfare: Social Welfare and Services in an International Context *(1990) with Doreen Elliott and T. D. Watts; and* Handbook on International Social Work Education *(1995) with Doreen Elliot;* Handbook on Social Work Theory and Practice *is in press. Doreen Elliott is professor of social work at the University of Texas at Arlington and currently serves as director of the doctoral program in this department. She teaches direct practice and social policy. Previously she served on the faculty of the School of Social Work at the University of Wales, Cardiff, U.K. Her published articles, chapters, and books cover the topics of comparative international approaches to policy and social work education. Recent coedited books include those cited above.*

International exchange has historically played an important part in the development of social work in the United States. This essay reviews the changing role of internationalism in the profession; it points toward a new model of greater and more equal exchange to enhance a worldwide common professional identity and empower the profession. Internationalism is presented as having three phases to date; the fourth phase is developed as a model for the new millennium and is discussed in terms of its application to social work practice, research, and education. These four phases are summarized in Figure 1.

Phases in Internationalism in Social Work

Phase One: The Early Pioneers (1880s–1940s)

For the 19th-century pioneers of the social work profession, the Atlantic Ocean was less of a barrier than it is today, despite our faster travel and electronic communication systems. The Settlement movement and the Charity Organization Society (COS) models were imported from England and established in many cities across the United States (Wenocur & Reisch,1989). There was much international exchange, as key figures in each movement visited each other's agencies and institutions of higher education.

Figure 1 summarizes this first phase, showing the direction of exchange as being predominantly from Europe to America;

Time Period	Predominant Direction of Exchange	Values	Model of Services
Phase I Early Pioneers 1880s–1940s	Europe to America	Paternalism Ethnocentricism Protectionism	Charity Philanthropy Social Control
Phase II Professional Imperialism 1940s–1970s	America to Rest of World Centrifugal	Paternalism Ethnocentricism Colonialism	Social Control Remedial Medical Crisis-Oriented
Phase III Reconceptualization and Indigenization 1970s–1990s	Within Regions Worldwide Centripetal	Regionalization Polarization Separation Localization	Developmental in Developing Countries Remedial in Western Industrial Nations
Phase IV International Social Development 21st century	International Networking	Globalization Transculturalism Multiculturalism Democracy, Diversity Social, Cultural, and Ethnic Interchange	Developmental in Rural and Urban Areas Worldwide

Figure 1 Phases in International Social Work Exchange

professional values were paternalism, ethnocentrism, and protectionism, and were based on service models of charity, philanthropy, and social control of the poor.

Phase Two: Professional Imperialism (1940s–1970s)

The next phase begins with developments in building theory and service delivery systems. It has been suggested that the great contribution of American social work is the establishment of the three interventive modes: casework, groupwork, and community practice (Midgley, 1981). America began to export these ideas to Europe, Britain, and throughout the English-speaking world. The vehicle of transmission was social work education. Schools of social work were established glob-

ally that based their curricula on the American model of professional education. (Watts, Elliott, & Mayadas, 1995).

The second phase is summarized in Figure 1 as that of "Professional Imperialism" (Midgley, 1981). Values remained predominantly ethnocentric and paternalistic. Indigenous cultures were set aside as a hindrance to progress. The remedial model of social welfare was exported with little adaptation for culture or economy. Practice interventions were individual-focused, despite the fact that social systems and values in the countries to which the model was exported were centered on the importance and predominance of the group. Curricula related to the needs of the West, and failed to include topics such as family planning or population studies.

Phase Three: The Reconceptualization and Indigenization of Social Work (1970s–1990s)
The lack of goodness of fit between the exported model and the needs of developing countries gave rise to questioning the relevance of the Western model and led to reform movements around the world during the 1970s. In South America, the *reconceptualization* of social work was inspired by dependency theory, liberation theology, social development, the ideas of Paulo Freire, and by radical political ideas arising out of the need to respond to poverty, underdevelopment, and exploitation (Resnick,1995). In the Middle East, India, and Africa, the *indigenization* of social work was under way within a different political and cultural context (Bose, 1992; Walton & El Nasr, 1988).

Figure 1 summarizes the predominant values of the third phase as regionalization, polarization, separation, and localization. Internationalism in social work lost popularity in America and federal funding decreased (Guzzetta, 1990; Kendall, 1995).

Phase Four: International Social Development in the 21st Century
In the last few decades, the developing world has recognized the shortcomings of the prevailing remedial and medical models of Western social work and has moved ahead to a forward-looking social development perspective. This paradigm shift has the potential to reestablish a basis for a new kind of international cooperation, which is no longer a one-way exporting of ideas, but is based on exchange and mutual benefit and the values set out in Figure 1 (Midgley & Toors,1992). It has considerable potential for bringing a fresh perspective on social problems in the West.

Social development is planned social change focused on promoting societal welfare in the context of economic development (Midgley, 1995). It is a deliberate, proactive approach that integrates social and economic development. The values of a social development approach are consistent with the values of social work—that is, social justice, cooperation, planning, prevention, participation and democracy, human dignity and worth, empowerment and institutional change (Falk, 1984; Midgley, 1995). It is consistent also with recent community development initiatives advocating a new, holistic ethnocultural paradigm (Glugoski, Reisch, & Rivera, 1994). Social development addresses the social, cultural, economic, and political levels of operation in social problems. It emphasizes a multicausal analysis of social issues and thus multilevel interventions, shifting away from the individual paradigm focus. It sees diversity as central because its context is multicultural. Although the social development paradigm is consistent in many ways with the macro tradition in social work, it does not exclude the clinical perspective. Rather, clinical practice within a social development framework is given a new dimension—for example, consideration of the economics of clinical practice conscientizes practitioners to the multibillion dollar health insurance industry behind the DSM (Elliott & Mayadas, 1996). They are more critical of the assessment process and pressure professional bodies to implement a generally recognized assessment process that adequately takes into account social, cultural, and economic factors. If we take a social development perspective, the economics cannot be ignored and we are forced to recognize the social costs of poverty. For example, the hidden social costs of the economic deprivation of the underprivileged are experienced by all, where the privileged resort to living behind "gated walls" to gain security, but at the cost of their freedom. Youth gangs and violence in the inner city and the alternate economy of the drug culture have far-reaching social costs; examples over and above the human costs to individuals and families are public health-care costs for the addict and for premature babies born to addicts; property damage; the deterioration of the inner city, and the cost to social freedom, in that the freedom of the individual to walk the streets of the inner city at night is severely constrained. Social work has so far supported the view that the abuse of drugs is an individual pathology rather than an economic problem in our society. Ignoring the economic factor ensures that an individual treatment approach predominates and the problem continues because the real causes remain unaddressed.

One much quoted and highly successful project illustrating the principles of social development is the Grameen Bank in Bangladesh. Mohammad Yunus, the bank's founder, named the three "C's" in banking—credit, collateral, and character—as the great divide between the have and have-nots in receiving loans. With the support of the World Bank, he established a policy of giving loans to individuals without a credit history or collateral securities, which has given economic independence to thousands of women, changing for the better the social and economic structure of villages in Bangladesh. In May 1995, Hillary Rodham Clinton met village women in Churankathi and Pancharabia near Jessore. Most of the women she met once lived by begging or working in rich homes as maids. Now they are self-reliant, generating their own income through loans that enabled them to buy cattle and poultry and run small businesses. The costs of the loans are low, and the repayment rate is above 98%. The average loan is $75. There are over 1 million female borrowers in 64,000 villages across Bangladesh. This example illustrates how social development projects can affect both the individual, where self-esteem and quality of life are improved, and also the environment, because the local economy benefits (Voice of America, 1995).

Another example of an integrated approach to social problems is the British "patch" system of service delivery. This involves the identification of a geographic area to which services are delivered through a team of social workers employed by a local government agency. Although the team has a mandatory requirement to respond to individual cases of child and adult protection, the goal is also to build an infrastructure of services, based on needs assessments and local participation. Services might be to enable the elderly to stay in their own homes as long as possible, or to provide day-care services for children at risk of abuse, and at the same time free women to participate in the labor market. This system marks the transition from remedial to developmental programs.

Yet another example may be seen in the work of the Office of the United Nation's High Commissioner for Refugees. In areas where local settlement of refugees was being carried out, services such as employment opportunities, schools, and clinics were provided for both local people and refugees. This meant that the stigma of dependence and "welfare" was reduced, the refugees were more accepted by the community because their presence brought development, and they were no longer viewed as liabilities.

An example from El Salvador illustrates how refugees returning to their repopulated village of Copapyo after the war were confronted with role changes. Women now faced more wage earning responsibilities. Social development principles were demonstrated in the organization of women's projects around small entrepreneurial groups. This facilitated the formalizing of the new roles, provided more equity and empowerment, and contributed to the sustainability of the economy (Juliá, 1992).

The Janashakthi Banking Society in Sri Lanka provides a credit and savings scheme for rural women. It is organized by urban women for rural women through the cooperation of a number of women's organizations to form a developmental program aimed to operationalize the values of human dignity, equality, and social justice through the provision of health care, education, and sanitation, as self-help projects, with the goal of achieving sustainable social development (Steven, 1994).

A social development approach has the potential to integrate the dichotomy between the micro and the macro and has application also for populations in the United States. It is commonly recognized that women who are abused by their spouses or partners remain in dysfunctional relationships because they are unable to support themselves and their children adequately. Single young women in the lower socioeconomic groups in Western societies often give up children for adoption for economic reasons. Appropriate adaptations of programs such as the Grameen Bank program relating to the social, economic, and cultural context in the West could have considerable impact in bringing about sustainable social change in Western industrialized nations. A combination of the British "patch" system of social services, and a social development approach might be applied to inner cities in the United States to address social and economic problems from a community perspective by improving the infrastructure of social services and offering incentives for employment opportunities. The UNHCR approach to community building and mobilizing the potential of people

temporarily dependent on others for help also has lessons for the welfare states of the developed Western world. The facilitation of sustainable social development as seen in the Janashakthi Bank project and in Copapayo, El Salvador, should inspire us in the developed world to more creative approaches to poverty in the inner city.

Social development represents both a theory and an ideology that is internationally recognized, and it offers a common ground to develop a stronger professional identity for the social work profession. Social work has a diffuse professional identity in this country and around the world. At present, social work means many different things, depending on the country in which it is practiced. A shared theoretical approach such as social development will help to foster recognition of common problems and increase reciprocity in addressing social problems and issues across the world. If we question the necessity of this, we question the value that international perspectives on social problems in the United States may bring, and imply that our system, which is based on a pathology model of assessment and a remedial, crisis-oriented approach to sevice delivery, is so superior that we do not need ideas from outside, thus illustrating the ethnocentrism of our present theory and practice. Many people in the United States are not clear what social workers do; those who do know may not recognize the role as it is practiced in France or Mexico. A shared theoretical perspective that brings common understandings, values, and interventive modes will strengthen its professional identity and improve the profession's ability to serve (Billups, 1994; Elliott, 1993; Mayadas & Elliott, 1995; Midgley, 1995). The ultimate goal of social development is world peace. Greater commonality among social workers around the world can contribute to efforts toward world peace.

This fourth phase is summarized in Figure 1, showing that a multidirectional exchange of ideas enriches practice through international networking. Democracy and diversity are key values, and the predominant concept of service shifts to a developmental model that incorporates economic, social, and cultural systems.

Implications of an International Perspective for Practice, Research, and Professional Education

Social Work Practice

What benefits does an international perspective bring to social work practice? What incentive is there for the profession to divest the dysfunctional myopia created by focusing only on regional or national issues, and on an interventive repertoire limited by the medical, remedial model? How much longer can the social service sector keep its head buried in the sands of isolationism, when the economic and business sectors have already established the "global economy" and "international marketplace" as household terms? The new internationalism of the 21st century will be different: We have argued that it will be a mutual exchange process, but for that to take place, we have to educate ourselves to be receptive.

It has been debated that the notion of the Third World as a distant, foreign place, obscures our ability to see the Third World under our noses, and that we should redefine the term as occurring in situations where poverty, deprivation, and exploitation exist (Midgley, 1990). This approach to social problems from an international perspective gives a new slant to social work practice. It puts back the "social" in social work, and opens the way for practice interventions where social justice

and empowerment play a central rather than a peripheral role.

Another lesson to be learned from international practice is the extension of community practice methods. The developing world is faced with problems such as high infant mortality, natural disasters, high incidence of poverty, lack of employment opportunities, and lack of access to adequate health care. The use of a large systems perspective emphasizes meeting human needs through institution building for economic self-sufficiency and through maximizing existing resources (Ginsberg, 1989). The level of expertise in these interventions is high in developing countries and has much to offer deprived rural and urban areas in the United States. Technology transfer of skills should be actively sought as a goal for social work in the 21st century (Kondrat, 1994).

The false dichotomy between the economic and the social is a function of the Western model of social work practice, where the socioeconomic linkages are not always recognized; for example, the DSM-IV is a system propped up by a multibillion dollar insurance industry; many women remain in abusive relationships for economic reasons based on the inequity of women's wages in the economic structure; social stratification is strongly biased according to racial origin; and racial conflict is heightened in adverse economic conditions— to illustrate but a few connections. Social work practice in the developing world integrates the economic and the social. Social services through the workplace are common in Mexico and India. Technology transfer could mean that by the 21st century, provision of child-care services in the workplace would be the social norm in industrialized nations.

An international perspective can assist our assessment techniques. Midgley (1992) illustrates the value of the international perspective with the example of AIDS. When the disease was first recognized, it was widely regarded as specific to the homosexual community. This perception resulted in discriminatory treatment of many people with AIDS, including myths that were widely propagated about the contagious nature of the disease. Recognition of its existence in the heterosexual population in other countries led to a greater recognition of its incidence beyond homosexual populations in the United States, and as knowledge of the disease improved, discrimination based on fear and myth lessened and national concern emerged.

Specific programs, well-established in other countries, may have much to offer the United States: Child-care policies in France ensure that the majority of preschool children enter government-funded day-care programs, and any stigma is eradicated by the universality of the provision. Sweden has a liberal and generous parental leave policy for childbirth and/or adoption; universal access to health care is provided free at the point of service delivery to everyone in Britain. Sound critical-thinking skills are needed in everyday practice to supplement formal research and evaluation in reviewing the strengths and weaknesses of such programs and their applicability for the United States.

Yet another benefit to be learned from international practice is the para-professional role in service delivery. Although social work assistants are currently used to some extent in the United States, training models from international examples could help to create more cost-effective and broadly based services.

An international perspective centralizes the role of culture. However, we do not have a mainstream social work practice model with cultural diversity as a central concept. Although content on human diversity is now required in social work curricula, it focuses on minority cultures in the United States. This parochial view is limiting and paternalistic and fails to normalize the concept of diversity. It further serves as an example of ethnocentricity and nationalism, which by their very essence, are antithetical to a world perspective. International social work promotes diversity as a normal human condition. It is time that Western models of practice allowed diversity to play a more central role in social work theories, policies, and applied research in order to facilitate international exchange of ideas, skills, and intervention strategies.

Social Work Research

If lessons learned from the global sharing of ideas are to be abstracted into universal theoretical principles and practice strategies with global application, then successful human service innovations must be analyzed and their transferability assessed. Gambrill (1994) points out the absence of specificity that currently marks social work research and suggests that it must be purpose-based and goal-driven.

Based on these criteria, international research networks must relate their investigations to identifying specific practice gains within countries and to how technology transfer can apply these interventions at a global level. For example, can the British "patch" system of social work service delivery be transported to inner cities in the United States? Similarly, can the structure of the Grameen Bank of Bangladesh be replicated to support social change in areas of economic deprivation in the United States?

The theoretical underpinning of international social work research in the 21st century should be based on the assumption that despite cultural and socioeconomic differences among nations, common social problems prevail that could benefit from a global exchange of strategies, ideas, and innovative practices.

In order to facilitate this knowledge transfer, channels for research findings need to be clearly structured and made more accessible. So far, Western journals publish very few articles from the developing countries (Midgley, 1994). Before technology transfer can occur, a structure for communication and dissemination is needed. A more proactive outreach is required to establish systematic access to learning about the management of social problems in the developing world and constructing models within which egalitarian international exchanges can occur. A by-product of these reciprocal exchanges could be studies related to perceptions of similar social problems by professionals from diverse cultures. Because human perceptions are culture-bound, studies such as these would sensitize professionals to a cross-section of world views and increase their tolerance and understanding of multicultural practice in international contexts. International research teams could provide a strong network for such global studies.

Internationalism can also be fostered through qualitative research. Because this methodology requires consideration of the cultural context, it is a helpful way of extrapolating alternative explanations for similar problems, as well as being consistent with social work values in recognizing human diversity.

Social Work Education

How should the social work curriculum reflect the global age? Requirements for accredited programs to include international content in the curriculum are noticeable only by their absence from the Evaluative Standards and the Curriculum Content Statements of the Council on Social Work Education (CSWE). This is indicative of the profession's regionalization and localization in phase three (Figure 1). The transition to phase four is evident in the proliferation of recent literature in the field of inter-

national comparative social policy, offering rich resources for extending the vision of the profession, but the policy statement requires no comparative international content. Although an international comparative perspective is now often reflected in the teaching of social policy, it is not similarly reflected in the teaching of human behavior or direct practice. Diversity teaching relates almost entirely to knowledge of different populations in the United States and not to how other countries deal with minority issues. Technology transfer in practice is not addressed. However, the importance of the international perspective is recognized through the work of the CSWE International Commission, and priority is given to influencing curriculum evaluative standards for accreditation. There is useful debate on integrating the international perspective in the social work literature, which provides evidence that many programs do include comparative studies of some kind (Estes, 1992; Garland & Escobar, 1988; Healy, 1988, 1992; Ramanathan & Kondrat, 1994). The profession is well-placed to move into phase four, but institutional change such as inclusion in the curriculum statement of CSWE is required to establish a global perspective for the profession in the 21st century.

Curriculum content should reflect the changing perspective of the profession. Across the world, the link between the social and the economic is evident, but social work has remained parochial. Social work programs would benefit from including a study of economics and the role they play in social problems, resulting in new approaches to clinical assessment. Social issues such as immigration policies and practices take on a different perspective when viewed within an international social development framework (Mayadas & Lasan, 1984). More consideration of cultural issues is needed in clinical assessment. Glugoski, Reisch, and Rivera (1994) propose three key areas for curriculum development for a diversity-and-development-centered curriculum: first, the reconceptualization of the etiology of social problems to include politics, ideology, and economics; second, "the development of a revised skill repertoire" for the empowerment of clients; and third, new teaching approaches to respond to an increasingly multicultural population. The adaptation of such proposals by CSWE could change curricula significantly. But first it seems, there is much work to be done in developing the theoretical base and a modified service delivery system to allow for the broader acceptance of a social development agenda in an international context.

Individual commitment can make a difference and help to establish this global vision. International organizations such as the International Association of Schools of Social Work (IASSW), the International Federation of social workers (IFSW), and the Inter-University Consortium for Social Development (IUCISD) are mainly member-supported. Social work educators can encourage student participation and membership, and encourage institutional memberships of their own schools. At present, both organizational and individual memberships of these organizations are biased in favor of the West. Currency exchange rates are to some extent responsible, but this should not preclude a proactive membership drive from those bodies. Greater collaboration and interchange with indigenous organizations would also serve to improve the global perspective.

Educational exchanges have traditionally been part of academia. Institutions such as the Fulbright Foundation have done much to develop internationalism. However, the social work profession needs a strong political lobby to increase its share of funding resources; to

date, engineering, science, and medicine take precedence over social issues.

The new technology, including electronic communication via the Internet, will become increasingly important as the World Wide Web grows. Distance education programs using the new technology will offer new opportunities and should be used creatively to foster the international perspective. Along with reciprocal academic credit for students taking overseas courses, distance education opens up new worlds of communication.

Conclusion

Here are five thoughts in conclusion. The international perspective:

- Challenges the false dichotomy between the social and the economic
- Places diversity and social justice as central to practice
- Requires an ideology that includes openness and sound critical thinking to evaluate applications
- Transcends and challenges regional and national allegiances
- Establishes social work as a human rights profession

REFERENCES

Billups, J. O. (1994). The social development model as an organizing framework for social work practice. In R. G. Meinert, J. T. Pardeck, & W. P. Sullivan (Eds.), *Issues in social work: A critical analysis*. Westport, CT: Auburn House.

Bose, A. B. (1992). Social work in India: Developmental roles for a helping profession. In M. C. Hokenstad, S. K. Khinduka, & J. Midgley (Eds.), *Profiles in international social work*. Washington, DC: NASW.

Elliott, D. (1993). Social work and social development: Toward an integrative model for social work practice. *International Social Work, 36*, 21–36.

Elliott, D., & Mayadas, N. S. (1996). Social development and clinical practice in social work. *Journal of Applied Social Sciences, 21*(1), 32–39.

Estes, R. (1992). *Internationalizing social work education: A guide to resources for a new century.* Philadelphia: University of Pennsylvania Press.

Falk, D. (1984). The social development paradigm. *Social Development Issues, 8*(4), 4I–14.

Gambrill, E. (1994). What's in a name? Task-centered, empirical and behavioral practice. *Social Service Review*, 578–599.

Garland, D. R., & Escobar, D. (1988). Education for cross-cultural social work practice. *Journal of Education for Social Work, 24*(3), 229–241.

Ginsberg, L. (1989). What the United States can learn about social welfare from Third World nations. In B. Mohan (Ed.), *Glimpses of international and comparative social welfare* (pp. 161–168). Belconnen, Australia: Informational Fellowship for Social and Economic Development, Inc. (IFSED).

Glugoski, G., Reisch, M., & Rivera, F. (1994). A wholistic ethno-cultural paradigm: A new model for community organization teaching and practice. *Journal of Community Practice. 1*(1), 81–98.

Guzzetta, C. (1990). Interaction. In K. A. Kendall (Ed.), *The international in American education.* Proceedings of an International Symposium, Hunter College, School of Social Work, New York.

Healy, L. (1988). Curriculum building in international social work: Toward preparing professionals for the Global Age. *Journal of Social Work Education, 24*(3), 221–228.

Healy, L. (1992). *Introducing international development content in social work curriculum.* Alexandria, VA: CSWE.

Juliá, M. (1992). The changing status of women: social development in a repopulated village. *International Social Work 37*(1), 61–73.

Kendall, K. (1995). Foreword. In D. Elliott, T. Watts, & N. S. Mayadas, (Eds.), *International handbook on social work education.* Westport, CT: Greenwood.

Kondrat, M. E. (1994). Culture and power in technology transfer: Perspectives from a critical sociology of knowledge. *Social Development Issues, 16*(3), 45–67.

Mayadas, N. S., & Elliott, D. (1995). Developing professional identity through social group work: A social development systems (SDS) model for education. In M. D. Feit, J. H. Ramey, J. S. Wodarski, & A. R. Mann (Eds.), *Capturing the power of diversity.* New York: Haworth.

Mayadas, N. S., & Lasan, D. B. (1984). Integrating refugees into alien cultures. In C. Guzzetta, A. J. Katz, & R. A. English (Eds.), *Education for social work practice: Selected international models.* New York: IASSW/CSWE.

Midgley, J. (1981). *Professional imperialism: Social work in the Third World.* London: Heinemann.

Midgley, J. (1990). International social work: Learning from the Third World. *Social Work, 35*(3), 295–301.

Midgley, J. (1992). The challenge of international social work. In M. C. Hockenstadt, S. K. Khinduka, & J. Midgley (Eds.), *Profiles in international social work.* Washington, DC; National Association of Social Workers.

Midgley, J. (1994). The challenge of social development: Their Third World and ours. 1993 Daniel S. Sanders Peace and Social Justice Lecture. *Social Development Issues, 16*(2).

Midgley, J. (1995). *Social development: The developmental perspective in social welfare.* Thousand Oaks, CA: Sage.

Midgley, J., & Toors, M. (1992). Is international social work a one-way transfer of ideas and practice methods from the United States to other countries? In E. Gambrill & R. Pruger (Eds.), *Controversial issues in social work*. Boston: Allyn & Bacon.

Ramanathan, C. S., & Kondrat, M. E. (1994). Conceptualizing and implementing a social work overseas study program in developing nations: Politics, realities and strategies. *Social Development Issues, 16*(2), 69–85.

Resnick, R. S. (1995). South America. In T. D. Watts, D. Elliott, & N. S. Mayadas (Eds.), *Handbook of social work education*. Westport, CT: Greenwood.

Steven, L. D. (1994). Credit as a women's issue in social development: The Janashakthi Banking Society in Sri Lanka. *Social Development Issues. 16*(1), 107–113.

Voice of America. (1995). Correspondent report #2-176500, 4/3/95.

Walton, R., & El Nasr, A. (1988). Indigenization and authentization in terms of social work in Egypt. *International Social Work, 31*(2), 135–144.

Watts, T., Elliott, D., & Mayadas, N. S. (Eds.). (1995). *International handbook on social work education*. Westport, CT: Greenwood.

Wenocur, S., & Reisch, M. (1989). *From charity to enterprise: The development of American social work in a market economy*. Chicago: University of Illinois Press.

B. Practice Issues

Each of the ten essays in this section addresses a particular area of concern for social workers. All have policy implications, just as the essays in Section A of Part II have practice implications. We have placed the essay on prevention at the very beginning to highlight its important but often neglected role. As Steven Schinke points out, prevention is a concept with which few social workers disagree. In the long term, prevention can be less costly not only in terms of avoiding distress to individuals but in monetary terms as well. However, it is often difficult to convince legislators and other funding sources of these potential long-term benefits. Steven Schinke describes some of the preventive research endeavors within social work, as well as challenges to preventive planning, including restrictions on funding and difficulties in identifying possible relationships between current programs and future effects. He highlights the importance of empirical investigation of the effectiveness of preventive efforts and of a clear definition of goals to allow for careful evaluation of outcomes. He calls on social work educators to take on part of the burden for improving the prospects for prevention by highlighting prevention opportunities as a regular part of the social work curriculum.

In their essay, "Prospects for Community Organization," Stanley Wenocur and Steven Soifer discuss the development of community organizing efforts. They argue that many social movements that started in the 1960s never really ended. They note that community organizers have become more sophisticated about fund-raising and that community organization efforts have shifted away from challenging the establishment to a more collaborative strategy involving partnerships between community groups, government officials, and corporate leaders. They point out that the groups left behind in the inner cities often form their own indigenous organizations based on communities of interest. They highlight the ineffectiveness of local governments to resolve community problems due to limited resources and urge citizens to participate in pursuing needed changes. However, they believe that without the strong hand of government, citizens have little hope of controlling the policies of private corporations that influence everyday life in cities. Their ending message is positive, calling for a conference bringing together leadership from many interested parties at diverse levels, further experimentation with new community models, and collection of a database of organizing efforts.

Jane Isaacs Lowe describes a social-health model that, she argues, should serve as the paradigm for social work and health care. She recommends a community-based approach in which health problems are placed in their environmental context and health promotion and prevention is emphasized. She calls on social workers to develop partnerships with managed care organizations to create and evaluate programs implementing the model. She argues that this model will encourage an increased range of social work roles, including opportunities for partnerships with community and health-care organizations and an extension of primary care responsibilities (e.g., quality assurance, marketing, public health). She describes implications of this model for social work education, including breaking down artificial divisions in the curriculum (e.g., between health and family specializations and micro and macro practice).

In her essay, "Opportunities for Social Workers in the Law? The Jury Is Out," Mary Ann Mason describes a variety of ways in which social workers could become more active in the legal system. Areas she discusses include child custody, child abuse and neglect, juvenile and adult offender programs, mental illness and incompetence, and advocacy for immigrants. She calls on social work educators to include content related to the law that bears on social work practice. This essay, as well as the one by Ira Schwartz in Section A of Part II, calls on social workers to become more active in the criminal justice system.

In "Occupational Social Work Practice," Beth Lewis presents an overview of the expansion of occupational social work and describes areas commonly addressed by occupational social workers. She discusses the implications of changes in demographics (e.g., age, ethnicity, and gender) for occupational social work. She also discusses the relationship between work and family life, work and structural organization, and changes in rates of unionization. She calls on social work educators to pay more attention to the influence of social policies on the world of work and to focus more on helping clients to get jobs. She believes that occupational social work will continue to expand in the next century.

In her essay, "Social Work Practice with Marginalized Populations," Nancy Cook Von Bretzel highlights the strains and tribulations of frontline social work staff as they confront clients struggling with a system that has insufficient resources. She asks, "What is the role of social workers when there are no resources available?" Dysfunctional reactions she describes include rationalizing, becoming numb, blaming the victim, and avoiding client contact. She suggests guidelines for compassionate relationships with clients in impossible conditions. Practical and ethical problems and issues that arise in agencies in which resources are scarce are also addressed by other authors in this book (see, for example, the Burton Gummer essay in Section A of Part III).

In "Multicultural Community Organizing," Lorraine Gutiérrez suggests multicultural community organizing as an alternative vision for practice in the 21st century. This type of organizing refers to a method of practice that forwards the development of communities of color by creating vehicles for interaction and change. As in many essays in this book, there is a call for increased attention to community-level programs, as well as a concern with those who are disadvantaged. She describes the importance of developing ethnic-sensitive and culturally competent approaches to social service organizations and programs. She defines an ethnic-sensitive approach as an adequate response to the disenfranchisement and inequality experienced by communities of color. Gutiérrez highlights the importance of focusing on communities and not on individuals in recognizing discrimination and oppression and recommends that social work education include the development of specific skills to address power deficits and develop more powerful resources.

Over the last few years there has been a renaissance of interest in establishing links between communities and schools. Stephanie Hochman discusses what she views as missing links in her essay, "School–Community Collaboratives: The Missing Links." She argues for the importance of school–community collaborations, gives examples, and highlights missing links. She, as well as many other authors in this book, emphasizes the importance of helping clients to influence social, economic, and political factors that contribute to the problems that clients confront. Hochman emphasizes that lack of involvement of families, community leaders, and front-line personnel is one way that school–community collaboration fails. She highlights the importance of involving school personnel in programs and the need for schools to be willing to change their usual ways of educating students to make room for collaborative efforts. She calls for a broad definition of community, including all those organizations and individuals that influence problems focused on. Hochman highlights the lack of resources available for addressing social and personal problems and the tendency to blame the poor for the problems. She calls on social workers to take a major role in educating funders about the importance of supporting school- and community-based efforts that tackle fundamental problems rather than funding piecemeal service programs.

Ram Cnaan provides descriptive data concerning the involvement of religious organizations in the provision of services and calls on social workers to take a more active role in working collaboratively with religious organizations. He discusses both the historical and philosophical role of religious congregations and denominations in social welfare and describes the results of a recent survey he conducted concerning services offered by religious organizations. He highlights the commitment of religiously based organizations to enhancing the quality of life for residents in their communities and calls on social workers to conduct research related to religiously based services.

In "Social Workers as Advocates for Elders," Iris Carlton-LaNey notes the growing population of the elderly, provides a brief historical overview of related services, and argues for an advocacy stance in providing services. She offers an overview of advocacy approaches for elderly clients and suggests some future roles in relation to families, work, and leisure.

All the essays in this section have implications for social work education. Many of these will decrease fragmentation of social work curriculums (e.g., between micro and macro practice and health and family areas of specialization). They all also have implications for research. For example, Steven Schinke's essay emphasizing preventive efforts calls for research investigating the effectiveness of different policies and programs in preventing personal and social problems.

Recommendations made have different degrees of feasibility. For example, to what degree can social workers create jobs for the unemployed? Many essays in this volume encourage a community approach. How much power is it possible for community members to exercise?

In her classic book *The Death and Life of Great American Cities* (1963), Jane Jacobs argues that only if neighborhoods have connections with wider districts, and only if these wider districts have connections with city, state, and perhaps federal agencies that influence what happens in neighborhoods, can residents influence conditions in their locales. Only if we take a candid look at what is possible at different levels of organization and action are we likely to identify ways of organizing services across different levels that may be successful in making desired changes and preventing unwanted ones at the neighborhood level.

Prospects for Prevention

Steven P. Schinke

This essay provides an overview of prevention in social work. Although prevention is emphasized by many, little systematic attention has been devoted to the subject. Steven Schinke describes some of the preventive efforts in social work and suggests future directions. Steven P. Schinke is a professor in the School of Social Work at Columbia University. He has focused his research on developing and testing interventions to prevent social, behavioral, and health problems among children and adolescents. His publications include Substance Abuse in Children and Adolescents: Intervention and Evaluation *(Thousand Oaks, CA: Sage, 1991).*

Prospects for Prevention

Prevention is a concept with which few social workers disagree. To prevent problems, most agree, is better than treating the consequences of those problems after they happen. Indeed, considerable evidence from social work and other fields supports the practical wisdom that an ounce of prevention is not only cheaper but is also more humane and predictably effective than many pounds of treatment and rehabilitation (Gilbert, 1982; Weissman, 1991). Why prevention works is worth considering. Equally interesting is the role of prevention in the panoply of social work practice. Perhaps even more intriguing is how social workers can infuse preventive services into their practice, now and in the future. This essay will address these and other topics regarding prospects for prevention as social work moves into the next century.

Prevention in Social Work

Preventive services in social work are usually construed as those programs, policies, and clinical efforts aimed at helping clients avoid future problems. Thus, child management training for new parents is preventive if it keeps the children of those parents from abuse and neglect (Morgan, Nu'Man-Sheppard, & Allin, 1990). Job skills training for teenage mothers is preventive if it allows young parents to avoid welfare dependence (Gilchrist & Schinke, 1985). Preventive services are also illustrated by programs that target at-risk youth and seek to equip those young people with the wherewithal to reach their full potential and not fall prey to problems of delinquency, school failure, and drug abuse (Epstein, Botvin, Diaz, & Schinke, 1995; Roosa, Gensheimer, Ayers, & Short, 1990; Work, Cowen, Parker, & Wyman, 1990).

Although these and other instances of prevention in social work imply direct programs and clinical services, prevention is also potently delivered through social policies that promote healthy functioning and facilitate future problem avoidance. For example, policies that encourage responsible sexual behavior, including condom distribution and use, among high school students will exert a preventive influence if they result in a lower incidence of sexually transmitted diseases and unplanned pregnancy (Gilchrist & Schinke, 1983). Policies that create healthy workplaces, homes, and schools are preventive when the people who reside in those settings realize improved health and social functioning as a result of their environmental improvements.

Admittedly, none of the aforementioned preventive efforts are solely in the ken of professional social workers. Prevention can be and is done effectively by members of other social and mental health helping professions and by most health-care workers. But social workers have a peculiar role in the planning, execution, and study of prevention programs not enjoyed by professionals from other fields. More than other human services professionals, social workers are involved in the range of program design, implementation, and evaluation of preventive efforts aimed at client populations. Whereas other professionals in the behavioral and social sciences may be occupied primarily with one of these stages of preventive intervention, social workers routinely are confronted with all three stages.

The peculiar role of social workers in prevention programming is illustrated by an example from the author's work in a child development center. All members of the interdisciplinary teams in the center—composed of social workers, nurses, pediatricians, neurologists, psychologists, educators, occupational and physical therapists, nutritionists, and endocrinologists—were charged with assessment tasks. Subsets of fewer of these professionals then developed treatment plans, which usually included prevention programs to help at-risk youths and their families avoid serious problems later. Fewer still professionals implemented the programs. When the prevention programs required evaluation, new professionals were called in to design questionnaires, collect data, and analyze the results. But social work staff were engaged at every step of the prevention programming process.

At the child development center, social work professionals functioned as diagnosticians, service providers, and evaluators of prevention programs. At the assessment stage, the social workers identified variables associated with future problems that were thus suitable for preventive intervention. Once they constructed the intervention protocols, the social workers delivered the prevention programs to children and, as necessary, to their parents and significant others. Evaluation procedures to empirically determine the efficacy of the prevention program were also designed and executed by social workers at the child development center. At this stage of the prevention process, the social workers often employed single-case methodologies, whereby clients served as their own controls for outcome evaluations.

As the foregoing illustration shows, social workers are ideally positioned to develop responsive prevention programs that address the everyday realities of clients' lives. Social workers are also well placed to determine if extant prevention services are meeting their originally stated objectives and if those programs need revision or even abandonment. Mindful of social work's special role in human services prevention, the current status and future directions of preventive services are worth discussing. A review of the challenges to prevention programming faced by social workers sets the stage for that discussion.

Challenges to Prevention Programming

Regrettably, the practice wisdom of prevention in social work has not translated into widespread funding for and adoption of preventive intervention programs. Funds for prevention programs are in short supply, in part because efforts to help people avoid problems are expensive relative to programs aimed at treating problems after they start or aimed at rehabilitating victims of problems once they become serious or have wrought their consequences. Implementation of prevention programs is difficult because of the difficulty of identifying appropriate target populations without labeling or singling out particular individuals for services, because of the intricacies of designing effective intervention programs, and because of challenges to determining whether prevention programs work. Among these challenges are obstacles to tracking and following up recipients of prevention programs over the long term to measure beneficial effects that may not be known for many years.

Social workers may take cold comfort in not being the only helping professionals that neglect prevention in favor of treatment and rehabilitation. Across the behavioral and social sciences and in medicine as well, prevention is not given the priority it warrants if professionals are to earnestly address problems before their serious effects emerge. The only field in which prevention has taken dominance over treatment is public health (Gordon, 1983; Schinke, Bebel, Orlandi, & Botvin, 1988; Schinke & Gilchrist, 1985). An explanation for public health's adoption of a commitment to prevention is likely found in the impressive gains seen over the decades in efforts to combat communicable illnesses, environmental hazards, and socially transmitted diseases. Even so, current failures in the public health sector to prevent the spread of HIV infection attest to the continued lack of ease in promoting prevention as a primary means of combating avoidable sources of morbidity and mortality.

Reconciling the potential of prevention with the realities of its current lack of widespread support and adoption in social work requires grappling with issues at the core of prevention services. Those issues include: a clear understanding and articulation of the assumptions of preventive services in social work; a rationale for planning and delivering efficacious and cost-effective preventive services; and a means through which responsive and potent interventions can be designed for the problems and populations targeted by prevention programs.

Questioning the assumptions behind preventive services in social work reveals an often implicit belief that problems of the human condition are avoidable. If only people had the necessary resources, skills, and opportunities—the argument goes—they would choose to avoid problems rather than to experience the untoward consequences of those problems. Yet, is that argument grounded in fact? Nowhere in the empirical literature are data to substantiate basic human instincts for preventing our problems before they start.

Indeed, much of our literature documents repeated instances of clients encountering again and again the same problem situations through dysfunctional patterns of behavior. Illustrative are such problems as substance abuse, family violence, unemployment, and school failure. Despite social workers' best efforts to make clients aware of problem behavior patterns, many individuals appear unable to break a maladaptive cycle. The evidence favoring a natural inclination toward a preventive lifestyle, therefore, is scant.

Equally scarce are data supporting the existence of the root causes of problems to which preventive interventions could be salubriously applied. Albeit such conditions as poverty, child abuse, teenage pregnancy, and family breakdown contribute to social and mental health functioning, these alleged causes of problems are elusive to specify. Even when specified, root causes of social and behavioral problems rarely lend themselves to facile solutions. Prevention as a solution to problems of human functioning is more easily embraced in the abstract than in the concrete.

Without a clearly defined target for preventive interventions, developing a rationale to plan and deliver effective prevention services is difficult. An instance of a poorly defined target that does not point toward successful prevention efforts is juvenile delinquency. Certainly an important social problem and one for which preventive services are suitable, juvenile delinquency is too broad a constellation of problem behaviors to foster focused intervention efforts (Feldman, Caplinger, & Wodarski, 1983). More responsive to prevention perhaps would be a subcomponent of juvenile delinquency, such as early childhood aggression or shyness (Kellam, Rebok, & Ialongo, 1994; Walker, Downey, & Nightingale, 1989). Alternatively, a preventive intervention aimed at juvenile delinquency could isolate family functioning variables toward improving youth's interpersonal and social behavior (Pearson, Ialongo, & Hunter, 1994). But targeting juvenile delinquency per se for a prevention program is futile and a recipe for failure.

As illustrated in the foregoing discussion of juvenile delinquency, social workers confront the inadequacy of their knowledge base about the origin of human problems when they craft interventions for prevention programs. That crafting usually reflects theory, data, or clinical wisdom about the potentially beneficial effects of providing clients with certain intervention content toward helping them avoid the target problems. Necessarily, interventions developed on the basis of such prior knowledge address proximate variables that are associated with the target prevention outcome. For example, a child abuse prevention program may focus on parenting and child management skills and not directly on adult violence against children (Schinke, Schilling, Barth, Gilchrist, & Maxwell, 1986). Prevention programs thus draw on current thinking among social workers and others regarding the loci of target problems through which interventions may be delivered.

That delivery of program content represents a final issue at the core of effective social work prevention services. Program delivery, in the present context, includes the means through which prevention programs reach target clients. Clearly, the delivery means will mirror the social environment surrounding clients for whom the program was designed. As with many aspects of prevention services, however, the concepts of program delivery appear deceptively easy. Operationally, program delivery is among the greatest challenges facing social workers involved in prevention services.

To deliver prevention services to the at-risk population, professionals must first identify, reach, and engage those clients. Identifying clients presumes that program planners know with some precision the risk characteristics of the target group. That precision is not only unavailable to most workers and agencies, but also it may mean singling out a particular group as in need of social work services. Reaching clients with prevention programs also poses difficulties. Consider, for example, a social work agency providing prevention services to youth at risk for sexually transmitted diseases. Where does that agency serve the target youth? How does it reach them with prevention services? What provisions can the agency take to avoid labeling target youth as sexually promiscuous or otherwise in need of its services? Last, prevention programs must engage clients in a program that the clients may not deem as necessary to their everyday functioning. Because programs that truly aim to help people avoid problems altogether will reach individuals who are not yet affected with the target problem, the credibility of the prevention service is at stake. Services that are not perceived by clients as valuable or even necessary are unlikely to be warmly greeted, embraced, and used.

Improving the Prospects

Mindful of the many challenges that face the development of meaningful prevention programs and the myriad obstacles to providing at-risk clients with those programs, social workers will wisely seek new directions for increasing the scope and impact of prevention services. One such direction is to locate opportunities for prevention that show promise as cost-effective ways of reducing social problems. Together with budgetary limitations, increasing demands for social programs that demonstrate their worth augur for prevention services that yield more than they consume.

For example, prevention programs that reduce the services clients use, increase clients' productivity, or improve the public welfare in a measurable economic manner will receive a warm reception from policymakers and funders. Illustrative are recent efforts by the state of Wisconsin to reduce rates of welfare dependency through prevention programs aimed at increasing school completion among teenage mothers, at improving the employment prospects of persons on public assistance, and at enhancing the job training of chronically unemployed and underemployed persons. Such prevention initiatives are embraced not only by policymakers who seek to reduce public spending on welfare services, but also by voters who wish to lower their tax burden for entitlements.

New prevention programs must also prove themselves effective scientifically. Prevention services in applied social work settings are not difficult to evaluate (Schinke, Gilchrist, Lodish, & Bobo, 1983). Programs that can withstand the scrutiny of scientific research will have an enhanced likelihood of support, whether through public or private venues. Similarly, social work prevention services must respond favorably to political influences and to community requirements for acceptance if they are to enjoy widespread popularity. Cognizant further of the political and funding realities of the 1990s, social workers will increase the likelihood that effective prevention programs will be implemented when these programs replace existing services. New prevention programs that supplement extant intervention or treatment efforts may not fare well in today's social services arena.

Instead, fresh approaches to prevention are needed that supplant current intervention, treatment, and rehabilitation programs in the social services. Those approaches will begin with the assumption that social and behavioral problems are preventable, just as are health problems. Social workers can take the forefront not only in making such theory-based and research-supported assumptions, but also in prospectively demonstrating the superiority of prevention relative to treatment as a mode for dealing with human problems. In defending such an approach, we can consider the problem of school failure. Once the problem is evident, too much time and momentum may have been lost to reverse the damage of early school failure. Youths may never compensate for years or even semesters of foregone educational progress. But a targeted prevention program to help young people avoid school failure before the problem is evident to anyone would pay off handsomely in gained progress for students and in increased productivity for society.

Methodological improvements are also overdue if prevention is to move into the mainstream of social work practice. In particular, more precise theories are needed to guide preventive intervention efforts. Among the more promising such theories are those that recognize social, behavioral, and environmental forces that guide human interactions (Prochaska, DiClemente, & Norcross, 1992). New technologies are also required to deliver preventive intervention services. These technologies may profitably include videotape, software, and interactive networking modes to reach clients in schools, agency sites, and workplaces (Moncher et al., 1989; Schinke & Orlandi, 1990; Schinke, Orlandi, Schilling, & Parms, 1992). Innovations can also improve the repertoire of evaluation tools social workers have to determine the efficacy of prevention programs. Without new and practical ways of measuring the impact of their preventive services, social workers cannot compete with those professions that are keeping pace with the latest research knowledge.

Educators, too, carry a burden for improving the prospects for prevention in social work. Across our degree programs, schools of social work have sorely neglected the inclusion of responsive courses on prevention. Curiously, this neglect occurs in the context of many and rich field placement opportunities for social work students, particularly at the M.S.W. level. Increasingly, field placements in prevention expose students to the realities of program development, implementation, and evaluation. Yet, educators are not keeping up with this movement in the field. More and better courses, independent tutorials, and research projects on prevention topics must be introduced into schools of social work. Going beyond training for social work practice, those curriculum additions should also help doctoral-level students gain skills for prevention program design and research.

Educational initiatives for prevention training at all levels of professional social work practice can make better use of applied field experiences to understand and acquire the requisite program planning, implementation, and evaluation skills. In collaboration with field placement instructors, for example, academic classroom teachers could mount joint projects to engage social work students in actual prevention programs. Those programs could involve students in the many tasks and roles of preventive social work, depending on the student's level of training. For example, whereas M.S.W. students could implement a program, Ph.D. students could evaluate it. Students at all levels could participate in prevention program design.

Finally, social work practitioners will wisely gain needed capacity for prevention services. Today's human services industry is faced with competition from within, as social workers, psychologists, educators, and health-care workers vie for the chance to deliver the same services to the same clients. Outside pressure from managed-care providers, government bodies, and regulatory agencies are urging those professionals to deliver their services to more people and at lower costs. Unless social work practitioners keep abreast of the potential efficacies and cost efficiencies of prevention programming, they find themselves in an invidious competitive environment with their human services colleagues.

Admittedly, determining the efficacy of a prevention program—or of any social work service, for that matter—is difficult. Considerable investment must be made in specifying the nature of the service and in locating suitable evaluation protocols before empirical data can be available on social work prevention services. Even after that investment is made, outcome results from social work program evaluations are notoriously flawed by the real-world constraints of measuring variable levels of services with transient and refractory client populations. At best, efficacy evaluations can only suggest the impact of prevention services on a particular group and within a constrained set of circumstances.

For social workers who can rise to meet the challenges of planning, delivering, and evaluating prevention services in a thoughtful, dispassionate manner, the future is bright. For those social workers who believe that simply by implementing prevention programs that are well intentioned, they are carrying out their mandates and serving their clients, a promising future in prevention is less certain. Social work professionals can and must take on the several and difficult issues facing the design and execution of relevant, sensitive, and effective prevention programs. They will take on those issues not by hastily conceived prevention efforts that address the immediate concerns of a client population, agency program, or referent funding agency. Rather, social workers will accept and meet the challenges of prevention programming by thoughtful, carefully laid, and impeccably executed efforts that attempt to reconcile the needs of all involved parties. The future of our profession's credibility in the prevention field and of the clients and constituencies we serve with prevention programs depends, in part, on the outcomes of those efforts.

REFERENCES

Epstein, J. A., Botvin, G. J., Diaz, T., & Schinke, S. P. (1995). The role of social factors and individual characteristics in promoting alcohol use among inner city minority youths. *Journal of Studies on Alcohol, 56*, 39–46.

Feldman, R. A., Caplinger, T. E., & Wodarski, J. S. (1983). *The St. Louis conundrum: The effective treatment of antisocial youths.* Englewood Cliffs, NJ: Prentice-Hall.

Gilbert, N. (1982). Policy issues in primary prevention. *Social Work*, 293–297.

Gilchrist, L. D., & Schinke, S. P. (1983). Teenage pregnancy and public policy. *Social Service Review, 57*, 307–322.

Gilchrist, L. D., & Schinke, S. P. (Eds.). (1985). *Preventing social and health problems through life skills training.* Seattle: University of Washington Press.

Gordon, R. S., Jr. (1983). An operational classification of disease prevention. *Public Health Reports, 98*, 107–109.

Kellam, S. G., Rebok, G. W., & Ialongo, N. S. (1994). The course and malleability of aggressive behavior from early first grade into middle school: Results of a developmental epidemiologically-based prevention trial. *Journal of Child Psychology and Psychiatry and Allied Disciplines, 35*, 259–281.

Moncher, M. S., Parms, C. A., Orlandi, M. A., Schinke, S. P., Miller, S. O., Palleja, J., & Schinke, M. B. (1989). Microcomputer-based approaches for preventing drug and alcohol abuse among adolescents from ethnic-racial minority backgrounds. *Computers in Human Behavior, 5*, 79–93.

Morgan, J. R., Nu'Man-Sheppard, J., & Allin, D. W. (1990). Prevention through parent training: Three preventive parent education programs. *Journal of Primary Prevention, 10*, 321–332.

Pearson, J. L., Ialongo, N. S., & Hunter, A. G. (1994). Family structure and aggressive behavior in a population of urban elementary school children. *Journal of the American Academy of Child and Adolescent Psychiatry, 33*(4), 540–548.

Prochaska, J. O., DiClemente, C. C., & Norcross, J. C. (1992). In search of how people change: Applications to the addictive behaviors. *American Psychologist, 47*, 1102–1114.

Roosa, M. W., Gensheimer, L. K., Ayers, T. S., & Short, J. L. (1990). Development of a school-based prevention program for children in alcoholic families. *Journal of Primary Prevention, 11*, 119–141.

Schinke, S. P., Bebel, M. Y., Orlandi, M. A., & Botvin, G. J. (1988). Prevention strategies for vulnerable pupils. *Urban Education, 22*, 510–519.

Schinke, S. P., & Gilchrist, L. D. (1985). Preventing substance abuse with children and adolescents. *Journal of Consulting and Clinical Psychology, 53*, 596–602.

Schinke, S. P., Gilchrist, L. D., Lodish, D., & Bobo, J. K. (1983). Strategies for prevention research in service environments. *Evaluation Review, 7*, 126–136.

Schinke, S. P., & Orlandi, M. A. (1990). Skills-based, interactive computer interventions to prevent HIV infection among African-American and Hispanic adolescents. *Computers in Human Behavior, 6*, 235–246.

Schinke, S. P., Orlandi, M. A., Schilling, R. F., & Parms, C. A. (1992). Feasibility of interactive videodisc technology to teach minority youth about preventing HIV infection. *Public Health Reports, 107*, 323–330.

Schinke, S. P., Schilling, R. F., Barth, R. P., Gilchrist, L. D., & Maxwell, J. S. (1986). Stress-management intervention to prevent family violence. *Journal of Family Violence, 1*, 13–26.

Walker, E., Downey, G., & Nightingale, N. (1989). The nonorthogonal nature of risk factors: Implications for research on the causes of maladjustment. *Journal of Primary Prevention, 9*, 143–163.

Weissman, G. (1991). Prevention for women at risk: Experience from a national demonstration research program. *Journal of Primary Prevention, 12*, 35–48.

Work, W. C., Cowen, E. L., Parker, G. R., & Wyman, P. A. (1990). Stress resilient children in urban settings. *Journal of Primary Prevention, 11*, 3–17.

Prospects for Community Organization

Stanley Wenocur and Steven Soifer

In their comprehensive analysis of the prospects for community organization within social work in the next century, Stanley Wenocur and Steven Soifer of the University of Maryland begin with the observation that "social work may be the only profession in the United States whose Code of Ethics enjoins us to promote the general welfare of society." Yet, although social workers have been involved in various aspects of community organizing for over a century, it has never been defined as the mainstream activity by the profession due to the inherently conservative bias of professionalization. Wenocur and Soifer argue that the focus around services is the distinguishing characteristic of community organizing within social work. In order to maintain this focus in the years ahead, however, community organizers will have to develop a "values-driven agenda" and create broad-based coalitions that transcend class, race, and geographic lines. They sketch out an ambitious agenda for the future that includes greater collaboration among various centers for the education of community organizers, ongoing experimentation with new community organizing models, the development of a national and international database of community organizing efforts, and research on the relationship of funding sources to the empowerment of community participants.

Stanley Wenocur is professor of social work and Steven Soifer is associate professor of social work at the University of Maryland at Baltimore, where they teach courses on community organization, social action, and social change. Dr. Wenocur is active in a variety of community organizations and community planning projects. Among his many publications, he

is the co-author (with David Hardcastle and Patricia Powers) of a new book on community-based practice entitled Community Practice: Theories and Skills for Social Workers *(New York: Oxford University Press). Dr. Soifer has organized low-income housing and trailer park residents and has written widely on organizing methods. His publications include* The Socialist Mayor: Bernard Sanders in Burlington, Vermont.

Introduction

What are the prospects for community organizing (CO) in the 21st century or, more modestly, maybe for the first decade of the new era? To answer that question, we need to briefly review the current state of CO and the social, political, and economic conditions that are now shaping it and may continue to exert influence into the future. Because no profession holds a monopoly on who practices or benefits from community organizing work, our discussion includes CO in social work, but necessarily goes beyond it as well. Finally, although our special interest in this essay is on grassroots organizing, we define CO inclusively to apply to social planning, community development, and social action work in all its variations.

A Few Words About CO in Social Work

Social workers have always been involved in community organizing in many different ways, from neighborhood-based organizing and community development to social planning, service coordination, fund-raising, advocacy, and social action. Social work in the United States began to take shape as a profession during a period of progressive reform—that is, from around 1900 to the start of World War I. The notion of helping poor individuals *and at the same time* reforming the conditions that contributed to poverty and human misery were built into social work's mission, largely a legacy of the settlement house movement. This mission was strongly reinforced in the Depression years during the battles to create a federal system of social protections, the basics of the modern welfare state (Wenocur and Reisch, 1989). It was re-energized during the War on Poverty and the social movements of the 1960s. These three periods, the Progressive Era, the Depression years, and the Civil Rights era, generated the greatest amount of reformist community organizing effort within social work (and outside of it) (Trattner, 1984). As a result, social work may be the only profession in the United States whose Code of Ethics enjoins us to promote the general welfare of society: by advocating for policies and legislation that improve social conditions and promote social justice; by struggling to ensure equal access to resources, services, and opportunities; and by acting to eliminate discrimination and promote respect for diversity (*NASW News*, January 1996).

Nevertheless, within the social work profession, CO has never been a mainstream activity. Professions in the United States have a conservative bias. In a capitalistic society, they seek to advance the financial security and status of their practitioners by creating and controlling a market for services that only they are licensed to provide (Larson, 1977). To do this, professions must attend to the requirements of their legitimators and financial supporters. Because the legitimacy and salaries of social workers depend heavily on governmental and philanthropic support, this means a predilection for operating within the dominant values of their funders, values that emphasize individual responsibility for failure over systemic deficiencies and injustices. Consequently, social work primarily trains and supports professionals who will provide services to individuals and families rather than professionals who will work to change the system (Wenocur and Reisch, 1989).

Nevertheless, the profession has always managed to keep a spark of reform alive, and will probably continue to do so in the future. Many social workers are attracted to the field because of its humanist ideals. But also, it is in our self-interest to maintain a reformist thrust. In order to develop and maintain human service organizations in which social work expertise (i.e., an MSW or BSW degree) is required as a condition of employment, it behooves the profession to train some of its members to advocate for the retention of existing services in the face of threatened cutbacks and to get new services established, organized, and funded to meet emerging needs—hence, to train community organizers.

Schools of social work have trained community organizers since their earliest years, as, for example, with past training for Community Chest (now United Way) and health and welfare council work. And although professional positions in these types of organizations no longer fall almost exclusively to MSW social workers, as they once did, community organizers presently still work in this arena, as, for example, with United Way staff employed in social planning, government relations, and fund-raising positions. They also work, alongside similarly employed non-MSWs, in many other local, state, and federal level organizations, whose efforts center basically around advocacy, planning, coordination, and development of various types of human services and safety net protections. Some examples might be a national children's advocacy organization like the Child Welfare League of America, or a state project to plan for the deinstitutionalization of residents of state-administered facilities, or a city or county Department of Homeless Services. These sorts of services, provided mainly by governmental and private nonprofit organizations, span many fields of practice, such as aging, family and children, health and mental health, occupational social work, education (school social work), and corrections.

The focus of community organizing around services is probably the feature that most distinguishes CO in social work from CO outside of it. At the local level, service provision and social action often combine within the same organizations and even the same social workers. Hyde (1992) refers to these organizations as "social movement agencies," a hearkening back to the settlement house, in which "the explicit pursuit of social change is accomplished through the delivery of services" (p. 122).

Social work–trained community organizers also work in a large assortment of local and state level, community-based citizen organizations, aimed at neighborhood preservation and development, cultural understanding, social and economic development, and liberal and radical social reform. Their organizational forms include: neighborhood and civic associations and coalitions of these groups; parish organizations; broad-based church-sponsored organizations; community, housing, and tenant organizations; human relations agencies; labor unions; community development corporations; political campaigns; and social movement organizations such as civil rights, welfare rights, environmental protection, and peace.

Post-1960s Conservatism and Community Organizing

Richard Nixon's election in 1968 on a law and order platform heralded a political shift to the right in the country, especially a growing mistrust of "big government." This direction has continued to the present with few deviations, even with Democratic presidents and/or a Democratic Congress. In the early 1970s, an electorate, weary of a decade of turmoil and social protest, began to express its disapproval over challenges to the time-tested values of family, hard work, and self-reliance. Many also took offense at a perceived governmental favoritism toward minorities and poor people. By the 1980s and 1990s, influenced by an increasingly powerful religious and intellectual right wing and discouraged by a steady drop in the standard of living (recall the anomaly of rising inflation and rising unemployment, dubbed "stagflation, of the mid-1970s), many voters expressed their resentments by supporting legislation aimed at cutting taxes, limiting and cutting expenditures for social programs, deregulating the private corporate sector, restricting immigration, and denying affirmative action. Followed to their conclusion, Republican proposals in the 1990s would unravel much of the national welfare state and return the country to a pre-1930s system of state welfare.

In the conservative aftermath of the 1960s, many observers thought that community organizing was likely to be as dead as the War on Poverty. With the fading of the student movement and cuts in programs such as Peace Corps and VISTA (except during the Carter administration), it became harder to recruit young people into organizing jobs, and with reductions in funds for all sorts of social programs, indeed fewer jobs were available. Schools of social work experienced a decline in federal grant monies for social work training of any kind, as well as a drop in interest in their community organizing programs (though not a drop in general enrollment). But community organizing was far from finished. According to one estimate (Delgado, 1994), "There are currently over 6,000 community organizations in operation in the U.S. Most are local, unaffiliated groups, initiated out of local residents' need to exert control over development of their communities" (p. 12). When other types of CO groups with liberal political aims are taken into account—as, for example, local, statewide, and national advocacy organizations to improve child care and protect consumers, the rights of mental patients, and community development corporations (CDCs)—the numbers are much higher. How can we account for all of this effort in conservative times? We suggest at least five important reasons for the continuation and growth of CO over the last 25 years.

First, many social movements rooted in the 1960s never really ended. Those that continued spread beyond the narrow confines of the college campuses (Boggs, 1995; Flacks, 1990). Some fall under the rubric of "new social movements"; these characteristically are organized around "communities of interest" or geography, focus more on cultural and identity struggles than class issues, and "reject hierarchically based forms of social interaction" in public and private relationships and structures, such as the family, business, and the state (Fisher and Kling, 1994, p. 9). Accordingly, national and local movement groups (e.g., peace, environment, gay rights, feminist, communitarian) multiplied, addressing a range of diverse issues with a broad mix of ideologies and strategies: direct action, empowerment and community self-help, internal consciousness-raising, and alternative lifestyles and value changes. All in all, in the last 25 years, probably millions of people mobilized to get governmental and corporate action on issues like toxic waste dumping, nuclear power plants, utility rates, home mortgage loan discrimination, nursing home abuse, abortion rights, civil rights, gay rights, women's rights, AIDS policies and programs, homelessness, neighborhood preservation, rights of the handicapped, nuclear disarmament, war and oppression in Central America, and apartheid in South Africa. All these movements centered in some way around basic "social contradictions (class, bureaucratic, patriarchal, ecological, and racial) that permeate advanced capitalist societies" (Boggs, 1995, p. 349). These movements had practical and far-reaching effects on American life, and internationally. They

> catalyzed the formation of alternative institutions (cooperatives, alternative media, bookstores, clinics, etc.); they have helped sustain electoral coalitions with progressive agendas; they have given rise to a new critical discourse and a radical intelligentsia both within and outside the universities, and they have stimulated the rebirth of student activism in the late 1980s. (Boggs, 1995, p. 350)

They led to legal and symbolic reforms and greater government and corporate accountability. Although they did not alter the distribution of income, perhaps it is fair to say that they helped to make "empowerment" a watchword for the 1990s.

Second, community organizing in the 1970s and 1980s built its own support system and, in so doing, took a major step toward defining itself as a profession. Here we refer to the creation by 1992 of some two dozen national and regional *organizer training centers* or "intermediaries" (Delgado, 1994). Often connected spiritually and intellectually to the ideal of participatory democracy espoused during the 1960s, many centers were formed by 1960s activists to create and refine different models of community organizing, to spread CO activity by providing training and technical assistance, and in some cases to build a network of organizations with sufficient mass and resources to promote initiatives beyond the local neighborhood level. Some of the best known and most influential centers were formed long before the 1960s but have gone through growth and change within the last 25 years—for example, the Industrial Areas Foundation established by Saul Alinsky in 1940 and the Highlander Folk School, now the Highlander Research and Education Center, begun by Myles Horton in 1932 and incorporated in Tennessee in October 1934. Some other well-known centers include the Midwest Academy; the Center for Community Change; the Institute for Social Justice (a training arm for ACORN); the National Training and Information Center (a training arm of National People's Action); the Center for Third World Organizing; the Pacific Institute for Community Organizing; and the Education Center for Community Organization, a project of the Hunter College School of Social Work in New York City. Training centers vary as to their models of organizing, their aims, their issue or constituent focus, and their scope, and often they compete with one another for clients or turf, resources, and public renown. Still, they have begun to lay an institutional foundation under community organizing work.

Third, community organizers became more sophisticated about fund-raising. With cutbacks in governmental funds for community organizing and human services of all kinds, managers of nonprofit organizations, including CO groups, in a now highly competitive resource environment, were forced to learn marketing and fund-raising skills. The establishment of several liberal foundations also helped CO and advocacy organizations generate resources. The fund-raising strategies that evolved—ever more dependent on computer technologies—included grant writing, special events, direct mail, phonathons, membership drives, forming

"alternative funds" to United Way, competing for workplace dollars through payroll check-offs, and others (Flanagan, 1982). The growing alternative fund movement has been especially important for women's groups, environmental groups, African-American groups, and other social change–oriented organizations, all of which have formed separate alternative funds in a number of local urban communities to support their special interests. Today, alternative funds operate in almost every state, and in 1994 they raised more than $158 million through payroll deductions (*Responsive Philanthropy*, Spring 1995).

Two additional fund-raising strategies developed in the 1970s also bear special mention here: door-to-door canvassing and religious institutional contracting. The former, adopted by Citizen Action, applied the technique of door-to-door product sales to soliciting broad-based support for the Citizen Action agenda and organization. Canvassing requires a whole separate "sales" staff to solicit nightly in selected neighborhoods with strict dollar quotas that must be met. The high costs of maintaining a separate canvassing operation and the requirements for education and coordination with the community organizing program are drawbacks of this strategy.

The latter approach, religious institutional contracting (our name), was developed by the Industrial Areas Foundation (IAF). Under this arrangement, national IAF staff members develop a contract with an interdenominational sponsoring committee of religious institutions (churches, synagogues, mosques) in a prospective community. The sponsoring committee must be committed to addressing community issues through building a broad-based interdenominational, culturally diverse organization. The contract provides funding for three years (from $150,000 to $250,000) for an IAF-trained lead organizer and/or other organizers,

IAF supervision and consultation, and IAF national and local training of organization leaders on an ongoing basis (IAF, 1990).

The significance of an approach that proceeds from a base of institutional support is (1) the organization can concentrate on winning issues rather than on fund-raising, (2) it weaves powerful connections into the organization's fabric, and (3) it supports a slow and careful leadership development and organization-building process. Using its institutional strategy, the IAF has developed an extensive national network of IAF organizations and a professionalized organizational structure and staff of decently paid organizers who can maintain community organizing as a lifetime career choice. The drawback of this approach, as with any resource dependency, is that the organization may need to avoid issues that its sponsors find too difficult to confront.

Fourth, some community organization efforts shifted away from "challenging the establishment" to more collaborative strategies involving partnerships between local community groups, government officials, and corporate leaders. A primary strategy was the formation of community development corporations (CDCs), which took root in very small numbers in the 1960s but grew to several thousand by the mid-1980s. CDCs vary greatly in size and focus, but they share several features: (1) Almost without exception they are incorporated as nonprofit, tax-exempt organizations; (2) their boards are usually controlled by residents of the communities targeted for development activity; (3) they all undertake some form of economic development, such as housing rehabilitation, construction and management, starting businesses, creating jobs for local residents, and/or operating services—all with the aim of sustaining and regenerating the social, physical, and economic life of the community; and (4) they all target their activities to a clearly defined geographic area with a high level of low-income residents (Pierce and Steinbach, 1987).

CDCs gained a strong foothold during the Carter administration (1976–1980) with the creation of the Office of Neighborhood Development and some dozen other federal programs that provided support for local staff and projects. The Reagan administration cut back these programs severely, including dismantling the most significant source of CDC support, the Community Services Administration. CDCs, however, continued to thrive, having become more savvy about putting together funding streams from a variety of nonfederal sources—liberal foundations, municipal and state programs, private corporations and banks, sweat equity, and the like.

Fifth, in the last 20 years, middle-class people moved out of inner cities in large numbers. They left behind majority populations of color and greater diversity, and were replaced by new immigrant groups. These varied populations often developed their own, indigenous organizations based on "communities of interest" that tended to be centered around "a combination of racial solidarity and concern about a specific set of issues" (Delgado, 1994, p. 46). Organizations in communities of color range along the CO spectrum from single- and multi-issue groups to social movement groups to CDCs. They have tended to develop apart from the organizing centers mentioned earlier and to share a worldview based in race relations. Their organizers are typically indigenous to the community in which they are working (Delgado, 1994).

Whither CO in the 21st Century?

It is hard to tell whether the conservative climate of the last 25 years will follow us into the 21st century. Much depends on how the dramatic restrictions in social programs come to be interpreted—whether as a nation we come to see the public good narrowly in terms of how "I" am doing or whether we come to see good as a function of how "we" are doing as an interdependent whole. In the latter part of the 20th century and the first decade of the 21st century, community organizing will have an important part to play in the struggle to define and redefine fundamental American values.

This struggle will be complicated by significant changes in the political economy that are already at work. One of the most pervasive of these changes is the shift to a postindustrial service economy and its globalization. Economists agree that the standard of living has actually been dropping since the 1960s and that we have seen an ever-widening gap between rich and poor reach a point where the middle class may be disappearing altogether (Cassidy, 1995). Although the "causes" for this economic situation are multiple, complex, and interrelated, among the often identified reasons are the growth of national and multinational corporations and a concomitant inability to regulate them, the availability of cheap foreign labor for manufacturing in underdeveloped countries, effective foreign competition from developed countries, the decline of the labor movement in the face of American deindustrialization, the availability of cheap new immigrant labor, the advance of computer technology and requirements for computer literacy, and the lack of opportunities for retraining unemployed and underemployed workers.

Another change, mentioned earlier, has been the abandonment of our central cities by the middle classes, especially whites. There are lots of reasons for this as well. Real estate development, a cornerstone of the market economy, and the businesses that revolve around it—banks, shopping malls, builders, and so on—invest heavily in promoting the American dream of a house in the suburbs. Older, decaying cities, dependent on taxes on declining property

values, do not have the constitutional power to generate the resources they need to rebuild their physical and social infrastructure—buildings, parks, schools, social services, police protection, and so on. Consequently, inner city communities are increasingly turning into majority populations of color, largely Black or Hispanic, and a diverse mix of other immigrant groups and poor and working-class whites.

Conservative control of government obviously exacerbates all of these trends. It generally implies cutting federal resources for social entitlements and social and economic development programs, selling a survival of the fittest ideology, and deregulating business competition and social and environmental protections.

What are some of the implications for community organizing? One of the more apparent implications is that local governments, which are often the targets of CO action, will be increasingly unable to respond in any significant way. They simply do not have the necessary resources by themselves. Stated differently, municipal power to effect community change is limited—ironically, at a point in time when racial and ethnic minority group members have been able to gain control of many larger city governments. Solutions to inner city problems will have to be dealt with on a regional level (Rusk, 1996) and/or a state level, and, unfortunately, this is a political formula pregnant with class and racial politics. From an organizing perspective, we all live locally and experience life through a web of local relationships, but local institutions are less and less subject to local control. Therefore, community organizers will have to learn how to create cross-neighborhood, citywide, city–county, and statewide organizations. This means creating interracial, interdenominational, and transclass organizations—coalitions, in all likelihood, with their own special knowledge and skill requirements. Cultural, racial, and identity politics, fraught with conflict as they are, make this task exceedingly challenging. The glue here will have to be something that transcends local issues, most likely a values-driven agenda. Broad-based IAF organizational models that proceed from this direction may have some potential to show the way.

The ineffectiveness of local governments to solve community problems should not turn citizens away from local governmental participation, nor from electoral participation at any level. Indeed the Right has gained political influence by increased participation in the electoral process with a good deal of attention to the grass roots. If action is devolving more and more from federal to state governments, then we need to be able to influence state decisions. Moreover, despite the valiant efforts of nonprofit organizations such as Greenpeace and Amnesty International, only government has sufficient power to counter and regulate the excesses of national and multinational corporations. The *delegitimization* of government is a right-wing agenda item aimed at *relegitimizing* private enterprise and voluntary organizations as the solution to social and economic problems. Without the strong hand of government, citizens have little hope of controlling the policies of private corporations. Nor does the voluntary sector have the resources to be able to make up for loss of public human services, or to create replacement jobs and job retraining, or to rebuild the supply of affordable housing. In this regard, CDCs remain useful for small-scale solutions and as important instruments for learning. In our view, however, they should not be seen as an alternative to governmental intervention. If government is to regain its proper place in civic life, future community organizing will have to pay a lot of attention to political and economic education, to the re-creation of civic sensibility, and to electoral politics. A number of national organizing networks, such as ACORN and Citizen Action, have experi-

ence with electoral politics that should be further developed and shared.

The labor movement should be an important member of any progressive coalition. Labor unions have a great deal of institutional power by virtue of their location in the economy and the legislation that protects their activities. This legislation needs to be strengthened. Prospective and current organizers need to become familiar with the labor movement. For many young organizers, labor unions have simply not been part of their reality or, if they are, unions have been tainted with the negative stamp of the Reagan era. In France in the fall of 1995, when the government proposed a reactionary social welfare, the public-employee unions went on strike until more acceptable alternatives could be negotiated. Why couldn't that happen in the United States? Maybe it will in the 21st century. Currently, new AFL-CIO leadership is making a significant reinvestment in labor organizing and political education. Citizen Action grew out of a citizen–labor–energy coalition that began in 1977. The IAF has some local projects in conjunction with labor unions. Can these experiences and relationships be expanded? How can that coalition be rebuilt and strengthened?

As we approach the 21st century, community organization has the potential, as it has not had before, to create a national—even international—progressive, organizing agenda, with the people power to put it into action. To get it started would take a major conference to bring together the leadership of national and regional CO training centers and leaders from various movement organizations, schools of social work, CDCs, and other interested parties. Perhaps a megadose of right-wing politics and policies will generate enough unity of purpose for such an event to happen.

Several positive results could come out this kind of conference. First, it would help build and strengthen the links between community organizing networks, various intermediary training centers, community development corporations, and schools of social work. Given the past distance between many of these community organizing networks and schools of social work, reinforcing these connections could be beneficial to all parties. Second, the conference could help pave the way for the possible confederation of the various community organizing networks in the United States. Although personal rivalries, turf struggles, and different models and styles of organizing permeate the community organizing movement, certainly these issues are no greater than those faced by the American Federation of Labor (AFL) and the Congress of Industrial Organizations (CIO) prior to their merger in 1955 (Peterson, 1963). Movement in this direction in the 21st century is imperative if the community organizing networks are to achieve their maximum potential influence.

Third, by involving schools of social work, an atmosphere could be created to impel more schools to implement community organizing/community development concentrations or tracks. A survey (Soifer, 1996) of the roughly 120 MSW programs across the country indicate that about 15 have full-fledged community organizing concentrations (though many offer at least some content or a course on the topic) and only a handful have community development concentrations or courses (Soifer, 1996).

We believe that three other directions should also be taken at the beginning of the 21st century. One would be to continue the experimentation with new community organizing models. The Alinsky organizing model, which is used in one form or another by all the major community organizing networks, has many strengths but also some key weaknesses, such as a tendency to avoid coalitions not of its own making. So, for example, an alternative approach, the so-called feminist organizing model, championed by the Education Center for Community Organization (ECCO) at Hunter College School of Social Work, holds much promise and should be developed further. Because this approach addresses women's fundamental self-interests, it has potential for overcoming barriers that keep many women from political activism. At the same time, it is not so exclusive that diverse coalitions could not be developed. Definitive characteristics of feminist organizing include (1) analysis of problems and issues through a gender lens; (2) attention to the process aspects of practice; (3) consciousness raising; (4) a grass-roots, bottom-up approach; (5) efforts to overcome differences that separate women and celebrate diversity; and (6) a holistic approach that integrates and uses both rational and nonrational elements of human experience (Guttiérez and Lewis, 1994). Other new or hybrid kinds of community organizing models should also be fully explored, including transformative approaches such as study circles and base ecclesial (of the church) communities (BECs)—communities of faith built around participation in church liturgy and reflection leading to action (Bradshaw, Soifer, and Gutiérrez, 1994; Hanna and Robinson, 1994; Reilly, 1994).

Second, it is imperative that a national (and ideally international) database of community organizing efforts since, at least, the 1960s should be compiled. There have been many different community organizing efforts over the last three decades, most of which have not been properly documented or even documented at all. Before this history is lost forever, efforts should be made to collect oral histories and/or case studies of these groups and catalogue them along a number of different criteria (e.g., local, regional, statewide, national, or international group; organizing model[s] used; paid or voluntary staff; issues worked on; significant accomplishments; period of existence, and so on).

Third, we need to study the relationship of funding (sources, strategies for securing funds) to the empowerment of the actors/participants. Lack of stable funding is a primary reason why many community organizing efforts fail. New information may lead us in new directions for supporting change-oriented organizations and movements. Furthermore, despite the current conservative tenor of the times, we should not assume a conservative future will follow, and therefore we should not assume that the enormous potential of the federal government for encouraging and funding progressive community-building programs cannot be recaptured.

Conclusion

This essay has suggested that, as we approach the new millennium, community organization practice is alive and well and should continue to thrive. The kind of impact CO will have on the larger political economy, however, is far from certain. Much will depend on the ability of CO practitioners to use small-scale organizing projects as building blocks for the creation of a more encompassing and enduring vision of society. To move in this direction, community organizers need to create opportunities for relationships and national and international discourse through journals, organizations, conferences, media, and perhaps the Internet—inclusive discourse that transcends but does not exclude the interests, concerns, and ideas of our many diverse, organized constituencies. One hopeful sign in this direction has been the formation of the National Organizers Alliance in Washington, D.C. Ultimately, community organization needs a national, as well as an international, political, and social agenda. Ideally this agenda will help to generate and guide the political and economic change that is sure to come in the 21st century in the direction of a more just and more peaceful national and global community.

REFERENCES

Boggs, C. (1995). Rethinking the sixties legacy: From new left to social movements. In S. M. Lyman (Ed.), *Social movements: Critiques, concepts, case-studies*. New York: New York University Press, 331–355.

Bradshaw, C., Soifer, S., & Gutiérrez, L. (1994). Toward a hybrid model for effective organizing in communities of color. *Journal of Community Practice, 1* (1), 25–41.

Cassidy, J. (1995, October 16). Who killed the middle class? *The New Yorker*, 113–124.

Delgado, G. (1994). *Beyond the politics of place: New directions in community organizing in the 1990s*. Oakland, CA: Applied Research Center.

Fisher, R., & Kling, J. (1994). Community organization and new social movement theory. *Journal of Progressive Human Services, 5* (2), 5–23.

Flacks, D. (1990). The revolution of citizenship. *Social policy, 21* (2), 37–50.

Flanagan, J. (1982). *The grassroots fundraising book*. Chicago: Contemporary Books.

Guttiérez, L. M., & Lewis, E. A. (1994). Community organizing with women of color: A feminist approach. *Journal of Community Practice, 1* (2), 23–44.

Hanna, M. G., & Robinson, B. (1994). *Strategies for community empowerment: Direct-action and transformative approaches to social change practice*. Lewiston, NY: Edwin Mellen Press.

Hyde, C. (1992). The ideational system of social movement agencies: An examination of feminist health centers. In Y. Hasenfeld (Ed.), *Human services as complex organizations*. Newbury Park, CA: Sage.

Industrial Areas Foundation. (1990). *IAF 50 years: Organizing for change.* Chicago: Industrial Areas Foundation.

Larson, S. M. (1977). *The rise of professionalism: A sociological analysis.* Berkeley: University of California Press.

NASW News. (1996, January). Proposal: Revision of the code of ethics. Washington, DC: National Association of Social Workers, *41* (1), 19–21.

Peterson, F. (1963). *American labor unions: What they are and how they work.* New York: Harper and Row.

Pierce, N. R., & Steinbach, C. F. (1987). *Corrective capitalism: The rise of America's community development corporations.* New York: Ford Foundation.

Reilly, M. M. (1994). Social change from a faith perspective: Community organizing with liberation theology. Unpublished paper.

Responsive philanthropy. (1995, Spring). Newsletter of the National Committee for Responsive Philanthropy. Washington, DC: NCRP, 11–12.

Rusk, D. (1996). *Baltimore unbound: A strategy for regional renewal.* Baltimore, MD: Abell Foundation.

Soifer, S. D. (1996). Survey of M.S.W. programs regarding community organizing and community development curricula content. Unpublished.

Trattner, W. I. (1984). *From poor law to welfare state: A history of social welfare in America.* 3d ed. New York: Free Press.

Wenocur, S., & Reisch, M. (1989). *From charity to enterprise: The development of American social work in a market economy.* Urbana: University of Illinois Press.

A Social-Health Model

A Paradigm for Social Work in Health Care

Jane Isaacs Lowe

This essay by Jane Isaacs Lowe, assistant professor of social work at the University of Pennsylvania, presents a social-health model that is grounded in community-oriented practice. Its focus is on the empowerment of individuals and groups and the development of strong, healthy communities. The model is designed to provide a framework for educating social workers in health-care practice. Lowe argues that, although social workers have long been involved in the health-care field, issues of community and public health have been neglected for decades. The practice paradigm she develops in this essay can redirect the profession's efforts and enable social workers to play leadership roles in the rapidly changing health-care field in the years ahead.

Dr. Lowe, who earned her MSW from Columbia University and her Ph.D. from Rutgers, is also a Senior Fellow at the Leonard Davis Institute of Health Economics at the University of Pennsylvania. With many years of professional experience in medical centers, her current research focuses on the delivery and design of social-health services at the community level. She is co-editor (with Michael Austin) of Controversial Issues in Communities and Organizations.

There is a long and well-documented history of the origins and development of social work practice in health care (Carlton, 1989a; Nacman, 1977). Over the decades this practice has evolved, based on changing definitions of dis-ease and treatment, social and organizational systems, and service and professional orientations. The social work role in health care has consistently concentrated on practice issues based on the social health needs and problems of individuals, families, and populations at risk (Rosenberg, 1983).

However, whereas social work in health established itself as a key player in hospital-based care and management, the focus on community and public health was neglected. As a result, several conflicts emerged within health-based practice: the provision of discharge planning vs. clinical services, inpatient vs. outpatient locus of care, individual vs. family intervention, hospital-based care vs. community-based care, prevention and primary care vs. high-tech tertiary intervention, and specialist vs. generalist practice. Although these issues have been discussed widely, the field has been unable to shift its practice to be responsive to new and rapidly changing directions in the health-care environment.

Today, social work in health is facing an uncertain future. It is confronted with the reorganization of health services into networks that reflect a continuum-of-care model, changing sources of revenue and financing, and the increasingly competitive market for health-care providers and professionals. These changes have placed the entire future of social work in health in question as it scrambles to survive and to redefine its place in the ever-broadening field of health.

Out of all these changes, several salient questions emerge: What are the roles for social work in health care? Should social work continue to view this as an area of specialization? Is there a paradigm for redefining social work in health? Social work in health care is at a crossroads. Although the answers to these questions are being debated within the field and within academic settings, one approach that offers the greatest potential for social work is the return to community-based practice in the delivery of both health and social services.

There are many different definitions of communities. For the purpose of this paper, a community is defined as "that combination of social units and systems that perform major social functions" essential for meeting the needs of people on the local level (Warren, 1978:9). Thus, a community can be a group of people who share a common set of beliefs, activities, location, and/or institutions. Community-based social work practice should be designed to increase community competence—that is, the ability of the members of the community to identify needs and solve problems to achieve goals (Fellin, 1995:5). Social work's focus on community practice in the 1960s (Brager and Purcell, 1967) and on prevention and primary care in the 1970s (Bloom, 1980; Miller, 1983) provides a theoretical background for utilizing professional knowledge and expertise to improve the health of people where they live and work.

Underlying this community-based approach is a social-health model for practice, education, and research. This conceptual approach places both individual and population health needs and problems into a social context. It looks for solutions within the individual, the environment (e.g., community and organization), and social-health policy (Falk, 1995; Ger-

main and Gitterman, 1980; Netting, Kettner, and McMurty, 1993; Rehr, 1982). In adapting this model to social work in health care, the goal is to link individuals, families, and groups to a range of health promotion, prevention, and treatment services that no longer fall solely within the health-care system. This essay presents an overview of the changing context of social work practice in health, develops the social-health model, and discusses its implications for education, practice, and research.

The Changing Context for Social Work Practice in Health

Several trends have emerged over the last decade that have had a profound impact on social work in health care. First, prospective payment and DRGs have had a significant impact on service delivery and length of hospital stays. Managed care has also emerged, as a mechanism to slow the growth of health-care costs by controlling the way health-care dollars are spent. Employers and federal and state governments have all participated in encouraging these new models in an attempt to stem the cost of health care (Cornelius, 1994).

One of the most obvious impacts of managed-care delivery has been on the organization of service delivery. This has included the transition from single, free-standing health-care institutions to integrated networks of providers, as well the move from hospital-based care to ambulatory care settings. Thus, the health-care marketplace is in transition from traditional indemnity plans to capitated health care through various forms of managed care.

Second, the aging of the population and the increasing numbers of chronically ill individuals have had a profound impact on health care. The elderly comprise approximately 11% of the American population, but they utilize the largest percentage of health-care services (U.S. Select Committee on Aging, 1991). Yet, as the elderly live longer, their illnesses are increasingly chronic as opposed to acute. In addition, with advances in technology, many illnesses (e.g., heart disease, juvenile diabetes, AIDS, and other long-term conditions) that were once viewed as fatal, can now be managed for extended periods of time, thus increasing the numbers of chronically ill in younger age groups. The health-care needs of the elderly and chronically ill can be viewed on a continuum from health promotion and prevention to long-term management of their aging and/or illness. The acute care model does not work well for these populations because what they require for successful care is continuity and education rather than episodic care.

Finally, there is growing concern about the "medicalization" of social problems, which continues to raise health-care costs (Dayaranta, 1992; Hurowitz, 1993; Schwartz, 1994). Society's social welfare and health policies have not dealt with the relationships among poverty, inequality, and health. Thus, the sequelae of social problems, such as domestic abuse, homelessness, substance abuse, and violence, end up being treated in hospital emergency rooms, intensive care units, and physicians' offices. By looking to the medical system for solutions to these problems, the social and economic factors that create them are ignored. To improve the overall health of individuals and population groups, an understanding of the socioeconomic variables that lead to poor health outcomes as well as new approaches for intervention must be clearly formulated.

In the move toward capitated managed care, maintaining the health of the community will be financially rewarded. Within this changed environment, social work's understanding of the impact of social issues on the physical health of populations becomes a valu-able asset. The next section will discuss social work's opportunity to take the lead in developing a more comprehensive community-based model for addressing social-health problems. This model has the potential to return social work to its community-based roots, as well as meet the demands of a fiscally driven and resource-scarce health-care system.

Social-Health Model

This model reconceptualizes the domain of social work practice in health from one that is based solely in the medical care system to one that places health needs within the context of the larger social welfare system. It is a model that draws together the theoretical constructs of person-in-environment (Coulton, 1979; Germain and Gitterman, 1980), prevention (Bloom, 1980; Siefert, Jayarante, and Martin, 1992), and community organization and development (Chavis, 1992; Rothman, Erlich, and Tropman, 1995). This social-health model requires that the "case" be viewed not only as a person, but also as the group, the organization, and/or the community. Therefore, this model recognizes that health promotion, and the prevention, treatment, and control of physical and mental illness represents a complex constellation of service delivery systems.

Social work practice in health care can no longer be viewed as specialized practice within an acute hospital. Rather, it becomes an approach that fully integrates micro and macro services and that transcends settings. Social work in health, therefore, requires the delivery of broad-based social-health services to individuals, families, and populations within a range of settings such as schools, workplaces, and community social-health agencies to promote social well-being.

The social-health model is based on the assumptions that (1) health, both physical and mental, is a function of human biology, social and physical environments, personal lifestyles, behavior, and access to health care; (2) there are inextricable links between socioeconomic status and health, and between the social and biological components of health and illness (Kitagawa and Hauser, 1973; Laveist, 1993); and (3) social problems, such as teen pregnancy, violence, substance abuse, and the effects of poverty are seen not as medical problems but as community problems to be treated at their points of origin. Given these assumptions, a four-point social-health model of practice emerges.

First, community social problems and their relationship to health and illness must be identified. Although many of these problems will span the boundaries of various communities, it is important for each community to arrive at interventions that best meet their own unique needs. This requires that social workers work in partnership with community residents and organizations to help them identify and analyze their social-health needs and concerns, as well as their strengths. An empowerment model of social work practice (Gutiérrez, Glen-Maye, and DeLois, 1995; Zippay, 1995) can be used to ensure that community members have the capacity (e.g., knowledge and resources) and authority (e.g., power) to make the decisions and choices required for this process. For example, community-based social-health organizations must not only involve community residents in all stages of needs assessment and program planning, but also must be willing to develop and implement programs that support the cultural beliefs, practices, and overall strengths of the community. This may require reconfiguring traditional community and organizational relationships so that they ensure the active participation by all constituency groups in service delivery.

Second, interventions must be designed to improve and maintain the social functioning of individuals, groups, organizations, and communities. For individuals, this means facilitating their capacity to meet basic needs, form positive relationships, and grow personally. For groups, organizations, and communities, social functioning can be enhanced by "developing resources, promoting harmony among members and creating dynamic opportunities for growth and change" (DuBois and Miley, 1996:66). Therefore, interventions to promote social functioning must be designed to improve or change the system itself or to create changes in other social structures.

Further, service programs must be universal, comprehensive and integrated, accessible, and accountable in order to support the overall well-being of the community and its constituencies (Specht and Courtney, 1994). For example, teen pregnancy, substance abuse, truancy, family violence, and physical and mental illness are often interrelated social-health issues faced by children, adolescents, and adults within communities. Thus, it is essential that these be addressed as a unit rather than as individual issues. For example, multiservice center programs that are built from within the community, are targeted to more than one age group, and are school- or community-agency–based are more likely to be effective in preventing many of these social-health problems and in promoting individual and community change (Dryfoos, 1994; Family Impact Seminar, 1991; Kahn and Kamerman, 1993).

Third, interventions must be designed to focus on prevention, health promotion, diagnosis, treatment, and rehabilitation, as well as on social action. Given that communities face a range of social-health problems in various stages of development, social workers need to be prepared to intervene along a continuum of service delivery. This requires that social workers understand how social problems are defined, and recognize the resulting contradictions in the financing and allocation of social-health resources. For example, over the past several years, violence has been identified as a significant social problem. Yet, the allocation of resources to address this problem has been focused on diagnosis and treatment of the problem in the criminal justice and medical care systems rather than on prevention through the educational, employment, and housing systems. Therefore, social workers must be active partners with the community and its organizations to identify these inherent contradictions in order to advocate for more appropriate interventions. Community organizing, coalition building, and employing community residents where appropriate as outreach workers are several approaches that support working partnerships.

Fourth, monitoring and evaluating the process of identifying and resolving social-health needs and problems is essential. Social workers have a wealth of practice experience that informally provides information about services that work and don't work both on the client, community, and organizational levels. However, as social-health services are increasingly privatized and as resources become scarcer, it becomes imperative that the outcomes of interventions be formally documented and systematically evaluated.

More social-health services are being provided in schools, workplaces, neighborhood agencies (e.g., senior centers, community centers), housing projects, and churches. As a result, there will be new opportunities to develop integrated service delivery systems. These systems will largely comprise community-based social-health agencies that are linked to the larger health-care system. For

example, the elderly and other individuals with chronic care needs and their families require a range of supportive services from home care to meal preparation, to counseling, to adult day care, to respite care, to acute and long-term care. To meet these needs adequately, services must be integrated to create a system of social-health care that is accessible and incorporates all the elements necessary to ensure the highest possible level of functioning for all population groups (Kaplan, 1989).

Although the social-health model can be carried out within the changing and expanding health-care system, changes in the reimbursement of social work services requires that social workers understand federal, state, and local budgetary processes in order to maximize resources. For example, by combining basic health services (Maternal and Child Health block grants) with case-management for high-risk children and their families (Child Protective Services), substance abuse prevention (Drug-Free Schools), and violence prevention (Centers for Disease Control), a comprehensive package of social-health services can be provided in schools, workplaces, and/or community-based agencies.

Further, social workers have an opportunity to demonstrate to the managed-care companies the importance of psychological and social interventions in primary care. There is a strong body of knowledge that suggests that psychosocial problems are highly prevalent among patients in primary care settings (Azzarto, 1993; Mechanic, 1980; Padgett, Patrick, Schlesinger, and Burns, 1993). These problems are often overlooked by providers and can often result in overutilization of medical services. Social workers bring to the managed-care environment the expertise to manage these individual problems, as well as to promote social change in systems that interfere with optimal social functioning.

Developing partnerships with managed-care organizations to pilot the implementation of the social-health model is essential for maintaining a biopsychosocial approach to care, particularly given the increasing tendency to split the physical and behavioral components of care. Also, other innovations in financing and implementing an integrated social-health model of service delivery can be developed with Departments of Human Services and state Medicaid programs for children and their families.

Implications for Social Work

The adoption of the social-health model provides some clear guidelines for practice, education, and research. These topics—although discussed separately in the following sections—are very much interrelated.

Practice

The changes in social work practice that will occur in implementing this model include an exciting combination of familiar and unfamiliar roles. One familiar role for social workers is that of activist and community organizer (Brager, Specht, and Torczyner, 1987). A less familiar role is the development of entrepreneurial approaches that take advantage of opportunities for partnerships with community and health-care organizations. Being a social work entrepreneur requires risk taking and a constant scanning of the external environment to capture opportunities for innovative service design. Examples of social-health service innovations include the creation of community health advisor programs, community-based resource and support centers for families, economic redevelopment programs, and the development of alternative agencies (Health Resources and Services Administration, 1995; Perlmutter, 1994).

Further, social workers must understand and be able to work within for-profit medical and behavioral organizational structures while maintaining social work values and ethics that specifically protect vulnerable populations and individual dignity. Issues of confidentiality of client information, inequitable distribution of societal resources, and the declassification (hiring less skilled workers at lower salaries) of professionals are but several examples of value conflicts that social workers confront in the current health-care environment.

In addition, as social workers move into primary care settings, they will find themselves in roles that span case management, behavioral health, quality assurance, marketing, community organizing, and public health. In performing these roles in different community arenas, social workers need to be able to move across community and organizational boundaries, scan the environment, work in interdisciplinary teams, and facilitate timely and effective service delivery. For example, as health-care organizations partner with school systems to provide both preventive and primary social-health services to children and their families, social workers need to be able to work with teachers, community residents, and the other professionals in reorganizing and transforming service delivery. Further, they must move between a range of organizations, such as schools, businesses, churches, clinics, and government agencies. This requires an array of social work skills from writing and public speaking to strategic planning to coalition building to program development to clinical practice. Thus, flexibility and adaptation to changing contexts for practice are essential.

Education

The implications of the social-health model for education for the 21st century involve three major curriculum revisions. First, a model of practice that melds micro and macro skills is essential for practice in the social-health arena (Carlton, 1989b; Watkins, 1985). In an increasingly complex social-health service delivery environment, the profession can no longer afford to have only individuals who are educated for clinical practice or for administrative practice. Social workers in health need and use both kinds of knowledge and skills in their daily practice.

As managed physical and behavioral care, the cross-training of staff, and the privatization of social-health services accelerates, students need a new array of skills that allow them to intervene at whatever level is necessary. These include an understanding of the key concepts involved in the financing and organization of social-health services in both the not-for-profit as well as for-profit sectors; skills in conflict resolution, including mediation and negotiation; an ability to work in a variety of organizational teams, community coalitions, and groups; and an understanding of interventions with culturally diverse populations.

Second, the artificial split between health and family specializations should be eliminated by developing content that encompasses knowledge relevant for a social-health practice paradigm (Olson, 1986). This knowledge, incorporated during the two-year Masters' program, would include epidemiology (Whitman and Hennelly, 1982), training in prevention and health promotion (Siefert, Jayarante, and Martin, 1992; Wittman, 1977), and community development that would focus on building and maintaining the social capital of communities (Putman, 1993 and 1995). Rather than focusing solely on family or health policy, there should be an emphasis on social-health policy that focuses on improving the overall health status of individuals, families, groups, and communities (Hurowitz, 1993; Rehr and Rosenberg, 1991). Such a focus calls attention to the rela-

tionship between the creation of jobs, housing, education, and overall health, and the resolution of social problems through nonmedical means. Thus, by eliminating the concept of specialization, students are given a broader framework—one that enables them to understand and practice across interrelated systems to build a broad knowledge base of social-health needs throughout the life cycle, and to conceptualize health in relation to socioeconomic variables.

Third, approaches need to be designed to bring up to date the knowledge and skills of social workers currently in the field. These social workers need to develop enhanced competencies in the innovative uses of technology in the workplace and in the treatment of clients, the restructuring of organizational and community service delivery systems, and the development of new roles for practice within a capitated social-health care system. Graduate schools of social work should be developing continuing education programs, which are on-site as well as available through distance learning and the Internet, that combine the realities of the field with the theoretical knowledge to adapt to the changing context of social work practice in health.

Research

Most community-based agencies do not carry out research initiatives. Yet, as social-health services continue to move to the community and social workers are called upon to demonstrate the effectiveness and outcomes of community-based services, research becomes more critical. Coulton, noting that our knowledge about community functioning has been sparse, calls for research that addresses "how communities work and how their capacities can be built . . . and how communities, including their formal and informal networks, care for vulnerable individuals" (1995:438). Clearly, these areas are critical to understand in order to address how best to intervene in social-health problems.

One approach is to develop collaborative academic-field partnerships, where the field can be defined as community-based agencies or as the broader community (Coulton, 1995; Johnson, 1994; Poole, 1991). An example of a collaborative community-based research method is the Participatory Action Research (PAR) model (Whyte, 1991). This model requires that the academic researcher and community (e.g., social work practitioner, community leaders, or community groups) engage in defining and setting the research agenda, in implementing the research, and in ensuring that the results be of use to the community for facilitating action. By training social work students in this model, a cadre of practitioners will emerge who are comfortable with participating in social-health research at the community level. They will bring to the process a broader perspective that transcends settings and specializations and is of potential use to the community. However, in order for this approach to research to work, faculty must be willing to engage the community as knowledgeable participants in research. Further, this approach requires that faculty adopt a "hands-on" community rather than "hands-off" institutional model of inquiry and be willing to take the time required to develop community partnerships that encourage and support such research efforts.

Conclusions

The introduction to this essay posed a number of questions about the future of social work in health care. The development of the social-health model of practice provides a theoretical framework in which to formulate the answers. The reorganized health-care system, although posing a major threat to traditional roles in social work in health care, provides exciting opportunities for social workers to take the lead in areas of community and organizational practice that play to social work's strengths. For example, as health-related social problems continue to demand significant resources, social workers can use their community organizing and planning skills, and their knowledge and experience in working with individuals and complex family and organizational systems, to intervene in these problems in a variety of social-health settings. This requires that social workers identify themselves as primary care providers who possess expertise in the development and provision of effective services to individuals, families, and groups on the community, organizational, and policy levels.

As this essay attests, strict boundaries between micro and macro practice models or between health and family specializations, inhibit innovation and change. There needs to be a broader definition of what constitutes health as well as what constitutes social work practice in health. A number of different paradigms are being suggested as health care recreates itself. What this paper has discussed is one such paradigm, rooted in community-based practice, that recommends a set of skills for social workers so that they can develop leadership roles in meeting complex individual, family, and community needs across a continuum of service delivery.

REFERENCES

Azzarto, J. (1993). Socioemotional needs of elderly family practice patients: Can social work help? *Health and Social Work*, 18(1), 40–48.

Bloom, M. (1980). *Primary prevention*. Englewood Cliffs, NJ: Prentice-Hall.

Brager, G., and Purcell, F. (Eds.). (1967). *Community action against poverty*. New Haven: College and University Press.

Brager. G., Specht, H., and Torczyner, J. L. (1987). *Community organizing*. New York: Columbia University Press.

Carlton, T. (1989a). Education for health social work practice: Reconciling past, present and future. *The Mt. Sinai Journal of Medicine*, 56(6), 468–471.

Carlton, T. (1989b). Education for health social work: Opportunities and constraints in schools and hospitals. *Health and Social Work*, 147–152.

Chavis, D. (1992). *Supporting urban community development: Renovating the social infrastructure*. New Brunswick, NJ: Center for Social and Community Development, Rutgers University.

Cornelius, D. (1994). Managed care and social work: Constructing a context and a response. In G. Rosenberg and A. Weissman (Eds.), *Social work in ambulatory care: New implications for health and social services*. New York: Haworth Press, 47–64.

Coulton, C. (1979). A study of person-in-environment fit among the chronically ill. *Social Work in Health Care*, 5(1), 5–18.

Coulton, C. (1995). Riding the pendulum of the 1990s: Building a community context for social work research. *Social Work*, 40(4), 437–439.

Dayaranta, S. (1992). *Social problems and rising health care cost in Pennsylvania*. Camp Hill, PA: Pennsylvania Blue Shield Institute.

Dryfoos, J. (1994). *Full-service schools: A revolution in health and social services for children, youth and families*. San Francisco: Jossey-Bass.

DuBois, B., and Miley, K. K. (1996). *Social work: An empowering profession* (2d ed.). Boston: Allyn and Bacon.

Falk, H. (1995). Rediscovering our community roots. *Social Work Administration: The Newsletter of the Society for Social Work Administrators in Health Care*, 1, 3–9.

Family Impact Seminar. (1991). *Promoting adolescent health and well-being through school-linked, multi-service, family-friendly programs*. Washington, DC: American Association for Marriage and Family Therapy Research and Education Foundation.

Fellin, P. (1995). *The community and the social worker* (2d ed.). Itasca, Ill.: F. E. Peacock Publishers.

Germain, C., and Gitterman, A. (1980). *A life model of social work practice*. New York: Columbia University Press.

Gutiérrez, L., GlenMaye, L., and DeLois, K. (1995). The organizational context of empowerment practice: Implications for social work administration. *Social Work*, 40(2), 249–258.

Health Resources and Services Administration. (1995). *Models that work*. Washington, DC: U.S. Government Printing Office.

Hurowitz, J. (1993). Toward a social policy in health. *NEJM*, 329(2), 130–133.

Johnson, A. (1994). Linking professionalism and community organization: A scholar/advocate approach. *Journal of Community Practice*, 1(2), 65–85.

Kahn, A., and Kamerman, S. (1993). *Integrating services integration: An overview of initiatives, issues and possibilities*. New York: National Center for Children in Poverty, Columbia University.

Kaplan, K. O. (1989). Social well-being: The future of the social and health care systems. *The Mt. Sinai Journal of Medicine*, 56(6), 483–489.

Kitagawa, E. M., and Hauser, P. M. (1973). *Differential mortality in the United States*. Cambridge, MA: Harvard University Press.

Laveist, T. (1993). Segregation, poverty and empowerment: Health consequences for African-Americans. *The Milbank Memorial Quarterly*, 71(1), 41–64.

Mechanic, D. (1980). The management of psychosocial problems in primary medical care: The potential role for social work. *Journal of Human Stress*, 6(4), 16–21.

Miller, R. S. (Ed.). (1983). *Primary health care: More than medicine*. Englewood Cliffs, NJ: Prentice-Hall.

Nacman, M. (1977). Social work in health settings: A historical review. *Social Work in Health Care*, 2(4), 7–23.

Netting, F. E., Kettner, P., and McMurty, S. (1993). *Social work macro practice.* New York: Longman.

Olson, M. (1986). Beyond specialization: Social work education and practice for health care and family life. *Journal of Social Work Education,* Spring/Summer, 30–37.

Padgett, D. K., Patrick, C., Schlesinger, H., and Burns, B. (1993). Linking physical and mental health services in medical care utilization. *Administration and Policy in Mental Health,* 20(5), 325–341.

Perlmutter, F. (1994). *Women and social change.* Washington, DC: National Association of Social Workers Press.

Poole, D. (1991). Broadening the definition of scholarship: Practice and action research. *Health and Social Work,* 16(4), 234–236.

Putman, R. (1993). The prosperous community: Social capital and public life. *The American Prospect,* 13, 35–42.

Putman, R. (1995). Bowling alone: America's declining social capital. *The National Voter,* 45(1), 9–11.

Rehr, H. (Eds.). (1982). *Milestones in social work and medicine: Social-health care concepts.* New York: Prodist.

Rehr, H., and Rosenberg, G. (Eds.). (1991). *The changing context of social-health care: Its implications for providers and consumers.* New York: Haworth Press.

Rosenberg, G. (1983). Advancing social work practice in health. *Social Work in Health Care,* 8(3), 30–44.

Rosenberg, G., and Weissman, A. (Eds.). (1994). *Social work in ambulatory care: New implications for health and social services.* New York: Haworth Press.

Rothman, J., Erlich, J., and Tropman, J. (1995). *Strategies for community intervention.* Itasca, Ill.: F. E. Peacock Publishers.

Schwartz, L. L. (1994). *The medicalization of social problems: American's special health care dilemma. Special report.* Washington, DC: American Health Systems Institute.

Siefert, K., Jayarante, S., and Martin, L. (1992). Implementing the public health social work forward plan: A research-based prevention curriculum for schools of social work. *Health and Social Work,* 17(1), 17–27.

Specht, H., and Courtney, M. (1994). *Unfaithful angels: How social work has abandoned its mission.* New York: Free Press.

U.S. Select Committee on Aging. (1991). *Aging America: Trends and projections.* Washington, DC: U.S. Government Printing Office.

Warren, R. L. (1978). The community in America (3d ed.). Chicago: Rand McNally.

Watkins, E. (1985). The conceptual base for public health social work. In A. Gitterman, R. B. Black, and F. Stein (Eds.), *Public health social work in maternal and child health: A forward plan.* Rockville, MD: Bureau of Health Care Delivery and Assistance, Health Resources and Services Administration, U.S. Department of Health and Human Services, 17–33.

Whitman, B., and Hennelly, A. (1982). The use of epidemiologic methods as the bridge between prevention and social work practice. *Social Work in Health Care,* 7, 27–38.

Whyte, W. (1991). *Participatory action research.* Newbury Park, CA: Sage.

Wittman, M. (1977). Application of knowledge about prevention in social work education and practice. *Social Work in Health Care,* 3(1), 37–47.

Zippay, A. (1995). The politics of empowerment. *Social Work,* 40(2), 263–267.

Opportunities for Social Workers in the Law?

The Jury Is Out

Mary Ann Mason

This essay suggests a variety of opportunities for social workers to participate more actively in a variety of legal settings, including child custody, child abuse and neglect, juvenile and adult offenders, mental illness and incompetence. The author notes that these new career tracks in the law could be both professionally satisfying and financially attractive. Mary Ann Mason is associate professor in the School of Social Welfare at the University of California at Berkeley. She has been a family law practitioner and has written on issues such as women, children, and related concerns. Recent publications include From Fathers' Property to Children's Rights: A History of Child Custody in America *(New York: Columbia University Press, 1994); and* Debating Children's Lives *(Newbury Park, CA: Sage, 1994) with Eileen Gambrill.*

The American legal system is overwhelmed. Parties may wait months, and sometimes years, for their day in court. More efficient and less costly ways of serving justice are being considered in virtually all jurisdictions—and they include possible new roles for social workers. Social workers are already in the courtroom, and they work with the police and officers of the court on a daily basis. They appear as witnesses, expert witnesses, or petitioners. However, these roles could be expanded. Social workers could take on the quasi-judicial roles of hearing officers in juvenile, civil commitment, workers' compensation, and other administrative hearings. Outside the courtroom, mediation in divorce and custody matters are growing alternatives to litigation. Social workers are well placed to extend their skills into this arena. Finally, for many of the populations normally served by social workers—the poor, disabled, elderly, and mentally ill—the world has become an increasingly complicated legal tangle. Social workers must increase their role as guides and advocates for clients making their way through the maze of new regulations.

These new career tracks in the law could be professionally satisfying and financially attractive, but they will not be realized unless social workers are prepared to assume them. Currently, social workers are not poised to act, and, in fact, some of the traditional employment roles of social workers in court-related activities are being gradually appropriated by other professionals. Psychologists, in particular, are taking over jobs as expert witnesses in child custody and other family matters that were previously assigned to social workers. In new areas, such as AIDS and disability rights, lawyers are assuming some of the advocacy and courtroom roles that could better be served by social workers. Organized vigilance and active promotion of social worker roles in the legal system are critical to prepare for the changes of the 21st century. Who is taking on this challenge?

Child Custody

The courtroom stilled, waiting for the judge to make his decision. It had been a complicated custody trial. The mother was an opera singer who traveled a good deal, and the father was a corporate lawyer who worked long hours. Their daughters were 3 and 5. Both wanted custody of the girls. The mother and father had each presented expert witnesses—one a clinical social worker, the other a clinical psychologist—who testified as to the nature of the relationship each had with the girls. The court had employed its own evaluator, a social worker. The court social worker was also called at trial to testify about the recommendations that she had submitted in her report.

This scenario is not futuristic; it happens every day in courtrooms across the country. According to my own study, since the 1960s the utilization of experts hired by mothers and fathers has risen from 10% to 38% of all trials (Mason, 1992). And judges routinely order their own expert evaluations. Changes in the law have removed the clear legal rules that previously guided judges in awarding custody—for example, a preference for the mother when the child is of "tender years." The standard now is usually a vague "best interest" test, forcing judges to rely upon experts to tell them what is in the best interest of the child (Mason, 1994).

The future will not reverse this trend, but it may offer opportunities to increase the role of social workers. This will occur in two ways. First, individuals and the courts may come to prefer social workers over clinical psychologists as expert witnesses because the former can better understand family dynamics as a whole. Although clinical psychologists are trained to treat individual problems and individual relationships, social workers are trained to understand the social context. Social workers are better able to evaluate the total environment in which a child spends his day—the other caretakers, the quality of the school, and peer relationships. For many children of working parents, time spent with their parents is only a fraction of their day.

The second way in which the role of social workers may increase in resolving custody disputes is in the practice of mediation. Many states have rushed to endorse mediation as either a mandatory or voluntary alternative to litigation. Although mediation has its own set of rules, and its own training protocols, social workers are particularly well suited by their training to facilitate this nonadversarial approach. Social work family interventions are already based on a cooperative model of dispute resolution (Fineman, 1988).

Mediation is also growing in popularity as a voluntary, nonadversarial approach to the entire divorce process—from division of property through custody arrangements and the attendant support issues. Increasingly, couples are choosing to settle the matters themselves, with the guidance of a single mediator, rather than allowing two lawyers to fight it out for them in court. Here also social workers, with the unique skills they offer, could establish a strong foothold in this burgeoning new field. It is also increasingly common for a social worker to team up with a lawyer. As a unit, they can handle the counseling and the legal aspects of divorce for both parties. With mediation, it is possible (although not always practiced) to involve the children in the process—to listen to their needs and desires in a manner that the adversarial process does not normally allow (Erickson & Erickson, 1988).

Child Abuse and Neglect

The courtroom is filled with lawyers. In this juvenile court hearing regarding the alleged neglect of Kevin, age 2, and Walter, age 5, the parents are represented by a public defender. County counsel represents Children's Protective Services. The children are represented by a lawyer appointed by the judge. The judge listens to the lawyers in a distracted manner, but pays close attention when the social worker from Children's Protective Services presents the facts of the case and offers a recommendation. The social worker offers specific evidence of the neglect charges—lack of nutrition and medical care—and suggests that the children become wards of the court. The social worker also offers a detailed plan for the parents to follow if they are to be reunited with their children.

This scenario currently occurs in courtrooms across the nation. Social workers are already the key players in abuse and neglect hearings. They normally initiate the petitions to bring, the action to court, and the judge looks to them, not to the attorneys, for evidence and guidance. They are also the key figures in following through with services to the families under court supervision, sometimes for several years. The prominence of social workers in dependency proceedings began with the inauguration of the first juvenile court in 1899. That Illinois court set the character of future juvenile courts by assigning several social workers to the court to provide services to the families (Axinn & Levin, 1992).

But there could be other roles here for social workers as well. In a few jurisdictions, social workers now serve as judges, or juvenile commissioners, as they are usually called. Because juvenile court hearings are usually informal, foregoing many of the usual procedural requirements, a commissioner need not have the trial experience or extensive legal knowledge usually required for becoming a judge. As the courts strive for belt-tightening efficiency,

social workers are well placed to take advantage of this possible new career track (Salzman & Proch, 1990).

As the case progresses, the parents may or may not have fulfilled the requirements laid out in the plan. Other hearings will be held to determine whether to reunite the parents and children, or otherwise make permanent plans for the children's future. At these hearings, a social worker may testify about the progress the parents have made but, typically, no one speaks for the child. As in most court proceedings, the children have no voice.

Some courts, however, have adopted a *guardian ad litem* model, appointing a special advocate for the child. It makes sense for this role to be filled by a social worker rather than a lawyer or a volunteer. A social worker is uniquely trained to best evaluate all aspects of the child's life. In England, under The Children Act of 1989, a child has the services of both a social worker and a legal advocate at any court proceeding that affects her or him. Under the English model, a child is guaranteed a voice. Social workers should promote this child-centered model in this country. It not only provides a voice for the child, but it offers another avenue by which a social worker can be a child advocate in the courtroom (Pugh, 1993).

Later that day, in another courtroom down the hall, a man is standing trial on the criminal charge of sexually abusing a child. With such a crime there is usually no corroborating evidence. The only evidence may be the child's testimony, and this may be weak or inconsistent, or the child may be too young to testify. In these cases, the courts have increasingly turned to expert witnesses, most often social workers or clinical psychologists, to explain to the court and to the jury the characteristics of sexually abused children. Social workers are uniquely qualified for this kind of testimony because they are the principal protectors of abused children. Social workers are the professionals most likely to counsel abused children and to work with their families (Mason, 1991b). In this trial, however, no social workers are to be seen. The only expert, a witness for the prosecution, is a clinical psychologist. The psychologist is reciting a litany of characteristics usually seen in a sexually abused child. In my study of expert testimony in cases of sexually abused children (Mason, 1991a), I found that psychologists are gaining on social workers as experts called to testify in child sex abuse cases. This is the same trend that was noted above in child custody cases. Social workers must be vigilant to the loss of opportunities for which they are best suited.

Juvenile and Adult Offenders

In another juvenile courtroom, the judge is sentencing a 16-year-old girl for a second petty theft offense. The girl stole about $45 worth of makeup from Walgreens, stuffing it into big pockets in the inside of her coat. The girl's probation officer is sitting with her. The judge sentences the girl to 100 hours of community service and tells her she must check in every week with her probation officer.

Who is this probation officer? It could be someone with a background in police work or security, but it is not usually a social worker. Why not? Working with troubled teens is part of the training and practice of social work. No other profession is as well-equipped to take on the probation officer's tasks. Unfortunately, with the rise of juvenile violence, the social model of rehabilitation for teen offenders, the intent of the original juvenile court, has been replaced by a deterrence model. Political pressure now dictates that public safety rather than child welfare become the primary consideration in dealing with juvenile offenders (Schwartz, 1989). Only a strong child welfare

lobby, akin to the child-saving movement that helped launch the juvenile court at the turn of the century, could affect this trend. Social workers should be the leading voice in this movement to reintroduce rehabilitation as the standard for juvenile offenders.

In the same courthouse, an adult offender may be about to receive his sentence for burglary. In this court, a social worker may be called upon—not as an expert witness, who testifies about specialized knowledge—but as a witness who knows pertinent facts about the case. In this instance, the social worker will testify as to his experience with the defendant while the defendant was on probation from a previous burglary conviction. The social worker was not his probation officer, but he supervised the defendant in a back-to-work program. His testimony regarding the defendant's willingness to find a job, and any work experience, will weigh heavily in the sentencing decision (Salzman & Proch, 1990).

Social workers already play important roles in the counseling and rehabilitation of convicted criminals, both inside and outside prison, and they sometimes serve as probation officers. Unfortunately, corrections is an extremely expensive growth industry, and taxpayers are sometimes reluctant to pay highly trained personnel to perform these services for convicted criminals. Deterrence with minimal maintenance, rather than rehabilitation, has become the popular political viewpoint in this arena. As with juvenile offenders, effective professional advocacy advocating prevention and rehabilitation are necessary to reverse this trend.

Mental Illness and Incompetency

Social work is one of the major professions that serves the mentally ill, the developmentally disabled, and the incompetent elderly.

The legal system has become increasingly activist in promoting the rights of these groups. Family members or doctors are no longer allowed to make decisions for them. Civil commitment hearings, conservatorship hearings, and hearings relating to forced drug-taking for serious disorders are now routine. Social workers can and do play an important role as patient advocates in these hearings, but they could expand their roles here, as in juvenile court, by serving as hearing officers as well. In a related arena, they are well-qualified to sit on the proliferating bioethics boards of hospitals and other institutions where agonizing decisions regarding the right to live and the right to die are decided (Christoffel, 1982).

Legal Advocacy

A client who is HIV positive claims he was fired from his position as a chef when his employer learned of his condition. Another client is in trouble with the Immigration and Naturalization Service and dreads deportation. This client will not come in for prenatal care because she fears disclosure of her illegal status. Every day social workers are faced with a wide variety of legal problems that confront their clients. Although a social worker cannot expect to become expert in all areas of the law, a basic knowledge of key areas will aid the social worker in his or her role as an advocate (Wood, Marks, & Dilley, 1990).

A few of the greatly expanding areas of the law where social workers could serve as effective advocates and troubleshooters for their clients are in the area covered by the Americans with Disabilities Act (ADA) and in the areas of domestic violence, sexual harassment, and immigration law.

In 1992, America enacted a comprehensive and complex law, the Americans with Disabili-

ties Act, which protects the right of disabled Americans from discrimination in employment, public accommodations, transportation, and telecommunications. Many social workers find their disabled clients, and those with serious illness such as AIDS or cancer, facing everyday discrimination. Unfortunately, the administrative courts charged with enforcing the broad new law are already seriously backed up with cases. And, in most instances, the client may be too timid to take his case to the EEOC, or the Justice Department. A social worker with an understanding of the law can support a client in bringing a claim to the proper agency, or finding an appropriate nongovernmental support group to pursue the claim through the proper channels. Sometimes a social worker can simply help the client stand up to the source of discrimination. Confronting an unfair employer with the threat of enforcement may be all that is necessary. If the HIV-positive client exhibited his knowledge of the law and made it clear to his employer that he would pursue legal remedies if not reinstated, the matter might be resolved immediately (Wood, Marks, & Dilley, 1990).

Similarly, the laws relating to domestic violence and rape have grown tougher and more protective of victims in nearly all jurisdictions. A clear knowledge of the enforcement mechanisms and the penalties will aid a social worker in advising and protecting a client. Sexual harassment in the workplace and the classroom and, in its most sinister form, as sexual stalking have also received expanded legal protection and remedies. Women clients who are victims of violence now have effective weapons to fight back, if they are guided to use them.

And increasingly clients seeking social services are part of the huge new wave of immigrants, some of them illegal. Immigration law is complex, and some states, like California, have passed special laws that restrict services to illegal immigrants. A social worker who tries to help immigrants must understand both their real and unfounded fears of the law, and serve as their personal advocate.

Legal advocacy skills are critical as well for the populations of homeless clients that social workers have longed served. Sometimes the courts are the only avenue for asserting clients' rights to basic requirements of adequate food and shelter and some form of rehabilitation.

Agenda for the 21st Century

It is not at all evident that social workers will be prepared to handle expanding legal challenges. Without preparation, not only will career opportunities be lost, but social workers will play an increasingly marginal role in their clients' lives. Social services and psychotherapy are not sufficient to help clients face their real worlds of juvenile court, domestic violence, and deportation. A plan for the future must be formulated on at least two fronts: the classroom and professional organizations.

Classroom Skills

Professional social work education should, as a minimum, include a strong introduction to each of the following areas of law and procedure:

- Juvenile court law
- Mental health law
- Health and disability law
- Family law
- Discrimination law
- Laws relating to domestic violence
- Aging law
- The role of experts in court

In addition to a basic introduction to these areas, students pursuing a specialty, such as children and families or mental health, should be required to complete an in-depth course covering the important legal issues in that specialty and the range of legal roles the social worker might fill there.

Professional Advocacy

Professional social work organizations such as NASW (National Association of Social Workers) should protect and foster the career tracks of MSWs in the legal system, as they do with any other bread and butter issue. Activities promoting social workers in court should include lobbying with the legislature, judges, state bars, and other legal organizations regarding the superior qualifications of social workers as expert witnesses, hearing officers, and administrative court judges. Professional organizations should also engage in continuing education opportunities for social workers to develop and expand their legal knowledge and courtroom skills.

It is also the business of professional organizations, at both the national and local levels, to lobby for changes in the legal system to promote the interests of their clients. As noted in this article, changes in the juvenile justice system that promote rehabilitation rather than deterrence are most likely to result from forceful social work advocacy. Similarly, social workers deal with populations, such as the frail elderly, the homeless, and the mentally ill for whom there are few other advocates. Clients and the legal system will be well served if social workers become more active participants in this arena in the 21st century.

Will the social work profession rise to the challenge of an expanded role in the 21st-century legal system? The verdict is awaited.

REFERENCES

Axinn, J., & Levin, H. (1992). *Social Welfare: A History of the American Response to Need*. New York: Longman.

Christoffel, T. (1982). *Health and The Law*. New York: Free Press.

Erickson, S,. & Erickson, M. S. M. (1988). Don and Linda: A typical divorce case. *Mediation Quarterly 21*(3), 4–25.

Fineman, M. (1988). Dominant discourse: Professional language, and legal change in child custody decision-making. *Harvard Law Review 101*(4), 720–805.

Mason, M. A. (Fall/Winter 1991a). A judicial dilemma: Expert witness testimony in child sex abuse cases. *Journal of Psychiatry and Law*. 185–219.

Mason, M. A. (1991b). The McMartin case re-visited: The conflict between social work and criminal justice. *Social Work 36*(5), 391–395.

Mason, M. A. (1992). Patterns of appellate court decisions in custody disputes: 1920, 1960, and 1990. Paper delivered at Law and Society, Philadelphia, May 1992.

Mason, M. A. (1994). *From Father's Property to Children's Rights: A History of Child Custody in America*. New York: Columbia University Press.

Pugh, G. (1993). *Thirty Years of Change*. London: National Children's Bureau.

Salzman, A., & Proch, K. (1990). *Law in Social Work Practice*. Chicago: Nelson Hall.

Schwartz, I. (1989). *Injustice for Juveniles*. Lexington, MA: Lexington Books.

Wood, G., Marks, R., & Dilley, J. (1990). *AIDS Law for Mental Health Professionals*. Berkeley, CA: Celestial Arts Press.

Occupational Social Work Practice

Beth Lewis

At the close of the 20th century, the world of work is changing more rapidly than at any time since the early years of the Industrial Revolution. These changes will have a direct and multifaceted impact on workers and their families and will require social workers to develop new directions in service delivery, education, and research. This essay on occupational social work by Beth Lewis, DSW, ACSW, a social worker at Yale-New Haven Hospital and assistant clinical professor of social work in medicine at Yale University, analyzes the significance of current workplace changes for social work practice and presents a variety of alternative models through which social workers can expand their role in this field in the future. Lewis concludes that future practice and education in occupational social work must synthesize research on human needs, policy analysis, direct practice methods, and an ethos of distributive justice in order to be effective.

Lewis's perspective comes from rich experience as a practitioner, researcher, and educator. She has worked in the Yale Occupational and Environmental Medicine Program since its inception in 1979, and has also taught on the faculties of the University of Connecticut, Southern Connecticut State University, Fordham University, Smith College, and Hunter College. Her research has focused on the experiences of workers who apply for workers' compensation and the social situation of workers who have developed work-related diseases.

The changes now occurring in the world of work, and projected to continue at a more rapid pace into the 21st century, are of great magnitude, with broad significance for social work practice in this arena. Changes in rates of unionization of the workforce, the shift from an industrial to a service economy, growing numbers of part-time and temporary workers, high rates of chronic unemployment, and an erosion of health benefits constitute only a partial representation of the total ongoing and projected structural changes in the workplace affecting workers and families and shaping practice strategies for the future. Expansion of social work programs to meet the needs of the workers in this changing milieu will be necessary as we move forward with training and service delivery in this vital field of practice.

This essay will address the multifaceted nature of change in the world of work and examine the implications of these changes for social work practice. Based on a review of historical perspectives and an overview of current practice in the field, it will then outline the future needs and areas for growth and development in service delivery, education, and research.

Current and Future Trends in the Workplace and Workforce

Trends in the world of work having major implications for future practice in the field may be grouped under four major headings, each comprising overlapping areas of change in the workforce and among work organizations: demographic changes, access to vocational training and educational opportunities, changes in industrial structure, and workplace health and safety.

Demographic Changes: Aging, Feminization, and Diversity in the Workforce

There are currently approximately 128 million workers in the United States, with projections of 151 million—a 19% gain—by the year 2005 [U.S. Department of Labor (U.S. DOL), 1994].

In the year 2000, there will be about 55 million adults age 55 and older compared to 51 million just 10 years ago. Given the trend toward longer life expectancy, higher age of retirement—retirement age is projected to be 67 in the 21st century (Stuen & Worden, 1993)—and lower birth rates since the post-WWII era, we will see a continued aging of the workforce. These combined trends will bring about the likelihood of increased competition among older workers for middle- and upper-level jobs, coupled with a shortage of younger workers to fill entry-level jobs (Lieberman, 1983) and increasing need among the elderly for continued employment in and/or reentry to the workforce. Further, subgroups among the population of older workers suffer disproportionately from the effects of discrimination, with older women and people of color more highly represented among the groups working in jobs at the lower end of the pay scale (Crawley, 1992).

Increasing attention must be paid by the profession to gerontological occupational social work as a subspecialization, advancing programs in pre- and post-retirement counseling, increasing services to retirees, and assisting with job reentry and/or training for older workers, as well as providing education aimed at dispelling harmful myths about older workers that affect their employment opportunities (Crawley, 1992).

The rate at which women are entering the workforce continues to grow rapidly. From 1969 to 1993, the percentage of the workforce that was female rose from 38% to 46%, and this rate is expected to continue to rise (U.S. DOL, 1994). The trend toward feminization of the workforce calls for continuing consideration of work and family life, issues that will grow in importance into the 21st century. As women commonly assume the caregiver role, dependent care—child care and elder care—will continue to predominate among the unmet needs of the workforce, with difficulties inherent in managing conflicts between work and family life continuing to frame the broad area of need that must be addressed by social workers in occupational settings of the future.

The ethnic and racial composition of the workforce will become increasingly diverse in coming years. African Americans now account for 14 million workers, or 11% of the total workforce, and are projected to comprise 12% by 2005. Hispanic workers currently number 10 million, or 8% of the workforce, and are likely to comprise 11% by 2005. Asian and other minorities will increase in percentage of the workforce from 4% to 6% by the year 2005 (U.S. DOL, 1994). Net immigration is expected to average 880,000 persons annually, with an expected increase in the portion of the workforce that is of Hispanic, Asian, and Pacific Islander descent. The need to assist work organizations by the development of policies that are reflective of considerations of ethnic diversity among the workforce and supportive of nondiscriminatory hiring and promotional practices is paramount among the issues facing the profession.

Access to Vocational Training and Educational Opportunities

Trends in employment and employment opportunities will continue toward increasing segmentation (Ozawa, 1980; Stafford, 1985). An increasing share of openings will occur in high-paying jobs requiring college training, although many jobs will become available that pay below-average wages and do not require a college education (Rosenthal, 1995; U.S. DOL, 1994). The widening gap between levels of skill in the population and the demand for skills in the fast-growth industries coupled with the lack of job and educational preparation among poor and minority youth have combined to create a workforce in which workers with low educational levels are confined to occupational fields with poor growth prospects, where both remuneration and benefits tend to be below average (Fiske, 1989; U.S. DOL, 1994). Although there has been an increase in employer-sponsored education and reorganization programs, recent studies have indicated that organizations that have undertaken these efforts are predominantly in the manufacturing sector, employ 200–500 or more employees, offer more generous wage and benefits packages, are more likely to promote from within, and—among the service sector—are less likely to be unionized (Bassi, 1995). Workers in smaller workplaces and in the service industries, therefore, are less likely to benefit from workplace education programs and "reorganization" initiatives. The need for access to worker education and a coordinated approach to developing new models of teamwork, inclusive of the broad spectrum of job categories, must be addressed by social workers in occupational settings, with an emphasis on creating opportunities for those who may benefit the most from participation in these initiatives.

Changes in Industrial Structure: Access to Benefits, Unemployment, Unionization, and Job Security

The days when the manufacturing sector dominated growth in the American work economy are rapidly receding into the past. Job growth in manufacturing reached an all-time high in 1979 but has declined since, and is projected never to return to its former higher level. Jobs in the service industries (business and health), on the other hand—now comprising 28% of all employment—will account for practically all of the total anticipated growth of 26.4 million jobs, and create most of the growth in new wealth between now and the year 2005 (Johnston, 1987; U.S. DOL, 1994). As these jobs will demand much higher skill levels than the jobs in service industries demand today, social workers may play a role in advocating for adequate educational and training opportunities for first-time job seekers, as well as for those who seek opportunities to maintain employment in their present place of work.

Generally speaking, workers in unionized workplaces are far more likely to have health-care benefits than workers in nonunion workplaces—95% versus 75% (Wiatrowski, 1990). Therefore, the decrease in employment in the more highly unionized manufacturing industries (only 1 in 4 workers in 1990 compared to 2 in 5 in 1960), has led to a loss of workplace benefit coverage among the workforce as a whole. Only six in ten workers currently receive health benefits and the proportion has been steadily declining over the past decade. Among those that do receive coverage, the amount that employees have been required to contribute toward their health-care plan has been steadily increasing (Wiatrowski, 1990).

The growth in part-time and temporary employment has, in addition to lowering wages, also affected access to work-based benefits. Only 16% of part-time workers (currently 17% of the labor force) receive benefits, and the vast majority of temporary workers (three times the rate in 1984, and expected to continue to rise) are employed in workplaces that do not offer benefits to any of their workers (Wiatrowski, 1990). Further, changing conceptions of "family" have not been reflected in benefit policies affecting dependent coverage: Unmarried partners, same-sex partners, adopted or foster children, parents, or family members other than spouse are typically not included in dependent coverage plans. An understanding of the impact of inadequate income and benefit coverage on the well-being of workers and their families constitutes another area for future emphasis, at all levels of practice.

Unions have lost, and continue to lose, much ground among the workforce, with recent collective bargaining agreements yielding lower average percentage pay increases, overall, than at any time in the recent past (Muhl, 1995; Williamson & Brown, 1995). In contrast to unionization rates in 1945, when unionization of the workforce was at its height (36% of the workforce), in 1993 only 17% of the workforce was organized (Wiatrowski, 1995). Should the current trend in union membership decline continue, it is projected that private-sector union membership will fall to 5% by the year 2000 (McDonald, 1992). Factors that have been found to be significant in contributing to non-unionized workers' desire for unionization—pay, job security, and the handling of promotions, among others—will continue to form the basis for job dissatisfaction among workers who desire unionization (Robinson, 1988). Professional practice in both employer- and labor-sponsored settings must incorporate recognition of the importance of these basic areas of perceived need among the workforce into practice in occupational settings.

Future projections point toward high rates of long-term, permanent, and chronic unemployment that will persist and continue to grow among the least skilled and among ethnic minorities. Today's unemployed worker is older and more likely to come from a minority group. Three-fifths of the long-term unemployed are men; one-fifth are African American and one-ninth are Hispanic. The alarmingly high differential between unemployment rates for whites and persons of color has changed little over the past several decades: jobless rates for African Americans (12.9%) have consistently remained 2 to $2^1/2$ times—and rates for Hispanics (10.6%), more than $1^1/2$ times—that of whites (6%) (U.S. DOL, 1994). Middle-aged, midcareer workers who lost their jobs, due either to plant closings during the early 1980s, or, more recently, to downsizing, have fared poorly in efforts to reenter the workforce (Sherraden, 1985; Leana & Feldman, 1992). As noted in earlier writings, work with the unemployed, including both the provision of supportive services to individuals and families, as well as advocacy for full employment, remains a compelling, and largely neglected, area for expanded professional practice (Briar, 1980).

Workplace Health and Safety

Projections for the future of workplace health are grim, with advocacy for strengthened governmental regulatory function in this sphere representing another area of professional emphasis for the future. Workers, in general, lack information about the effects of hazards and are likely to be exposed to more than one hazardous substance (Selikoff, 1989). Higher rates of temporary and part-time employment, with less likelihood of access to a range of benefits, and increasing employment in small workplaces and nonunionized plants, coupled with deregulation of workplaces, have led to a lowering of activities aimed at early detection and follow-up of the effects of hazardous exposures (Landrigan and Selikoff, 1989).

The incidence of violence in the workplace has escalated. An increasing number of work-related deaths and injuries are due to higher rates of homicide, violent acts, and assaults. Increasing rates of repetitive trauma (impairment in physical functioning caused by repetitive strain), particularly among women, are also of concern (Stout et al., 1996; U.S. DOL, 1994). Social work practice in work organizations must embrace a comprehensive model of service delivery to work-injured and work-diseased workers, augmented by workplace education and policy development in injury and illness prevention, and continuity in employment and income replacement.

Historical Overview: Conflicting Perspectives

Historical accounts of social work in this field include varying perspectives on the role of professional practice that emerged concurrently with the growth of industrialization and unionization in the United States.

Controversy regarding the field's ability to maintain a professional focus within the historical context of a corporate auspice has been the focus of concern of several authors who have chronicled the history of occupational social work (Abramovitz & Epstein, 1983; Bakalinsky, 1980; Googins, 1985; Popple, 1981). According to this perspective, the direct service model, or EAP, has been identified as having its roots in the corporate alcoholism programs of the 1940s (Blomquist, 1979, cited in Abramovitz & Epstein, 1983; Wyers & Kaulukukui, 1984) or, alternatively, in the earlier role of the "welfare secretary," who was

employed by management in the beginning decades of the 20th century (Mor-Borak et al., 1993; Popple, 1981). In making a range of services available to workers and their families, the role of welfare secretary fulfilled the function of social control of the workforce, aiding in employers' efforts to avoid unionization of the workforce (Popple, 1981).

Perspectives on the role of the profession vis-à-vis the labor movement have focused on the changing nature of social work's relationship with organized labor throughout the century, beginning with the period of union formation, through to the development and expansion of social work practice within labor organizations. This history has been distinguished by both shared goals and periods of conflict, with fluctuation in the nature of this relationship described as owing to labor's perception of social work as having primary allegiance to management goals (Karger, 1988; Straussner & Phillips, 1988).

In describing the development of practice in this field, other authors have traced its roots to the social reform movement, documenting need among the growing, largely immigrant, industrial labor force and paving the way for the passage of legislation aimed at improving the social and work conditions of this population (Lewis, 1990; Mulloy & Kurzman, 1993).

Current Practice in the World of Work

Currently, professional social workers with MSW and/or DSW degrees and eligibility for state licensure have emerged as the predominant provider (Kurzman, 1993) in what has been termed "the best known and most rapidly developing model of practice in the World of Work"—Employee Assistance Programs and Member Assistance Programs (EAPs and MAPs) (Smith & Gould, 1993).

NASW's efforts in 1985 to compile a mailing list of social workers practicing in this field resulted in the self-identification of 2200 individuals as occupational social workers and revealed that 614 licensed social workers were members of the Association of Labor Management Administrators & Consultants on Alcoholism (ALMACA) (Kurzman, 1993). In the area of social work education, a survey conducted in 1985 that looked at the prevalence of occupational social work training received positive responses from 39 schools of social work. Respondents identified the private sector work organization as the most common field setting of occupational social service delivery (Maiden & Hardcastle, 1985, cited in Straussner, 1990).

Estimates of the number of EAP-model programs currently in operation in work organizations across the country range from 5500 (Wyers & Kaulukukui, 1984) to 10,000 (including MAPs) (Akabas, 1993). A recent study looking at EAP prevalence among private, nonagricultural work settings, utilizing a stratified national probability sample of more than 6400 private, nonagricultural U.S. worksites with 50 or more full-time employees, revealed approximately 33% of 3200 respondents offering EAP services—an increase of 8.9% since 1985 (Hartwell et al., 1996). Yet, despite their numbers, no comprehensive study of social services offered in private industry exists to date (Abramovitz & Epstein, 1983). In carrying out a survey of 60 work sites, some of which were known to offer social services, authors Wyers and Kaulukukui questioned the extent to which previous studies of industrial social work practice critically analyzed the function, nature, and scope of services. The authors found considerable differences between unionized and nonunionized and between small and large corporations in the emphasis each places on such issues as the need for day-care services and employee financial problems (Wyers & Kaulukukui, 1984).

Social work practice carried out under the auspice of labor organizations has more readily lent itself to quantification and description, with estimates of 14 unions out of the total of 77 internationals nationwide (*Labor Union Directory*, 1996) providing jobs for 79 social workers at the end of 1989 (Straussner & Phillips, 1988). The union-based member assistance program—a model of service initiated in 1943 in the National Maritime Union under the direction of Bertha Reynolds—gained considerable ground during the 1970s and 80s, most notably in unions representing textile, automobile, hospital, and public sector employees, among others (Mulloy & Kurzman, 1993).

Direct services offered in both labor- and employer-sponsored settings to working and retired individuals and family members include linkage to entitlements and other public and private resources; short-term counseling with a full range of job-related and non–job-related psychosocial and health/disability concerns; and specialized and emergency services in the areas of substance abuse, disability management, and mental health care (Mulloy & Kurzman, 1993).

Identifying and addressing the needs of special populations within the world of work has been an area of increasing emphasis in both employer-sponsored and labor-sponsored settings and is reflective of the changing demographics and needs of the workforce. Such populations include older workers and retirees (Mor-Borak & Tynan, 1993; Safford, 1988); disabled (Mudrick, 1991); chemically dependent (Bacharach, Bamberger, & Sonnenstuhl, 1994; Heyman, 1971; Weiss, 1980); relocated workers (Anderson & Stark, 1988; Gaylord, 1979); women (Gerstel & Gross, 1987; Gruber & Bjorn,

1982; Soine, 1995); unemployed, dislocated, and underemployed (AFL-CIO & Hunter College School of Social Work, 1985; Auslander, 1988; Berenbeim, 1986; Briar, 1980; Cobb et al., 1966; Cowdry, 1991; Ensminger & Celentano, 1988; Ezzy, 1993; Krystal et al., 1983; Leana & Feldman, 1992; Linn et al., 1986; Riches & Ternowetsky, 1990; Sharlach et al., 1991; Sherraden, 1985; Stafford, 1985; Strauss, 1951); ethnic and racial minorities (Crawley, 1992; Gray & Barrow, 1993); workers exposed to hazardous conditions (Balgopal, 1989; Balgopal & Nofz, 1989; Jankovic & Dotson, 1981; Lawson, 1987; Lewis, 1989; Meiss, 1991; Robinson, 1988; Shanker, 1983; Walker, 1989), and mental health (Austin, 1977; Madonia, 1985).

Professional social work practice in the world of work is carried out within a broader social context characterized by a lack of integration between the corporate and public welfare systems and the basic inadequacies of each in meeting the needs of workers and their dependents (Gerstel & Gross, 1987; Kammerman & Kahn, 1987). Dilemmas encountered in practice in this field, as with practice in other host settings, are particularly defined by the characteristics of employing organizations—and of the nature of work production—in our society. Acknowledgment of these features of the host setting has led to the development of practice models that address the structural context of employee needs. For example, in her discussion of social work practice in the area of work-related stress, Donovan noted the relative efficacy of models of group organization aimed at identifying and eliminating "stressors" in the workplace, compared to an emphasis on individual coping mechanisms, in alleviating occupational-related stress (Donovan, 1987).

Earlier writings addressing these issues have focused on the need to conceptualize practice in

this field as a "continuum" of services, moving from "micro" interventions, aimed at providing a variety of services to the workforce, to "macro" interventions, aimed at affecting corporate policy in all areas of decision making (Ozawa, 1980). Authors Kurzman & Akabas have stressed the importance of maintaining a focus on "achieving the more person-oriented goals of the profession" within the setting of the work organization, eventually moving toward policy and program development that is responsive to both work and community need (Kurzman & Akabas, 1981). More recent writings have highlighted the difficulties inherent in efforts to "integrate the person-centered approach and the structural change model," in the context of direct service provision in the setting of the labor or workplace organization (Ramanathan, 1992). These authors have pointed to the usefulness of an ecological model in addressing problems of the work organization that contribute to, and often underlie, the presenting problem of the individual worker, particularly in the case of workplace injury (Balgopal, 1989; Balgopal & Nofz, 1989).

Directions for the Future: Expansion of the Social Work Role

Drawing on previous work in the field, Straussner has developed a typology of five models of occupational social work (Straussner, 1990) that may be useful as a guide in outlining and summarizing future areas of emphasis for practice in the world of work:

1. *Employee Service Model*: The broad range of social, psychological, vocational, and financial needs of workers and their families will continue to form the basis for direct service delivery in workplace and labor-sponsored settings. Education and training toward the

goal of increasing supervisory and management sensitivity to the needs of new employees and special populations will continue to present areas of opportunity for social workers in small and complex organizations.

2. *Employer/Work Organization Service Model*: Changes in the workforce and structure of work organizations will require an expanded role for social workers in the area of policy development and program planning. Social work consultation to organizations will increasingly be aimed at influencing work organization policy in the areas of health and safety practices, conflict mediation, benefit structures (including child and elder care), training and development, and affirmative action.

3. *Consumer Service Model:* Less emphasis has been given within the field to program development in the area of consumer need, as compared with employee and employer need. As populations at risk experience increasing barriers to accessing private and public sector services, entitlements, and advocacy, the skills of the occupational social worker can be well utilized in efforts to identify consumer need and devise programs that encourage equitable access to workplace products and/or services. For example, the occupational social worker practicing in a health organization may be called upon to conduct a needs assessment among a population in the community who may be experiencing difficulties accessing adequate care, assisting the organization in developing programs that may correct inequities in service delivery.

4. *Corporate Social Responsibility Model*: Linkage of work organization resources to the wide range of community need will play an increasing role in the activities carried out by occupational social workers in the future. Social workers must broaden their activities within work organizations to include the use of community organization skills in networking, needs assessment, and program development within the community, in tandem with the more traditional roles of advisement and consultation in corporate giving endeavors.

5. *Work-Related Public Policy Model*: Policy planning and analysis in the world of work has been identified as an area requiring further emphasis and development (Mor-Borak et al., 1993). The trends in the workplace and among the workforce identified in this essay frame the areas for further social policy development in the world of work, including—but not limited to—analysis of training and educational needs within a given community or among the working-age population as a whole; the impact of differing models of management within work organizations on employee productivity; the effect of workplace production processes on employee and community health; and the degree to which work organization human resource and health benefit policies meet the needs of a changing workforce and family structure.

Conclusions

The adherence to ethical principles of distributive justice, undergirding professional practice in the world of work (Kurzman, 1983), forcefully argues for a continued and expanded role for social work in the coming years, through the provision of services to those in greatest need. Included among this group are those who—without adequate resources—have been and will continue to be effectively "locked out" of occupational opportunity and/or consigned to work in the most menial and unstable jobs. The need to evaluate current and future approaches to practice—what services will be offered, where, and to whom—will become more critical as the gap between the "haves" and "have-nots" in workplaces and surrounding communities widens and unmet needs intensify. Social work in labor and management settings will need to address the significant differences that exist in both the numbers of programs, as well as in the range of non–work-related services offered to workers and their families, dependent on size of the workforce and organizational type. Services provided to injured workers must incorporate a focus on their rehabilitative and work-reentry needs, encouraging the development of workplace policies that ensure job security for the work-disabled population. Linkages must be made between workplace health promotional activities and the development of organizational policies focused on prevention of work-related injury and disease (Walsh, et al., 1991).

Future emphasis in curriculum development must reflect educational needs in the areas of social policy, preparing students to carry out change on the organizational level as well as in the provision of services (Mor-Borak et al., 1993). Increased opportunities for practice with youth job-entry programs (Eder, 1989), as well as vocational rehabilitation and training programs, emerge as a critical need, providing a focus for professional activity that is inclusive of the needs of the under- and the unemployed. Also, social work education must seek to broaden the profession's knowledge base to include the system of entitlements and protective legislation affecting older workers and retirees.

Research in this field must play a role in describing the needs of special populations and in evaluating programs designed to address these needs. The needs of ethnic and racial minorities, women, the elderly, and the disabled, and programs addressing the mental health needs of workers require particular emphasis (Googins, 1993); likewise, variations in the outcomes of different approaches to addressing problems of chemical dependence among workers require continuing evaluation (Bacharach et al., 1994; Dover, 1990; Walsh et al., 1992).

In summary, occupational social work practice will continue to expand in the direction of meeting the needs of workers—those within the workplace, those seeking entry to the workplace, and those who have been uprooted from the workplace. An understanding of the current and future social and economic trends affecting work and workers is essential to the continuing agenda of promoting practice that is responsive to needs and capable of addressing areas for change within work organizations and the broader social context of work.

REFERENCES

Abramovitz, Mimi, and Epstein, Irwin. The politics of privatization: Industrial social work and private enterprise. *Urban and Social Change Review*, Vol. 16, No. 1, Winter 1983, pp. 13–19.

Akabas, Sheila. Introduction. In Paul Kurzman & Sheila Akabas, eds., *Work and Well-Being: The Occupational Social Work Advantage*. Washington, DC: NASW, 1993, pp.xvii–xxiv.

Akabas, Sheila, & Kurzman, Paul, eds. *Work, Workers and Work Organizations*. Englewood Cliffs, NJ: Prentice-Hall, 1982.

American Federation of Labor and Congress of Industrial Organizations. *The Changing Situation of Workers and Their Unions: A Report by the AFL-CIO Committee on the Evolution of Work*. Washington, DC: AFL-CIO. Publication No. 165. February 1985, pp. 1–34.

American Federation of Labor and Congress of Industrial Organizations (AFL-CIO) & Hunter College School of Social Work—Jack Kamaiko Fund. Presentation: A dialog on "serving workers who have lost their jobs." 1985.

Anderson, Charlene, & Stark, Carolyn. Psychosocial problems of job relocation: Preventive roles in industry. *Social Work*, Vol. 33, No. 1, January 1988, pp. 38–41.

Auslander, Gail. Social networks and health status of the unemployed. *Health and Social Work*, Summer 1988, pp. 191–200.

Austin, Michael, & Jackson, Erwin. Occupational mental health and human services: A review. *Health and Social Work*, Vol. 2, No. 1, February 1977, pp. 92–118.

Bacharach, Samuel, Bamberger, Peter, & Sonnenstuhl, William. *Member Assistance Programs in the Workplace: The Role of Labor in the Prevention and Treatment of Substance Abuse*. Ithaca, NY: ILR Press, 1994.

Bakalinsky, Rosalie. People vs. profits: Social work in industry. *Social Work*, Vol. 25, No. 6, November 1980, pp. 471–475.

Balgopal, Pallassana. Occupational social work: An expanded clinical perspective. *Social Work*, September 1989, pp. 437–442.

Balgopal, Pallassana, & Nofz, Michael. Injured workers: From statutory compensation to holistic social work services. *Journal of Sociology and Social Welfare*, Vol. 16, 1989, pp. 147–164.

Bassi, Laurie. Upgrading the U.S. workplace: Do reorganization, education help? *Monthly Labor Review*, May 1995, pp. 37–47.

Berenbeim, Ronald. *Company Programs to Ease the Impact of Shutdowns*. New York: The Conference Board, 1986.

Briar, Katherine. Helping the unemployed client. *Journal of Sociology and Social Welfare*, Vol. 7, 1980, pp. 895–906.

The Coalition of Labor Union Women. *Bargaining for Family Benefits*. Washington, DC: AFL-CIO. Publication No. 0-228-0491-5.

Cobb, Sidney et al. The health of people changing jobs: A description of a longitudinal study, *American Journal of Public Health*, Vol. 56, No. 9, September 1966, pp. 1476–1481.

Conrad, Peter, & Walsh, Diana. The new corporate health ethic: Lifestyle and the social control of work. *International Journal of Health Services*, Vol. 22, No. 1, 1992, pp. 89–111.

Cowdry, Kenneth. Training inner-city youth to work. *Personnel Journal*, October 1991, pp. 45–48.

Crawley, Brenda. The transformation of the American labor force: Elder African Americans and occupational social work. *Social Work*, Vol. 37, No. 1, January 1992, pp. 41–46.

Donovan, Rebecca. 1987. Stress in the workplace: A framework for research and practice. Social Casework, Vol. 68(5), 1987, pp. 256–266.

Dover, Michael. Labor-management programming: Critical issues. In E. Dante & R. McConaghy, eds., *Employee Assistance: Programs for the Future*. Englewood Cliffs, NJ: Prentice-Hall, Spring 1990.

Eder, Doris, ed. *A Partnership in Caring: A Blueprint for the Hunter College School of Social Works's Development Until the Year 2000*. New York: Hunter College School of Social Work, 1989, pp. 28–30.

Ensminger, Margaret, & Celentano, David. Unemployment and psychiatric distress: Social resources and coping. *Social Science & Medicine*, Vol. 27, No. 3, 1988, pp. 239–247.

Ezzy, Douglas. Unemployment and mental health: A critical review. *Social Science & Medicine*, Vol. 37, No. 1, 1993, pp. 41–52.

Fiske, Edward. Impending U.S. jobs "disaster": Work force unqualified to work. *New York Times*, September 25, 1989, p. 1.

Gaylord, Maxine. Relocation and the corporate family: Unexplored issues. *Social Work*, Vol. 24, No. 3, May, 1979, pp. 186–191.

Gerstel, Naomi, & Gross, Harriet, eds. *Families and Work*. Philadelphia: Temple University Press, 1987.

Googins, Bradley. Work-site research: Challenges and opportunities for social work. In Paul Kurzman & Sheila Akabas, eds. *Work and Well-Being: The Occupational Social Work Advantage*. Washington, DC: NASW, 1993, pp. 61–78.

Googins, Bradley, & Godfrey, Joline. The evolution of occupational social work. *Social Work*, Vol. 25, No. 5, September-October 1985, pp. 396–402.

Gray, Muriel, & Barrow, Frederica. 1993. Ethnic, cultural and social diversity in the workplace. In Paul Kurzman & Sheila Akabas, eds., *Work and Well-Being: The Occupational Social Work Advantage*. Washington, DC: NASW, 1993.

Gruber, James, & Bjorn, Lars. Blue-collar blues: The sexual harassment of women autoworkers. *Work and Occupations*, Vol. 9, No. 3, August 1982, pp. 271–298.

Hartwell, Tyler, & Steele, Paul et al. Aiding troubled employees: The prevalence, cost and characteristics of employee assistance programs in the United States. *American Journal of Public Health*, Vol. 86, No. 6, June 1996, pp. 804–808.

Heyman, Margaret. Employer-sponsored programs for problem drinkers. *Social Casework*, November 1971, pp. 547–552.

Jankovic, Joanne, & Dotson, David. Social work response to problems of occupational health. *Journal of Sociology and Social Welfare*, March 1981, pp. 62–69.

Johnston, William. *Workforce 2000: Work and Workers for the Twenty-first Century*. Indianapolis: Hudson Institute, 1987.

Kammerman, Sheila, & Kahn, Alfred. *The Responsive Workplace: Employers and a Changing Labor Force*. New York: Columbia University Press, 1987.

Karger, Howard. The common goals of labor and social work. In Howard Karger, ed., *Social Workers and Labor Unions*. Contributions in Labor Studies, number 26. New York: Greenwood Press, 1988.

Kilborn, Peter. Why labor wants the tired and poor. *New York Times*, October 29, 1995, p. E3.

Kochan, Thomas, ed. *Challenges and Choices Facing American Labor*. Cambridge: The MIT Press, 1986.

Krystal, Esthe et al. Serving the unemployed. *Social Casework*, Vol. 64, No. 2, February 1983, pp. 67–76.

Kurzman, Paul. Ethical issues in industrial social work practice. *Social Casework*, February 1983, pp. 105–111.

Kurzman, Paul, & Akabas, Sheila. Industrial social work as an arena for practice. *Social Work*, Vol. 26, No. 1, January 1981, pp. 51–60.

Kurzman, Paul, & Akabas, Sheila, eds. *Work and Well-Being: The Occupational Social Work Advantage*. Washington, DC: NASW, 1993.

Labor Union Directory. Famighetti, Robert, ed. *The World Almanac and Book of Facts 1996*. Mahwah, NJ: Funk & Wagnalls, pp. 156–157.

Landrigan, Philip, & Selikoff, Irving. *Occupational Health in the 1990's: Developing a Platform for Disease Prevention*. Annals of the New York Academy of Science, vol. 572, 1989.

Lawson, Billie. Work-related post-traumatic stress reactions: The hidden dimension. Health and Social Work, Vol. 12(4), 1987, pp. 250–258.

Leana, Carrie, & Feldman, Daniel. *Coping with Job Loss*. New York: Lexington Books, 1992.

Lewis, Beth. Social workers' role in promoting occupational health and safety. In Shulamith Straussner, ed. *Occupational Social Work Today: Employee Assistance Quarterly*, Vol. 5, No. 1, 1990, pp. 99–118.

Lieberman, Cheryl. A perspective on managing new workforce issues. Keynote presentation, Second Annual Conference on Industry and Mental Health. Sponsored by Boston University School of Social Work, June 6, 1983, Boston, MA.

Linn, Margaret et al. Effects of unemployment on mental and physical health. *American Journal of Public Health*, Vol. 75, No. 5, May 1986, pp. 502–506.

Madonia, Joseph. Handling emotional problems in business and industry. *Social Casework*, December 1985, pp. 587–593.

McDonald, Charles. U.S. union membership in future decades: A trade unionist's perspective. *Industrial Relations*, Vol. 31, No. 1, Winter 1992, pp. 13–30.

Meiss, Kathleen. *Work, Welfare & Social Work Practice.* Stockholm Studies in Social Work 6. Stockholm: Almqvist & Wiksell International, 1991.

Mor-Barak, Michal, & Tynan, Margaret. Older workers and the workplace: A new challenge for occupational social work. *Social Work*, Vol. 38, No. 1, January 1993, pp. 45–55.

Mor-Borak, Michal et al. A model curriculum for occupational social work. *Journal of Social Work Education*, Vol. 29, No. 1, Winter 1993, pp. 63–77.

Mudrick, Nancy. An undeveloped role for occupational social work: Facilitating the employment of people with disabilities. *Social Work*, Vol. 36, No. 6, November 1991, pp. 490–495.

Muhl, Charles. Collective bargaining in state and local government, 1994. *Monthly Labor Review*, June 1995, pp. 13–20.

Mulloy, Daniel, & Kurzman, Paul. Practice with unions: Collaborating toward an empowerment model. In Paul Kurzman, & Sheila Akabas, eds. *Work and Well-Being: The Occupational Social Work Advantage*. Washington, DC: NASW, 1993, pp. 46–60.

Ozawa, Martha. Development of social services in industry: Why and how? *Social Work*, Vol. 25, No. 6, November 1980, pp. 464–470.

Ozawa, Martha. Economics of occupational social work. *Social Work*, Vol. 25, No. 5, September-October 1985, pp. 442–445.

Popple, Philip. Social work practice in business and industry, 1875–1930. *Social Service Review*, June 1981, pp. 257–269.

Proceedings. Conference on Social Work Practice in Labor and Industrial Settings. Sponsored by NASW, Hunter College School of Social Work, & Columbia University School of Social Work, June 7–9, 1978, New York City.

Ramanathan, Chathapuram. EAP's response to personal stress and productivity: Implications for occupational social work. *Social Work*, Vol. 37, No. 3, May 1992, pp. 234–239.

Riches, Graham, & Ternowetsky, Gordon, eds. *Unemployment and Welfare: Social Policy and the Work of Social Work*. Toronto: Garamond Press, 1990.

Robinson, James. Workplace hazards and workers' desires for union representation. *Journal of Labor Research*, Vol. 9, No. 3, Summer 1988, pp. 237–249.

Rosenthal, Neal. The nature of occupational employment growth: 1983–93. *Monthly Labor Review*, June 1995, pp. 45–54.

Safford, Florence. Value of gerontology for occupational social work. *Social Work*, Vol. 33, No. 1, January-February 1988, pp. 42–45.

Selikoff, Irving. Keynote address. In Philip Landrigan & Irving Selikoff, *Occupational Health in the 1990's: Developing a Platform for Disease Prevention*. Annals of the New York Academy of Science, Vol. 572, 1989, pp. 4–9.

Shanker, Renee. Occupational disease, workers' compensation and the social work advocate. *Social Work*, Vol. 28, 1983, pp. 24–27.

Sharlach, Andrew et al., eds. *Elder Care and the Workforce: Blueprint for Action*. Lexington, MA: Lexington Books, 1991.

Sherraden, Michael. Chronic unemployment: A social work perspective. *Social Work*, Vol. 25, No. 5, September-October 1985, pp. 403–408.

Smith, Michael, & Gould, Gary. A profession at the crossroads: Occupational social work—present and future. In Paul Kurzman & Sheila Akabas, eds., *Work and Well-Being: The Occupational Social Work Advantage*. Washington, DC: NASW, 1993, pp. 7–25.

Soine, Lynne. Sick building syndrome and gender bias: Imperiling women's health. *Social Work in Health Care*, Vol. 20, No. 3, 1995, pp. 51–65.

Stafford, Walter. *Closed Labor Markets: Underrepresentation of Blacks, Hispanics and Women in New York City's Industries and Jobs*. New York: Community Service Society, January, 1985, pp. i–xvi.

Stout, Nancy et al. Occupational injury mortality rates in the United States: Changes from 1980 to 1989. *American Journal of Public Health*, Vol. 86. No. 1, January 1996, pp. 73–76.

Strauss, Emilie. The caseworker deals with employment problems. *Social Casework*, Vol. 32, 1951, pp. 388–392.

Straussner, Shulamith. Occupational social work today: An overview. In S. Straussner, ed., *Occupational Social Work Today*. New York: The Haworth Press, 1990, pp. 1–17.

Straussner, Shulamith, & Phillips, Norma. The relationship between social work and labor unions: A history of strife and cooperation. *Journal of Sociology and Social Welfare*, Vol. 10, No. 1, March 1988, pp. 105–118.

Stuen, Cynthia, & Worden, Barbara. The older worker and service delivery at the workplace. In Paul Kurzman & Sheila Akabas, eds., *Work and Well-Being: The Occupational Social Work Advantage*. Washington, DC: NASW, 1993, pp. 256–275.

U. S. Department of Labor. *Report on the American Workforce*. Washington, DC: U.S. Government Printing Office, 1994.

Walker, Bailus. Social and economic determinants of occupational health policies and services. *American Journal of Industrial Medicine*, Vol. 16, 1989, pp. 321–328.

Walsh, Diana et al. Health promotion versus health protection? Employees' perceptions and concerns. *Journal of Public Health Policy*, Vol. 12, No. 2, Summer 1991, pp. 148–164.

Walsh, Diana et al. Treating the employed alcoholic: Which interventions work? *Alcohol Health & Research World*, Vol. 16, No. 2, Spring 1992, pp. 140–149.

Weiss, Richard. *Dealing with Alcoholism in the Workplace*. New York: The Conference Board, 1980.

Wiatrowski, William. Family-related benefits in the workplace. *Monthly Labor Review*, March 1990, pp. 28–33.

Wiatrowski, William. Who really has access to employer-provided health benefits? *Monthly Labor Review*, June 1995, pp. 36–44.

Williamson, Lisa, & Brown, Phyllis. Collective bargaining in private industry, 1994. *Monthly Labor Review*, June 1995, pp. 12.

Wyers, Norman, & Kaulukukui, Malina. Social services in the workplace: Rhetoric vs. reality. *Social Work*, Vol. 29, No. 2, March-April 1984, pp. 167–172.

Yamatani, Hide. Client assessment in an industrial setting: A cross-sectional method. *Social Work*, Vol. 28, No. 1, pp. 34–37.

Social Work Practice
with Marginalized Populations

Nancy Cook Von Bretzel

This essay by Nancy Cook Von Bretzel, a front-line social worker in the Emergency Department at San Francisco General Hospital since 1988, explores some of the ethical and emotional issues about practice that social workers rarely discuss publicly. It examines the responses of social workers who are battered on a daily base by draconian social policies and clients' rage, including violence. Von Bretzel, who is one of the founders and the clinical director of the Critical Incident Debriefing Program for the Department of Public Health for the city of San Francisco, suggests some ways for social workers to minimize the damage to clients and themselves from this battering and to lessen the possibility of "compassion depletion" in the profession. These suggestions require the development of new clinical techniques, new strategies for community organizing, and new ways to educate subsequent generations of social workers.

In addition to her work in the only public hospital in San Francisco, Von Bretzel is an ongoing project organizer for the International Research and Exchange Board, a consultant to the National Family Violence Prevention Fund, and a lecturer and field instructor in the School of Social Work at San Francisco State University. In 1995, she received the Rhoda Sarnat International Award from NASW for her work in Bulgaria on behalf of the Gypsy community.

Introduction

This essay is about the professional, ethical, and emotional dilemmas confronted by social workers who work on the front lines with marginalized populations at this time of enormously reduced public spending on programs to aid those most in need. Many ethical issues arise when social workers are called upon to implement draconian policies. Not only are they increasingly expected to communicate and implement such policies, which are objectively against the interests of their clients; they also frequently become targets of the rage and desperation the cutbacks evoke in their clients (Bates, 1996; Moskal, 1994; Newhill, 1995).

This essay will examine the responses of social workers resulting from dealing with that rage, including violence. It will suggest practical methods for minimizing the damage to clients and thereby to social workers themselves, both of whom are victimized today. It will conclude with suggestions for how to minimize "compassion depletion" within our profession, and discuss the implications for social work education. These observations and proposals have two sources. The first is my own experience for the past decade as a social worker in the emergency department of San Francisco's only public hospital. The second is the observations of graduate students attending the classes I teach in the School of Social Work at San Francisco State University, who are interning in the public sector.

A belief implicit in this essay is that the sense of rage, hopelessness, and helplessness shown by marginalized populations can be so overwhelming that contact and interaction with this degree of human suffering, even when confined to 8 hours a day in a professional setting, can have dehumanizing effects upon the social worker. It is the social workers in the public sector who must deliver messages of impossible criteria, ineligibility, rejection, and refusal of service to those highly stigmatized individuals seeking assistance upon which their survival depends.

When social workers are seen and experienced as adversary, not advocate, many of our marginalized clients simply go away in defeat, and we are just one more link in a chain of betrayals. But some clients don't turn their rage inward; rather, they direct it toward those representing the system. Sometimes that is us, the social workers. This can be such a distressing experience that our contacts for the rest of the day or the rest of the week with nonhostile clients can be affected with emotional reverberations. Such hostile encounters can cause havoc within the social worker, raising tremendous self-doubt, or tremendous anger against the clients, or questions about the meaning of our work. It is extremely painful for social workers who joined the profession to be of assistance to our fellow human beings to find ourselves perceived as the enemy of those we want to serve (Hawkins, 1995). This shift is so stressful that without training and support, our responses are not automatically compassionate or constructive.

There are in every agency outstanding social workers who do much more than is required to try to make up for the constrictions in the system, but these social workers need recognition and support. If we fail to offer this, our caring front-line workers will either leave the public sector or be at risk for becoming embittered, cynical, and burned out adversaries of the marginalized clients they had originally aimed to serve.

To begin to address this dilemma we must face the question: Should any principled social worker take a front-line position where the social worker has little opportunity to operate justly and fairly? How is such a role compatible with the National Association of Social Workers (NASW) definition of social work practice as "the professional activity of helping individuals, groups or communities to enhance or restore their capacity for social functioning and creating societal conditions favorable to this goal" (NASW, 1994)? Or the NASW Code of Ethics: "The social worker should act to prevent practices that are inhumane or discriminatory against any person or group of persons" (NASW, 1994)?

The urgency of this problem is unfortunately increasing more than at any time in recent U.S. history because the numbers of people who are becoming marginalized by the current dismantling of the social contract on which they have been forced to depend are greater than ever before.

This is a process that has been unfolding since the early eighties, when the cutbacks in social services promulgated by the Reagan administration first began to make it seem acceptable for Americans to express attitudes of indifference or contempt toward the poor. Now, in the last half of the nineties, the process is well under way—yet this is only the prelude. By the 21st century, the annihilation of social services may be complete. Even now, throughout the public sector, social workers are turning people away by the thousands.

What IS the role of the social worker when there are no resources available? This is the elephant in the room that no one mentions. This question epitomizes a major change in the social worker/client paradigm—a 180° turn. Should we as a profession call upon social workers to refuse these positions? Or is there any possibility for the exercise of compassionate judgment and action that would make it important for a client to have a committed and caring social worker in such a position rather than a burned out bureaucrat? In an era of a shrinking job market for social workers, the answer to these questions is not an easy one.

Over one-third of social workers nationally are employed in the public sector in local, state, and federal social service agencies (Gibelman and Scherbish, 1993). These are equal opportunity agencies, and the staff members of such agencies are far more ethnically and racially diverse than those of many non-profits and other agencies not directly run by the government (Gibelman and Schervish, 1993, p. 59). Frequently, these are the jobs most available to newly graduated social workers because there are no prerequisites. In order to get financing for their education, many graduate students had to contract to work in the public sector. They are frequently students of color and others with least access to financial resources. Can we really tell all these people not to take the only jobs that might be available with decent pay and benefits? Condemning them for taking such jobs would also objectively push them further out of the profession. Instead, I suggest that we need to recognize the painful reality of their situations and provide them with education about alternative ways to maintain their integrity in these positions.

Dysfunctional Emotional Responses

What are the dangers to the integrity of the social workers who are forced to violate their own sense of fairness and justice on a daily basis? How do social workers deal with the fact that they joined the profession to help and empower people, and instead find themselves the object of hatred because they are functioning as the official representatives of a punitive and unjust system? The dysfunctional responses discussed below are typical reactions that develop over time, and they characterize the burned-out caregiver.

Rationalizing

As has been well documented by organizational theorists, it is common to try to view one's own activities in the best possible light, to look for ways to justify or rationalize one's conduct. No one wants to think they are imposing unfair criteria. Over time, then, there comes to be a blurring of one's clear vision; what at first seemed undoable—turning needy people away—happens so frequently that it is no longer shocking, but commonplace. The rules and regulations that at first were clearly unacceptable and absurd become internalized. Clients declared ineligible come to be perceived by the worker as undeserving. Identification with the institution or agency replaces one's original conscience, and rather than a defender of the marginalized, the social worker has become a collaborator in attacking the very existence of the marginalized.

The following true examples, taken from a variety of public social work settings, illustrate the dysfunctional ways social workers can respond to the stress created by the present lack of resources.

Becoming Numb

In a public hospital emergency room, workers had to tell more and more ill homeless men during the last year that there were no shelter beds they could arrange for them. This meant the patients would have to go into the streets with their illnesses. Social workers had to do this so frequently, they stopped thinking about what they were doing because they couldn't bear it.

Blaming the Victim

If the client is a drug addict, social workers can begin to rationalize their actions by thinking, "Well, I didn't put that needle in your arm so don't blame me that your welfare check is in your veins and not available for housing." It becomes easier to think it is the client's fault, that the client is undeserving, than that the worker is representing an inhumane system. How easy it then becomes for the worker to forget that there are fewer and fewer beds in drug recovery programs for the indigent and that even the most committed homeless addicts in recovery can't stay clean long when they are living on the street. Even more significantly, social workers can come to forget by what act of socioeconomic fate it was that the client and not *them* became exposed to drugs, at what age and in what neighborhood. If one can feel judgmental toward the victim, that somehow lets the worker off the hook. The workers aren't being cruel, just "detached" and "professional."

Identifying with the Rules and Regulations

In Oakland, where the unemployment rate for black males is very high, a new Child Protective Service worker tells an African-American male just out of prison without a home that he can have custody of his children as soon as he gets a home and a job. The worker no longer sees herself doing anything but implementing reasonable, client-centered reunification criteria. The worker ignores the fact that the client is an ex-felon, without job skills, in a very down-turned job market. Contradictions between the reality of the human being and the Kafkaesque unreality of the requirements are no longer apparent to the worker. When, upon hearing the impossible criteria, the client becomes verbally aggressive, the worker tells herself that this lack of impulse control is what got the client into prison in the first place, so his dilemma is of his own making.

Avoiding Client Contact

A welfare department worker tells a homeless alcoholic woman who has been raped twice in the streets over the last 5 years that she will get no welfare grant this month because she didn't show up for her workfare detail. Therefore, her temporary subsidized housing is canceled and she is back in the streets. The rules require workfare. If there is no work done, there is no welfare grant. If there is no grant, then eviction is the result. The punishment does not exactly fit the crime. Should indigent alcoholic women be forced to live on the streets because they manifest the irresponsibility of their disease? Does anyone really think this will induce sobriety? Is there any guiding intelligence here? The worker does not make eye contact, but just keeps repeating "I'm sorry, it's the rules." When the woman starts talking about her fear of being raped again, the worker says, "There is no point in you explaining all this to me because I won't be able to change the policy." In the face of the woman's protests, the worker asks security to escort the client out when she refuses to leave. "It's just a job. I don't like doing it but I only have 4 years before retirement," the worker says to herself.

These are just a few real-life samples of what is going on between worker and client on a daily basis throughout the public sector social service delivery system.

Burn-out and Abandonment of the Public Sector

In the face of these seemingly impossible conditions under which to practice social work in its true meaning, many choose instead to go into less brutal jobs. They may even flee direct service in the public sector altogether in favor of less stressful client populations. But social work jobs where there are actually sufficient resources to meet client needs are not plentiful these days. Going into private practice within the context of HMOs may become a growing opportunity, but one that takes the clinical social worker farther away from those who are most desperately in need.

I don't think we can blame social workers for burning out or fleeing the field unless we are willing to take a long and honest look at the conditions of their work. It is incumbent upon our schools to prepare students for these new and brutal realities and to develop methodologies with which to respond to the crisis of the clients and the stress of the workers who confront their desperation.

What follows are some suggestions based on my work with clients, staff, and students.

Guidelines for Social Worker Survival in Difficult Conditions

The professional and ethical dilemma for the social worker arises because he or she is pitted against the client. To resolve this dilemma the social worker must realign himself or herself on the side of the client. In interactions with the client, social workers can take certain measures that make it clear to themselves and their clients that they are not in accord with the harsh and punitive direction of the agency or policy they must communicate.

1. Social workers should feel free to distance themselves from decisions they don't agree with. In compliance with the NASW code of ethics, when social workers disagree with a policy they have to implement, they should feel free to identify to the client what they think is unjust and why they think so. Social workers should not feel they have to justify or defend the indefensible just because it is institutional policy. Of course, depending on the openness of the institution or the social worker's supervisor, these messages can be overt or covert.

2. More than ever before, social workers need to become as informed as possible about alternative resources and courses of appeal and action. Social workers should encourage and help clients to file appeals or complaints if the clients so desire.

3. Despite the repetitive nature of client requests and the difficulty of time demands, client/social worker interactions will be much less stressful for both if the worker takes the time to make personal contact with each client. Just two more minutes can make all the difference in the overall tone of the interaction. Often social workers don't hear their clients out because they know that regardless of what the client says, the worker will have to say no. It is very important to hear as much of the story as time allows, and let the client know that his or her specific situation or plight has been understood. Perhaps the worker can help once they hear the client out. If the worker can't help, at least the client will know the worker's answer came after the worker recognized his or her situation and was not just an automatic, indifferent rejection.

4. It is important for the social worker to make every effort to serve the marginalized clients, even if it might seem futile. Ask clients what else they can suggest for the

worker to do to help them, such as phone calls the worker could make or letters the worker could write, and do this if possible. This includes running interference where that might help, which requires being on good terms with other agencies and sources of help so that the worker can call upon them in the most urgent circumstances.

5. As implausible as it might seem, utilizing what is called the "strengths perspective" is especially useful with marginalized clients. The strengths perspective is an approach to a client or client system that focuses on the strengths the client manifests in his or her life. This is in contrast to focusing on problems, pathologies, and deficits in the client and his or her environment.

   Learning how to eat any kind of food (from meal programs or garbage dumpsters), sleep anywhere (on a door stoop, in a park, or in a noisy, frightening shelter), and meet basic needs (through panhandling, recycling aluminum cans, or accepting a stranger's kindness) requires competence and mastery of survival skills (Sheridan, Gowen, and Halpin, 1993).

   At times, the external configuration of the client's life circumstances may appear to the worker to be so devastating that the strengths inherent in the client's environment are not immediately apparent. However, much to the worker's surprise, seemingly marginalized clients may have developed very ingenious mechanisms for survival. For example, a 60-year-old, severely arthritic, incontinent African-American homeless wheelchair patient lived in a van outside of the house he once rented. Although he was far from restroom and food facilities and could not get in and out of the van by himself, he resisted all

social work efforts to get him more services and a "better" placement. He insisted that all he wanted was medical attention for a fever and cough he had. Further dialogue with the client revealed that his former neighbors bathed him, washed his van, emptied his commode, and left him food. He was a member of a community and no impersonal placement could replace that. Workers need to remember that people have been surviving long before they meet us. If the clients have some kind of homeostatic system, don't mess with it, don't be intrusive, don't meddle—don't act "like a social worker." Just do what the clients ask, if you can, and respect and value their judgment.

6. Workers shouldn't expect clients to tell them the truth in this day and age. It is most often not in the client's interest to do so. Remember that a worker inherits the image of every social worker and eligibility worker the client has seen before, and the client may have little reason (even less now) to trust a new worker. For example, general assistance grants in most cities in the United States today are not sufficient to cover both the client's subsistence and housing needs. Because the client *is* surviving, there may be other sources of revenue. These may or may not be legal. If the client reports any additional revenue, his or her grant will immediately be reduced. There are some things the worker is better off not knowing.

7. Social workers need to know what protest activities, hearings, or meetings are going on in which the client can participate. It is useful to have petitions or declarations of protest about unfair policies for the client to

sign. Social work offices should be stocked with leaflets and resource materials directing clients to these events and sites as well as to advocacy organizations in the community.

8. Although it may seem like a far cry from the help the social worker wished to be able to provide, don't undervalue the potential meaning to the marginalized client of encountering just one worker who treats him or her with respect. This may be an island of validation in a sea of rejection and abandonment. For many of the marginalized, it may be the first real conversation they have had in weeks. The compassionate social worker can know that at least for the period of that encounter, the client found a caring human being.

9. Despite the best style of work and a clear advocacy stand, if the worker cannot grant a client's request, some clients will be so explosive that they cannot hear the worker or distinguish a worker on their side from a worker who is indifferent. It is important for social workers to receive training in crisis intervention and how to defuse and "talk down" an agitated client. Explosions should be avoided, as they frequently result in more trauma for both the client and the worker. When clients do "go off" on a caring worker, workers need to know that it is not personal, that they didn't make the rules.

In summary, social workers will not feel their work is a betrayal to either their clients or to their own professional code of ethics if they remain allied with the interests of the client. As indicated in the suggestions above, in order for the client to understand that the social worker is on his or her side, the social worker must manifest this solidarity in a wide variety of ways.

Ways to Prevent Compassion Depletion in Social Workers

Historically, psychiatric doctors, nurses, and social workers have received training to prepare them to handle violent patients. No one took such violence personally; it was part of the diagnosable and documented psychiatric illness of the patient. Violence from clients and patients toward workers in the helping professions is an increasingly frequent occurrence today, but with one major difference. Today's patients aren't suffering from a mental illness; they are not diagnosable; they are enraged. How are we as a profession to make sense of such a contradictory phenomenon in the midst of our desire to help? How can we assist individual social workers to keep their bearings as client advocates and at the same time handle such disturbing events?

Caught in a situation of chronic entrapment, in a job he or she can't afford to leave, delivering negative responses to clients in grave need, and absorbing their volatile responses can be a profoundly disturbing experience. It is important that we as a profession take measures to assist the tens of thousands of social workers thus affected to maintain their sanity and their desire not to abandon the goals of the profession but to maintain a compassionate stance in the face of great difficulties. This problem can be addressed from a number of angles, but first social work as a profession must bring it out into the open. We can no longer ignore the shift in our role from helpers to gatekeepers. We must begin to address the psychological toll upon social workers of being the recipient of the despair and/or fury of clients. We must acknowledge the chronic entrapment and helplessness experienced by front-line social workers, who are caught in the dilemma of abandoning their clients.

Social Work Education

Courses to prepare future social workers have a responsibility to address the changes in the social work environment since the birth of our system. It will not do to exhort social workers to avoid jobs that at times pit them against the clients' interests. The obligation of the educators in the profession is to recognize reality and develop tools to help the worker respond to the present crisis with integrity, remaining a client advocate. This includes teaching all generalist social workers how to develop programs to fill gaps, how to write grants, how to build coalitions, how to apply public pressure on policymakers. At the same time, the mental health of the workers must also be addressed, for the stress of their position is extremely intense.

Preparatory courses that help students anticipate these realities are necessary. Interpersonal techniques for deescalating violence and attending to client crisis must be explicitly taught. Courses concerned with strategies and tactics of social action to address the sources of the clients' rage need to be integrated into the possibilities for front-line social worker practice. In fact, by gearing our professional educational efforts toward the workers who are enmeshed in the present devolution of the social contract, the profession can begin to hammer out a front-line response to the current crisis. This is one reason why having social workers located at the heart of the crisis can be an important position from which to fight the current trends.

Social Action Measures

In addition to the intrinsic value of fighting the present punitive social policies, social workers themselves can encounter their clients from a position as allies if they know themselves to be active on behalf of clients' rights. To the extent that the social worker takes steps to express opposition to the current policies, which are destructive to the well-being of the client, the social worker will feel united with the clients and the clients in turn will perceive this.

Front-line social workers are in an ideal position to bear witness to the social injustices they see around them and in which they are forced to work. They can use their position to testify to the particularities of how the present shift in policy is playing out. Social workers can join client-initiated demonstrations, hearings, and organizing efforts and can lend their professional voice (if requested). And social workers need not be afraid to "drop a dime"— that is, to call the news media when a particularly horrific situation comes before them. Depending on the institutional environment in which the social worker is located, these activist activities may have to be pursued discreetly in order not to jeopardize employment. However, there are all kinds of ways to lend help to the efforts to implement more humane social policies. Social workers can form or join organizations or caucuses of social workers advocating for an alternate domestic social agenda. Social workers can use their training in community development and social action to start groups or initiate programs to fill in the gaps in the system. This, however, requires that part of every social worker's training include basic organizing skills such as program development.

The more deeply involved in community efforts for self-defense against the current attacks on the disenfranchised, the less torn the social worker will feel.

At the Workplace

In order for workers to maintain their sanity, it is important to have a macro-level understanding of why the hostility and frustration of the clients is so intense in the present period. This is important information and an important perspective to share with the rest of the staff. Educationals that provide a broader view of the present situation will help workers to be more empathetic with the clients and will begin to address the atmosphere of the institution or agency in relation to the client population. For example, it is easy to become disgusted and frustrated with drug addicts appearing to manufacture illnesses as they seek narcotics at public health facilities. However, in order to maintain a professional stance, it is important for staff to be aware of the paucity of resources or programs available for those thousands of addicts seeking treatment daily who are without funds.

Finally, it is important that social workers be active in fighting for their rights at the workplace through their unions. Unions can be effective in forming coalitions with service provider agencies to press public policymakers for additional resources and better working conditions. Unions can write workload limits into contracts with public agencies so that social workers' client loads do not make it impossible to give a client minimal respect and attention. Unions can also lobby for the rotation of front-line positions so that workers get a break periodically from dealing directly with the public.

Psychological Well-being

Social workers are not saints, nor should we strive to be. We did not enlist to be the scapegoats of the system. We bleed, we get our feelings hurt, we get angry, we sometimes get provoked. We need to be able to work in an atmosphere of support and understanding if we are to offer the same to our clients. We should not be abused, and we have a right to protect ourselves from abuse, and to attend to our own needs if such incidents occur.

It is important to develop debriefing protocols for especially traumatic incidents so that residue from such interactions does not build up. It is not healthy to bury our reactions to a difficult interaction with a client; it is very helpful to talk to co-workers who have similar views about an upsetting confrontation. For this to be useful, it is important to share experiences with workers who will not justify dysfunctional and unprofessional responses to client abuse, and who see the macro picture of why such tension is accumulating.

In Conclusion

Our profession has much work to do to prepare us to defend and embody our principles and ethics as we go into the 21st century. We must develop new clinical techniques as well as new strategies for community organizing. Our work with marginalized clients impels us to bridge the gap between individual- and community-oriented social work practice so that all of our accumulated wisdom can come to bear as we struggle to serve this population adequately.

Finally, before closing, let me direct the reader's attention to a related issue. I think we as a profession now have to be much more proactive in coming up with program designs and proposals that will really meet the needs of our marginalized clients and that can be defended. One of the tragedies of the current attack on the social contract is that we who have been working within the bounds of the "entitlement programs" have known that they were deeply flawed. For example, classifying addiction as a disease was progressive. However, then giving cash grants to addicts once a month was cruel and destructive. It became a way to give money to drug dealers through the bodies of our patients and clients. We have known that, in many other cases as well, grants had the opposite effect from what we intended. We have known that we have been institutionalizing dependency and passivity and that programs that really succeed in helping people to reclaim their lives and their self-reliance have been few. In fact, social welfare has played the role of social control by giving just enough to pacify potentially challenging sectors of the population who have been excluded from receiving their share of the wealth of our country.

Sadly, instead of cleaning our own house and coming up with programs that are more humane and more effective, we have been developing huge holes in the side of our ship. That has enabled the whole social service system to be sunk by conservative critics. Although some of these critics are truly mean-spirited and racist, many ordinary people are fed up with the irrationality of the system and its well-publicized flaws. Instead of defending those programs and saying that the flaws constitute only a small percentage, we should take a harder, more honest look and use our vast knowledge and hopefully accumulated wisdom to be the designers of a new social service system in the 21st century.

REFERENCES

Bates, James. (1996, March 15). U.S. guidelines target workplace violence. *Los Angeles Times*, Home Edition, p. D-3.

Gibelman, Margaret, and Schervish, Philip H. (1993). *Who we are: The social work labor force as reflected in the NASW membership*. Washington, DC: NASW Press, p. 56.

Hawkins, Denise B. (1995, May 4). The experience at the front line: Social workers at work. *Black Issues in Higher Education*, pp. PG.

Moskal, Jerry. (1994, May 10). Social workers duck bullets, fists as part of their jobs. Gannett News Service.

National Association of Social Workers. (1994). Code of ethics of the National Association of Social Workers. Washington, DC.

Newhill, Christina E. (1995). Client violence toward social workers: A practice and policy concern for the 1990s. *Social Work*, 40, pp. 631–636.

Sheridan, M. J., Gowen, N., and Halpin, S. (1993). Developing a practice model for the homeless mentally ill. *Families in Society* 74, pp. 410–421. Quoted in K. Miley, M. O'Melia, and B. Du Bois (1995), *Generalist social work practice: An empowering approach*. Needham Heights, MA: Allyn & Bacon, p. 64.

Multicultural Community Organizing

Lorraine Gutiérrez

Lorraine Gutiérrez, associate professor of social work and psychology at the University of Michigan, sees multicultural community organizing not merely as a tool to enhance services to racial and ethnic minorities, but as a means to respond proactively to a broad set of economic and social challenges that face the nation as a whole at the end of the 20th century. Gutiérrez defines multicultural organizing within an "ethno-conscious" approach to practice, which aims at the "development of communities of color while creating mechanisms for greater intergroup interaction and change." It requires an emphasis on the process of empowerment, particularly those aspects that focus on education, participation, and capacity building, and suggests new roles for social workers. Her essay presents this alternative vision for practice and discusses some of its challenges and contradictions.

Dr. Gutiérrez' research focuses on multicultural issues in communities and organizations. Her current research includes an evaluation of gender and ethnically relevant AIDS prevention programs, the identification of multicultural issues in community and organizational practice, and the definition of culturally competent mental health practice. She has published on topics such as empowerment, multicultural practice, and social work practice with women of color.

The late 20th century challenges us to examine our profession's role and purpose. This is particularly true in the United States, where large economic transformations have contributed to a society in which fewer and fewer individuals are gaining direct benefit from economic growth (Murdock & Michael, 1996). No longer are jobs secure, higher education affordable, or income supports adequate to help those displaced by these broad societal changes. The role of social work in addressing these issues is particularly controversial, as our profession has been identified by some as contributing to the current sense of crisis.

What is the role of community organization within this context? How can we take an active role in confronting and immobilizing those social and economic trends that increase inequality while removing the tattered remnants of the social safety net? Given the growing diversity in our society, I propose that a multicultural approach to community practice can be one avenue for responding to these challenges in a proactive manner. Creating methods to develop communities while building coalitions between them is one strategy for working toward greater social justice. It proposes a way to work in partnership with communities to confront the assaults experienced by individuals, families, and communities.

In this essay, the focus will be on defining the concept of multicultural community organizing and on ways in which it can provide an alternative vision for practice in the 21st century. However, the development of multicultural practice involves its own challenges and contradictions. Therefore, this essay will also focus on some of these issues and ways in which they can be addressed. Only by focusing on our potentials and challenges can we engage in creative and positive change.

Understanding Multicultural Community Organizing

Multicultural community organization (MCO) refers to methods of practice that work toward the development of communities of color while creating mechanisms for greater intergroup interaction and change (Gutiérrez, Alvarez, Nemon, & Lewis, in press). It is work that attempts to address the central challenge of living in a diverse society: How do we respect diversity and reduce inequality while working toward a common good? MCO is built on a pluralistic foundation, while going beyond pluralism to recognize and work to eliminate social injustices and oppression based on group membership (Gutiérrez & Nagda, 1996; Jackson & Holvino, 1988).

Methods of MCO are grounded in an "ethno-conscious" approach to practice (Gutiérrez, 1992). Social work approaches to working with communities of color can be located on a continuum ranging from ethno-centric to ethno-conscious perspectives. These approaches have differed in their perspectives regarding the culture and social status of communities of color.

The ethnocentric perspective places the Euro-American tradition as central and judges the experiences of others from that particular perspective. It is likely to locate problems existing in communities of color as arising from their values or traditions (Chau, 1991; Gallegos, 1982; Gutiérrez & Nagda, 1996; Morales, 1981). This perspective has been the dominant orientation of social services. It was reflected in the development of the social services by predominantly upper-class men and women who created programs that often reflected classist, racist, and nativist social mores (Wenocur & Reisch, 1989). Historically, ethnocentrism has manifested itself in the social services through the provision of segregated services (Stehno, 1982), the deportation of "aliens," or in "Americanization" programs that resulted in the loss of culture and community (Carpenter, 1980; Sanchez, 1995). It is currently present in our society in movements to deny social services to immigrants and to eliminate programs for affirmative action.

Organizing by communities of color led to the development of ethnic *sensitive* and *culturally competent* approaches to practice (Gallegos, 1982; Scott & Delgado, 1979). This movement has led to the development of programs and organizations that will be more responsive and responsible to the culture of people of color. For example, the language, location, and methods used are developed with the needs and values of cultures in the community. It is based on a pluralistic vision for social work that suggests that positive gains can result from learning about different cultural groups and incorporating cultural values into organizational procedures, structures, and services (Devore & Schlesinger, 1987; Gallegos, 1982; Green, 1995).

The ethnic sensitive approach is an inadequate response to the disenfranchisement and inequality experienced by communities of color. By focusing on individual change and cultural factors, it ignores the role of power in the social order and in social work practice (McMahon & Allen-Meares, 1992). In addition, by focusing solely on cultural factors, these approaches may not recognize the diversity that exists within ethnic and racial groups and may serve to reinforce stereotypes. Research suggests that if ethnic sensitive services do not lead to structural changes in organizations and a greater participation of people of color in the governance of the agency, efforts toward change can be mostly symbolic and marginal (Gutiérrez & Nagda, 1996).

The *ethno-conscious* approach, which combines an ethnic sensitive orientation and an empowerment perspective on practice, holds promise for creating services, programs, and organizations that will work to reduce inequality. The ethno-conscious approach is based in an appreciation and recognition of the strengths existing in communities of color (Gutiérrez, 1992; Pinderhughes, 1989; Solomon, 1976). At its center is a concern with power and confronting social inequality through work with individuals, families, groups, organizations, and communities. It involves methods for partnership, participation, and capacity building. In all work, people of color are active agents in individual and social change.

Like other methods of social work practice, community organizing can take place on any point on this continuum. For example, an ethnocentric community organizing perspective would locate difficulties with organizing within the community itself and with the predominant culture of the community, rather than looking at structural barriers to participation or ways in which cultural traditions could be used to mobilize for change. An ethnic sensitive perspective would utilize cultural traditions but would not focus on social justice or inequality. Although this approach could be successful in reaching or mobilizing a specific ethnic community, it would not address larger issues of inequality and injustice.

Ethno-conscious practice through MCO can begin to address the challenges of the 21st century by creating social environments that support social justice through influencing policies,

program development, or local governance. Although the target of change is the community or larger society, the forum for change will involve individuals, families, groups, or organizations (Bradshaw, Soifer, & Gutiérrez, 1993; Burghardt, 1982). Specific tactics reflect current community practice and can range from short and focused activities such as public hearings to long and sustained projects such as the development of alternative services (Mondros & Wilson, 1994; Rivera & Erlich, 1995).

MCO is based in our understanding of empowerment: ways in which social workers can work with individuals, families, groups, and communities to become more powerful (Gutiérrez & Nurius, 1994). Gaining power would involve developing the means to have influence over one's life and social environment on the personal, interpersonal, or political levels (Gutiérrez, 1994; Pinderhughes, 1989). It involves both changes in one's self-perception and in the ability to act on the social world. This perspective on power and empowerment is centered on understanding how individuals develop a sense of personal control and the ability to affect the behavior of others and on an understanding that power is not necessarily a scarce commodity but one that can be generated in the process of empowerment (Gutiérrez, 1994; Kieffer, 1984; Rappaport, 1987; Zimmerman, in press).

Research suggests that the process of empowerment can take place when practice methods are focused on *education, participation,* and *capacity building* (Gutiérrez, DeLois, & GlenMaye, 1995; Parsons, 1991). It suggests a role for the organizer as catalyst or facilitator of change rather than leader or educator. If MCO is to contribute to the empowerment of communities of color, it needs to use these methods to develop organizing strategies. The following discussion uses examples from the People of

Color Against AIDS Network (POCAAN) in Seattle to demonstrate how these methods can be woven into multicultural community organizing work.[1]

Educational methods focus on helping participants develop the ability to understand and act upon the social environment. The focus of these methods is on understanding one's situation and community and on developing skills to increase one's interpersonal or political power.

Consciousness raising can take place in groups in which members share their common histories through discussion and other educational channels. The process of consciousness raising is important because it helps individuals, families, or communities understand the nature of their problems. This understanding can also clarify possible responses or solutions to difficult situations (Freire, 1972; Wallerstein, 1992).

An effective power analysis is one element of consciousness raising. This exercise involves identifying one's own sources of power and methods for increasing power resources (Burghardt, 1982; Bradshaw et al., 1993). It requires that organizers fully comprehend the connection between the immediate situation and the distribution of power in society as a whole and see the potential for power and influence in every situation. Sources of potential power can include such things as individual skills, personal qualities that could increase social influence, members of past social support networks, and other organizations.

Education also involves developing specific skills to address power deficits and to develop the resources to be more powerful (Gutiérrez et

POCAAN has developed methods of education that are based on the understanding and experiences of community members. Because it is a multiethnic coalition, this has meant tailoring prevention education to the realities of different communities and subcommunities. This was most effectively done by facilitating the development of programs within specific communities to reach their own members. Educational efforts combine consciousness raising about AIDS with information about HIV transmission and prevention.

An example of this was a media campaign by POCAAN that attempted to confront misinformation and stereotypes regarding HIV infection. The theme of this campaign was "famous last words"—such as "AIDS is a White Man's Disease—famous last words." These messages were tailored to different communities by the use of language, "myths" to be challenged, the use of music and other media, and the medium used to carry the message. For example, fotonovellas and radio novellas have been used to reach the Latino community.

al., 1995; Mondros & Wilson, 1994). These skills can include formal training on information such as tenants rights or on skills such as conflict resolution. When teaching these skills, the organizer should operate as a consultant or facilitator rather than instructor, so as not to replicate the power relationships that the worker and client are attempting to overcome (Sherman & Wenocur, 1983; Solomon, 1976).

Participatory methods require working collaboratively with community members. These

[1]Information regarding POCAAN was taken from specific program materials and interviews with volunteers and staff. This organization can be contacted by writing to People of Color Against AIDS Network, 1200 S. Jackson, Suite 25, Seattle, WA 98144.

involve recognizing and sharing one's own power in order to develop the power of others. For example, within POCAAN, organizers take the role of consultant and facilitator, working with members of community-based agencies in order to help them design, develop, and run their own educational programs. When doing this work, we must perceive ourselves as enablers, organizers, consultants, or compatriots of the community in an effort to avoid replicating the powerlessness the community experienced with other helpers or professionals. It presumes that we do not hold the "answers" to problems, but that in the context of collaboration, community members will develop the insights, skills, and capacity to resolve their own situations (Bricker-Jenkins & Hooyman, 1986; Pinderhughes, 1989; Solomon, 1976).

The context of this interaction is influenced by the person of the organizer in relation to the community (Rivera & Erlich, 1995). If the organizer is a member of the community, then primary contact is appropriate. Primary contact involves intimate and personal grassroots work with the community. In contrast, an organizer who is of a similar ethnic or racial background but not of the community would be involved at the secondary level. This level would involve participation as a liaison or linkperson between the community and the larger society. The tertiary level of contact would be most appropriate for those who are not members of the group on any dimension. They can provide valuable contributions to the community through consultation and the sharing of technical knowledge. Therefore, awareness of one's own similarity to and difference from a community is critical for defining work roles and understanding how one might be seen by others (Rivera & Erlich, 1995).

Participation suggests ways in which community members are involved in governance of

POCAAN describes itself as an organization that seeks to make fundamental change through community participation and leadership. Community members are active participants in the governance of the organization, in the staffing of projects, and in the planning process. In this way communities have considerable power regarding the methods and goals of organizing.

A central aspect of POCAAN's community education program has been peer education. This has involved enlisting members of different communities to develop and implement culturally competent and well-grounded methods for AIDS/HIV education. In some communities, peer educators have been involved in participatory action research, organizing mutual aid networks, conducting safer sex parties, and working with clergy to reach church members. These programs have been effective in reaching a broadbased and diverse population within communities of color.

the organizing effort. This can range from collaboration in analyzing community conditions to representation on the board of directors. The degree to which participation translates into actual power over the organizing effort will determine the level of empowerment.

An equally critical aspect of participation is the process of praxis. If active involvement is to contribute to empowerment, participants should be encouraged to reflect upon and analyze their experience. The results of this analysis can then be integrated into the development of future efforts (Burghardt, 1982;

Freire, 1972; Keefe, 1980; Longres & McLeod, 1980; Wallerstein, 1992).

Capacity building refers to methods that build from individual and community strengths rather than on working to correct problems or difficulties. Building from strengths means first identifying areas of positive functioning and using those to develop new skills (Kretzmann & McKnight, 1993; Saleebey, 1992). Building from strengths often mean recognizing and validating skills and capacities that may often go unnoticed and unrewarded. It is crucial that we recognize that many communities been involved in a process of struggle against oppressive structures and that this has required considerable strength. By analyzing elements of the struggle, strengths can be more easily identified, communicated, and used as a basis for future work.

This requires recognizing how community leaders have worked to improve conditions within their communities through the involvement of community networks (Ackelsberg & Diamond, 1987; Gilkes, 1983; Gutiérrez & Lewis, 1994; Medoff & Sklar, 1994). For example, the movements for equality and civil rights within communities of color during the mid- and late-20th century build upon existing relations within churches, voluntary organizations, and the workplace (Evans, 1980; Muñoz, 1989; West, 1990). In urban communities today, grassroots organizations continue to use these informal networks to work on issues such as education, housing, safety, and immigration reform (Medoff & Sklar, 1994; Rivera & Erlich, 1995).

This discussion and the examples have focused primarily on how MCO methods can be used within communities of color. This is not to imply that the development of methods for cross-cultural or multiethnic coalitions are not also the focus of this practice. Instead, the development of unity in diversity arises from a

> Capacity building for POCAAN has meant recognizing how some of the barriers to AIDS/HIV education in communities of color can be overcome by using existing strengths. For example, exclusionary attitudes of clergy toward gay men or injecting drug users can prevent them from seeing the AIDS epidemic as a community problem. POCAAN has dealt with these attitudes by confronting them directly—engaging in dialogue with clergy about ways in which they view their role in relation to the community. By recognizing their role as leaders and engaging in open dialogue, POCAAN was able to garner the support of community leaders. By recognizing and building upon the informal networks in communities of color, the ability to confront the AIDS epidemic was bolstered.

critical understanding and application of the processes discussed here. Only by building effective and viable organizations within communities of color can coalitions that unite communities around common issues be developed. By understanding one's own place and one's own community, individuals can begin to reach out and work with others.

Again, the work of POCAAN illustrates how this can be done as highlighted in the box on page 255.

This discussion and examples from the field identify ways in which these methods, though discussed separately, are interlocking and mutually reinforcing in increasing individual and community power. Participating in programs within an organization can be educational and can build on strengths. When participants and communities are not seen as competent, they will not be treated as equal partners. A focus on education can guide the ways in which strengths are developed and participation is structured. Therefore, multicultural organizing methods comprise a holistic approach to community practice.

Challenges in Multicultural Community Organizing

Multicultural organizing, like all community work, is challenging and difficult. It involves diving into those conflicts that exist in our society and being able to take a stand on controversial issues. In order to do this work, organizers require supportive supervision, education, and leadership (Gutiérrez, Glen-Maye, & Delois, 1995). When this work is successful, it can be particularly gratifying and rewarding for the organizer and community at large. This following section outlines some of the challenges to be met if we are to engage in effective multicultural community work.

Multicultural organizing requires organizers skilled in all aspects of community work. Rather than working from one framework of practice, the focus is on ways to mix and phase different approaches to community organization according to the community, its needs and strengths, and the resources available (Bradshaw et al., 1993). Of particular importance is the ability to learn from the community. This involves self-awareness regarding one's own understanding of the community, finding ways to learn more about the local community through key informants, working as partners to develop local leadership, and focusing on ways to build cohesiveness within and between ethnic communities. The critical role of the organizer is that of a learner who approaches the community to understand and facilitate

The work of POCAAN has been centered on a four-level strategy requiring work within and between different communities. The four levels have the following foci:

- Identifying issues within specific communities

- Motivating behavioral change in individuals engaging in high-risk behavior

- Organizing individuals within communities

- Mobilizing community-based organizations and public institutions to work together to break down barriers to health care

This form of public/private partnership requires the involvement of the entire community in Seattle to be concerned about AIDS/HIV prevention in communities of color. It is based both on working within communities to provide education and support for AIDS/HIV prevention and on mechanisms to bring communities together to advocate for larger system change. Building strong, culturally relevant organizing efforts within specific ethnic and racial communities has been seen as providing a base for engaging other communities.

change (Bradshaw et al., 1993; Green, 1995; Rivera & Erlich, 1995).

Multicultural organizing calls for understanding the significance of social location in shaping human experience (Green, 1995; Gutiérrez, Rosegrant Alvarez, Nemon, & Lewis, in press). This includes a valuing of one's own class, gender, and cultural heritage and having respect for and interest in the heritage of others (Green, 1995). By realizing where one is situated and what values and worldviews one holds, the dynamics of intergroup relationships become more apparent. Without seeing one's own position, it is impossible to really grasp the position of others (Green, 1995).

Gaining knowledge of the history, traditions, and values of other groups is also essential. Because ethnicity is formed from historical and social influences, learning about these external and internal factors helps to understand the problems and strengths of different communities. Respect for others means that one not only acknowledges the importance of the others' cultures but takes an interest in gaining knowledge about the differences. Through ethnic competence, multicultural organizers can cultivate a respect for diversity among the different groups in order to facilitate cooperation and break down the barriers between cultures. They must also be able to use this knowledge effectively so that the potentials of each group can be maximized through coordinated efforts with other groups.

Multicultural organizers must act as both facilitators and learners (Green, 1995; Gutiérrez & Lewis, 1994). The process of empowerment requires that individuals and groups develop their own strengths and solutions. Through a facultative approach, the multicultural organizer can foster positive collaborations. In order to do this, an effective facilitator must be open to others and recognize his or her own limitations. Through this cooperative interaction between the organizer and the community, consciousness is raised and solutions are generated (Rivera & Erlich, 1995).

Recognizing and working with inter- and intragroup conflict is critical for MCO: It requires breaking down existing social boundaries to build alliances to recognize and embrace the conflict that characterizes cross-cultural work. Conflicts arise both within organizations that have been successful in reaching a diverse group and between the organization and a larger community that may be threatened by these multiracial and ethnic coalitions. In some respects, the emergence of conflict indicates that meaningful multicultural work is taking place. However, the sources and resolution of conflict will affect the outcomes. The extent to which the organizer can anticipate and use conflict constructively determines whether the efforts are successful (Gutiérrez & Lewis, 1994; Ristock, 1990; West, 1990).

Work on MCO is currently limited by a lack of systematic research to evaluate its methods. The field of research on evaluating community organization methods has focused primarily on the effectiveness on changing individual-level outcomes such as health behaviors, educational attainment, or employment (O'Conner, 1995). Research on community practice has been primarily descriptive, focusing on describing methods for practice or forms of participation (MacNair, 1995). Only recently has research begun to look specifically at the effectiveness of methods for engaging citizens in community-level efforts or on strengthening community institutions (Maton & Salem, 1995). If we are to understand methods of MCO and their ability to improve community life, research is needed that looks more specifically at ways in which MCO can be made most effective.

This brief discussion of the challenges of MCO suggests that barriers to engage in this form of practice are daunting. It requires consistent and appropriate education and support, a focus on the inter- and intrapersonal aspects of community practice, skills in conflict management, and understanding of how difference and inequality affect interpersonal and community interactions. Such challenges will require a greater investment in community practice and research in schools of social work. The capacity of our profession to meet this challenge may be limited, but perhaps the inability to meet these challenges may doom us to limited impact on emerging and critical issues.

Conclusion

In what ways can multicultural organizing influence the trends identified at the beginning of this chapter? The demographic changes in our society will proceed regardless of how we respond. We currently face a choice between working for social justice and equality in an increasingly diverse world or working to reinforce current calls for social control. Will our role be focused on using ethnic sensitive community education methods to encourage the construction of larger and stronger prisons or to develop multicultural methods to question the use of prisons to solve problems of economic dislocation (Dressel, 1994)? The path we take will be affected by the direction of our professional mission as well as by our ability to engage in multicultural organizing within our profession and our community.

In order for our profession to contribute to the empowerment of communities of color, we need to recognize our role within the society and identify ways in which we can work more effectively as allies to the communities that we serve (Frumkin & O'Conner, 1985; Reisch & Wenocur, 1986). We need to maintain a positive focus both on the strengths and possibilities that exist in our world and on our own strengths and possibilities as a profession.

Reaching the objectives of multicultural organizing will require a social transformation toward the development of equitable and just intergroup relationships. In this process, diversity must be understood, respected, and utilized while unity must be forged. Through unity in diversity and social change, multicultural community organizers can be instrumental in promoting greater equity.

This chapter has highlighted issues involved in the definition, practice, and implementation of MCO. If we are to engage in MCO, we need to recognize and act upon multiple dimensions of social work education, research, and practice. Without these changes in the structure of social work and the education of practitioners, effective MCO will not take place. As we enter the next century, we must take a critical look at our roles and mission and find ways to work together with our colleagues, clients, and communities for a more equitable society.

REFERENCES

Ackelsberg, M., & Diamond, I. (1987). Gender and political life: New directions in political science. In B. Hess & M. Feree (Eds)., *Analyzing Gender: A Handbook of Social Science.* Newbury Park: Sage.

Albrecht, L., & Brewer, R. (1990). *Bridges of Power: Women's Multicultural Alliances.* Philadelphia: New Society Publishers.

Bradshaw, C., Soifer, S., & Gutiérrez, L. (1993). Toward a hybrid model for effective organizing in communities of color. *Journal of Community Practice, 1,* 25–42.

Bricker-Jenkins, M., & Hooyman, N. (1986). *Not for Women Only: Social Work Practice for a Feminist Future.* Silver Spring, MD: NASW.

Burghardt, S. (1982). *The Other Side of Organizing.* Cambridge, MA: Schenkman.

Carpenter, E. (1980). Social services, policies, and issues. *Social Casework, 61,* 455–461.

Chau, K. L. (1991). Social work with ethnic minorities: Practice issues and potentials. *Journal of Multi-cultural Social Work, 1*(1), 23–39.

Devore, W., & Schlesinger, E. (1981). *Ethnic-Sensitive Social Work Practice.* St. Louis: Mosby.

DiNitto, D. (1996). The future of social welfare policy. In P. Raffoul & A. McNeece (Eds.), *Future Issues for Social Work Practice.* Boston: Allyn & Bacon.

Dressel, P. (1994). . . . And We Keep on Building Prisons: Racism, Poverty and Challenges to the Welfare State. *Journal of Sociology and Social Welfare, 21*(3), 7–30.

Evans, S. (1980). *Personal Politics.* New York: Vintage Books.

Fighting back: Frances Sandoval and her mother's crusade take aim at gangs. (1988, October 16). *Sunday Chicago Tribune Magazine,* pp. 10–24.

Freire, P. (1972). *The Pedagogy of the Oppressed.* New York: Seabury.

Frumkin, M., & O'Conner, G. (1985). Where has the profession gone? Where is it going? Social work's search for identity. *The Urban and Social Change Review, 18*(1), 12–19.

Gallegos, J. (1982). The ethnic competence model for social work education. In B. White (Ed.), *Color in a White Society* (pp. 1–9). Silver Spring, MD: NASW.

Gilkes, C. (1983). Going up for the oppressed: The career mobility of Black women community workers. *Journal of Social Issues, 39*(3), 115–139.

Green, J. (1995). Cultural Awareness in the Human Services. (2d ed.). Needham Heights, MA: Allyn & Bacon.

Gutiérrez, L. (1992). Empowering ethnic minorities in the 21st century: The role of human service organizations. In Y. Hasenfeld (Ed.), *The Organization of Human Services: Structure and Processes.* Beverly Hills: Sage.

Gutiérrez, L. (1994). Beyond Coping: An Empowerment Perspective on Stressful Life Events. *Journal of Sociology and Social Welfare, 21*(3), 201–220.

Gutiérrez, L., DeLois, K., & GlenMaye, L. (1995). Understanding empowerment practice: Building on practitioner based knowledge. *Families in Society, 76*(9), 534–542.

Gutiérrez, L., GlenMaye, L., & DeLois, K. (1995). The organizational context of empowerment practice: Implications for social work administration. *Social Work, 40*(2), 249–258.

Gutiérrez, L., & Lewis, E. (1994). Community organizing with women of color: A feminist approach. *Journal of Community Practice, 1*(2).

Gutiérrez, L., & Nagda, B. (1996). The multicultural imperative for human service organizations. In P. Raffoul & A. McNeece (Eds.), *Future Issues for Social Work Practice.* Boston: Allyn & Bacon.

Gutiérrez, L., & Nurius, P. (1994). *Education and Research for Empowerment Practice.* Seattle, WA: Center for Social Policy and Practice, University of Washington.

Gutiérrez, L., Rosegrant Alvarez, A., Nemon, H., & Lewis, E. (In press). Multicultural community organizing: A strategy for change. *Social Work.*

Hirsch, K. (1991). Clementine Barfield takes on the mean streets of Detroit. *Ms. The World of Women, 1*(4), 54–58.

Jackson, B., & Holvino, E. (1988). *Multicultural Organizational Development.* Ann Arbor: Program on Conflict Management Alternatives.

Keefe, T. (1980). Empathy skill and critical consciousness. *Social Casework, 61,* 387–393.

Kieffer, C. (1984). Citizen Empowerment: A Developmental Perspective. In J. Rappaport, C. Swift, & R. Hess (Eds.), *Studies in Empowerment: Towards Understanding and Action.* New York: Haworth Press.

Kretzmann, J., & McKnight, J. (1993). *Building Communities from the Inside Out: A Path Toward Finding and Mobilizing a Community's Assets.* Evanston, IL: Center for Urban Affairs and Policy Research, Northwestern University.

Longres, J., & McLeod, E. (1980). Consciousness raising and social work practice. *Social Casework, 61,* 267–277.

MacNair, R. (1995). *A Research Methodology for Community Practice.* Annual Program Meeting, Council on Social Work Education, March 1995, San Diego, CA.

Maton, K., & Salem, D. (1995). Organizational characteristics of empowering community settings. *American Journal of Community Psychology, 23*(5), 631–656.

McMahon, A., & Allen-Meares, P. (1992). Is social work racist? A content analysis of the recent literature. *Social Work, 37*(6), 533–539.

Medoff, P., & Sklar, H. (1994). *Streets of Hope: The Fall and Rise of an Urban Neighborhood.* Boston: South End Press.

Mondros, J., & Wilson, S. (1994). *Organizing for Power and Empowerment.* New York: Columbia University Press.

Morales, A. (1981) Social work with third world people. *Social Work, 26,* 48–51.

Muñoz, C. (1989). *Youth, Identity and Power: The Chicano Movement.* London: Verso.

Murdock, S., & Michael, M. (1996). Future demographic changes: The demand for social welfare services in the 21st century. In P. Raffoul & A. McNeece (Eds.), *Future Issues for Social Work Practice.* Boston: Allyn & Bacon.

O'Conner, A. (1995). Evaluating comprehensive community initiatives. In J. Connell, A. Kubish, L. Schorr, & C. Weiss (Eds.), *New Approaches to Evaluating Community Initiatives: Concepts, Methods & Contexts* (pp. 23–63). Washington, DC: The Aspen Institute.

Parsons, R. J. (1991). Empowerment: Purpose and practice in social work. *Social Work with Groups, 14*(2), 27–43.

Pinderhughes, E. (1989). *Understanding Race, Ethnicity, & Power: The Key to Efficacy in Clinical Practice.* New York: Free Press.

Rappaport, J. (1987). Terms of Empowerment/ Examples of Prevention: Towards a Theory of Community Psychology. *American Journal of Community Psychology, 15,* 117–148.

Reisch, M., & Wenocur, S. (1986). The Future of community organization in social work: Social activism and the politics of profession-building. *Social Service Review 60*(1), 70–91.

Ristock, J. (1990). Canadian feminist social service collectives: Caring and contradictions. In L. Albrecht & R. Brewer (Eds.), *Bridges of Power: Women's Multicultural Alliances.* Philadelphia: New Society Publishers.

Rivera, F., and Erlich, J. (1995). *Community Organizing in a Diverse Society.* (2d ed.). Needham Heights, MA: Allyn & Bacon.

Saleebey, D. (1992). The strengths perspective in social work practice. New York: Longman.

Sanchez, G. (1993). *Becoming Mexican American: Ethnicity, Culture, and Identity in Chicano Los Angeles, 1900–1945.* New York: Oxford University Press.

Scott, J., & Delgado, M. (1979). Planning mental health programs for Hispanic communities. *Social Casework, 60,* 451–456.

Sherman, W., & Wenocur, S. (1983). Empowering public welfare workers through mutual support. *Social Work, 28*(5) 375–379.

Solomon, B. (1976). *Black Empowerment.* New York: Columbia University Press.

Stehno, S. (1982). Differential treatment of minority children in service systems. *Social Work, 27,* 39–45.

Wallerstein, N. (1992). Powerless, empowerment and health: Implications for health promotion programs. *American Journal of Health Promotion, 6*(3), 197–205.

Wenocur, S., & Reisch, M. (1989). *From Charity to Enterprise: The Development of American Social Work in a Market Economy.* Chicago: University of Illinois Press.

West, G. (1990). Cooperation and conflict among women in the welfare rights movement. In L. Albrecht & R. Brewer, (Eds.), *Bridges of Power: Women's Multicultural Alliances* (pp. 149–171). Philadelphia: New Society Publishers.

Zimmerman, M. A. (In press). Empowerment: Forging new perspectives in mental health. In J. Rappaport & E. Seidman (Eds.), *Handbook of Community Psychology.* New York: Plenum Press.

School–Community Collaboratives

The Missing Links

Stephanie Hochman

In response to harsh economic and fiscal realities, school–community collaborations have become increasingly popular in the delivery of services to children. Yet, according to Stephanie Hochman, LCSW, a program director for Bay Area Community Resources in Richmond, California, a non-profit agency engaged in school-based collaborations in several counties of the San Francisco Bay Area, there are currently several "missing links" in this model that hinder its effectiveness in addressing the many nonacademic needs of youth and their families. Hochman describes these gaps and analyzes current economic and social trends that are obstacles to the success of collaborative efforts. She argues that future collaborative models must incorporate attacks on the root causes of the problems of youth, focus on change-oriented strategies and activities, and involve all the stakeholders in program development and implementation in order to succeed. Social workers can play key roles in this model as bridge-builders, program facilitators, educators, and community mediators.

Stephanie Hochman is a faculty member at San Francisco State University School of Social Work, where she teaches social change strategies and gender issues.

I stand outside an inner-city elementary school in one of California's most impoverished cities. Under the Chevron refinery's watchful eye (and plume of smoke), I hand out questionnaires written to parents in English and Spanish for a hopeful Healthy Start program proposal. "What will make this school a better place for your child? What do you think? Your input is very important." I wonder what will really come of all this.

In another neighborhood, I visit a church two blocks from the local elementary school to inquire about the relationship between the two institutions. The minister asks me, "What's the name of that school again?"

In the faculty lounge during lunch time, teachers complain that they are being asked to do things that are not their jobs, "You take care of these difficult kids—take them off my hands!!!"

What is the relationship between schools and communities? Can we expect schools to address the myriad nonacademic needs of youth and their families? What are successful models for addressing these needs? Moving into the 21st century, the landscape of public responsibility for the care and cultivation of our society is changing and these questions become even more salient.

Programs that integrate community services and school programs, often called "school–community linked" or "school–community collaboratives" have been a focus in both the literature and the funding worlds. Adapting to the harsh economic realities in the upcoming decade and beyond, school–community collaborations are prominent in the field of youth services now and will undoubtedly continue to be. This essay will discuss some of the missing links and relevant economic and social trends that are hindering the true success of many collaboratives.

School and community collaborations have much to offer. Programs that bring community social services into schools can increase accessibility and can integrate a broad range of services. However, these programs, as they exist, cannot pretend to be the solution to the complex problems and deep needs that our youth and families experience. Among these many issues are job insecurity, economic dislocation, racial tension, youth violence, drug abuse, and reduced funding for health and welfare benefits. More all-encompassing, proactive, economic, and social solutions must be cultivated to effectively solve the problems that school–community linked programs are now attempting to solve.

Although the discussion here does not include a detailed analysis of every school-linked program in the country (see Chavkin and Brown, 1992; Franklin, 1992; Kahn and Kamerman, 1992; Levy and Shepardson, 1992), the essay will focus on general cross-cutting issues drawn from a review of the literature and references to specific programs in California, in which the author has had direct participation over the past seven years.

What Is School–Community Collaboration?

Franklin and Streeter (1995) differentiate school–community linked programs into five categories, based on the quality of the linkage. These categories range from "Informal Relations," defined as school referrals to community services, such as a traditional school social worker might do, to "Integration," which identifies fully integrated collaborations between community service agencies and the school.

The majority of new collaborative models for joining school and community services, like the Healthy Start model in California, fall under Franklin and Streeter's fourth category of "collaboration" models. This category is defined by the coming together of school and human service agency personnel to jointly develop common goals and strategies for addressing problems. Services begin to be merged as both the school and the agency share resources and actually work together. An example would be the running of psychoeducational substance abuse prevention groups by teacher–counselor teams. This might also include school personnel involved in service delivery planning.

The Integration schema in Franklin and Streeter's model is unique in its vision of a high degree of formal administrative and political collaboration from both state and local levels. The Integration category is defined by a high degree of commitment and shared ownership by the school as well as by the many participants. This requires significant commitment at all levels. Community agencies and leaders and school faculty should be involved in the planning and implementation processes. The Integration model also requires a redistribution and redefinition of resources from both community and school constellations. Integration necessitates a commitment from both systems to undergo significant reform in their staffing, operation, and missions.

> This is the most radical approach to linking public schools with human services in that it moves beyond collaboration to actually merge the two systems into a single, integrated service delivery system. (Franklin and Streeter, 1995, p. 778)

The "one-stop shopping" model of school-based programming seeks to locate a variety of services at school sites. Health, mental health, public health, and employment services may be some of those that are provided. This type of programming may result in state-mandated or state-supported school clinics or health-care centers that are integrated with a school's academic programs (Franklin and Streeter, 1995). (It is interesting to note that nowhere in the literature is posited the option of total school ownership of a social service program, such as an in-house social services department as part of the school. This may be because none exist, but one wonders whether this would be a good option.)

Why School–Community Collaborations?

Public schools and non-profit human service agencies are being challenged to create integrated programs that enhance children's lives and address the challenges that they and their families face. Many community-based organizations exist that address these challenges, and programs that integrate school efforts and community efforts are emerging. Schools are a natural venue for human services programs for a variety of reasons. Most often cited is that public schools provide natural access to youth and their families (Franklin and Streeter, 1995). Schools are a universal point of intervention because everyone must attend them.

Secondly, schools have a vested interest in the well-being of the student, and "if supportive services can help ensure educational success and self-sufficiency, then the institution responsible for education should have a part in the provision of those services" (Levy and Shepardson, 1992, p. 46).

A third reason for the collaboration that is not often mentioned is that the school *is* the community or, at least, one of the communities of youth. School is where young people develop their social relationships and become socialized to the world outside of their families. It is often the first social environment where a young person begins to make her or his mark, to be an activist in the world. Therefore, school-based programs intervene not only at the point of access, but also at the point of potential strength for youth. Combining the grassroots understanding and social context of community-based support with the educative environment and resources of schools, these collaboratives have an opportunity to enhance resiliency and develop leadership as youth begin their journey of impacting the world.

Fourthly, the school is a neighborhood institution. It can be a focal point, not only for services, but for community gathering. Along with places of worship, schools can potentially be the heart of a neighborhood. For these reasons, school–community collaboratives can be effective.

Actually, schools have been a locus for mental health and social services since the 1920s. Progressive education reformers advocated for the inclusion of a variety of social services in the public schools. The progressive reformers conceived of these "comprehensive schools" as a vital link between the school, home, and the community. Some of their programs resemble those of today: lunch programs, health clinics, and a full range of services to ameliorate the effects of poverty and to respond to human needs. Social workers and nurses would provide health, safety, and sex education (Tyack, 1992).

Unfortunately, the vision of comprehensive schools was never quite fulfilled. Schools and their programs became more bureaucratized, and programs were consolidated rather than expanded. This contraction caused schools to become insular, closed systems and school social workers narrowed their role to that of specialized caseworker rather than the home–school–community liaison once envisioned (for more history, see Tyack, 1992).

Since the narrowing of the 1950s–1980s, the connection between educational reform and social service delivery has once again become closely linked. Educational reform is broadening its focus to include family involvement, the fostering of positive cultural expression, and an educational perspective that takes into account the emotional state of the child. The author is familiar with a number of schools that have successfully used state Compensatory Education funds, intended for academic development, for mental health and other prevention activities. Schools know that you cannot separate the two.

Clearly, the ideals of today's school–community collaboration movement are not new. How then do we ensure success this time around? How do we create meaningful programs for the needs of today and tomorrow? The answers to these questions lie in a critical analysis of the shortcomings of school–community collaboratives and of some future trends that compound the impact of these inadequacies.

Some Missing Links

The author knows of an attempt to rid a Harlem high school and its students of the difficult problems that beset them: low school achievement, behavioral problems, gangs, disobedience—common inner-city school problems. Money flooded into the school and state of the art social service programs were implemented. In addition, a nearby corporation adopted the school, pumping in more money and notoriety to create an innovative attempt to reform the educational conditions. However, the school is still floundering, with high levels of absenteeism, low academic achievement, and acting-out behaviors.

Why has there been no change? Perhaps because the critical conditions in which these youths live and the future which they imagine has not changed very much. As wonderful as the school and its innovative program may be, poverty, racism, substance abuse, deepening economic dislocation, and bleak tomorrows all conspire to undermine the best attempts at the narrowly focused remediation that characterizes school-linked programs. Many collaborations neglect asking the most critical questions: What are the fundamental problems? What are the values that underlie our assumptions and perspectives? What are we really trying to accomplish? And therefore, what are the most efficacious solutions?

Chevron in Richmond, California, helps 6th graders with reading while fumes from their refinery waft over the playground. Across America, corporations allow employees time to be mentors to youth. But when these corporations do not hire the neighborhoods' adults, which would help mothers, fathers, aunts, and uncles be mentors to their own children, they have not changed the economic landscape of the community.

To effect real changes, programs seeking to address the academic, emotional, and social needs of youth must reach out beyond the educational environs of the schoolyard. Most programs target the enhancement of individual skills (e.g., tutoring, job development, teen parenting, and so on) (Levy and Shepardson, 1992), but do not target enhancing one's ability to impact the larger social, economic, and political problems that are the root causes of the troubles that our youth face. School–community collaborations must begin with the understanding that many of the problems of youth and their families are community/society problems and not only problems of the individuals (Dupper, 1993). Youth, families, and community members must define the problems. Programming can follow from that.

Now, let us look at ways that these programs fall short of their own missions of addressing the needs of youth and families. Lack of involvement of families, front-line school personnel, and community leaders is one way that school–community collaborations fail in their stated missions.

Family Issues

Schools can be both safe havens and oppressive nightmares for youth and their families. Schools are often not the friendly, open, nurturing places that we imagine them to be. Many parents/guardians are alienated from their child's school, not feeling welcome or accepted. The marginalizing that occurs in the larger society for those who do not "fit in" is replicated daily in the schools for both students and their caretakers. This is especially true with students for whom education is not easily accessible for academic or other reasons. Often parents, especially low-income parents, are seen not as partners with the school and teachers, but as adversaries, who are only tolerated. In an educational era that reveres "parent involvement" from above, these parents are dissuaded from real participation in many institutionalized and not so subtle ways.

Parents of disenfranchised youth may be more disenfranchised from the school than are parents for whom the educational environment is familiar. Some may be less active due to an unfamiliarity with formal and informal mechanisms for participation, because of prior negative experiences with schools or other institutions, and cultural and language barriers. PTA,

Back to School Nights, and other school events often do not include translators for non–English-speaking parents. In the future, these problems will be compounded. The Census Bureau estimates that by the year 2000, 33% of school-age youth will be students of color, as will be the majority of adults in the Western states (Chavkin and Brown, 1992). It is imperative that the school system remove cultural and language barriers for student success and family participation.

Many school–community programs call for the inclusion of parents and community in their design. However, this inclusion often ends before implementation. Many programs incorporate consultation of parents at the planning phase or provide parent workshops, but do not involve parents in the provision or control of services, or in the leadership of the school. This is an important missing link.

School Issues

School personnel also need to be involved in an intimate way in school–community collaboratives. They are sometimes involved in the planning and development of a program but not its implementation and maintenance. School personnel have knowledge of and access to the school district and school perspectives that community agencies cannot have. The school is its own community and as such has indigenous leaders, stated and unstated norms, and power relationships. Active leadership from the front-line school staff is critical. Anyone who has worked in a school knows that the secretary and custodian are valuable resources concerning the needs of the community and youth.

A school representative or two integrated throughout the life of a program is vital to making it holistic and proactive. Staff participants are representatives to and of the school faculty and staff. They communicate, influence, inspire, and involve the rest of the staff through their active representation. This person or persons can represent other staffs' ideas and concerns, encourage involvement, and transfer information of program goals and needs. However, leadership from school administrators and structured allocation of time and resources are crucial for successful participation. If collaborative responsibilities are experienced as "add-on" duties for already overworked teachers, resistance and refusal will ensue.

In one multiservice program in which the author worked, teacher staff development was a component. However, it was also one of the first services to fall away. One reason for this was that any staff development plans that were developed by the committee's faculty were repeatedly postponed by the principal. Without leadership from above, the committee and therefore the staff development program withered. It is important to note that this same neglect was visited upon the parent involvement committee, which listed "Leadership of school must be committed to parent involvement" as its first recommendation for improving parent involvement. The principal never implemented any of the 25 recommendations from that committee. Not surprisingly, the committee no longer exists. Another new multiservice program proudly claims that parents and youth are partners in identifying needs and program priorities. However, to date, parents have been separated into a "parent group" that is segregated from the major decision-making body of the program. This has resulted in their having very little actual input.

The school as the locus of remediation is rarely addressed in school–community service programs. The school is seen as the receptacle for services but not as the target of change. What are the ways that the school itself hinders students' development? As this author has seen, tracking, labeling, insufficient teacher development, crowded classes, poorly funded schools, and punitive rather than therapeutic disciplinary procedures and structures are all examples of systemic school mechanisms that are harmful to youth and that are rarely change targets in youth enhancement programs.

Until schools look at the institutionalized ways they create obstacles to the growth of youth and families, they cannot become partners in school–community collaboratives that will truly make any difference. As social workers, we are commanded to help promote systems change. In creating the school–community collaboration goals, social workers can play a key role in initiating organizational and school program analysis as an integral part of the process. We must facilitate the evaluation of the institution's weaknesses in relation to educating and serving youth and families. Furthermore, we can help parents and youth develop the skills necessary to negotiate and participate in the educational and political systems, thereby increasing their power. By so doing, we facilitate schoolwide changes that will better serve the child.

Finally, schools must be willing to change their normal way of educating to make room for collaborative projects. Communication and decision-making structures of a school need to be changed to creatively involve parents and community. This requires all those affected to create the mechanisms for involvement. As mentioned, time must be allotted to school personnel to allow for meaningful participation.

Community Issues

One major flaw in typical school–community collaboratives is the narrow definition of community. The "community" being referred to is predominantly community agencies and community social service programs—not neighborhood, grassroots community members. Community agencies do not necessarily represent the community at all. Community agencies are often staffed with well-intentioned professionals from outside the community, who bring skills and training, but often do not have insight into the community's problems or relevant solutions. Therefore, some paid staff in these agencies (as well as in the schools) need to represent the communities served.

This same lack of representation is seen in the reemerging use of volunteers as an important strategy in providing services and will continue as dollars continue to shrink. Volunteers are often white middle-class professionals or college students who have the best of intentions but usually lack the essential knowledge and life experience to be most effective. The challenge is to also recruit and train parents, community elders, and teenage youth who are hanging out on the streets, to mentor, tutor, play ball, and interact with youth in myriad ways.

Furthermore, community service agencies rarely strive for the eradication of the most fundamental problems of the community or for changing the usual structures and power dynamics that guide social relations. Community service agencies tend to be fairly traditional in the kinds of programming they provide. Funders continue to favor service-based programs with focused service outcomes; social work schools continue to produce liberal reformers who focus on changing individual and family behavior.

Programs can become more change-oriented by directly addressing the issues and root problems that youth, families, and even schools face. For instance, change-oriented programming can organize for true multiculturalism, eradicating racism both in society and in our institutions. It can work toward overturning poverty and the economic forces that perpetuate unequal distribution of resources in society by organizing for increasing the minimum wage, universal health care, or economic development. Programs can focus on teaching skills to youth and families so that they can intervene in the bureaucracies that impact their lives. Youth can be taught to be critical thinkers, able to reflect on and act on the forces around them, rather than adapting to the existing system.

Additionally, change-oriented programs should involve clients on their boards and in program planning and evaluation processes. In one school–community program in which the author worked, 4 parents (out of a group of 40) were prominent members of the governing board. Although only 10% participated, the groundwork was laid for increasing parent governance. Unfortunately, the foundation funding dwindled to nothing and only vestiges of the program remain.

Future Trends

As of 1992, one in five young people lived in poverty—an increase of 5 million since 1973 (Carnegie Council on Adolescent Development, 1994). Every day 1870 teens drop out of high school (Klopf, Shedlin, and Zaret, 1989). Young people are dying from violence at a steadily increasing rate—in this decade, the rate has grown from 62.4 to 69.3 deaths per 100,000 (Melaville and Blank, 1993). These are only a few of the future trends that will exacerbate many of the issues already raised. The current dismantling of social welfare ideology and programs nationally is creating a deepening scarcity of resources available for human needs. The gorge that exists between rich and poor is widening and so are the disparities between those with resources and those without.

This resource chasm also affects the disparities between students who are able to have successful school experiences and those who are not. We are now firmly planted in the information age, where some schools have personal computers on every desk, and others are lacking even the most basic educational supplies, such as up-to-date textbooks or paper enough for teachers to copy assignments. Academic achievement has never been as important as it now is. The job market of the 21st century will require literate and semi-skilled workers (Melaville and Blank, 1991). Because funding for schools is still determined by local tax bases, opportunities and resources are allocated disproportionately from community to community and from school to school. Furthermore, poorer communities are less able to support additional programs. For instance, many schools in West Contra Costa County, an impoverished area of Northern California, have no PTAs. In addition to fostering parent involvement in schools, PTAs are long known for their fund-raising activities. Their funds are often instrumental for supplemental school programs, such as tutoring and after-school recreation.

The continuing reduction of federal dollars for services, the weakening of the Department of Education, and block granting to states reduces the federal mandate for programs and lessens state accountability for education standards and the social safety net. The Department of Education is on the edge of being dismantled as part of the Contract with America, and states are trimming allocations to education. This year in California, a 17% reduction in the State Compensatory Education funding is feared; federal Drug-Free Schools allocations, which fund many support service programs, have been reduced steadily in the past several years, losing 40% from 1993–4 to 1994–5, and an additional 14% from 1994–5 to 1995–6. This next year's allocation is still uncertain (Chan, 1996). In 1995, the final year of a 3-year Department of

Education school–community collaborative grant was eliminated across the country—with no explanation, no apologies, and no replacement funding. This grant, called The Future Is Ours, began a process it did not finish. The schools and community were bereft, wondering what happened to the Future.

Not only are academic and special support programs being reduced or cut completely, but also there are fewer and fewer public opportunities for a broad range of programs for youth. Many traditional sources of support for all children, such as neighborhood, government, and religious organizations and other kinds of services, are fragmented at best and nonexistent at worst (Klopf et al., 1989).

The disintegration of society's economic base has been accompanied by a growing tendency to blame the poor for their problems. This tendency has reduced the tolerance for social programs while economic conditions have increased the need for more thorough support programs for all youth. We cannot continue to marginalize those in need by ignoring the environmental forces that create the need. "We need to develop comprehensive preventive strategies to deal with the stresses and obstacles affecting all children, directly or indirectly" (Klopf et al., p. 4). Historically, school–community linked services have identified specific youth and their families as having social service needs (e.g., counseling, case management, and so on). Now, changes in society necessitate a shift in the programs offered by school-linked services. This shift calls for resiliency-enhancing programs like leadership development and peer tutoring.

In addition to reduced funding and increasing poverty, growing racism is a dangerous trend with which to contend. Swelling poverty and racism have led to increased social dislocation, disenfranchisement, and the widening dissociation of certain groups and communities from others. The dream of eradicating segregation through busing in schools has proven to be ineffective. Schools and neighborhoods are more segregated rather than less (Eaton, 1993). This trend will continue to increase as middle-class "baby boomers" continue to remove their children from the public schools. Tyack discusses the risk of complete school segregation with the advent of a school voucher program where "well-informed, middle-class and prosperous parents of students with few special needs would send their children to schools with similar background pupils" (Tyack, 1992, p. 29). Teaching respect for diversity and differences must be enforced for all students, school personnel, and administrators.

The Coalition for PRIDE in San Marcos, Texas, emphasizes its multiethnic collaboration among community, business, university faculty, community-based organizations and agencies, parents, and school personnel to prevent drop-outs.

> The success of the coalition can be directly attributed to the emphasis on multiethnic family-school-community collaboration. Not only does the program have broad multiethnic representation on its advisory council, but it also receives input from a wide variety of educators, parents, businesses, and community agencies that reflect the ethnic composition of the community. . . . People cannot talk about community collaboration unless they talk about multiethnic collaboration. (Chavkin and Brown, 1992, p. 164)

Collaboratives must include culturally specific services and diversity training in their programs.

Following is a trend in programming that institutes some of the issues that have been delineated. This example is certainly not all-inclusive; it is simply an example with which the author is familiar.

One trend in youth programming that has the potential to build community, strengthen communities and schools, empower and enliven youth, and make real social change is programs that incorporate community activism. Perhaps inspired by Clinton's Americorps program, a number of organizations (Youth Power, Teen Outreach Program [TOP], and Bay Area Community Resources, for example) are developing community service projects where youth become service providers and community organizers. In these programs, young people acquire the skills that enable them to identify a need in the community (or school) and to create projects that respond to it. Examples of projects vary from peer tutoring to developing a teen pregnancy prevention program to organizing the restoration of a decrepit neighborhood park to changing smoking laws in the community. What is important is that the youth decide; they identify the problems; they identify and implement the solutions. Community service projects have the promise of reenergizing, skill building, and mobilizing youth into meaningful activity. Those involved gain skills and confidence that can catapult them into future activities. Rather than producing passive service recipients, youth power programs cultivate actors.

Conclusion

This essay has discussed some ways that school–community collaboratives can improve upon their structure and activities to make them relevant to the lives of those they attempt to serve. Only by addressing the root causes of the problems of youth, by focusing on change-oriented strategies and activities, and by truly incorporating all the stakeholders into program development and implementation can school–community collaboratives have a chance to meet the needs of youth.

Social work skills are key to addressing and affecting this potential. Because social workers understand the interactions among the external economic and political environment, the internal school environment, and the individual family's relationship to these, we can build bridges among school, community, and families. We must decry the external forces that chip away at the sovereignty of youth and families. Then we must facilitate the creation of programs that provide the skills and opportunities for people to speak out, to help one another, and to make changes in the school and larger social environments.

Social workers must educate funders to the importance of supporting school and community-based efforts that tackle fundamental problems, rather than funding piecemeal service programs. We must see our role not as the community agency school-based counselor or case manager who ensures that a child is discussed in the Care Team meeting; rather, we must see our role as bringing together all those who should have a voice and ensure that they are heard. When we talk about school–community integration, we must look beyond community service agencies and how well they are integrated into service provision in the schools. We need to create ways to truly integrate community members into shaping schools and to mobilizing for community and social change. We can facilitate the clasping together of all the links—the strengths of the educational arena, the active voice of parents and youth, and the knowledge and diversity of community leaders—to create effective, broad-based, change-oriented collaboratives.

REFERENCES

Bruner, Charles. *Thinking Collaboratively: Ten Questions and Answers to Help Policy Makers Improve Children's Services*. Washington, DC: Education and Human Services Consortium, 1991.

Carngie Council on Adolescent Development. *A Matter of Time: Risk and Opportunity in the Nonschool Hours*. New York: Carnegie Corporation, 1992.

Center for the Future of Children staff. "Analysis." In *The Future of Children*, 2(1), Spring 1992, pp. 6–18. Center for the Future of Children, David and Lucile Packard Foundation.

Chan, Dennis, West Contra Costa Unified School District. Personal conversation, 1996.

Chavkin, Nancy Feyl, and Brown, Karen. "School Social Workers Building a Multiethnic Family–School–Community Partnership." *Social Work in Education*, 149(3), July 1992, pp. 160–164.

Dupper, David R. "School–Community Collaboration: A Description of a Model Program Designed to Prevent School Dropouts." *School Social Work Journal*, 18, Fall 1993, pp. 32–39.

Eaton, William J. "Segregation Creeping Back in U.S. Schools." *Los Angeles Times*, December 14, 1993, p. A1.

Franklin, Cynthia. "Alternative School Programs for At-Risk Youths." *Social Work in Education*, 14, 1992, pp. 239–251.

Franklin, Cynthia, and Streeter, Calvin L. "School Reform: Linking Public Schools with Human Services." *Social Work*, 40(6), November 1995, pp. 773–782.

Gardner, Stanley L. "Key Issues in Developing School-linked Integrated Services." In *The Future of Children*, 2(1), Spring 1992, pp. 85–94. Center for the Future of Children, David and Lucile Packard Foundation.

Jehl, Jeanne, and Kirst, Michael, Ph.D. "Getting Ready to Provide School-linked Services: What Schools Must Do." In *The Future of Children*,

2(1), Spring 1992, pp. 95–106. Center for the Future of Children, David and Lucile Packard Foundation.

Kahn, Alfred J., and Kamerman, Shiela B. *Integrating Services Integration: An Overview of Initiatives, Issues, and Possibilities.* New York: Columbia University School of Public Health, National Center for Children in Poverty, 1992.

Klopf, Gordon J., Shedlin, Allen Jr., and Zaret, Esther S. *The School as Locus of Advocacy for All Children.* New York: Elementary School Center, 1989.

Levy, Janet E., and Shepardson, William. "A Look at Current School-linked Service Efforts." In *The Future of Children,* 2(1), Spring 1992, pp. 44–55. Center for the Future of Children, David and Lucile Packard Foundation.

Melaville, Atelia I., and Blank, Martin J. *What It Takes: Structuring Interagency Partnerships to Connect Children and Families with Comprehensive Services.* Washington, DC: Education and Human Services Consortium, 1991.

Melaville, Atelia I., and Blank, Martin J., *Together We Can: A Guide for Crafting a Profamily System of Education and Human Services.* Washington, DC: Office of Educational Research and Improvement, 1993.

Outland-Mitchell, Chiquetta, and Anderson, Richard J. "Involving Parents of At-Risk Chil-dren in the Educational Process: A Literature Review." *School Social Work Journal,* 17, Fall 1992, pp. 17–24.

Tyack, David. "Health and Social Services in Public Schools: Historical Perspectives." In *The Future of Children,* 2(1), Spring 1992, pp. 19–31. Center for the Future of Children, David and Lucile Packard Foundation.

Recognizing the Role of Religious Congregations and Denominations in Social Service Provision

Ram A. Cnaan

For historians ought to be precise, truthful, and quite unprejudiced, and neither interest nor fear, hatred nor affection, should swerve them from the path of truth whose mother is history, the rival of time, the depository of great actions, the witness of what is past, the example and instruction of the present, and the monitor of the future.

Miguel de Cervantes, *Don Quixote*

Historically, religious organizations have provided a range of services to those in need. This essay explores this role. The extent and range of services are described and a call made for increasing cooperation between religious organizations and other providers of services. Ram A. Cnaan is an associate professor at the University of Pennsylvania School of Social Work. He focuses on volunteers in human services, voluntary action and organizations, community mental health, community organization from an international perspective, religiously based social service delivery, and policy *practice. Professor Cnaan has published numerous articles in these areas and serves on the editorial board of seven journals. He is chairperson of the editorial board of* Nonprofit and Voluntary Sector Quarterly.

Author note: This paper is based in part on a study carried out with major support from Partners for Sacred Places (the national center for the sound stewardship and active use of America's older and historic religious properties) and by the Research Fund at the University of Pennsylvania School of Social Work and the Lilly Endowment. I also want to thank Robert J. Wineburg, University of North Carolina, Greensboro, and Gaynor Yancey, Greater Philadelphia Food Bank, for helpful comments on earlier drafts of this chapter.

Introduction

As Cervantes has suggested, history should be precise, truthful, and unprejudiced, yet how we interpret the past is often shaped by our ideologies, beliefs, and philosophies. According to Glassie (1982), history is a cultural construction, a way that people organize reality and interpret that reality on their own terms. Modern scholars recognize that history is not carved in stone; it is not a matter of right or wrong. Rather, it is seen as a field of conflicting approaches. More than one hero, hailed in the past, has been later described as a cruel and heartless villain. Similarly, even interpretations of past events are now being recast, refined, and revised by today's scholars. In some cases, what is being taught in schools today differs from what was taught a few years ago and what will be taught in the future. Thus, the unprejudiced pursuit of truth, where mother is history, is when one wants to predict the future.

This raises the question as to whether social work truly understands its own history. I believe that the answer is not only negative, but we are actively avoiding it. I contend that the role of religious organizations in social service provision is little understood and requires serious critical review. I claim that the role of religious congregations and denominations in social service provision has been consistently downplayed in the social work literature over the past 30 years, except in religiously affiliated schools of social work. Harris (1995), for example, noted that "little attention has been paid to the welfare contribution of religious congregations" (p. 53). This separation of social work from its roots not only jeopardizes its moral foundation and public support basis, but also makes it difficult for the profession to chart its future course. I, for one, see that future as one in which social work reconnects with its origin: religiously based organizations.

The purpose of this paper is to argue for broad and full cooperation between social work and religious groups so that we may better serve those in need in the coming century. I strongly believe that based on the enormous welfare provision by religious congregations and denominations and current social and political climate in the United States, serving people in need will depend on a full and mutual alliance between social work and religiously based social services. It will take some careful ideological compromises and bold leadership, but these religiously based social services are

our historical as well as future allies. In this essay, I will not elaborate on the form that this collaboration should take, rather I will focus on the need to see religiously based social services as historical and current allies.

Before presenting my arguments, several terms require explanation. I have used the term *religiously affiliated social service* as a broad concept that includes a few elements. The first element is local congregational welfare programs. Examples include food pantries, provision of space for AA meetings, clothing closets, volunteer visitors, day care for children or the elderly, free transportation, soup kitchens, or in-home assistance. The second element is community-wide religiously affiliated services. Examples include Jewish Family and Children's Services, Catholic Charities, Salvation Army, Lutheran Youth Services, Episcopal Adoption Agencies, and interfaith coalitions. Agencies such as these have similar characteristics. They are social service agencies officially affiliated with religious denominations; their boards of trustees consist of clergy or lay leaders from the relevant denomination; they receive some financial support from the religious parent body either directly from a citywide headquarters (such as a diocese) or through local congregational fund-raising; and they were started by members of the religious order (Netting, 1982). The third element consists of national projects and organizations under religious auspices. Examples include the Catholic Bishops' Committee, the Salvation Army, and Habitat for Humanity. The final element is religiously affiliated international organizations. Examples include the Catholic Relief Committee and the Friends Committee, which provided assistance in the Rwandan and Somalian famines; and the Joint Distribution Committee, which supports Jews in Ethiopia and Eastern Europe. In addition, I have used the terms *social welfare* and *social service provision* interchangeably to denote the myriad of human services provided under religious auspices that respect and adhere to spiritual and religious needs and preferences of clients.

To address the question of what the future of social work will be, this essay begins with a review of the social work/social welfare literature on social services provided by religious congregations and denominations. The findings from this review suggest that, with a few exceptions, the role of religious congregations and denominations in providing social services has been overlooked. The next section briefly examines the historical and philosophical roles of religious congregations and denominations in social service provision. The third section reviews anecdotal and empirical evidence of current religious congregational and denominational involvement in social service provision. The final section offers suggestions as to why and how social work and religious organizations should unite in the future to help those in need. The purpose of this essay, therefore, is to pave a way for reestablishing the link between religiously based social services and social work so that each will relegitimize the other and assume mutual cooperation in alleviating human misery.

Religious Social Service Provision in Social Work Literature

Three methods were used to assess the extent to which social work research and education deals with religiously based social welfare. The first method involved content analysis of 1500 abstracts of papers presented in the Annual Program Meeting (APM) of the Council on Social Work Education (CSWE) for the years 1990–94. The analysis found that less than 2% of these papers dealt with religiously based social service provision. Of these, most were historical in nature, such as a discussion on Charity Organization Societies (COSs) in various cities. Only two papers discussed services currently provided through religious organizations or congregations.

The second method involved two steps. The first was compiling a list of the 20 books most often used in courses of social policy and social welfare history and philosophy. The second step was performing a content analysis of these books. The analysis found that, in 14 of the books, there was no mention of any congregational or sectarian aspect of social work, with the exception of the obligatory COSs, which was the basis for Mary Richmond's work and the origin of scientific philanthropy. The other 6 books, most notably those by Morris (1986), Loewenberg (1988), and Magnuson (1977), referred to sectarian-related social work, but the references were mostly historical and ended with the Great Depression and the Social Security Act of the 1930s.

The third method involved content analysis of 50 social welfare course outlines posted at the 1993 APM meeting. Of these, five papers (10%) mentioned religiously affiliated social service provision, but mostly in the context of the history of the profession or the threats to social work from the extreme religious right.

The following example is indicative of the bias toward religiously based social service provision that can be found in the social work literature. In most texts and course outlines, Jane Adams and the Chicago settlement houses are hailed as pioneers for the innovative settlement house model. In fact, no other settlement houses are mentioned. These books and course outlines fail to mention that, at the same time, "the Salvation Army launched a program of slum work in which teams of two 'slum sisters' lived in depressed areas year-round" (Tice, 1992, p. 66). It is also of interest that in "Army homes" they never spoke of "fallen women" but always "sisters," never "cases" but always "our girls" or "sisters who have stumbled" (Magnuson, 1977, p. 86). This, however, is rarely mentioned in any social work textbook.

This blatant neglect of religiously based services is not altogether surprising due to the constitutional separation of state and church in the United States. Yet, in a World Value survey (conducted 1990–93), more people in the United States defined themselves as religious people (82%) than in any other country (*The Economist*, 1995). Furthermore, a 1993 CNN/USA Today/Gallup poll reported that 71% of Americans claim to be members of a church or synagogue, and 41% report having attended church or synagogue in the seven days prior to the survey interview (McAneny & Saad, 1993). Given that the majority of the American people define themselves as religious and belong to religious congregations, the gap in the literature regarding religiously based social service provision deprives social work educators, scholars, and practitioners alike of the opportunity to consider important facts and trends that are critical to the future of the profession.

The Historical and Philosophical Roles of Religious Congregations and Denominations in Social Welfare

Provision of services to the poor, orphans and widows, sick and disabled, prisoners and captives, travellers, and to neighbors in times of calamities was both emphasized and fostered in the early Jewish and Christian traditions (Loewenberg, 1995; Hinson, 1988). Thus, social service provision by religious bodies in keep-ing with religious doctrine was already prevalent in the 4th century.

The link between social services and health care and religion has been very strong in America since the 17th century. Tocqueville, for one, noted some 150 years ago that "religion, which never intervenes directly in the government of American society, should therefore be considered as the first of their political institutions, for although it did not give them the taste for liberty, it singularly facilitates their use thereof" (1835/1969, p. 292). Rosenberg (1987) noted that in the 18th century: "American communities had grown proud of their hospitals; ethnic and religious groups saw their institutions as symbols of community identity and respectability" (p. 8).

In 1832, Leonard Bacon summed up the concept of religiously based service to others in a sermon entitled "The Christian Doctrine of Stewardship in Respect to Property" that he gave at the Young Men's Benevolent Society. In this sermon, which was later published and widely circulated, Bacon said that people must actively seek out ways to do what God expects of them. Such actions must extend to all aspects of life and link voluntary service and personal philanthropy as a means of doing God's will. In his sermon, Bacon provided a moral and religious basis for voluntary organizations that ran counter to the Jeffersonian and Jacksonian thinking on the role of religion and voluntary groups in social life and social welfare. What is most important for our discussion here is that, for many, Bacon answered the moral question "Lord, what wilt thou have me do?" For Bacon it was "the BUSINESS OF DOING GOOD" (sic).

Thus, Bacon's sermon gave impetus to the rise of church-affiliated civic associations that raised money to spread the word of the Lord and simultaneously do good for others. These religiously based associations increased the scope of charitable efforts; piety and evangelical missions were merged into a business where personal property was used in doing good. In many ways, Bacon laid the moral ground for religiously based philanthropy.

For over 250 years, nearly all organized social services in the United States were religiously based. In 1897, Reverend Samuel H. Gurteen began the Buffalo Charity Organization Society (COS), based on the London COS (Leiby, 1984). The latter originated in the work of Reverend Thomas Chalmers in Glasgow and London and in his philosophy of parish responsibility to its neediest people (Schweinitz, 1943). The principle was a simple one: Members of the congregation, together with the wealthy members of the community, had an obligation to meet the needs of the poor. Church deacons visited the poor, counseled them, and supervised their use of the funds allocated for them. Samuel H. Gurteen later added the concept of parishioners visiting the needy ("friendly visitors"), a major feature of what later came to be called the new benevolent gospel. It was through the COSs that social services left their community-religious base for one that was citywide, temporal, and professional (Magnuson, 1977; Tice, 1992). It was through the efforts of the COSs that social services became less arbitrary and more systematic, and it was through the efforts of Mary Richmond in the first two decades of the 20th century that social work and welfare became secular.

The case of the First Baptist Church in Philadelphia may illustrate the development of welfare under congregational auspices. In 1839 an organization of Baptist women was formed in Philadelphia (The Evangelical Sewing Society) whose primary activity was sewing for the poor. In 1873 the same congregation launched its campaign to establish what later became known as the Baptist Children's Services and, at the time, was the Baptist Orphanage. A few years later, members of this congregation established the Philadelphia Home for Incurables, operating until today as a most advanced center for people with severe handicap and mobility problems under the name Inglis House (Thompson, 1989)

Social services and welfare developed within a religious framework not only in the United States but also internationally. American missionaries carried not only the "word of God" to all parts of the world; they brought health care and social services long before UNICEF was conceived. In China, for example, the country's first mental health hospital was founded in 1898 by John Kerr, an American physician and Presbyterian missionary, in Canton (Tucker, 1983).

Social Service Delivery by Religiously Based Organizations

The full extent, depth, and range of religiously based welfare activity in the United States has yet to be addressed in the social work literature. Nevertheless, there is much anecdotal and descriptive evidence which suggests that many services are provided through religious auspices and that welfare work constitutes a major part of clergy and lay leader activity. In this section, I will highlight a few such examples as well as findings from my own study.

An important corollary to understanding religiously based social service provision is understanding that people with religious commitment tend to contribute to charities of all kinds. The Russ Reid Company (1995), in conjunction with the Barna Research Corporation, carried out a study of donors (those who gave money to a nonprofit organization other than a church or place of worship in the past 12 months). They found that "the best predictor of a person's giving behavior relates to the intensity and nature of their spiritual commitment . . . 82% of the people who give to nonprofit organizations also give to churches or places of worship" (p. 2). They went on to state that "no other characteristic is so predominant or defining [donors] as religious giving" (p. 3). Among the regular donors in the study, 60% attended a church or other religious service in the past month; 37% volunteered at their place of worship in the past month; and 84% agreed that religious faith was very important in life. This high correlation between giving to welfare and social nonprofits and involvement in religious organizations is not coincidental. The reason is that, for many people, giving to others is central to their religious beliefs. Yet, social welfare services, unless under religious auspices, tend to ignore these findings and concentrate instead on the secular aspects of what they do. Other findings also suggest that many religious people are willing to help others in need, and that their support to nonprofit organizations goes beyond financial contributions.

One example of the role played by religiously based organizations in the social welfare arena is in the field of homelessness. On May 17, 1994, the federal government released its report: "Priority: Home! The Federal Plan to Break the Cycle of Homelessness." Although acknowledging the government's lack of significant progress in alleviating the problem, the report gave credit to the nation's churches, synagogues, and other not-for-profit organizations that, in the early 1980s, responded to the crisis long before the federal government even conceded that there was a problem (Alliance, 1994). A specific example may illustrate this trend. New York City's Partnership for the Homeless was founded in 1982. Its creators were a handful of religious leaders from the city's major faith traditions who were distressed by the

paucity of available services to meet the burgeoning needs of the homeless. The Partnership became one of the premier service organizations of its kind, mobilizing some 150 churches and synagogues and more than 11,000 community and congregational volunteers to provide a new community of comprehensive care for the homeless (Cohen & Jeager, 1994).

Another important role played by religious organizations is in the field of day care. This service is extremely important to single mothers who want to become self-sufficient. The availability of day care is very limited and would be even more so if not for congregations, which are the largest single landlord for day-care programs in the nation. As much as one-third of all day-care services in the United States are provided under religious auspices. Half of these programs are provided by the congregations themselves; the other half operated by independent, usually not-for-profit, organizations (Lindner, Mattis, & Rogers, 1983; Trost, 1988).

Another area of religiously based social service is housing for the poor and elderly. Efforts by congregations range from simple renovating to rehabilitating an entire block. This activity is relatively new and is intended to help the community and its members (Mares, 1994). A specific example is provided by Sengupta (1995), who reported on the work of the Allen A.M.E. church in Queens, New York. This church-building record includes a 300-unit apartment complex for the elderly built 15 years ago with federal housing loans, about 4 dozen two-family homes that the church's real estate arm is helping to build with city and state housing dollars, and 76 more houses that the church acquired or developed and sold to private home buyers. "Just below the school, the church also owns a strip of shops and offices: a pizzeria, a beauty shop, and a home health care agency" (Sengupta, 1995, B1). Sengupta concluded that "in the church world, Allen A.M.E.'s real estate ventures are nothing new. . . . Over the last decade, many black churches have taken up the task of building housing and running neighborhood businesses at a time when the federal government has largely abandoned urban economic development" (B1).

Another example is provided by Wittberg (1994), who noted that in 1990 Catholic orders alone maintained some 645 orphanages and at least 500 hospitals in the United States. Also noted in the literature are reports by Filinson (1988), who documented how a mental health center trained and used church volunteers from an interfaith coalition to provide services to people with Alzheimer's disease and one by Hendrickson (1987), who reported health screening services provided by church volunteers.

An example of the scope and breadth of religiously based social service provision can be found in a study conducted by the Community Workshop on Economic Development (1991) based on a random sample of 152 synagogues and churches in Chicago. Findings showed that 77% of the sample housed at least one community program or organization; 59% housed two or more. The average religious congregation had two programs and served 400 persons per month, 70% of whom were not church members. Most congregations (83%) provided space free of charge to other groups, such as AA and food and/or clothing distribution centers. More than half of the congregations (59%) funded their own human service programs. These programs included meals for the hungry or frail elderly; counselling; youth programs such as latch-key programs, tutoring for immigrant children, and sport programs; and day-care programs. Similar findings were found for Philadelphia by Nowak (1989). This study

found that 92% of AA groups, 80% of all Police Athletic Leagues, and 55% of Boy Scout troops are housed in religious congregations.

Hodgkinson and colleagues (1993), in the only national survey of local congregations, found that in 1991 nearly 92% of congregations reported one or more programs in human services and welfare; 90% reported one or more programs in health (mostly visitation of the sick); 62% reported involvement in international relief. These congregations also reported programs for public or societal benefits (62%); educational activities (53%); activities in arts and culture (50%); and programs for the environment (40%). In the same year, these congregations alone spent $4.4 billion for human services, $4.0 billion on health and hospitals, $1.3 billion for arts and culture, $0.7 billion on human justice and community development, $0.5 billion for environmental programs, $0.5 billion for international welfare, and $2.1 billion on other programs to benefit the community. Similar findings have been reported by La Barbera (1991), Salamon and Teitelbaum (1984), and Wineburg (1990–91, 1994).

Finally, there is the work of the Society of Friends, whose doctrine of the "inner light" means that all persons are of immense value and should be treated accordingly. This egalitarianism has been evidenced in Quaker support of pacifism, care for the poor, prison reform, and opposition to slavery. The American Friends Service Committee, perhaps the best known Quaker social service committee, was founded in 1917 to provide assistance for conscientious objectors and to send relief workers overseas. In 1947, the organization received the Nobel Prize for its outstanding work with refugees following the Second World War (Leonard, 1988).

In addition to the examples presented above, I offer findings from a survey I conducted in 1995. These findings provide empirical evidence for what many had long suspected—namely, that long-established places of worship (predating 1940) serve as the core of their communities because of the wealth of services they provide. Although the buildings themselves are neutral, they serve as the focal point for the congregations, whose service to others is rooted in both their religious beliefs and a strong tradition of social involvement. Without the presence of these congregations, social and community activities in many Philadelphia neighborhoods would be significantly curtailed.

The Philadelphia area was selected as the survey site because it is representative of other major cities in that it has many long-established neighborhood churches and synagogues. The sample included all Philadelphia religious congregations housed in places of worship built before 1940 ($N = 698$). It is important to note that virtually all of these congregations bear heavy financial burden in maintaining these older buildings. The study instrument consisted of a mailed questionnaire in which respondents were asked to identify up to four services they provided and the recipients of these services. The response rate was 26.3% ($N = 181$).

Respondents indicated that they are significantly involved in a wide range of programs. Most frequent are programs for children and teens (69.1% of the studied congregations), providing space for numerous community groups and other organizations (58.6%), food distribution (soup kitchens/food pantries) (39.2%), and a variety of services for people with many types of addictions (31.5%). Most congregations made their services and space available to nonmembers. Those who received assistance were required neither to join the congregation nor to contribute financially. Each program served, on

the average, 39 congregational members and 91 nonmembers: a 1 to 2.33 ratio in favor of serving others.

Space provision by these congregations is extremely important because most neighborhoods have few, if any, facilities that are available to community organizations at relatively low rent or rent-free. Furthermore, few local facilities have kitchens where food can be prepared for the hungry, the elderly, or children in day care. There are even fewer such facilities whose owners are willing to make them available at low or no cost for such purposes. These congregations therefore attract programs that care for or feed large numbers of adults and children.

Several findings from this study also merit mention. First, most of the projects were not only run by congregations, but also funded by them through individual donations, in-kind contribution, or the operating budget. Second, space provided to others was provided free or at a nominal cost—usually far below market price. Third, the congregations had little or no interest in obtaining public funds for their programs. Fourth, these projects were initiated by the clergy or lay leaders rather than publicly initiated, often in response to the changing social environment and the decrease in public services. Finally, a majority of the recipients of service were needy people in the community rather than members of the congregation. In sum, the overwhelming majority of the studied congregations (87%) are involved in provision of services that are not mandated by their religious doctrine. Furthermore, it is important to note that 48.9% of the responding congregations reported at least four social and community programs (the highest number possible on the mailed questionnaire).

As noted above, these findings clearly indicate that local religious congregations should not be viewed solely as member-serving organizations but as other-serving organizations committed to improving the quality of life in their communities. This commitment extends to matters of cost and income as well. No matter how conservative the calculations, I found that the costs to the congregations (in providing both space and programs) far outweigh the income. In many cases, congregations open their doors to worthy community groups and causes at little or no charge despite the fact that building use involves wear-and-tear as well as utility costs. The practice of charging rent is quite uncommon lest it compromise the congregation's charitable tax status. Thus, the provision of these services is clearly not to benefit members. It seems as if service is as important for the members of the congregation as it is for those benefiting from it.

The role of local religious congregations as a social and community pillar was well documented in my study. It should be noted, however, that this study, which was limited to Philadelphia, had a relatively low rate of return and tended to overrepresent mainline Protestant denominations. Yet, the findings were significantly similar to those found in a study on Greensboro, a small city in North Carolina (Wineburg, 1993), and those of Hodgkinson and colleagues (1993) in a national survey. Furthermore, the methodological drawbacks in my study indicate that the findings should be viewed as an emerging trend rather than as a final picture. However, if the trend is representative of our urban reality, many questions arise. For example, how long can congregations carry the double burden of paying for the upkeep and maintenance of their properties and making them available to their communities? How much more can be expected from local religious congregations in terms of serving their needy neighbors? Why is it that religious congregations assume the role that, in many other countries, is often undertaken by the government? These and many other questions need further examination and careful study.

In light of the above discussion, one interesting development is of relevance here. Currently, Mississippi, under the leadership of Governor Kirk Fordice, is experimenting with a new welfare reform called "Faith and Family." The program is based on Marvin Olasky's (1992) idea that charities and voluntary organizations, many of them churches, are better equipped than government to deal with helping the poor. Governor Fordice, not without influence from Newt Gingrich, has pushed for this program, in which 5500 congregations are being asked to adopt poor families and help them get off public assistance by helping them find jobs after initial job training. The congregational volunteers help welfare families with transportation, résumé preparation, child care, loans, personal advice, and other needs, but are not expected to proselytize. Harrison (1995) reported that none of the welfare families helped by one Mississippi Baptist church had been asked to attend worship services, yet all had chosen to do so. Currently, 165 families and 55 congregations are actively involved in the program, out of 59,343 eligible families and 5500 religious congregations. Small as these numbers are, they are sufficient to be a trendsetter in a new mode of welfare delivery and an important indicator to social work that not only are religious communities welfare involved, but that government will increasingly seek out their help in providing social welfare services. Along with this trend, we can look at Michigan's new initiative. Governor John Engler of Michigan "advocates for shifting the responsibility for helping the poor from the hands of the government to civil institutions—particularly religious ones—that can address the underlying moral and cultural aspects of chronic dependency. Engler has approved a multimillion-dollar contract with the Salvation Army to care for the state's homeless population" (Sherman, 1995, p. 58).

The Future of Social Work Research and Religiously Based Social Service Provision

Steinfels (1995) noted that "the new wisdom in Washington is this: Religious institutions, along with other charitable organizations, can provide the nation with a social and economic safety net as well as moral and spiritual one" (p. 11). The question is: Where is social work in all of this?

Social work is not unique in its failure to acknowledge the positive contributions of religious organizations to social welfare. Psychiatry, for example, once treated religion as evidence of neurosis, immaturity or escapism. Yet, the DSM-IV now categorizes religious and spiritual problems as a category distinct from any mental disorder (Lukoff, Lu, & Turner, 1992). In like manner, the study of voluntary action ignored the importance of religious congregations (Smith, 1983), and only in the past few years has serious attention been given to this field of study. As in other fields, it is now time for social work to reevaluate and reassess its position vis-à-vis services provided under religious auspices.

There has been little or no attempt to present religiously based social service provision as an option or part of the research agenda. Yet, the lack of research cannot mask reality. The reality is that in every community in the United States, people in need of basic goods and services are turning to religiously based organiza-

tions and services for help. The reality is that the American safety net is, to a large extent, being provided and financed by religious congregations and denominations. These groups help provide soup kitchens and food pantries; shelters for the homeless; and child welfare and family services. And on the international scale, their help extends to care of victims of war, famine, and other disasters. Yet, we in the social work field persist in our ostrichlike approach and pretend that religiously based social service provision does not exist.

Elsewhere I have speculated on why social work divorced itself from its roots and now distances itself from religiously based social services (Cnaan, 1994). The reasons are varied. They range from the quest for a scientific approach to social work to the quest for professional status. However, the secular values of social work can also be viewed as antithetical to institutional religions. For example, social work and religion can differ significantly in assessing who is worthy of assistance. Further, social work agencies often rely on government for financial support, whereas religious bodies wish to remain independent. Finally, there are ideological differences in that social work promises solutions where the religious approach believes in the continual persistence of need and has no claim to eradicate poverty or need but to alleviate pain and misery. These are but a few reasons for the rift between social work and religiously based social services, yet the reality is that the two overlap to such a degree that the rift must be bridged—and soon.

Many of us in the academic ivory tower of social work are captive to the "social security thesis." In most Western European countries, social service provision is legally mandated, but in the United States the first such legislation was the 1935 Social Security Act. Although social security coverage has been expanded, little other federal social service legislation has followed. Thus, social welfare scholars use Europe as a model for social services guaranteed by law. In contrast, social services in the United States are given little legal protection and can be quickly eliminated through governmental budget cuts. The perception, then, is that social services supported by legislation are superior to voluntary services. Accordingly, many books that deal with the evolution of social welfare in America take the view that success comes only when the government guarantees the service for all who need and when one can go to court to demand service. This approach is contrary to that of religiously based social service, which is limited in scope, not guaranteed even to current clients, and cannot be challenged legally. Thus, social work, in its advocacy for national health insurance, better public education, and institutional support for the poor and needy, attempts to secure these services through legal and nonreligious avenues. What these scholars are missing is the fact that social service system in the United States, more than that of any other country, is predicated on voluntary services, many of which are religiously based. An example of this approach can be found in Michael Katz's work. Katz (1983), in talking about the "war on welfare," argued that public programs always have been more important and more supportive in guaranteeing social welfare than private relief or voluntary efforts. He stated that "voluntarism never was and never will be an adequate answer to the problem of dependence" (pp. xiii and 291). Katz further asserts that, even in the 19th century, more people were helped by public relief than by private charities and that the latter relied heavily on public finds. For Katz, this proves that real support for poor and needy people can come only from the government.

However, this approach is more ideological than pragmatic. It is based on what many social workers want to hear rather than on what actually is going on in the real world. The facts are these: namely, that more and more social work is being provided under religious auspices and that regardless of which party controls Capitol Hill, public allocation for welfare will not increase in the immediate future, and is more likely to be cut back further. Yet, there is also a growing demand for services in relatively new areas such as homelessness and AIDS. Another fact that must be taken into consideration is that new trends in social service delivery are appearing. I previously noted the examples of Mississippi congregations being asked to take on official welfare service and of Michigan's contract with the Salvation Army to care for all the state's homeless people after welfare payments were cut. Another example is a $50 million federal grant for Habitat for Humanity and other organizations that build homes for the poor. This legislation was introduced by Representative Rick Lazio (R-NY) and supported by Newt Gingrich. In similar vein, Senator John Ashcroft (R-Mo) proposed that states contract directly with religiously based charities for delivery of social services to the poor through a federal block grant. This money would go directly from the U.S. Treasury to local charities, and no federal agency would be involved. These are but a few indications as to the widening role and public and political expectations of religious organizations in the field of social service delivery.

What then must the response of social work be to these facts if the concern for the well-being of all Americans is really its guiding principle? I firmly believe that the response must be one of reconciliation and cooperation with the other force in society that is also concerned with the well-being of the neediest. The current segmentation of welfare by religious and secular groupings is costly and unwarranted.

Even more disturbing is the division taking place in the field whereby religiously based services are meeting basic human needs and social work is losing its historical role as the protector and service provider for the poor. The reason for this division is that, as social work has become professionalized and has gradually shifted its focus from helping the poor to helping more affluent and capable segments of our society, the churches have stepped up their role in serving the poor. Furthermore, as government support for social services has decreased, congregations are taking on more of the services once provided by the state.

Social work is now finding itself in a troublesome situation. It is no longer the primary advocate of the poor and needy; it is losing its holding in the public sphere; and it is ignoring the one ally that has proven its commitment to those in need and with whom social work should be working in concert. A strong collaboration with all types of religiously based services, from local congregations to international welfare endeavors, may enable us to renew our commitment to changing social structures and provide the poor, the minority, and the needy full participation in society.

It is true that there may be value conflicts between social work and religiously based services. The latter may wish to recruit new members or to save clients' souls. There may be disagreements about the role of contraceptives and/or abortion, but these differences are small when we compare them to what mutual cooperation between social work and religious auspices may achieve. The two combined can and should collaborate to advocate for and provide services to the neediest in our society.

No one can predict the future of social work with certainty, but it is my contention that we can successfully prepare for that future by recognizing trends in social service delivery that, to date, have been ignored in the literature. I refer specifically to the fact that religious groups are fully involved in serving the neediest in our society. Social work should, therefore, collaborate with these religiously based services in serving and championing clients. Such a move will take bold leadership—leadership that is more concerned with clients than with defense of a professional turf. It is my prediction that, if efficiency of services and best interests of the clients are the guiding forces in our profession, then aligning ourselves with religiously based services is a top priority for both the survival and optimization of social work in the future. However, for this to take place, we first ought to make sure that our research and education do not swerve us "from the path of truth whose mother is history, . . . the example and instruction of the present, and the monitor of the future."

REFERENCES

Alliance: A Publication of the National Alliance to End Homelessness, 10(3), July 1994, 1–3.

Bacon, L. (1832). *The Christian doctrine of stewardship in respect to property.* New Haven: Nathan Whiting.

Cnaan, R. A. (1994). The neglect of religious congregations and denominations in social service provision in social work texts and education. Paper presented at the 23rd annual meeting of the Association for Research on Nonprofit Organizations and Voluntary Action, Berkeley, CA, October.

Cohen, D., & Jeager, A. R. (1994). Urban congregations and philanthropy. *NY Ragtimes,* Summer, 7–10.

Community Workshop on Economic Development. (1991). *Good space and good work: Research and* analysis of the extent and nature of the use of religious properties in Chicago neighborhoods. Chicago: Inspired Partnerships Program of the National Trust for Historic Preservation in the United States.

The Economist. (1995). The counter-attack of God. *The Economist,* July 8, 19–21.

Filinson, R. (1988). A model for church-based services for frail and elderly persons and their families. *The Gerontologist, 28*(4), 483–486.

Glassie, H. (1982). The topography of past time. In *Passing the time in Ballymenone: Culture and history of an Ulster community.* Philadelphia: University of Pennsylvania Press.

Harris, M. (1995). Quiet care: Welfare work and religious congregations. *Journal of Social Policy, 24,* 53–71.

Harrison, E. (1995). Churches given welfare role: Mississippi families are adopted out. Some say the state's out of line. *Philadelphia Inquirer,* September 10, Section A, p. 15.

Hendrickson, S. L. (1987). Churches as geriatric health clinics for community cased elderly. *Journal of Religion and Aging, 2*(4), 13–24.

Hinson, E. G. (1988). The historical involvement of the church in social ministries and social action. *Review & Expositor, 85,* 233–242.

Hodgkinson, V. A., Weitzman, M. S., Kirsch, A. D., Noga, S. M., & Gorski, H. A. (1993). *From belief to commitment.* Washington, DC: Independent Sector.

Katz, M. B. (1983). *Poverty and policy in American history.* New York: Academic Press.

La Barbera, P. A. (1991). Commercial ventures of religious organizations. *Nonprofit Management & Leadership, 1,* 217–234.

Leiby, C. (1984). Charity organization reconsidered. *Social Service Review, 58,* 523–538.

Leonard, B. J. (1988). The modern church and social action. *Review & Expositor, 85,* 243–253.

Lindner, E. W., Mattis, M. C., & Rogers, J. R. (1983). *When churches mind the children: A study of day care in local parishes.* Ypsilanti, MI: The High Scope Press.

Loewenberg, F. M. (1988). *Religion and social work practice in contemporary American society.* New York: Columbia University Press

Loewenberg, F. M. (1995). Financing philanthropic institutions in Biblical and Talmudic times. *Nonprofit and Voluntary Sector Quarterly, 24,* 307–320.

Lukoff, D., Lu, F., & Turner, R. (1992). Toward a more culturally sensitive DSM-IV: Psychoreligious and psychospiritual problems. *The Journal of Nervous and Mental Disease, 180,* 673–682.

Magnuson, N. (1977). *Salvation in the slums: Evangelical social work, 1865–1920.* New York: Scarecrow Press.

Mares. A. (1994). Housing and the church. *Nonprofit and Voluntary Sector Quarterly, 23,* 139–157.

McAneny, L., & Saad, L. (1993). Strong ties between religion commitment and abortion views. *The Gallup Poll Monthly,* No. 331, 35–43.

Morris, R. (1986). *Rethinking social welfare: Why care for the stranger.* New York: Longman.

Netting, E. F. (1982). Secular and religious funding of church-related agencies. *Social Service Review, 56,* 586–604.

Nowak, J. (1989). *Religious institutions and community renewal.* Philadelphia: The Delaware Valley Community Reinvestment Fund and The Philadelphia Historic Preservation Corporation.

Olasky, M. (1992). *The tragedy of the American community.* Washington, DC: Regenry.

Rosenberg, C. E. (1987). *The care of strangers: The rise of America's hospital system.* New York: Basic Books.

Russ Reid Company. (1995). *The heart of the donor.* Pasadena, CA: Author.

Salamon, L. M., & Teitelbaum, F. (1984). Religious congregations as social service agencies: How extensive are they? *Foundation News, 5,* B2–G4.

Schweinitz, K. de (1943). *England's road to social security.* New York: A. S. Barnes.

Sengupta, S. (1995). Meshing the sacred and the secular: Floyd Flake offers community development via church and state. *New York Times*, November 23, B1, B12.

Sherman, A. L. (1995). Cross purposes: Will conservative welfare reform corrupt religious charities? *Policy Review*, Fall, 58–63.

Smith, D. H. (1983). Churches are generally ignored in contemporary voluntary action research: Causes and consequences. *Review of religious research, 24*, 295–302.

Steinfels, P. (1995). As government aid evaporates, how will religious and charity organizations hold up as a safety net for the poor, the sick and the elderly? *New York Times*, October 28, p. 11.

Thompson, W. D. (1989). *Philadelphia's first Baptists*. Philadelphia: First Baptist Church of Philadelphia.

Tice K. (1992). The battle for benevolence: Scientific disciplinary control vs. indiscriminate relief—A case study of the Lexington Associated Charities vs. the Salvation Army. *Journal of Sociology and Social Welfare, 21*(2), 59–77.

Tocqueville, A. de (1969). *Democracy in America*. New York: Vintage. (Originally published 1835)

Trost, C. (1988). Debate over day-care bill spurs odd alliances and raises issue of church-state separation. *Wall Street Journal*, August 29, p. 32.

Tucker, S. W. (1983). The Canton hospital and medicine in 19th century China (1835–1900). Unpublished dissertation, Indiana University.

Wineburg, R. J. (1990–91). A community study on the ways religious congregations support individuals and human service network. *Journal of Applied Social Sciences, 15*(1), 51–74.

Wineburg, R. J. (1993). Social policy, service development, and religious organizations. *Non Profit Management & Leadership, 3*, 283–299.

Wineburg, R. J. (1994). A longitudinal case study of religious congregations in local human service delivery. *Nonprofit and Voluntary Sector Quarterly, 23*, 159–169.

Wittberg, P. (1994). *The rise and fall of Catholic religious orders: A social movement perspective*. Albany, NY: SUNY Press.

Social Workers as Advocates for Elders

Iris Carlton-LaNey

By the middle of the 21st century, 22% of the total U.S. population will be elderly. Growth rates in this demographic category will be particularly striking among racial and ethnic minority groups. This essay by Iris Carlton-LaNey, associate professor in the School of Social Work at the University of North Carolina at Chapel Hill, discusses the unique potential contribution of social workers in improving the quality of life for older Americans, particularly those who will be economically, socially, psychologically, and physiologically vulnerable in the decades ahead. Social work practice in this area, she asserts, will need to combine micro and macro approaches and take into account the growing roles that both work and leisure will play for the elderly in the next century.

Professor Carlton-LaNey chairs the Concentration on the Aging and Services to Their Families. In addition to a monograph entitled Elderly Black Farm Women as Keepers of the Community and the Culture, *Dr. Carlton-LaNey has written several book chapters and articles about aging African-American women in the South, the education of homeless children, and African-American social welfare history. She has served on several boards and task forces that deal with issues regarding services to the elderly, particularly in the areas of health care and nursing homes.*

Social workers face a number of challenges as we move into the 21st century. One of those challenges is to provide appropriate, timely, and sensitive social services to the elderly. In a country that cherishes the vigor of youth and evades allegorical and tangible reminders of human mortality, this is a primal challenge. The population of Americans age 65 and older is growing. The absolute and proportional increases in the elderly population are projected to continue into the 21st century. In 1990 there were 32 million elders living in the United States. That number is expected to double and total 65 million by 2030 (Dunkle and Norgard, 1995). By 2050 the American population of elders will have grown to 68.5 million, or 22.0% of the total population (Atchley, 1994).

The number of elders of various racial, religious, and ethnic backgrounds is also increasing dramatically. Racial and ethnic groups were 10% of the elderly population in 1990. This group will grow at a rate of 247% for African Americans, and 395% for Hispanic elders by 2030. The growth rate for Whites is expected to reach 92% by that same year (Bellos and Ruffolo, 1995). The Asian-American population of elders is the fastest growing group, as well as the most diverse, including Chinese, East Indian, Hawaiian, Japanese, Korean, Malaysian, Southeast Asian, and Thai. American Indian elders comprise the smallest group of elders and experience tremendous poverty throughout their lives (Zuniga, 1995).

Many of these elders will be socially, economically, psychologically, and physiologically vulnerable, with problems that affect their families, communities, and the broader society. A large number will also be healthy, well-educated, and employed either full or part-time (Hooyman and Kiyak, 1993). The group of elders who are age 85 and older will show the most rapid increase (Walker, 1996). Most will be in need of some type of social work intervention. Accessing these services will be a challenge for many of these elders. The large number of elders who lack knowledge about how to get needed services makes them a population of major concern to social workers. The problem is even more pronounced by the shortage of professionally trained social workers available to serve elders and their families. With social work's emphasis on helping people to interact successfully with their environment, meeting the needs of underserved populations, and engaging in social work advocacy, the profession is in a unique position to improve the quality of life for older Americans.

Historical Overview of American Services for the Elderly

Elder care has traditionally been the sole responsibility of the aging individuals themselves, their families, and/or neighbors. Throughout history, elders have been expected to prepare for their "twilight years" through thrift and piety. Successful preparation for old age was a testimony to their "worthiness." If individuals did not save and prepare, their personal care was left to family members. When families, because of their obligations to their nuclear unit, were unwilling or, more often, unable to care for the indigent elder or when there were no family members available, the elder's lot fell to some public interest. In colonial America, elder care was usually in-kind and outdoor. When indoor relief was available,

it was usually humanely and compassionately provided. Unlike able-bodied paupers or vagrants, elders were not held in contempt by overseers of the poor. Their age and decrepit state were indicators that they deserved some level of community care. As Americans reversed their ideas about the community's responsibilities to paupers, both young and old and worthy and unworthy, the almshouses and other forms of indoor relief of the late 19th century became oppressive and feared shelters. During the early 1900s, almshouses quickly became the primary means of caring for indigent elders (Haber, 1983).

During the first three decades of the 20th century, the growth of racial-ethnic homes, ethnic mutual aid, and ethnic charities combined to reduce the number of aged in almshouses (Carlton-LaNey, 1989). Those worthy elders who remained in almshouses were an unwelcome reminder that America was not living up to its obligation to care for its once contributory citizenry. Agitation for state public assistance to the indigent aged grew. The first "old-age pension" program became law in 1915 and, by 1929, seven additional states had enacted such laws. The pensions were meager and inadequate. Based on the country's methods of serving elders, it is apparent that policies for elder care have been piecemeal and sporadic. Reliance on private sector altruism has dominated, whereas governmental intervention has developed slowly and begrudgingly. It was not until 1935 with the enactment of the Social Security Act that meaningful intervention took place regarding elder care. The Social Security Act, through the old age assistance entitlement program, replaced public and private services by providing cash assistance to the aged on a federal level (Kutzik, 1979).

In 1965, the Older Americans Act (OAA), through the creation of an administrative arm, the Administration on Aging (AoA), became a significant universal mechanism for serving all older Americans. Together, the Social Security Act and the OAA have become the core components in the complex network of services to elders in this country. These two legislative acts account for the myriad of programs and services forming the aging network. The AoA, through ten regional offices, has initiated state and local public and private agencies charged with providing a system of coordinated and comprehensive local programs for America's elders. The AoA network's programs consist of in-home and community-based services, including home care, protective services, information and referral, senior center programs, congregate meals, health and wellness promotion, respite services, and nursing home ombudsmen (Bellos and Ruffolo, 1995).

In 1991 an Elder Care Campaign was initiated through AoA to help elders at risk of losing their independence. The campaign was designed to build public awareness, increase organizational involvement, and create community coalitions (Bellos and Ruffolo, 1995). The Elder Care Campaign responded to the new ageism that has emerged. The new ageism is characterized by focusing on the least able elders, who are seen as powerless and dependent, and by encouraging the development of services that fail to enhance the elder's independence (Hooyman and Kiyak, 1993).

Given the increased initiatives and funding in services to elders, one may assume that elders are being well cared for in contemporary America. Furthermore, we are informed that elders are also more financially secure in much larger numbers. Kart (1994) indicates that the aged have been a favored social welfare constituency and have done relatively well in the public policy arena. Increased spending for this group had resulted in the phrase the "graying

of the federal budget." Proponents (Crystal and Shea, 1990) suggest that this spending is necessary and imperative whereas opponents (Torres-Gil and Puccinelli, 1995) argue that generational tensions may force younger groups to suffer as programs for elders increase. Essentially, elders are being blamed as "greedy geezers" who are responsible for the increased poverty rates of younger age groups (Torres-Gil, 1992).

Although it may seem that services for elders are being well funded, the new initiatives in recent fiscal years are not adequate indicators of the overall expansion of services and programs. Binstock (1991) noted that OAA funds, when adjusted for inflation, have actually declined substantially since 1981. We also see a decline in terms of total dollars when measured as a percentage of the gross national product (Hooyman and Kiyak, 1993). Essentially, OAA funding is insufficient to support its broad and comprehensive network of programs; this has resulted in what can be called a symbolic gesture of commitment to elders. As the population of elders increases and becomes more diverse and as available resources dwindle, the need for social work advocacy will become even more apparent.

Social Work Advocacy Is Political

The social work profession has a rich legacy of advocacy for vulnerable people. The degree and extent of social work agitation has varied throughout the years from colonial times to today. We have moved from seeing the aged as merely part of the larger homogenous group of indigent to recognizing their unique place as consumers and contributors. As a profession, however, we have not fully embraced the role of advocate to the extent necessary to serve this group.

Haynes and Mickelson (1991) suggest that social work has failed to take a position of leadership in social reform advocacy, which is inconsistent with its historical background. The rollback in social spending during the Reagan and Bush years has resulted in further devastation for historically disadvantaged groups such as the elderly. The profession's relative inactivity and failure to speak out against these injustices is incongruent with a belief in the worth and dignity of human beings (Haynes and Mickelson, 1991; Reisch, 1986; Thompson, 1994). On the other hand, Edwards (1995) indicates that social workers are being increasingly effective advocates. He notes that both the National Association of Social Workers (NASW) and the Council on Social Work Education (CSWE) are more politically sophisticated, and he cites NASW's growing and impressive legislative staffs as evidence of the organization's involvement.

Clearly there is disagreement about the profession's role in the political arena and the extent to which it fulfills that role. Conservatives argue that for social work to be politicized is unprofessional (Bardill, 1993). Others (Abramovitz, 1993; Haynes and Mickelson, 1991; Rees, 1991) contend that social work is and should be political. In response to the profession's need to accept a political role, the University of Houston has developed a concentration in political social work for the MSW program. The concentration has both micro and macro emphases (Fisher, 1995).

Given the fundamental mission of the profession, the phrase "political social work" seems redundant and somewhat superfluous. Social work's ethical responsibility to society is political. To act to prevent and eliminate discrimination, to ensure that all people have access to opportunities, to promote conditions that encourage respect for diversity, to advocate changes in policy and legislation to improve social conditions, and to promote

social justice are all political acts. It is impossible to separate social work from the political process. It is likewise impossible to produce competent practitioners who have no understanding of the relationship between social work practice and the policies that influence and affect practice decisions. Whatever position one takes regarding social workers' past and present involvement as political advocates, there seems to be agreement that the role of advocate is demanded and that having a sound understanding of practice relative to the American polity is imperative.

Overview of Advocacy in Social Work Practice with Elders

In social work with elders, social work advocacy should take a micro and macro perspective as case advocacy or social advocacy. Case advocacy is action on behalf of a single individual and social advocacy is action for an aggregate population of clients (Rothman, 1994). Because of the diversity of the aging population, professional social work advocacy must also be diverse in its approach in order to be effective. Social advocacy should be neither color- nor gender-blind. The lifestyles of various racial and ethnic groups require that their unique needs be highlighted and served. Older men and older women have different problems and issues of concern. Elders who live in rural areas face hardships that distinguish them from their urban counterparts and vice versa. In our zeal to be supportive and helpful, social workers must avoid the detrimental effects of the new ageism and concentrate on identifying and building on strengths. We have to rely on current empirical research data, both quantitative and qualitative, to inform us of the unique needs of various groups of elders. Gaps in those data make it difficult for social work advocates to understand and respect the heterogeneity of the aged population in program development and service delivery. Where these data are incomplete, we are also ill equipped to advocate for legislative acts and policy decisions that best serve the divergent needs of elders.

Social work advocacy for clients needs to exist in concert with professional self-interest. Legislation that addresses licensure and vendorships, for example, is beneficial to the profession because it puts the professional social worker in a more strategic position for both case and group advocacy. Ewalt (1994) notes that "advocacy that benefits social work and advocacy that benefits clients interact, each lending credibility to the other" (p. 342). She further notes that matters that deal with credentials are important in helping legislators to be better informed about social work education and the work that social workers perform. When congressional representatives perceive of us as credible, our involvement in the political process is enhanced.

Schools of social work have a key role in both teaching and promoting social and case advocacy in service to America's elders. Social work programs must place a greater emphasis on the need for advocacy in competent practice with oppressed and disadvantaged groups such as the elderly. One strategy for encouraging effective advocacy practice with elders is to promote among students a greater awareness of the aging population in America. Yet, there is still concern in social work education that the curriculum gives only symbolic representation of the later phase of life (Brody and Brody, 1974) and that materials about adulthood and later life are squeezed in at the conclusion of the course. Although this observation was made over 20 years ago, it remains a valid concern in social work education. Morales and Sheafor (1989) suggest that all schools of social work would do well to institute required courses in social gerontology. This would not only stimu-

late interest in the aged, but would provide meaningful practical information. Browne and Broderick (1994), in discussing issues of practice and education for work with Asian and Pacific Island elders, suggest that a social work curriculum that includes topics related to historical background, levels of acculturation and assimilation, nativity, and the role of ethnicity in aging can promote greater knowledge of the elderly. Similarly, content about other groups of elders can also be added to the curriculum. This will not only fill some knowledge gaps, but may also attract students to the field of gerontological social work and better enable us to respond to the proliferation of jobs that will be available in the next century.

According to Rees (1991), good social work is being political, focusing on power, gaining knowledge, and learning skills from the micro through macro levels, as well as linking policy to practice. Tower (1994) observes that most social work students graduate with a clear awareness of their ethical responsibility to advocate for their clients, but lack strategies for performing this function within the confines of their agencies. Providing the essential knowledge to advocate for elders is significant if "good social work" is to be practiced. Teaching strategy and providing support for those who engage in advocacy is paramount if the social work profession is to take its place as a leader among elder care professionals.

Social Work with Elders in the 21st Century

Current trends in aging suggest that 21st-century social work advocates should be prepared to work with healthier and more socially skilled elders as well as with a sizable proportion of old-old who are incapacitated, frail, and poor. Social scientists (Hooyman and Kiyak, 1993; Raffoul and McNeece, 1996) project that changes in medicine and medical technology, marital status and family structure, work and leisure, and government intervention, will ensure that elders of the 21st century are older and healthier. They will also be active participants in ensuring a high quality of life for themselves and for others. As society shifts away from its youth orientation, we will view elders as both consumers and resources. Their power base will increase as they move into positions of control and become an integral part of daily social system activities.

Families

The future for elders will see family structures altered as the traditional nuclear family continues to change. The divorce and remarriage rates will increase, which will reshape social support systems. By the year 2000, approximately four million people will have had three or more marriages. Many women will remain single throughout their lives, not remarry after divorce, or experience a second divorce after remarriage. Reduced fertility and delayed childbearing until one's 30s or 40s will have a profound effect on family structure (Hooyman and Kiyak, 1993; Kart, 1994; Raffoul and McNeece, 1996), leaving fewer children to fill the caregiver role.

For gay men and lesbians, issues of aging include many of the same concerns that heterosexual couples experience. On the other hand, sexual orientation and the discrimination and stigma associated with it greatly influence the way that gay and lesbian elders experience aging (Friend, 1991). Gay men and lesbian elders may assume, based on a history of ostracism, rejection, and differential treatment, that they cannot expect their immediate families to care for them in old age. They are, therefore, likely to develop "surrogate families" to

replace or to supplement natural kin systems. The presence of a strong and supportive gay community may also provide many social, cultural, economic, political, and religious opportunities for this population (Friend, 1987).

Other elders who live great distances from family may also have established an additional support system of neighbors, church families, and friends who replace or reinforce family networks. Fictive kin networks and/or "surrogate families," as well as individuals related by bloodline and marriage, will all form communities of mutual support for elders of the 21st century. The kinship networks will, by necessity, become more diffuse and complex, resulting in myriad family types, including blended, extended, and fictive families. Complex family issues resulting from multiple marriages, multiple divorces, and fictive kin and/or surrogate families, gay and lesbian families, and never-married heterosexual women and men will require new social work intervention that is nonjudgmental, supportive, and creative.

Work and Leisure

For women, employment will form a significant and meaningful part of their lives in old age. They will continue to work after their male counterparts retire (Dychtwald, 1989; Wellons, 1996). Today's elders find that they are spending over 20% of their adult life in retirement (Hooyman and Kiyak, 1993). This trend is expected to continue for a great many retirees. Existing work and retirement practices will change, however, because elders will be dissatisfied with the current system and so will the public at large. With no mandatory retirement policies, and impending labor shortages, older workers will become more attractive. Their skills and services in the labor force will become more valuable, forcing employers to accommodate their needs and wishes with more flexible work plans, part-time employment, and phased-in retirement programs (Moon and Hushbeck, 1989). Some companies will also encourage older workers to move into second or third careers, which may mean returning to school. For many women, the family crisis brought on by divorce also encourages them to seek formal training for new careers. The phenomenon of "a graying of the university" suggests that the number of elders making the decision to return to college, graduate, or professional schools will continue to increase (Hooyman and Kiyak, 1993).

Leisure for elders of the 21st century will be closely tied to work rather than compartmentalized as a separate stage of life. The image of the leisure activities of the wealthier senior housing development is only one very important, but isolated, look at planned leisure. Future elders will experience more balance between productive work and recreation and will experience leisure as a continuation of their leisure activities of previous years. According to Kunkel (1989), they will "reinvest the extra eight hours a day" in those activities popular throughout their life course. These elders will also find pleasure in leisure activities that are both meaningful and goal-oriented. They will fashion for themselves an identity that is more complete and that is based on personal qualities instead of roles and activities (Kunkel, 1989; Atchley, 1988).

How can social work advocates prepare for this new population of elders? As stated above, understanding and incorporating the meaning of advocacy within a political framework will form the foundation of their work with elders of the 21st century. Kart (1994) and Wellons (1996) suggest that the titles "geriatric social worker" or "elder care generalist" best describe the social work advocate who will be prepared to work with elders in the next century. This social worker will be a master's-prepared professional with a broad range of knowledge and expertise in elder care, including an understanding of ecological systems (Kart, 1994; Wellons, 1996). Wellons (1996) suggests that serving future elders will involve greater participation from the private sector with the formation of an effective public-private partnership. That partnership will involve the Area Agency on Aging network, the corporate structure, the university, and senior citizens centers. Wellons (1996) identifies social work as having a significant and intricate role as these partnerships unfold.

The corporate arena, as noted above, will find that responding to the needs of older workers will ensure a more productive and happier work force. Social workers will be involved in several aspects of this environment, from helping workers extend their job readiness to providing direct clinical services to workers and their elderly family members (Walker, 1996). For problems that affect work performance, they will provide services directly to employers via counseling and clinical intervention. Such problems may include employers' caretaking responsibilities toward employees' elderly family members. As corporate families relocate, elderly family members are increasingly being included in the scenario. Providing adult day care as well as day care for children will become an important benefit to the corporate world's morale. Identifying other community resources and services, such as long-term care facilities, will be an important and necessary service for family-friendly corporations to provide to their workers. As corporations increasingly envision themselves as part of the total community in which they are located, they will seek opportunities to engage in social programs and to provide community support. The volunteer spirit of their workers can best be harnessed if the workplace encourages and supports their work with other community entities, such as schools, YMCAs, YWCAs, senior centers, and so on. Social workers will be active in developing and administering these programs. Furthermore, social workers will find that they must interact with other systems to be effective within the corporate world, to best serve workers, and to ensure that elders maintain a high quality of life.

Other corporate opportunities for social workers include private, nonprofit, and/or for-profit businesses that provide services directly to elderly clients in an effort to keep them independent and living in their own homes for as long as possible. This may involve, for example, the social worker who works with a home health-care organization or with a case management service (Wellons, 1996). Corporations that provide housing alternatives for elders, from the elegant and costly to the most affordable, will also find that they can best attract and service elderly residents with professional social workers on their staff who are involved from the initial phases of needs assessment and site selection to designing the housing and determining the amenities available (Walker, 1996).

Much of the work that corporations engage in as they support their workers will also involve developing relationships with colleges and universities (Wellons, 1996). University-based gerontology centers will continue to form contractual relationships with corporations and with state agencies to provide training, consultation, and technical assistance to many different groups. These university-based organizations will also disseminate information, conduct policy analysis, and carry out applied research to support service providers who work with older adults. Social workers will be part of the staff of these university-based centers. The Center for Aging Research and Education Services (CARES) at the University of North Carolina at Chapel Hill is an example of such a university-based organization. In addition to the above, this organization's mission is to focus on the need for elderly and disabled adults to lead satisfying lives that enrich their families and communities. Through organizations like CARES, universities are becoming major employers of social workers who have macro and micro skills and expertise in gerontology.

Action research is one of the roles that universities will increasingly take in service to elders. The following case example is a good illustration of action research that helped to create both social services and social change and ultimately helped to better serve vulnerable elders at risk of nursing home placement.

In 1985, Hunter College School of Social Work entered into a contractual agreement with Local 1199 to do a needs assessment for the union's newest workers, home care aides. The personal needs of these workers, who were mostly women of color, African American, and Hispanics, were especially acute in the areas of housing and health care. In their collective bargaining on behalf of these workers, the union used the research data that the university had gathered. At the same time, the university established a union-funded member assistance program to provide ongoing supportive services for the home care workers (Donovan, Kurzman, and Rotman, 1993). This is one way that educational institutions can use action research to identify avenues for service delivery. Social workers must be vigilant and flexible in order to recognize and respond to new opportunities for advocacy and service delivery.

Similar flexibility is demanded of the Area Agency on Aging (AAA). This aging network must adopt a proactive attitude in order to be prepared to function in the 21st century. Wellons (1996) indicated that AAA will begin to expand the participation of private industry in servicing elders by recruiting private industry participants, coordinating public-private efforts, and defining needs and designing services. It will become the coordinating partner with private industry and will link industry to other service providers. A local utility company in North Carolina has developed such a public-private partnership with AAAs, senior centers, local departments of social services, and other components of the aging network in their service area. The utility company's public-private initiative is called the "Gatekeeper Program" and is designed to encourage employers to "keep an eye out" for senior citizens while they carry out their usual work activities. The workers are trained to identify danger signs in elderly customers and to contact the aging network to alert them to the perceived problems. This is a very important service for elders who live alone and are isolated. Social workers will increasingly find that they are playing a major role in providing the training to workers like these utility workers, as well as conducting research and planning and designing services that encourage collaborative work among corporations, universities, senior centers, and members of the aging network.

Finally, as we advance into the 21st century, the need for long-term care for elders will become more obvious, with 9 million elders expected to need such care by the year 2000 (Dunkle and Norgard, 1995). Expectations that female family members should assume more responsibility for elders in need of long-term care are not realistic. Given trends in family type, availability of caregiver, and economics, it is not likely that families will have the resources to keep chronically ill elders at home. A major debate of the future will be over who will assume responsibility for long-term care: the family, the private sector, or some governmental entity (Hooyman and Kiyak, 1993). Social workers will be likely participants in that future debate. Our role as advocates for residents of long-term care facilities will encourage us to work to ensure that residents' rights are not violated and to attend to the psychosocial needs of residents. In our role as elder care generalists, we will also advocate for such things as appropriate staff-to-resident ratios, greater attention to issues of oversedation, failure to exercise the resident, and elder abuse/neglect (Hancock, 1990). As the number of elders in long-term care increases, more skilled and committed social workers will be needed. The inadequate number of professionals interested in work with elders will become more of a problem. Education, exposure, and competitive salaries will help to increase our ranks among professionals who serve elders.

This essay has attempted to identify some of the areas of importance to social workers who will advocate for elders in the next century. Our preparation for competent social work with this population requires that social workers be political and educated to understand the significance of advocacy to our professional mission. Furthermore, we need to recognize the importance of our expertise as it fits within the existing framework of American society. As elder care generalists in the 21st century, we must have a firm knowledge base for work with this population. We must be creative, nonjudgmental, proactive, and strategic in our work in the aging network as we encourage a public-private partnership and provide the linkages among universities, senior centers, and other agencies/organizations serving elders. Macro and micro skills will be essential as we embrace the primacy of social work advocacy in our service to a rapidly growing and diverse population of elders in the next century.

REFERENCES

Abramovitz, M. (1993). Should all social work students be educated for social change? Pro. *Journal of Social Work Education, 29,* 6–11, 17–18.

Atchley, R. (1988). Finding meaning in the leisure of retirement. *The Aging Connection, 9,* 12.

Atchley, R. (1994). *Social forces and aging: An introduction to social gerontology* (7th ed.). Belmont, CA: Wadsworth.

Bardill, D. (1993). Should all social work students be educated for social change? Con. *Journal of Social Work Education, 29,* 11–17.

Bellos, N., & Ruffolo, M. (1995). Aging: Services. In R. E. Edwards (Ed.) *Encyclopedia of social work* (pp. 165–173). Washington, DC: National Association of Social Workers Press.

Binstock, R. (1991). From the great society to the aging society: 25 years of the Older American Act. *Generations, 15,* 1–18.

Brody, M., & Brody, S. (1974). Decades of decision for the elderly. *Social Work, 19,* 544–554.

Browne, C., & Broderick, A. (1994). Asian and Pacific Island elders: Issues for social work practice and education. *Social Work, 39,* 252–259.

Carlton-LaNey, I. (1989). Old folks' homes for Blacks during the progressive era. *Journal of Sociology and Social Welfare, 16,* 43–60.

Crystal, S., & Shea, D. (1990). Cumulative advantages, cumulative disadvantages, and inequality among elderly people. *The Gerontologist, 30,* 437–443.

Donovan, R., Kurzman, P., & Rotman, C. (1993). Improving the lives of home care workers: A partnership of social work and labor. *Social Work, 38,* 579–585.

Dunkle, R., & Norgard, T. (1995). Aging overview. In R. E. Edwards (Ed.), *Encyclopedia of social work* (pp. 142–152). Washington, DC: National Association of Social Workers Press.

Dychtwald, R. (1989). *Age wave: The challenges and opportunities of an aging America.* Los Angeles: Tarcher.

Edwards, R. (Ed.). (1995). Introduction. *Encyclopedia of social work.* Washington, DC: National Association of Social Workers Press.

Ewalt, P. (1994). Federal legislation and the social work profession. *Social Work, 35,* 341–342, 480.

Fisher, R. (1995). Political social work. *Journal of Social Work Education, 31,* 194–203.

Friend, R. (1987). The individual social psychology of aging: Clinical implications for lesbians and gay men. *Journal of Homosexuality, 14,* 308–331.

Friend, R. (1991). Older lesbian and gay people: A theory of successful aging. *Journal of Homosexuality, 20,* 99–118.

Haber, C (1983). *Beyond sixty-five: The dilemma of old age in America's past.* Cambridge: Cambridge University Press.

Hancock, B. (1990). *Social work with older people.* Englewood Cliffs, NJ: Prentice-Hall.

Haynes, K., & Mickelson, J. (1991). *Affecting change: Social workers in the political arena* (2d ed.). New York: Longman.

Hooyman, N., & Kiyak, H. (1993). *Social gerontology: A multidisciplinary perspective.* Boston: Allyn and Bacon.

Kart, C. (1994). *The realities of aging.* Boston: Allyn and Bacon.

Kunkel, S. (1989). An extra eight hours a day. *Generations, 13,* 57–60.

Kutzik, A. J. (1979). American social provisions for the aged: A historical perspective. In D. E. Gelfand & A. J. Kutzill (Eds.), *Ethnicity and Aging: Theory, Research and Policy.* New York: Springer.

Moon, M., & Hushbeck, J. (1989). Options for extending work life. *Generations, 13,* 27–30.

Morales, A., & Sheafor, B. (1989). *Social work: A profession of many faces*. Boston: Allyn and Bacon.

Raffoul, P., & McNeece, C. (Eds.). (1996). *Future issues for social work practice*. Boston: Allyn and Bacon.

Rees, S. (1991). *Achieving power: Practice and policy in social welfare*. North Sidney, Australia: Allen and Unwins.

Reisch, M. (1986). From cause to case and back again: The reemergence of advocacy in social work. *The Urban and Social Change Review, 19*, 20–24.

Rothman, J. (1994). *Practice with highly vulnerable clients*. Englewood Cliffs, NJ: Prentice-Hall.

Thompson, J. (1994). Social workers and policies: Beyond the Hatch Act. *Social Work, 39*, 457–465.

Torres-Gil, F. (1992). *The new aging: Politics and change in America*. New York: Auburn House.

Torres-Gil, F., & Puccinelli, M. (1995). Aging: Public policy issues and trends. In R. E. Edwards (Ed.), *Encyclopedia of Social Work* (pp. 159–164). Washington, DC: National Association of Social Workers Press.

Tower, K. (1994). Consumer-centered social work practice: Restoring client self-determination. *Social Work, 39*, 191–197.

Walker, R. (1996). Caregiving stress, long-term care, and future social work practice. In P. R. Raffoul & C. A. McNeece (Eds.), *Future issues for social work practice* (pp. 125–137). Boston: Allyn and Bacon.

Wellons, K. (1996). Aspects of aging in the twenty-first century. In P. R. Raffoul & C. A. McNeece (Eds.), *Future issues for social work practice* (pp. 117–124). Boston: Allyn and Bacon.

Zuniga, M. (1995). Aging: Social work practice. In R. E. Edwards (Ed.), *Encyclopedia of social work* (pp. 173–183). Washington, DC: National Association of Social Workers Press.

Part III

Theories, Knowledge, and Values and the Social Work Profession

A. Theories, Knowledge, and Values

The essence of a profession is the alleged possession of unique knowledge in relation to certain problems. The discussion of what is knowledge and how to get it is central to any profession, and social work is no exception. The question "What is knowledge?" has been considered for thousands of years. There is a spirited debate about different ways of knowing in the social work literature. Different views have different consequences for both professionals and clients. Epistemology involves exploring different definitions of knowledge—what it is and how to get it. Social workers have drawn on related literature in a piecemeal fashion. For example, they often refer to Thomas Kuhn's relativistic closed circle view of knowledge, but rarely present critiques of this view (see, for example, Bartley, 1990; Munz, 1985). Relativistic positions assume that only those within a certain paradigm can evaluate the soundness of arguments. The result of this view is that there can be no criticism from outside the circle. This view removes the possibility of the growth of knowledge through error elimination. As Munz (1985) suggests, such protectionism serves useful functions (e.g., encouraging cooperation and avoiding critical appraisal of shared beliefs).

Different kinds of knowledge include functional knowledge, inert knowledge, irrelevant knowledge, and false knowledge. Functional knowledge refers to information that decreases uncertainty about how to attain valued outcomes. Inert knowledge refers to knowledge that is unaccompanied by related performance skills and so remains unused. Peter Munz (1985) uses the concept of false knowledge to refer to beliefs that are not true and that are not questioned. He emphasizes the importance of false knowledge in maintaining social bonds among members of a group. Does false knowledge exist in social work? If so, what kinds and what functions does it serve? (For example, does it serve professionals and/or clients?) Functions may change as circumstances change. What consequences flow from what kinds of false knowledge to different parties (e.g., clients, social workers)? Tomi Gomory presents an incisive description and critical review of current approaches to knowledge and describes the implications of different views. Bruce Thyer, Alicia Isaac, and Rufus Larkin call for a closer integration of research and practice, and draw out the implications of doing so versus not doing so. In "Social Work Education: Current Concerns and Possible Futures" Eileen Gambrill highlights some current problems in social work education, such as indoctrination rather than education, suggests causes for them, and offers some remedies.

Jerome Wakefield forecasts an increasingly close working relationship between social workers and psychiatrists based on the conceptual foundations of each particular profession. The essays by Jerome C. Wakefield and Tomi Gomory (see Part II) provide contrasting views of the wisdom of a close connection between psychiatry and social work. In his essay "Social Work and Psychiatry," Wakefield argues that social work and psychiatry will (and should) increasingly work together because of a diagnostically based partnership. In Part II, Section A, Tomi Gomory argues that, based on a critical appraisal of basic concepts such as mental illness and treatment efficacy studies, there should be no relationship.

Ethical issues in social work practice are addressed by both Frederick Reamer and Burton Gummer. Reamer draws on the past (e.g., the increased recognition that some social workers engage in unethical activities and misconduct) to suggest changes for the future. He describes ethical challenges associated with technological advances such as confidentiality concerns related to electronic communication systems. He highlights the recurring debate concerning the balance between individual well-being and concerns about social justice, social change, and social action. He calls on social work educators to prepare students to speak the language of ethics and be familiar with its vocabulary and ways of thinking. Concerns about scarce resources are raised by many essayists in this volume, including Burton Gummer, who argues persuasively that the NASW Code of Ethics has nothing to say about the daily decisions social work administrators confront in allocating scarce resources. Many essayists emphasize the changes in the resources available to meet clients' needs and the dilemmas this poses in pursuing the profession's social justice mission.

REFERENCES

Bartley, W. W., III. (1990). *Unfathomed knowledge, unmeasured wealth: On universities and the wealth of nations*. LaSalle, IL: Open Court.

Kuhn, T. S. (1970). The structure of scientific revolutions (2nd ed.). Chicago: University of Chicago Press.

Munz, P. (1985). *Our knowledge of the growth of knowledge: Popper or Wittgenstein*. London: Routledge & Kegan Paul.

Social Work and Philosophy

Tomi Gomory

There is perhaps no other more heated topic of discussion in social work than what knowledge is and how to get it. Currently, there is a celebration of relativism in the social work literature that claims that all ways of knowing are equally valid. Tomi Gomory first describes different dominant approaches to knowledge, noting the similarities between a logical positivist and a so-called heuristic approach, and argues for an alternative—evolutionary epistemology. He calls on social workers to consider the consequences for clients of accepting different views.

Tomi Gomory, MSW, is currently completing his doctoral studies in the School of Social Welfare, University of California at Berkeley. He is the recipient of a National Institute of Mental Health Doctoral Fellowship. His current areas of research include a critical review of outcome claims of PACT-type community programs that target the "severely mentally ill," conceptual and situational analysis of the historical changes in the public mental health system, and an evaluation of the impact on social work of justificationary philosophic frameworks—logical positivist: heuristic paradigm, postmodernism, relativist versus a fallabilist critical rational evolutionary epistemology. Mr. Gomory's practical experience includes directing the San Francisco component of the federal model project The Homeless Family, cosponsored by the Robert Wood Johnson Foundation.

A philosophically inclined social worker reviewing the current intellectual notions prevalent in the field of social work about scientific practice will find two dominant paradigms.

The first is the long-defunct system generally known as logical empiricism or positivism, originated by Wittgenstein in his Tractatus, refined—or, more properly, fiddled with—by the Vienna Circle, the members of which group largely constituted the logical positivists (Munz, 1985). This approach is associated with "hard data crunchers," those social scientists involved with controlled experimental models and complex statistical analyses using "objective facts" based on empirical observations.

This research program postulated the theory-free direct observation of the out there—called facts—by an unbiased observer, defined such facts as scientific, based on these direct observations by the senses, and proposed a kind of logarithm of deductive reasoning that, if properly applied, would inevitably lead to truth. It further claimed that the securing of the truth by experimental research depended on finding more and more support (verification) by repeated and accumulated confirmations of explanatory hypotheses. This approach is justificationary because the accumulation of confirming evidence is used by this school of thought as proof or justification of the hypotheses being evaluated.

The logical positivists recognized that there were some difficulties with their claims—for example, with the "problem of induction." First addressed by David Hume back in 1739, it concerns the logical impossibility of conclusively proving any general law from discrete, confirming observations, regardless of how many, because general laws or statements are always underdetermined by the observed "facts." A universally true statement, to be fully justified, would have to demonstrate that all observational evidence about that statement confirms it. This cannot be done because we cannot guarantee that we have looked at each and every piece of evidence bearing on the statement without overlooking any. This leaves our justifications always incomplete and leaves open the distinct possibility that one of these yet-to-be-discovered observations will provide the counterevidence for disconfirming an apparently well-justified theory. Another difficulty for the logical positivists was the discomfiting result of Einstein's theoretical musings—later to be corroborated empirically—about the influence of the observer on the observed when measuring data, contradicting the logical positivists' claim that our senses are reliable witnesses impartially reporting the objective facts and nothing but such facts. They explained these problems away by suggesting that some statements called "basic observation statements," logically mirror in some way the world out there, that they express direct information from the senses about the outside world and not an interpretation (Hattiangadi, 1987). Also, they claimed that scientific research is probabilistic at best and guaranteed truth can't be guaranteed. Like some Las Vegas gamblers, they felt that the more frequent the success of a hypothesis, the higher the odds of it reoccurring—the sun rising each day, for example—and being probably true (Meehl, 1993).

The second philosophic perspective, relativism, was well aware of the various problems of the logical positivist research program. In addition to those already mentioned, its proponents identified a few more, such as the dilemma of the mind–body debate and the Kantian claim that we impose on the "bloomin' buzzin' noise" out there the mind's own innate categories to make sense of it all—thus subjectifying, as it were, the physical (and, of course, the social) world. We, the relativists proclaimed, subjectively and socially "construct" our various realities. This trivial truism holding for certain aspects of our world—tradition, penal codes, sexual mores or social custom, for example—led these true believers to assert the complete absence of objective knowledge and, as a result, also the impossibility of absolute truth (Gellner, 1985; Munz, 1985; Pieper, 1989). Further, based on the multiple realities thus asserted, they then claimed that there are many truths, many, many ways of knowing, all dependent on the particular cultural or societal frame of reference used to explore various problems of interest.

This alternate paradigm, which I've suggested falls under the general rubric of relativism, is currently making the intellectual rounds as postmodernism, an ephemeral movement consisting of the sociology of knowledge, fideism, hermeneutics, meaning and linguistic philosophy, deconstructualism, and perhaps others, forming a rather untidy package of theoretical constructs (Gellner, 1992). I point this out so that we will not be confused or intimidated by these apparently different systems of analysis, which in social work are marketed, as in other social sciences, as various possible routes to scientific knowledge—the many ways of knowing, of "problem solving"—when in fact only the rhetoric differs. The fundamental regulative idea is one and the same among them: a hostility

> to the idea of unique, exclusive, objective, external or transcendent truth. Truth is elusive, polymorphous, inward, subjective . . . and perhaps a few other things as well. Straightforward it is not. (Gellner, 1992, p. 24)

Some proponents of relativistic theories in social work go as far as to claim that they are no such creatures (relativists, that is), but are by "personal preference" (a relativistic phrase if I ever heard one) "qualified realists" instead (Pieper, 1994, p. 76). It's just that they are very catholic in their philosophic tastes and like to invite all parties to sup at Science's horn of plenty.

> Both relativism and realism are heuristic choices and, as such, are encompassed within the heuristic paradigm[1] although they neither define nor exhaust it. (Tyson, 1995, p. xxv)

The question left unanswered by such a claim is, How, if this paradigm encompasses relativistic approaches as well as those that deny them, does it maintain theoretical coherence? Either one version or the other of reality is true; both cannot logically coexist.

These two philosophic approaches pretty much cover the field, with an occasional rare mention, generally in mistaken association with the logical positivists, of Karl Popper. His philosophy, however, is usually quickly dismissed as perhaps interesting, but fatally flawed (Tyson, 1995, p. 116). This is the same Popper who has, I believe, decisively critiqued and refuted both logical positivism and the various relativistic approaches to the doing of science, while simultaneously offering his own alternative to both of the preceding research programs: his fallabilistic critical rationalism (Popper, 1959, 1965, 1983).

In what follows, I will summarize the important claims of both the logical positivists and the relativists, and then offer some criticism alleging that both positions are untenable. I will further argue that the debate in social work about these positions is a waste of time. Whatever the differences between them, perhaps even formally correct, are nevertheless pseudo problems because both approaches are justifica-

tionary approaches claiming scientific validity on inductive grounds—an approach both logically and empirically without merit (Popper, 1959, 1965, 1979, 1983). More particularly in the case of relativism, its approach is unscientific, fideistic, irrational, and very dangerous for a democratic society. I will conclude by briefly outlining critical rationalism—an evolutionary epistemology (Radnitzky & Bartley, 1987; Munz, 1993)—which is based on a strict deductive methodology using trial and error correction. It consists of progressively more comprehensive guesses or bold conjectures about our world that are put to severe tests, in attempts at falsification. I claim and hope to demonstrate— not dogmatically but with critical argument— that this approach solves the problems of the previous two philosophies.

Assumptions and Difficulties of Logical Positivism

Assumptions:

1. All that we can talk about and test are "facts" or data that are directly perceivable by our senses.

2. Sense data guarantee truth. Content and theory are valid only when connected to such physical observations by logical structures.

3. Sense data are mirror images of the world out there, unencumbered by subjective bias.

4. There is a basic correct pattern of scientific explanation, consisting of two parts: First, the explicandum, the sentence describing the phenomenon to be explained, and, second, the explicans or class of sentences that are produced to account for the *why* of the phenomenon in the explicandum. The explicans contains sentences describing the antecedent conditions (such as the nature and circumstances of the situation or sub-

---

[1]The heuristic paradigm is the latest if not the greatest new "meta-theory" to surface in social work. It is explicated in painful detail over slightly less than 600 pages by Katherine Tyson, an acolyte of the paradigm's inventor, Martha Heineman Pieper, in *The Heuristic Paradigm* (1995).

jects) and the general laws of consequence (hypothesized universal laws of causality). In order for such an explanation to be sound, the explicandum must be logically deducible from the explicans, and the general laws of the explicans must be required for the derivation of the explicandum. The explicans must have empirical content—that is, it must, in principle, be capable of a test by either observation or experiment—and the sentences representing the explicans must be true (Hempel, 1988). This is often called the covering law model.

Difficulties:

1. The claim of assumption 1, of course, eliminates all theoretical entities such as atoms, subatomic particles, electromagnetic forces, cells, molecules, and so on, that are not directly available to human perception but appear to be real and are fundamental to scientific explanation.

2. As Hume and others have demonstrated, all universal generalizations are underdetermined by data or individual observations. No matter how many observations of white swans we may make, the very first observation of a black swan—assuming it is a swan—falsifies the putative universal generalization that all swans are white. This holds for all attempts at justification of general theories by discrete "facts." Universal laws never can be proven. But they may be falsified (Miller, 1994; Popper, 1983).

3. Assumption 3 has been proven false by experimental demonstrations of the fallibility of our senses—for example, by optical illusions. What we observe to a larger or smaller degree is filtered and shaped by the nature of our cognitive equipment.

4. Some suggest that the formal theory-testing methodology in assumption 4 collapses under the demonstration of the subjective component of observations. Also, this formal, almost logarithmic, methodology must assume that the universe is governed by causality and is made possible by assumed laws of nature—asserting the *immutability of natural processes*. These assumptions are not necessary, and are not testable; they are metaphysical, and their truth claims are unknowable, demonstrating the failure of this approach (Miller, 1994).

These sum up the principle claims and critiques leveled at this philosophic position. There is a general consensus among philosophers of science that this research program is a failure, and it has been retired in most serious areas of research although it apparently is alive and well in social work (Bloom & Fisher, 1982; Hudson, 1978; Klein & Bloom, 1995; Tyson, 1995). There the battlefield is active and rather bloody.

The Relativist Position

The nature of the conflict in social work is sometimes obscured by the reformulating of this dispute as being between what is broadly speaking called quantitative research, equated with the logical positivist position, and qualitative research, serving as a proxy for the relativist position. This has led to scores of unnecessary scholarly articles proving or debunking the scientific seaworthiness of one methodology or the other, or to articles mediating this debate, suggesting a cease fire or a peace settlement (Klein & Bloom, 1995; Tyson, 1995; Wakefield, 1995). Because both types of methodologies may be "scientific," depending on the question to be answered, all of these articles, although inflating various résumés, seriously miss the point at issue: whether doing science differs from doing such things as literature or music or art. Is there scientific truth—

objective truth, empirical truth—or not? This is of consequence because I am assuming that social work interventions and processes presuppose empirical impact. They are expected to be effective, to work, to promote change "scientifically." If nothing distinguishes science from these other intellectual enterprises, we have a moot discussion.

Let's look more closely at the relativists in social work. They are a curious group. Their claims appear to be models of democratic, or better yet, egalitarian reasoning, fitting well into social work's long-time commitment to "social justice"[2] and its accompanying norms for social and ethnic sensitivity. Ann Hartman's (1990) statement is representative:

> This editor takes the position that there are many truths and there are many ways of knowing [presumably these many truths]. Each discovery contributes to our knowledge, and each way of knowing deepens our understanding and adds another dimension to our view of the world. . . . There are indeed many ways of knowing and many kinds of knowers; researchers, practitioners, clients. Some seekers of truth may take a path that demands distance and objectivity, whereas others rely on deeply personal and empathic knowing. Some will find the validation of their findings through statistical analysis and probability tests. Others will find it through the intensity and authenticity of "being there" (Geertz, 1988) or through public and shared consensus in what has been called "practice wisdom" (Siporin, 1989). Some truth seekers strive to predict, whereas others turn to the past for an enhanced understanding of the present. (pp. 3–4)

This seemingly amiable, gently accepting ecumenical worldview is clearly based on the refutation of the hard-core empiricist position of the logical positivists. If no assurance of objective data gathering is possible and many affirmations of a hypothesis are not proof enough of an objective truth claim, then all claims and subjective reports must gain full

and equal employment status in the work effort of the sciences, validating various truths in various situations, to be determined by the various values and standards of individual communities or societies. Is this right?

The key issue of contention, it seems to me, is what we mean by knowledge. As Hartman quite rightly suggests in her quote, but not in the way she intends, there may be many ways of knowing and various forms of knowledge. We can include among these religious, spiritual, or aesthetic knowledge—that is, forms of knowledge that are not open to intersubjective scrutiny to determine what is true or what is false, primarily because the knowledge we may acquire and use in these areas is concerned with preference and taste, like and dislike, faith and not fact. In these matters, relativism is a fact and no impediment precisely because we are not really interested in answers to such questions as, Who was the greater composer, Beethoven or Mozart, or who painted better portraits, Picasso or Van Gogh? Questions like these are not germane to enhancing our knowledge about music and art, and answers to them are ultimately subjective decisions determined by our tastes not empirical necessity. Hartman and others (Tyson, 1995) are not asserting this,

---

[2] Social justice, upon careful analysis, turns out to have many different definitions, representing all things to all people, ultimately therefore becoming meaningless. More importantly, as Hayek has pointed out in his comprehensive discussion of this concept,

> "Social" justice . . . came to be regarded as an attribute which the "actions" of society, or the "treatment" of individuals and groups by society ought to possess. . . . The results of the spontaneous [self] ordering of the market were interpreted as if some thinking being deliberately directed them, or as if the particular benefits or harm different persons derive from them were determined by deliberate acts of will, and could therefore be guided by moral rules. This conception of "social" justice is thus a direct consequence of that anthropomorphism or personification by which naive thinking tries to account for all self-ordering processes. (1976, pp. 62–63)

perhaps obvious, point, but rather that there are multiple versions of *scientific* knowledge and truth—an arena where, I claim, we should know what is more effective, a better explanation, more successful or simply true.

The social work relativists' contemporary position is well expressed by a recent ideologue of the field, Martha Heineman Pieper, the inventor of the heuristic paradigm of research in social work,

> [The] advantage of the heuristic paradigm is that investigators in different areas, such as public policy and family therapy, need no longer argue about whose work is more scientific, more valuable or more empirical. Rather, each researcher can see that no focus is inherently superior and that other researchers legitimately have defined important problems in differing ways. All arguments about whether it is better to study individuals, families, groups, political entities, or public policies are in principle undecideable because, at bottom, they are conflicts about competing values. That is, since we can't know with certainty either the truth or the best way to approximate it, decisions about how to proceed are subjective or value judgments. If we realize the futility of pursuing *the* answer, then we become grateful for any explanation or intervention that promises to help with the question. (Pieper, 1989)

But if one kind of test is no better than any other for that determination, but is merely one of many possible value judgments, how do we decide that an explanation or intervention helps (I assume here that help means that an intervention is found to work).

Relativism leaves us bereft of any way of choosing or testing helping interventions or policies because by definition no "objective facts"—intersubjectively corroborated information or observations—are recognized as such. Such observations are asserted to be no more privileged, no more objective, and just as biased—as are, for example, the personal subjective conclusions of social workers about the

services they provide to clients (Tyson, 1995, p. 217):

> . . . no facts are privileged: that is, no one category of facts is inherently better at telling us about reality than another category of facts. (Tyson, 1995, p. 211)

The falsification of the logical positivist paradigm seemingly has led to nihilism (Gellner, 1992, pp. 49–50), anarchy, and to the Kuhnian concept of epistemic authority (Kuhn, 1970). Epistemic authority is the idea that what is to be taken as scientifically correct or truthful knowledge is to be determined by a power elite who speak for the scientific community. A similar idea was expressed by the less well known Hungarian philosopher/scientist M. Polanyi prior to Kuhn (Polanyi, 1964). In our case, the epistemic authority would be constituted by the social work elite who control what is or is not proper and acceptable for social work practice and theory—perhaps a group like NASW or large institutional funding authorities like the National Institute of Mental Health (defining what is and is not mental illness). Pieper again helps to articulate this concept when she states in Tyson's book,

> If you conclude that your research results are substantively significant, then the evaluation process will shift to the true test of any results, namely utility and acceptance by the field over time. (Tyson, 1995, p. 217)

Here she argues, if I read her correctly, that in fact there are *not* many ways of scientifically knowing—thus contradicting her entire paradigm's overarching claim—but just one, through the authority and acceptance of the field. This illuminates the authoritarian antidemocratic nature of relativistic thinking. Either we are free to choose any datum we want, with no explanations needed to support our position—a process best described as anarchy because no particular type of "fact" is privileged and therefore any choice must be arbitrary—thus making way for those who are the most powerful to determine from all that is arbitrary what is to become scientifically sublime. Or we can genuflect and fall in line, accepting the authority of the field as the "true test"—ascertained by divine right perhaps—because no objective tests are recognized for determining what is scientifically the best intervention or process to solve a particular problem in social work. Facts for the relativists may be any phenomenon any researcher wishes to call a fact. No criteria exist to distinguish among them, and all one needs are facts that may be considered "clinically credible":

> Clinical credibility . . . can rest on the comprehensive, detailed, well-conceptualized presentation by a single practitioner of her or his conduct and understanding of a specific treatment process. (Tyson, 1995, p. xxiv)

I beg to differ. What a breast cancer patient (or any other person looking for professional help) wants is a treatment that has demonstrated its effectiveness by being put to severe tests and passing such tests—reducing or destroying malignancies, for instance—in many cases, and not simply a "credible" report of one professional asserting success.

Be that as it may, either option means no more and no less than accepting a form of totalitarian control over science—albeit sugarcoated à la Tyson, Pieper, and Hartman—with its attendant restrictions on intellectual freedom. Having demonstrated that the justificationist philosophic stance of the logical positivists is refuted and that the major alternate paradigm of relativism[3] is a nonstarter, are we therefore existentially condemned to a scientific twilight zone with no way out? If the relativists correctly critique the logical positivists, but they themselves are incoherent, is there an alternative to both? Yes! Let's examine Karl Popper's critical rationalism.

Critical Rationalism: A Fallibilistic Evolutionary Epistemology

Popper stands alone among 20th-century philosophers in that he has found an antidote for Hume's problem. Although no amount of confirming evidence can fully justify a general theory, just one falsifying observation can logically refute a theory. Thus, Popper proposes that if truth is what we are after—and he claims, and I agree, that there is absolute truth as a regulative idea (Miller, 1994)—then all hypotheses must submit to severe criticism, to various rigorous tests that they must pass to remain in the realm of science. If they fail such tests, they are to be expelled from the hard knocks school of science (Miller, 1994).

Let's back up a moment and argue a bit more for the ideas of objective truth and reality that the relativists claim are mirages. I believe that they don't for a moment actually practice what they preach, but because they are justificationists and inductionists they have placed themselves in a philosophic paper bag from which they are unable to intellectually punch their way out.

No relativist doubts, for example, that planes fly because they are constructed in accordance with the objective, scientific laws—laws applicable anywhere and anytime in our world—of aerodynamics, gravity, metallurgy, and thermodynamics. I further assert that such a person would not get on a "plane" created by an origami artist, even if that artist was very talented. Why? Because "real" planes are scientifically developed and tested using objective

[3]Relativists, as it happens, are all also justificationists and inductionists, falling prey to all of the criticisms leveled at the logical positivists when they actually look for—as opposed to just dogmatically assert—evidence to support their hypotheses. They differ from logical positivists only in their method of justification. Relativists use the epistemic authority of the elite or the ideas of the most powerful, instead of "covering laws," to determine what is scientifically justifiable.

data; origami planes, being art constructions, are not. That is, the "real" plane's design evolved by trial and error methods. Various alternate designs might have been proposed, beginning with drawings, then proceeding to building models conforming to scientific laws, which were then tested. Some passed the progressively more severe tests and others didn't. Those passing were put to further tests, with some again passing and others failing; these latter were then discarded. Over time, the best design emerged by passing the most tests. These methods are intersubjectively testable and replicable. An airplane must conform to such objective laws, and even relativists would want to know that they do, before departing on one.

The relativists, with all their broad-minded philosophic notions about what passes for facts (see Tyson, 1995, p. 209), would also not place hemlock on their health salads—unless they were in a Socratic mood of course. Why? Because hemlock is poison. How do I know that? Trial and error research has demonstrated objectively that it will kill human beings.

I use these examples to point to the absurdities inherent in the "many ways of scientifically knowing" school of social work. We have an objective world and we can identify and gather objective data, but unfortunately we can only use them in attempts to falsify hypotheses, not to prove them. But how can I claim that observations, those that are intersubjectively evaluated, are objective, having acknowledged in my criticism of the logical positivists that all observations are theory-based and subject to the natural limitations of human cognitive structures? Such limitations prevent *Homo sapiens* from directly observing the out there.

Popper provides a startlingly simple but provocative solution as he develops his early critical rationalist philosophy into a Darwinian selectionist evolutionary epistemology (Popper, 1979):

I uphold the ancient theory of truth . . . [in] which truth is the agreement with the facts. . . .

It so happens that . . . my thought about human knowledge is *fallibilism* and the critical approach; and . . . I see, . . . that human knowledge is a . . . special case of animal knowledge. My central idea in the field of animal knowledge . . . is that it is based on *inherited* knowledge. It is of the character of unconscious expectations. It . . . develops as the result of modification of previous knowledge. The modification is . . . a mutation, . . . it is of the nature of a trial balloon, it is intuitive or boldly imaginative. It is . . . of a *conjectural* character: the expectation may be disappointed . . . all the information received from outside is eliminative, *selective*.

The special thing about human knowledge is that it may be formulated in language. . . . This makes it possible for knowledge to become conscious and to be *objectively criticizable* by arguments and by tests. (Popper, 1983, pp. xxxi, xxxv) (Italics mine)

In the preceding quote, Sir Karl Popper, in his usual concise and crisp manner, provides the answer to how human (especially scientific) knowledge actually grows. He boldly conjectures—to use the famous Popperian terminology—that this takes place through Darwinian random mutation and natural—in science, rational theory—selection. Here I will follow the argument that has been most daringly presented by a former student of Popper's, historian Peter Munz, in his *Philosophical Darwinism* (1993).

If one accepts Darwinian evolution and the existence of a universe of which we are a part, then those facts will lead us to search for theories that explain more and eliminate inconsistencies. That is to say, because we are part of a universe and the universe consists of subsystems and those subsystems must be compatible with each other, then those theories that eliminate more of the inconsistencies and explain more, will be preferred and will be better progressive approximations to the truth by correspondence (Munz, 1993, p. 206). Evolutionary epistemology or, more particularly, philosophical Darwinism, I believe, successfully answers the age-old problem of minds and whether they refer to a real world out there (empiricism) or simply contain internal mind dramas of their own making (idealism or rationalism). This dual tension owes much to Descartes' separation of the knower from the known—the objective world. His speculations about the inadequacy of a mind to be ever certain of seeing an objective reality has plagued us right to the present, as I've noted in my earlier analysis of the logical positivists. The philosophical representation of (scientific) knowledge as modeled on physics, which is used by both of the research programs examined previously, has no room for a conscious subject. The arena of evaluation there is the physical universe: "Physics is how an atom appears to an atom; not how it appears to a conscious subject" (Munz, 1993, p. 187).

However, with the advent of biology, we change the whole philosophic texture of our understanding:

> With . . . living matter, biology has introduced us into a world which is full of self-reflection. . . . Through chance mutation and selective retention [evolution], the physical world has generated a biological world in which one part of the world reflects another part. . . . In this world, one part contains knowledge about the world because living matter evolves by the acquisition of knowledge. If there are photons and light, there will be parts of the world which are sensitive to photons and light. . . . Biology has opened a new perspective because, biologically, the eye is not caused by photons, but selected by photons. (Munz, 1993, p. 191)

With the emergence of evolutionary biology, we have cleared up an age-old dilemma. We can be fairly assured that what we see is "really" out there. We, as organisms with vision, have adaptively survived better than those without, precisely because there are things out there to be seen. Sight is only valuable—adaptive—in a world that can be observed. This evolutionary development does not end with our physical processes but continues with our cognitive processes. As suggested above, what constitutes our observations (facts) about the world bears a strong verisimilitude to reality. Our cognitive processes have evolved, and we have survived in the environment due to the fact that our cognitive equipment fits the environment better than the cognitive equipment of other creatures who did not survive. Munz's great contribution, I believe, is in linking, and thereby expanding, Popperian epistemology, the evolution of physical organisms to the evolution of the growth of scientific knowledge. He suggests that we create theories about the world, which he wishes to call "disembodied organisms," in a relatively random fashion, and these theories are then exposed to the environment, which "tests" these theories and selectively retains a very few that are adaptive and "verisimilitudinously" true.

His use of the concept of organisms, including humans, being embodied theories about the environment that are tested by the environment for fit and are naturally selected for survival, and the complementary idea of theories being disembodied organisms that are evaluated by a rational process, have great explanatory significance. The first concept, of course, is the theory of Darwinian evolution; the second explains the dynamics of theories. Theories are replaced as more adaptive or more verisimilitudinous theories are found (conjectured and criticized) (Munz, 1993, p. 213). The selection of theories is based on the greater explanatory power of the replacing theory. That is, the more powerful theory explains all that the other (replaced) theory did and something more. The rationale for such a selection process is what Munz calls his minimal ontology. This ontology holds that evolution is a fact, and this fact entails two distinct characteristics that the universe must possess:

> First, there must be regularities. Organisms which are adapted must be adapted to regularities. Second, all regularities must be compatible with each other. . . . Third, it follows from the second contention . . . that disembodied organisms (theories) will tend towards progressive elimination of incompatibilities, so that the evolution of knowledge will appear to be unilinear rather than cumulatively circular. (p.173)

The preceding description of how scientific knowledge grows by the use of a fallabilistic evolutionary epistemology, I think, clears up the apparently unsolvable difficulties presented by the two contending current paradigms in social work. Neither the logical positivists nor the relativists have a way to overcome their induction-driven justificationary methodology and, as a result, are left either to quietly fade away—the apparent long-term fate of the logical positivists—or to pretend to umpire a research game without rules, as apparently is being done by the relativists.

Popperian critical evolutionary methodology frees us from having to use internal group authority to protect our various Kuhnian incommensurate, closed-circle scientific paradigms (Kuhn, 1970, pp. 149–150, 198–202) from outside evaluations, critical arguments, or hard environmental tests. We are no longer stuck as to how we can choose between competing explanations about the world. The solution is clear and compelling. Evolution has made us into creatures capable of speculating about our world—because of the evolution of consciousness—and has made us capable of creating better and better-fitted theories that seek to explain our world more comprehensively. The criterion of theory selection is the greater explanatory power of a theory over its rival theories.

By eliminating more and more inconsistencies with fewer and more unified explanations, we do, in fact, make progress, progress from the more primitive. This progress is unilinear in its direction and we are assured contra Kuhn (Kuhn, 1970) of never returning in our cognitive development to an Aristotelian scientific worldview. It is quite true that we never see the world as "raw" facts—no direct knowledge is possible due to the design of our nervous system and the theory-based nature of all observations, as discussed earlier. But the fact that we are the result of evolution and, as a consequence, fit our environment relatively well suggests that the world we observe is pretty much the world out there. This is so precisely because our cognitive equipment was selected over other possibilities by the environment for its better fit or, to put it another way, its observational capabilities are verisimilitudinous with nature.

Although we may not always possess effective scientific interventions or true theories and could not comprehensively prove them to be so even if they were, we are assured as social workers that we do have an objective approach that will identify those that are scientifically untenable. This may not seem like much for those who believe in absolute knowledge or in utopian worldviews. But absolute knowledge is not possible for mortals—all three schools of thought discussed here agree to that—and utopian dreams are, by definition, fated to remain that way, and should, because my utopian dream may be your fascist nightmare. All utopias, unfortunately, suffer the shortcoming of having to be imposed on those of us who might wish to live otherwise.

Because of these difficulties, we will have to settle for the much frailer version of knowledge that is possible. This is a tentative type of knowledge, best called conjectural knowledge (Popper, 1979, ch. 1), always on its guard for correcting human error through criticism, which we should use to make small piecemeal progress in our very real, objective, and troubled world.

REFERENCES

Bloom, M., & Fisher, J. (1982). *Evaluating practice: Guidelines for the accountable professional.* Englewood Cliffs, NJ: Prentice-Hall.

Geertz, C. (1988). *Works and lives.* Stanford, CA: Stanford University Press.

Gellner, E. (1985). *Relativism and the social sciences.* Cambridge: Cambridge University Press.

_____. (1992). *Postmodernism, reason, religion.* London: Routledge.

Hartman, A. (1990). Editorial: Many ways of knowing. *Social Work, 35,* 3–4.

Hattiangadi, J. N. (1987). *How is language possible? Philosophical reflections on the evolution of language and knowledge.* La Salle, IL: Open Court.

Hayek, F. A. (1976). *The mirage of social justice.* Chicago: The University of Chicago Press.

Hempel, C. G. (1988). Studies in the logic of explanation. In E. D. Klemke, R. Hollinger, & A. D. Kline (Eds.), *Introductory readings in the philosophy of science* (pp. 91–108). Buffalo, NY: Prometheus.

Hudson, W. (1978). First axioms of treatment. *Social Work, 23,* 65–66, 518–519.

_____. (1982). Scientific imperatives in social work research and practice. *Social Service Review, 56,* 246–258.

Klein, W. C., & Bloom, M. (1995). Practice wisdom. *Social Work, 40,* 799–807.

Kuhn, T. (1970). *The structure of scientific revolutions.* Chicago: The University of Chicago Press.

Meehl, P. E. (1993). Philosophy of science: Help or hindrance? *Psychological Reports, 72,* 707–733.

Miller, D. (1994). *Critical rationalism: A restatement and defence.* Chicago: Open Court.

Munz, P. (1985). *Our knowledge of the growth of knowledge: Popper or Wittgenstein?* London: Routledge & Kegan Paul.

_____. (1993). *Philosophical Darwinism: On the origin of knowledge by means of natural selection.* London: Routledge.

Pieper, M. Heineman. (1989). The heuristic paradigm: A unifying and comprehensive approach to social work research. *Smith College Studies in Social Work, 60,* 8–34.

_____. (1994). Science not scientism: The robustness of naturalistic clinical research. In E. Sherman & W. J. Reid (Eds.), *Qualitative research in social work.* New York: Columbia University Press.

Polanyi, M. (1964). *Personal knowledge: Towards a post-critical philosophy.* New York: Harper & Row, Harper Torchbooks/Academy Library.

Popper, K. R. (1959). *The logic of scientific discovery.* New York: Basic Books.

_____. (1965). *Conjectures and refutations: The growth of scientific knowledge* (2d ed.). New York: Basic Books.

_____. (1979). *Objective knowledge: An evolutionary approach.* Oxford: Clarendon Press.

_____. (1983). *Realism and the aim of science.* Totowa, NJ: Rowman & Littlefield.

Radnitzky, G. & Bartley, W. W. (Eds.). (1987). *Evolutionary epistemology, rationality, and the sociology of knowledge.* La Salle, IL: Open Court.

Siporin, M. (1989). Metamodels, models, and basics: An essay review. *Social Service Review, 63,* 474–480.

Tyson, K. (1995). *New foundations for scientific social and behavioral research: The Heuristic paradigm.* Boston: Allyn and Bacon.

Wakefield, J. C. (1995). When an irresistible epistemology meets an immovable ontology. *Social Work Research, 19*(1), 9–17.

Integrating Research and Practice

Bruce A. Thyer, Alicia Isaac, and Rufus Larkin

I wish that I could make all women fall in love with scientific reasoning. It doesn't suffocate the voice of the heart but augments it and supports it.

Maria Montessori (in Wallace et al., 1981, p. 544)

Concerns about basing practice on practice-related empirical literature have long been a part of social work. The authors make a well-reasoned argument, both on ethical and practical grounds, for basing practice decisions on related empirical literature. They discuss what they view as hindrances to progress, including postmodernistic views of knowledge, and suggest guidelines for enhancing integration of research and practice. Bruce A. Thyer, Ph.D., is professor of social work and adjunct professor of psychology at the University of Georgia and associate clinical professor of psychiatry and health behavior at the Medical College of Georgia. Dr. Thyer is the founder and editor of Research on Social Work Practice, *a peer viewed quarterly journal. Alicia Isaac, DPA, is an assistant professor at the University of Georgia. Rufus Larkin is a doctoral student in social work at the University of Georgia.*

The relevance of integrating research and practice with regard to the effective delivery of social services has long been recognized as an important issue for social work (see Todd, 1920; Preston & Mudd, 1956). Indeed, the continuing existence of the profession may reside in our ability to develop replicable and reliably effective social services, and to implement them on a widespread scale. Anticipating contemporary conservative political views, Edith Abbott said, 65 years ago, that: "the failure in the past to apply scientific method and scientific leadership to the needs of the poor has wasted the taxpayers' money and left behind a trail of good intentions and futile efforts" (in Dunlap, 1993, p. 293).

When the January 1996 issue of the *NASW News* came across our desks, we read of massive shakeups in the social work departments of the nation's veterans' hospitals. Here is one comment:

> The profession must do a better job of compiling data to demonstrate the effectiveness of social work in health care. . . . We have to think in terms of measuring what we do. Anecdotes that show that social work has a place in health care don't work anymore. They want hard, cold facts. (Smith, 1996, p. 3)

To some extent, we have been successful in demonstrating that certain forms of psychosocial interventions provided by social workers are effective in alleviating selected problems of social or interpersonal importance (see, for example, MacDonald, Sheldon, & Gillespie, 1992; Reid & Hanrahan, 1982; Thyer, 1995), but our general field seems to lack a sufficiently credible foundation of empirical research support to justify the billions of dollars expended in social work and welfare services. Thus, public support and private capital (e.g., managed care corporations) are eroding their commitment to our field.

Why is this? In our opinion, a major culprit has been the profession's initial and continuing adoption of theoretical perspectives that are neither empirically supported nor conducive to the development of effective interventions. The dominance of psychoanalytic theory and its metastasized grandchildren (object relations theory, ego psychology, attachment theory, *ad infinitum*) continue to exert a stifling influence on present-day clinical practice, and the "let's-pretend-we-are-as-scientific-as-cybernetics-or-ecology" pseudotheories of systems theory and the ecosystems perspective as applied to social work have yet to produce effective social work practices or policies. One highly regarded theoretical text in social work practice (Dorfman, 1988) contains chapters on "psychodynamic theory," "Adlerian theory," the "eco-systems perspective," "existential social work," the "constructivist-developmental paradigm," and "cybernetic epistemology." Why? To our knowledge, not one of these approaches has ever yielded demonstrably effective methods of helping social work clients.

Another hindrance to progress has been our field's mindless adoption of so-called postmodernist (a.k.a. intellectual Luddites') views pertaining to scientific philosophy and epistemology, the promotion of "many ways of knowing," while ignoring the most important form of critical analysis there is: of knowing truth from falsehood, fiction from fact. Some social work writers advocate an intellectual solipsism, claiming that there is no such thing as objective reality, only social constructions of individualized perceptions. In this misguided view, understanding "meaning" is seen as more important than either ascertaining the facts of the case or social workers taking active responsibility to work with clients to alleviate the problems they bring to us. Try telling that to the homeless woman shivering in the cold, to the unemployed man, to the client with bipolar disorder, or to the child with AIDS. Some social workers have forgotten the insights of Bertha Capen Reynolds, one of social work's true pioneers:

> I believe that it is possible to understand scientifically the movement of social and economic forces and to apply our strength in cooperation with them. . . . At first glance it seems unnecessary to state that, if we believe in a *non-capricious and objectively reliable universe,* such belief also includes social and economic forces with which we can cooperate. Actually, we constantly deny this reliance on *objective reality* in favor of wishful fantasies. (Reynolds, 1963-1991, p. 315; italics added)

Our perspective on the future of social work, however, is an optimistic one. The vacuity of invalid, traditionally taught and subscribed-to human behavior and practice theories is gradually becoming apparent to the majority of dispassionate observers in the field, and their several generations of social work devotees are dying off, leaving the field to others more interested in promoting truth than ideology. The machinery of behavioral science continues to formulate and test theoretical propositions, coming ever closer to a valid understanding of the complexities of social problems and of individual pathologies. Applied researchers are constantly evaluating a variety of psychosocial interventions, and undeniable progress has been made in developing truly helpful ways to help clients. Social workers have been at the forefront of some of these developments—Janet Williams and the refinements of the *Diagnostic and Statistical Manual*; Gail Steketee and the treatment of clients with obsessive compulsive disorder; Christine McGill, Gerald Hogarty, and the development of effective psychoeducational interventions for the chronically mentally ill; Myrna Weissman and advances in psychiatric epidemiology, and her work in interpersonal psychotherapy for depression; Stephen Wong and positive behavioral treatment for schizophrenia; Sheldon Rose and his dozens of demonstrations of the value of social work in group contexts; and Steven Schinke's prevention studies in cancer, adolescent pregnancy, and drug abuse—to name but a few of the sterling practitioner-researchers in our field.

McMahon, Reisch, and Patti have rightly noted that:

> As never before, social work needs better, more demonstratively effective intervention technologies to use with client populations that present increasingly chronic and difficult problems. Professional practitioners simply require more usable information about what works with whom, under what circumstances. (1991, p. 5)

Well, such developments really are occurring, both within and without professional social work! Organized psychiatry and psychology are busy at work developing empirically based practice guidelines for helping clients with various so-called mental disorders. Clients are coming to be seen to have a right to effective treatment, where such knowledge exists, with "effective" implying psychosocial interventions that well-crafted clinical research has shown to be helpful. A new membership organization has been formed, the Society for Social Work and Research, dedicated to furthering the empirical knowledge base of our field, and new journals have been established

(e.g., *Research on Social Work Practice*, published by Sage Publications) that are explicitly dedicated to publishing empirically based outcome studies of relevance to social work practice and to practitioners.

Progress is also occurring on the practice evaluation front, with respect to individual social workers using single system research designs (SSRDs). Studies have shown that clients readily accept the use of this form of practice evaluation (e.g., Campbell, 1988, 1990), and SSRDs are being used by greater numbers of practitioners in ever more diverse areas of practice and in the evaluation of many forms of intervention (e.g., Gerdes, Edmonds, Haslam, & McCartney, 1996; Kazi & Wilson, 1996). To date, literally hundreds of social work articles, books, and chapters illustrate the use of SSRDs in clinical, community, and policy practice; these also add to the empirical foundations of our field.

What Can Be Done to Further the Integration of Research and Practice?

The Task Force on Social Work Research, sponsored by the National Institute of Mental Health, published a plan for research development within social work that contained useful proposals. If implemented, these practices would go far toward promoting our field as an empirically based human services profession. Among their recommendations to the Council on Social Work Education were the following (all italics added):

> Require that all areas of the foundation curriculum, including practice methods, be based on knowledge derived to the fullest extent possible from *research* in social work and from related professions and disciplines . . . should require that textbooks for practice methods courses be based to the fullest extent possible on *research-based knowledge* from social work and allied professions and disciplines. (Task Force, 1991, p. 82)

Both BSW and MSW programs should:

> increase significantly the attention given to *research-based knowledge* in the teaching of practice methods and to the *use of research methods* to examine practice effectiveness (p. 85)

and

> Faculty members should take increased responsibility for *incorporating research-based information* in the teaching of practice methods. (p. 90)

Remarkably, the National Association of Social Workers' Code of Ethics Revision Committee has put forth some proposed standards that bode well for the integration of research and practice. Among these are the following (all italics added):

> Social workers who function as educators, field instructors for students, or trainers should provide instruction based on the *most current information and knowledge* available in the profession. [pp. 21–22] . . . Continuing education and training should address *current knowledge* and emerging developments related to social work practice. . . . Social workers should base practice on *recognized knowledge, including empirically-based knowledge*, relevant to social work practice. . . . Social workers should critically examine and keep current with emerging knowledge relevant to social work and fully utilize *evaluation and research evidence* in their professional practice. (Code of Ethics Revision Committee, 1996, p. 22)

We support the Task Force's recommendations, as well as the above proposed changes to the NASW's Code of Ethics. Such initiatives support our belief that the profession is generally heading in the right direction. Flogged on by the whips of managed care companies to demonstrate our effectiveness; prodded by the harpies of evolving ethical standards of quality care; stimulated by research studies that demonstrate that selected psychosocial interventions are effective (and that some are not)—the social work oxcart trundles on toward the Elysium of empirical practice. Some are pulling the cart forward, others push it ahead, and a few have their feet hard on the brakes. Nevertheless, progress is being made. Here are some additional practices to hasten the good work.

Constructive Steps for Students, Practitioners, and Teachers

Practitioners and students really should insist that the practice methods they are taught in graduate school and in continuing education programs are those with a strong degree of credible empirical support, where such exists. There is little role for continuing to teach methods of social work practice that lack significant scientific support, particularly as favorable evidence mounts relating to the efficacy of other approaches. At present, virtually every major area of social work intervention *does* have some empirical literature of value to practitioners, in terms of providing guidance on helping clients. It is almost criminal not to formally adopt the professional ethic that we should rely, first and foremost, on these scientific findings.

In keeping with the Task Force's report, social work education should begin clearly mandating that the professional curriculum *must* teach theories of human behavior and methods of social work intervention that have credible amounts of scientifically credible empirical support with respect to their validity and usefulness, *where such knowledge already exists*. Outmoded and scientifically invalidated theories and practice methods have little place in the training of professional social workers. Schools could adopt as a graduation standard the requirement that students provide scientifically credible evidence that they have helped *at least one client*. Curiously, we find our colleagues often laugh when exposed to this latter suggestion. Why is it amusing?

Constructive Steps for
Social Work Researchers

Talented and experienced clinicians and other social work practitioners should be recruited into training programs focusing on services research. Talented and experienced researchers can spend sabbaticals doing social work practice, enriching both areas. Over time, the profession needs to build a much larger cadre of doctoral-level social workers trained as practitioners and as researchers. Moreover, a special kind of research training is called for, that of conducting outcome studies (see Montgomery & Thyer, 1988). Research content on conducting surveys and correlational studies should be deemphasized in favor of much more extensive training in using single-system research designs and small-scale group designs to conduct clinical and program evaluations at the agency level. Doctoral programs should make greater use of research practica and clinical-research internships. Many more doctoral graduates need expertise in evaluative/services research focusing on empirically testing the outcomes of social work interventions. As such studies get published, practitioners will naturally turn to this much more functional, journal-based literature for guidance.

Conclusions

Within the professional lifetime of the authors of this chapter, social work has made significant strides toward becoming an empirically based profession, guided of course by the traditional values and ethical commitments of the field. Considerable advances have been made in developing practitioner and client-friendly assessment methods useful in the initial appraisal of the client-in-environment and in monitoring the outcomes of practice. When these are combined with the use of SSRDs, each practitioner has the minimal tools needed to empirically demonstrate whether his or her client/system is improving over the course of social work intervention. Truly effective psychosocial interventions have been developed and can be used on a widespread scale, if we choose to adopt them. Large-scale contingencies being imposed by managed care companies, insurance carriers, and governmental agencies are hastening the integration of research into practice, and practice into research. Almost 80 years ago, Winston S. Churchill wrote to Lloyd George on the day after Christmas in 1918:

> I hope that you will gather together all forces of strength and influence in the country and lead them along the paths of science and organization to the rescue of the weak and the poor. (in Addison, 1993, p. 198)

Social work is in a better position now to fulfill Churchill's Christmas wish than ever before. To the extent that we provide evidence of effective, cost-saving, and humane social services, these will be gladly supported by the citizenry.

REFERENCES

Abbott, E. (1931). *Social welfare and professional education*. Chicago: University of Chicago Press.

Addison, P. (1993). *Churchill on the home front: 1900–1955*. London: Pimlico.

Campbell, J. A. (1988). Client acceptance of single-system evaluation procedures. *Social Work Research and Abstracts, 24*(2), 21–22.

Campbell, J. A. (1990). Ability of practitioners to estimate client acceptance of single-subject evaluation procedures. *Social Work, 35*, 9–14.

Code of Ethics Revision Committee. (1996, January). Proposal: Revision of the Code of Ethics. *NASW News, 41*(1), 19–23.

Dorfman, R. (Ed.). (1988). *Paradigms of clinical social work*. New York: Brunner/Mazel.

Dunlap, K. (1993). A history of research in social work education: 1915–1991. *Journal of Social Work Education, 29*, 293–301.

Gerdes, K., Edmonds, R. M., Haslam, D. R., & McCartney, T. (1996). A statewide survey of licensed clinical social workers' use of practice evaluation procedures. *Research on Social Work Practice, 6*, 27–39.

Kazi, M. A. F., & Wilson, J. (1996). Applying single-case evaluation methodology in a British social work agency. *Research on Social Work Practice, 6*, 5–26.

MacDonald, G., Sheldon, B., & Gillespie, J. (1992). Contemporary studies of the effectiveness of social work. *British Journal of Social Work, 22*, 615–643.

McMahon, M. O., Reisch, M., & Patti R. (1991). *Scholarship in social work: Integration of research, teaching, and service*. Washington, DC: National Association of Deans and Directors of Schools of Social Work.

Montgomery, D. F., & Thyer, B. A. (1988). Doctoral research on social work practice. *Journal of Social Work Education, 24*, 107–114.

Preston, M. G., & Mudd, E. H. (1956). Research and service in social work: Conditions for a stable union. *Social Work, 1*(1), 34–39.

Reid, W. R., & Hanrahan, P. (1982). Recent evaluations of social work: Grounds for optimism. *Social Work, 27*, 328–340.

Reynolds, B. C. (1991). *An uncharted journey*. Silver Spring, MD: NASW Press. (Originally published in 1963)

Smith, R. (1996, January). VA shake-up signals a role shift. *NASW News, 41*(1), 3.

Task Force on Social Work Research (1991). *Building social work knowledge for effective services and policies: A plan for research development*. Washington, DC: National Institute of Mental Health.

Thyer, B. A. (1995). Effective psychosocial treatments for children and adolescents: A selected review. *Early Child Development and Care, 106*, 137–147.

Todd, A. J. (1920). *The scientific spirit and social work*. New York: Macmillan.

Wallace. I., Wallace, A., Wallechinsky, D., & Wallace, D. (1981). *The intimate sex lives of famous people*. New York: Delacorte.

Social Work Education

Current Concerns and Possible Futures

Eileen Gambrill

*It is through social work education that profession-
als are assumed to acquire the knowledge, skills,
and values uniquely related to the profession. How
well are we doing our job? How can the present
inform the future? The author calls on social work
educators to move from a current emphasis on
indoctrination of students to one emphasizing the
education of students and suggests a problem-
focused model of practice emphasizing critical
thinking. Eileen Gambrill is professor of social welfare, University of California at Berkeley. Recent
publications include* Critical Thinking in Clinical
Practice *(1990),* Critical Thinking for Social Workers: A Workbook *(with Leonard Gibbs) (1996),*
Debating Children's Lives *(with Mary Ann Mason)
(1994), and* Social Work Practice: A Critical
Thinker's Guide *(1997). Her areas of interest
include professional decision making, professional
education, and social skills training.*

Educators in professional programs bear a
heavy burden. They have an obligation to
encourage values, knowledge, and skills that
help professionals to provide services that are
most likely to help clients and not harm them.
The possession and use of specialized knowledge and skills is basic to a profession. Society
allots unique privileges to members of a profession based on the supposition that they possess and use certain kinds of expertise others do
not have. The Council on Social Work Education identifies educational standards and re-

views departments of social work to determine
if they are adhering to these standards. Based
on these reviews, accreditation is offered,
renewed, or removed. This process assumes
that there is specialized knowledge and that
accreditors can determine if this knowledge is
being transferred to students.

Thinking carefully about educational
aims, content, and formats is important not
only because of professional obligations to the
users of services, but also because of obligations to students to provide an education.
How is social work education faring today?
Does it produce well-educated social workers
who bring to their work the knowledge, skills,
and values that are most likely to help them
achieve outcomes pursued? If not, why not?
Does anyone know the extent to which this
aim is achieved? This would require clear
identification of tasks related to outcomes
sought via task analyses and systematic investigation of the degree to which different skill
levels relate to different outcome levels. There
are no shortcuts. This research has not been
done for reasons suggested later in this essay.
Does the quality of education for social workers matter? One condition under which it
would not is if the problems clients confront
are not solvable and therefore social workers
cannot help clients other than to support them
in their difficult situations. But if this is so, do

we need professional education? In *House of Cards* (1994), Robin Dawes argues that research shows that nonprofessionals are as helpful as professionals with many problems clients confront. Is social work education just a house of cards? In this essay, I will first suggest what is wrong with social work education. Then I will suggest reasons and remedies.

What's Wrong with Social Work Education

As Sir Karl Popper (1972, 1992) has argued, we can only move forward through criticism, through subjecting even our most cherished views to careful scrutiny. The concerns raised here are in this spirit.

Indoctrination Rather Than Education

The main concern I had as a social work student many years ago remains a key one today: indoctrination rather than education. In my master's social work education, I encountered claims asserted on the grounds of authority as well as criticism for questioning such claims. (Exceptions included the excellent research courses I took and the course on social services.) There was a clear expectation that we, the students, should be satisfied with the pronouncements of authorities and that if we were not, something was wrong with us. I found this remarkable and upsetting.

Differences between education on the one hand and schooling/indoctrination on the other highlight the emphasis on students learning to think critically for themselves in education rather than relying on authority. Education is conjecture-based rather than belief-based. It is reason-based rather than authority-based. All claims, no matter who makes them, are subject to critical testing and discussion. It is contextual rather than parochial. It is self-corrective. Education requires presenting alternative views on subjects, critically appraising arguments for claims/positions, accurately describing alternative points of view, and questioning accepted views. Knowledge is viewed as tentative, ambiguous, and hard to get. Students as well as instructors are *critically* reflective (not just reflective). Understanding is emphasized rather than memorizing. Discordant points of view have quite different fates in education compared with indoctrination. They are welcomed in the former and punished or censored in the latter. Education seeks to inform, to enlighten, to deepen understanding. In contrast, in authority-based programs, ignorance of alternative views and related evidence is promoted through propagandistic methods such as disregarding relevant evidence, appealing to self-interest, and encouraging beliefs and actions with the least thought possible (Ellul, 1965).

The Active Promotion of Ignorance

Ignorance is actively promoted in social work in a number of ways. One way is through punishment of criticism (e.g., ridiculing questions about popular views). Another is through censorship (e.g., telling students not to read outside of social work), not presenting arguments and evidence against popular points of view, and covering up scandals (e.g., harming clients in the name of helping). Previous literature may be ignored. For example, descriptions of the "strengths perspective" rarely mention the constructional approach described in *Social Casework: A Behavioral Approach* by Schwartz and Goldiamond (1975). When I taught at Michigan from 1967 to 1970, all students had to take courses in social deviance, and basic behavioral principles. This is no longer true. I think we have moved backward in some important ways in social work education.

Encouraging antiscience is another way ignorance is promoted. Knowledge can advance only through criticism. Students are too often exposed to a variety of competing theories, with little concern about whether they are contradictory or the extent to which related predictions have been critically tested. Although intuition is an invaluable source of ideas and how to critically test them, other methods are needed to test them, such as controlled experimental studies that consider multiple sources of bias and rival views. Antiscience is rife in academia as well as without (Burnham, 1987; Gross & Levitt, 1994). We proclaim we want to help clients, yet argue that all ways of knowing are equally valid (see the essay by Tomi Gomory in this section). Ignorance is also promoted through pseudoscience [i.e., material that makes sciencelike claims but provides no evidence for them (Bunge, 1984)]. This produces faith and belief but not knowledge; claims are not critically tested. Quackery flourishes in the helping professions, including social work. This refers to the promotion and marketing of untested, often worthless, and sometimes dangerous health products and methods either by professionals or others for a profit (Jarvis, 1990).

Ignoring the Results of Educational Research
Sporadic calls for taking advantage of research regarding what educational methods work best for what purpose in educating social workers have largely fallen on deaf ears. Lack of integration of research findings about learning in the design of educational formats is troubling in professional programs in which there is an obligation to offer clients high-quality service. A rich data source exists about learning (e.g., Gagne, 1987; Voss, 1989). However, this information has not been drawn on in the design of social work programs. Literature related to the acquisition of new skills indicates that repeated opportunities to observe expert models is important. Yet students have few opportunities to watch experts conduct interviews (Barth & Gambrill, 1984). Often, if not typically, feedback offered both in the classroom and in the field is indirect and vague. Such feedback is not the best kind to enhance expertise.

Not Assessing Competencies and Outcomes
Because few instructors evaluate acquisition of values, knowledge, skills, and outcomes attained, no one knows if hoped for outcomes increase, decrease, or do not change (Kameoka & Lister, 1991; Wodarski, Feit, & Green, 1995). Rarely do social work educators assess students' background knowledge and provide ongoing assessment of learning outcomes as students move through educational programs. For all we know, students graduate with more inert knowledge (material that is relevant but is not used because of a lack of accompanying performance skills), more irrelevant knowledge (knowledge that does not contribute to problem solving), and more false knowledge (beliefs that are not true and that are not questioned) than when they started their programs. This removes valuable opportunities to prepare individually designed learning programs that maximize acquisition of competencies and help students develop self-assessment skills they can use to update knowledge over their careers.

Prevalence of Fads and Rituals
Like other professions, social work is subject to fads—short-term infatuations with an idea or method with little or no critical testing of conjectures. Disseminating untested methods is not a benign event. It may result in false promises and harm to clients, as illustrated by the history of facilitated communication (Jacobson, Mulick, & Schwartz, 1995) and

repressed memory therapy (Offshe & Watters, 1994). Abandoning interest usually does not rest on selection of more abstract theories that can account for a broader range of events; this would be all to the good.

Ritualistic practices that presume to address a goal but do not are common in social work. Consider the task of identifying practice competencies. This requires task analyses in which those who are successful in achieving valued outcomes are observed and specific related patterns of behavior are identified, including their sequence and contexts. The relation of these behaviors to attainment of valued outcomes must be systematically investigated. Instead, competencies are often identified by asking social workers what they believe is important. This is just the beginning, not the end. Many have pointed out the fashions and fads in academia and the need to align one's self with reigning fashions to get ahead. Consider, for example, the moving account of William Bartley in the introduction to *Unfathomable Knowledge* (1990): "I learned that it is prudent for someone who wishes to prosper within the halls of academe to align himself with the reigning fashion. If he does so, dropping the right names and the right slogans, he may say, discretely and indirectly, almost anything he wants—including any nonsense" (p. xvii).

Other Concerns

We expect our students to continue to upgrade their knowledge and skills over their careers, yet do not help them acquire effective self-directed learning skills. There is little integration of knowledge in social work education or coordination of teaching. The curriculum is broken into individual parts—policy, methods, research—with few efforts to integrate them.

There is a lack of integration between class and field. There has long been an "add-on" approach in social work education, in which we simply add new content, resulting in an unintegrated and (often) undigestible mix. This fragmentation gets in the way of learning (e.g., seeing the interrelationships among different areas). Obscurantism abounds. The more obscure, the more profound content may be viewed (Armstrong, 1980). Key aims espoused often remain undefined. For example, the term *social justice* is often accepted as understood and as a good thing to pursue. Hayek (1976) argues that because there are different views about what social justice consists of, pursuing vague, related outcomes inevitably involves imposing some people's view of social justice on others.

Causes of Lost Opportunities for Education

An economic perspective on knowledge encourages us to think about production costs. Educating students requires considerable time and effort on the part of faculty (e.g., reading and critically evaluating competing views of topics and related empirical studies—not just secondary reports, but the original studies). Indoctrination takes much less time and effort on the part of both students and faculty. Simply making pronouncements about what is or what is not saves time. (No time for criticism or for acquiring accurate understanding of competing views is needed.) Think what time is saved by a relativist position in which all ways of knowing are viewed as equally valid.

Many writers have noted the changes in universities. In Philip Reiff's (1985) view of higher education: "Less and less is taught by more and more managers of the false knowledge industry or by gurus of experimental life, who help nothing by their teachings" (p. 97). Fiscal concerns rather than knowledge development may be uppermost. Prestige may be based on the amount of research funds one has rather than on the extent to which the results of research programs add to understanding. Hersen and Miller (1992) note that a typical question asked of colleagues is: "How large is your grant?" rather than, "What are you investigating?" The pressure on academics to publish as well as teach, serve on committees, design curriculum, press faculty for time. Obscurantism lessens time pressures, as does teaching within, rather than about, frameworks. The Institute of Medicine (1989) concluded that, "Not only does the pressure to publish lead to the practices of repetitive publication, trivial work, and loose authorship, but it may also tempt researchers to engage in serious misconduct to achieve publishable results" (p. 32). Criticism that is so central to education and knowledge building conflicts with the social bonding functions of false knowledge, such as cooperation and protection of shared beliefs from critical review (Munz, 1985). By false knowledge, Munz refers to beliefs that are not true and that are not questioned. Protectionism and anticompetition decrease production costs and also provide security. Bartley (1990) argues "that individuals working in educational institutions are as self interested as businessmen, but that the organizational framework in which they operate—the network of incentives, constraints, and sanctions—tends to work against public benefit, and does so just because educational and professional institutions work contrary to market principles" (p. 100). Bartley argues that there is a great deal of "anti-competitive activity by intellectuals" (p. 102) and notes that the view that one discipline may not stand in judgment of another is anticompetitive. As Bartley points out, academics may even use slogans such as "intellectual freedom" or "the free market of ideas" to maintain a protectionist environment that is quite the opposite.

Attachment to theories gets in the way of their critical examination. William Bartley (1990, p. 253) refers to a quote from the Buddha, which states, "Even this view, which is so pure and so clear, if you cling to it, if you fondle it, if you treasure it, if you are attached to it, then you do not understand that our teaching is similar to a raft, which is for crossing over, and not for keeping hold of" (Trenckner, 1960–1964, p. 160). The evolutionary influences of ranking and status also pose an obstacle. Maintaining rank as an authority may be viewed as more important than forwarding knowledge (Gilbert, 1989). Confusing political and educational aims creates an obstacle to education. Criticism of questionable claims and requests for clarification of their real-life consequences is often viewed as politically incorrect rather than as a quest for knowledge. A view of education as therapy is an obstacle. Misunderstanding of science is yet another obstacle. There are pretensions to greater scientific status than exist in many social work reports. The problems that social work addresses are difficult if not unsolvable, and "there are the social constraints forced by the pretense of maturity" in a field in which there is not maturity (Ravetz, 1996, p. 366). As Ravetz suggests, "the situation becomes worse when an immature or ineffective field is enlisted in the work of resolution of some practical problem." In such contexts, especially when political passions are intense, the function of "knowledge" may be not to advance understanding "but to offer comfort and reassurance for some body of believers" (see also Munz, 1985).

Proposals for the Future

Suggested changes for the future are discussed in the following sections.

Shift to a Problem-Focused Educational Model Emphasizing Critical Discussion

I suggest that we can best pursue education rather than schooling or indoctrination by shifting to a problem-focused teaching model emphasizing critical discussion and testing and the importance of transferring useful competencies to the field (Gambrill, 1997). The problem-solving nature of social work practice has been emphasized for some time, however related scientific literature has been ignored. It is time we take advantage of this. Problem-focused education in which the entire curriculum is organized around learning via problems clients confront has been explored in medicine for many years (e.g., Barrows, 1994). "Problem-led" learning in social work has recently been introduced in England (Burgess, 1992). The model suggested here emphasizes the importance of taking advantage of scientific research related to problem-solving, professional decision making, critical thinking, and education. It emphasizes knowledge development through criticism and the importance of drawing on problem-related scientific literature in making practice decisions. There is a rich literature on problem solving and decision making lying in many different fields (see, for example, Gambrill, 1990, 1997) that has not been integrated into social work even though many authors emphasize its problem-solving nature.

A problem focus grounds content squarely on practice concerns, highlights key decisions and related questions and options, and links curriculum areas in a manner that reflects everyday practice concerns (e.g., research and practice, policy and practice, knowledge about human behavior and the environment, and

practice decisions). It highlights common errors in different decision phases and how we can avoid them, as well as resources needed. It emphasizes the unstructured and uncertain nature of problem solving and provides many opportunities to help students develop skills for this. Focusing on problems of concern to clients and/or significant others in no way implies that client strengths are overlooked. It would be a poor problem solver indeed who did not take advantage of both personal and environmental resources. If students do not have a field work placement, examples could be drawn from the literature or presented via interactive computer programs. A curriculum focused on problems that clients confront provides multiple opportunities to integrate knowledge from different domains (e.g., human behavior and the social environment, practice methods, research, policy) and to transfer knowledge to real-life practice contexts.

Value Criticism as the Key Route to Knowledge

We must shift from being believers to being questioners. Discussions in social work are too often *within* frameworks rather than *about* them (Popper, 1994). Criteria such as authority, tradition, anecdotal experience, and popularity are often relied on to support claims. Pronouncements are made without accompanying argument or evidence. Only through criticism of our guesses about what is helpful in solving problems (critical discussion and testing) can we discover errors, learn more about problems, and take timely corrective action. Principles that Karl Popper (1992) highlights as the basis of every rational discussion include the following:

1. The principle of fallibility; perhaps I am wrong and perhaps you are right. But we could easily both be wrong.

2. The principle of rational discussion: we want to try, as impersonally as possible, to weigh up our reasons for and against a theory: a theory that is definite and criticizable.

3. The principle of approximation to the truth: we can nearly always come closer to the truth in a discussion which avoids personal attacks. It can help us to achieve a better understanding; even in those areas where we do not reach an agreement. (p. 199)

How different this is compared to reliance on authority—the acceptance of claims based on what someone pronounces as true.

Karl Popper (1994) defines truth as the correspondence of statements with facts. Valuing truth over prejudice and ignorance entails critically testing claims and conclusions. If a community organizer says, "I helped this community," this statement should correspond with the facts (e.g., residents report that they have been helped because there is a new park, a new recreation center, a citizen's advisory center, and a day-care facility for toddlers.) Only through evaluation of plans, programs, and policies can we discover if they achieve valued goals. If a program developer says my plan will help clients find housing, we should carefully examine whether this is accomplished. Given the inevitability of unintended consequences from any policy, plan, or program, we can never predict with certainty what will occur. Evaluation is but a small and necessary cost compared to lost opportunities to discover unwanted effects and correct them at an early point. As Karl Popper (1994) emphasized, relying on unexamined claims about what is true reflects an arrogance that is at odds with a compassion for others. "It is important never to forget our ignorance. *We should therefore never pretend to know anything, and we should never use big words. What I call the cardinal sin . . . is simply taking hot air, professing a wisdom we do not possess"* (Popper, 1992, p. 86). We have "the obligation

never to pose as a prophet" (Popper, 1992, p. 206). The "prophet motive" (Jarvis, 1990) will be difficult to resist given the public's interest in soothsayers.

Critical thinking values, knowledge, and skills should be infused throughout the curriculum to achieve a community of inquiry that is responsive to real-life problems of clients (Lipman, 1991). In a community of inquiry, there is:

- a focus on critical discussion and testing of claims rather than on justifying them

- an awareness that we are all equal in our vast ignorance

- a valuing of truth over ignorance and prejudice

- an appreciation of errors and mistakes as learning opportunities

- a discarding of authority as a sound basis of knowledge

- a view of knowledge as hypothetical/ tentative

- a valuing of clashing points of view as invaluable for discovering approximation to the truth.

Those in a community of inquiry recognize the value of clashing of points of view and their careful consideration in relation to specific problems. We should offer educational units on propaganda analysis, in which students learn to recognize propagandistic human service advertisements and to avoid their influence (Gibbs & Gambrill, 1996). We can conduct research ferreting out common errors in social work decision making and create aids for avoiding them. We can determine the ratio of inert to functional knowledge in each course. We can apply a propaganda/scholarship index to any course, sequence of courses, or entire curriculums to determine the ratio of propaganda to scholarship (Gambrill, 1992). Moving to a falsification approach to knowledge that emphasizes that we can only discover what is false would have a number of benefits, such as encouraging correct appraisals of current approximation to truth. The impossibility of arriving at knowledge via induction has been well argued by Karl Popper.

Take Advantage of the Results of Educational Research

We can use teaching methods that research suggests are most likely to help students acquire knowledge and skills (see, for example, Brookfield, 1990; Gagne, 1987; Nickerson & Zodhiates, 1988) and evaluate the effectiveness of our teaching. For example, we could test whether a case-based, problem-focused model emphasizing critical thinking enhances (or detracts from) acquisition of valued outcomes. Teaching formats that could be explored include peer learning, self-paced learning through interactive computer programs, apprenticeships in selected content areas (e.g., clearly defining outcomes to focus on), and multiple opportunities for self-assessment of learning.

Identify Competencies That Influence Outcomes Attained

There has long been an interest in identifying competencies in social work (see, for example, Clark, Arkava, & Associates, 1979). To the extent we can identify value, knowledge, performance, and outcome competencies—what skilled social workers in a certain area should know, be able to do, value, and achieve—we are in a better position to teach this content and review the extent to which we have succeeded. Identifying professional competencies required to achieve valued outcomes is an important goal. However, this will require systematic

investigation as discussed earlier. Here at Berkeley the opinions of child welfare staff and others are sought to identify competencies. These opinions are not expert opinions (they are not from people with a known track record of success in achieving certain outcomes). There are no shortcuts to this knowledge.

Other Steps

We will be more likely to chart a successful course for the future if we understand the influence of the context (universities and their external environment) in which social work programs exist and rearrange contingencies to encourage a community of inquirers in contrast to a community of believers. Valuing criticism as the route to knowledge will require creating contingencies that promote knowledge development and education through criticism of ideas. We can arrange for ongoing assessment of educational outcomes and help students acquire effective learning skills they can draw on over their careers. We can integrate field and class more closely.

The National Association of Social Workers should take a more active role in encouraging systematic investigation of the accuracy of claims and a more active role in disseminating what is known and what is not about methods used by social workers. They should take a major role in disseminating critical reviews of specific service methods and sponsor incisive reviews. (See, for example, reports from the Cochrane Collaboration.) NASW could provide awards for the best critical reviews of the year. The Council on Social Work Education could develop an index permitting accurate description of the extent to which effective teaching formats are used in social work programs. This index could be created based on the results of systematic research concerning the effectiveness of different methods. Reviews could be based on a random sample of formats used in classrooms. They could give yearly awards for the best designed studies of the effectiveness of given educational formats. Accreditation teams talk to students and thus get hearsay evidence. They review course outlines. Why not test a random sample of students to determine the extent to which values, knowledge, and skills have been acquired (or lost). Students' evaluations may reflect the popularity of teachers rather than what is learned (Brookfield, 1990). They could explore how the ratio of inert, irrelevant, false, and functional knowledge changes as students move through a program. Perhaps students acquire more inert, false, and irrelevant knowledge compared to functional knowledge during their educational experience in social work. CSWE review teams could evaluate the extent to which students move from a justificationist point of view, in which they seek support for their views, to a falsification one, in which they critically examine their beliefs. They could evaluate the extent to which students move from an approach to knowledge in which they think *within* theories to an approach in which they think *about* them.

Summary

Planning for the future offers opportunities to reflect on where we have been and where we want to go. It provides new opportunities to regroup and explore new directions. Looking back, we can see lost opportunities in social work education. Social work could take the lead in developing a problem-focused model for uncertain helping situations and developing educational formats and tools for teaching and continuing to refine it. We can develop interactive computer programs, flow-charts, and visual aids that help students acquire valuable skills and make the best decisions possible in their everyday work. The future offers an opportunity to create communities of inquiry in which critical discussion and testing of claims is valued and demonstrated. Both clients and students deserve more than rhetoric. We can take advantage of natural opportunities to conduct experimental studies regarding practice and educational questions. We can work together to create communities of inquiry in which criticism is valued as the route to knowledge. We can value truth over certainty, ignorance over prejudice. We can work together as colleagues in a community of questioners to create and maintain high-quality educational programs that truly prepare social workers for the work that awaits them. Only if social work turns toward education and away from indoctrination does the future bode well, especially for consumers of social work services. There must be no sacred cows in a profession dedicated to helping clients, especially when the sacred cows get in the way of helping clients and avoiding harm.

REFERENCES

Armstrong, J. C. (1980). Unintelligible management research and academic prestige. *Interfaces, 10,* 80–86.

Barrows, H. S. (1994). *Practice-based learning: Problem-based learning applied to medical education.* Springfield, IL: Southern Illinois University School of Medicine.

Barth, R. P., & Gambrill, E. (1984). Learning to interview: The quality of training opportunities. *The Clinical Supervisor, 2,* 3–14.

Bartley, W. W., III. (1987). Alienation alienated: The economics of knowledge versus the psychology and sociology of knowledge. In G. Radnitzky & W. W. Bartley, III (Eds.), *Evolutionary epistemology, rationality, and the sociology of knowledge* (pp. 423–451). LaSalle, IL: Open Court.

Bartley, W. W., III. (1990). *Unfathomed knowledge, unmeasured wealth: On universities and the wealth of nations*. LaSalle, IL: Open Court.

Brookfield, S. D. (1990). *The skillful teacher*. San Francisco: Jossey-Bass.

Bunge, M. (1984). What is pseudoscience? *The Skeptical Inquirer, 9*, 36–47.

Burgess, H. (1992). *Problem-led learning for social work: The enquiry and action approach*. London: Whiting and Birch.

Burnham, J. C. (1987). *How superstitition won and science lost: Popularizing science and health in the United States*. New Brunswick, NJ: Rutgers University Press.

Clark, F. W., Arkava, M. L., & Associates. (1979). *The pursuit of competence in social work*. San Francisco: Jossey-Bass.

Cochrane Collaboration Center. Summertown Pavilion. Middle Way, Oxford, U.K. 0X2 7LG.

Dawes, R. M. (1994). *House of cards: Psychology and psychotherapy built on myth*. New York: Free Press.

Ellul, J. (1965). *Propaganda: The formation of man's attitudes*. New York: Vintage.

Gagne, R. M. (Ed.). (1987). *Instructional technology: Foundations*. Hillsdale, NJ: Erlbaum.

Gambrill, E. (1990). *Critical thinking in clinical practice: Improving the accuracy of judgments and decisions about clients*. San Francisco: Jossey-Bass.

Gambrill, E. (1992). Scholarship and propaganda: What's the difference? Paper presented at the 12th Annual International Conference on Critical Thinking, Santa Rosa, CA.

Gambrill, E. (1996). Thinking critically about social work education in a time of scarce resources. Presented at the annual program meeting of the Council of Social Work Education, February, 1996.

Gambrill, E. (1997). *Social work practice: A critical thinker's guide*. New York: Oxford University Press.

Gibbs, L., & Gambrill, E. (1996). *Critical thinking for social workers: A workbook*. Thousand Oaks, CA: Pine Forge Press.

Gilbert, P. (1989). *Human nature and suffering*. New York: Guilford.

Gross, P. R., & Levitt, N. (1994). *Higher superstitition: The academic left and its quarrels with science*. Baltimore, MD: Johns Hopkins University Press.

Hayek, F. A. (1976). *Law, legislation and liberty*. Vol. 2: *The mirage of social justice*. Chicago: University of Chicago Press.

Hersen, M., & Miller, D. J. (1992). Future directions: A model proposal. In D. J. Miller & M. Hersen (Eds.), *Research fraud in the behavioral and biomedical sciences* (pp. 225–243). New York: John Wiley.

Institute of Medicine. (1989). *Report of a study: The responsible conduct of research in the health sciences*. Washington, DC: National Academy Press.

Jacobson, J., Mulick, J. A., & Schwartz, A. A. (1995). A history of facilitated communication: Science, pseudoscience, and antiscience. Group on facilitative communication. *American Psychologist, 50*, 750–765.

Jarvis, W. T. (1990). *Dubious dentistry: A dental continuing education course*. Loma Linda, CA.

Kameoka, V. A., & Lister, L. (1991). Evaluation of student learning outcomes in MSW programs. *Journal of Social Work Education, 27*(3), 251–257.

Lipman, M. (1991). *Thinking in education*. Cambridge: Cambridge University Press.

Lloyd, J. E. (1985). Selling scholarship down the river: The pernicious aspects of peer review. *The Chronicle of Higher Education*, June 26, 1985, p. 64.

Munz, P. (1985). *Our knowledge of the growth of knowledge: Popper or Wittgenstein*. London: Routledge and Kegan Paul.

Nickerson, R. S., & Zodhiates, P. P. (1988). *Technology in education: Looking forward toward 2020*. Hillsdale, NJ: Erlbaum.

Offshe, R., & Watters, E. (1994). *Making monsters: False memories, psychotherapy, and sexual hysteria*. New York: Scribner's.

Popper, K. R. (1972). *Conjectures and refutations: The growth of scientific knowledge* (4th ed.). London: Routledge and Kegan Paul.

Popper, K. (1992). *In search of a better world: Lectures and essays from thirty years*. New York: Routledge.

Popper, K. (1994). *The myth of the framework: In defense of science and rationality*. London: Routledge.

Ravetz, J. R. (1996). *Scientific knowledge and its social problems*. New Brunswick: Transaction Publishers. (Originally published in 1971)

Reiff, P. (1985). *Fellow teachers: A culture and its second death*. Chicago: University of Chicago Press.

Schwartz, A., & Goldiamond, I. (1975). *Social casework: A behavioral approach*. New York: Columbia.

Trenckner, V. (Ed.). (1960–1964). *Majjhima-nikaya*. London: Pali Text Society.

Voss, J. F. (1989). Problem solving in the educational process. In A. Lesgold and R. Glaser (Eds.), *Foundations of a psychology of education*. Hillsdale, NJ: Laurence Erlbaum.

Wodarski, J. S., Feit, M. D., & Green, R. K. (1995). Graduate social work education: A review of 2 decades of empirical research and considerations for the future. *Social Service Review, 69,* 108–130.

Social Work and Psychiatry

Toward a Conceptually Based Partnership

Jerome C. Wakefield

The author explores the past relationship between social work and psychiatry and suggests that the relationship between these two professions will become more closely linked in the future. He suggests that this increasing intertwinement will occur based on the conceptual foundations of the two professions. Jerome C. Wakefield is professor in the School of Social Work at Rutgers University and also in the Institute for Health, Health Care Policy, and Aging Research at the same university. He also is lecturer in psychiatry at the College of Physicians and Surgeons of Columbia University. He has published extensively in the areas of defining mental disorder, distributive justice, and epistemology.

What can we expect—and hope for—in the next century in the long-evolving relationship between social work and psychiatry? The relationship is already an intimate one, to the point of provoking controversy about whether psychotherapy is swallowing up the broader social work field (Specht, 1990; Specht & Courtney, 1994; Wakefield, 1992c, 1992d). Nonetheless, I will argue that in the next century, we can expect to see social work and psychiatry enter into an even more integrated relationship than now exists, and one that is much more of an equal partnership. The professional "team" concept will, I believe, take on a new and more profound meaning, and the relationship between the two professions, while retaining many of its present elements, will have an additional, qualitatively different, complementary component. Not only is this likely to happen, but there are reasons why it should happen.

This further intertwining of social work and psychiatry will occur, I maintain, not primarily for reasons of professional self-interest, turf wars, status, reimbursement incentives, or even cost-containment—although the fact that social workers are less expensive than psychiatrists will certainly play an important role—or because of any of the other usual suspects. The reasons go much deeper and are much more interesting than that, and concern the very conceptual foundations of the two professions. The American Psychiatric Association's *Diagnostic and Statistical Manual of Mental Disorders*, 4th Edition (DSM-IV) (American Psychiatric Association, 1994) is used throughout the mental health professions and is likely to remain dominant, in its future editions, through the next century. However, there is a fundamental conceptual problem at the very heart of *DSM-IV*'s approach to diagnosis, and this problem has implications that make it necessary and appropriate for social work and psychiatry to forge an even closer link than they now have.

The essential conceptual problem is this: *DSM-IV* specifies that psychiatric disorders must be caused by a dysfunction in some internal mental mechanism; that is, something must have gone wrong with the workings of the mechanism itself (Spitzer & Endicott, 1978). However, when it comes to diagnostic criteria, *DSM-IV* defines psychiatric disorders in terms of observable symptoms. Symptom-based criteria have been embraced of necessity, because they are the best way to achieve *DSM*'s goals of reliability (i.e., the criteria should lead to the same diagnosis every time, no matter who is using them) and theory neutrality (i.e., the criteria should not be based on concepts that are special to any one theory or approach). However, there turns out to be an unanticipated problem with symptomatic criteria—namely, they are not able to distinguish between genuine disorders (i.e., internal dysfunctions) and normal reactions to problems in living. The very same "symptoms" that may indicate a psychiatric disorder may instead indicate a normal response to an adverse social environment. For example, the same intense sadness that satisfies *DSM-IV* criteria for the diagnosis of Major Depressive Disorder could be indicative of a genuine depressive disorder in which there is something wrong with one's sadness-response mechanisms, or it could result from a normal response to a serious loss; the same antisocial conduct that satisfies *DSM-IV* criteria for the diagnosis of Conduct Disorder or Antisocial Personality Disorder could be indicative of a genuine mental disorder resulting from a dysfunction in, for example, the sense of empathy, or it could be the result of a normal response to adverse, deprived, or otherwise criminogenic environments; and the same intense anxiety that satisfies *DSM-IV* criteria for a diagnosis of Generalized Anxiety Disorder could be indicative of a genuine anxiety disorder that involves inappropriate triggering of anxiety response mechanisms, or it could indicate a normal response to overwhelming environmental demands. In these cases and many more, the "symptoms" of a normal

response to an adverse environment, where nothing is wrong with the workings of the internal mechanisms, can satisfy *DSM-IV* diagnostic criteria for the corresponding mental disorder. Yet, such normal responses are not true mental disorders in the medical sense that *DSM-IV* embraces. Thus, *DSM-IV* criteria often do not successfully distinguish between true mental disorders, which are within the domain of psychiatry, and problems in the interaction of persons and environments, which are within the province of social work.

In effect, this means that *DSM-IV* categories in fact (contrary to their medical intent) overlap substantially with social work's domain. This flaw in *DSM-IV* makes greater involvement of social workers in the mental health system inevitable. People with normal responses to adverse environments must be distinguished from people with breakdowns in internal mechanisms, whether or not they are incorrectly labeled as disordered for reimbursement purposes. Effective treatment depends on such a discrimination of causes; the alternative is chronic misdiagnosis and mistreatment of nondisordered clients. Yet, psychiatrists are neither motivated nor trained to deal with environmental diagnosis or treatment. As it becomes apparent that the symptoms that determine *DSM-IV* diagnosis do not indicate whether there exists a mental disorder or an interactional problem, it will become necessary to routinely involve social workers and psychiatrists in teams that can diagnose and treat both internal dysfunctional causes and interactional, environmental causes of a patient's symptoms.

Before I explore these points more systematically, note two caveats: First, I am saying that these changes will probably happen and that in any case they ought to happen. In order to avoid awkward repetition of "probably will or in any event should," the reader is hereby notified that, whatever specific words I use in a given sentence, I am offering both a prediction and a proposal. Second, there are obviously many other important fields of social work besides the mental health field. Controversies about social work's role in psychiatry are usually concerned with the degree to which mental health concerns are eclipsing traditional roles of social work. However, I am concerned here only with social workers who serve in the mental health system, not with the relative importance of such work within social work's overall mission. Everything that I suggest here with respect to the increasing involvement of social workers in the mental health field is compatible with an increasingly vigorous engagement in other areas of social work concern as well.

Professional Missions of Psychiatry and Social Work

Although many considerations enter into society's decisions to assign certain roles to a profession, the most fundamental consideration of all is the profession's basic mission and, to a lesser extent, the skills it possesses to pursue that mission. Even if a task is very much unlike other tasks pursued by a profession and requires quite different skills, it will still generally be given to a profession if it clearly falls within that profession's domain as defined by its basic mission. So, for example, although psychotherapy has very little to do with any traditional medical skills, the fact that psychotherapy is a technique for helping those with mental disorders has led to psychiatrists being trained in this specialty. Tasks that are assigned because they fit the purpose of a profession may be dubbed the "essential" tasks of the profession (Wakefield, 1988a, 1988b). Even when a task falls outside a profession's mission, if the task requires the profession's skills, then it is

likely to be given to that profession. Such tasks might be called "derived" tasks because they are derived from the skills the profession happens to possess rather than a direct outcome of the profession's mission (Wakefield, 1988a, 1988b). For example, even though large areas of cosmetic surgery have no relationship to health (e.g., nose jobs, breast augmentation, face lifts), the medical profession is, nonetheless, sanctioned to do such surgery because it possesses the requisite surgical skills. However, unless there are strong overriding reasons, a profession's mission usually takes precedence over other, more practical factors in determining professional tasks.

Psychiatry and social work clearly have very different overall missions, and their future relationship will largely be determined by these missions. Psychiatry is defined as a medical profession that deals with mental disorder. If psychiatry is indeed to be a viable medical discipline, it must distinguish mental disorders—that is, conditions where something has gone wrong with how the mind is supposed to work—from the many other problems of living with which human beings must contend. "Disorder," in the medical sense, refers only to those negative conditions caused by an internal dysfunction. A dysfunction occurs when something goes wrong with the functioning of some internal mechanism, so that it is no longer capable of performing its natural function, which is the function for which it was designed by natural selection (Wakefield, 1992a). For example, when the heart cannot adequately pump the blood to oxygenate the cells of the body, that is a dysfunction because the heart was naturally selected to pump the blood and oxygenate the cells; and when the eyes cannot see, that is a dysfunction because the function of the eyes is to make one capable of seeing. A mental disorder occurs when the dysfunctional mechanism is one of those that form the "mind," such as mechanisms concerned with motivation, perception, thinking, emotion, language, learning, socialization, and other basic psychological functions (these mechanisms are still largely unknown, but we can infer that they exist from human capacities). When such a mechanism breaks down and becomes incapable of performing its functions, that is a mental dysfunction; if the dysfunction causes harm to the individual, there is a mental disorder.

DSM-IV itself provides a definition of mental disorder that underscores these points. *DSM-IV* asserts that mental disorders, like all medical disorders, are distresses or disabilities resulting from internal dysfunctions (American Psychiatric Association, 1994, p. xxi).

Obviously, there are many ways that internal mental mechanisms can go wrong. For example, the mechanisms that mediate sadness responses can produce deep sadness reactions despite the lack of an appropriate environmental situation that would warrant the sadness, thus causing depression. The mechanisms that generate appropriate fear and anxiety responses to environmental dangers may fire inappropriately, leading to panic attacks and generalized anxiety (Barlow, 1988, 1991). The brain mechanisms responsible for producing rational thought may break down, leading to psychotic conditions. The mechanisms that allow children to be socialized and to internalize moral rules may not function properly, and thus some children may suffer from disorders of conduct. And, attentional mechanisms or learning mechanisms may not function properly, yielding attentional disorders and learning disorders, respectively. Just as physical mechanisms sometimes do not function as they were designed to function and thus cause physical disorder, so mental mechanisms may also break down and cause a mental disorder.

Note that nothing in *DSM-IV*'s definition of disorder in terms of internal dysfunction implies that all mental disorders must be physiological disorders. Just as computer software can malfunction even when the underlying hardware is functioning flawlessly, so, in principle, the mind's "programming" might become dysfunctional for reasons other than that there is a malfunction of underlying brain mechanisms. For example, a sequence of experiences ("inputs") might occur that the programming was not designed to handle, leading to dysfunctions in some mental processes, as in Post-Traumatic Stress Disorder.

DSM-IV's definition of mental disorder emphasizes that the distress, disability, or other harm must occur as a direct result of a dysfunction and not just because society disapproves of the person's condition or for other reasons originating in interpersonal or social conflict. This last requirement is meant to preclude the misuse of psychodiagnosis for sheer social control purposes. For example, the Soviet Union classified many political dissidents as mentally disordered, incarcerated them in mental institutions, and "treated" them with sedating drugs. Many of these "patients" were clearly not really mentally disordered, even though they were socially deviant and they were in distress and socially impaired in their functioning due to their refusal to accept the tyrannical nature of their state. *DSM-IV*'s definition of mental disorder explains why such cases are not genuine cases of mental disorder. These individuals' problems were not due to a breakdown in the designed functioning of some internal mental mechanism but to their normal-range reaction to an unjust and adverse environment. They suffered, not from internal dysfunctions, but from the consequences of their courage in a repressive environment. The definition of mental disorder is supposed to distinguish true disorders in the medical sense from such problems caused by a normal response to a difficult environment.

The mission of social work remains more controversial and vaguer than that of psychiatry, but certain points can be made with fair confidence. Social work is not a medical discipline; it is concerned primarily with nondisordered but nonetheless problematic human conditions of certain kinds. Specifically, social work deals with problems in the interaction between the person and the social environment that prevent the individual from obtaining basic needs. These interactive problems sometimes are side effects of internal mental or physical dysfunctions, but often they are not. Social work's primary purpose is not to treat disorders but rather to improve the individual's interaction with the social environment to the point where the individual's basic needs are met. Elsewhere, I have called the lack of basic needs due an inadequate relationship with social institutions "minimal distributive injustice" (Wakefield, 1988a, 1988b). An individual suffering from a mental disorder falls within the professional domain of psychiatry, whereas an individual whose basic needs are not being met due to an inadequate interaction with social institutions falls within the domain of social work. However, these problems often overlap, and this leads to the involvement of the social work profession in psychiatry-related activities.

Current Roles of Social Work in Psychiatry

Before considering how social work's relationship to psychiatry might be different in the future, it will be useful to remind ourselves of the multiplicity of roles that social workers now have in the mental health system, and the rationale for these roles based on professional mission and skills. Several of these roles concern problems that can arise in the interaction of mentally disordered individuals with other social systems or institutions that provide basic needs. Because mental disorders often impair social functioning, social workers have the responsibility of ensuring that people with mental disorders do not, as a result of their disability, fail to possess a minimal level of basic human needs. Such activities as discharge planning, finding housing, helping a patient to obtain food stamps or other welfare support, and other such social support tasks are associated with this role. Moreover, social workers traditionally have the role of working with the patient's family, which is the social institution that is often of most importance to the patient. Social workers mobilize family support for the patient, help the family cope with the consequences for them of the patient's problems, prevent family dysfunction from reigniting the patient's symptoms, help create a family environment that is optimally beneficial to the patient, and perform other such tasks in adjusting the interaction between patient and family so that the basic needs of both are met. Social workers also serve as intermediaries between the patient and medical and mental health institutions, attempting to ensure that the patient's need for mental health care is met. Social workers help patients to find, be integrated into, and remain in halfway houses or day treatment centers; they link the patient with therapeutic services, or even help the patient to be hospitalized or to seek release from the hospital. These and similar roles use traditional social work skills to link the patient to various resources so that the patient's basic needs can be met.

A second kind of psychiatric involvement of social workers is when they use psychiatric techniques or institutions to pursue social work purposes with mental patients or with other clients. Psychotherapy is a set of procedures for changing psychological processes that was originally developed for use with mentally disordered patients. However, often the easiest way to improve an individual's interaction with the social environment is to change the individual's psychological processes—for example, by increasing coping skills, increasing impulse control, or increasing social interactional skills—in a way that allows the individual to interact with the environment in a more effective manner. So, social workers commonly use psychotherapeutic techniques to accomplish social work's purpose. For example, clinical social workers use psychotherapeutic techniques to enable clients who are suffering from various problems in living to better cope with their social environments and to develop the social skills and impulse controls necessary to do so. Thus, the techniques of psychiatry can be used to achieve social work's purpose of promoting those psychological capacities that people need to function at a minimally adequate level in our society. I have elsewhere called the provision of such basic, needed psychological capacities "psychological justice" (Wakefield, 1988a, 1988b). In psychotherapy, these capacities are often provided to people who did not have a chance to develop them earlier due to abusive or otherwise inadequate family or social environments.

Such use of psychotherapeutic techniques to deal with nondisorders can apply to mental patients themselves. A mental disorder can cause severe disruption of social functioning, not only directly due to the disorder but also because of the patient's normal reaction to having the symptoms (e.g., sadness and demoralization because of one's misfortune, anxiety about experiencing the symptoms, constriction of one's activities in an attempt to avoid triggering symptoms). Social workers often use psychotherapeutic techniques to help

the patient develop alternative ways of coping with the symptoms that allow for more productive social functioning, despite the disorder.

Another, rather different way in which social work relies on psychiatry is through the reimbursement system. Because our society tends to be more generous in reimbursing for medical ailments than for other problems of living that might be equally impairing, there is tremendous pressure on social service agencies to diagnose their clients as having mental disorders, whatever the reason that brings them into the agency. Reimbursement pressure puts a premium on looking at cases through a psychiatric prism.

We now come to one of the most controversial psychiatry-related roles of social workers—namely, the provision of psychotherapeutic services to those who do have mental disorders for the purpose of ameliorating the mental disorder. From doing group therapy with the severely disturbed in mental hospitals to seeing less disturbed patients in private practice, social workers have become the major providers of psychotherapeutic services to those classified as mentally disordered. On the surface, this is not a social work task as judged by the criterion of professional purpose. The primary goal is not to improve social functioning so that basic needs are met, but to cure a mental disorder, which in principle is within the domain of psychiatry. So, why are social workers sanctioned to do this task?

The main reason that social workers do psychotherapy with the mentally disordered is obvious: There is a need, and social workers have the skill. Psychotherapy is ultimately a social influence process. As Freud pointed out regarding psychoanalysis, there is really no reason why a medical degree is necessary to be an effective therapist. Moreover, the reality is that most psychotherapeutic treatments help the patient to better cope with the mental problem rather than to cure it, and this is a matter of building skills at self-control and social interaction, a social work domain. Although psychotherapy aimed at curing the mentally disordered is, in principle, a medical intervention, that does not imply that physicians are uniquely or even best equipped to perform it, and there is no persuasive evidence that they are more effective psychotherapists. So, although curing the disordered is not an essential social work mission, for reasons of skill and social need, it is a derived social work task.

This derived task is carried on largely at arm's length from psychiatric practice. Either social workers themselves become licensed mental health practitioners and work in mental health centers or clinics under the supervision of psychiatrists, or they go into private practice. Psychiatrists call in social workers when they need discharge planning or family work, but consider themselves equipped to diagnose and treat standard *DSM-IV* mental disorders without the aid of social workers. There is not a true partnership or complementarity here in the approach to the mentally disordered individual; each profession simply has a right to treat the same problems. I suggest that the future relationship, while retaining all of the above essential and derived elements, will also contain a new dependence of the psychiatrist on the social worker to perform essential social work tasks in routine psychiatric diagnosis and treatment, for reasons to which I now turn.

The Inconsistency in *DSM-IV*

In addition to its function of listing and briefly describing the various mental disorders that clinicians and researchers might confront, *DSM-IV*, like *DSM-III* (American Psychiatric Association, 1980) and *DSM-III-R* (American Psychiatric Association, 1987) before it, has the additional function of operationally defining each disorder in terms of a set of diagnostic criteria that are supposed to provide necessary and sufficient criteria for correct diagnosis of the disorder. These criteria are tremendously influential in all areas of the mental health field. *DSM-IV* criteria for disorders are formulated in terms of specific symptoms and behaviors so that disorders can be reliably diagnosed.

However, there is a basic inconsistency in *DSM-IV*'s system. The problem is that, for many categories of disorder, the diagnostic criteria do not in fact fit the careful definition of mental disorder presented in the *Manual*'s own introduction. Although the categories themselves are generally perfectly good categories of mental disorder, the criteria used to identify people as having those disorders do not in fact distinguish the genuinely disordered, according to *DSM-IV*'s own definition of disorder, from the nondisordered. The source of the inconsistency between the definition and the criteria is what systems theorists call "equifinality"; many different causes can lead to the same effect. The goal of reliable diagnosis requires that *DSM-IV* criteria be composed of easy-to-assess symptoms and behaviors and not make references to unobservable internal processes. Yet, as we noted earlier, for the problem to be a genuine mental disorder, *DSM-IV*'s definition of mental disorder requires not only that there be symptoms but that the symptoms be caused by an internal dysfunction. But, *DSM-IV* criteria do not say much about how the symptoms were caused. So, *DSM-IV* criteria fail to distinguish symptoms that indicate genuine mental disorders (i.e., symptoms caused by an internal dysfunction) from symptoms that indicate normal reactions to adverse environments or other problems in living (Wakefield, 1992a, 1992b, 1993, 1996).

These problems occur in categories throughout *DSM-IV*. Let me offer just half a dozen examples [some of these descriptions are taken in part from Wakefield (1996), where fuller discussion may be found].

Separation Anxiety Disorder

Separation Anxiety Disorder is diagnosed on the basis of symptoms indicating inappropriate and excessive anxiety concerning separation from home or from those to whom the individual is attached, lasting at least four weeks. The symptoms (e.g., excessive distress when separation occurs, worry that some event will lead to separation, refusal to go to school because of fear of separation, reluctance to be alone or without major attachment figure) are just the sorts of things children experience when they have a normal, intense separation anxiety response. The criteria do not distinguish between a true disorder in which separation responses are triggered inappropriately and normal responses to perceived threats to the child's primary bond due to an unreliable caregiver or other serious disruptions.

Substance Abuse

Diagnosis of Substance Abuse requires any one of four criteria: poor role performance at work or home due to substance use; substance use in hazardous circumstances, such as driving under the influence of alcohol; recurrent substance-related legal problems; or social or interpersonal problems due to substance use, such as arguments with family members about substance use. Contrary to *DSM-IV*'s definition of mental disorder, these criteria allow diagnosis on the basis of conflict between the individual and social institutions such as police or family. Arguments with one's spouse about alcohol or drug use, or between a child and his

or her parent, is sufficient for diagnosis, as is being arrested more than once for driving while under the influence of alcohol or for possession of marijuana. These social problems and interpersonal conflicts need not be due to mental disorders.

Learning Disorders

DSM-IV diagnosis of Learning Disorders is based solely on achievement test results being "substantially below that expected." However, these criteria do not distinguish true learning disorders, in which some internal mechanism necessary for learning is dysfunctional, from problems of learning due to family problems, lack of motivation, lack of adequate language skills, or other acculturation issues.

Major Depression

Diagnosis of Major Depression is based on a set of symptoms indicating an extreme sadness response. The criteria correctly contain an exclusion for uncomplicated bereavement (i.e., one is not diagnosed as disordered if the symptoms are due to a normal-range response to having recently lost a loved one), but they contain no exclusions for equally normal reactions to other losses, such as a terminal medical diagnosis in oneself or a loved one, separation from one's spouse, or losing one's job.

Selective Mutism

DSM-IV diagnoses Selective Mutism on the basis of a child's failure to speak in certain settings, especially school. The criteria properly exclude the diagnosis of children who do not speak in school because they do not know the local language, or children who are quiet only during the first month of school. However, other children who are silent for nondisordered reasons do fall under the criteria. For example, a child who is frightened to speak because a violent bully has threatened to hurt the child if he or she speaks up in class, and many other similar normal reactions to environmental threats, would be diagnosed as disordered by *DSM-IV* criteria.

Antisocial Personality Disorder

The *DSM-IV* criteria for Antisocial Personality Disorder are the following: In addition to having been conduct-disordered before age 15, the adult must meet three or more of the following criteria: either inconsistent work history or failure to honor financial obligations, breaking the law, irritability and aggressiveness, impulsivity, deceitfulness, recklessness, and lack of remorse. These criteria do not adequately distinguish between career criminals and the mentally disordered. The criminal will satisfy the illegal activity criterion and possibly, or even probably, satisfy the work/finance criterion (criminal activity is not "work" as intended in this criterion), the deceit criterion (by the nature of a criminal career), and one or more of the impulsivity, recklessness, or irritability/aggressiveness criteria (by the nature of criminal activity).

Toward a New Conceptually Based Partnership

What we see in the preceding examples, and in many other criteria sets in *DSM-IV*, is a breakdown in the basic distinction between psychiatric and social work problems. That is, the criteria that are now universally used to diagnose mental disorders in fact diagnose either mental disorders or person–environment problems, and one cannot tell from the criteria themselves which category applies in a given case.

What are the implications of this fundamental problem for the relationship between psychiatry and social work? Because the nature and source of a problem is critical to effective treatment planning, there is no alternative but for patients to be routinely assessed for both internal dysfunctions and person–environment problems. This sort of joint assessment requires coordination, so psychiatrists must routinely work together with social workers as a team on virtually every individual case, if cases are to be properly understood and treated.

Ironically, the need for such radical integration of psychiatric and social work efforts is a result of psychiatry's attempt to define itself as a medical discipline different from social work. To do so, it attempted to formulate reliable diagnostic criteria for genuine mental disorders in terms of symptoms. The resultant diagnostic criteria, considered from a medical standpoint, possess flaws that yield false positives (i.e., they sometimes incorrectly diagnose nondisordered, normal responses as disordered). But, these same flaws make *DSM-IV* criteria of importance to social work because they mean that *DSM-IV* encompasses a large part of social work's domain.

There are powerful intellectual, historical, and institutional reasons for framing psychiatric diagnostic criteria in *DSM-IV*'s operationalized, symptom-based way. This practice is unlikely to change. Indeed, the equifinality problem in this area is so great that it is hard to envision any operational criteria that could distinguish true disorders from person–environment problems without detailed assessment of both kinds of possible causal factors. Thus, for the foreseeable future, psychiatric diagnostic criteria will continue to encompass social work problems, and psychiatry and social work will be even more deeply connected at a conceptual level than the traditional roles would indicate.

There are two more reasons worth briefly mentioning for the breakdown in professional boundaries between social work and psychiatry, one specific to *DSM-IV* and the other a more general one. First, those writing *DSM-IV* did perceive that there was a problem with validity and did attempt to deal with it. The main thing they did was to add to almost all the criteria sets in the *Manual* an additional requirement that the symptoms must cause clinically significant distress or impairment of social, academic, or occupational functioning. However, this was the wrong medicine for *DSM-IV*'s ailment. Normal responses to adverse environmental factors can also cause intense distress or impairment (for example, as *DSM-IV* implicitly acknowledges, normal bereavement can be as distressing and impairing as the disorder of Major Depression). In all of the given examples, the disorders and the corresponding nondisordered responses cause similar "symptoms." So, the central problem with *DSM-IV*'s validity is not that the criteria do not require enough symptomatic distress or impairment, but that such distress or impairment itself often does not tell you whether the condition is a disorder or a normal response. However, the distress or impairment requirement does have the effect of making explicit a central feature of *DSM-IV*, which is that the judgment of whether a condition is a disorder often depends largely on assessment of social functioning. There is a *DSM-IV* Axis for rating social functioning, but I am referring to something different here; the symptoms in the diagnostic criteria themselves often reflect issues in social functioning. Thus, the distress or impairment requirement further erodes the distinction between psychiatric disorders and those problems of social functioning that constitute social work's domain.

Second, there is a more general reason for a breakdown in the distinction between psychiatry's and social work's professional domains. Internal mechanisms are designed to operate in certain "expectable" environments. Indeed, that is the heart of evolution; the organism's

nature adapts to features of the environment. The concept of disorder is to some degree based on the simple idea that sometimes something goes wrong with an internal mechanism and it can no longer do what it was designed to do. However, there is a hidden presupposition here—namely, that the environment stays roughly the same in relevant ways, so that the internal mechanism could perform its functions if nothing were wrong with it. The problem with this assumption is that humankind is so radically altering the environment that it is becoming less clear when a problem is due to a breakdown in a mechanism and when it is due to changes in the environment that make it impossible for the mechanism to perform its function. For example, pervasive anxiety may be a disorder in which internal anxiety-generating mechanisms start firing inappropriately, or it may be the response of normal anxiety mechanisms to the unprecedented demands of modern life, which did not exist when humankind was evolving. These are not exclusive possibilities, of course. However, as the environment changes, it becomes more difficult to tell whether symptoms indicate true disorders or failures of the environment to provide what people need to function adequately. Again, this means that the traditional roles of psychiatry and social work are becoming conceptually harder to separate.

Psychiatrists have neither the training nor the motivation to explore the patient's environmental circumstances adequately to distinguish internal from external problem sources or to treat the environment when need be. Short of a radical shift in psychiatric training and practice, psychiatrists are not about to routinely do direct assessments of the family and community context of the patient's symptoms or intervene directly in those systems when the person–environment relationship is the source of a client's problem; these are the tasks of social work. Yet, if the above arguments are correct, such assessments are necessary to decide whether or not a patient meeting *DSM-IV* diagnostic criteria actually has a mental disorder or not, and such knowledge may be necessary to deal effectively and appropriately with the client's problem. Thus, the future of psychiatric diagnosis and treatment will have to involve teams of psychiatrists and social workers sorting out the social and internal factors determining the individual's problem and executing the psychiatric and social treatment strategies appropriate to the problem. By its very nature, psychiatric practice will have to be a team effort with social workers.

Granting that those meeting *DSM-IV* criteria are often not genuinely disordered and are suffering instead from normal reactions to problematic person–environment interactions, and granting that psychiatrists are not about to engage in social diagnosis and person–environment intervention on the scale required by the flaws in *DSM-IV*, why can't psychiatrists still just ignore these conceptual points and continue to treat as psychiatric disorders the entire range of disorders and social problems encompassed by *DSM-IV* criteria? The answer is that to do so would be unethical, for informed consent reasons if for no others. People care greatly about whether a problem is a normal problem of living or a genuine mental disorder; controversies often erupt when medical treatment is provided to those who are not genuinely disordered, in areas ranging from the use of hormone treatments to increase normal children's height to using Prozac to elevate normal patients' moods. It is even more problematic to label and treat normal people as disordered when they are not so. Given that *DSM-IV* diagnostic criteria do not correctly distinguish the normal from the disordered, it will eventually become apparent that a great wrong is being done to those

who are summarily dispensed psychotropic medication or psychotherapy without adequate differential diagnosis (including social diagnosis) to ensure that a genuine disorder exists. To take just one example, drug trials for Separation Anxiety Disorder using *DSM-IV* criteria risk giving drugs to children to suppress a normal separation anxiety response. The use of drugs to treat normal, nondisordered reactions is generally controversial and raises complex value questions, but it is particularly problematic to use drugs to treat normal reactions in children without proper social diagnostic assessment and thus without consideration of alternative environmental interventions. Such inadvertent errors can only be prevented if genuine disorders and normal reactions to environmental problems can be distinguished through the combined efforts of social workers and psychiatrists during the diagnostic phase of treatment. Indeed, it is the professional responsibility of social workers to insist that such errors not be allowed to continue.

In conclusion, I briefly recapitulate the main line of argument above: A genuine psychiatric disorder exists when symptoms are caused by a breakdown in the functioning of some internal mental mechanism. This is why anyone diagnosed with a psychiatric disorder is thought to need intervention into the internal workings of their mental mechanisms, whether through psychotherapy or drug treatment. However, this assumed connection between psychiatric diagnosis and internal dysfunction no longer holds. Psychiatry has embraced symptom-based criteria for mental disorders, for a variety of intellectual and institutional reasons. It turns out that the same "symptoms" (e.g., sadness, anxiety, antisocial behavior) that can be caused by internal dysfunctions can also be caused by normal responses to social problems. Therefore, psychiatry's symptom-based criteria inadvertently and incorrectly classify a large part of social work's domain as medical disorders. Moreover, it is impossible to tell from symptoms alone which seeming disorders are genuine disorders that require a change of internal functioning and which are normal responses to environmental problems that require social intervention. Thus, parallel social and psychiatric assessment is necessary if correct diagnosis and effective and appropriate treatment are to be achieved. It follows that social workers and psychiatrists must work together to respond to presenting symptomatic complaints. Such teamwork is necessary as long as psychiatry remains committed to symptom-based criteria and as long as psychiatrists are not trained or interested in doing what social workers now do, including direct family and community assessment and intervention. It is likely that both these factors will continue to exist long into the 21st century.

REFERENCES

American Psychiatric Association. (1980). *Diagnostic and Statistical Manual of Mental Disorders,* (3rd ed.). Washington, DC: Author.

American Psychiatric Association. (1987). *Diagnostic and Statistical Manual of Mental Disorders,* (3rd ed. rev.). Washington, DC: Author.

American Psychiatric Association. (1994). *Diagnostic and Statistical Manual of Mental Disorders,* (4th ed.). Washington, DC: Author.

Barlow, D. H. (1988). *Anxiety and its disorders: The nature and treatment of anxiety and panic.* New York: Guilford Press.

Barlow, D. H. (1991). Disorders of emotion. *Psychological Inquiry, 2,* 58–71.

Specht, H. (1990). Social work and the popular psychotherapies. *Social Service Review, 64,* 345–357.

Specht, H., & Courtney, M. E. (1994). *Unfaithful angels: How social work has abandoned its mission.* New York: Free Press.

Spitzer, R. L., & Endicott, J. (1978). Medical and mental disorder: Proposed definition and criteria. In R. L. Spitzer & D. F. Klein (Eds.), *Critical issues in psychiatric diagnosis* (pp. 15–39). New York: Raven Press.

Wakefield, J. C. (1988a). Psychotherapy, distributive justice, and social work: I. Distributive justice as a conceptual framework for social work. *Social Service Review, 62,* 187–210.

Wakefield, J. C. (1988b). Psychotherapy, distributive justice, and social work: II. Psychotherapy and the pursuit of justice. *Social Service Review, 62,* 353–382.

Wakefield, J. C. (1992a). The concept of mental disorder: On the boundary between biological facts and social values. *American Psychologist, 47,* 373–388.

Wakefield, J. C. (1992b). Disorder as harmful dysfunction: A conceptual critique of DSM-III-R's definition of mental disorder. *Psychological Review, 99,* 232–247.

Wakefield, J. C. (1992c). Is private practice a proper form of social work? In E. Gambrill & R. Pruger (Eds.), *Controversial issues in social work* (pp. 221–230). Boston: Allyn and Bacon.

Wakefield, J. C. (1992d). Why psychotherapeutic social work don't get no re-Specht. *Social Service Review, 66,* 141–151.

Wakefield, J. C. (1993). Limits of operationalization: A critique of Spitzer and Endicott's (1978) proposed operational criteria for mental disorder. *Journal of Abnormal Psychology, 102,* 160–172.

Wakefield, J. C. (1996). DSM-IV: Are we making diagnostic progress? *Contemporary Psychology, 41,* 646–652.

Ethical Issues for Social Work Practice

Frederic G. Reamer

Increased attention has been paid to ethical concerns in social work practice over the last decade. Using the past as a guide to the future, Frederick Reamer highlights what he views as some key concerns. Frederick G. Reamer is professor in the graduate program of social work, Rhode Island College. His books include: Social Work Values and Ethics, Foundations of Social Work Knowledge, The Philosophical Foundations of Social Work, Ethical Dilemmas in Social Service, *and* Social Work Malpractice and Liability, *all with Columbia University Press. He currently chairs the National Association of Social Workers Task Force, which has drafted a new Code of Ethics. In 1995 he received the Distinguished Recent Contribution to Social Work Education Award from the Council on Social Work Education.*

I engaged in an interesting and, ultimately, humbling exercise as I began my work on this essay. I imagined that I was seated at my desk exactly a century ago and was asked to speculate about ethical issues for social work practice in the *20th* century. This would have meant, of course, that I would be writing very nearly at the moment of social work's formal birth (and I wouldn't have been writing with the assistance of computer software).

What would I have said? Certainly it's hard to know for sure, but it's fun to guess. My hunch—judging in part from issues facing this fresh, new profession in the late 19th century— is that I would have commented on social work's relationship with and obligation to the poor, especially new immigrants to the United States. Most probably, I would have had something to say about possible clashes between social workers' and clients' values and, unless I had been able to rise above some of the less flattering biases of that era, I might have dwelled some on social workers' opportunities to enhance the moral rectitude of the people with whom they work. Had it been a particularly good day, I might have been smart enough to think ahead about confidentiality and privacy issues that arise in casework and about the nature and limits of clients' right to self-determination.

I doubt that I would have had much to say about social workers' ethical obligation to engage in ambitious social change efforts or about complicated ethical issues that arise in clinical work, agency administration, community organizing, the formulation of social policy, or research or evaluation. The profession simply had not matured to the point where such issues seemed pressing, and I'm pretty sure I wouldn't have been wise enough to forecast them. In addition, the political climate in the late 19th century was such that I doubt I would have exhorted social workers to engage in radical forms of social action as a way to fulfill their ethical duties.

But, oh, how times have changed. In the interim, social work has experienced an ethics metamorphosis, with the bulk of the transformation occurring within the past 15 years. Who could have prophesied in the late 19th century that today's social workers would need to wrestle with ethical issues pertaining, for example, to the use of computer networks, the transplantation of organs, clients' use of psychotropic medication, the AIDS pandemic, managed care, or counseling on the radio? It's hard for me to believe that any social worker in the late 1800s could have been so talented a soothsayer as to be able to anticipate these sorts of developments.

Thus, I approach the present task with considerable humility. Who knows what awaits us in the 21st century? I believe I have a reasonable grasp of some developments that may be around the *near* corner as we enter the next century, but I hesitate to assert with complete confidence what phenomena will appear under the heading of "ethics" on social work's 21st century agenda.

The Past as Prelude?

There does seem to be some truth to the claim that history, or at least some elements of it, repeats itself and, again to some extent, portends the future. Although I don't expect that social work's history concerning ethics literally will repeat itself—it better not, because we've made our share of mistakes along the way—I do believe that some themes and issues will persist, some of them taking on new and novel forms because of developments that right now are not within our ken. I also think it is important for social workers to have a reasonable grasp of the historical events that have shaped present circumstances and may shape future ones.

So, what lessons are to be learned from social work's encounters with ethics, particularly as they might pertain to the future? Following are the main themes, as I see them.

1. *Over the years, social work has moved away from a preoccupation with the ethics or, to be more precise, morality of clients (many once known as paupers) toward a deep-seated concern about the ethical issues facing, and the ethics of, practitioners.* Particularly during the end of the 19th and the beginning of the 20th centuries, much of the discussion of ethics in social work focused on the moral virtues and immoral failings of clients with which social workers should be concerned (Siporin, 1992). Thankfully, today we hear less of this rhetoric (although still too much for my taste) and, instead, are more likely to discuss complex ethical predicaments and choices that social workers face in practice. I think that's good news and that this trend will gain momentum as we move into the next century.

2. *During the last century or so, social workers have learned that there is more to social work ethics than reciting and accepting a superficial listing of professional values.* Let me make clear that I would never question the need for social workers to articulate core values on which the profession is based. I am not at all cynical about the profession's value base. It is, after all, the ballast in social work's ship and it has served us well during various storms at sea.

But at the front end of our careers, too many of us were led to believe that the profession's core values—and familiarity with important terms such as *client dignity, social justice, integrity,* and *self-determination*—are pretty much what there is to know about social work ethics. Now we know better. We now know that professional life is much more complicated ethically and that a competent professional needs some polished and refined intellectual tools in order to deal with complex ethical issues effectively (Loewenberg & Dolgoff, 1992; Reamer, 1990, 1995d; Rhodes, 1986).

3. *The secret to ethical decision making does not lie in the profession's principal code of ethics.* This may seem like an odd statement, particularly coming from the person who chaired the National Association of Social Workers task

force that wrote the new code of ethics voted on by the 1996 NASW Delegate Assembly. But I mean this. For too many years, social workers have assumed that when faced with complex ethical decisions—for example, whether to breach a client's confidentiality to protect a third party from harm, blow the whistle on an impaired or unethical colleague, or interfere with a client who wants to engage in some sort of self-destructive behavior—the primary or only reliable guide is the NASW Code of Ethics (clearly the most visible and consulted code among several that exist within social work).

However, any thoughtful student of codes of ethics knows that principles and standards contained within them can provide only a modest measure of specific guidance when complicated circumstances arise and that, in many instances, such principles and standards cannot resolve an ethical dilemma unequivocally (Kultgen, 1982). Codes can serve a terribly valuable service to the extent that they cite the issues and concepts that practitioners ought to factor into their thinking and decisions. But in many instances, codes of ethics cannot do much more than that. In the final analysis, social workers need to view the code of ethics as they view a road map when traveling to an unfamiliar destination via an unfamiliar route. The document can point you in the right direction, outline various possible routes, cite significant landmarks on the way, and keep you focused. However, it can't dictate which highway to take, where to stop, and how much time to take to get where you're headed, and it can't tell you whether what you'll find at the other end of the line will meet your needs.

In ethics, as in highway travel, social workers need to be able to conceptualize about where they are headed and why. In recent years, social workers have had available a rich array of resources to help them do just that,

resources that simply were not available to social workers before the early 1980s. I am referring specifically to literature, educational offerings, and other forms of training that draw on the rich body of knowledge that has developed related to ethical dilemmas and ethical decision making (Reamer, 1995b; Reamer & Abramson, 1982).

The not-so-good news is that social work is still in a rather early stage of development in this regard. That is, few practicing social workers, and only some current students, have had *substantial* exposure to concepts and literature related to professional ethics, ethical dilemmas and conflicts, and ethical theory. Although many agencies and social work education programs are taking this subject much more seriously than ever before, we still have a long way to go before we can say with a straight face that contemporary social workers are receiving the kind of in-depth, rigorous, and intellectually sophisticated education on these topics that will prepare them to deal with the ethical issues that dot the 21st-century's landscape.

4. *Some social workers are unethical and engage in misconduct.* This is one of the more painful lessons we've learned. During most of social work's history there was virtually no mention of this fact in the profession's literature. Even today there are only sporadic references to ethical misconduct and professionals' misbehavior (Berliner, 1989; Besharov, 1985; McCann & Cutler, 1979; Reamer 1992a, 1994, 1995c). Indeed, there are very few in-depth descriptions or analyses of social workers' ethical misdeeds.

We know, however, that social work, like all professions, has within its ranks a relatively small number of people who don't play by the rules and, in turn, abuse clients, colleagues, and others as they behave in ways that may meet their own "needs" but no one else's.

Forecasting the Future

Anticipating the ethical issues that are likely to emerge in the 21st century seems a lot like predicting the weather for a particular day three months in advance. It's a daunting task, one filled with considerable uncertainty. That's not to say there is nothing that is predictable, but, to use the language of statistics, most likely we will explain only a small portion of the variance in the dependent variable using the not-so-precise independent variables that appear in our equation. It's a bit like having a Delaware-based meteorologist say in September that in three months the weather most likely will be cold. That's a pretty reasonable prediction for December, but strange things can happen in December in Delaware. Lots of extraneous factors can rear their head and change the course of the weather in unanticipated ways.

So too with ethics. For example, I feel fairly confident predicting that in the 21st century social workers will face increasingly complex ethical issues involving the use of computers (privacy issues and the like). But for all I know, in 30 years, computers themselves will be obsolete, replaced by some form of technology that is being researched secretly in some out-of-the-way lab somewhere. That may seem farfetched, but wouldn't it have sounded comparably farfetched if, in the late 19th century, some social worker had speculated about storing information about clients on something called a hard drive or about confidentiality breaches that may result from social workers' use of cellular telephones (conversations can be monitored with a relatively inexpensive scanner) and facsimile machines (documents may be read by people for whom they are not intended)?

Having said all that, my sense is that social workers will need to be prepared to deal with four major phenomena that are likely to loom large in the 21st century, in addition to—not instead of—the already impressive array of ethical issues facing practitioners in the late 20th century.

First, social workers should anticipate dramatic changes in the resources available to meet clients' needs and to pursue the profession's time-honored social justice mission. We see the seeds being planted now. It is hard to bump into a social worker whose job has not been affected somehow by the onset of what is now typically dubbed managed care, where access to and provision of services are strictly controlled and limited. What are a social worker's ethical obligations to a client who seems to be in need of additional service but whose insurance benefits have run out? Are social workers morally obliged to continue serving such clients *pro bono*? What malpractice and liability risks do social workers face if they terminate services to such clients?

Managed care does not seem to be a fad, and the ethical implications are many (Reamer, in press). Social workers will need to understand the ways in which managed care policies introduce ethical choices concerning the allocation of scarce resources to people in need and the termination of services to people receiving them. Social workers will also need to understand more fully their ethical obligation to participate in the political process that influences policy and funding decisions in both the public and private sectors.

Another scarce resource challenge concerns social workers' involvement with the elderly. Nearly everyone in the profession has heard the litany of statistics concerning the anticipated rate of growth among the elderly in future decades, not only in actual numbers but as a percentage of the population (Dunkle & Norgard, 1995). We should expect that, commensurate with this trend, social workers will work with the elderly in increasing numbers.

These social workers will need to be prepared to deal with a number of enormously complicated ethical issues. In the clinical domain, social workers will need to be prepared to decide whether to participate in end-of-life decisions and, if so, in what ways. Should social workers be permitted to help clients decide whether to end their own lives, particularly if they are terminally ill or seriously infirm?

In addition, social workers will need to make very difficult ethical decisions about the extent to which elderly clients should be permitted to place themselves in circumstances where they may be at risk. I recently spoke to a social worker employed in a hospital whose client, an 82-year-old woman who had been admitted for renal care, wanted to be discharged to her home, where she has lived alone for many years. Both the social worker and the patient's daughter thought the patient should move to a nursing home, given the patient's frail health and occasional forgetfulness (the patient's daughter reported that her mother has been forgetting to take some of her medication and on occasion has left the oven gas on). To what extent should this patient be discouraged from engaging in what may be self-destructive behavior, especially since the hospital's psychiatrist has concluded that the patient is mentally competent? What obligation does the social worker have to respect the patient's right to self-determination, even if the patient's judgment seems flawed? Is any form of professional paternalism justifiable in a case such as this (Reamer, 1983)?

Second, social workers should anticipate enormous ethical challenges triggered by various technological advances. In recent years, many social workers have been stunned by the difficult ethical issues that have trailed the introduction of new technology. Examples include ethical decisions about the morality of transplanting an animal organ into an infant to replace an impaired organ; the rights people have to end their lives with medical paraphernalia (for example, Dr. Kevorkian's famous "suicide machine"); civil liberties issues involved when clients are monitored by electronic devices placed on their bodies (as is done in some social service programs); and privacy issues brought about by the existence of the World Wide Web, the information highway, electronic mail, and other computer-based means of communication. Should a hospital social worker encourage parents of an infant born with an impaired heart to consent to transplantation of an animal heart? Would it be morally permissible for a social worker to help a client locate Dr. Kevorkian and learn how to use his life-ending apparatus? What limits, if any, should be placed on social workers who want to provide counseling services via the Internet? This is only the tip of the proverbial iceberg, I suspect. Tomorrow's social workers will need to think about the intimate relationship between ethics and technology in ways that their predecessors have not needed to. We may not know what specific technological wonders await us, but we can keep our individual and collective antennae extended so that we are as prepared as we can be when new developments appear.

Third, as I suggested earlier, social workers need to expect that increasing attention will be paid to ethical misconduct, misbehavior, and negligence. In one respect, this is a mere sign of the times, and the sign is likely to increase in size in future years. Nearly all professions are finding themselves entangled in an increasing number of ethics complaints and lawsuits filed against practitioners.

It is not clear whether the increase in complaints and litigation is a function of an increasing incidence of misconduct and negligence, a greater willingness on the part of clients to assert themselves when they believe they have been wronged, or both. Whatever the determinants, most social workers have learned very little about the causes of ethical misconduct and negligence, the reasons why ethics complaints and lawsuits are filed, and how to prevent such untoward occurrences. This trend's trajectory will likely force social workers of the future to become serious students of these phenomena.

Finally, the most difficult ethical challenge is likely to focus on social work's primary mission, its fundamental moral purposes. Throughout social work's history there has been recurring tension and debate concerning social work's principal aims, particularly with respect to the balance between the profession's preoccupation with individual well-being (primarily in the form of clinical services) and concern about social justice, social change, and social action. Consider, for example, the thought-provoking, provocative, and sign-of-the-times claim in Specht and Courtney's (1994) *Unfaithful Angels: How Social Work Has Abandoned Its Mission* with respect to the profession's past, present, and future:

> We stand now at the end of a century of development of social services, in danger of losing the promise of the quintessentially American idea of social work and the hope for community solidarity that lay in the thinking behind the Charity Organization Societies, the Community Chest, the Social Security Act, and the developing American welfare state. That potential richness for community development may be spent on the kinds of frivolous, self-indulgent, and time-limited approaches to problem solving that are offered to us by the psychotherapy industry. (pp. 174–175)

In the 21st century, social workers are likely to face more intense debate than ever about the profession's relative emphases on "case" and "cause" (Billups, 1992; Popple, 1992; Reamer, 1992b). Social workers will need to be particularly vigilant if we are to preserve our long-

standing embrace of social justice and dedication to confronting issues of oppression (Gil, 1994).

Final Thoughts

It is not enough to speculate about the specific substantive ethical issues that await social workers who practice in the 21st century. What is more important, perhaps, is to outline for social workers what knowledge and skills they will need to have to manage, with a reasonable degree of competence and confidence, whatever ethical challenges emerge during the next century. For one thing, social workers will need to be able to identify an ethical issue or dilemma when they encounter one. This sounds simpler than it is. Although some ethical issues are patently obvious, sometimes it's not so easy to uncover a subtle ethical issue that is embedded in a complicated practice-based situation. This takes skill, much like the skill involved when a therapist searches for subtle clinical dynamics that need attention but are not obvious to the naked eye. Although good instincts help, there's also something to be said for more formal education about relevant concepts, theoretical perspectives, and analytical frameworks. This is knowledge that was not available in social work during most of the 20th century but will be essential during the 21st.

Social workers will need to speak the language of ethics and be familiar with its special vocabulary and ways of thinking. That's not to say that social workers need to obtain graduate degrees in moral philosophy; rather, social workers will need to set aside some time to grasp the basics, to understand the most relevant and core concepts (just as clinical social workers tend to master the central concepts contained in the American Psychiatric Association's *Diagnostic and Statistical Manual* without obtaining an M.D. and completing a psychiatric residency). Essential concepts include relevant theories of metaethics and normative ethics (what moral philosophers call deontological and teleological or consequentialist theories) and ethics decision-making models (Loewenberg & Dolgoff, 1992; Reamer, 1990, 1995b, 1995d).

How can social workers obtain this sort of knowledge? There are four ways. First, undergraduate and graduate social work education programs need to take much more seriously their obligation to provide students with ethics-related knowledge. The current Council on Social Work Education *Curriculum Policy Statement* makes it abundantly clear that social work education programs must teach students about value conflicts, ethical dilemmas, and ethical decision making. That's great. Unfortunately, relatively few social work education programs teach this material in an in-depth, comprehensive, and deliberate way (Black, Hartley, Whelley, & Kirk-Sharp, 1989). Although several social work education programs offer discrete courses on social work ethics, the vast majority do not. Most social work education programs introduce students to issues related to social work values and ethical norms, but most don't provide students with rigorous introductions to ethical theory and decision making.

Clearly, this dimension of social work education needs to be shored up. Social work educators need to take a hard look at where in the curriculum this content can be included, either in the form of discrete courses on professional ethics or as components of existing courses. Social work educators need to take deliberate steps to incorporate ethics content in practice, human behavior, research and evaluation, and policy courses. They must also work closely with field instructors to ensure that ethical issues are addressed in field placements. Superficial coverage of this content will no longer do.

To address this content adequately, social work educators need to cover four major topics.

1. *Professional values and conflicts among values.* Social workers have always embraced a core set of values. In his classic essay on social work's values, Gordon (1965) argues that for a social worker

> to "value" something is to "prefer" it. A measure of the extent of a preference is what price, effort, or sacrifice one will make to obtain what is preferred, whether article, behavior, or state of affairs. To identify a value held by an individual or a society, therefore, requires a description of "what" is preferred and some measure of the extent of that preference, that is, the price in effort, money, or sacrifice the individual will pay to achieve his preference, or the provision a society will make or the positive or negative sanctions it will impose to enforce the preference. (p. 33)

Commonly cited social work values are individual worth and dignity, respect of persons, client self-determination, the importance of human relationships, professional integrity, social justice, valuing individuals' capacity to change, providing individuals with opportunity to change, seeking to provide individuals with adequate resources and services to meet their needs, client empowerment, confidentiality and privacy, equal opportunity, organizational loyalty, and nondiscrimination (Abbott, 1988; Keith-Lucas, 1977; Levy, 1976; Pumphrey, 1959; Reamer, 1995d; Teicher, 1967). Considered together, such values constitute the profession's foundation.

Students need to be acquainted with the profession's core values and, in particular, the ways in which these values may conflict with each other and with those held by clients, employers, and the society at large. For example, how should a social worker respond when a client continually makes racist, sexist, or homophobic comments during their work together? What should a social worker do when a community group wants to use the social worker's community organizing expertise to develop a new shopping area, in order to revitalize the neighborhood, when it appears that a latent goal is to force low-income people of color from the area? How should a social worker who is "pro choice" on the abortion issue respond when her agency's administrator issues a directive forbidding staff to discuss abortion as an option in their work with clients?

2. *Ethical dilemmas.* Conflicts among values —and the professional duties and obligations that rise from them—are what create ethical dilemmas. In short, ethical dilemmas occur when various values, and related duties and obligations, bump up against each other, forcing some sort of choice among them. Social workers need to understand the ways in which professional duties and obligations can clash, thus presenting practitioners with hard ethical choices. These ethical dilemmas may pertain to direct practice (for example, conflicts between client confidentiality and protection of third parties); agency policy and administration, regulations, and community practice (for example, conflicts between agency policy and clients' interests, or conflicts between a community organizer's values and a community group's agenda); and relationships among practitioners (for example, the nature of social workers' obligations to address unethical conduct engaged in by a colleague).

3. *Ethical decision making.* Students must be acquainted with a wide range of ethical theories and conceptual frameworks related to ethical decision making. By the time students graduate, they should have at least a rudimen-

tary understanding of core concepts in ethical theory and some experience applying decision-making models to case material.

In addition, students should be aware of mechanisms that exist in various social service settings to facilitate ethical decision making. Most hospitals, for example, now have "institutional ethics committees" (IECs), whose mission is to help staff, patients, and families make difficult ethical judgments related to such matters as termination of life support, "Do Not Resuscitate" orders, and whether aggressive treatment of a patient would be futile (Conrad, 1989; Reamer, 1987). Also, many agencies have inaugurated ethics grand rounds to provide staff with an opportunity to reflect on ways to handle complex ethical circumstances (Glover, Ozar, & Thomasama, 1986). In addition, some social service agencies have used ethics consultants to help staff think through the handling of difficult cases (La Puma & Schiedermayer, 1991; Reamer, 1995a; Skeel & Self, 1989).

4. *Ethical misconduct.* Students need to be informed of the nature of professional misconduct and ways to prevent it. They should be introduced to the NASW Code of Ethics and be acquainted with data on ethics complaints and malpractice claims filed against social workers.

A second way to educate social workers is for social service agencies to place the subject of professional ethics on their in-service training agendas. Certainly, some agencies have done a good job of offering periodic training on ethical dilemmas, ethical decision making, and ethical misconduct. Other agencies, however, have been somewhat lax.

Third, the social work profession itself needs to be more assertive in its efforts to educate practitioners about this content. Conferences sponsored by organizations such as the National Association of Social Workers, the Council on Social Work Education, and various

---

clinical social work societies need to offer workshops and sessions on professional ethics.

Finally, social workers need to monitor and keep up with the profession's literature on social work ethics. This is easier said than done, of course. Most of us lead remarkably busy, jam-packed lives; many of us would need a shoehorn to pack in reading that extends beyond the immediate demands of our day-to-day responsibilities. I would argue, however, that we can't afford *not* to keep pace with developments and literature germane to professional ethics. In the final analysis, social work ethics defines who we are and how we practice. If we stray from our ethical duties and obligations because we neglected to keep current with prevailing standards, we expose both ourselves and our clients to considerable and indefensible risk.

Where we've been in social work does not necessarily foreshadow where we are headed (as stockbrokers say, past performance is not a guarantee of future results). However, our recent history in social work—during which we've made major strides in our efforts to confront the profession's ethical challenges—suggests that we are merely in the adolescence of this aspect of social work's maturation. As we anticipate the future, we must do what adolescence often requires—that is, clarify our identity to the extent possible, try to manage the turbulence, and equip ourselves with the concepts and skills that are necessary to negotiate life's next chapter.

REFERENCES

Abbott, A. A. (1988). *Professional choices: Values at work*. Silver Spring, MD: National Association of Social Workers.

Berliner, A. K. (1989). Misconduct in social work practice. *Social Work*, 34(1), 69–72.

Besharov, D. J. (1985). *The vulnerable social worker*. Silver Spring, MD: National Association of Social Workers.

Billups, J. O. (1992). The moral basis for a radical reconstruction of social work. In P. N. Reid and P. R. Popple (Eds.), *The moral purposes of social work* (pp. 100–119). Chicago: Nelson-Hall.

Black, P. N., Hartley, E. K., Whelley, J., & Kirk-Sharp, C. (1989). Ethics curricula: A national survey of graduate schools of social work. *Social Thought*, 15(3/4), 141–148.

Conrad, A. P. (1989). Developing an ethics review process in a social service agency. *Social Thought*, 7, 102–115.

Dunkle, R. E., & Norgard, T. (1995). Aging overview. In *Encyclopedia of social work* (19th ed., pp. 142–153). Washington, DC: NASW Press.

Gil, D. G. (1994). Confronting social injustice and oppression. In F. G. Reamer (Ed.), *The foundations of social work knowledge* (pp. 231–263). New York: Columbia University Press.

Glover, J. J., Ozar, D. T., & Thomasama, D. C. (1986). Teaching ethics on rounds: Ethicist as teacher, consultant, and decision-maker. *Theoretical Medicine*, 7, 13–32.

Gordon, W. E. (1965). Knowledge and value: Their distinction and relationship in clarifying social work practice. *Social Work*, 10(3), 32–39.

Keith-Lucas, A. (1977). Ethics in social work. In *Encyclopedia of Social Work* (17th ed., pp. 350–355). Washington, DC: National Association of Social Workers.

Kultgen, J. (1982). The ideological use of professional codes. *Business and Professional Ethics Journal* 1(3), 53–69.

La Puma, J., & Schiedermayer, D. L. (1991). Ethics consultation: Skills, roles, and training. *Annals of Internal Medicine*, 114, 155–160.

Levy, C. S. (1976). *Social work ethics*. New York: Human Sciences Press.

Loewenberg, F. M., & Dolgoff, R. (1992). *Ethical decisions for social work practice* (4th ed.). Itasca, IL: F. E. Peacock.

McCann, C. W. & Cutler, J. P. (1979). Ethics and the alleged unethical. *Social Work* 24(1), 5–8.

Popple, P. R. (1992). Social function and moral purpose. In P. N. Reid and P. R. Popple (Eds.), *The moral purposes of social work* (pp. 141–154). Chicago: Nelson-Hall.

Pumphrey, M. W. (1959). *The teaching of values and ethics in social work.* New York: Council on Social Work Education.

Reamer, F. G. (1983). The concept of paternalism in social work. *Social Service Review*, 57(2), 254–271.

Reamer, F. G. (1987). Ethics committees in social work. *Social Work*, 32, 188–192.

Reamer, F. G. (1990). *Ethical dilemmas in social service* (2d ed.). New York: Columbia University Press.

Reamer, F. G. (1992a). The impaired social worker. *Social Work* 37(2), 165–170.

Reamer, F. G. (1992b). Social work and the public good: Calling or career? In P. N. Reid and P. R. Popple (Eds.), *The moral purposes of social work* (pp. 11–33). Chicago: Nelson-Hall.

Reamer, F. G. (1994). *Social work malpractice and liability.* New York: Columbia University Press.

Reamer, F. G. (1995a). Ethics consultation in social work. *Social Thought*, 18(1), 3–16.

Reamer, F. G. (1995b). Ethics and values. In *Encyclopedia of social work* (19th ed., pp. 893–902). Washington, D.C.: NASW Press.

Reamer, F. G. (1995c). Malpractice claims against social workers: First facts. *Social Work*, 40(5), 595–601.

Reamer, F. G. (1995d). *Social work values and ethics.* New York: Columbia University Press.

Reamer, F. G. (in press). Managing ethics under managed care. *Families in Society.*

Reamer, F. G., & Abramson, M. (1982). *The teaching of social work ethics.* Hastings-on-Hudson, NY: The Hastings Center.

Rhodes, M. L. (1986). *Ethical dilemmas in social work practice.* London: Routledge and Kegan Paul.

Siporin, M. (1992). Strengthening the moral mission of social work. In P. N. Reid and P. R. Popple (Eds.), *The moral purposes of social work* (pp. 71–99). Chicago: Nelson-Hall.

Skeel, J. D., & Self, D. J. (1989). An analysis of ethics consultation in the clinical setting. *Theoretical Medicine*, 10, 289–299.

Specht, H., & Courtney, M. (1994). *Unfaithful angels: How social work has abandoned its mission.* New York: Free Press.

Teicher, M. (1967). *Values in social work: A reexamination.* New York: National Association of Social Workers.

Ethics and Administrative Practice

The Politics of Values and the Value of Politics

Burton Gummer

---

*The courage to act on one's own convictions arising from
a sense of self-engendered authority is a necessary
requisite for moral action.*

Kaaren Hedblom Jacobson (1993)

This essay draws social workers' attention to unrecognized ethical concerns in administrative practice (e.g., how to distribute scarce resources). Burton Gummer argues persuasively that the NASW Code of Ethics ignores these important issues, and he makes a persuasive case for increased attention to such concerns in the future. Burton Gummer is a professor of social welfare at the Nelson A. Rockefeller School of Social Welfare, University of Albany, State University of New York. He is the author of The Politics of Social Administration: Managing Organizational Politics in Social Agencies. *He has also written a number of articles in social welfare administration and finance. His "Notes from the Management Literature" is a regular feature of* Administration in Social Work, *of which he is an associate editor.*

The role that ethical considerations should play in the work of administrators of public and not-for-profit organizations is a topic that has received a great deal of attention over the past two decades. Starting at about the time of the Watergate break-in in 1972, there has been a growing demand for greater ethical accountability on the part of administrators and managers of those organizations whose products and services are provided in the name of the public interest. The question immediately comes to mind if this increased interest in administrative ethics reflects a rise in the actual incidence of unethical behavior on the part of these administrators. If so, it would be ironic because a major development in administration in all sectors—public, not-for-profit, and for-profit—has been the growth in the number of administrators and managers who have graduate degrees in their fields and who aspire to professional status.

More likely, the growing concern about unethical behavior is a result of increasing public resentment of and hostility toward government, and the greater opportunities for journalists and public interest groups to gain information about the internal workings of government. Negative public attitudes toward government have been part of the American political culture since the earliest days of our nation. It is not surprising, therefore, that Americans have seldom placed a high value on government service and have frequently reverted to a Jacksonian disparagement of experience and professionalism. These attitudes took a turn for the better in the post-World War II period, when the level of cynicism decreased and a more positive bond was built between the government and its citizens.

> But Vietnam, Watergate, and the economic failures of the past two decades have led to a decline in confidence in government. In reviewing the new realities of public opinion, pollster Daniel Yankelovich has concluded: "Perhaps the sharpest drift in American attitudes has been a steady erosion of trust in government and other institutions, falling from a peak of trust and confidence in the late fifties to a trough of mistrust in the early eighties." (Adams, 1984, p. 6)

Matters have been made even worse as the political scene continues to move to the right. The growing influence of conservative politicians and pundits has inflated our native distrust of government with an ideology which holds that government is *intrinsically* bad—as is often heard: "Government is the problem, not the solution." Social welfare organizations face double jeopardy. Because most are public sector organizations or what has come to be called "third-party" organizations—that is, those private sector organizations that are heavily financed and influenced by government (Salamon, 1981)—they are victims of the "government bashing" that is directed at all government agencies. But the new conservative ideology is not only antigovernment, it is also virulently antiwelfare and anticlient,

which means that these organizations are also the victims of "welfare bashing."

The growth of investigative reporting—another offshoot of the Watergate era—also contributes to the public's sense of a rise in unethical practices among this group of administrators. The proliferation of investigative reporting often decontextualizes the actions of social services agencies from their goals and their problems, including resource shortages.* (For a good example of how one administrator dealt with this problem, see Garner, 1987.) Not only are reporters more anxious to probe deeply into public affairs, they now have more tools than ever before. Legally, "sunshine laws" and other freedom of information provisions make it harder and harder for organizations to keep their dirty linen from being washed in public. The "information revolution" has produced an enormous increase in the types and amounts of information that are now available through databases that, more and more, can be easily accessed through the Internet. (I am reminded of the scene in the movie *All the President's Men* where we get a Library of Congress "dome's-eye" view of Robert Redford and Dustin Hoffman poring over thousands of library slips in search of clues to the burglars' identity. Now, they would just turn on their laptop computers, call up the Internet, and access any number of databases.) Whether the ethical behavior of administrators is getting worse, or whether this is an artifact of more sophisticated information gathering and reporting styles is a moot point. The fact remains that the public's *perception* is one of an increase in the incidence

---

*This important point was brought to my attention by the editors.

of corruption among those entrusted with the public's business (Adams, 1984; Posner & Rothstein, 1994).

Three Views of Administrative Ethics

Although the social work profession has its roots in the 19th-century administrators of the Charities Organization Societies, by the turn of the century the profession was largely given over to the practice of social casework (Lubove, 1969). In the contemporary field of social work (the post-World War II period), administration was not considered one of the profession's practice modalities until relatively recently. Starting in the late 1950s, schools of social work began to offer concentrations in administration and planning, and at present, most, if not all, schools of social work have such practice specialties. However, these concentrations typically account for less than 10% of a school's total enrollment. The small numbers of students opting to concentrate in administration reflect, in part, the difficulty social welfare administrators have in gaining the recognition of their colleagues as legitimate members of the profession, and the lurking suspicion that the practice of administration is not social work (Ezell, 1990; Gummer, 1987). One of the stickiest points in the debate over whether administrators are *really* social workers is whether social welfare administrators should be held accountable to the same code of ethics as the one followed by direct practitioners (Gummer, forthcoming).

In general, people take one of three positions in response to this question. (1) Yes, social work administrators should be held to the same code of ethics as any other professional social worker; this will be called the *professional ethics* position. (2) No, administrators cannot be held accountable to this, *or any other* code of

ethics; this will be termed the *neutral rationality* school of thought. (3) Yes, social work administrators can be held accountable to a code of ethics, but not the one put forth by the National Association of Social Workers; this position will be termed, following Cooper (1990), the *responsible administrator*.

Professional Ethics

Since the introduction of the Hippocratic Oath in the 5th century to govern the behavior of physicians, a code of ethics has become one of the hallmarks of a profession. Nowadays, every group with claims to professional status has its own code of ethics; these include, in addition to the traditional fields of law and medicine, contemporary fields such as public administration, social work, accounting, city planning, and teaching. The fact that a need is felt for a code of ethics separate from the prevailing religious codes and societal mores reflects the unique role of the professions. This uniqueness comes out of the independence that professionals claim as essential to the practice of their profession. This independence, or autonomy, is needed, in part, because the special knowledge base and training of the professional is such that their work can be supervised and evaluated only by other professionals. The second, and more important basis for the professional's claim to independence from societal supervision, is the nature of the professional–client relationship. This is, as physicians call it, a "sacred trust"; nothing should be allowed to interfere with the professional's ministrations to his or her patients or clients.

The Code of Ethics of the National Association of Social Workers is mostly concerned with the profession's responsibilities to its clients. If social welfare administrators *are* social workers, then they should be bound to the same ethical standards as are their colleagues, who provide services directly to clients. This position is clearly presented by Levy (1979):

> At the foundation of the administrative responsibility and relationships of every social worker, at every level of administrative hierarchy and in every social agency, is the ethical framework within which it is incumbent upon every social worker to operate. The ethical responsibility of the chief administrator will be different from that of the direct service practitioner, but both will carry it in some degree. As social workers, both will be bound by the code of professional ethics to which they will have subscribed, or which will be ascribed to them by custom and usage. (pp. 277–278)

In addition to being the official position of the social work profession, this position reflects the sentiments of, I think, most professional social workers.

Neutral Rationality

The contemporary managerial role , Katz and Georgopoulos (1971) suggest, is the quintessence of instrumental rationality and, as such, is no longer accountable to traditional ethical or moral standards.

> The very growth of bureaucratic systems helped to diminish absolutist values of a moral character. As conscious attempts to organize collective enterprises, organizations were guided by rational objectives and empirical feedback. Pragmatism replaced tradition. Results and accomplishment were the criteria rather than internal moral principle. . . . Rules and laws were the instruments of men to achieve their purposes and lacked any transcendental quality. They could be changed at will as situations and needs changed or they became ineffective. (Katz & Georgopoulos, 1971, p. 347)

This argument leads to drawing a sharp contrast between the ethical responsibilities of those in bureaucratic roles compared to the responsibilities we have as private individuals. Jones (1984), for example, characterizes private roles as those where expectations are not determined in advance but develop over time, and where behavior is not means-oriented but reflects the uniqueness of a particular relationship that grows and develops in an organic pattern. Public roles, by contrast, are goal-oriented, impersonal, and often require "an arms-length, calculating stance" (Jones, 1984, pp. 607–609). The expectations for public roles are spelled out in advance by a constitution or other document, and success is measured in terms of fulfilling those expectations: "What is chiefly looked for in the playing out of a public role is effectiveness" (Jones, 1984, pp. 607–608).

When one accepts the proposition that administrative roles are ethically neutral, the logical extension is that administrators—elected officials included—cannot be faulted for acting unethically; they should be judged only on the effectiveness of their actions. This position was sharply expressed in Jones' (1984) admonition that the condemnation of Nixon's handling of Watergate expressed in such language as "betrayal of trust," "dishonesty," and "lack of integrity" reveals a tendency to assimilate public roles to private roles; the underlying model is that of the close associate—spouse, friend, business partner, colleague—who has let the other member of the dyad down (p. 618). Jones implies that such judgments are simply mistaken, part of what he calls the "counterfeit privatization of many once public roles" (p. 618). What we should expect from presidents and administrators is simple effectiveness; "moral purists" who naively expect integrity or trustworthiness misapply expectations appropriate to friendship to the public domain.

The Responsible Administrator

The responsible administrator school of thought, which is the one the author subscribes to, holds that it is irresponsible to maintain that the administrative role is ethically neutral, for to do so would shift the whole ground of morality and redefine administrative and political virtue. Clearly, Jos and Hines (1993) argue,

> questions of personal integrity and trust are vital to those who serve in public roles and . . . this is especially so for administrators whose credibility is under attack. . . . [T]he public service presents employees with moral issues that require attributes often associated with our private lives—sensitivity, compassion, trustworthiness—as well as those generally regarded as appropriate to our public and professional lives—impartiality and effective attainment of . . . goals. (pp. 381–382)

Although administrators must be ethically accountable for their behavior, a central tenet of this school of thought is that ethical behavior can only be judged within the institutional structure within which that behavior occurs. As Hardin (1990) argues,

> one must be concerned with the way in which professional ethics depends on what is possible. As moral theorists of almost all stripes would say, ought implies can. If it is impossible for you to do something, it cannot be true that you ought to do it. (p. 529)

Administrators are powerfully constrained by their organizational settings and often presented with ethically ambiguous or contradictory choices (Reisch & Taylor, 1983). Although the setting constrains the behavior of all members of an organization to some degree, the impact on administrators is considerably greater. In an important sense, the organization is the administrator's "client." Being responsible for the operation of the agency as a whole, the administrator's effectiveness becomes syn-

onymous with the organization's overall performance. The direct service worker can claim to be a superior social worker who's stuck in a lousy agency; the executive director cannot.

Hardin (1990) looks at the impact of organizational setting on ethics in terms of "natural" versus "artificial" duties. The particular rules and policies governing the actions of members of a social agency are not derived from natural law but reflect the value preferences of the major stakeholders in that organization. They are "artificial" in the sense that a different set of stakeholders would most likely come up with different policies and rules. In the field of social welfare, moreover, our preferences for one policy over another depend on our vision of what Donnison (1955) calls the "social health" of our society:

> It is generally agreed that disease and burst pipes are undesirable. Physicians and plumbers are therefore employed to prevent or cure ills without having to think much about the purpose or social consequences of their prescriptions. . . . But in social work this is not so. There is no generally understood state of "social health" toward which all people strive; our disagreements on this question form the subject matter of politics the world over. (pp. 349–350)

To behave ethically, therefore, administrators must be able to identify what their value preferences are and present them in ways their constituents will support. In short, the ethical administrator must be a major actor in the struggle over who will determine the values of a social agency, which means that he or she will have to actively engage in organizational politics.

The Ethical Social Administrator

Frameworks for evaluating the ethical behavior of public officials can be profitably applied to social work administrators because both are responsible for the implementation of public social policies. Wilbern (1984), for example, identified six levels of public morality: basic honesty and conformity to law; conflicts of interest; service orientation and procedural fairness; the ethic of democratic responsibility; the ethic of public policy determination; and the ethic of compromise and social integration. The first three levels deal mainly with the administrator's personal morality, and the latter three address the ethics of both the substance of an administrator's decisions and the processes by which they are arrived at. Many discussions of professional ethics begin and end with the issue of personal morality. Even in social work, where 90% of the work takes place within complex organizations, the profession's code of ethics is mostly concerned with issues that arise between individual social workers and their clients. Administrators, however, have as great a need for ethical guidelines for actions that result from their organizational roles as they do for those that come out of their personal or professional beliefs.

One aspect of administrative work that creates a number of ethical concerns is the amount of discretion inherent in most administrative roles. Through administrative discretion, managers participate in making agency policy. Although administrators play an important role in determining what social programs will actually do, many do not admit to having this kind of power. They frequently resist the idea that they have an impact on policymaking, which, in their eyes, can be done only by those bodies duly authorized to do so. This line of reasoning is usually based on the fallacy that if legislatures and boards of directors have much power, then administrators have none. Not only is this reasoning fallacious, it is dangerous as well, "for it is always dangerous when the powerful are unaware of their own power" (Rohr, 1978, p. 40).

Although most administrators state that their actions are determined by the people to whom they are responsible for implementing policies and programs, in practice there is no way they can escape the necessity to make ethical choices based on their own values. The mandates of those who set policy will rarely be clear or univocal: "It will not be based on full knowledge, it will conflict in small or large degree with other persuasive and powerful normative considerations" (Wilbern, 1984, p. 105). The conflicts will be most severe when the policymaker's goals conflicts with the administrator's. Administrators often rationalize actions that differ from legislative or board directives on the grounds that they are doing what their superiors would want done if they had the same information available to them.

No matter how persuasive or eloquent these arguments are, however, the use of administrative discretion to modify or change agency policies inevitably raises questions of disloyalty or underhanded practices. Administrators often try to avoid this dilemma by working to influence the content of policies as they are being developed. The change in the conception of administrators from value-neutral technicians to policy and program advocates who actively seek to invest the programs they manage with their own beliefs, values, and professional philosophies, raises important questions regarding the administrator's ethical responsibilities for policy development.

The ultimate ethical test of a social program is what it accomplishes. Did the program produce benefits for its clients? Were the beneficiaries those most in need of the service? How were the costs of the program distributed? The way in which a program is administered will account for some of the variation in the answers to these questions. However, the most important determinant of the questions of who benefits and who pays is the substance

---

of the policies upon which the program is based. This, in turn, raises what is for many the most crucial ethical issue for administrators—namely, their responsibility to play an active role in promoting the policies they believe are correct and opposing those they think are harmful. This role leads them into political arenas and necessitates the development of political skills. The ethics of social welfare administrators are, ultimately, the ethics of people trying to promote their beliefs about the social good in an imperfect world.

REFERENCES

Adams, B. (1984). The frustrations of government service. *Public Administration Review, 44*(1), 5–13.

Cooper, T. L. (1990). *The responsible administrator: An approach to ethics for the administrative role.* 3d ed. San Francisco: Jossey-Bass.

Donnison, D. D. (1955). Observations on university training for social workers in Great Britain and North America. *Social Service Review, 29*(4), 341–350.

Ezell, M. (1990). The anti-management ideology in social work. Paper presented at the Annual Conferences of the National Association of Social Workers, Boston.

Garner, L. H. (1987). Using information to define problems: A new perspective on the administrator's role. *Administration in Social Work, 11*(1), 69–80.Gummer. B. (1987). Are administrators social workers? The politics of intraprofessional rivalry. *Administration in Social Work, 11*(2), 19–31.

Gummer, B. (Forthcoming). Is the code of ethics as applicable to agency executives as it is to direct service practitioners? Negative position. In E. Gambrill & R. Pruger (Eds.), *Controversial ethical issues in social work.* Boston: Allyn and Bacon.

Hardin, R. (1990). The artificial duties of contemporary professionals. *Social Service Review, 64*(4), 528–541.

Jacobson, K. H. (1993). Organization and the mother archetype: A Jungian analysis of adult development and self-identity within the organization. *Administration & Society, 25*(1), 60–84.

Jones, W. T. (1984). Public roles, private roles, and differential assessments of role performance. *Ethics, 94*, 603–620.

Jos, P. H., & Hines, Jr., S. M. (1993). Care, justice, and public administration. *Administration & Society, 25*(3), 373–392.

Katz, D., & Georgopoulos, B. S. (1971). Organizations in a changing world. *The Journal of Applied Behavioral Science, 7*, 342–370.

Levy, C. S. (1979). The ethics of management. *Administration in Social Work, 3*(3), 277–288.

Lubove, R. (1969). *The professional altruist: The emergence of social work as a career—1880–1930.* New York: Atheneum, pp. 22–54.

Posner, B. G., & Rothstein, L. R. (1994). Reinventing the business of government: An interview with change catalyst David Osborne. *Harvard Business Review, 72*(3), 133–143.

Reisch, M., & Taylor, C. L. (1983). Ethical guidelines for cutback management: A preliminary approach. *Administration in Social Work, 7*(3/4), 59–72.

Rohr, J. A. (1978). *Ethics for bureaucrats.* New York: Marcel Dekker.

Salamon, L. M. (1981). Rethinking public management: Third-party government and the changing forms of government action. *Public Policy, 29*(3), 255–275.

Wilbern, Y. (1984). Types and levels of public morality. *Public Administration Review, 44*(2), 102–108.

B. The Social Work Profession

The five essays in this section offer different views of the future of social work. James Leiby, a distinguished social work historian, provides a brief overview of the history of social work and suggests that the expansion of social work brought about considerable confusion in the profession, beginning with the question "What was professional about it?" He highlights the value of viewing the development of social work in relation to the development of other professions (see also the following essay by David Stoesz). Like other essayists in this volume, Leiby suggests that there is an important future for community organization; however, he believes that its future lies in its original form—getting various agencies together in a common cause. He highlights what he views as the original insight of social workers concerning the helping process: the intent to improve the practice of charity by supporting and enhancing the natural feelings of personal responsibilities of individuals for themselves and the social responsibility of family, friends, and neighbors for each other, and generally of the community for its members. He argues that the key contribution of social workers is recognizable technical competencies—in particular, continuing the "historic tradition of a profession that came to understand that the process of helping had a value as important as the particular relief or service."

Rosemary Sarri provides an international perspective on the future of social work, suggesting radical new formats for education and practice (e.g., holding classes in the community). She provides a much needed definition of international social work and points the way to possible routes to a more global perspective. Paula Allen-Meares and Yosikazu DeRoos suggest that governmental attempts to restructure social welfare will rekindle a spirit of social change, justice, and advocacy among social workers. They call on social work educators to take a preventative stance and to take advantage of advances in the biological and social sciences and computer technology.

The essays by David Stoesz, "The End of Social Work," and David Austin, "The Profession of Social Work," provide contrasting views of the future of social work. David Stoesz suggests that social work will be incorporated under a larger umbrella of human services professions, largely because of bad decisions and bad directions it itself has pursued. David Austin suggests that social work occupies a significant position in American society at a very critical time (social workers deal with many of the contentious social issues in our society on an everyday basis) and that it is a growth profession that will continue to develop as a major profession with an expansion both in membership and diversity of practice settings.

He suggests that the future of social work will be guided by the characteristics of the society in which we currently live and by how these characteristics are played out in the 21st century, and argues that related current conflicts are really about the form and pace of cultural change. For example, one issue concerns the extent of communally shared responsibilities for the welfare of children, elder adults, and persons with severe disabling conditions in a society that celebrates and rewards individualism and individual achievements. He suggests that deprofessionalization is likely to continue and to be the model in state- and county-controlled income maintenance and child welfare programs.

Social Work and Social Responsibility

James Leiby

This essay presents an incisive review of the history of social welfare and suggests needed directions for the future, emphasizing the role of personal responsibility. James Leiby taught history at the School of Social Welfare, University of California at Berkeley for 30 years. His History of Social Welfare and Social Work *(New York: Columbia University Press, 1978) was selected by the librarians' magazine* Choice *for its list of best academic books of that year.*

Professional social work took form in the 1890s as part of an effort to reform society by reorganizing its charities, which were religious in inspiration, along scientific lines. Its preoccupation with technical administration and social science gradually separated it from religion but proved to be compatible with the secular and public social services that grew into the welfare state. In the 1990s, opposition to the welfare state has reached a climax. Social work flourished in the advance; how will it fare in the retreat? I shall argue that history has clarified the functions and mission of social work and opened a promising prospect for the 21st century. My story will tell how the earliest social workers defined their mission in terms of a reciprocity between personal and social responsibility, how their successors adapted their methods to suit the changing circumstances of their practice, how other vocations have taken on functions of social work, and how present-day confusions about the functions and mission of professional social work may be clarified.

I

The call for a profession of social work first sounded among leaders in the charity organization movement. What look to us like feeble beginnings looked to them like the culmination of an extraordinary social movement—a cumulative awakening of conscience that over a century created thousands of voluntary charitable associations. Today we may label such associations as humanitarian or philanthropic, but they were in a religious tradition.

Although the charity organizers welcomed the outpouring of charity, they were also critical of it. They hoped by making it scientific to make it more efficacious and important. Scientific charity began with a distinction made in the 1830s by the Rev. Thomas Chalmers between natural and artificial charity. *Natural* charity flowed in spontaneous, informal ways from "four fountains": love of individuals for themselves, of families for their members, of neighbors for each other, and of community leaders for the local poor. In Christian theology it was the love of God that infused the community of the faithful; in experiential terms it was feelings of solidarity—personal and social responsibility, one for all, all for one—that was the proper foundation of social life. *Artificial* charity was help offered by associations that were, in today's lingo, formally organized and functionally specific. It supported or replaced natural or spontaneous charity as a crutch braced a weak leg.[1]

Artificial charity was especially necessary in large cities, where individuals and families were likely to be separated from what we now call "natural support groups." It was well intentioned but easy to abuse. Its supporters might be satisfied with a perfunctory gift—a coin to a beggar, a donation to a worthy cause—without taking pains to learn what the real need was or whether their act was really beneficial. Knavish beggars or wily fundraisers could easily take advantage of such sentimental good will and complacency. Proponents of scientific charity wanted to replace charity that was perfunctory, sentimental, and self-defeating with helping that was conscientiously rational, in the sense of deliberately relating the means and ends of helping.

The basic principle of scientific charity was that artificial charity should strengthen rather than weaken natural charity. It should help individuals, families, neighbors, and communities define and carry out their natural responsibilities. The first practical step was a Charity Organization Society (COS) that would unite the scores or hundreds of local charitable associations in a common cause. The COS would divide the city into districts for charitable administration. Each district would have a committee of concerned people, ordinarily those already active in good works, and a paid secretary. People who were asked for help would refer the mendicant to the district secretary, who would look into the case, refer the mendicant to local agencies, and follow up with (1) a case con-

ference of the district committee to make a long-range plan of help and (2) a friendly visitor to keep in touch. Whenever possible, the long-range plan would arrange assistance around the natural forms of charity, so that the helpers and the helped would have a personal acquaintance and feel a personal responsibility to each other. In addition to helping particular cases, the COS would collect information about local problems and agencies, so as to get at causes of pauperism and develop community resources to deal with it.

Professional social work developed around two methods practiced in the COS: *casework* and *community organization*. Casework began with the assumption that each case—each individual or family—had a distinctive pattern of needs and resources. What came to be called "social diagnosis" was a systematic way to collect evidence to identify the differential pattern. Moreover it was understood from the start that the responses of the individuals and those close to them were essential to a constructive plan of helping. Somehow the relationship of helper and helped, the process of helping, should encourage constructive responses and summon the latent responsibility and energy of the needy and their relatives and friends. Therefore the process of casework required a tactful, friendly, and trustworthy manner to get the facts and implement the plan. Casework was a means both to meet needs and to strengthen sentiments like acceptance, good will, mutual trust, purpose, and courage. The caseworker's interest in scientific psychology, growing more and more self-conscious, separated scientific charity and professional service from the amateur helpfulness of the volunteer.

Community organization began as a method to bring local charities together in a common cause. The executive of the COS and its board members had to work with the executives and

---

[1]This interpretation of the relation between "scientific charity" and professional social work rests on my article "Charity organization reconsidered," *Social Service Review* 58(4): 523–538 (December 1984).

board members of the variety of local charities. Most of these were sectarian or ethnic, exclusive or missionary, and dubious about one another: Catholics and Protestants, evangelicals and Unitarians, Irish and Germans and Italians, orthodox and liberal Jews, and so forth. To begin with, the COS wanted to know about their policy and program, so its district secretaries could make referrals and keep records of who helped whom, how. Beyond that the COS wanted to strengthen understanding and cooperation among the various boards, financial contributors, and volunteer and paid staff. The COS could not exert authority: Its leaders had to build understanding and good will on a basis of facts and objectives that people could agree on. The means—getting agencies together in the common cause, improving social responsibility—was as important as the practical solution of immediate problems.

Then, beginning in 1913, the charity organizers did get an authoritative influence, in the form of the community chest. A community chest was primarily a common fund-raising drive for all the local agencies, or at least the ones that were admitted to the chest. The community chest was supported by downtown businessmen because it minimized the annoyance of separate solicitations by a host of local charities. The chest's professional staff reviewed member agencies and certified that they met proper standards of organization, financial administration, and personnel, so that contributors to the chest could believe they were getting their money's worth. The chests also arranged for "social surveys" of the community's needs and resources, to help in mobilizing existing agencies and planning new ones.

A third professional method, group work, developed in settlement houses among leaders of clubs. The settlements encouraged all sorts of clubs, for recreation, informal education, or political action, but most were for children or young people, and after 1900 the method became useful in a variety of youth-serving character-building agencies—the YMCA, YWCA, Boy and Girl Scouts, 4-H Clubs, and so forth—and in the programs of big-city "institutional churches" that were similar to settlement houses. Club leaders came to realize that the activity of getting together, the process of merging individuals into a common endeavor, was as valuable as achieving the group's manifest purpose. In theory, the clubs were a microcosm of social life in a democracy, a matrix of personal and social responsibility.

By 1930, American practitioners of casework, community organization, and group work had a viable sense of a common past and mission. Their past was the effort to make charity scientific, to think critically about means and ends in helping. Whether they worked with cases, or groups, or representatives of groups, they believed that psychological factors—emotions, motives, and relationships—were the dynamic of personal and social responsibility, in the family, or the club, or the community, and that helping should consciously encourage a mutual spirit.

II

Meanwhile, professional social workers also found increasing employment in government agencies. In the 19th century these were called "public charities," but their formal legal basis, in America, was the "police power," the power of the state to act to protect the health, safety, and morals of the community.[2] It was the constitutional basis of public poor relief, law

[2]The doctrine and significance of the police power is discussed in my article "Moral foundations of social welfare and social work: A historical view," *Social Work* 30(4): 323–330 (July–August 1985).

enforcement, penal and correctional institutions, public health, public education, and much child welfare. Before 1900, American public agencies were typically debased by political parties, which used their jobs and contracts to reward party workers, but after 1900, European notions of civil service reform along technical and professional lines spread from the federal government to the states and municipalities. This was especially true in education (public schools and the new state universities) and in health (public hospitals and public health agencies). The chief supporters of civil service reform were business and professional men who wanted economy and efficiency. They, and especially their wives, daughters, and clergymen, were also the main social support of scientific charity in private agencies, the community chest, and professional social work. Social workers appeared in the courts, especially family or juvenile courts (probation), prisons (parole), hospitals and clinics (hospital, later medical, social work), mental hospitals and clinics (psychiatric social work), public schools (visiting teachers or school social work), and public recreation. The earliest strictly professional associations of social workers were formed among those employed in hospitals and schools because medical and educational bureaucracies relished specialization and certification. During the first World War, social workers organized the Home Service program of the Red Cross, which aimed to provide services to soldiers and their families in every local Red Cross chapter.

In the depression years after 1930, professional social workers often took charge of expanding public poor relief. After 1935, they headed the Bureau of Public Assistance of the new federal Social Security Administration, which tried to impose professional notions of administration and casework on the thousands of shambling local departments that came into being to administer old-age assistance, aid to the blind, and aid to dependent children. Even though professional social workers were proportionally few in this public assistance bureaucracy, it was a large new market for their services.

In the 1930s, the new federal programs—the New Deal—seemed to carry on the history of reform of the evils of industrial capitalism and its urban setting. This movement found political support in disadvantaged economic groups—workers and farmers—and also among many business and professional people who supported social agencies, especially those that helped women and children, immigrants, and the aged. The case for reform drew mostly on earlier Progressive arguments for economic and social legislation, and it also had religious support in the form of a "social gospel" that directed the churches toward the "salvation of society" as well as the conversion of individual sinners. Neither Progressives nor social gospelers had much use for 19th-century notions of charity, which by then seemed to manifest snobbish condescension (the charity balls and bazaars celebrated on the society page) rather than social justice. Consequently, the idea of scientific charity and methods based on it gave way to the concept of professional methods, like those of the physician, based on a commitment to democratic social service rather than charity.

World War II ended the depression, and thereafter political historians began to interpret the New Deal as a rudimentary version of "the Welfare State." This term was imported from England, where it signified a middle way between laissez-faire capitalism and socialism; specifically, it was supposed to provide a decent minimum of economic security as a right. It included medical care and housing, as well as education. By 1960, the American version was much criticized as below the standard of England, Sweden, and most of Europe.

Nevertheless, after 1945, the government expanded public assistance and spent increasing sums of money for hospital and medical care, mental health, education (elementary, secondary, and college), housing, the Bureau of Indian Affairs, and social services for the military. MSW's found jobs in all these agencies (the military, together with the Veterans Administration, became their largest employer). Meanwhile high income taxes stimulated tax-deductible contributions for charity and philanthropic foundations, so private or voluntary agencies also flourished in the Cold War. The market for social workers steadily improved, as did their associations, schools, and professional apparatus. By 1960, they were identified more with programs for health, mental health, and education than with poor relief.

III

Expansion brought out much confusion in the profession, beginning with the question, what was professional about it?[3]

In the 1890s, a "professional" person was, in American common speech, someone who did for money what others did for love. The term

[3]This interpretation of the history of professional social work follows the continuity of technical function and competence. It differs from that of most historians of the subject, who begin with (1) a sociological analysis of professions as a class of occupations and ask how social work developed the attributes of that class [e.g., Roy Lubove, *The professional altruist* (Cambridge, MA: Harvard University Press, 1965) and Stanley Wenocur and Michael Reisch, *From charity to enterprise* (Urbana: University of Illinois Press, 1989)] or (2) with the political history of legislation comprehended in the notion of a welfare state, and ask how professional social workers advanced or retarded the achievement of the welfare state [e.g. John H. Ehrenreich, *The altruistic imagination* (Ithaca: Cornell University Press, 1985)].

connoted a career, in contrast with "amateur." So a professional athlete coached the team, a professional musician led the choir, a professional undertaker prepared the body for burial, a professional charity worker served the board members and friendly visitors. Meanwhile, European notions of a "learned profession" were gaining currency. Learned professions—the clergy, law, and medicine—had an imposing literature in Latin and Greek that was best studied in a university. By 1900, however, the authority of Latin and Greek classics was giving way, especially in medicine, to science. Engineering and agricultural schools, which came to the fore to train experts in new technologies, taught science. Teachers' colleges prided themselves on a scientific "educational psychology."

Assuming that social work was a scientific profession, what was its basis in theory? Its early leaders were mostly either clergymen interested in Christian sociology or academic economists interested in "social economics." After 1900, the decisive trend in academic economics and sociology was away from philanthropic concerns and toward more theoretical rigor and empirical nicety. Alas, the academic refinement of economic and sociological theory was not much help to social workers interested in casework, group work, or community organization.

The science that most interested caseworkers was psychology, but academic psychology focused on the stimulus and response by studying rats in a laboratory. It did invent standardized tests of intelligence and personality that proved to be useful diagnostic tools, but didn't illuminate the helping process. Caseworkers, along with many other lay people, became fascinated by psychoanalytic psychology. It was especially helpful in the mental hygiene and child guidance clinics that were so exciting in the 1920s, and it was generally relevant to understanding the client's motives and creating a trusting and supportive relationship. Psychoanalysis did not, however, impress academic psychologists, or even the psychiatrists and neurologists, who dominated medical education and practice. Moreover, it had little appeal to social workers in group work and community organization. Those social workers found some theory in social psychology, but that subject was, in 1930, still an inchoate novelty in academic departments of psychology and sociology, remote from social work practice.

Apart from their interest in the psychology of casework, social workers in the 1930s claimed to be experts in the policy and administration of poor relief; the important School of Social Service Administration at the University of Chicago aspired to build the profession around those subjects. Its leaders studied the history and development of the poor law, to learn from experience. But academic expertise about policy and administration had already devolved upon departments of political science and economics because the main considerations were fiscal and budgetary, involving three levels of government and well-organized taxpayers. These policymakers were not interested in casework, group work, or the kind of community organization practiced in community chests and settlement houses. Social work practitioners, professors, and students, for their part, were not much interested in academic economics, political science, or policy analysis.

Another confusion lay in the fact that by the 1930s schools of professional social work had pretty much committed themselves to a two-year graduate program leading to the MSW. It was essential, they believed, for the grave responsibilities and delicate decisions of social work, which involved both academic learning and a deliberate skillful use of self in relating to clients. But most tasks to which professional social workers laid claim were in fact performed by people without professional training. In public assistance, few workers in eligibility or even in child welfare or protective services were MSWs. Few probation or parole officers or group workers had MSWs. Even in medical and psychiatric social work, many lacked the MSW. Why not authorize a professional undergraduate degree? Schoolteachers and military officers managed grave responsibilities and important personal relationships without graduate study; police officers and nurses got by with in-service training. Or why not, at least, combine prescribed third and fourth years of college with one year of graduate work for an MSW? What was the practical or substantial difference between an MSW and a non-MSW social worker?

Yet another confusion was between the professional techniques of social work and its mission. Most 19th-century charitable agencies were religious; to justify their work, they invoked the exhortations of the prophets. Donors and career and volunteer workers were serving God by serving the least of humankind. Many agencies were frankly missionary: They designed their helpful services to attract lost sheep into their fold. Career professionals were sometimes criticized for lacking the spirit of amateur volunteers. Then, as 19th-century charity gave way to 20th-century social welfare and social justice, a "social gospel" in religion inspired many social workers and their supporters to think of themselves as advocates of a grand political mission rather than mere technicians in a bureaucracy funded by the establishment. Unlike economists, political scientists, psychologists, sociologists, and lawyers, they had a quasi-religious commitment to social justice for their clients.

In the 1960s, the "war on poverty" dramatized these confusions. Its strategists perceived that public assistance and social services, including public schools and local public health and mental health services, were part of a tacit conspiracy for social control of the poor. They believed that professional education and status ordinarily desensitized social workers, along with teachers and health-care providers, to the needs and interests of the poor. They believed that casework in particular was irrelevant to the plight of the poor. They wanted the bureaucracies to open participation in policy-making and new careers for the poor, whose life experience was an essential qualification.

Radical doubts about the relevance of professional social service concurred with the findings of careful "evaluative research" into the costs and benefits and efficiency of interventions. Evaluative research was first worked out in public health and then applied to programs for social work and education. It fascinated policy wonks and budgetary decision-makers.

By 1972, the hopes of the 1960s lost coherence and direction. Since then, neoconservative academics and prophets of the religious right have denounced a rising rate of illegitimacy, drug abuse, and crime in an "underclass" that they blame on the welfare state. In Europe, victory over the communist empire and disappointment with the welfare state have enhanced arguments for market-oriented policies. Professional social work has even fewer friends among 1990s conservatives than among 1960s radicals.

IV

Meanwhile, a serious challenge to professional social work appeared in the proliferation of competing vocational specialties. After 1940, academic psychology and sociology grew vigorously and developed many practical applications. By 1950, clinical psychologists pushed beyond testing to counseling and therapy. Other psychologists devised curricula about child development; others took over the "industrial social work" of the 1920s and converted it to personnel management. Sociologists developed theoretical and practical interests in bureaucratic administration, family life, and deviant behavior; criminologists prepared specialists in group work as well as correctional policy and administration and law enforcement. Teachers' colleges arranged certifications in special education and educational and vocational counseling that might also apply to problem behavior (Carl Rogers earned his Ph.D. at Columbia University Teachers' College). The clergy, which had always engaged in pastoral counseling, very much expanded that side of its work—a form of mental health—and religious education also drew on ideas about mental health. Lawyers too had often counseled on personal as well as legal matters, and that side of their work developed with the increase in divorce and child custody cases. An overlap of social work and medical care appeared in rehabilitation, drug abuse, the treatment of sexual problems, and gerontology. Public health nursing and education overlapped "public health social work" and psychiatric nurses and various paraprofessionals in mental health worked beside social workers, along with an assortment of quasi-medical, quasi-religious purveyors of counseling.

Professional social workers in the 1930s could not have foreseen the future elaboration of programs for health, mental health, corrections, and education or the industrial personnel work that paralleled social work in the military. The proliferation of specialists whose functions and skills approximate social work is not something peripheral to the profession; the profession is not the center around which these specializations appear here and there. The proliferation is itself the significant historical trend.[4] Many academic disciplines and professions have found reason to engage in activities that were once the particular concern of professional social workers.

Competition in specific functions demands that the competitors define themselves in terms of their technical competence as well as their moral virtue. One and all must continually demonstrate by evaluative research that they are efficient and effective. The difficulty and complications of this business are shown in the history of any social work method and of the research method itself. Nevertheless, prospects for the 21st century depend on it.

V

Technical competence obtains in methods. What is the prospect for casework and group work? Psychotherapeutic casework suffers the perplexity of all psychotherapy, but there has always been much more to casework than psychotherapy. For 50 years, casework has been well established in (1) services to families and children, especially in connection with health and mental health, family breakdown, and public assistance; (2) services to youth in schools, courts, and corrections; (3) services to adults at work in the military and in business, as part of personnel management; (4) services to the elderly. These services generally involve

mental health. They require sensitivity to the client's situation and motives, as variously perceived by psychology and sociology, and training in personal relationships. They also require a practical acquaintance with organizations, policies, and programs—what is needed for information, referral, case management, and evaluative research. Group work is well established in its traditional venues of recreation and informal education, and increasingly supplements casework when "support groups" seem called for. To be sure, MSW and BSW programs have no monopoly on knowledge, training, and certification for these services, but the growth of competition is plain evidence of the continuing and growing demand for them.

With regard to the method traditionally called "community organization," in the forms of social policy and administration, the prospect is less favorable. The demand for social work services is now mostly in large service bureaucracies—income maintenance, health, mental health, education, the courts, corrections—and in personnel management in the military and large business corporations. In all these bureaucracies, general budgetary, managerial, and political considerations take precedence over the preferences of technical experts. Community organization in the form of political campaigning has not earned much historical credibility, although social workers may assist authentic campaigners such as union organizers, civil rights leaders, clergy, and politicians, much as they assist the executives of the service bureaucracies.

I believe there is an important future for community organization, however, in its original form: getting the various agencies together in a common cause. This was its role in the community chest and the community welfare council: to encourage the integration and development of local service delivery. Here the tradi-

---

[4]A sociological analysis based on this point is set forth by Andrew Abbott, *The system of professions: An essay on the division of labor* (Chicago: University of Chicago Press, 1988). Abbott was drawn to this analysis by his acquaintance with mental health professions; see p. xii. The most convenient way to trace recent developments in professional social work and its knowledge base, with bibliography, is in the successive editions of the *Encyclopedia of Social Work*.

tional social work focus on clients and their response, and especially on families, is the key. For the vast array of agencies, programs may be conceived as addressing phases and transitions in the cycles of individual and family life, as these have been analyzed in the courses in human growth and development and social organization that for two generations have been central to the MSW curriculum. In theory, the effects of these agencies and programs should be combined and cumulative: How individuals or families respond and manage in one phase may affect how they will respond and manage in another. Other professions offer particular services, without special attention to their combined and cumulative effects, but professional social workers have historically thought about *the helping process*, as well as material or personal relief. Their methods of case work, group work, and community organization have aimed to make the process of helping encourage personal and social responsibility.

Their original insight was intended to improve the practice of charity by supporting and enhancing the natural feelings of personal responsibility, of individuals for themselves, and social responsibility, of family, friends, and neighbors for each other, and, generally, of the community for its members. Charity was a religious commandment—none more sacred—but professional social workers were able to conceptualize it in terms of secular psychology, central to their methods and separate from theology. This professional value—that helping should build mutual responsibility— is different from what prophets say God wants, or what political philosophers say is social justice, or what economists say is efficiently productive, or what physicians say is health, or what educators say is academic achievement. Social workers ordinarily apply it in their everyday practice, but they may also apply it comprehensively to the vast array of programs that are now judged primarily by budgetary, managerial, or political considerations. In this perspective their judgment rests on the authority of experience. They are better prepared than ever before to codify and apply that experience.

The importance of this value has been brought out since World War II by the experience of third-world societies in social development. They sought investment for economic growth. They began with economic infrastructure; they learned that infrastructure means not simply a transportation system and a power grid, but a properly trained and motivated work force and the education, health, and social services necessary to sustain it. Their experience in social planning shows that individual development and social development are interdependent. Professional social work, which seemed in the 19th century to be part of a religious reform, and in the 20th century to be part of a political reform, may in the 21st century be part of the technical planning for social development.

For the time being, however, I think that leaders and educators in the profession should concentrate on the functions, tasks, and skills that have historically presented the market for social work services. This involves a practical familiarity with (1) psychological and sociological theories of individual and group behavior, the phases of psychosocial development, and the special significance of family life; (2) the variety of programs and their policies and administration; and (3) the forms of research to test theories and practice. There are many opportunities to differentiate levels of service and to integrate local service delivery, but the basis for these is recognizable technical competence in particulars—and the historic tradition of a profession that came to understand that the process of helping had a value as important as the particular relief or service.

The End of Social Work

David Stoesz

Only if we candidly examine the present can we plan most effectively for the future. In this essay, David Stoesz takes such a candid look at social work and suggests a gloomy prognosis unless we change our ways. David Stoesz holds the Samuel S. Wurtzel Chair of Social Work at Virginia Commonwealth University. His research interests include the proliferation of for-profit health and human service corporations, the role of think tanks in social policy contexts, and social work theory. He is the coauthor of American and Social Welfare Policy, Reconstructing the American Welfare State, The Politics of Child Abuse in America, *and* Small Change: Domestic Policy Under the Clinton Presidency.

Social work, a profession that evolved with industrialization, has failed to make the transition to the postindustrial era. The symptoms of professional decline are conspicuous in two spheres of activity: private practice and public social services. Although commercial clinical practice flourished during the 1970s and 1980s, social workers in private practice began to lose substantial ground to managed care by the early 1990s. Private practitioners might have anticipated corporate raids for a greater share of the human services market given ample warning (Stoesz, 1986a, 1989), but they blithely went about their business, exploiting what was to become an exhausted reserve of insurance benefits. In the public sector, social workers

continued to staff a welfare bureaucracy that had become an archaic institutional form, oblivious of indications that public sentiments ran toward downsizing government (Pinkerton, 1995). It seemed to matter little that public social services in the United States were managed in the same manner that the Soviet Union had produced tractors, except there wasn't any Soviet Union anymore. During the 1980s, social workers in the public sector suffered setbacks, but these paled compared to the intentions of the 104th Congress to devolve public welfare to the states.[1] In both of these instances, social workers seemed to suffer from an aggregate case of learned helplessness, watching from the sidelines as alien forces deconstructed the very institutions that had been the foundation of the profession.

The profundity of this development far exceeds that of earlier disputes within the profession. During the Depression, social work debated whether it should marshal resources to promote the "cause" of preventing poverty through community work, as demonstrated by the settlement houses, or focus on the "function" of providing benefits to individuals in need, as had the charity organizations (Axinn

---

[1]Even prior to the recent formal devolution of welfare programs from the federal government to the states, the proliferation of waivers for state welfare reform demonstrations had resulted in de facto welfare devolution.

and Levin, 1982, 156–158). Later, social workers disagreed about the extent to which professional practice was effective empirically (*Social Work Practice*, July 1992). Significantly, these disagreements assumed that social work had an essential social role to play; the ultimate value of the profession was not at question. By contrast, the forces currently conspiring to diminish social work are presenting a far more serious possibility: whether or not social work is even *relevant*.

This has not always been the case. Thirty years ago, social work commanded the entire vertical organization of social welfare, enjoying virtually complete control of the means of social administration, from the highest secretariats to the lowest direct service positions. Today, social work administrators are unprepared for the challenges of a postindustrial environment. Social work has not been a participant in the experiments to "reinvent government" (Osborne and Gaebler, 1992). The struggle of public social service administrators to recruit and retain professionally trained social workers has become legendary. Usually, recent social work graduates abandon public employment as soon as they meet the conditions of their stipends and can exit from government service. Those credentialed social workers continuing to practice in the public sector find themselves increasingly isolated in agencies besieged. Research and policy analysis functions have largely devolved from university-based social service programs to private research firms and policy institutes.[2] As social work has become less relevant, other occupational groups have prospered; increas-

ingly, human resources and personnel management are assuming responsibility for what had been social work functions.

A frank assessment reveals the magnitude of the profession's shortcomings. Insofar as American social work has been extant for over a century, its inadequacies are nothing less than astonishing. Consider the following.

1. Most of the knowledge generated for social work continues to be derivative of other social sciences or professions. Social work has yet to generate field-tested theories complete with articulated variables, intervention methods, and predicted outcomes. As a result, few (if any) schools of social work are associated with a viable theoretical orientation. By contrast, American sociology, a discipline that evolved parallel to social work, evidences multiple "schools of thought" that mark the evolution of sociological knowledge. Social work's clientele does *not* explain away this responsibility. The Manpower Demonstration Research Corporation (MDRC), for example, has mounted field experiments of the welfare poor, yielding significant data on the employment prospects of recipients of the Aid to Families with Dependent Children program (Gueron and Pauly, 1991). The research record in child welfare, a societal assignment assumed by social work for a century, is skimpy by comparison (Costin, Karger, and Stoesz, 1996).[3] Indeed, research in social work had so stagnated that in 1988 the director of the National Institute of Mental Health was provoked to goad social work to come up to speed with other disciplines regarding research productivity (Austin, 1992, 313). Would such a request

[2]The University of Wisconsin's Institute for Poverty Research is an exception. Its existence provokes the question, why have not dozens of comparable research centers evolved with the graduate social work programs in the United States?

[3]Evaluations, such as *Putting Families First* (Schuerman, Rzepnicki, and Littel, 1994), are the exception. Rather than the standard, such studies are rare. Their paucity makes the point.

have been necessary to prompt other disciplines, such as psychology, to become minimally productive vis-à-vis research?

2. Few Masters-prepared practitioners view themselves as the source of knowledge that enhances the skills of the professional community. The Council on Social Work Education (CSWE) accreditation standards notwithstanding, social work research courses are watered down to be palatable for students who are unable to view research as integral to professional practice. The tendency of graduate programs to contrive single-subject research designs as a substitute for more rigorous and adequate research methods diminishes the capacity of professionals with the terminal practice degree to inform the professional community about optimal ways to improve service. Such diluted content would not suffice in other disciplines, academic or applied; whereas the social sciences educate graduates to be "generators" of knowledge, social work is content for its graduates to be "consumers." In its failure to insist on a research standard comparable to other social sciences, CSWE effectively condones flaccid research content. As inadequate research becomes normative for social work, the accreditation authority functions as nothing less than an "occupying army"[4] of mediocrity. Not surprisingly, few graduate programs offer, let alone require, a research thesis for students.[5] As a result, the research generated by MSWs in the field and published in the professional literature remains a novelty.[6]

3. Despite the profession's extensive service in government, it has been largely unable to present budget and program alternatives to a society that insists on reducing its support of public welfare. There is, to my knowledge, no requirement in *any* school of social work offering a graduate specialization in social administration that students pass even elementary courses in accounting or finance, let alone demonstrate the more advanced budgetary skills necessary to manage the multimillion dollar budgets typical of many social programs. Unskilled in fiscal management, social work administrators are simply incapable of conceiving viable alternatives to traditional, bureaucratic methods of service delivery. Whereas health maintenance organizations have emerged in health care and charter schools in education, comparable innovations have failed to emerge in social services, largely because social work managers lack the skills to prepare revenue and cost analyses. If a welfare reform initiative proposed capitating income maintenance and putting the service out to bid, could a social worker write the RFP, or respond with a competitive proposal?

4. Even though most social work education programs are underwritten by tax dollars, social work educators have neglected to generate the most basic information necessary for effective service delivery. In the United States, there are no reliable data on the cost/unit-of-service under varying arrangements of service provision. This omission diminishes the public credibility of the profession. When public officials insist on better returns for tax expendi-

[4]Telephone interview with Howard Karger, November 30, 1995.

[5]The Council on Social Work Education (CSWE) does not have data on the number of graduate programs offering or requiring a research thesis for graduate students, nor the number MSWs who complete a research thesis (per conversation with Rosalee Salinas, November 7, 1995).

[6]An exception is Gerald Hogarty, professor of psychiatry at the School of Medicine of the University of Pittsburgh. Equipped with an MSW and an inquisitive mind, Hogarty has generated an impressive legacy of research and publications, mostly in the psychiatric literature.

tures, and social work managers are unable to identify more efficient methods of service delivery, the situation is ripe for critics of social welfare spouting nostrums such as privatization. For example, when New Jersey officials announced plans to contract out the state's child welfare system (budgeted at $225 million and serving 46,000 children) to a for-profit case management firm, the dean of the school of social work in the state was unable to cite research that would counter the initiative (Pulley, 1996, 25).

Much of the fault here can be attributed to social work faculty who have neglected to do the basic, small-scale research that could generate research grants which would then subsidize the education of graduate students specializing in social administration. Incredibly, social work, despite its lip service about the primacy of the client, has generated no longitudinal surveys of the consumer perceptions of social services they receive (Popkin, 1990).

5. The primary organs for disseminating knowledge to the professional community, the professional journals, have such lumbering publication procedures that they retard the response of the profession to new developments. To write for the professional journals is to inter one's work in the occupational archives. Typically, social work journals publish articles more than a year after submission, whereas more competitive professions will publish seminal works within three months of submission (Stoesz, 1986b). Such editorial ineptitude is self-defeating.

Elizabeth Hutchison's unfortunate experience typifies the problem. After she had won the Breul Memorial Prize for best manuscript from *Social Service Review*, she submitted an article to *Social Work* exhorting human service professionals to urge Congress to enact the family support and preservations provisions of proposed legislation and renew the Child Abuse Prevention and Treatment Act (Hutchison, 1993). The effort was to little avail, not because the article failed to be published, but because it took so long to get into print that the legislation had already been signed by President Clinton by the time it appeared. In a scathing review of journal editorial practices, Fraser (1994) examined studies of the research of editors of social work journals, concluding that editors often lacked the necessary competence to judge research articles submitted for publication.

6. Despite the significance of the service they provide, social workers commonly assume responsibility for programs for which the fate of service recipients is either unknown or worsens. In many jurisdictions, child welfare workers have lost track of children they are mandated to serve. In the District of Columbia, child welfare workers were unable to locate one in four children in foster care. Despite several efforts to bring the District's child welfare program up to standard, a federal judge put the program into receivership, under a court-appointed director (Locy, 1995). Thus, the District joined 21 state child welfare agencies that are under court supervision. But service deterioration is far worse in child protection. Nationwide, between 30% and 50% of child deaths attributed to abuse are cases known to child protective service agencies (Besharov, 1987). When a Pulitzer Prize-winning journalist recalled her investigation of child homicides, she noted that state children's services administrators either did not have information on children who died from abuse or refused to release it based on some perverse interpretation of confidentiality. The journalist concluded that many state child welfare administrators were covering up a scandal in child welfare (Costin et al., 1996).

The media are quick to affix blame in the most graphic lapses in child protection. After a New York City girl was tortured to death, the *Washington Post* editorialized about "the shocking failure of a social welfare system to protect its most vulnerable charges" ("The Murdered Brooklyn Child," 1995, A22). Journalists investigating this incident discovered that "as of May 1994, more than 80 percent of the 31,405 pending child abuse and neglect investigations had not been completed in the time required by law" and that in 1993 "14,000 cases had been pending more than six years" (Toy, 1995, 51). Thus, the very agencies mandated to protect abused children have failed to do so, and social workers are implicated in this tragedy.

7. Social workers in the public sector often strive to meet organizational requirements even when that means failing to honor their professional and ethical obligations to clients. Social workers in public service routinely ration care in a manner that endangers client safety rather than taking more assertive action. Social workers faced with compromising professional standards might be expected to challenge existing policies individually and reap the consequences. By way of illustration, journalists usually cite professional standards as a basis for refusing to divulge sources to the courts, and go to jail as a result. Confronted with circumstances of comparable gravity, social workers tend to opt for discretion over valor, redoubling their efforts to provide deteriorating care.

Under conditions in which benefits, services, and opportunities are denied to entire classes of clients, social workers might be expected to react collectively. Yet, even group action seems beyond the comprehension of social workers. A report on child welfare in Milwaukee revealed that "social workers today have caseloads of 100 children, five times the national average, and have to abandon them all to an unstaffed 'vacant zone' if they leave the agency" (Bernstein, 1995, 26). How can professional social workers condone such conditions without taking decisive action to correct them?

When collective bargaining units of public employees are faced with such circumstances, they often respond with a range of counteractions from the "blue flu" to a wildcat strike. Yet, social workers rarely engage in such actions (Karger, 1988). Social work exceptionalism is often attributed to some special obligations that workers have toward their clients, but this is untenable. Public employees engaged in public safety and emergency health care—police officers and nurses—routinely employ job actions, even when they are legally prohibited from doing so. NASW maintains a legal defense fund and a $5000 biennial whistleblowers award, yet the assistance available to support social worker litigants—in 1995, $25,500 for seven cases with a maximum award of $5000—is hardly enough to jar derelict agencies in the direction of more adequate care ("Grants Bolster Seven Legal Battles," 1995).

8. Even though social work has extensive experience using tax dollars to promote the public welfare, the profession has failed to make more than token inroads in electing members to public office. Although more than half of the federal budget is expended for social programs, only three social workers—Barbara Mikulski, "Ed" Towns, and Ron Dellums—serve in Congress (of 535 members). NASW has been successful at increasing the number of social workers in elected office; from 1991 to 1995, the number of social workers elected to local, state, and federal offices increased from 113 to 199 ("Social Workers Serving in Elective Offices" 1995; personal communication with

Toby Weismiller, 1995). Lest the profession congratulate itself, however, there are about 500,000 elected offices in the United States, so the number of social workers that NASW can account for in elected office for 1995 represents an infinitesimal 0.04%. Given the substantial portion of governmental budgets dedicated to social programs and the legacy of the profession, the numbers of social workers elected to public offices should be greater by a factor of ten (and even then it would be less than 1%).

9. Despite the increasing diversity of American culture, social work education insists on essentially frivolous responses to the opportunities presented by this development. A range of substantive responses might be deployed to ensure that social work is consonant with diversity, beginning with requiring training in a language other than English for undergraduate and graduate students. Conceivably, specializations in cultural practice would include language proficiency, preparatory work in anthropology and immigration studies, social work courses in social action research and community development, and internships with advocacy organizations. Given the latitude that social work education programs have in their curricula, one would expect to see specializations in cultural practice sprouting up around the country, yet these are the exception. Instead, CSWE allows minimalist responses vis-à-vis curriculum accreditation requirements, expecting little more than implanting benign references to diversity in course syllabi.[7]

10. As a method for identifying leadership, social work commonly selects its elders for recognition instead of accelerating the careers of exceptional young professionals. Leadership recognition in social work has come to mean the bestowing of some lifetime achievement award at an annual dinner. Instead of mounting a formal leadership program, social work relies on the individual initiative of extraordinary young professionals who are perseverant enough to wend their way up through the ranks. At best, the profession designates a handful of scholarships to a small number of students in any given year—presently four $4000 grants are available through the Gosnell Memorial Scholarship Fund and a fund in memorial to Verne Lyons is seeking contributions—yet, NASW does not have a structured program to promote the leadership of young professionals.[8]

A nationwide leadership program might have been synthesized from honors courses extant in most universities and civic leadership programs that evolved in many metropolitan areas. However, the implementation would have required collaboration between NASW and CSWE, as well as the dispersion of financial and personnel resources that have been centralized in the Washington, D.C., metropolitan area. Rather than disperse resources to states and localities, NASW maintains the plush trappings of an imperial national office in Washington, D.C.

In a competitive post-industrial environment, a profession that fails so substantially on so many fronts faces extinction. The continual erosion of private practice and public social

[7]A review of "Summary Information on Master of Social Work Programs" reveals that only a handful of the more than 115 accredited graduate programs indicate references to specific populations: Columbia University, immigrants and refugees; Our Lady of the Lake, minorities of the Southwest; University of Connecticut, Puerto Rican studies and the African-American experience; Gallaudet University, the deaf; University of Minnesota, Duluth, American Indians; Yeshiva University, Jews. Probably the strongest candidate for a specialization in cultural practice would be the University of Puerto Rico, though work with the Hispanic population is not identified as such. Few programs perceive concentrations as culturally specific (Council on Social Work Education, 1995).

[8]Conversation with Billie Langston on December 12, 1995.

services contrasted with the growth of human resources management, indicate that social work is approaching a nadir. As this downward trajectory continues, social work will be tempted to commit already scarce resources in the effort to salvage its future. But for the reasons cited above, this is unlikely to be successful. Had social work taken its mission seriously, invested its resources strategically, demanded competence on the part of practitioners, insisted on accountability of programs it managed, and displayed courage by living its ethics, social work would be a respected profession today. Having done little of this, the profession finds that it is increasingly superfluous in a swiftly changing context. The most prudent decision the profession could make would be to merge with other disciplines to construct a "human services" discipline that corrects for the inadequacies of industrial era social work. Within the educational arena, prototypes already exist in "human ecology" at Cornell University and "human resources" at the New School of Social Research. In practice settings, Employee Assistance Programs, Health Maintenance Organizations, and Children's Service Authorities suggest models to pursue.

Professional responses to human need have unfolded in American culture over time. Prior to the New Deal, much social welfare was offered through settlement houses and charity organizations. What we now call "social work" developed parallel to the American welfare state, late in the industrial era. As social structures in education and health care are reinvented to meet the requirements of the postindustrial era, it becomes evident that this must occur in social welfare also. Unfortunately, social work has failed to make the transition to the postindustrial environment. The corporate rationing of services through managed care and privatization of the public social services are symptomatic of occupational fail-ure. Given social work's poor performance during the industrial era, it is not a good candidate for meeting future social needs. Rather than insist on an antiquated occupational form, we should evolve a profession that meets the requirements of the coming millennium. Having botched *social work,* we would be more successful working with other disciplines to develop a new profession—*human services.*

REFERENCES

Austin, D. (1992). Findings of the NIMH Task Force on social work research. *Research on Social Work Practice, 2*(3), 311–322.

Axinn, J., & Levin, H. (1982). *Social Welfare: A History of the American Response to Need.* New York: Harper & Row.

Bernstein, N. (1995). Are welfare cuts a foster care burden? *New York Times* (November 19), A1, 26.

Besharov, D. (1987). Contending with over-blown expectations. *Public Welfare,* (Winter), 7–8.

Costin, L., Karger, H., & Stoesz, D. (1996). *The Politics of Child Abuse in America.* New York: Oxford University Press.

Council on Social Work Education. (1995). *Summary Information on Master of Social Work Programs.* Alexandria, VA: Author.

Fraser, M. (1994). Scholarship and research in social work: Emerging challenges. *Journal of Social Work Education, 30*(2), 252–266.

Grants bolster seven legal battles. (1995). *NASW News* (November), 9.

Gueron, J., & Pauly, E. (1991). *From Welfare to Work.* New York: Russell Sage Foundation.

Hutchison, L. (1993). Mandatory reporting laws: Child protective case finding gone awry? *Social Work 38*(1), 56–63.

Karger, H. (1988). Social Work and Labor Unions. New York: Greenwood.

Locy T. (1995). Ruling shakes judge's takeover of D.C. child welfare system. Washington Post. (November 1): D3.

The murdered Brooklyn child. (1995). *Washington Post* (November 30), A22.

Osborne, D., & Gaebler, T. (1992). *Reinventing Government*. Reading, MA: Addison Wesley.

Pinkerton, J. (1995). *What Comes Next*. New York: Hyperion.

Popkin, S. (1990). Welfare: Views from the bottom. *Social Problems 37*(1), (February).

Pulley, B. (1996). New Jersey considers privatizing its child welfare. *New York Times* (March 2), 25.

Schuerman, J., Rzepnicki, T., & Littel, J. (1994). Putting Families First: An Experiment in Family Preservation. New York: Aldine de Gruyter.

Social Work Practice. (July 1992). "Social Workers Serving in Elective Offices." (1995). Internal NASW document. Washington, DC: NASW.

Stoesz, D. (1986a). Corporate health care and social welfare. *Health and Social Work* (Summer).

_____. (1986b). Time capsule. *Social Work* (November–December).

_____. (1989). A theory of social welfare. *Social Work* (March).

Toy, V. (1995). Mayor backs bid to shrink care caseload. *New York Times* (December 3).

The Future of the Social Work Profession

Paula Allen-Meares and Yosikazu DeRoos

This essay takes a critical but optimistic view of the future of the social work profession. Paula Allen-Meares and Yosikazu DeRoos focus on the potential impact on social work of several major external influences: the restructuring of the nation's welfare system, the educational transformation of the liberal arts and social sciences, developments in the biological sciences and health/mental health care, and the effects of computer technology. Although these developments will pose significant challenges for practitioners and educators, the authors argue that social workers can infuse a humanizing element into each of these trends. This will occur, however, only if the profession maintains a dual focus on individuals and the environment.

Paula Allen-Meares is dean of the School of Social Work at the University of Michigan and former dean of the School of Social Work at the University of Illinois at Champaign-Urbana. She has published widely on social work research, school-based social work, and the social work profession, and has held leadership roles in several national organizations. Yosikazu DeRoos is assistant professor at New Mexico State University whose research interests include clinical decision making, computer technology in education, and family preservation program effectiveness.

Introduction

We address only a few of several possible themes that will emerge in the future concerning the social work profession. This selection was difficult to make for a variety of reasons. Foremost is the fact that the profession of social work does not exist in a vacuum. A variety of internal and external forces have driven it in various directions at specific times in its evolution.

If one traces the history of the profession, it becomes all too clear in view of these forces why it has been so difficult to achieve a consensus on its definition and focus. However, the values and the dual emphasis of the profession on both the person and environment/society have provided the stabilizing foundation from which to respond to changing social needs, new knowledge from the disciplines, and technological advancements.

In its early beginnings during the 19th century, some questioned accepting social work as a profession (Flexner, 1915). Some saw it as a scientific approach to charity; others called upon it where there were socioeconomic ills. More recently, there are those who blame the profession for contributing to the growth of the welfare state, while offering too few solutions for the eradication of poverty, violence, and other problems. Society has responded to the profession with considerable ambivalence. In fact, we would characterize the current political environment as hostile toward both the profession and those at-risk populations we care about. These shifting political attitudes could impede the development of the profession unless we respond with united, forceful action. Now, as we approach the 21st century, many of the issues that social work has been addressing throughout its history continue to beset individuals and society. This essay will focus on some of those areas of concern and on some responses, both by society and by the profession. Because of the pervasiveness of changes that we expect to see, it is not possible to address them all. However, there are several areas that we believe will have particular relevance to social work. Therefore, this essay will focus on the implications to social work and to society of welfare reform and of changes in liberal arts education, the social/biological sciences, health, and technology.

These are areas in which we expect to see significant activity in the future. Not all of the activity will originate in social work, of course. In fact, much of it will arise in a manner that will make it necessary for social work to respond to such activity because of the likely negative effect if we do not do so. In other areas, the potential is to improve or enhance the nature of social work practice, client well-being, or societal functioning.

Futurists are almost always wrong. The clarity of hindsight attests to that. Thus, in trying to characterize the nature of social work in the 21st century, one probably mixes one part hope, one part apprehension, and another part that reflects one's own interests in the topics discussed. The mixture will almost certainly be more wrong than right and reveal a great deal about the one doing the predicting. Nevertheless, it seems we are impelled to try to envision our future, and we suspect that however lofty we may characterize the motivations for such activity, it is very likely to be primarily motivated by basic existential concerns.

Restructuring of Welfare

If we are to make a guess about social work in the 21st century, the soundest predictions will be those that extend from current knowledge, events, and trends. Therefore, one can look at our society and our profession today and try to characterize how they might reasonably appear 10, 20, or 50 years in the future.

We predict that the welfare reform movement—"efforts to change the way social welfare programs are administered, funded, and used" (Barker, 1995, p. 406) in the United States, will rekindle in the profession the strong sense and spirit of social change, social justice, and advocacy. We also believe that the economic restructuring of the country will continue to expand the gap between the poor and those with incomes to support themselves. Children, women, and minorities will continue to be disproportionately affected (Danziger & Gottschalk, 1993). The boundaries between the public and private human service systems will become even more ambiguous. The pendulum will swing back to an emphasis on the transformation of society/community empowerment, more similar to the 1960s and 1970s. According to Frumkin and Lloyd (1995), as we approach the 21st century, a number of important issues will require systematic thought and action if we are to advance social work education. They advocate the following goals: Make explicit the domain of professional social work and education; develop a curriculum that takes into account a diverse society; accentuate social work research as a political instrument in the definition and solution of social problems; and rekindle the relationship among practice, social work education, and community in an effort to promote social change.

According to Ewalt (1994), social work education can influence welfare reform in three respects: advocacy, training, and curriculum development. To accomplish these goals, we will need to emphasize even more strongly the importance of research findings as a "tool" to counteract irresponsible generalization and attitudes, as well as condemnatory statements about social welfare and those populations that are vulnerable. There is no place for emotionality in the age of knowledge/information. Reisch (1994) recommends that schools of social work engage in systematic research on socioeconomic conditions affecting children and families and the differential impact of various welfare reform proposals on their well-being. Social justice should be a central theme within the curriculum that prepares our social work workforce. Social justice can be defined as "the embodiment of fairness (whether people are dealt with reasonably), equity (whether similar situations are dealt with similarly), and equality (whether people and situations are dealt with in the same manner)" (Flynn, 1995, p. 2176); as an ideal condition in which all members of a society have the same basic rights, protection, opportunities, obligations, and social benefits (Barker, 1995, p. 254). According to Garvin (1995), the objective of social work education is for students to recognize that we live in a society in which many parts of the population are oppressed by virtue of their social status (e.g., race/ethnicity, gender, sexual orientation, economic status, and disability), and to develop a critical consciousness of these circumstances and strategies to remember them.

Our curriculum must move from being too "hi-touch" (i.e., an overreliance on impressions, feelings, and interventions that are not empirically validated) to a balance between "hi-touch" and "hi-tech," or data driven. Data from either quantitative or qualitative approaches can provide useful information in social advocacy and intervention. Of considerable importance is the inclusion of a prevention orientation and a deemphasis on remediation in social work education and practice. A preventive orientation is defined as "action taken by social workers and others to minimize and eliminate social, psychological, or other conditions known to cause or contribute to physical and emotional illness and sometimes socioeconomic problems. Prevention includes establishing those conditions in society that enhance the opportunities for individuals, families, and communities to achieve positive fulfillment" (Barker, 1995, p. 292). Welfare expenditures and social/emotional/health problems such as poverty, violence, depression, AIDS, and drug abuse will continue to escalate if we continue to respond to the victims of troubled systems/institutions with a too-little, too-late orientation.

Other dichotomous issues must also be resolved. For example, Coates (1994) suggests that because interpersonal practice and policy have been taught in separate classrooms, we have undermined their integration. This removes policy practitioners from individual problems and leaves micro practitioners helpless in altering macro issues. To achieve the transformation, all social workers must have a strong understanding of the interconnectedness of micro and macro.

Further, others suggest that two different theories of instruction be combined to advance our instructional objectives (Kramer & Wrenn, 1994). Rather than relying on the "art and science of teaching children" or "pedagogy," which translates into providing practical experience and related opportunities, we need to adopt "andragogy," the art and science of helping adults learn in our curriculum, to prepare social workers.

Liberal Arts and the Social Sciences

According to Shapiro (1995), president of Princeton University, liberal arts will become increasingly important if we want to prepare students to recognize the common humanity, distinguish self-interest from community interests, and value democratic principles. We need quality social work practitioners, educators, and researchers who ask important and thoughtful questions that inform this multifaceted profession. We need thinkers as well as doers. "We need to better understand ourselves and discover and understand the grand traditions of thoughts that have informed the hearts, minds and deeds of those who came before us. And we need to make moral and/or political choices that will give our individual and joint lives greater and more complete meaning" (Shapiro, 1995, pp. 6–11).

While liberal arts education is undergoing major rethinking, the social sciences are also undergoing a slow and interesting transformation. As you know, the social sciences and the profession of social work are analogous to hand and glove. The human service profession draws upon the social and behavioral sciences for fundamental knowledge about human nature and human behavior at all levels—from individual to societal (see Gulbenkian Report, 1995). It is the profession's charge to study, generate, transfer, and apply this knowledge. Similarly, the social and behavioral sciences are significantly dependent on the profession as a window through which aspects of the human and social condition can be highlighted. The "professions" are more engaged in interactions with the social and political realities of those who are the subject of study by social scientists. We hear the voices of the poor and disenfranchised.

A report by the Gulbenkian Commission (1995) entitled "Open the Social Sciences: The Restructuring of the Social Sciences" suggests that new quasi-disciplines are evolving that ignore disciplinary boundaries, that a reconfiguration of the social sciences is occurring. The report also suggests that the complexity of today's social dynamics needs to be taken more seriously and that the major issues facing a complex society cannot be solved by decomposing them into small parts but rather by attempting to understand these problems in their complexity and interrelations (p. 90). The report acknowledges emerging groups of social scientists and nonsocial scientists around thematic areas (e.g., health, culture, and cognition) as well as groupings around the level of analysis (e.g. long-term social processes). The dissident voices of feminists are cited, challenging the ability of the social sciences to account for their current perception of reality and urging openness to the full spectrum of cultural realities in order to achieve objectivity (p. 57). We will need to evaluate the utility of new quasi-disciplines for our mutual purpose of advancing the profession and must participate in the transformation in order to bring knowledge to bear on social ills and conditions. Our challenge will be to update our curriculum and research agendas with appropriate abstractions from these new quasi-disciplines.

Biological Sciences and Health/Mental Health

Another arena of relevance to social work in which one can make reasonable predictions is related to the burgeoning activities in biochemistry, neuroscience, and biotechnology. These areas, as extensive as they may appear today, are in their infancy (Freeman, 1995). The significance of biochemistry, neuroscience, and biotechnology for social work lies in the tripartite nature of how we have come to characterize social work—as a biopsychosocial field. Social work's history has been characterized by its psychosocial focus. While the profession has actively debated the merits of a psychological versus a social orientation and of how we might effectively embrace both simultaneously, biological content has been increasingly taking its place alongside the other two. It is evident, for example, in the increased biological content in HBSE courses in schools of social work and particularly in such courses as "Brain and Behavior," taught at a prominent school of social work in the Southwest.

As health and human service professions continue to blur boundaries and overlap in more and more activities, the role of social work will expand to include more of what we today consider activity in the biological realm. In part, this will be because there will be a better understanding of the interrelationships among the biological, psychological, and social spheres of functioning, and how they influence changes and outcomes.

This increased awareness of biological factors in social work practice is currently most evident in the areas of health social work, in which health problems, whether brought on by disease or injury or issues of dying and death among the elderly, often create the conditions on which social workers focus. It is also evident in mental health today that biochemistry has revolutionized treatment (Kaplan & Sadock, 1995; Sederer, 1991) and social workers have had to respond accordingly, by becoming familiar with psychopharmacology and medication side effects, as well as continuing to work on related psychosocial issues. In practice with problems of substance dependency, awareness of the biochemistry of dependency and the cognitive, emotional, and behavioral correlates are essential for effective social work practice.

However, in the 21st century, the health and mental health issues that will confront social workers will be far more likely to involve matters of biochemistry, neuroscience, and biotechnology than they do today (Roobeek, 1995). For example, as it becomes increasingly possible to prolong life, issues of the quality of elderly life will become more salient. At the federal level, laws or regulations about euthanasia will be introduced, specifying when it is and is not allowed and who will have input in the decision. However distasteful it may be to some, such regulation of life termination is inevitable. Such an issue is clearly biopsychosocial in nature. The current practice of portraying the decision to terminate life as a medical one will eventually lead to a debacle similar to what is already occurring in Holland, where physicians are sanctioned to unilaterally decide on and perform euthanasia on their patients. Life termination cannot be made simply a medical decision. When such a decision is made, it must be one that considers the full range of biopsychosocial concerns for the client and significant others, and with an appreciation for its implications for society.

Another health outcome of the development of biochemistry and neuroscience is the possibility of saving, sustaining, and significantly prolonging life through biotechnology, thus allowing retirees to live as long in retirement as they did during their preretirement work years (Banta, 1995; Freeman & Robbins, 1995; Nichols, 1988). This raises the specter of lives profoundly devoid of meaningful activity. Social work will have a role to play here by helping to address the most fundamental, most profound questions that arise in one's life—questions about the nature and meaning of existence. The profession will help clients who have had the opportunity to live long, fulfilling lives to continue to develop lives that fully engage their knowledge, skills, and accumulated wisdom. Such lives can enrich clients themselves and others in society who can learn from those who have amassed such experience. Social work in the 21st century will find a role for the elderly in society that focuses less on issues of death and dying and more on issues of living and growing.

Another example of the effects of 21st-century biochemistry and neuroscience in the area of mental health is in the development of psychopharmacological agents that can fundamentally alter cognition, affect, and behavior. One drug that has had a profound effect on many of those for whom it has been prescribed is Prozac (Kramer, 1993). It is more powerful and specific in its actions than previous psychopharmacologic agents used for similar purposes. Its clear benefits (Kaplan & Sadock, 1995, pp. 2056–2061) mask the insidious intrusion of such agents into the psychosocial functioning of everyday life. Even with current technology, it is possible to design drugs with a particular molecular structure to work at particular types of sites. In the 21st century, the technology will be available to design psychopharmacologic agents that will not only profoundly affect cognition, emotion, and behavior, but will be able to alter the structure of an individual's personality—that is, an individual's patterns of thinking, feeling, and behaving, which emerge developmentally and are assumed to be stable over time and across situations. Drugs, for example, will become available that will be able to induce and control emotions and their intensity and duration far beyond what is available today.

The most challenging task for social work lies not in the benefits such agents provide but in their harm, both individually and societally. There will be dependency problems, of course, with such drugs, and social work will have a role in their treatment. However, a more profound issue for social workers in a society confronted with these drugs lies in defining what constitutes human personality or human nature. If one is restructuring one's personality with psychopharmacologic agents, where do we draw the distinction between the person and the chemical agents? When we speak of the right to self-determination, what will that mean in an age in which drugs will be able to change the character of what constitutes the self? Also, given the power of such psychopharmacologic agents to fundamentally affect personality—

one's cognitions, emotions, and behavior, and that which underlies them—there will arise the nightmarish scenario that the pharmaceutical companies will hold the equivalent of patents on aspects of people's personalities. Such developments will clearly test our professional values and our actions, as well as test our definition of what it means to be a person.

Some aspects of social workers' roles under such conditions may be profoundly different. Will social workers engage with clients in personality selection counseling? Will social workers assist a client in selecting the right psychological profile for an upcoming interview or job? Will social workers, given the unhappy state of a client, persuade the client that it is no longer necessary to be unhappy because the right psychopharmacologic agents are now available that will permanently eliminate such unhappiness? (For a promotion of such a position, see Pearce, 1995.) Given the availability of such methods, many clients will want to resort to them. Will social workers critically appraise the impact of such drugs on society and on what it means to be a person and respond accordingly, or will we act simply on the basis of what the client (and possibly society) wants? Will we acquiesce to the notion that human personality is infinitely malleable and therefore should be open to such manipulation if one chooses, or will we argue that there are aspects of what we are as human beings that should not be altered, even when the means for such alterations are available? As the role of social workers is expanded to include fully the biopsychosocial realm, social work principles as well as methods will be profoundly tested.

Computer Technology

Another area of importance to social work in the new century will be related to the use of computer technology. The advent of computer technology in the present century can be characterized as revolutionary. It is revolutionary in the same sense as the industrial revolution in the 19th century. The same effects that occurred then—increased productivity, the creation of monopolistic enterprises, job displacement—are happening again with the computer revolution, and this new revolution is just beginning. The impact of computerization will be even more dramatic than the industrial revolution because the computer revolution will subsume existing technology, including industrial technology, within its realm (Pancucci, 1995). This revolution is in its infancy. The impact of computer technology in the 21st century will be so pervasive that it will remake large sectors of society, just as the industrial revolution did in the 19th century. This new technology will create problems for social work to address—problems similar to those faced by social workers under similar circumstances during other periods of rapid change: homelessness, hunger, unemployment, and mass migration. Just as millions moved to the cities from the farms during the 19th and 20th centuries in search of work and shelter, resulting today in only 3% of the population in the United States being engaged in farming activities, the 21st century will see millions move out of the industrial centers because only a small percentage of the population will be necessary to maintain the industrial base of the country. We are already seeing that movement away from industry and toward the service sector, where job growth will be in the future. Again, as during the industrial revolution, there will be too many workers and not enough jobs, resulting in poor pay, poor working conditions, and the creation of an ever-growing subsistence class. History will repeat the trends of the 19th and 20th centuries in the 21st century. Social work involvement will be in great demand at that time, as society once again tries to cope with millions of unemployed and underemployed adults living through a new revolution brought about by computer technology.

Within the social work profession itself, computer technology will play an increasingly important role in the 21st century. Today, we see the application of computer technology in recordkeeping, data analysis, and matters of accountability; in communication, including audio- and video-conferencing; in distance education; and some beginning efforts at the use of such technology for training, including the use of virtual training environments (Traub, 1991). All of these activities will continue to increase in sophistication.

Also, as computer technology becomes more powerful, social service agencies will be able to perform many of the functions currently being performed by schools of social work. For example, the creation of "virtual arenas," in which workers or student-workers will be immersed in lifelike social work practice scenarios will change the nature of practice training. With the burgeoning of such training arenas, the need for university-based schools of social work will either change or diminish. It is possible that schools will extend beyond the bounds of a university and directly into the community and into social service agencies, something that is now possible in a limited sense with distance technology, but which is seldom done because of maintenance of outmoded notions about what constitutes a university. As computer technology becomes more available and as workers and students gain ready access to education, training, and skills databases throughout the world, something seen on a small scale with the current Internet access, one will begin to remotely access universities as needed. Schools of social work will decrease their direct educational role and increase their consultative role for social service agencies. The technology will create a significant shift in the balance of power between schools and agencies as the latter gains the ability to increasingly educate and train workers.

Social work practice will be affected by computer technology. In addition to the enhancement of recordkeeping and budgeting, worker accountability will be a primary area of computer technology development. Such applications raise ethical questions and questions of professionalism that social workers will have to address.

It will become possible to regularly monitor where the worker is, what the worker is doing, and to transmit data to and from the worker via wireless links (a capability that already exists). Workers will also have sophisticated interactive, computerized knowledge systems that will provide them with a means for accessing client and resource information and for making or verifying worker decisions. Such systems will be able to interact with the worker and even warn of critical decisions and outcomes. It will even be possible to override the worker's decisions when necessary. Such an override capability exists today on machinery. Fifty years from now, it will be routinely incorporated into social work decision making.

The scenario just envisioned raises interesting questions about the role of the worker vis-à-vis the computer. Decision making will take on a different character as social workers begin to interact with computers as part of their routine activity. For example, there already exist programs to assist in determining child neglect and child abuse and for assisting in child placement decisions (J. Rycraft, personal communication). As the power of computers and the programs they run increase, they will play an increasingly larger role in social work activity, including social work practice decision making. Of course, such programs do not operate on their own; they will be used by social workers and will embody the knowledge or skill of social workers or related professionals, particularly those who are most highly knowledgeable or skilled.

Nevertheless, for many social workers today, this probably appears as a nightmare scenario. Worries about technology taking over some roles, some functions of social work practice is seen not only as troubling because dehumanizing, but is viewed by many as a poor practical solution given how social work has elected to address personal and societal concerns. Although we would like to guarantee that such technology will not be used inappropriately, no such guarantee can be given. It will become an activity of the profession to monitor such technology to ensure that it is being used properly. Also, there is no assurance that such technology will not become all-pervasive within the profession. In fact, we assume that it will enter increasingly into more fields of social work practice. What we must ensure is that such technology is used to enhance the profession's effectiveness. If it is used merely for financial efficiency, then we run the risk of undermining the nature of social work practice. However, if we are willing to work with such technology, we can only enhance our practice.

Such technology need not be seen as dehumanizing. Few think it is dehumanizing to drive a car rather than to walk, to talk by telephone rather than face to face. The reason it is not dehumanizing is that we recognize that in interacting with the machinery, we control the machinery and not vice versa, and that we can use it to enhance our performance. The same holds true for computer technology. As long as we ultimately control the technology, it will be another tool to enhance our performance.

We must remain aware that political and economic considerations will affect the application of such technology. Politically, there will always be those who insist that our profession invoke a social control function. The increasing power of such technology will make it easier to use it for such purposes. However, such technology does not have imbedded within it a value dimension. This technology is neither good nor bad. To characterize it in such a way is to imbue it with human characteristics, something that is unfortunately too common today. It is the role of the professional and the profession to resist pressures to misuse such technology and to develop means by which we can ensure that its use promotes individual well-being and societal functioning.

There will also be economic pressures related to such technology. There will be those whose concern will be to use such technology simply to reduce costs. Others will argue that such technology ought not to be used because it is too expensive. Both arguments relegate as secondary the effectiveness of the technology. Although cost considerations will always be of concern, we must find a way to use such technology that is both effective and efficient. If it is right to use the technology, and we certainly believe it is, let us find a way to finance its use. Its long-term benefits will enhance individual well-being and societal functioning and therefore will result in long-term financial benefit for all. For social workers, as labor-intensive as the profession is, such technology will increase their efficiency. Therefore, if efficiency is an issue, it will be seen that it is more efficient to employ the technology.

Implications for Social Work

Given all we have discussed, what are the implications if we do not respond to such changes and do not incorporate such changes. We believe the consequences will be severe.

Social work does not exist in a vacuum. As much as any profession, social work activity is woven into the very fabric of society. Social work acts and reacts to that which transpires in society. The very responsiveness of social work to personal and social concerns and its transformation as a profession as society itself is transformed is a reason why some find it hard to define social work. Social work action must embody the manner in which individuals or society is receptive to such social work action. It must not only do the right things but do them in a manner appropriate for that setting or environment.

In fact, social work has never really maintained the status quo. If it had done so, it would not exist as a profession today. It continues to exist and will continue to do so because of its responsiveness to the needs of individuals and society. Social work practice will continue to change, not only in its practice technology or knowledge base but in its definition of what constitutes social work practice. That it will still be addressing seemingly intractable problems such as poverty, hunger, and oppression does not mean that the manner of that response will be the same 25 or 50 years from now.

Social work education will also continue to evolve, both in its characteristics and in the manner in which one is educated. Social work education, as it always has, will continue to be influenced by individual and societal concerns. It will respond to those concerns and be transformed through its responses. We have no doubt that social work education will be responsive to the needs of individuals and society. Wherever such education takes place in the future, as long as we as a profession maintain our dual focus on individuals and the environment and educate and act in line with that dual focus, the social profession will continue to play an important role in society.

As we stated previously, futurists are almost always wrong—but perhaps this essay can be used as a benchmark to assess change in the areas we discussed. Perhaps, a few decades from now, someone will contend that our predictions were just that—predictions.

ADDITIONAL READING

Axinn, J., & Levin, H. (1992). *Social welfare: A history of the American response to need* (3d ed.). New York: Longman.

Chatterjee, P. (1995). Technology transfer. In R. Edwards (Ed.), *19th encyclopedia of social work* (pp. 2392–2397). Washington, DC: National Association of Social Workers.

Helsel, S. K., & Roth, J. P. (Eds.). (1991). *Virtual reality: Theory, practice, and promise.* Westport, CT and London: Meckler.

Jacobson, M. (1993). *Foundations of neuroscience.* New York and London: Plenum.

Marcarov, D. (1991). *Certain change: Social work practice in the future.* Silver Spring, MD: NASW Press.

Popple, P. R., & Leighninger, L. (1990). *Social work/social welfare, and American society.* Needham Heights, MA: Allyn & Bacon.

Specht, H., & Courtney, M. (1994). *Unfaithful angels: How social work has abandoned its mission.* New York: Free Press.

REFERENCES

Banta, H. D. (1995). Some social implications of diagnostic applications of biotechnology. In M. Fransman, G. Junne, & A. Roobeek (Eds.), *The biotechnology revolution?* (pp. 385–391). Oxford and Cambridge, MA: Blackwell.

Barker, R. (1995). *The social work dictionary.* Washington, DC: NASW Press.

Coates, J. (1994). Education for social transformation. *Journal of Teaching in Social Work, 10*(42), 1–17.

Danziger, S., & Gottschalk, P. (1993). *Uneven tides: Rising inequality in America.* New York: Russell Sage Foundation.

Ewalt, P. (October 1994). *Welfare reform and social work education.* Paper presented at the meeting of the National Association of Deans and Directors of Schools of Social Work, Myrtle Beach, SC.

Flexner, A. (1915). Is social work a profession? Proceedings of the National Conference of Charities and Correction (pp. 576–590). Chicago: Hildman Printing.

Flynn, J. (1995). Social justice in social agencies. In R. Edwards (Ed.), *19th encyclopedia of social work* (pp. 2173–2179). Washington, DC: NASW Press,

Freeman, C. (1995). Technology revolutions: Historical analogies. In M. Fransman, G. Junne, & A. Roobeek (Eds.), *The biotechnology revolution?* (pp. 7–24). Oxford and Cambridge, MA: Blackwell.

Freeman, P., & Robbins, A. (1995). The promise of biotechnology for vaccines. In M. Fransman, G. Junne, & A. Roobeek (Eds.), *The biotechnology revolution?* (pp. 174–183). Oxford and Cambridge, MA: Blackwell.

Frumkin, M. & Lloyd, G. (1995). Social work education. In R. Edwards (Ed.), *19th encyclopedia of social work* (pp. 2238–2246). Washington, DC: NASW.

Garvin, C. (September 1995). *Social justice in the social work curriculum.* Paper presented at the Retreat of the School of Social Work, the University of Michigan, Ann Arbor.

Gulbenkian Commission (August 1995). *Open the social sciences: The restructuring of the social sciences* (pp. 1–121). Binghamton: Binghamton University, State University of New York, Fels and Braudel Center.

Kaplan, H. I., & Sadock, B. J. (1995). *Comprehensive textbook of psychiatry/VI.* Baltimore: Williams & Wilkins.

Kramer, B. J., & Wrenn, R. (1994). The blending of andragogical and pedagogical methods in advance social work practice courses. *Journal of Teaching Social Work, 10*(42), 43–64.

Kramer, P. D. (1993). *Listening to Prozac*. New York: Viking.

Nichols, E. (1988). *Human gene therapy*. Cambridge, MA: Harvard University Press.

Pancucci, D. (May 11, 1995). Looking into the future. *Computer Weekly, 42*.

Pearce, D. (June 2, 1995). *The hedonistic imperative*. BLTC Research: http://www.pavilion.co.uk/david-pearce/hedab.htm.

Reisch, M. (October 1994). *Welfare reform and social work education*. Paper presented at the meeting of the National Association of Deans and Directors of Schools of Social Work, Myrtle Beach, SC.

Roobeek, A. J. M. (1995). Biotechnology: A core technology in a new techno-economic paradigm. In M. Fransman, G. Junne, & A. Roobeek (Eds.), *The biotechnology revolution?* (pp. 62–84). Oxford and Cambridge, MA: Blackwell.

Sederer, L. I. (1991). *Inpatient psychiatry: Diagnosis and treatment*. Baltimore: Williams & Wilkins.

Shapiro, H. (October 1995). *Changing in the world of change: The university and its publics* (pp. 1–13). Address given at the University of Michigan, Ann Arbor.

Traub, D. C. (1991). Simulated world as classroom: The potential for designed learning within virtual environments. In S. K. Helsel & J. P. Roth (Eds.), *Virtual reality: Theory, practice, and promise*. Westport, CT and London: Meckler.

International Social Work at the Millennium

Rosemary Sarri

Rosemary Sarri, professor of social work at the University of Michigan, poses some important questions about the international dimensions of social work in the 21st century. She argues that because of increasing global interdependence, effective international social work in the next century must be collaborative, rather than dominated by the models developed by affluent, industrialized nations. She presents four advantages for infusing a greater emphasis on internationalism in the social work profession: (1) greater understanding of alternative economic, political, and social welfare systems; (2) enhanced appreciation for diverse cultures; (3) exposure to comparative options for addressing economic and social issues; and (4) increased possibilities for innovation and change in practice and education.

Rosemary Sarri is professor emeritus, School of Social Work, University of Michigan, and a faculty associate at the Institute for Survey Research of the University of Michigan. Her research interests include the criminal justice system, focusing especially on women, international social work, and participatory community organization. Her recent publications include The Trapped Women: Catch-22 *(Thousand Oaks, CA: Sage, 1987).*

The world today is increasingly interdependent in terms of economic, political, social, communication, and mobility characteristics such that peoples and countries are intertwined in innumerable ways. Often, this interdependence is not recognized, as people and nations continue to act in ad hoc independent ways that result in conflict and exploitation. In recent years, the world has undergone several major social transformations. Eastern Europe and the former Soviet Union witnessed the overthrow of Communist government. Africa has experienced transformation resulting from serious tribal and religious wars, disease epidemics such as AIDS, as well as the lifting of white dominance in southern Africa.

Economic development has been the driving force of transformation in Asia, but there have also been many political repercussions, and not all countries or people have shared equally in the growing prosperity. The Americas also are experiencing transformation, as United States dominance is challenged by Canada and a rapidly developing Latin America, and as concern with global environmental change grows. It is within this context that there has been a growing awareness of and interest in international social work among social workers in various parts of the world (Ramanathan and Kondrat, 1994).[1] Effective

[1] The growing size and influence of the four major international social work organizations is a reflection of that interest, as is the content of papers presented at the various international conferences. Social workers also are increasingly involved in the work of the United Nations and as participants in the international conferences on social development, on the environment, and on population.

international social work for the 21st century needs to be collaborative.

Unidirectional influence, from developed affluent countries to the developing world and the areas that have undergone social transformation following the overthrow of Communist states, will fail to meet the goals that are being sought.

Historical Development

International social work is not a new field of endeavor, having been around since the mid-19th century when Western European governments established social services in the colonies they governed. Early colonial administrations and Christian missions established social service systems in many countries of Asia, Africa, and the Americas. These services were primarily charitable and focused on the individual and the family, and much less on the community. This focus on child and family welfare programs is still visible in many states of the United States.[2] Developments in U.S. social work were also influenced by a tendency to develop and use only U.S. service strategies and intervention technologies. As a result, there was limited borrowing of social intervention methodologies. Following World War II, the United States directed the development of many facets of the Japanese social security system while it occupied the country, but that was done with little consultation with other countries and that work seems to have had little or no impact on developments in our domestic social security system. This isolationism may distinguish the United States

[2]One exception was the work of Jane Addams and her colleagues in Chicago. They visited many public and private social programs and Europe and then adapted them in their work at Hull House. Some of that work subsequently became a model for settlement house programs in many parts of the United States.

from Canada and Western European countries, where there has been a longer interest in collaborative international social work.

The latter half of the 20th century witnessed a rapid growth in international social work in both the public and the private sectors in most regions of the world (Hokenstad, Khinduka, and Midgley, 1992). A number of important events provided the impetus for this growth. *First*, world and regional wars and conflicts, as well as terrorist activities, produced millions of refugees and immigrants who were in desperate need of social services. Drought, dislocation, and poverty further contributed to the situation. The internationalization of social problems continues unabated as the century closes, but the arena has shifted from Western Europe to the Mediterranean area and to developing countries in the southern hemisphere. *Second*, social problems associated with dramatic population growth in countries such as the Philippines and Kenya have resulted in increased poverty, malnutrition, and poor health despite the efforts of the United Nations and many private relief organizations. *Third*, and closely related to the increases in birth rate, is the rapid aging of the population in many countries. These latter two changes place special demands on social security and health-care systems, especially on those established on a basis of contributory social insurance.

Fourth, economic globalization, along with deregulation and entrepreneurialism, required significant shifts in resource utilization, but it also increased labor opportunities in Asia. At the same time, there have been serious costs in structural unemployment and loss of industry in other countries. *Fifth*, the increasing impoverishment of women and children as well as the increases in single-mother families resulted in homelessness and child neglect in most regions of the world. *Sixth*, the growth of the United Nations as an effective international body has increased opportunities for many types of international social work in organizations such as UNICEF, WHO, ILO, and UNCHR (Healy, 1995). The U.N. International Children's Emergency Fund (UNICEF) accomplished much with its advocacy of child immunization, health care, poverty reduction, education, and improved nutrition (Grant, 1993). *Lastly*, the growth of several international professional social work organizations resulted in more communication among professional social workers. There also are now many more opportunities for intercountry exchanges, which are of benefit to all participating countries (Ramanathan and Kondrat, 1994).

Studies of welfare systems in other countries increased awareness of a variety of solutions to social problems as well as the development of a broader range of intervention methodologies. The preparation of rich data sets on development patterns and outcomes provided the basis for systematic comparative analysis of development (Human Development Report, 1996; World Resources Institute, 1996). All of the above factors support the assumption that education for international social work is vital for the future.

What Is International Social Work?

Social work is a profession whose primary mandate is the development and delivery of a broad range of social welfare policy and human services in the public and private sectors. Because of the pluralistic ways in which it developed, international social work is often not clearly understood or distinguished from other human services. Midgley (1990) defines it simply as exchanges between social workers from different societies and cultures. Such a definition, however, is probably too inclusive to be meaningful. Others refer to it as a field of practice within the social work profession that is primarily concerned with social work practice between nations or cultural groups, as well as practice in international social service organizations. As such, it has explicit goals and objectives but can be expected to vary among nations and cultures because of their different histories, situations, and needs. Sanders (1984) suggests that social welfare and social work must be considered together because one implies the other. He defines international social welfare as the arena of activity for human resource development efforts, services, and activities of governments and private organizations that cut across national boundaries and are designed to control or contribute to the meeting of human needs and the resolutions of social problems. Complementarily, he defines international social work as the core functions and specialized helping services performed by social workers in their professional capacity that transcend national boundaries and deal with varying cultural, socioeconomic, and political contexts.

Social work as it is practiced today by U.S. social workers, even in international settings, is often practiced from an intranational perspective. Many believe that social work is a profession that is to be taught to social workers in other countries from the unidirectional perspective of U.S. ideologies, institutions, and technologies (Midgley, 1990, 1995). Because these social workers often lack knowledge about social conditions, values, and ideologies, as well social welfare developments, in other countries, they fail to benefit from the experience and programs of other countries (Almanzor, 1990).

At one time, there was close collaboration and exchange between Latin American countries and the United States in the training of social workers, but Latin America withdrew from this exchange when it became apparent that the United States saw the influence going only from North to South. As a result, innovative developments that occurred in each hemisphere were not known or exchanged with the other. In Latin America these developments included the "base community" organizations associated with liberation theology, the training of indigenous health and social service workers as outreach personnel, and the development of innovative programs in employment, community health services, nutrition education, and the education of women by women so that issues of gender inequality could be further examined.[3]

There are a diverse number of reasons why we are interested in seeing that social workers have greater knowledge of international social work practice as well as greater skill in working in other countries or in working with international populations within the United States. Consider the following reasons for greater emphasis:

1. An international cross-cultural social welfare education can broaden one's horizons about alternative economic, political, and social welfare systems. There is at present considerable dissatisfaction among U.S. social workers with a human services system that is unresponsive, stigmatizing, and ineffective. Many practitioners are attempting exciting innovations that could be aided by knowledge of some of the effective alternative services and technologies that are being employed in other countries. The need for change in the practice and organization of human services in the United States is obvious (Adams and Nelson, 1995). Resources are decreasing

rapidly and public services are being terminated or contracted to nongovernmental agencies on the basis of competitive contracts. Managed-care systems have grown beyond health care to child welfare, corrections, services for the disabled, and special education. Thousands of social workers from other countries have been brought to the United States to study, but very few social workers have studied social work in other countries, particularly in developing countries where some of the greatest challenges are there for study, both in the classroom and in the field.

2. A cross-cultural emphasis helps one to understand and appreciate diverse cultures from other countries, but also to gain added insight about one's own values, ideologies, and cultural preferences. The United States is truly a "rainbow country," with citizens from every corner of the globe. With the current strategies of empowerment and multiculturalism, the past policy of homogenization is no longer acceptable because it has usually resulted in oppression of immigrant groups, women, and persons of color.

3. An international approach exposes one to divergent thinking so that one can view social policies and services more critically and in a comparative perspective because there usually are alternative options. In business and industry, much effort and many resources are dedicated to critical analysis of markets, consumers, and suppliers. Social workers in the United States, more than in other sister countries, seldom use a critical comparative analysis as a basis for introducing new policies and services. This is particularly apparent with respect to child and family services, in criminal justice, and in community development with active citizen involvement.

[3]*Base community* was the term used in Latin America to refer to local grassroots organizations in poor areas that were developed to aid the residents in understanding their conditions, its causes, and solutions. Base community organizations were initially developed by worker priests associated with the liberation theology movement.

4. Cross-national collaboration between social workers and other human service professionals opens up many possibilities for innovation and change. Given the many serious problems that face the world, international collaboration is essential if we are to have any possibility of success. Such collaboration will require team structures that include several different professionals to complement each other. In recent years, such teams have functioned quite effectively in the droughts and conflicts in Africa, as well as in Eastern Europe and in the Bosnian-Serbian conflict. Opportunities for social workers are available through international organizations, both public and private, as well as in governmental agencies.

Significance for Practice, Education and Professional Development

Programs in international social work have the potential to enhance the profession in a variety of ways, including:

1. *Knowledge development.* Disciplines seek the development of knowledge as their primary goal; thus, the disciplinary aspects of international social welfare/social work address the development and testing of knowledge that is useful for policy and practice in the international arena. Innumerable possibilities for comparative research and theorizing seek to identify conceptual dimensions and relationships that cut across societies/nations, which vary in their economies, polities, cultures, demographic and geographic characteristics, histories, and forces that influence stabilization and destabilization (Estes, 1988). Comparative social welfare research to date has been wide ranging, covering various aspects of social policies and services, but the knowl-

edge gained provides insight that is useful in education, policy development, and planning, as well as in program evaluation (Balbo and Nowotny, 1986; Dixon and Macarov, 1992; Ferge and Kolberg, 1992; Midgley, 1995; Titmuss, 1974). The changing global situation raises many problems, but it also raises new possibilities for cooperation, collaboration, and exchange.

2. *Education.* The development of an international and comparative perspective is desirable for all BSW and MSW graduates, argues Boehm (1984) because most problems that social workers address can no longer be viewed exclusively in national terms. Such an approach would require that courses which focus on social welfare and the profession of social work must indicate commitment to international affairs. For those wishing to specialize in international practice, knowledge and skill in working with varied ethnic populations in different geographical contexts is essential. There also needs to be a focus on global and regional influences on social welfare and social work. Education can take place collaboratively among nations, including practical training, exchanges, and work in international agencies. Ramanathan and Kondrat (1994) present a detailed proposal for international exchanges in practicum training.

3. *Research.* Cross-national collaborations in applied research, development, consultation, and action are presently under way in many areas and are providing knowledge for application within and between countries. When such research recognizes and respects local needs, values, institutions, and practices, it has the potential for creating the foundations for more effective social institutions throughout the world.

Participation in Social Work Development

Effective international social work for the future needs to be collaborative rather than unidirectional from developed to developing countries. The latter can teach those from developed countries to question the whole-hearted acceptance of Western models of development, modernity, and industrialization that have been so destructive of the world's resources and environment, as well as of family and cultural values. The dominance of clinical social work in the United States may or may not be appropriate here with our societal value of individualism, but few would argue that it should be exported to other countries interested in social and economic development to meet basic human needs for food, shelter, clothing, health care, education, and so on. The power of Western institutions such as the World Bank and the International Monetary Fund over national economies must be reconsidered, because their rigid prescriptions for economic development have resulted in serious suffering in many countries in health care, child welfare, education, and similar programs. Moreover, there have been repeated, unsuccessful efforts with centralized approaches to resolving major social problems that are said to be ineffective because the target populations are not directly involved in the effort. Dames (1992) describes the many problems that have emerged as the U.S. federal government has dealt very bureaucratically with the people of Guam and some of the other Pacific island trust territories.

New models for social work intervention are required that will involve targeted local populations directly in the entire process of development. Poverty and violence are two of the most intractable problems in the world today, and they are unlikely to be resolved without a comprehensive effort that directly involves the poor and the victims of violence in the process of change. Taylor (1994) points out that community development must accompany any effort of violence reduction and social reconstruction. The case of South Africa is particularly relevant because so much of the recent violence involves young people who previously were active participants in the fight for independence. Now, they find themselves without an education or employment so the movement to violence and alienation is not surprising.

Consider the application of Freire's models of critical thinking and empowerment in situations like these (Ankrah, 1990; Burstow, 1991). Paulo Freire argues that fundamental change toward human betterment will occur when people understand the factors producing their situation and the actions that are necessary to change it. He speaks of the "indigenization" of social work as a necessary step. By that he means that the methods, philosophies, policies, and values must have relevance to the persons toward whom an effort is directed. There is ample evidence with regard to family planning that women must be educated and see that controlling their fertility is in their own interest if policies and programs are to succeed permanently. The Freirian model has been successfully implemented in South and East Asia, in Africa, as well as extensively in Latin America. What is less well recognized is what Western developed countries can learn from those who have successfully implemented the Freirian model in developing countries, but it is clear that there are a number of potential benefits. Social workers can learn greater sensitivity to cultural issues and to empowerment strategies (Gutiérrez, 1996).

Cross-national collaboration among human service professionals with nongovernmental organizations, as well as with United Nations agencies, can provide special benefits to developing innovative policies and services, as has been amply demonstrated with respect to social development, child health and welfare, population planning, women's well-being, and implementing sustainable environmental programs (Midgley, 1990). Almanzor (1990) reports on the successful results of a project supported by the International Association of Schools of Social Work, which emphasized the indigenization of social work in the Philippines. The Pacific regional projects involved 20 schools of social work in several Asian countries in the early 1980s, but its effects are still seen at the end of the century. One particular facet of the development in the Philippines was the holistic approach to the resolution of the multiproblem family. Students were placed in "floating" agencies that served rural areas, city slums, and deprived communities in agro-industrial areas (Almanzor, 1990). Students lived in and immersed themselves in the life of the community. Most schools in Asia today, Almanzor (1990) reports, now use this practicum method. More recently, California State University at Los Angeles reported that it was now successfully using this approach in social work education (Better and Bender, 1995). In fact, the school has taken it one step further in that classes are also held in the community, so that the school can become integrated into the effort at community development in South Central Los Angeles, an area where life is not vastly different from that in other urban centers in impoverished developing countries. Bibus (1995) from the Center for Global Education in Minnesota reports on a successful exchange between his social work students with social workers in Cuernavaca, Mexico.

> The current exchanges between social workers in the U.S. and Mexico must continue to grow and what we learn mutually from those exchanges must be documented and passed on

through our practice, writing and teaching. Using a tree as a metaphor for international social work that bridges the presumed dichotomy between helping individuals adjust to their environment and building more just communities, we will be simultaneously nurturing its roots while securing its branches to sustain people. And by doing so we will connect our practice to the heritage of social work at its best. (251)

International social work will continue to grow in the foreseeable future as a parallel development with the globalization of the economies and polities, and as changes occur in commitment to the welfare state ideology. Many Western countries are now questioning whether they can continue to have the welfare state benefits they now have due to globalization, changes in demographic characteristics that produce increasing demands for social services, and because of ideological opposition to taxes and other forms of income redistribution. At the same time, social work is being developed in Russia and several republics of the former Soviet Union, in Eastern Europe, and in China, Thailand, and other countries where it was not formerly practiced. In many of the latter countries, there is much enthusiasm toward social work and extensive collaboration between professional schools, professional organizations, private and public agencies, and grassroots organizations (Kelly, 1996).

A Tentative Agenda for the Early 21st Century

In preparation for the International Conference on Social Development in 1995, the United Nations examined a number of key indicators before formulating several recommendations. Representatives from 118 countries and 2400 private and public organizations representing (civil society worldwide proposed a plan of action with provisions that look toward the eradication of poverty, full employment, equality and equity between the sexes, universal access to education and health-care services, peace and just solutions to conflict, and sustainable development that protects the environment as well as the people living in it (Human Development Report, 1996). Children, the disabled, and the elderly deserve special attention because of their dependent status and the fact that they are often the most disadvantaged in society. Achievement of these objectives will require active citizen participation and consumption patterns in affluent countries that do not jeopardize the environment or victimize those from poorer nations. At a time when the widest gap in income inequality in over 40 years is reported by the U.N., there must be immediate efforts to reduce this gap if peace and justice are to prevail (Human Development Report, 1996).

This agenda is highly relevant for international social work, but its implementation will require a shift away from the traditional modes of practice with individuals to community and organizational action to effect social structural change. Social workers can be prepared to work in participatory and popular education programs in which all citizens are encouraged to be involved. Ankrah (1990) challenged social workers to address a number of pertinent questions:

1. How genuinely committed are we to the principle of people's participation?

2. How should we critically examine our relationship with the people with whom we work?

3. Are we close enough to the people to know how to guide and assist them in their development?

4. What skills are needed for creative and self-sustaining change?

5. What potential leverage do we have with the resource power brokers or donors to bring about approaches and directions in development that are in the interest of the most vulnerable population groups, and provide them opportunities for genuine participation?

Answering these questions is essential for one to be effective in international social work, but they are provocative and challenging. The old ways of doing things will need to change and the search is on for distinct combinations and more comprehensive approaches in addressing the social problem domains of particular concern to social work. It will require interdisciplinary and interprofessional approaches and partnerships that involve grassroots organizations, social agencies, and governmental and nongovernmental organizations.

REFERENCES

Adams, P., and Nelson, K. (Eds.). (1995). *Reinventing human services: Community and family centered-practice.* New York: Aldine.

Almanzor, A. (1990). Poverty, social welfare and the university. Lima, Peru: Proceedings of the International Conference of IASSW, 39–47.

Ankrah, M. (1990). Popularizing popular education and participation in Africa. Lima, Peru: Proceedings of the XXV International Conference of IASSW, 34–38.

Balbo, L., and Nowotny, H. (1986). *Time to care in tomorrow's welfare systems.* Vienna: European Centre for Social Welfare.

Better, S., and Bender, G. (1995). Social development in the Los Angeles area. Los Angeles, CA: California State University at Los Angeles, Department of Social Work.

Bibus, A. (1995). Reflections on social work from Cuernavaca. *International Social Work,* 38, 243–252.

Boehm, W. (1984). International and comparative social work in the undergraduate and graduate curriculum. In D. Sanders and P. Pedersen (Eds.), *Education for international social welfare.* Honolulu: University of Hawaii Press.

Burstow, B. (1991). Freirian codifications and social work education. *Journal of Social Work Education,* 27:2, 196–207.

Campfens, H. (1992). The new reality of poverty and social work interventions. *International Social Work,* 99–104.

Dames, V. (1992). Political status, citizenship and dependency: The children of the U.S. insular areas. *Children and Youth Services Review,* 14:3/4, 323–346.

Dixon, J., & Macarov, D. (1992). *Social welfare in a socialist country.* London: Routledge.

Estes, R. (1988). *Trends in the world social development: The social progress of nations, 1970–1978.* New York: Praeger.

Ferge, Z., and Kolberg, J. E. (Eds.). (1992). *Social policy in a changing Europe.* Boulder, CO: Westview.

Grant, J. (1993). Children and women: The Trojan horse against mass poverty. Washington, DC: Proceedings of the 1993 International Development Conference.

Gutiérrez, L. (1996). Macro practice for the 21st century: An empowerment perspective. In D. Tucker, C. Garvin, and R. Sarri (Eds.), *Integrating knowledge and practice: The case of social work and social science.* New York: Greenwood (forthcoming).

Healy, L. (1995). International social work: Organizations and activities. *Encyclopedia of Social Work.* Washington, DC: National Assn. of Social Workers, 1499–1510.

Hokenstad, T., Khinduka, S., and Midgley J. (Eds.). (1992). *Profiles in international social work.* Washington, DC: NASW.

Human Development Report. (1994). United Nations Development Programme. New York: Oxford University Press.

Human Development Report. (1996). United Nations Development Programme. New York: Oxford University Press.

Kelly, E. (1996). *Social Work in Russia.* Washington, DC: NASW.

Midgley, J. (1990). International social work: Learning from the Third World. *Social Work,* 35:4, 295–306.

Midgley, J. (1995). International and comparative social welfare. *Encyclopedia of Social Work.* Washington, DC: NASW, 1490–1499.

Ramanathan, C., and Kondrat, M. (1994). Conceptualizing and implementing a social work overseas study program in developing nations: Politics, realities and strategies. *Social Development Issues,* 16:2, 4–21.

Sanders, D. (1984). Developing a graduate social work curriculum with an international crosscultural perspective. In D. Sanders and P. Pedersen (Eds.), *Education for International Social Welfare.* Hawaii: University of Hawaii Press, 10–20.

Taylor, V. (1994). Social reconstruction and community development in the fact of violence and conflict in South Africa. *Community Development Journal,* 29:2, 123–131.

Titmuss, R. (1974). *Social Policy.* London: Allen and Unwin.

Vernon, R. (1990). Same planet, different worlds. In W. Brock and R. Hormats (Eds.), *The global economy: America's role in the decade ahead.* New York: W. W. Norton, 15–40.

World Resources Institute. (1994) *World resources: A guide in the global environment.* New York: Oxford University Press.

The Profession of Social Work

In the Second Century

David M. Austin

As social work enters its "second century," the debate over the profession's mission and goals has intensified. David M. Austin, the Bert Kruger Smith Centennial Professor at the School of Social Work, University of Texas at Austin, believes that suggestions to define the profession's future in terms of its past are misguided. Instead, he argues that "a real vision for the future of social work must be rooted in the actual characteristics of the society that we are [now] living in . . . and the real characteristics of the profession . . . as it exists today." These characteristics include a continuing devolution of governmental authority and responsibility from federal to state levels, a continuing growth of joint public-private measures in the provision of human services, and the globalization of the economic system. They will pose difficult choices for social workers "in defining the boundaries for our concerns about social justice." In making these choices, Austin urges social workers to keep in mind the following "central and critical elements" of the profession: its contemporary societal significance; long-standing focus on service; recent and projected growth; distinctive emphasis on the problems of women and children; demographic diversity; and historic involvement in public controversy.

Dr. Austin holds graduate degrees from Western Reserve University and the Florence Heller School at Brandeis University. He has also been a member of the faculty at Brandeis University, the University of Tennessee, and Case Western Reserve University. The author of The Political Economy of Human Service Programs, he served as chair of the NIMH Task Force on Social Work Research from 1988 to 1991. In 1997, he received the CSWE Lifetime Achievement Award.

This is a crucial moment for the profession of social work. The mid-1990s are the beginning of social work's second century. It was during the economic crisis of the early 1890s that charity organizations and other voluntary philanthropic social welfare organizations expanded their services to help desperate families survive. It was a period when social scientists and leaders in voluntary social welfare agencies began to talk about "scientific philanthropy"— the development of general principles that could increase the effectiveness, and efficiency, of charitable activities. This period also brought the beginnings of systematic training for charity workers, who soon after the beginning of the 20th century began to call themselves "social workers," and also first steps toward defining such workers as members of a new profession (Broadhurst, 1971).

Several writers have suggested that the organized profession of social work, and social work education, as they exist in the 1990s have "lost their way" (Karger, 1989; Specht, 1990; Specht & Courtney, 1994; Wenocur & Reisch,

1989). The message of Harry Specht and Mark Courtney in their book, *Unfaithful Angels* (1994) is that the profession should be reorganized and restructured with a new/different definition of mission and an entirely different approach to professional practice. They argue that we should look back to the early beginnings of social work in the 1890s for guidance in defining the mission for social work in the 21st century.

Mary Richmond and, in particular, Jane Addams are cited by Specht and Courtney (1994) as historic exemplars for the profession, in their call for "the profession" to turn away from "popular psychotherapies," "private practice," and professionalization, and to focus only on community-level interventions. Specht and Courtney argue that the mission of social work, based on its past, should be "to build a meaning, a purpose, and a sense of obligation *for the community* [emphasis added]. . . . We call for a social work practice that abandons individually oriented psychotherapeutic work and develops an adult education approach to helping people solve their problems" (pp. 27, 29).

The debate between the clinical practice wing of social work and the communitarian/social reform wing has a long history. This has included very different ideas about the appropriate settings for social worker practice. This debate has often been confused by an overly simplified interpretation of the actual historical development of the professionalization of social work and of professional education (Kirschner, 1986). In particular, most historical accounts focus only on the contributions of a few key individuals but give little attention to the processes through which practicing social workers, mostly women, struggled to gain public recognition as professionals and to make a living in a hostile society in which the few women who sought to be independent and

self-supporting were systematically blocked from entrance into the "male professions," including academic teaching careers and business leadership positions. These accounts also ignore the fact that the settlement house movement, although it included persons with a commitment to fundamental social changes, was largely a creation of middle-class reformers intended to facilitate the assimilation of immigrants into the existing social and economic system (Karger, 1987).

Although there are interesting parallels between the events of the 1890s, including the events that shaped the beginnings of social work, and events of the 1990s, recommendations that social workers and social work educators of today should look to the 1890s to define the future mission of the profession and the relation of the profession to the field of social welfare and the rest of American society is *bad advice*. A real vision for the future of social work must be rooted in the actual characteristics of the society that we are living in as we approach the beginning of the 21st century, and in the real characteristics of the profession of social work as it exists today.

A currently popular conservative writer, Professor Martin Olasky, provides a telling example of the possible results when one takes selected examples from the past and uncritically applies them to our current society. It is Professor Olasky's argument, set forth in his book *The Tragedy of American Compassion* (1992), that it is indeed the Mary Richmond model of private philanthropy that should shape the future of social welfare in the United States. Government programs that provide assistance to persons in poverty should be demolished; private charity and churches should be expected to meet all needs for temporary assistance. Moreover, social welfare program administrators and social work practitioners, from the point of view of Professor Olasky, are parasites on the system, enriching themselves while families in poverty receive little assistance. Like Richmond and many other early social welfare leaders, he believes strongly in the personal model of charity—that is, in a direct and personal connection between the charitable giver and the charity receiver.

The observations that follow begin with an examination of what I perceive to be certain critical characteristics of United States society in the immediate future, the society in which social workers will actually be practicing. This is followed by a look at important characteristics of contemporary social work practice—that is, the actual professional practice context of those persons who constitute the organized profession of social work: the tens of thousands of professional practitioners, primarily women, who are engaged in making their living in social work practice day in and day out. And, finally, I draw some conclusions about the future nature of the profession. This is not a statement of personal preferences. As in all forms of serious professional practice, a realistic assessment of the real situation, whether at an individual or societal level, is the first step in the development of a relevant form of action.

Social work as an organized profession occupies a significant position in American society at a very critical time because social workers deal every day with many of the most contentious social issues in our society. The period immediately ahead of us will be *a period of increasing political tension,* with some similarities to the period of 100 years ago, which was also a period of intense political conflict. Indeed, the intensity of emotions over ethnic identity reflected in the reactions to the outcome of the O. J. Simpson trial and the debate over affirmative action have their parallel in the intensity of the conflict 100 years ago over religion—in particular, the conflict in many com-

munities between the dominant and controlling Protestant majority and Roman Catholic immigrants.

Similar to the period 100 years ago, the most politically contentious issues of today are actually about the form and pace of cultural change more than they are about policies shaping the economic order or the structure of the American governmental system. Even when economic issues, or the definition of federalism, are being debated, political alignments are largely defined by opposing views on cultural issues.

Current hot button political issues do not really involve "class warfare." They are instead a series of conflicts over cultural issues within the broad "middle class." The hot button conflicts are over such issues as cultural diversity, affirmative action, civil rights of immigrants—legal and illegal, English as the official national language, lifestyle diversity, religious diversity, school prayer, charter schools and home schooling, abortion, gun control, property rights, and traditional and nontraditional "families."

Many of these conflicts reflect cultural forces that are changing the respective social and economic roles of men and of women. They grow out of the fact that the traditional paradigm of political and cultural dominance by white men, cutting across "class" or economic lines, is breaking down. But there is no consensus on what form of unifying social order will replace it. The "new conservatives" would like to return social and cultural conditions to the period of the 1950s, or, indeed, to the 1920s before the New Deal. Also involved are conflicts over the extent of communally shared responsibility for the welfare of children, older adults, and persons with severe disabling conditions in a society that celebrates and rewards individualism and individual achievements.

Around these cultural conflict issues, a fundamental restructuring of traditional political alignments is rapidly taking place. The white, male, traditional values, economically conservative, Southern states wing of the Democratic Party has moved en masse into the Republican Party. This has been particularly dramatic in Texas, where the *New York Times* reports that 39 local and state officials who were formerly Democrats have joined the Republican party, the largest such group in any one state in the country. Texas also now has two conservative Republican senators and a Republican governor. This process of political shift is also reflected in the retirement decisions of long-time conservative Democratic officeholders like Senator Sam Nunn of Georgia. The shift reflects a perception by this constituency of conservative white men that they have lost their traditional control of the organizational machinery of the Democratic Party in the South and that the Party nationally does not support the conservative values they believe in.

The constituency of traditional Democratic voters in the South who are now voting Republican in local elections as well as in presidential elections will not return to the ranks of the Democratic party, regardless of any effort by the Democratic leadership to recapture that constituency by moving "to the center." This shift in political labels is not a direct result of the Clinton presidency although the Clintons and the Clinton presidency have become demonized symbols of the cultural changes that are the object of attack by the "New Right."

The culture conflict issues that are shaping national political alignments are much more difficult to compromise in political platforms and pronouncements than economic issues and governmental funding issues. That is why a compromise "political center" is largely unavailable for candidates, including both centrist Democrats and centrist Republicans, and

why a compromise solution to the 1996 federal budget conflict has been so difficult to find. The battles around these cultural change issues—figuratively and, in some cases, literally—are likely to continue to be very bitter. The recent actions by Congress on welfare reform and immigration simply mean that the battles over the specifics in these two policy areas have been shifted from the federal level to the state level—a preelection outcome that suited both the Republican and Democratic leadership at the federal level.

The Democratic Party will be restructured beginning with activity at the precinct and community level, without a large portion of the constituency of traditionalist men, particularly in the South and West. This could result in a political party structure that is much more polarized at state and local levels than the current pattern of two versions of one "political party of the center." For example, in the state of Georgia in this Congress there are only African-American Democrats and white Republicans—there are no traditional white Democratic male representatives. This polarization is also illustrated by the "Liberal Democrat Wanted" poster put out by the Republican Party, which consisted almost entirely of the pictures of women, African-American, and Hispanic members of Congress, targeted for political elimination.

In this period of political tension, social work may well be identified with many of the contentious issues—for example, "welfare" for teenage unmarried mothers and protection of the rights of gays and lesbians—in which the attacks are really not about economic issues or about individual rights and community rights, but about lifestyles that contradict traditional patterns of marriage and community. For some political leaders, the entire voluntary nonprofit sector is identified with these contentious issues, as reflected in the efforts in Congress to put such organizations into a public policy straitjacket by curtailing their ability to take a public position on any social policy issue.

In the period ahead, there will be a continuing *downshifting of government authority and responsibility for domestic programs from federal to state levels*. In a federated structure like the United States in a period without a clearly perceived external crisis, available resources, including both money and program control, tend to move from the central authority to the constituent units in the federation. Popular identification of the federal government—Congress, the presidency, and the federal courts—with many of the contentious cultural changes now taking place in our society is intensifying this process.

There is an implicit assumption, on the part of cultural conservatives, that state political processes and state governments will be more culturally conservative than the federal government—or at least that individual states with culturally conservative majorities will be able to protect conservative cultural values within their borders without federal interference. In the case of the federal government, this downshifting of money and authority means reducing the national budget and allocating federal funds to state governments (but not to cities) through block grants. Equally important, it also means shrinking the administrative structure at the federal level so that the ability to enforce compliance with those uniform rules and regulations that are still intended to apply to all citizens, including the regressive mandates now being considered, is seriously compromised.

The combination of downshifting of money and of authority to the states and the weakening of the federal capability to monitor state performance means that the pertinent political arenas for policy issues dealing with such issues as income maintenance, health care through Medicaid, and child welfare will be at the state level. There may be very limited ability to affect those policies through advocacy at the federal level. This means that it is advocacy at the level of the state chapter that becomes the critical arena for public policy initiatives in these areas by the National Association of Social Workers.

In the immediate future there will be a continued expansion of a mixed economy system in the provision of human services—that is, a system of services in which the roles of government, voluntary nonprofit, and for-profit organizations overlap. The most dramatic changes in the institutional structure of human services for the immediate future are occurring in the provision of health care and mental health care services through "managed care" systems—that is, through the "commercialization" of health and mental health services. Nonprofit organizations are competing with for-profit organizations for participation in health-care/mental health-care networks that may be put together by insurance companies, mega health care/ hospital corporations like Columbia HCA, large employers, existing nonprofit health-care providers, or by individual entrepreneurial professionals, including social workers.

Government funds are being used to purchase services through such service networks for persons covered by Medicaid and Medicare, as well as for those persons eligible for publicly funded mental health services. Nonprofit service organizations are likely to become more dependent on support from for-profit corporations, including both contributions and contracts, as government funding is cut back. And some entrepreneurial voluntary nonprofit organizations may look more and more like wheeling-and-dealing for-profit firms, with high salaries for executives and sizable reserve funds—the only distinction being that there are no stockholders, and members of the policy board do not receive any direct financial benefits.

In this mixed economy pattern, one of the clear advantages for public bodies in contracting out for service production with both nonprofit and for-profit organizations is that a range of organizations representing diverse positions on contentious cultural change issues may be included, allowing the funding agency to avoid taking a single policy position. Moreover, if a particular contract agency becomes the object of cultural attack, the funding agency can be protected by dropping that organization from the contract list.

Traditional distinctions between public, voluntary nonprofit, and for-profit organizations in human services will become blurred. Indeed, it may be difficult for United Way campaigns to identify what is a true voluntary service organization deserving of support through community contributions when the majority of funding for many traditional agencies may come from a combination of insurance reimbursements and government contracts.

Many of the traditional distinctions between agency-based practice and private practice in social work will also become blurred. Many traditional private practitioner social workers will become "contract" employees within managed behavioral care networks, whereas other practitioners will become staff members in an organization that has a contract with a managed behavioral care company to provide EAP services to the local branch of a large multinational corporation. Other social workers will become part of the primary care/intake component in a for-profit health-care system, or become case managers or designers of coordinated health-care systems, for both profit and nonprofit components, or potentially become health-care executives.

Indeed, social workers in the future are more likely to work directly with low-income households through health/mental health/substance abuse service networks than through traditional public social service programs, particularly as de-professionalization is likely to be the model in state- and county-controlled income maintenance and child welfare programs if there are no federal quality control standards. In some settings, mental health care may be folded into a general health-care network with access through primary care physicians; in other settings, mental health care may be "carved out" and subcontracted to behavioral management firms. A strong professional organizational structure with an ability to monitor the performance of social workers in health-care systems and behavioral management systems may be an absolute requirement for protecting quality standards in services under this competitive marketplace model of health and mental health services.

The immediate future will also bring further developments in *the "globalization" of the economic system.* The United States economic system is no longer a "closed system." We cannot deal with social welfare issues as though it were a closed system. Banking and investment have been internationalized for some time. Manufacturing is rapidly becoming internationalized. Through the Internet and the World Wide Web, academic and scientific communication is becoming internationalized. Many national nonprofit social welfare service organizations are part of international associations or have a mission that includes societies outside of the United States.

The legislative events of the 1930s and the social and economic changes of the 1950s and 1960s, including the movement of several million African-American citizens from the rural South to the urban North and the elimination of legal forms of discrimination, resulted in a widespread redistribution of economic opportunities and political power within the United States. In a similar way, the current economic internationalization is redistributing both economic opportunities and relative political power on a worldwide scale.

Diminished economic opportunities in heavy industry in the United States for men with limited formal education is not primarily a result of a weak economy. The U.S. economy is, in fact, quite vigorous. These diminished opportunities for men, for example, have been accompanied by increased economic opportunities for women in light industry in the United States and in many other parts of the world. A large U.S. corporation announces that it will cut back on civic contributions in its home community and on benefits for retired employees in order to compete financially with other companies in a worldwide marketplace. Simultaneously, it is also creating new economic opportunities for men and women in many other countries of the world.

For social workers, this poses difficult choices in defining the boundaries for our concerns about social justice. In the fall of 1995, I traveled to El Paso every two weeks to teach MSSW students. The social policy class primarily looked at the effect of social policy choices on families living in El Paso and in the poverty-stricken colonias in the Lower Valley that are part of the larger El Paso community. But what about the effects of U.S. social policies, such as the intensified INS enforcement of the border crossing restrictions, on men and women and children living in the city of Juarez, Mexico, spread across the hillsides to the south, including children who are U.S. citizens by virtue of having been born in an El Paso hospital? Some of these families are literally 50 feet away from the border of El Paso across a narrow river. Some of the adults living in Juarez work every day in homes in El Paso, and some children cross the river every day to go to school in the United States. The internationalization of the economy makes the question of "who is one of us?" in the social work concern for social justice, a very immediate issue.

These and other characteristics of the immediate future—continued increase in ethnic/cultural population diversity in the United States; the increasing number and longevity of older adults; increased diversity in family structures; increased polarization of public attitudes along both gender and ethnic lines; redefinition of the primary causes of chronic and severe mental illness as being biological rather than psychological; a two-tier labor force with limited crossover from unskilled and semiskilled nontechnical jobs to skilled, technical, managerial, and professional jobs—will make the second century of social work very different from the present, and very different from the social work beginnings 100 years ago. This very complicated future includes both challenges and opportunities for the profession and for professional education.

In order for the organized profession of social work to respond to these challenges and opportunities, there must be a realistic analysis of the actual characteristics of the social work profession of today—that is, the characteristics of today's social work practitioners and the nature of their professional practice. The following are, for me, central and critical elements of contemporary social work.

■ *Social work today is a major profession.* It includes a diverse, complex, multidimensional model of professional practice. It includes intervention models that deal with individuals and households, with communities, with organizations, and with social policy. Sociological analyses, such as that published by Amitai

Etzioni in *The Semi-Professions* (1969), that label social work and other professions in which women predominate, as "semiprofessions"—a phrase that is repeated all too often by social work authors—are incorrect. A much more thoughtful discussion of the structure of organized social work is presented by Andrew Abbott in the December 1995 issue of *Social Service Review*.

As members of a major profession, social workers work in all types of communities, serving individuals and households from all economic levels, from all types of cultural and social backgrounds. One of the major changes from the society of 100 years ago is that the work settings of social workers are not limited primarily to nonprofit agencies, as they were during the first two decades of this century. Social work includes practitioners in private practice and those providing professional services in for-profit firms. Social work practice is not limited to one type of community or one economic group of service users.

■ *Social work is a service profession.* Social work professional practice does include the critical analysis of social policies that impact the lives of individuals, families, and communities. In order to increase the impact of such analyses by social workers, there must be much greater attention to the economic dimensions of such policies. But social work is not primarily a profession of policy analysts nor a profession of full-time policy advocates. Social work shares the processes of policy analysis, and social action and advocacy, with many other groups in society.

Social workers are predominantly direct service practitioners who provide helping services directly to individuals and households, as well as to groups and communities. Fundamentally, social work, like other major social institutions, is shaped by the pattern of finan-

cial resources. That is, social work practitioners actually practice in those settings in which they can make a living. The users of social work services include many victims of unjust social policies and economic exploitation, but they also include individuals at all income levels who are struggling with personal sources of pain and families and communities at all economic levels that are directly involved in self-destructive behavior.

■ *Social work is a growth profession.* The membership of NASW and other professional associations in social work is growing, with some 160,000 NASW members currently. There is an increase in the variety of settings in which social workers practice, including contemporary forms of private practice and practice in and through for-profit businesses. There has been a dramatic expansion of the institutional structure of social work education, with more educational programs and more students—in spite of occasional dire predictions that "if something isn't changed, social work will disappear." However, the growth of the profession is not the result of the application of a single "unique" social work method of intervention, nor of an intellectual campaign to persuade the general public that social work meets the 1915 Flexner criteria for being a true profession. The growth of the profession and, in turn, the growth of the social work education enterprise are a result, in substantial part, of the aggressive, self-interested political push by NASW over the past two decades for public recognition and sanction through licensing and vendorship.

■ *Social work has a distinctive focus on the problems of women and children.* Social work in the 1990s, like social work 100 years ago, is distinctive because its major practice arenas focus heavily on the issues affecting women and children, cutting across economic and cultural distinctions. Indeed, social work emerged 100 years ago in substantial part because other types of professional services, primarily staffed by men, paid little attention to the problems of women and children. Although there is frequent reference to social work's historic commitment to the "poor," it was the really desperate conditions of *poor women and children* that the early social workers were primarily involved with. Early social workers had little involvement with either the labor union movement or the social insurance movement, both of which were primarily concerned with the economic situation of employed men.

Indeed, if one examines the often criticized practice of psychotherapy in social work (Specht & Courtney, 1994), it becomes evident that psychotherapy, which certainly takes many different forms in the absence of definitive clinical research, provides an inclusive framework through which women from all walks of life, from all types of background, have sought professional assistance with critical problems of personal and family survival. These are problems that have been largely overlooked in the practice domains of other major professions.

■ *Social work is also distinctive among major professions in that the majority of practitioners are women and the majority of leadership positions in the profession are increasingly being held by women, while there continues to be substantial participation by men.* The majority of leadership positions in social work professional associations are held by women, but not exclusively by women. Fifty percent of the deans and directors of accredited and in-candidacy graduate social work education programs are women (1995) and a majority of undergraduate directors are women. Two-thirds of the social work doctoral students, the primary source for future faculty members and deans and directors, are women. And an increasing number of women are organizational executives in both nonprofit and government social service organizations, and the proportion is likely to continue to increase.

■ *Social work is a profession of diversity.* The diversity in modes of intervention and in practice settings has resulted in a growing number of specialized collegial associations around areas of common professional interests: public health, oncology, private practice, gerontology, group work, management, school social work, community practice, and many more. This diversification has now begun to be recognized by the creation of special interest sections within NASW. This is a development that is compatible with a continued identification by social workers with the profession as a whole through NASW as an inclusive professional association. The emergence of these practice constituencies is also reflected in the variety of symposium groups that meet at the Annual Program Meeting of the Council on Social Work Education.

Social work is also very diverse in the cultural and ethnic backgrounds of its practitioners, and this has resulted in an increasing number of special interest constituencies within the profession that cut across differences in settings and in modes of intervention and across geographic boundaries. In addition, social work education programs are being established in institutions that represent an increasing diversity of intellectual and cultural traditions.

■ And *social work continues to be involved in public controversy.* Social work today, as 100 years ago, is identified in the public mind with unpopular social problems that many members of the general public wish would just "go away." Because many of those persons whom social workers serve are the subject of public criticism and attack—teenage unmarried mothers, victims of the AIDS epidemic, undocumented immigrants—the profession of social work is also attacked, as it was in the 1994 U.S. Senate debate on the crime control bill. Indeed, the funders of philanthropic causes may often be suspicious of the role of social workers because of their frequent association with contentious and controversial issues.

Moreover, because social work is historically an open and inclusive occupation, social work practitioners include many individuals who are identified with constituencies in the general community that are the object of public criticism and attack. These practitioners are often very visible spokespersons on issues that directly affect themselves and other persons in like circumstances. Because many of the persons who identify with particular special interest constituencies are also active leaders within the profession and members of social work faculties, social work professional organizations often take policy positions that are politically unpopular, and they are frequently on the losing side in political controversies.

And what of the future for social work?

As the second century of social work gets under way, it is interesting to trace linkages with the society of 100 years ago, the society of the 1890s. But it is essential to recognize that much more important than any historical analysis is analysis of the implications of current societal developments for the future of the profession.

Social work will continue to develop as a major profession, with an expansion in membership and in the diversity of practice settings. The central practice focus of social work on the interface between individuals/families and the social environment will continue to be relevant to a wide range of human problems. The rate of cultural, technological, and demographic change, and the persistence of economic inequality within our society, will continue to create a high level of individual and family distress, and a demand for both preventive services and treatment services. However, the level of social work influence at management and program development levels, particularly in large service organizations, may be limited as recruitment for such organizational positions increasingly places more emphasis on directly applicable educational preparation than on clinical training and prior clinical experience.

The practice methods used by social workers will be directly affected by the constraints created through managed health care, with their emphasis on intensive, short-term interventions for a wide range of mental illness conditions, and on increased use of group procedures as well as individual treatment methods. There may also be an expanded within-the-system advocacy role for social workers as the gap between the service needs of many persons with chronic and persistent illnesses and managed health-care procedures becomes increasingly obvious. All of these developments will slowly filter back into professional education curriculums.

The policy environment will continue to be turbulent, with state political processes becoming the critical arena for domestic policy. Organized social work can have an important impact in particular policy debates in collaboration with those individuals most affected by regressive policy proposals. However, the influence of the profession on the processes of policy development may be quite limited as long as attention within the profession is given almost exclusively to normative criteria and general principles in evaluating policy alternatives rather than to technical analysis of policy implementation alternatives, including economic analysis and the application of research-based knowledge. Moreover, an increasing polarization of political perspectives in the society may result in social work and social workers becoming even more of a target in political battles.

The degree and range of diversity within the membership of the profession and in the sponsorship of professional education will continue to increase. There is likely to be increased diversity among schools of social work, particularly at the graduate level, with different advanced practice curriculum emphases emerging in different schools, and with a concentration of doctoral education in a limited number of schools. Indeed, diversity of specialization in professional education is essential if social workers are to play a leadership role in the many different arenas of professional practice.

With the growth in numbers and in diversity, there may well be a greater diversity in social and political perspectives among professional practitioners and within schools of social work among both faculty and students. In turn, there may be an increasing level of internal controversy over public policy positions taken by professional associations, as well as within faculties of schools of social work. Social work policy perspectives will never match the perspectives of the general public, reflecting a broad consensus on fundamental values by persons who choose to enter the profession, but there is also less likelihood in the future that there will be be a single inclusive consensus within the profession on all major issues of public policy.

The fit between the institutional development of organized social work and the human needs of the most deprived and exploited individuals and families in this society will continue to be an issue. Historically, social workers have often been found in the front lines of the "war on human misery." But social workers also have practiced and will continue to practice in other settings as well. The dynamics of the admission process of schools of social work and of the employment market for social workers will be the primary forces that shape the practicing profession in the future. The language of historically grounded mission statements in schools of social work can be important, as can the content of the social work education experience. But it is finally only as schools of social work recruit, and actually admit, a much more culturally diverse cohort of students than is currently happening that the historical connections of social work with the most desperate human conditions in our society can be maintained or expanded.

In many ways, the early 21st century may be a very uncomfortable time for many citizens of the United States, even while the economy is strong. The organized profession of social work will face expanding opportunities, while individual social workers will share the discomforts of the larger society. The history of social work can serve as a source of inspiration, but to master the events of the future it is essential that strategic planning for the profession be "grounded" in an understanding of the forces that are actually shaping this society and the profession of social work within it.

REFERENCES

Abbott, A. (1995). Boundaries of social work or social work of boundaries? *Social Service Review, 69,* 545–562.

Broadhurst, B. (1971). *Social thought, social practice, and social work education: Sanborn, Ely, Warner,*

Richmond. New York: Columbia University School of Social Work. Unpublished dissertation.

Karger, H. J. (1987). *The sentinels of order: A study of social control and the Minneapolis settlement house movement, 1915–1950.* Lanham, MD: University Press.

Karger, H. J. (1989). Private practice: The fast track to the shingle. *Social Work,* 34 (November 1989), 479.

Kirschner, D. S. (1986). *The paradox of professionalism: Reform and public service in urban America, 1900–1940.* New York: Greenwood Press.

Olasky, M. (1992). *The tragedy of American compassion.* Washington, DC: Regnery Gateway.

Specht, H. (1990). Social work and the popular psychotherapies. *Social Service Review,* 64, 345–357.

Specht, H, & Courtney, M. E. (1994). *Unfaithful angels: How social work has abandoned its mission.* New York: The Free Press.

Wenocur, S., & Reisch, M. (1989). *From charity to enterprise: The development of American social work in a market economy.* Chicago: University of Illinois Press.

Index

American Association for Retired
People (AARP), 71, 76
American College of Life
Insurance, 146
American dilemma, 4, 40
American Friends Service
Committee, 277
American Indians. *See* Native
Americans
American Red Cross, 362
Americans with Disabilities Act
(ADA)
employee assistance programs
(EAPs) and, 138
legal advocacy under, 223
Americorps program, 268
Amott, Teresa L., 30
Anderson, Charlene, 231
Anderson, Norman B., 159
Ankrah, M., 392, 394
Anorexia, 168
Antiscience, encouragement
of, 319
Antisocial Personality Disorder,
329, 336
Area Agency on Aging, 291, 293
Arenson, K. W., 76
Arkava, M. L., 324
Armstrong, J. C., 320
Artificial charity, 359–360
Ashcroft, John, 281
Asia, economic development
in, 387
Asian Americans, 9
economic status of children, 20
in elderly population, 285
out-marriage by, 45
population growth rate, 9, 13
in workforce, 227
Assertive Community Treat-
ment, 166
Assimilation, 41
Association of Labor
Management
Administrators &
Consultants on
Alcoholism, 231
Atchley, R., 291
AT&T, 31
Attention deficit disorder
(ADD), 168

Attkisson, C., 167, 169
Au Claire, P., 105
Auslander, Gail, 232
Austin, David M., 357–358, 369,
396–407
Austin, Michael, 232
Axinn, June, 52, 57, 81, 82, 84,
221, 374
Ayers, T. S., 190
Azzarto, J., 213

B
Baby Boomers. *See also* Social
Security
demographics of, 146–147
Bacharach, Samuel, 231, 234
Bacon, Leonard, 274–275
Bakalinsky, Rosalie, 230
Balbo, L., 391
Balgopal, Pallassana, 232
Balkin, S., 65
Ball, Michael A., 135
Bamberger, Peter, 231
Bane, Mary Jo, 51, 54
Bangladesh, Grameen Bank
in, 178
Banks
failures, 33
Grameen Bank, Banglaesh, 178
Janashakthi Banking Society,
Sri Lanka, 179
Banta, H. D., 380
Baptist Children's Services, 275
Barancik, Scott, 86
Bardill, D., 288
Barer, M. L., 159
Barker, R., 377, 378
Barlett, Donald, 83, 84, 85, 86, 87
Barlow, D. H., 331
Barna Research Corporation,
275–276
Barrow, Frederica, 232
Barrows, H. S., 322
Barth, R. P., 110, 193
Bartley, William W., III, 168, 298,
302, 320, 321
Base community organiza-
tions, 390
Base ecclesial communities
(BECs), 206
Bassi, Laurie, 228

Bates, James, 239
Battered women shelters, 129
Bay Area Community Resources,
268
Bebel, M. Y., 192
Becerra, R. M., 42
Beck, Ulrich, 53
Bellah, Robert, 83, 87
Bell Curve, 49
Bellos, N., 285, 287
Bender, G., 393
Bendick, M., Jr., 72
Bennett, William, 52–53
Bentall, R. P., 169
Berenbeim, Ronald, 232
Berk, R. A., 132
Berlin, G., 139
Berliner, A. K., 342
Bernstein, J., 109, 138
Bernstein, N., 372
Berrick, J. D., 100, 110
Besharov, D. J., 342, 371
Better, S., 393
Bezold, C., 155
Bibus, A., 393
Billups, J. O., 179, 345
Binstock, R., 287
Biological sciences education,
379–381
Births and deaths
child abuse deaths, 371
percentage distribution of, 15
population increase and, 14
Bjorn, Lars, 231
Black, R. N., 346
Blaming the victim, 242
Blank, Martin J., 266, 267
Bloom, M., 210, 211, 303
Blue-collar workers
layoffs, 31
race and job loss, 51
Bluestone, Barry, 31, 37, 52, 60, 61
Blumenthal, D., 157
Blumenthal, Sidney, 84, 85, 86
Bobo, J. K., 194
Boehm, W., 391
Boettner Institute, 146
Boggs, C., 201
Bose, A. B., 177
Bosnian-Serbian conflict, 391
Bottomore, Thomas, 90

research and, 391
Crystal, S., 287
Cultural amalgamation, 43
  racism and, 45
Cultural competence, 42, 250
Cultural conflict issues, 398–399
Cultural relativity, 41
Cultures, 44. *See also*
  Multiculturalism
Cunninggim, M., 75
Curriculum Content Statements,
  Council on Social Work
  Education, 182
Cutler, J. P., 342
Cutler, Neal E., 97, 143–151
Cybernetic epistemology, 312
Cycle of violence theory, 128

D

Dames, V., 392
Danziger, S. K., 102, 109, 111, 377
Daro, D., 100
Darwinian evolution, 307–309
Davis, Allen F., 82, 90
Davis, B. J., 169
Dawes, Robin, 318
Dayaranta, S., 211
Dean, W. R., Jr., 423
De Anda, D., 42
*The Death and Life of Great Ameri-
  can Cities* (Jacobs), 189
Deaths. *See* Births and deaths
Decline of social work, 368–375
The Declining Significance of Race
  (Wilson), 51
Deconstructualism, 301
De Hoyos, G., 42
Deindustrialization, 30–31, 204
Delevan, S. M., 62, 65
Delgado, G., 201, 203
Delgado, M., 250
Dellums, Ron, 372
DeLois, K., 212, 251, 255
Democratic Party, 82, 399
  as organizational entity, 86
Demographics, 8–27. *See also*
  Population
  Baby Boomers and, 146–147
  child welfare system and, 110
  early retirement and, 148–149
  economic status

of children, 19–22
of population, 21, 22
labor force and, 227
poverty and, 55
Demone, H. W., Jr., 72
Denton, Nancy, 49, 51
Department of Homeless
  Services, 200
Dependency ratio, 16–19
Depression
  DSM-IV diagnosis of, 335
  unemployment and, 35
Deregulation, 34, 388
DeRoos, Yosikazu, 357, 376–386
Descartes, R., 308
Deschner, J. P., 129
Desowitz, R. S., 111
De Tocqueville, Alexis, 274
Developing countries. *See* Third
  World
Developmental forms of social
  work, 65
Devitt, James, 86, 87, 88
Devore, W., 42, 250
Dewar, H., 154
*Diagnostic and Statistical Manual of
  Mental Disorders, 4th
  Edition. See DSM-IV*
Diagnostic and Statistic Manual
  (Williams), 313
Diamond, I., 254
Diaz, T., 190
DiClemente, C. C., 195
Dilley, J., 223
Disability insurance, 53
Discrimination. *See* Racism and
  discrimination
Diversity profession, social work
  as, 404, 406
Dix, Dorothea, 164, 165–166
Dixon, J., 391
Doh, J., 100, 101, 103, 106, 108
Dolgoff, R., 341, 346
Dollars and Sense, 37
Domestic violence. *See* Family
  violence
Donnison, D. D., 354
Donovan, Rebecca, 232, 292
Dorman, R., 312
Dotson, David, 232

Douglas, J., 70
Dover, Michael, 234
Dow Jones average, 33
Downey, G., 193
Downsizing, 31
  poverty and, 52
Doyle, K. O., 146, 147
Dressel, P., 257
Drug-Free Schools alloca-
  tions, 267
Drugs. *See also* Substance abuse
  psychopharmacological agents,
    development of, 381
Dryfoos, J., 212
DSM-III-R, 334
DSM-IV, 168–169
  Antisocial Personality
    Disorder, 336
  definitions in, 329, 331
  ethical issues, 345–346
  inconsistency in, 334–336
  international social work
    practice and, 180
  Learning Disorders, 335
  Major Depression, 335
  meeting criteria for diag-
    nosis, 338
  religious and spiritual
    problems, 280
  Selective Mutism, 335–336
  Separation Anxiety
    Disorder, 335, 338
  social work and, 336–337
  Substance Abuse, 335
  use of, 328
DuBois, B., 212
DuBois, W. E. B., 2, 4
Due process, 95
  in juvenile justice system, 124
Duke, David, 84
Dumpson, J. R., 107
Duncan, G. J., 110
Dunkle, R. E., 285, 293, 343–344
Dunlap, K., 311
Dupper, David R., 264
Dychtwald, R., 290

E

Early retirement, 145, 147
  demographics of, 148–149
  financial literacy and, 149–150

Food pantries, 278
Ford Foundation, 75
Fordice, Kirk, 279
For-profit health services, 157–158, 400
  social-health model and, 214
Foster care, 100
  California, AFDC foster care in, 104
Foster Higgens, 155
France, 181
Frank, Robert H., 52
Frankel, Max, 87
Franklin, Cynthia, 155, 261–262
Fraser, M., 105, 371
Fraser, S., 49, 56, 82, 84, 85
Freeman, M. A., 158, 159
Freeman, P., 380
Freeman, R. B., 109
Freire, Paulo, 177, 252, 254, 392
Freud, S., 333
Freudenheim, M., 74, 153, 155
Freund, P. E. S., 157
Friedman, E. A., 16
Friend, R., 290
Friends Committee, 272
Frumkin, M., 257, 377
Fulbright Foundations, 183
Fundamentalism, 56
Fund-raising
  community chest programs, 361
  community organizing and, 202–203
  in politics, 87

G

Gaebler, T., 369
Gagne, R. M., 319, 324
Gallegos, J., 250
Gambling addiction, 168
Gambrill, Eileen, 28, 181, 298, 317–327, 322, 323, 324
Gangs, 177–178
Garland, D. R., 182
Garner, L. H., 351
Garvin, C., 378
Gault decision, 95, 121, 124
Gay persons. *See* Homosexuals
Geertz, C., 304

Gelles, R., 128
Gellner, E., 301, 305
Gender discrimination, 29–30
Generalized Anxiety Disorder, 329
General Motors, 31
General paralysis of the insane (GPI), 169
Genital mutilation, 127
Gensheimer, L. K., 190
Georgopolous, B. S., 353
Gerdes, K., 313
Geriatric social worker, 291
Germain, C. B., 159, 210, 211
Gerontology. *See* Social gerontology
Gerstel, Naomi, 231, 232
Gerstle, Gary, 56, 82, 84, 85
Gibbs, L., 323
Gibelman, Margaret, 72, 157, 241
Giddens, Anthony, 53
The Gift Relationship (Titmuss), 68–69
Gil, D. G., 69, 100, 103, 345
Gilbert, N., 69, 72, 190
Gilchrist, L. D., 190, 191, 192, 193, 194
Gilkes, C., 254
Gillespie, J., 312
Gingrich, Newt, 69, 279, 281
Ginsberg, L., 180
Gitterman, A., 159, 210, 211
Glassie, H., 271
GlenMaye, L., 212, 251, 255
Globalization, 388. *See also* International social work
  challenges of, 60–62
  effects of, 401
  family violence, global response to, 132
  opportunities of, 62
  population and, 61
  relevance of social work to, 63–66
  social problems of, 60–62
  social work and, 59
Global restructuring, 31–32
Glover, J. J., 347
Glugoski, G., 182–183, 184
Gold, S., 109

Gold exchange standard, 31
Goldiamond, I., 318
Goldsmith, J. C., 156
Gomez, E., 43
Gomory, Tomi, 98, 163–174, 299, 300–310, 319
Goode, R., 71
Googins, Bradley, 230, 234
Gordon, David M., 30, 33, 34, 37
Gordon, R. S., Jr., 102, 192
Gordon, W. E., 346
Gorin, Stephen, 97, 152–162
Gorski, H. A., 71
Gosnell Memorial Scholarship, 373
Gottschalk, P., 109, 377
Gould, Gary, 230
Gould, K. H., 45
Government. *See also* Politics
  big government, mistrust of, 200
  health care, role in, 154
  history of social work and, 81–83
  juvenile justice system, 122
  nonprofit organizations and, 72–74
  religion and, 274
  shifting attitudes, 87–88
  third-party organizations, 351
Gowen, N., 244
Grameen Bank, Bangladesh, 178
Gray, Muriel, 232
Great Britain. *See* Britain
Great Depression, 35, 53, 273
  resources in, 368–369
The Great U-Turn: Corporate Restructuring and the Polarizing of America (Harrison & Bluestone), 37
Green, J., 250, 255
Green, J. W., 42
Green, R. K., 319
Greenberg, Stanley, 84, 85, 86, 87
Greenstein, Robert, 33, 109
Gregg, D. W., 144, 146
Grob, G., 165, 166
Gronjberg, K. A., 69
Gross, Harriet, 231, 232
Gross, P. R., 319

Gross Domestic Product
(GDP), 82
Group work, 3461
Growth of profession, 403
Gruber, James, 231
Guam, 392
Guardian ad litem model, 221
Gueron, J., 369
Gulbenkian Report, 379
Gummer, Burton, 187, 299, 350–356
Gun control, 398
Gurteen, Samuel H., 275
Gutiérrez, Lorraine, 187–188, 206, 212, 249–259, 392
Guzzetta, C., 177

H

Haapala, D. A., 105
Haber, C., 286
Habitat for Humanity, 272, 281
Hagstrom, Jerry, 84, 85, 86
Hajnal, Zoltan L., 54
Hall, A., 18
Halpin, S., 244
Hancock, B., 293
Handler, Joel F., 54, 112
Hanna, M. G., 206
Hansmann, H. B., 70, 77
Hardin, R., 354
Hardy-Fanta, C., 42
Harris, M., 272
Harrison, Bennett, 31, 37, 52, 60, 61
Harrison, E., 279
Hartley, E. K., 346
Hartman, Ann, 45, 304, 306
Hartwell, Tyler, 231
Harvey, P. L., 111
Hasenfeld, Y., 112
Haslam, D. R., 313
Hatch, R., 65
Hattiangadi, J. N., 301
Hauser, P. M., 211–212
Haveman, R., 114
Hawkins, Denise B., 240
Hayek, F. A., 167, 170, 304, 320
Hayes, C., 108
Haynes, Karen, 81, 83, 89, 288
Head, S., 154

Health care, 97–98. *See also* Health maintenance organizations (HMOs); Managed health care; Mental health; Social-health model
capitation, 158
community-based care, 158–159
context for social work in, 210–211
corporate medicine, 155
current trends in, 153–154
education in, 379–381
elderly persons and, 289–290
for-profit health services, 157–158
future of, 154–157
government's role, 154
health promotion and disease prevention, 159
international social work practice, 180
medicalization of social problems, 211
prevention programming and, 192
scenario one, 156
education in social work under, 159
social work under, 157–158
scenario two, 156–157
education in social work under, 159
social work under, 158–159
single-payer plan, 156–157
social work and, 152–162
at state level, 400
in unionized workplaces, 228
Health insurance, 153. *See also* Heath maintenance organizations (HMOs)
early retirement and, 149–150
erosion of employment-based insurance, 153–154
family policies, 229
Health Insurance Plan of New York (HIP), 153
Health Maintenance Organization (HMO) Act, 153

Health maintenance organizations (HMOs), 98, 136, 374
in scenario one for health care, 155
in scenario two for health care, 156
single-payer plan with, 157
Health Security Act, 154, 156
Healthy People 2000: National Health Promotion and Disease Prevention Objectives, 157
Healthy Start program, 260, 261
Healy, L., 63, 64, 72, 182, 389
Hempell, C. G., 303
Hendrickson, S. L., 277
Heneghan, A. M., 106
Henly, Julia R., 94–95, 100–119
Hennelly, A., 215
Henwood, Doug, 31
Hermeneutics, 301
Herrnstein, Richard J., 49
Hersen, M., 321
Heuristic paradigm, 302
Heyman, Margaret, 231
Hicks, E., 127
Highlander Research, 202
High school graduates, earnings of, 23
Hill, H., 84, 85, 86
Himmelfarb, Gertrude, 52–53
Hines, S. M., Jr., 354
Hinson, E. G., 274
Hispanic Americans, 9
births and deaths, 14, 16
child poverty, 102
economic status of children, 20
in elderly population, 285
out-marriage by, 45
population growth rate, 9, 13
unemployment rates, 229
in workforce, 227
HIV. *See* AIDS
Hochman, Stephanie, 188, 260–270
Hodgkinson, V. A., 71, 73, 74, 277, 279
Hogan, D. P., 110
Hogarty, Gerald, 313
Hokenstad, M. C., 65
Hokenstad, T., 388

Holvino, E., 250
Homelessness, 281. *See also*
    Marginalized populations
    Department of Homeless
        Services, 200
    international dimensions of, 62
    mental health system and, 168
    religious organizations
        and, 276
Home schooling, 398
Home Service program American
    Red Cross, 362
Homosexuals
    elder care, 290
    politics and, 85
Hooyman, N., 253, 286, 287, 289,
    290, 291, 293
Hopkins, B. R., 70, 71, 75
Horton, Myles, 202
Horwitz, S. M., 106
Hospitals. *See also* Managed
        health care
    institutional ethics committees
        (IECs), 347
House of Cards (Dawes), 318
Houses of Refuge, 120–121
Huckfeldt, Robert, 84, 85, 86
Hudson, W., 303
Hull House, 388
Human resources program-
    ming, 137
Human wealth span, 144
Hume, David, 300–301, 303
Humphrey-Hawkins Act, 36
Hunter, A. G., 193
Hunter, J. D., 45
Hunter, Robert, 2
Hunter College School of Social
    Work
    Education Center for Commu-
        nity Organization, 202, 206
    elder care needs, 292
Hurowitz, J., 211, 215
Hushbeck, J., 291
Hutchison, Elizabeth, 371
Hyde, C., 200

I

Ialongo, N. S., 193
IBM, 31

Iglehart, A. P., 42
Iglehart, J. K., 153
Illegal immigrants
    legal advocacy and, 223–224
    treatment of, 61
Illig, D. C., 100
ILO, 389
Immigrants and immigration. *See*
        Illegal immigrants
    births and deaths, 15
    civil rights of immigrants, 398
    legal advocacy and, 223
    population increase and, 14
    poverty and, 55
    in workplace, 135
Immutability of natural pro-
        cesses, 303
Income. *See* Earnings
Income taxes, 33
India
    indigenization of social
        work, 177
    workplace, social services
        through, 180
Indigenization of social work,
    177, 392
    in Philippines, 393
Individual aging, 144
Individual Retirement Accounts
    (IRAs), 114
Industrial Areas Foundation,
    202–203
Industrial research, 135
Industrial social work, 365
Infant mortality, 110–111
    international social work
        practice, 180
Inflation, 28–29
    elderly persons and, 287
Inglis House, 275
Insane asylums, 166
Institute for Poverty Research,
    University of Wisconsin,
    369
Institute for Social Justice, 202
Institutional ethics committees
    (IECs), 347
Interest rates, 28–29
Internal Revenue Service (IRS),
    70–71

International Association of
    Schools of Social Work, 66,
    72, 183, 393
    Women's Caucus, 132
International Conference on
    Social Development, 1995,
    393–394
International credit, 60
International Federation of Social
    Workers, 72, 183
*Internationalizing Social Work
    Education: A Guide to
    Resources for a New Century*
    (Estes), 64
International Monetary Fund,
    60, 392
International social work,
    175–185. *See also* Cross-
    national collaboration
    agenda for 21st century,
        393–394
    definition of, 389–391
    development in 21st century,
        177–180
    diversity teaching, 182
    early pioneers in, 175–176
    education, 182–183
    historical development,
        388–389
    indigenization of social
        work, 177
    knowledge development, 391
    in latter half of 20th century,
        388–389
    at the millennium, 387–394
    para-professional, role of, 181
    participation in development,
        392–393
    phases in, 175–180
    practice, 180–181
    professional imperialism
        phase, 176
    reconceptualization phase, 177
    research, 181–182
Internet
    distance education pro-
        grams, 183
    internationalization of
        communication, 401
    privacy issues, 344

Multiculturalism, 4, 39–46. *See also* Multicultural community organizing
  critique of, 42–44
  cultural amalgamation and, 43
  future of, 44–45
  meaning of, 40–41
  satisfaction and, 43
  social service response, 41–42
  societal context of, 39–40
  theoretical support for, 41
Muoz, C., 254
Munz, Peter, 298, 300, 301, 307, 308, 321
Murdock, S., 249
Murphy, K. M., 23
Murray, Charles, 49, 52
Myrdal, Gunnar, 4, 40

N

Nacman, M., 209
Nagda, B., 250, 251
NASW News, 311
National Association for the Advancement of Colored People (NAACP), 71
National Association of Social Workers (NASW). *See also* Code of Ethics
  accuracy of education, investigation of, 324
  diversity of profession, 404
  ethics conferences, 347–348
  internationalization and, 64–65
  leadership program, 373
  marginalized populations, working with, 240
  political sophistication, 288
  professional advocacy by, 224
  public policy initiatives, 400
  twinning chapters of, 64
  whistleblowers award, 372
National Crime Victimization Survey, 128
National Incident-Based Reporting system, 128
National Institute of Mental Health (NIMH), 170, 305
  research productivity for social work, 369–370

Task Force on Social Work Research, 313–314
Nationalism, 59
National Labor Relations Board (NLRB), 34
National Maritime Union, 231
National Organizers Alliance, 207
National People's Action, 202
National Resources Planning Board, 36
National Rifle Association (NRA), 87
National Training and Information Center, 202
Nation of Islam, 56
Native Americans, 9
  ethnic struggles, 40
  melting pot theory and, 45
  population growth rate, 9
Natural disasters, 180
Neckerman, Kathryn M., 51
Nelson, K., 390
Nemon, H., 250, 255
Neo-social Darwinism, 49
Netting, E. F., 210, 272
Neurosyphilis, 169
Neutral rationality in administrative ethics, 353
New Deal, 50, 52
  coalition, 85
  public charities in, 362
  social work profession and, 872
The New Field Guide to the U.S. Economy: A Compact and Irreverent Guide to Economic Life in America, 37
Newhill, Christina E., 230
Newhouse, J. P., 155, 156
New Right, 399
New School of Social Research, 374
New York House of Refuge, 120
New York School of Philanthropy, 135
Nichols, E., 380
Nickerson, R. S., 324
Nightingale, N., 193
Nihilism, 305
Niskanen, W. A., 164
Nixon administration, 82

government, mistrust of, 200
health maintenance organizations (HMOs) in, 153
impeachment proceedings, 88
Watergate, 353
Nofz, Michael, 232
Noga, S. M., 71
Nonprofit organizations, 68–79
  charitable organizations, 71
  cutbacks in funds, 74
  entrepreneurial organizations, 400–401
  federal funding, 74
  future of, 76–77
  government supporting, 72–74
  independent sector, 71
  lobbying and advocacy, 75–76
  private sector organizations and, 74–76
  Reagan administration and, 72–73
  traditional distinctions between public and, 401
  types of, 70
Norcross, J. C., 195
Norgard, T., 285, 293, 343–344
North American Free Trade Agreement (NAFTA), 30, 32
Nowak, J., 277
Nowotny, H., 391
Nu'Man-Sheppard, J., 190
Nunn, Sam, 399
Nurius, P., 251

O

Occupational Safety and Health Administration (OSHA), 34
Occupational social work, 226–238
  consumer service model, 233
  corporate social responsibility model, 233
  current and future trends, 226–227
  current practice, 230–232
  directions for future, 232–233
  employee service model, 232–233

Politics (continued)
    views changing on, 87–88
Poor Law Act, 165
Popkin, S., 371
Popper, Karl R., 167, 171, 172,
        302–303, 306–310, 318,
        322–323, 324
Popple, Philip R., 81, 230, 345
Population
    change by race and Hispanic
        origin, 13
    demographic change affecting
        economic status of, 21
    dependency ratio, 16–19
    expected growth of, 9
    globalization and, 61
    percentage distribution
        by age, 11
        by race and Hispanic
            origin, 12
    projections by age, race, and
        Hispanic origin, 10
Population aging, 144
Porter, R., 165
Positivism, 300
Post-Traumatic Stress Dis-
        order, 331
Poverty, 48–57
    age, rates by, 24
    average poverty ratio of
        population, 21
    California, child poverty in, 103
    child poverty, 23, 25, 102
    cultural framework and, 53
    cultural justification, 49
    demographic change and,
        19–20
    elderly persons, 102
    family and, 53
    future of, 55–56
    international social work
        practice, 180
    managed poverty, 49–50
    moral constitution of the poor,
        48–49
    19th century views, 48–49
    politics of, 53
    postindustrial explanation of,
        50–51

postmodern poverty, 51–54
prevention programming,
        192–193
ratio by age, race and Hispanic
        origin, 20
religious organizations,
        services of, 276–277
school-community
        collaboratives and,
        267–268
surge in rate of, 22–23
unemployment and, 33
Practice. See Social work
Praxis, process of, 253–254
Pressman, B., 128
Preston, J., 153
Preston, M. G., 311
Prevention, 190–197, 378
    and at-risk population,
        193–194
    challenges to, 191–194
    improving prospects for,
        194–196
    methodological improve-
        ments, 195
    social-health model
        interventions, 212–213
Prigogine, I., 155
Probation officers, 222
Problem-focused educational
        model, 322
Proch, K., 221, 222
Prochaska, J. O., 195
Professional imperialism
        phase, 176
Professional journals, 371
Profession of social work,
        396–407
Profiles in International Social Work
        (Hokenstad, Khinduka &
        Midgley), 65
Progressive era, 48
    charities in, 362
    community organizing in, 199
    government, role of, 81
    juvenile justice in, 121
    schools in, 262
Property rights, 398
Prozac, 338, 381

Psychiatry, 328–339. See also
        DSM-IV
    conceptually based partnership
        with social work,
        336–339
    distinction between social work
        and, 336–337
    integration of research and
        social work practice,
        311–316
    missions of social work
        and, 329
    psychotherapeutic techniques,
        333–334
    role of, 332–334
    team concept and, 328
Psychoanalysis, 333
Psychodynamic theory, 312
Psychopharmacological agents,
        development of, 381
Psychotherapeutic techniques,
        333–334
Public assistance. See Welfare
        system
Public charities, 361–363
Public Health Service, 157
Public sector. See Marginalized
        populations
Puccinelli, M., 287
Pugh, G., 221
Pulley, B., 371
Purcell, F., 210
Putman, R., 215
Putnam, Robert D., 86, 88

Q
Quakers, 277
Quetel, C., 169
Quinn, J. R., 18

R
Race. See also Multiculturalism
    concept of, 45
    of elderly population, 285
    exploitation and, 51
    poor/non-poor schism
        and, 54
    in workforce, 227
Rachlis, M., 156

Racial-ethnic composition of
population, 8, 9, 13
differential rates of change,
causes of, 13–16
economic status of children
and, 22
Racism and discrimination, 45
immigration and, 61
income gaps and, 29–30
school-community
collaboratives and,
267–268
unemployment and, 32
Radnitzky, G., 302
Raffoul, P., 289, 290
Raheim, S., 65
Rainwater, L., 20, 25
Ramanathan, Chathapuram, 182,
232, 387, 389, 391
Rappaport, J., 251
Rationalizing, 241
Ravetz, J. R., 321
Reagan administration
community development
corporations (CDCs), 203
deregulation and, 34
mythology of simplicity, 87
nonprofit organizations under,
72–73
PATCO workers, 34
social welfare programs, 33
Real World Macro, 37
Real World Micro, 37
Reamer, Frederick G., 158, 299,
342, 344, 345, 346, 347
Rebok, G. W., 193
Recidivism, 123
Reconceptualization of social
work, 177
Rees, S., 288, 289
Reformatories, 121
Refugees
globalization and, 61
United Nations service,
178–179
Registered Retirement Savings
Plans (RRSPs), 114
Rehr, H., 210, 215
Reich, R. B., 139

Reiff, Philip, 320–321
Rein, M., 20
Reinhardt, U. E., 155, 158
Reisch, Michael, 6–7, 28, 69,
80–92, 175, 182–183, 184,
199, 250, 258, 313, 354, 363,
378, 396
Relativism, 301–302, 303–306
objective facts in, 305
Religious diversity, 398
Religious organizations, 271–284
base ecclesial communities
(BECs), 206
and community organiz-
ing, 277
community organizing
and, 361
delivery of social services by,
275–280
education and research in
social work, 273–274
elderly, services to, 276–277
examples of, 272
Faith and Family, 279
future of social work by,
280–282
historical role of, 274–275
homelessness and, 276
melting pot theory and,
44–45
missionary agencies, 364
in Philadelphia area, 278
philosophical role of, 274–275
poor persons, services to,
276–277
social responsibility and,
359–360
social values of Catholic
church, 55–56
space provided to community
groups, 277, 278
Relman, A. S., 153, 156–157
Remilitarization, 31–32, 33
Repressed memory therapy, 320
Republican Party, 399
Revolution of 1994, 83, 85
Research
accreditation standards for
research programs, 370

on Aid to Families with
Dependent Children
(AFDC), 369
constructive steps for
researchers, 315
cross-national collaboration
and, 391
elder care, 292
on ethnic sensitive services,
250–251
ignoring results of, 319
industrial research, 135
integrating practice and,
311–316
international social work,
181–182
in multicultural community
organizing, 256
in occupational social
work, 234
religious organizations and,
273–274
single system research designs
(SSRDs), 313
social-health model and,
215–216
*Research on Social Work
Practice*, 313
Residual services in family
preservation movement,
107–109
Resnick, R. P., 63
Resnick, R. S., 177
Retirement. *See also* Early
retirement; Elderly persons
age for, 18
biotechnology and, 380
wealth span and, 144
work and retirement practices,
290–291
Reves, R., 157
Reynolds, Bertha Capen, 88, 312
Reynolds, Beth, 231
Riches, Graham, 232
Richmond, Mary, 2, 63, 273,
397, 398
Rifkin, Jeremy, 85, 139, 154
Right-wing economic policies,
33–34

Shedlin, Allen, Jr., 266
Sheldon, B., 107, 312
Shepardson, William, 261,
    262, 263
Sheridan, M. J., 244
Sherman, K. W., 132
Sherman, W., 252
Sherraden, Michael, 112, 229, 232
Shore, D., 166, 172
Short, J. L., 190
Shroyer, J. A., 160
Siefert, K., 211, 215
Simbi, P., 72
Simon, Barbara Levy, 83
Simon, J., 70
Simpson, O. J., 398
Singer, S. J., 153
Single-parent families, 110
Single-payer health care plan,
    156–157
Single system research designs
    (SSRDs), 313
Siporin, M., 304, 341
Sivarajan, L., 155
Skeel, J. D., 347
Sklar, H., 254
Skocpol, Theda, 53, 54
Skultans, V., 165
Slogans of multiculturalism, 43
Smeeding, T. M., 20, 25
Smith, D. H., 280
Smith, Michael, 230
Smith, R. M., 84
Smith, S. R., 69
Smithey, R. W., 158
*Social Casework: A Behavioral
    Approach* (Schwartz &
    Goldiamond), 318
Social constructivism, 41
Social development approach,
    177–180
Social diagnosis, 360
Social Diagnosis (Richmond), 2
Social gerontology, 143
    coursework on, 289
    defined, 144
Social-health model, 209–218
    assumptions of, 211–212
    community organizing
        and, 213

context for, 210–211
education and, 214–215
empowerment model, 211–212
implications for social work,
    214–216
interventions, design of, 212
managed health care and,
    213–214
monitoring and evaluating
    process, 213
Participatory Action Research
    (PAR) model, 216
practice and, 214
prevention, interventions for,
    212–213
research and, 215–216
theoretical constructs, 211
universal, comprehensive and
    integrated services, 212
Social insurances, 53–54
Social isolation, 51
Social justice, 304, 341
    as central theme, 378
    resources for pursuing, 343
    in social work education, 320
The Social Meaning of Money
    (Zelizer), 53
Social movements, 201. *See also*
    Community organizing
Social reform, 42–43
Social responsibility, 359–367
    casework and, 360
    charitable organization
        movement, 359–360
    community organizing and,
        360–361
    group work, 361
    industrial social work, 365
    missionary agencies, 364
    public charities, 361–363
    techology and, 366–367
    war on poverty and, 365
Social sciences education,
    378–379
Social Security, 50, 54, 111–112,
    143, 273. *See also* Early
    retirement; Medicare
aging patterns and, 144
expansion of benefits, 82
poverty of elderly and, 111–112

as share of total income, 146
as success story, 145–146
Social Security Act of 1935,
    36, 286
Social Security Administra-
    tion, 362
Social Service Review, 403
Social work. *See also* International
    social work; Law career
    tracks; Occupational social
    work; Religious
    organizations; Social-
    health model
community organizing in,
    198–200
developmental forms of, 65
distinction between psychiatry
    and, 336–337
DSM-IV, 336–337
end of, 368–375
future of profession, 376–386
and health care, 152–162
immigrant ethnic minorities,
    services to, 61
international context of, 59–67,
    62–63
juvenile justice system and,
    125–126
mission of, 332
multiculturalism and, 41–42
partisanship and, 89
prevention in, 190–197
profession of, 396–407
psychotherapeutic techniques
    in, 333–334
role of, 332–334
and workplace, 134–142
Social work education, 317–327
    accreditation teams, 325
    add-on approach to, 320
    administration, graduate work
        in, 370
    antiscience, encouragement
        of, 319
    competencies and outcomes,
        assessment of, 319, 324
    computer training, 382–383
    criticisms, valuing, 322–324
    curriculum, 320
    fads, prevalence of, 319–320

World Wide Web
  distance education programs, 183
  internationalization of communication, 401
  privacy issues, 344
Wrenn, R., 378
Wright, L., 45
Wyers, Norman, 230, 231
Wyman, P. A., 190

Y
Yancey, Gaynor, 271
Yates, Michael D., 37
Yegidis, Bonnie L., 95–96, 127–132
YMCAs/YWCAs
  elder care, 292
  group work in, 361
Youth correction system. *See* Juvenile justice
Youth Power, 268

Yuan, Y. Y., 105, 106
Yudkowsky, B. K., 153

Z
Zaret, Esther S., 266
Zelizer, Viviana, 48, 53
Zimmerman, M. A., 251
Zodhiates, P. P., 324
Zuniga, M., 285

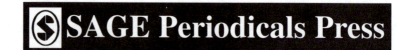